THE OLD PROVINCE OF QUEBEC

LONDON : HUMPHREY MILFORD
OXFORD UNIVERSITY PRESS

A Bird's-Eye View of the Old City of Quebec

[Photograph of a painted wooden model executed, on a scale of 24 feet to the inch, by Lieutenant J. B. Duberger of the Royal Engineers. The drawings were begun in his lodgings in 1795, and the model was finished in the ballroom of the Castle of St. Louis in 1809. Four years later it was taken to Woolwich Arsenal in England. In 1910 the British government presented it to the Public Archives of Canada.]

THE
OLD PROVINCE OF
QUEBEC

BY

ALFRED LEROY BURT

Professor of History in the
University of Minnesota

MCMXXXIII
THE RYERSON PRESS • TORONTO

THE UNIVERSITY OF MINNESOTA PRESS
MINNEAPOLIS

TO
MY FORMER COLLEAGUES
AND STUDENTS
IN THE
UNIVERSITY OF ALBERTA

FOREWORD

I did not intend to write this book. My original purpose was to produce a study of the dual nationality of Canada, where public questions have so often been seen out of focus because viewed with only one eye — French or English. But when I essayed the task, the inadequacy of the secondary authorities on the crucial period treated in this volume drove me to the Public Archives of Canada. There, before I knew it, I found myself engaged in the work which is just finished. Had I known how many years it would take, I might not have begun it. But I could not leave off once I had started. The annual summer's pilgrimage to the chief shrine of Canadian history, alternating with a winter's "mulling" over the material then gathered, became too strong a habit.

For making it easy to indulge in this habit, I am indebted to the University of Alberta, where the greater part of this volume was written, and to the University of Minnesota, where it was completed. For making it pleasant and profitable, I owe much to the unfailing courtesies of the Canadian Public Archives staff and to the stimulating intercourse with other students of Canadian history with whom I have forgathered in Ottawa. No one can appreciate how much this means unless he has spent at least part of a summer delving in the Canadian Archives. Nor can any but an author imagine my gratitude to the University of Minnesota Press for countless improvements of the text. Finally, no man can understand how much I am obliged to my wife's forbearance during the years I have devoted to this work.

A. L. B.

September, 1933.

CONTENTS

XI. A REACTIONARY GOVERNMENT

XII. A WAR OF RAIDS AND SURPRISES

XIII. THE SHADOW OF THE WAR

XIV. THE SHADOW OF THE PEACE

XV. THE LOYALISTS

XVI. A RISING STORM

XVII. CHIEF JUSTICE SMITH AND LORD DORCHESTER

XVIII. TRADE, EDUCATION, TENURES, AND FINANCE

XIX. THE END OF THE OLD PROVINCE OF QUEBEC

ILLUSTRATIONS

MAPS

CHAPTER I

THE COLONY SURRENDERED

THE Canada that Governor Vaudreuil surrendered to the British commander-in-chief on September 8, 1760, was as large in territory as it was small in population. It extended down the Ohio, it included the Great Lakes, and no one knew how far it reached toward the setting sun. Most of this country land was still as wild as it was on the day two centuries earlier when Jacques Cartier first sailed from St. Malo to discover the land that was to be New France. To gather furs and to block the English, the French had flung their posts far and wide. But in all the great heart of the continent their only settlements were at Detroit and on the Mississippi in what was known as the Illinois country, and these were very feeble. Detroit, which belonged to Canada, contained only a thousand persons. The other community, an offshoot from Louisiana, may have had a few more. Most of the people living in these two places were limited to a primitive existence, for they had little contact with the outside world.

Only on the lower St. Lawrence had the French planted themselves in any numbers. There some sixty-two thousand Canadians inhabited a long narrow colony that stretched for two hundred and fifty miles from the southwest to the northeast. Checked by the rapids on either side of the Ottawa's mouth, settlement had climbed no farther up the St. Lawrence River than Cedars; downstream, it died out in the harsher climate of Kamouraska, which lies more than two degrees farther north. The band of settlement had no breadth except at the upper end, where it spread across the fertile islands of Jesus and Montreal and over to the right bank of the Richelieu, which runs nearly parallel to the St. Lawrence until it empties into it at Sorel. Below this point, settlement clung to the banks of the great river, here and there thrusting a little arm five or six miles up a tributary stream. On either side the river the wandering line of white cottages, built of stone or of rough-hewn timber, with now and then a church and a mill, presented the appearance

1

of an interminable village, for the habitants' farms were squeezed together along the water's edge. Only the lower ends were cultivated. The rest of the land was left a wilderness, because it was less fertile and less accessible from the river, and, more important still, because there was no need to bring it under the plough. There was little market for agricultural produce; the seignior's dues were very light; the church's tithe was only one twenty-sixth; and there were no taxes. Most habitants, therefore, though they had large families, raised small crops. A surplus would have been a superfluity.

They led a primitive life, though not quite so primitive as that of their brethren farther west. They sold little and bought little, for almost all their food, clothing, and furniture were of home manufacture. Nor was their independence confined to material things. They knew nothing of the weight of civilization which bore so heavily upon the lower orders at home. No deep social gulf separated them from their feudal lords, the seigniors, and many of these, indeed, were little better off than themselves. European travelers had already observed that they "breathed from their birth the air of liberty," and that "even the ordinary habitants lived in greater ease and comfort than did thousands of the gentlemen of France," for privilege sickens whereas freedom and equality thrive in a pioneer atmosphere. The habitants' relations with the church were friendly and intimate, because the parish clergy were drawn mostly from their own ranks. And the church itself, imbued with the missionary zeal of frontier life, preserved a pure spirit that inspired the wholehearted devotion of its worshipers.

Their attitude toward the government was likewise happy, on the whole, being very much that of a child toward a parent. English-speaking people generally have such a prejudice against paternalism that they are somewhat blind to its good side, its human quality. The government of New France was neither a vague abstraction nor an impersonal machine. It had a heart as well as an intelligence, and was like a wise father who knows how to humor his children. The principal agent of the government in each locality was the captain of militia. With few exceptions, there was only one in each parish, and he was never of seigniorial rank. He was usually the most responsible and respected habitant of the community. Legally he received his powers from above; practically he derived his authority from below. Though he secured his commission from the governor, he really owed his appointment to the people, for they were regularly consulted and their approval was considered necessary. This informal election, generally held at the church after the Sunday service, seems to have resulted in the selection of a truer representation than do most of our formal elections. An honored seat in the church, a larger piece of holy bread than the other habitants received at the celebration of the Mass, the right to wear a sword, an occasional gift of powder and shot from the governor, and the great respect of his fellows, constituted his only rewards. The laws and orders of the government he read out to the people at the church door on Sundays, and none could plead ignorance, for they all attended divine service regularly. Coming through him,

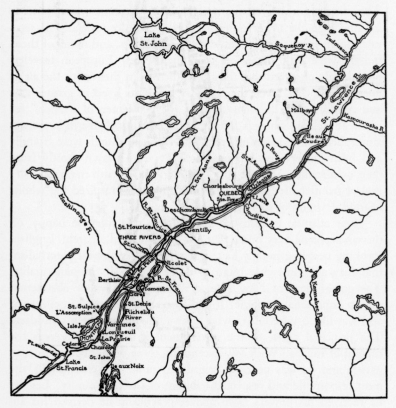

THE ST. LAWRENCE RIVER

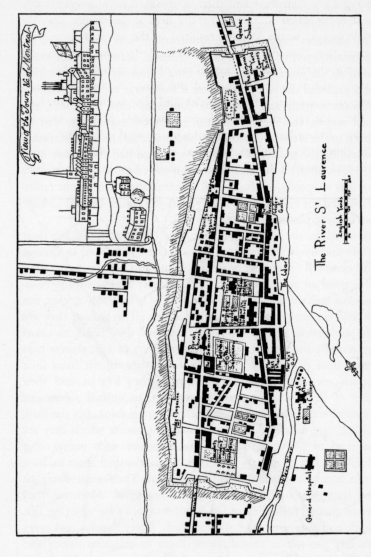

The City of Montreal in 1760

[Redrawn by Forrest Burt from a contemporary engraving in the possession of the Public Archives of Canada]

the commands of government were commonly obeyed; but if they were not, he reported to the governor or the intendant, who, after careful investigation, might impose a fine upon the delinquent.

The habitants' regard for the government was also fostered by the administration of justice. Every criminal accusation was made privately to the *procureur du roi,* or king's attorney, who thereupon secretly explored the case to discover if there was sufficient evidence to warrant a trial; and unless he concluded that there was, the accused was never apprehended and might not even know that he had been under a cloud. Such a method protected the innocent without shielding the guilty, as it might have done had the colony been larger. The courts were numerous and sat twice a week. Indeed, justice was so speedy, so cheap, and so sound that men sought rather than avoided the courts, and litigation might almost be said to have been a favorite pastime.

As a people, the Canadians were then, as now, noted for their sprightly and lively character. A British officer who came to Quebec in 1768 observed [1] that "the peasantry salute and bow to one another with as good an air as people of higher rank; they testify no bashfulness nor awkwardness in any company of what rank so ever, but speak and act with great ease and freedom. This indeed they are taught and habituated to from the moment they begin to crawl about, and, by the time they are fourteen years of age, possess it as much as their parents. . . . Their vivacity they inherit from their European ancestors, to which the climate they live in, and their manner of feeding more upon vegetable than animal substances, may contribute." They were not given to strong drink, but the men, he added, "are much addicted to smoking tobacco, which they are accustomed to from mere boys." In common with many other English-speaking people of that time, he condemned them as lazy. But this accusation is easily explained away. Their wants were no greater than their needs, and nature was bountiful. Moreover, they possessed that enviable genius, an infinite capacity for enjoying life. At work and play they sang and laughed. Every Sunday and every saint's day the parish church drew them to religious duties and social pleasures. The long winter months were never dreary but were always filled with good cheer. The river valley rang with the joy of young and old, skating, horseracing, or driving carioles, for they had horses in plenty. Indoors there was an endless round of festivity. Cards were a thief of time, and dancing feet sped away the hours. Around the stove, tongues wagged in gossip and retailed stories that made sides rock or hair stand on end. The folk songs and folklore of old French Canada are eloquent testimony that no children of the earth ever had a gayer or more wholesome existence.

Such was the normal life of the great majority of the Canadians. Only a small minority dwelt in the towns. Of these there were only two, for Three Rivers was but a straggling village of hardly a hundred houses. Montreal was surrounded by a wall and a ditch, but was counted a place of no strength. It was less than a mile long, running from the present McGill Street to Cartier Square. At its widest it was only three hundred and fifty yards across. Along the north ran the creek, which has since disappeared under Craig Street; on the south the town was bounded by the St. Lawrence and by St. Peter's River, over which Ste. Ann's Market was later built. There were only two thoroughfares traversing the town, the modern Notre Dame and St. Paul streets, and the former was interrupted by the old parish church on the Place d'Armes. The population, which may have been five thousand, had outgrown the walls to form the Quebec Suburb at the east end, the Récollet Suburb at the other extreme, and the St. Lawrence Suburb across Craig Street Creek along the road leading to Sault au Récollet. The General Hospital, which the Grey Nuns had taken over in 1755, also lay outside the walls, just south of the little St. Peter's River. As a reminder of the heavenly origin of the town, so charmingly related by Parkman, one-fifth of its area was occupied by the houses and gardens of various religious organizations, the Jesuits, the Sisters of the Congregation, the Seminary of St. Sulpice, and the Récollet friars. The rest of the town was built for the service of Mammon, Montreal being the capital of the North American fur trade, and the lay population was obviously infected by the devil-may-care spirit which that traffic has usually engendered. Some might adduce this as the cause of the frequent fires that had preyed upon the place and led to the substitution of stone structures for wooden buildings.

Quebec was a very different sort of place. It was a staid town, for it was far removed from the contagion of the fur trade and was the seat of the bishop, the capital of the colony, and the Gibraltar of America. Perched on the cliff, three hundred feet and more above the river, stood the bastion of Cape Diamond. This was the highest, the strongest, and the most southerly point of the triangular town inclosed on the north by the St. Charles, on the east by the St. Lawrence, and on the landward side by the line of fortifications, which ran north-northwest. Along the northern half of the eastern side of Quebec the cliff did not plunge right into the river. Here, just above the water level at high tide, was a little narrow shelf on which the dwellings, warehouses, and shops of the Lower Town lay huddled together. Trade had not yet contaminated the proud Upper Town, which belonged wholly to God, the king, and a few gentry. Here were the spacious college of the Jesuits, the seminary that Laval had founded, the Hôtel Dieu, the houses of the Récollets and the Ursulines, and two other convents, the parish church, which served also as a cathedral, the Bishop's Palace, and, just across the way, the Castle of St. Louis, the abode of the governor. On the northwest corner, just outside the walls, was the suburb of St. Roch. To the east of this stood the Intendant's Palace, and three-quarters of a mile to the west, on the southern bend of the St. Charles, lay the General Hospital.

In further contrast to Montreal, which had been surrendered whole, without a blow, Quebec was a town of ruins, so badly had it been battered by the British guns. Lying off by itself, the General Hospital was mercifully preserved unscathed, but not a building in the town had escaped the deadly work of shot and shell. The bare walls were all that was left standing of the parish church. One-third of the houses were completely destroyed, and many more were so shattered that they had to be pulled down. The streets were cumbered with fallen beams and piled with broken masonry. In 1754 the population had been computed at eight thousand, but no more than thirty-five hundred were recorded by the census taken shortly after the conquest. Truly it was a stricken city.

The blight of war had also hit the countryside. Around and below Quebec many a charred heap marked the site of a once happy cottage, for the invaders had been driven to use the sternest methods to prevent the habitants from taking up arms against them or bearing succor to the beleaguered garrison. And throughout the colony the people were more or less exhausted by the protracted strife. The whole community was suffering from economic pleurisy, for the ever growing volume of paper currency had long since driven all sound money out of circulation. The merchants had been forced to part with their wares and the habitants to yield their flour and grain, their horses and cattle, in return for the notes of a bankrupt government. The government which had thus impoverished them had also worn them out in countless corvées and endless militia service, until they could stand the strain no longer. All these sacrifices had been in vain, and as the final crisis was clearly approaching, with the British closing in on Montreal, the habitants had deserted the hopeless struggle, thereby precipitating the fall of their country.

The fall of Quebec on September 18, 1759, though it sealed the

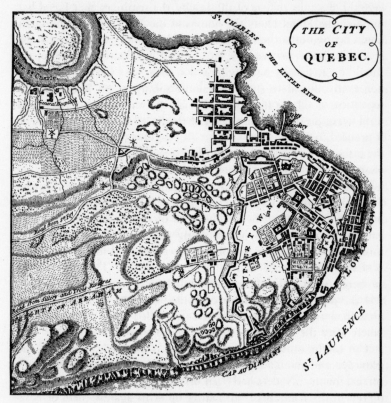

THE CITY OF QUEBEC IN 1760

[From the inset on the map reproduced on pages 84 and 85]

a. Palace Gate. b. St. John's Gate. c. St. Louis's Gate. d. Potasse Bastion. e. St. John's Bastion. f. St. Ursula's Bastion. g. St. Louis's Bastion. h. La Glacière Bastion. i. Cape Diamond Bastion. k. Fort St. Louis. l. The Parish Church. m. The Seminary. n. Church of the Lower Town. o. Hôtel Dieu. p. The Bishop's Palace. q. The Jesuits. r. The Ursulines. s. The Récollets. t. Royal Battery.

doom of Canada, was only the surrender of one fortified place. The articles that the British Admiral Saunders and General Townshend and the French commander De Ramezay signed on that day were, therefore, short and few, only eleven in all. The members of the garrison were allowed to "march out with their arms and baggage, drums beating, matches lighted, with two pieces of French cannon, and twelve rounds for each piece," and were to be "embarked as conveniently as possible, to be sent to the first port in France." The rest of the artillery and military stores were yielded up with the town. Before the delivery of the gate the British had to post soldiers to safeguard "the churches, convents, and principal habitations." Upon laying down their arms the residents were guaranteed the possession of their private property, and until their future condition should be settled by a treaty of peace, they were not to be removed nor even obliged to quit their houses, for neither side wished a repetition of the Acadian tragedy. Moreover, article six stated that until a treaty was negotiated "the free exercise of the Roman religion is granted, likewise safeguards to all religious persons, as well as to the bishop," who had retired to Montreal. He was to be allowed "to come and exercise, freely and with decency, the functions of his office, whenever he shall think proper."

The document that Vaudreuil, the Canadian governor, and Jeffrey Amherst, the British commander-in-chief, signed on September 8, 1760, is commonly called the Capitulation of Montreal, but it should be known as the Capitulation of Canada. Because it involved very much more, it has five times as many articles and is eight times as long as the Capitulation of Quebec. The military provisions, which were most explicit, occupy the forefront of the document. Denied the honors of war, all troops whether in Montreal or elsewhere were to lay down their arms, to be transported to France free of charge, and to take no more part in the war. Similarly, the governor and the intendant, with their staffs of officials, were to be carried home. Nor was any obstacle to be placed in the way of private individuals who wished to retire to France. All, whether civil or military, were to be allowed to carry with them their families and effects. They were also permitted to carry off their official papers, except charts and plans of the country and such archives as might be necessary for the government of the colony. But Vaudreuil demanded and Amherst promised that the registers of the supreme council of Quebec and all other documents belonging to that and other offices, including seigniorial and notarial records, "that may serve to prove the estates and fortunes of the citizens," should remain where they were. All property except that belonging to the government, which of course was surrendered, was to be left untouched in the hands of its owners, who were given full liberty to sell it and take away the produce "in bills of exchange, furs, specie, or other returns." No Canadian was to be molested in any way, but Amherst would not agree to extend any guarantee to the few Acadians who had come to the country. Inspired by the sad history of these people, Vaudreuil also tried to extract a promise that the Canadians who remained in the country should never be required to bear arms against France or her allies. Amherst, however, insisted that they become the subjects of the British king. There had been too many half-subjects down in Acadia. Nor would he give any more explicit answer to Vaudreuil's demand that the old laws be preserved by the new government.

So much has been made of the provisions touching religion that it is necessary to examine them closely. Article twenty-seven reads in part as follows: "The free exercise of the Catholic, Apostolic, and Roman religion, shall subsist entire, in such manner that all the states and the people of the towns and countries, places and distant posts, shall continue to assemble in the churches, and to frequent the sacraments as heretofore, without being molested in any manner, directly or indirectly." Amherst agreed to this wide stipulation, but to the further demand that the new government continue the legal obligation of the tithe he replied that this "will depend upon the king's pleasure." The secular clergy were to retain all their rights and functions. The communities of nuns were to remain inviolate in all their privileges, but Amherst withheld a similar promise from the Jesuits, the Récollets, and the Sulpicians "till the king's pleasure be known." They were, however, guaranteed their property. Even the Indians were to be included in this covenant of religious liberty and were to retain their missionaries.

But however large were the promises of the British, there was one thing that threatened to undermine them all. There was no bishop in the land, for Pontbriand, whose functions had been guaranteed in the capitulation of Quebec, had died on May 8, just four months before Montreal was surrendered. Without a bishop no priest could be ordained, and death might slowly rob the people of their clergy and their religion. If the British promises were to mean anything, there must be a succession of priests, and for this there must be a bishop. The great question was how to get him. Though invested by the pope, he had been nominated by the king. This method had been possible as long as Canada belonged to France, but it became impossible the moment the country was transferred to Britain. A Roman Catholic king might pick a Roman Catholic bishop, but a Protestant king certainly could not. Vaudreuil suggested therefore that the French monarch retain his right to nominate to the see of Quebec. Of course there were also political motives behind the proposal, and they must have leaped to Amherst's eye. By imposing his veto he left the great question unsolved.

Only comfortable critics at Versailles could condemn the surrender of the country upon these terms. They were just and generous, and do equal honor to the Canadian governor and the British commander. Vaudreuil demanded everything that was essential to the honor of the troops and the welfare of the people, and Amherst denied nothing that he could possibly have granted, except the honors of war to the garrison. This exception was but a detail of the moment. The only thing that really mattered in the transaction signed on September 8, 1760, was the transfer of a country and its people from one empire to another for a period at least and possibly for all time.

Many tears have been shed over these foundlings on the banks of the St. Lawrence, exhausted materially and physically by a bankrupt government and a vain war, deserted by an unnatural and extravagant mother, and endangered spiritually by falling under the yoke of an alien and heretical government. Even heaven seemed to have betrayed them in their hour of trial by stealing away their bishop. This pitiful picture of these people in 1760 is of more than ephemeral interest. It is one of the most important and abiding things in Canadian history, for the glorious contrast presented by the condition of their children in successive generations has been and will continue to be the chief inspiration of the French Canadian race.

But the pathos of their plight on the morrow of the conquest must not be overdrawn. New France was already separated from Old France by more than the Atlantic. The country that gave birth to the colony was not the same country when she lost it, for she was sickening with the disease that was soon to shock the world.

Nor had the colony stood still. Like the English colonies, it had been quietly drifting away from Europe and may even have drifted further, for immigration to Canada had ceased two generations before, whereas English recruits were still pouring into the colonies to the south. Thus cut off, and living under very different conditions from Frenchmen at home, the Canadians tended to become conscious that they were a distinct people. The historic antipathy between Montcalm and the Canadian-born Vaudreuil was tragic testimony to the growing estrangement. Although the final separation did not come in hate, there was a drop of bitterness in the cup whenever Caandians drank to the health of their lost mother, for had not France really abandoned them to their fate? This touch of resentment went far to neutralize the romantic feeling that the severance of the tie added to their filial affection.

The chief love of the Canadians was for Canada and not for France. The fortunes of war revealed this truth and the blessings of peace were to emphasize it. Never was a people more war-weary than were the Canadians in 1760. For generations they had been fighting, first redskins and then white men, until they could fight no more. Now, in a great revulsion from war, they reverted to type, as far as was possible in the New World, and struck ever deeper roots into the soil. Paradoxical as it may seem, they had been forced to live an unnatural life under governors of their own blood, but under rulers of an alien race they were to find themselves.

One other important factor in their situation at this time was long obscured by the legend of a social decapitation. It used to be said that the better classes as a whole retired to France after the conquest, leaving behind only a helpless and hopeless mass. This tradition was doubly false. In the first place, most of the so-called better classes clung to the colony. In the second place, these were not the real leaders of the people. Although the wealthier seigniorial families lent grace to the society of the towns, chiefly Quebec, and many of the noblesse had distinguished themselves in numerous campaigns and more numerous forays, the real leaders of the people were two classes of men who sprang from their own midst and remained in daily and intimate contact with them — the curés and the captains of militia. They were the true shepherds, and they never for one moment dreamed of deserting their flocks.[2]

CHAPTER II

THE FIRST WINTER OF THE BRITISH IN CANADA

THE military heel has ground out groans from conquered people in many lands. But the rule of the soldier, though proverbially heavy, was particularly light in Canada during the first few years of British rule. These years are known as the military régime or the *règne militaire*. Until permanently ceded by treaty, Canada was only a temporary possession of uncertain future and, in accordance with the customs of war, was occupied and administered by the victorious army. But the Peace of Paris, which was signed on February 10, 1763, did not terminate this régime at once. It had to be continued until a regular civil government was established, which was not until August 10, 1764. This date was fixed inferentially by one of the terms of the treaty, which gave all Canadians the right to retain their French allegiance by withdrawing from the colony before that time. For eighteen months after the treaty, therefore, the population of Canada could not be regarded as wholly and finally British. Thus the military régime lasted for nearly five years in the district of Quebec and for nearly four years in the rest of the country.

During this period the colony had three governments, each quite independent of the others. The first, that of Quebec, arose immediately after the capital of Canada was captured on September 18, 1759, almost a year before the governments of Montreal and of Three Rivers were established. In his secret instructions Wolfe had been directed to appoint a governor for the place when it fell.[1] This duty now devolved upon General Monckton, who had sufficiently recovered from his wound to resume the command from Townshend. As the latter did not wish to remain, the offer of the governorship was naturally made to the next senior officer, Brigadier General James Murray, who accepted the honor. His appointment was arranged in a "council of war" on September 21,[2] but was not actually made until October 23.[3] At the same time, Monckton appointed Lieutenant Colonel Ralph Burton to be lieutenant gov-

13

ernor, and Murray selected Captain Hector Theophilus Cramahé as his secretary. Burton, the son of a Yorkshire attorney, was to leave no impression as lieutenant governor of Quebec, and even though he became military governor of Three Rivers and later of Montreal, and then succeeded to the command of the troops in the colony on the establishment of civil government in 1764, he remains little more than a shadow.[4] Cramahé, on the other hand, became a very much better known figure in the life of the country with whose government he was intimately associated for nearly twenty years as secretary, councilor, acting receiver general, judge, and lieutenant governor. In him Murray made an excellent choice, for he was a businesslike officer, and his French blood, much stronger than the faith he inherited from his Huguenot ancestors, bound him in deep sympathy to the Canadians.

James Murray, as military governor of Quebec and later as the first British governor of Canada, was to leave a much greater mark on the history of the country. He was born in January, 1721, the fifth son of the fourth Lord Elibank of the Scottish peerage. His formal schooling, which lasted until he was fifteen years old, was probably very thorough, for it was all in Scotland, and the letters he wrote in later life bear the stamp of a fine education. There is a family tradition that he was originally destined for the bar, and this may very well be true, for two of his elder brothers entered the army and the other two went into the navy and the church. He left school, however, the year after his father's death, to commence his military career as a cadet in a Scottish unit in the Dutch service, to which he was drawn by family connection. At the age of nineteen he received his first commission in the British army. The time was most auspicious, for Britain was beginning that series of wars that filled the middle years of the eighteenth century and were marked with British victories all over the world. After serving in the West Indies and on the continent of Europe, Murray came to America in 1757 with the rank of lieutenant colonel and shared in the capture of Louisburg in the following year. He was one of the three brigadiers under General Wolfe, who had a high regard for him. He commanded the left wing of the army in the battle on the Plains of Abraham.

There was not a drop of cold blood in the veins of James Murray. His forceful personality fired men with either love or hate, and he returned their sentiments with equal warmth. Even in this distant day, those who bury themselves in the correspondence of that time feel the spell of his character and have to guard against the temptation to be for him or against him. He had all the pride of a soldier and of a Highlander, and this pride frequently touched off his explosive temper. Some might say that he was ill tempered, but this would hardly be fair, because noble feelings quite as often roused his ire. His sense of justice was as delicate as his pride, and the welfare of those who were placed under his charge was much dearer to him than his own interests. Indeed, the strongest passion which this forthright man was to manifest during his seven years in Canada was pity for the whole Canadian race. This pity was deep-rooted, for he knew more than their tongue: he knew their hearts, and they quickly learned to love him.[5]

The first year of the military government of Quebec was quite different from the following four years. Murray's primary duty was military — to hold what Wolfe had won — and this was no holiday task. With a garrison of seventy-three hundred, of whom less than forty-nine hundred rank and file were fit for duty, he had to maintain the wreck of a city against French forces that might outnumber him several times. Moreover, he was in a hostile country whereas his enemies were at home. More formidable still was the winter, which was doubly his foe. It was to him what the British fleet was to the French, a barrier that cut off all hope of relief. It also laid close siege to all his men, particularly the Highlanders, and wrought great havoc among them, for their scanty garments and their excessive duties exposed them unduly. Having received no issue of clothing that year, they were reduced to such expedients as cutting up blankets for mittens, stockings, and shirts; and to keep from freezing in their billets they had to toil like horses in harness, drawing endless loads of fuel from the neighboring woods. These grim "sleighing parties" cost hundreds of toes. Because proper provisions for the men's sustenance were also lacking, a diet saturated with salt sent hundreds of men to the hospital and even to their death. French, frost, and food reduced the effective rank and file to thirty-five hundred by March 24, 1760. A month later, when the Chevalier de Lévis mustered nine thousand to retake Quebec before the British fleet came up the St. Lawrence, Murray could place only three thousand on the field of Ste. Foy.

This battle of April 28, 1760, was his one military blunder. His only justification for attempting a pitched battle was a desire to emulate Wolfe. He was in a very different position from that of Montcalm in the previous September. A victory in the field was unnecessary and would have cost him more than it was worth. But instead of victory he found defeat, and he lost more than a third of his remaining effectives. He nearly lost much more than that, for the defeated soldiers, falling into a panic, threatened to ruin what was left of the town and themselves by breaking open stores and houses and draining all the liquor they could seize. Fortunately for the British, the French let slip this alcoholic opportunity. "Had they followed their blow on the 28th, 29th, or 30th, before the soldiers recollected themselves," said Captain Knox, "I am strongly inclined to think, notwithstanding the active zeal and spirit of the governors and officers in general, Quebec would have reverted to its old masters." Murray restored order by hanging a man "*in terrorem,* without any trial," and by spilling the spirits to be found in the Lower Town.[6] The arrival of the frigate "Lowestoffe" on May 9 reinforced the morale, though not the numbers, of the besieged, for it was the harbinger of the approaching fleet. Eight days later, fearing to be caught in a trap, Lévis and his army scuttled away up the river.

Murray, who had just received confirmation from home of his appointment as governor, was now undoubted master of the lower part of the colony, but still his first concern was military — to carry out the previous year's plan for taking the whole country. Accordingly he embarked on July 14 and proceeded up the St. Lawrence by easy stages,[7] receiving the submission of the inhabitants as he went along, to place himself under the immediate command of General Amherst. He reached Montreal at the same time as his superior but did not remain with him. As Vaudreuil surrendered promptly, Murray returned at once to Quebec, and thenceforth his chief business was government.

Though military considerations were paramount during this first year, they did not close Murray's mind to the needs of government. Indeed, they quickened his appreciation of something that was all-important — the attitude of the inhabitants. Their hostility might ruin him and his little army, and therefore they must be won over. This narrow calculation was not the only cause of his large view. He saw clearly "that the conquest of the land, if bereaved of its inhabitants and stock, would be of little value," [8] and he felt deeply for the Canadians, who, he said, were "plundered and oppressed" by their own army. Only two months after the capture of Quebec, in a letter to Amherst, Murray struck the keynote of his Canadian career. "Everybody will inform you how powerful and how flourishing this colony was, and how formidable it might be under any other government than that of Monsr. Vaudreuil. *En bonne politique,* it should be perhaps destroyed, but there may be reasons why it should remain, as it is a guarantee for the good behaviour of its neighbouring colonies. It is not with me to judge, I know, it is in your power now to decide the fate of Canada. Until I have the honour to receive your orders, I shall follow the natural disposition of my heart, which dictates clemency. This conduct can do no hurt, because the effects of it may be undone in one week. It may have a permanent advantage. The Canadians have been taught to look upon [us] as barbarians whose only view was their destruction; hence the obstinate resistance they have made, and the eagerness they shewed to take up arms against us. They begin now to be astonished with our conduct, will soon be convinced that there was no deceit in it, and hardly will hereafter be easily persuaded to take up arms against a nation they admire, and who will have it always in their [power] to burn or destroy. Sufficient examples they have [had] this summer of the horrors of war. They were n[ever] treated tenderly before we had the good fortune to [take] Quebec. They will remember that no doubt and it [may] be supposed they will not forget any instances of [humanity] and generosity that may be shewn them since [they] have been entirely in our power." [9]

Murray was giving voice to more than his own thoughts. He was expressing the feelings of the army under him. Although some soldiers were tempted to continue the war on their own account by plundering the natives, they were exceptions, and at least one of them was hanged as an example to the others. With the fall of Quebec, the barrier of hostility between French and British crumbled. At once the inhabitants of Beauport received the happy soldiers with open arms and made them happier still with wine and such other refreshments as they possessed, and the people generally began to flock in to surrender their arms and make their submission. Just one week after the capitulation, Captain Knox recorded in his journal: "it is with the utmost satisfaction that I have daily ocular experience of the most distinguished humanity and generosity in our worthy soldiers; they not only share their provisions with the distressed Canadians, but even their small allowance of rum: today I saw above twenty of our men assisting those poor people in cutting and binding their sheaves of corn; they being within the district of the post where I was on duty, I went towards them, and, asking the soldiers what they were to get for their labour, they replied, 'They sought not any thing; what they did was out of good will to the poor creatures, who had little enough for themselves.' One of them added, 'It would be rank murder to take any thing from the poor devils, for they have lost enough already.' While I stood reflecting on the matchless goodness of our honest Britons, with the oddity of the foregoing speech, I saw a peasant take from his pocket a sealskin pouch, which they all refused: one of them instantly produced a rusty iron box that was also filled with tobacco, and tendered it to the Canadian, saying, 'When it is out, I know where to get more; perhaps that is not your case, poor man!' " [10] Nor was the new-found harmony between conqueror and conquered confined to men in the harvest field, as may be inferred from the general orders that were issued shortly to stop soldiers from marrying the inhabitants.

Although a few hearts may have been blighted by this command, countless other hearts were delighted by another command in these same general orders. It enjoined all officers, on meeting religious processions in the streets, "to pay them the compliment of the hat, because it is a civility due to the people who have chosen to live under the protection of our laws"; or, if their Protestant consciences were too sturdy, they were to retire on the approach of any procession.[11] Though the few Jesuit fathers were turned out of their college that it might be used as a storehouse and barrack, the hundred nuns of the General Hospital, the Hôtel Dieu, and the Ursuline Convent were very differently treated, for they were true sisters of mercy to the British garrison. Perhaps prudery as well as pity inspired Ursuline fingers to knit stockings for bare-legged Scots,[12] but no such mixed motives led the inmates of the three houses to care for the sick, whose numbers grew daily until they were well over two thousand. By their tender nursing these sisters did more than save hundreds of British lives. They did much to heal the spiritual wounds that war inflicts, and perhaps contributed more

than any other influence to the friendly relations that drew conqueror and conquered together.

In pity for their poverty as well as in gratitude for their Christian
services, Monckton gave the nuns of the General Hospital four
hundred pounds before he departed, and throughout the winter
Murray issued provisions to the three communities and saw that
they were supplied with fuel. One incident illustrating their spirit
and the governor's attitude is worth special mention. While sitting
at a table in the Ursuline Convent, Murray signed the death warrant of a soldier who had broken through the guard protecting the
General Hospital and tried to enter the convent. He did not die,
however, for the nuns interceded in his behalf and the general pardoned the culprit. Murray's memory, which all the communities of
Quebec still cherish, is a touching reminder of the countless civilities
that passed at this time.[13]

Murray first strengthened his hold over the country parishes by
dismissing to their homes, as soon as they were disarmed and had
taken an oath of allegiance, all the militia who had been serving in
the town. His next step was to issue a circular letter to the curés
and captains of militia to take a census of their respective parishes.[14]
The information thus gathered was soon to aid in the discovery of
absentees, who were presumably with the opposing army. He also
sent a circular order through the countryside requiring the people in
each locality to deposit their arms with the captain of militia and
making him responsible for their custody. To complete the submission of the population, he used detachments of his own troops.

The instructions to Captain Leslie,[15] who led a party of two
hundred down the south shore during December, illustrate how this
was done. Taking the census with him, he was to oblige each captain of militia to submit a list of those who were still with the
French colors. All their effects, cattle, sheep, and corn, were to be
lodged with this local official, who was to be answerable for them
until the troops returned on their upward journey, and then were
to be destroyed or carried off. Two men in each parish, whom the
curé was to nominate and for whose good conduct he was to be
responsible, were to keep their guns for purposes of the chase, but
all other arms were to be confiscated. Leslie was also to administer
an oath of allegiance to the inhabitants and to enjoin obedience by
requiring each curé to read a public manifesto and then paste it

upon his church door. To make doubly sure that obedience would be secured, he was to bring back one hostage from each parish. Lest such an expedition defeat its own end, Leslie was to pay for carriages and all other contingencies, and was to "be particularly careful to ma[ke] the troops under his command observe strict [discipline] and a just decorum towards the inhabitants, tha[t they] may be sensible of the equity of our government."

The party was to have proceeded to the end of settlement, but it did not enter the lower parishes because they had been so completely burned that the men could have found no lodging. When they returned to Pointe Lévis on Christmas Day, every one of them had been bitten by the frost. But otherwise they were able to give a good account of their expedition.

The following entry in Murray's diary on the last day of 1759 is a pleasing retrospect: "Much had been done here within these three last months, if rightly considered. Quebec had only capitulated for itself, but now the province from the Cap Rouge on the northern and from the Chaudière on the southern shore had submitted; the inhabitants had taken an oath of fidelity, and surrendered their arms; my orders were obeyed everywhere within this extent, and the parishes within reach of the garrison assisted to carry in our wood; they furnished bullocks for our use, hay, straw and oats for the draft cattle." Since he was in so strong a position, it may seem surprising that Murray did not spare his troops by forcing the habitants to cut and draw all the necessary fuel for the garrison, but his concern for "the equity of our government" stayed his hand. Instead of compelling them, therefore, he only invited them to provide fuel, and for their services, even in supplying the General Hospital, he promised to pay full value.

To retain the people in their duty, as he said, Murray also established a civil jurisdiction among them. Early in December he appointed a judge for the near-by parishes of Charlesbourg, Beauport, and Petite Rivière.[16] Toward the end of January he did the same for the south shore, which he divided at Berthier (*en bas*).[17] Unfortunately little is known about these courts. Only one commission [18] has been found, that of Allier, who was criminal and civil judge for the district between Berthier and Kamouraska, and the only records that have survived are those of the other south-shore court.[19] They are all in French, and the judgments are supported by the signatures of three French names, Saillant, Frémont, and Lajus. The north-shore judge bore the name of Cugnet and was probably Joseph Etienne Cugnet, who had been a member of the old superior council and was soon to be given another appoint ment by Murray.

Though the people in the country parishes were left pretty much to themselves, except in so far as was necessary to insure their submission, a closer regulation was needed within the town of Quebec. Here Murray anticipated his creation of the first country court by nearly four weeks. On November 12, 1759,[20] he established a civil jurisdiction for the inhabitants of the capital, appointing Colonel John Young chief judge. In this capacity Young sat in his lodgings, near the Castle of St. Louis, every Tuesday and Friday morning, and was apparently assisted by Canadians. In the placard announcing this appointment, Murray included several orders for the proper policing of the place. All communication within the walls was free; only at the gates were people liable to be stopped by sentries. Every inhabitant receiving anyone from the country had to report him at once to the governor's secretary that he might be examined. This measure, however, was not directed against those who might bring in provisions, for they were to be encouraged. Lights in all houses had to be out by nine o'clock, and no civilian could venture on the streets after nightfall without carrying a lantern, a regulation that was to cause amusing trouble some months later. Every inhabitant suffering the least injury or insult from a soldier was directed to apply to the nearest guardhouse, the officer of which was ordered to arrest and hold the accused for trial. About this time, also, all the tinsmiths in the army were busy with their tools turning out lamps to be hung at the corners of the streets and in other convenient places, and by the middle of December Quebec had its first street-lighting system, maintained by the various regiments.[21]

Two days after the posting of the placard already mentioned, Murray issued another important order. "As drunkenness and theft continued to reign predominant vices in the garrison," runs his diary for November 14, "I recalled all licenses and ordered for the future every man who was found drunk to receive twenty lashes every morning till he acknowledged where he got it, and forfeit his allowance of rum for six weeks." Within the next week he had two women who belonged to the army whipped through the streets for

selling rum to the soldiers, and a short time afterwards he had the
same penalty inflicted on a couple of inhabitants "for appearing
abroad at an unseasonable time of night, without a lanthorn, contrary to repeated orders." [22] Though such punishment seems harsh,
it was seldom imposed [23] and was probably justified. As the French
outposts were close at hand, the safety of the garrison depended
upon the utmost vigilance. At all costs the governor had to preserve
the sobriety of his troops and to prevent possible enemies prowling
around under cover of the night.

When the French forces led by De Lévis advanced for a last
great effort to save the colony by retaking its capital, Murray was
driven to adopt the much more drastic measure of ordering all the
inhabitants to clear out of the town. But even then, such was his
consideration, he gave them three days to move, he allowed them to
carry their effects with them, he appointed the Récollet Convent as
a repository for all the belongings they left behind, he invited them
to choose two of their number to remain as guardians of this property, and, for greater security, he mounted a special guard over the
depot. [24]

Of the economic problems that pressed upon the harassed governor, the one of most immediate importance was lack of funds.
His first impulse was to issue a paper currency, [25] but he soon saw
that hard cash was necessary in a country already flooded with
paper. The British merchants who accompanied the army as sutlers
might have been able to relieve his necessity if they had not found
means to smuggle money up to Montreal for the purchase of furs.
Therefore he had no other recourse than to a public appeal, which
he made in a proclamation on November 25, offering five per cent
interest and the personal security of his own and Burton's signatures. Of the eight thousand pounds which he thus secured, one-
quarter came from the noncommissioned officers and privates of one
regiment, the Highlanders. [26] Many of the soldiers in the other units
may have regretted their public spirit, for they received no pay
between October and the following summer.

The first economic regulation that Murray issued, on November
23, was a currency ordinance. [27] Bigot's paper was still in circulation, and in addition to this many coins now made their appearance,
having been imported with the army or tempted out of Canadian
hiding-places. The value of the paper was very doubtful and the

value of the coins very uncertain, for they were of various origins, British, French, Spanish, and Portuguese. The result was growing confusion and increasing disputes. Murray therefore stopped the use of paper, which he branded as "a manifest imposition on the public" — words suggesting that he acted from political as well as economic motives — and he fixed the value of each of the other kinds of money. The scale he adopted gave to each a greater than its intrinsic value. This appreciation was in general accord with colonial practice, which arose out of the difficulty of preserving a sound currency in new countries. The guinea was to pass for one pound three shillings and fourpence, and all other coins in proportion. For example, the Spanish dollar, a much commoner piece in America, was to be reckoned as five shillings instead of four shillings and sixpence, its equivalent in sterling. This particular rate, for there was no uniformity throughout the colonies, was that which had been established in Massachusetts and then adopted in Halifax, and was therefore to be known in Canada as Halifax currency. In spite of later efforts to dislodge it, this was to remain the customary standard in the colony.

After settling the circulating medium, the next problem was that of high prices. Though it was now illegal to pay or receive the old paper, the effect of this inflated currency lingered, supported by the general scarcity of goods. To remedy the evil, both British and French traders were summoned to consult with Colonel Young. Apparently the prices of many commodities were then fixed and published, but the details are unknown, for the only extant record of this proceeding is a general reference in Captain Knox's journal.[28] Ten days later Murray issued an order to regulate the prices of grain and flour, which had become exorbitant.[29] Though he made a naïve entry in his diary implying that this order might discourage those who could supply the market, he had some hopes that it would keep down the price of bread. In this he was disappointed, for some bakers sold "black bread, badly baked" at more than a shilling a pound. This abuse drew from him two further ordinances,[30] one for the British and one for the Canadians, in which he also dealt with the butchers. The best white bread was to sell for fivepence or ten sous a pound, the "middling sort" for fourpence or eight sous, and brown bread for threepence or six sous; butchers were to retail beef at fivepence or ten sous a pound, and mutton and veal at sixpence or twelve sous. Every butcher and baker had to take out a license from the governor's secretary. The penalty for failing to procure a license, or for selling above these prices, was a fine of five pounds or one hundred livres for the first offense and for the second offense imprisonment if the culprit were British, corporal punishment if he were Canadian.

Apparently there was no regular market until the end of May, when the whole situation had changed as a result of the retirement of the French army and the arrival of the British fleet. Then a daily market was established in the suburb of St. Roch, where the country people brought fresh meat, fish, eggs, butter, and milk. Every morning, from sunrise until noon, a quartermaster was stationed there "to see proper order observed, and justice done to the people that come from the country," and sentries were posted to prevent anyone, particularly officers' servants, from going out to buy of the country folk on their way to market. Murray's chief concern was lest Quebec supply the French army with provisions, of which it was very short, and therefore, though he allowed officers and soldiers to barter salt provisions for fresh, he forbade all others giving anything but money in exchange.[31]

In the latter part of May, five or six days after the siege of Quebec was raised, Murray was presented with another problem by the surrender of the King's Posts down the river. These were at Malbaye, later Murray Bay; Tadousac, at the mouth of the Saguenay; Chicoutimi, about a hundred miles up that stream; the Iles Jérémie, on the north side of the St. Lawrence almost opposite Father Point; and the Sept Iles, more than a hundred and fifty miles below. Except the first, which had a farm, these were merely fur-trading establishments, but they were different in character from the posts around the Great Lakes. The Indians who frequented them were particularly improvident and generally inferior, and therefore could not be treated in the same way as the redskins farther west. Realizing this, the old government had wavered between two policies. Sometimes it had leased these posts for six or seven hundred livres per annum, but at the end it had been managing them as a part of the public domain. In return for supplies advanced by the clerk at each post, the natives gave half their furs to the king; the rest were purchased at stated prices. The appearance of the British fleet in 1759 interfered with the furnishing of the posts, so that the

French who were employed at them and the Indians who visited them were nearly famished. One of the establishments, Sept Iles, was abandoned, and Murray feared that the others might be; if that happened, the new government would lose a possible source of riches. Therefore he appointed an agent on June 23 to take charge of the posts. He was ordered to collect the furs in the hands of the clerks, but the navy anticipated him by seizing the magazines. By Lord Colville's orders, the contents were judged lawful prize and sold for fifteen hundred pounds, and Murray could only protest that the furs really belonged to the king. This untoward incident did not wreck the governor's plan, for he had already enlisted the interest of the merchant whom he had chosen as agent by giving him a temporary monopoly of the trade at those places. This merchant, it is interesting to observe, was Thomas Ainslie, who had served Murray before either of them had set eyes on Canada and was soon to attain prominence in the colony as the collector of customs, an office which he held until his death more than a generation later.[32]

Shortly before leaving to cooperate with Amherst in the reduction of Montreal, Murray was troubled by a ghost that he thought he had laid some months before. When denouncing the old paper in his currency ordinance of November 23, he had been unaware that the French government had anticipated his action after its own fashion. On October 15, 1759, a royal decree had suspended payment on Canadian paper. As soon as this was known in Montreal, where Vaudreuil and Bigot were still exercising their offices, they issued a circular on June 15, 1760, informing the people of the suspension and also of the royal promise to redeem the paper by degrees after the war was over. In less than a fortnight a copy of this pronouncement reached the governor of Quebec, and he published a counterblast, to be read by the militia captains at the doors of all the churches, ridiculing the idea of France ever meeting these obligations.[33] As in the previous November, he was moved by a sound political instinct which sought to turn the minds of the Canadians away from France and toward Britain. Until the surrender of the colony, it was good propaganda to discredit the value of this currency, but then a new attitude became necessary, as will appear in the following chapter.

CHAPTER III

THE CANADIANS UNDER MILITARY RULE

WHEN Amherst became master of the whole country on September 8, 1760, he faced the problem of how to hold it securely. The first essential was a garrison. In arranging this he apparently sought to interfere as little as possible with the existing organization of the troops. Most of the line regiments that he had led into the colony he stationed in or around Montreal, while to Quebec he allotted all of Murray's units except two, one of which he detached to occupy Three Rivers.[1] It will be observed that this garrison comprised only regulars. All the provincials he sent away within a week of the capitulation. Two hundred rangers under Major Robert Rogers, who bore letters from Vaudreuil, set out to receive the surrender of the upper posts. The other colonials went off first to finish the works at Chambly on the Richelieu and at Fort William Augustus [2] and Oswegatchie on the upper St. Lawrence, and later to proceed home.

The removal of the colonial troops was a great blessing, for their minds were stained with many bloody memories of partisan warfare. The line regiments were much more welcome guests, and the *rapprochement* between conqueror and conquered that Murray had witnessed in Quebec, Amherst observed throughout the colony on his tour of inspection before he departed for New York. The soldiers and the inhabitants on whom they were quartered commonly shared their provisions and ate together at the same board. Indeed, when any of the men were moved to be nearer the rest of their units, it was not unusual for the Canadians with whom they had been living to plead that they might keep their new-found friends.[3]

Amherst had also to provide the colony with a government, for the conquest was followed immediately by an administrative decapitation. All the old salaried officials retired to France with the defeated army. Their withdrawal was natural, since they were not natives of Canada and they hoped for new preferments at home or in other parts of the French empire. Their departure may also have been sped by the attitude of the victorious commander-in-chief, who had flatly refused to continue the old form of government. To fill the void he had no thought of erecting a whole new system. That was a task for the home government when the time should come. His duty was merely to find a temporary substitute. What was needed was something that could be started right away and could be worked easily — a simple scheme.

It has sometimes been said that Amherst cut the colony into the three parts, over each of which he placed an officer as governor. But Amherst did not divide the colony. He simply continued a division that had been in existence in the French régime — the three administrative districts of Montreal, Three Rivers, and Quebec, the first two meeting at Berthier on the north shore and Yamaska Bay on the opposite side of the St. Lawrence, and the second two joining at Ste. Anne on the north and St. Pierre de Bequets on the south. On September 16 he appointed Burton to the "vacant" government of Three Rivers,[4] and six days later he placed Brigadier General Thomas Gage over the more important district of Montreal.[5] Apparently he had no thought of superseding Murray, who had received a royal commission as governor of the town, the lines and fortifications, and the dependencies of Quebec. There was some doubt, however, about the extent of the authority thus conferred. Therefore on October 3 Amherst appointed Murray governor over the remainder of the old district.[6] Incidentally, no other military governor received a royal parchment, but the only difference this made was that Murray drew an extra pound a day and carried his head a little higher.

Amherst has sometimes been called the first British governor of Canada, but this is not true. The only titles he used at this time were those of governor of Virginia and commander-in-chief. It was solely in the latter capacity that he exercised any authority over the whole of the newly conquered country. Theoretically he ruled the colony from his headquarters in New York; practically the military governors ruled it according to the general directions he laid down in the beginning. Though they wrote regular reports to him, his subsequent interference, except in purely military matters, was negligible. Nor did the home government interfere, though at least Murray corresponded directly with civil officials in London.

Another feature of the French régime Amherst did more than continue; he developed it to be the pivot of the government in each locality. This was the captain of militia, who was transformed into a British functionary by the receipt of a new commission, his old one having become invalid with the cession of the country. At once he was ordered to assemble the male inhabitants to disarm them and to administer the oath of allegiance. He himself, however, was allowed to retain a firelock to assist in preserving good order and discipline in his village, for he was to be its policeman.[7] He also became its magistrate.[8] This new function he acquired as a consequence of Amherst's desire to have all disputes between the inhabitants settled, as much as possible, among themselves and by their own laws. Of course there were bound to be some cases too difficult to be determined by this general factotum of the government in each parish; and these, according to Amherst's orders, were to be brought before the British officer commanding in the locality, who in turn was to submit them when necessary to the military governor. The jurisdiction of the captain of militia also stopped short of serious crimes, such as theft and murder, for which, as might be expected, the commander-in-chief prescribed military law.

Amherst's concern for the Canadians appears in the following injunction, which he issued to Murray, Gage, and Burton. "As the inhabitants of this country are now as much His Majesty's subjects as any of us, and so long as they remain deserving of it, are entitled to the same protection, I would have you particularly give it in charge to the troops under your command to live in good harmony and brotherhood with them and to avoid all differences whatsoever." The same feeling is more fully revealed by a document [9] which he prepared for the enlightenment of the people. This document bears the date September 22, and is known as a "placard," because it was posted up all over the country at the doors of the churches. While proclaiming the disarmament of the population, it invited all who desired arms for hunting to apply to their respective military governors, or their deputies, for permits to enjoy this privilege. It announced the continuance of their old captains of militia and the new authority with which these officials were invested. Other paragraphs conveyed the information that the army of occupation, being provided for in kind, was to give cash for everything procured from the inhabitants. Carriage services were to be paid for at the rate of ten shillings a day in New York currency for each cart or sleigh and three shillings for each horse. Another tariff was issued for masters of posthouses, an old institution continued without question, and they were instructed to furnish only those who bore written orders. The next sentence, though long, is worth quotation in full: "The meagre support which Canada has received from France during the last two years having exhausted her wealth, provisions and necessaries, we have for the common good of the troops and the inhabitants requested by our letters to the different governors of the English colonies nearest to Canada that they have posted up and published notices to their colonists to repair hither with all kinds of commodities and provisions, and we flatter ourselves that there will be no delay in carrying out this plan for you, and when it is done, every person will be notified in order that he may participate in it at current prices and without duty." Commerce was declared free to all. Traders were required to obtain passports from the governors, but these were to be furnished gratis. The placard concludes with a passage which matches that from the instructions to the military governors quoted above: "As it is specially enjoined on the troops to live with the habitants in harmony and good fellowship, we likewise recommend the habitant to receive and treat the troops as brothers and fellow-citizens." The rest of the passage promised the Canadians "the same privileges as the ancient subjects of the King," if they obeyed those who were placed in authority over them.

Amherst's plan for the administration of the colony suggests at first glance that he drew upon Murray's year of experience in governing Canadians. But the two men had scarcely met in Montreal before they parted company, and Murray, on his return to Quebec, wrote back to his chief pleading for guidance and beseeching him, "I wish to God you would come down yourself." [10] Amherst, moreover, formulated his scheme before he left Montreal, and no one then seems to have observed any connection with what the governor of Quebec had done. If any credit had been due Murray, he would have been the first to claim it, for that was his nature, and Amherst would probably have given it ungrudgingly, for he was very tender of the feelings of his junior. The similarity between the work of the two men arises, in all probability, from the simple fact that they were both using ordinary common sense under somewhat similar circumstances.

The home government gave its blessing to all Amherst's arrangements in Canada. The blessing was conveyed in a letter Amherst received from Lord Egremont, Pitt's successor as secretary of state, written on December 12, 1761.[11] The letter did not stop with an expression of approval but went on to observe that "nothing can be more essential to His Majesty's service than to retain as many of the French subjects as may be." Therefore, continued the secretary of state, the commander-in-chief was to press upon the different governors "the conciliating part" of their instructions, and to "recommend it strongly to them to employ the most vigilant attention and take the most effectual care that the French inhabitants . . . be humanely and kindly treated, and that they do enjoy the full benefit of that indulgent and benign government which already characterizes His Majesty's auspicious reign and constitutes the peculiar happiness of all who are subjects to the British Empire." He was also to see that the governors "give the strictest orders to prevent all soldiers, mariners and others . . . from insulting or reviling any of the French inhabitants, now their fellow subjects, either by ungenerous insinuation of that inferiority which the fate of war has decided, or by harsh and provoking observations on their language, dress, manners, customs, or country, or by uncharitable reflections on the errors of that mistaken religion which they unhappily profess." The pertinent passages in this letter were copied in New York and forwarded to Canada, where they were given the wide publication they deserved. Needless to say, such orders were obeyed ere ever they were issued, but they are of value as an expression of the attitude of the British government toward the conquered race.

When Amherst departed from Quebec on October 5, 1760, he was really passing out of Canadian history, though his claim to the Jesuits' estates was to be a troublesome ghost in later years. Of the military governors whom he left behind and now left pretty much to themselves, Murray and Burton have already been noticed, but the ruler of Montreal has been only mentioned. Thomas Gage was of the same age as Murray, but he had an English temper even though his father was an Irish peer. Having come to America with Braddock, he had lost some blood and gained some honor in the disaster which overwhelmed that unfortunate general. In October, 1763, he was promoted to succeed Amherst in New York, where he remained till 1772. Two years later, as governor of Massachusetts, he returned to this continent, where the rising revolution soon reduced his reputation. The government, however, was juster than fate, for he was promoted to the full rank of general five years before his death in 1787. The Canadians as a whole were happy under their military governors, but none seems to have been more acceptable to them than was this man during his three years' stay in Montreal. Indeed, he had not been long in this place before they paid him a delightful compliment in a pun upon his name. They said that Amherst had left *un Gage précieux* [12] of his goodness toward them.

More important in the history of Canada was another individual who presided over the government of Three Rivers from May, 1762, to March, 1763, when Burton was off campaigning in Cuba, and seven months later received the appointment of military governor of that district when Burton stepped up to fill Gage's place in Montreal. This was Frederick Haldimand. A French Swiss born at Yverdun in the canton of Neuchâtel in 1718, he had chosen, like many of his countrymen, the career of a soldier of fortune. After some years of knocking about Europe in the Sardinian, the Prussian, and the Dutch armies, he entered the British service on the eve of the Seven Years' War. He was attracted by the offer of a commission as lieutenant colonel and the command of a battalion in a regiment to be raised from among the foreign Protestants in America, a regiment known first as the Royal Americans and later as the Sixtieth Foot. Crossing the Atlantic, he wandered up and down the old colonies recruiting his unit, and then he plunged into the fray. At Ticonderoga in March, 1758, he won distinction at the price of a slight wound. In the following summer he rebuilt Fort Oswego and repelled a combined force of French and savages under St. Luc de la Corne, and finally he accompanied Amherst down the St. Lawrence to Montreal, where he remained as second in command until he first relieved and then replaced Burton at Three Rivers. It is not in this capacity, however, that he is chiefly remembered, but as the governor of Canada during and after the American Revolution and as the industrious collector of all the documents upon which he could lay his hands. The two hundred and thirty-two volumes of Haldimand manuscripts in the British Museum are one of the richest quarries for students of Canadian history.

Of the four men who had charge of the three military governments,[13] it is important to observe that none was separated by the bar of language from the people over whom he ruled. Indeed, Murray could be as eloquent in French as in English, which is saying a great deal, while Haldimand was still so little master of the English tongue that Gage sometimes preferred to address him in French. The officers whom these four chose as their secretaries, and through whose hands all the details of administration passed, were no less familiar with the language of the Canadians. They all bore French names — Cramahé, Maturin, Bruyères, and Gugy. Of the second, who served Gage, and the third, who moved with Burton to Montreal, little is known except that they were, like Cramahé, of French families settled in the British Isles. These two appear only as names during the military régime and then they vanish. Conrad Gugy, on the other hand, was a French Swiss like his master Haldimand, and, though he never attained Cramahé's prominence, he became quite a person in the colony, settling down as seignior of Machiche, where he later took charge of the first loyalists who sought a refuge in Canada.

The government, which was thus partly French above, was entirely French below, for the whole of the administration was carried on through the agency of the Canadian militia officers. They were the hands, the eyes, the ears, and the mouth of the government. On Sundays, after listening to the words of God from the curé, the habitants heard the words of the government from the captain of militia, just as in the days of old. According to custom, also, these orders of man were posted on the church door to stimulate rather than to refresh the memories of the people, for most of them were unlettered; and the lay official's duty, like that of the curé, was to see that the commands he uttered on Sunday were observed on week days. In this he seems to have been quite effectual, for, though he could not threaten eternal punishment, he was the local instrument of temporal authority.

The administration of justice during the military régime was not exactly the same in the three governments, though in all the captains of militia served as justices of the peace, and appeals lay to British army officers, according to Amherst's directions. In Quebec,

Murray was obviously influenced by the old régime when he established a superior jurisdiction. In an ordinance of October 31, 1760,[14] which abolished his previous courts, he announced that he would sit in the Castle of St. Louis every Tuesday morning for the hearing of criminal and civil cases — just as did the intendant before the conquest. In practice he rarely exercised the power he thus asserted. Most of the cases that might have been brought before him he preferred to leave to the military council, for which the same ordinance also provided.

This provision was in accord with another of Amherst's instructions, which called for a council of as many field officers as he thought proper. But Murray did more than obey orders when he created this body two days later.[15] He called it *une cour et conseil supérieur,* and he gave it seven members — the very name of the old institution that had possessed much the same authority, and the exact number that had formed its quorum. Nor did his imitation stop here. He appointed Jacques Belcourt de la Fontaine attorney general for the south shore and Joseph Etienne Cugnet attorney general for the north shore.[16] These individuals had been members of the old council and their functions were simply those of two old officials, the king's attorney general and the king's attorney for the Quebec district, added together and then divided geographically. Like the former they were attached to the council, and like the latter they were guardians of the property of unprotected minors and absentees. As a final touch in his partial reconstruction, Murray appointed Jean Claude Panet,[17] a former royal notary, to be chief clerk of the council, "with the rights, emoluments, honours and prerogatives attached thereto." This phrase, which he also used in commissioning De la Fontaine and Cugnet, is further proof, if any be needed, that the governor of Quebec was endeavoring to restore rather than to create. No record has yet come to light of his attempting to improve upon this system.

In the government of Montreal, Gage followed a different policy, being guided more by the present and less by the past. This was perhaps necessary in that richer and more progressive part of the colony. His first experiment was made on October 26, 1760,[18] when he combined all the militia captains of the town to form one court, which met every Tuesday. There can be no doubt that this strengthened the administration of justice in the town and provided a favorable contrast with the system in the country, where each captain of militia still held his own little court. A year later, after an investigation into conditions in the rural parishes, Gage extended this reform over the whole government,[19] dividing the country into five districts centering around Pointe Claire, Longueuil, St. Antoine, Pointe aux Trembles, and Lavaltrie. In each of these places a court of not less than five nor more than seven militia officers was to sit twice a month, all the officers in each area arranging among them their turn of duty. At the same time Gage created three appeal districts with centers at Montreal, Varennes, and St. Sulpice, where courts or councils of British officers were to be held monthly. He, of course, might hear appeals from any of their judgments.

This reform limited but did not destroy the judicial power of the single captain of militia. He was not deprived of the right to determine suits involving any sum up to twenty livres, subject to the revision of the militia chamber. He also became the executive officer of the chamber, enforcing its judgments by arrest or by seizure of property. Apparently he had not possessed sufficient criminal jurisdiction, for each chamber was required to deal with "vagabonds and villains" by sentencing them "to the lash, prison or fine, according to the requirements of the case." No change, however, was made in proceeding against those charged with "atrocious crimes such as murder, rape or other capital offences." The reform that Gage effected in the Montreal district was presumably wholesome, for Haldimand copied it in Three Rivers a few months later, and in both governments there was no further change until the establishment of civil rule.

The system that Haldimand set up on June 5, 1762, shortly after he relieved Burton, differed in minor detail from that after which it was modeled. Outside the town of Three Rivers, where two militia officers held court every Monday, there were four chambers of from three to five militia officers each, sitting at Champlain, Rivière du Loup, St. François, and Gentilly. Appeal courts of British officers met regularly in Three Rivers, Ste. Anne, Maskinongé, and St. François. "Vagabonds and rascals," who were probably scarcer than in the Montreal government, were all to be brought to Three Rivers.[20]

The militia captains performed their judicial functions gratis until they were organized in chambers. Then a fund was created for the support of each chamber by imposing upon unsuccessful suitors penalties varying from half a dollar to twenty dollars, according to the amount of the suit, and by adding the fines collected for the infraction of ordinances issued by the government. The expenses of maintaining the court were first deducted from the fund and the remainder was divided among the various officers according to the distance each had to travel and the number of sessions he attended.

The Canadians were such a litigious race that the administration of justice was a vital feature in their lives, and the system in vogue during the military régime fitted them admirably. One might expect this to be true of the jurisdiction exercised by the militia officers, their natural leaders, who knew only their own tongue and the laws with which they were familiar. That it was also true of the courts of British officers may be seen in the volumes of records they have left behind. All these courts had Canadian clerks and other Canadian assistants. Except when both parties to a suit spoke English as their native tongue, the proceedings were conducted almost entirely in French. Indeed, one unfortunate Englishman named Anderson who was sued by a Canadian in the Quebec court in September, 1761, had to ask for a copy of the case against him that he might get it translated into English. The judges, his own countrymen, granted his request but ordered him to submit his replies in French, for that was the language of the country.[21] The courts of British officers also took over and applied the laws of the country as they found them. Here the courts' Canadian advisers were indispensable.

This legal continuity may seem surprising after Vaudreuil had demanded it and Amherst had evaded the issue by replying that the Canadians became the subjects of the king. But none of the military governors had the slightest thought of introducing English law. That was something beyond their powers. One reason for their conservatism was the uncertain future of the colony. Was it to be retained or restored? "Wishing in these times of uncertainty to follow the former practices," runs the preamble to one of Gage's decrees.[22] But this was not the only reason. It could not be, because it disappeared with the treaty of peace, whereas the old laws were continued without question for another year and a half. A further explanation was advanced by Gage more than a year after the signing of the Peace of Paris.[23] According to him, they acted on the "maxim held by all civilians that no government can subsist without law [and] that in conquered countries the laws of such countries subsist till it shall please the conqueror to give them new laws." In other words, only the home government could make a change.

In the light of this principle, Amherst's reply referred to above did not necessarily mean the abolition of the existing laws. Indeed, when Murray was establishing his superior jurisdiction he quoted this article of the capitulation as if it bound him to preserve the old laws. Throughout the military régime the new authorities were scrupulous in their obedience to Canadian precedent. One good illustration of this may be found in the records of the Montreal court of officers for August 22, 1762.[24] On that day the court annulled one of Gage's recent decrees because it conflicted with a judgment delivered by a French judge in Montreal six years before the surrender of the country. The pathetic legend of the Canadians shunning these military courts gives a false picture of what was happening at this time. The contemporary records show that the number of cases that came before the Montreal council of officers sitting in appeal rose steadily to the end of the military period. In the Quebec court, which in form was copied from the old régime and which was therefore more likely to inspire confidence, over thirty cases were heard during the first month. All but two were brought by Canadian suitors, and they involved even such trivial matters as the possession of a feather bed.

In theory the military governors may have been autocrats whose will was law, subject of course to the revision of the commander-in-chief. In fact the relation between their will and the law was the very reverse. Their will was expressed in proclamations, ordinances, orders, decrees, and commissions.[25] But these names, except the last, were used rather indiscriminately, for the military governors' training and position made them careless of the civilian's distinction between the judicial, the administrative, and the legislative functions of government. Many of these public documents issued by Murray have not been found, but the loss is probably of no great moment. The corresponding documents for Montreal and for Three Rivers have been preserved, and to these two collections, between which there is very little difference, the surviving Quebec fragments bear a close resemblance. In the absence of any contrary evidence, therefore, one may presume that Murray exercised his authority in much the same manner as did the other military governors. Through all these documents one leading motive runs, the preservation of Canadian society as it was found on the morrow of the conquest. Not only the laws but also the customs that held this society together were maintained with as little change as possible. This effort of the military governors brought two important results. One is political and will be discussed at the end of the chapter. The other is photographic. The documents which these men promulgated form, when pieced together, a picture of Canadian life at that time. True, some parts of the picture are missing and some appear only in dim outline, but many are filled in with a mass of intimate detail.

Under the French régime the intervention of the intendant had been necessary to keep the feudal system working properly. Now that he was gone, who was there to take over this function unless it was the military governor? This question faced Gage almost at once, and he did not hesitate to assume the intendant's power. For some years the growing inflation of the currency had been lifting the burden of feudal dues. When real money appeared on the morrow of the conquest, seigniors naturally objected to tenants getting rid of their pecuniary obligations and their worthless paper at the same time. An appeal to the military governor of Montreal roused Gage's sense of justice. On January 22, 1761, he published a general order [26] requiring all seigniorial *rentes,* and also *lods et ventes,* to be paid in metallic currency, except where contracts stipulated otherwise. All inhabitants were to "repair on the day to the place and at the hour, which will be notified to them by the captains of the respective seigneuries, with their contracts and last receipts, for the purpose of paying the arrears of rent, which they may owe, on pain of proceedings against the defaulters, as is customary." The presumption is that his word was obeyed, for it was not repeated, as were some other decrees that were difficult to enforce.

As might be expected, the habitants of the Montreal district were not the only ones who sought to ease their feudal burden by using the old paper. In the previous November the Quebec court, on receiving a petition transmitted by Murray, had already decreed that *cens et rentes* be paid in hard cash. Similar action may have been taken in Three Rivers, though there is no record of it. In the spring of 1762, again on seigniorial appeals, Gage applied the fifty-year-old *Arrêt* of Marly, under which habitants lost the holdings they failed to occupy and to improve within a year and a day of their concession. He gave the delinquents anywhere from six months' to a year's warning. Sometimes this was effective. Sometimes it was not, and then, on the local militia captain's certifying that the proper notice had been read and posted at the parish church with no result, the governor issued a final decree.[27]

It is not known whether the new rulers of Three Rivers and of Quebec also put this old law into operation. Possibly the abandonment of conceded holdings was confined to the upper district, where the lure of the fur trade had an unsettling influence.[28] In both Montreal and Three Rivers the governors were besought to carve out new seigniories from the uncultivated lands, and to avoid trenching on any ancient grants they ordered all who had French titles to uncleared fiefs to present these titles on pain of forfeiture.[29] In Quebec, Murray also faced the demand for new seigniories, and throughout the colony homage was performed as before the conquest. Nor were the feudal rights of the crown forgotten. To discover all the mutation fines that might fall due — the *quint* on fiefs and the *lods et ventes* on land held of the king *en roture* — the notaries of Montreal and of Three Rivers, and possibly also those of Quebec, were ordered to submit copies of all sales and transfers for which they supplied the necessary instruments.[30]

These notaries constituted another essential feature of Canadian society. They drew up all conveyances of land and other property, bonds for the payment of money, deeds of partnership, marriage contracts, and generally all written agreements intended to be legally binding. Their houses were offices of record where all the original documents were deposited. Though only attested copies were given to the interested parties, such copies had as great validity in Canadian courts as the originals would have had in English courts. These men were not private individuals but public functionaries commissioned, though not paid, by the government, and therefore they were officially known as royal notaries. They were scattered all over the country in almost every parish, and as a body they formed the corner stone of private property throughout the colony. Being Canadians, they did not follow the higher officials back to France, and very quickly the new rulers of the country saw that they were indispensable. Just a week after his appointment to the government of Montreal, Gage began issuing new commissions to the old notaries,[31] and shortly afterward Murray did the same in Quebec.[32] If Burton did not do the same in Three Rivers, he omitted only a formality. Having heard that certain unqualified individuals had taken upon themselves to draw up deeds, he issued a proclamation on May 17, 1761, forbidding "all persons whatsoever, within the limits of this government to meddle with drawing up the deeds, which custom requires to be drawn up before the public notaries, under penalty of fine in favour of the notaries, or even of more severe punishment, if the case warrants it. . . . Exception is nevertheless made of contracts of marriage, which may, as formerly, be made before the curés, they being required to enter them at the Court at Three Rivers within the period of two months from their date." [33]

Like the notaries, the land surveyors had been commissioned by the government of New France and therefore were called "royal." They too were continued by the new government, at least in Montreal, where Gage had to add to their number.[34] He also decreed that judicial sales of property "must be made in the customary manner," [35] and he filled the old office of king's auctioneer — with an Englishman, however, Joseph Howard.[36] Another and more interesting survival is recorded in Three Rivers, where Burton, scarcely three months after he had assumed the government, ordered the nurses of illegitimate children to report "to receive their usual compensation . . . and to engage to continue their services" [37] — welcome evidence that unfortunate women were still protected and their offspring still cared for at public expense according to one of the most humane laws of the French régime.

Roads, bridges, ferries, and posthouses were maintained much as they had been. Now that there was no single government for the whole country, the *grand voyer,* who had possessed jurisdiction over all the highways, disappeared. In Quebec, Murray invested each attorney general with the powers of the old *grand voyer,* but apparently there was no regular substitute in Montreal or in Three Rivers, where the governors issued orders directly to each locality.[38] Acting on the advice of Canadian militia officers, or of British army officers with engineering experience, they commanded the construction of new roads that seemed necessary, or countermanded the building of roads that had been ordered but now appeared unnecessary. On the complaint of travelers between Quebec and Montreal, Burton decreed that the highway through his government should be ditched and crowned and made thirty feet wide.

Though Gage made all carters and carriers travel with picks and shovels in their sleighs to repair any sections that winter conditions had made impassable,[39] this was an exceptional order. The general rule was exactly what it had been before the conquest. Each parish was responsible for all roads and bridges within its own boundaries and might be fined if they were not in proper condition. The necessary work was done under the direction of the captain of militia, who, if need be, was backed by higher authority. In the spring of 1762 the militia captain of Chambly complained "that several inhabitants of the place refuse to work on the King's road and that several who have tenants forbid them obeying . . . and that, in addition, some of them remove the wheels from their carts and sell them to avoid being called upon." Thereupon the military governor published an ordinance threatening rigorous punishment, and the resisters seem to have bowed to his will and their old obligations.

When the master of the Montreal-Longueuil ferry complained that various inhabitants were invading his rightful monopoly, Gage interfered by making each of them liable to a fine of one dollar to be collected by any militia captain and paid to the aggrieved ferryman. The governor also issued a warning that he would impose severer penalties if this would not suffice.[40] In Three Rivers, Burton established a new ferry over the St. Maurice and fixed the tariff of charges.[41] For the convenience of couriers and ordinary travelers, he also recommissioned the old masters of posthouses and allowed them, under the supervision of the militia captains, to select their own assistants, whom they were to pay out of the fares collected from regular passengers and the money received monthly in exchange for the notes left by official couriers.[42] Nor was the governor of Montreal behind his brother of Three Rivers in maintaining this system of public conveyance. Finding a gap of half a league just below the Repentigny River, he filled it by appointing a new postmaster near that river and requiring him to provide the necessary horses and carriages, in return of course for the customary monopoly.[43]

The regulation of navigation was a problem for Murray alone, because few ships passed above Quebec. The river for nearly two hundred miles below this port hid many perils through which no vessel from the high seas could pass safely without a pilot at the helm. As the secret dangers of these waters were known only to Canadians,[44] Murray naturally turned to them. Selecting one who had guided Saunders up the stream and another whom he could likewise trust, the governor commissioned them to examine the competence of the others who claimed to know the way. On the report of these two, he issued certificates over his own signature, and to the holders of these papers he gave the sole right to serve as pilots. At Bic or at the Ile au Coudres they were picked up by incoming ships to be dropped later at the same stations by outbound vessels. Murray made the system self-supporting by requiring all masters, except of river or coasting craft, to pay according to a schedule he had drawn up. Those who preferred the risk to a pilot, who was not compulsory, might avoid sunken reefs but they could not escape payment. They were charged half rates. Each pilot received three-quarters of the dues collected from the vessels he conducted. The remainder, together with all the half dues, went to the official in charge of the whole service, for he had to maintain a small vessel at his own expense.[45]

The fresh air of country life blows through many of the documents of the other two governments. Three Rivers was such a purely rural community that Haldimand suspended the sittings of all law courts for more than five weeks while everybody went harvesting.[46] Many other decrees also carry the modern reader out into the open, where livestock roamed free and where the habitant followed the chase or slipped off to meet the redskins and gather their furs. By the law of the land, all cattle had to be inclosed between seedtime and harvest, but from Michaelmas until the coming of spring they might wander at will. No one thought of interfering with this ancient custom of *abandon,* but errant beasts and their erring masters were a problem during the growing season. Apparently Gage was forewarned, because he cautioned the inhabitants in November, 1760, to seize the leisurely opportunity of the winter to cut wood for their fences.[47] In Three Rivers, Burton issued new orders every spring reminding the people that their own crops were sown and that owners of stray cattle were liable to a fine.[48]

These two governors had regard also for the fowls of the air, for they enacted a closed season for partridge.[49] During four months in each year it was now illegal to kill, snare, or sell these birds. The preamble to Burton's decree is so naïve that it deserves quoting: "Having been informed that, from March 20 to July 15, a great destruction of partridge takes place and notably during the time of their mating, by the facility with which they may be killed, they disclosing where they are by the flapping of their wings, and to prevent the continuation of this abuse from which will infallibly result the entire destruction of these birds, which would deprive the public of a great comfort of life." In both governments all who violated the closed season were subject to heavy fines, half of which went to the informer and half to the poor of the parish or to the *fabrique* of the church.

Hunting was such an important factor in the life of the community that Burton relaxed the disarmament regulation. In addition to allowing firearms to all the seigniors, curés, and militia officers, he sent a number of guns and hunting licenses, usually anywhere from six to ten, to each parish. These guns and permits were at the disposal of the captain of militia, who was to see that they were lent impartially to all who could use them, "taking care nevertheless to leave them longest, preferably, to those who are poorest." [50] Many were such keen Nimrods that they were careless of their neighbors' fields. They trampled down growing crops and ripening hay, and the governor had to issue a general order to all militia captains to stop hunting across meadows and sown fields.[51]

Another temptation to many individuals in the government of Three Rivers was to go up the rivers in the spring to meet and trade with the Tête de Boule tribe on their way down with a winter's harvest of furs. This traffic actually forestalled the descent of the redskins in 1761, to the injury of both the red and the white communities. The traffic was also objectionable because it opened a door for anti-English propaganda among the savages. Burton therefore forbade anyone to go or to send merchandise into the wilds. He insisted that the natives must be allowed to come all the way down to Three Rivers to exchange their peltries. Thenceforth every May when the season drew near for the interesting visit of the Indians the governor repeated this prohibition and issued minute orders to regulate the trade according to established custom. On the arrival of the dusky hunters, their furs were "deposited in bulk at the top of the hill opposite the house of Mr. de Francheville." Their outstanding accounts were settled and registered at the secretary's office, and then the public crier announced to all and sundry the opening of the public market. Until it closed no one was allowed to give the red men strong drink, though it might be traded for furs, and the governor arranged that all merchants and others who wished to buy from the Indians might secure equal amounts of gunpowder at cost price.[52]

The larger trade of Montreal was managed very differently. Instead of waiting there, the traders went up to the Great Lakes in the spring to procure furs from the Indians, who hunted over the heart of the continent. Under the French this commerce had been the privilege of the few; under the British it became the right of all. Amherst decreed it and Gage proclaimed it. In addition to the passport which the former had required, the latter ordered every trader to leave a statement of the merchandise and the number of canoes he was taking and also the names of the men whom he had employed to go with him. In the Indian interest he limited the alcoholic cargo to the internal needs of each party, and in the British interest he forbade the export of furs to France.[53]

The military governors also had an eye on the local trade through the countryside. Gage granted liquor licenses only to those who were well recommended as responsible persons able to furnish good lodging for man and beast,[54] and he warned the militia captains against allowing any new purveyor of other wares to settle down without a covering permit.[55] Toward the end of the military régime, to stop disorders in several parishes of his government Haldimand summoned all who were licensed to sell wet or dry goods to appear in person, and he instructed the captains of militia that only those whose licenses were then renewed might continue their business.[56] In both Montreal and Three Rivers the military governors tried to stop wandering merchants from buying up supplies. They further ordered the arrest and the confiscation of the goods of every peddler with a pack and without a permit. This was more than a simple police measure; it was designed to protect the simple habitants from clever rascals, of whom there seem to have been not a few.[57]

The ruts of custom confined the activities of life in the rural districts more than they did in the urban centers and the latter consequently stood in greater need of special regulation. Three Rivers, however, was not in the same category as Quebec and Montreal. Though called a town, it was so far from being a town that it had no regular market when Burton arrived. Yet it was something more than a mere village, for its inhabitants wanted a market and their new ruler believed that they should have one. Therefore in November, 1760, he sent a circular to all the militia captains to encourage the country people to bring in their surplus produce for sale. That there was such a surplus he concluded from the number of traveling traders who, in defiance of his orders, were purchasing provisions in the rural districts of his government.[58] This circular apparently brought only a moderate response, for in the following June its author issued another [59] which was more explicit. Now each captain was to order the people "to bring from time to time to this town the largest quantity of supplies they are able, such as veal, mutton, fish, butter, eggs and other commodities for the use of troops and other persons." He also allotted "the edge of the water, opposite the old gate, as a market place," declared the market hours to be from seven until nine o'clock in the morning, and posted an officer or sergeant "to prevent soldiers or citizens from possessing themselves of the said commodities without paying for them."

It would be interesting if we could follow in detail what Murray did for the well ordering of the economic life in the colony's old capital. Unfortunately the loss of most of his ordinances makes this impossible. Still, in turning over the pages of the Quebec court register, one may catch fleeting glimpses that are very suggestive. On November 22, 1760, the clerk entered the results of public bidding which the governor had invited when decreeing the establishment of a slaughter house, and a fortnight later he recorded a prosecution for selling wheat above the legal price.[60]

In Montreal, one of Gage's earliest enactments struck at all who monopolized provisions or merchandise.[61] Offenders were to suffer imprisonment or confiscation of their goods, or if they were newly arrived merchants — that is, those who spoke English as their native tongue — they were to be banished from the government. Three weeks later,[62] so determined was he to protect the Montreal market for the inhabitants of both town and country, the governor forbade anyone from going out to meet the canoes or vehicles of country folk coming in, and he prohibited the purchase of country provisions for resale. For the former offense he decreed a fine; for the latter, a month in prison and the loss of the goods. That he achieved his main purpose may be inferred from the overcrowding of the market, which led him, a year later, to confine it to the sale of provisions and to appoint the parish square for the sale of forage and wood.[63]

Evidently the general community was thriving. Indeed, the speculative spirit was very lively in Montreal during the military régime. Many artisans and others who had been living on wages set up in business for themselves. Their competition threatened many of the regular traders and merchants with ruin. By deserting their old employments they produced a scarcity of labor that forced their senior rivals to pay higher wages. They, on the other hand, paid none, for they were operating in a small way. Moreover, they conducted their affairs right out in the open on the streets, the squares, and the shores of the town, and thus they escaped the burden of overhead charges which those with permanent establishments had to bear. To stop this economic revolution, which threatened to drag down the commercial level of the place, Gage interfered, in August, 1763.[64] He ordered that no one should be allowed to sell anything on the squares, streets, shores, or even in the suburbs of the town under pain of confiscation of his stock. He excepted, however, the manufactures of the artisans of the country, such as earthenware and copper utensils.

Like Murray in Quebec, the Montreal governor also followed the Canadian tradition of fixing prices. On the request of the chamber of militia officers in October, 1761, he limited the price of hardwood to nine livres or a dollar and a half a cord.[65] The reduction in the price of fuel benefited the bakers, who continued to demand four livres a quintal for converting their customers' flour into bread, the rate they had charged on the eve of the conquest, when the cost of wood was high. Therefore in October of the following year Gage cut this rate to less than half, but allowed the bakers to take somewhat more than half if they gave form to the bread. As they also bought their raw material and sold the finished product, the governor at the same time decreed the price and weight of bread — tenpence and four pounds for the white loaf, and twelvepence and six pounds for the brown.[66] In November, 1763, again on the advice of the militia chamber, he reduced these prices to seven and nine sous, respectively, which was a little more than half what they had been. In this decree [67] he also regulated the price of beef at three sous and a half per pound for the next five months, and then, for the spring and early summer, at four sous and a half. The carters likewise sought to charge heavy rates and to carry light loads, and therefore in December, 1760, Gage enacted a more specific tariff than Amherst had laid down, and he fixed the load for one horse at three barrels and for a team at five barrels.[68]

The control of street traffic was then, as now, a real problem. In September, 1761, two people were condemned for galloping horses in the narrow thoroughfares of Quebec, and until they paid their fines, which were to go to the poor of the town, they were ordered off to prison and their horses and charettes into custody.[69] In Montreal, furious driving in the streets and the confused crowd of horses and carriages at the church doors on Sundays and on holy days caused some distressing accidents. To protect pedestrians and worshipers from these wild men and beasts, Gage issued a decree in January, 1763, prohibiting the standing of vehicles at church doors, the galloping or fast trotting of horses in the streets and suburbs of the town, and the harnessing of teams with reins on only one horse. The penalty for infringing any of these regulations was a fine of twenty livres, half of which was to go to the informer and the other half to the poor of the town.[70] But pedestrians still walked in peril and worshipers still found the inside of a church safer than the out-side, for Burton had to repeat and enlarge this ordinance in the following December. He insisted on drivers turning to the right as the rule of the road, and he ordered that only one vehicle at a time come before the door of a church. The others were to be in a line moving clockwise around the edifice. After a heavy snowfall, the Jehus of Montreal hunted foot passengers even on the sidewalks, where the going was easier than in the middle of the road. The result was to be expected — more accidents and still more disputes. Therefore Burton issued another edict. This forbade driving along the sidewalks. Very justly it added a prohibition for pedestrians; they were not to wander along the middle of the road.[71]

Montreal could not have been as sweet smelling then as it is now. In October, 1760, Gage decreed: "Let every person take care, every day, to have gathered together in front of his property, the dung and other refuse which is there, put them in a heap, and have them carried to the water's edge to be thrown into the river, under penalty of ten livres fine." [72] In the following April he repeated this order with the following addition: "As several persons who have had their closets cleaned, have the filth thrown over the town walls, we order that all who do so henceforth shall pay 20 livres fine, and further order that those who have done so shall have the filth carted away without .delay to the water's edge, under penalty of double fines." [73] Pigs must also have been very plentiful both in the town and in the suburbs. They became such a nuisance that their owners were ordered to shut them up. Careless persons had to face a fine, a bill for damages, and the loss of their animals. Anyone was legally free to shoot an illegally free pig, a privilege which the inhabitants of Three Rivers enjoyed along with those of Montreal.[74]

In cold weather the wood fuel blazing far up the flues caused many a fire, which entertained the eternal small boy but occasioned serious danger and heavy loss to the people of the community. To reduce the risk to a minimum, Gage published several regulations [75] during his first autumn in Montreal. Every tenant or proprietor of a house had to have his chimneys cleaned once a month or pay a fine of six livres. If one of them caught fire, either he or the sweep whom he had employed, according as the conflagration was more or less than a month since the last cleaning, had to pay a fine of double this amount. On the outbreak of any fire in the town or suburbs, all the inhabitants were compelled to gather with axes and buckets on pain of a six livres fine. In Three Rivers, Burton required a fortnightly cleaning during the winter months, and he appointed a public sweep whose pay was collected by the militia officers. During the warm season, however, the inhabitants of Three Rivers were made responsible for taking the necessary precautions.[76] One of the worst conflagrations which broke loose in this little town occurred on July 4, 1762, when the greatest efforts could not prevent the flames from devouring five houses with their sheds and other outbuildings and all their contents. Burton thereupon issued a public appeal [77] to assist the stricken proprietors and tenants, and he doubtless hoped for considerable success, because the destroyed buildings, all lying next the beach, had "served as a resting place for the inhabitants of the country when their business drew them to town."

In approaching the currency question, Burton followed blindly in Murray's footsteps. Within a few days of his appointment to the government of Three Rivers he forbade paying or receiving in payment the old paper, which he dubbed "imaginary money." [78] This was the last official effort to destroy all faith in the preconquest circulating medium. No denunciation was ever issued in Montreal, where Amherst advised caution, and both in Quebec and in Three Rivers the governors relented from their stern attitude. The surrender of the country transformed what had been good propaganda into bad politics. Now the military governors naturally sought to foster the welfare and to cultivate the good will of the people under their care. Had they continued to insist that this money possessed no value, they would have been working to wipe out the capital of many and the savings of all. Moreover, they would have been putting themselves in a false position, for this money still had some value, small though it might be, based on the promise of deferred payment. But they could not establish any equivalence between this doubtful paper and the other currency, the value of which rested on the bullion it contained. Such official action would have disturbed the economic life of the colony, and it might have incurred the risk of involving the British government in the obligations of the French government. Therefore, with the exception noted below, they held aloof from the whole business, leaving the people free to accept this paper for what they might think it was worth. The courts, however, could not shut their eyes to its daily use. Sitting in judgment upon cases of debt incurred in terms of the old currency, they had to insist upon payment in paper or its market value in coin. After some fluctuations, the discount settled at about eighty-five per cent, at which rate not only Canadians but also English-speaking merchants who had followed in the wake of the army were glad to receive the paper. From them it passed into the hands of London merchants, who naturally pressed their government to insist upon the French government redeeming its obligations.

This discussion of the matter during the peace negotiations in 1762 raised hopes of justice in Canada and of profit in London. Seeing the conflict between these two hopes, the military governors threw their weight in favor of the former by trying to dissuade the Canadians from parting with their paper at a sacrifice. In this year one of the London schemers, an army contractor named Arnold

Nesbit, was so brazen that he wrote to Murray offering to share the profit on thirty thousand pounds worth of Canadian paper which he contemplated purchasing because he had private information from Paris that some liquidation was contemplated. The insulted governor at once summoned the leading Canadians, and to them he read the letter, adding many an eloquent comment of his own. The immediate result of this disclosure was that paper jumped two hundred per cent in the local market, and the permanent effect was that Murray incurred the undying hatred of many British traders.[79] In the following year, when the French plenipotentiary signed, along with the treaty, a declaration promising payment, the military governors published it throughout Canada and called upon all holders of paper to register it according to the procedure stipulated by the French government. The registration was performed gratis.

In regulating the metallic currency, the governors of Three Rivers and of Montreal did not follow Murray's example. In place of the Halifax standard of five shillings to the dollar, which he had adopted and now maintained, they accepted the New York system of eight shillings to the dollar, which Amherst introduced by implication in his famous placard. That York currency, as it was commonly called, should prevail in these two governments was natural, because their business connection was largely with New York over the Lake Champlain route. It also had the advantage of coinciding with the division of the Spanish dollar into eight *reals,* or "bits." The convenience of this reckoning in the two upper governments was probably greater than it would have been in Quebec, where there seems to have been a greater variety of coins.

In addition to British and French money, the dollar is the only piece that Gage mentioned in monetary decrees, and though Burton also referred to the half Johannes he did not call it by its proper name.[80] In Three Rivers and in Montreal it was common to cut dollars into eight "bits," but some enterprising persons in the latter government tried to make easy money by cutting them into nine, ten, or even eleven shillings. This drew from Gage an ordinance [81] threatening such rascals with prosecution as money-clippers and warning the public against their too clever tricks. In Three Rivers the fifth of a dollar appeared in circulation, but this had a legitimate origin in the neighboring government of Quebec, where it was a regular shilling, and therefore it was recognized by Burton.[80] In

Canada, French coins and those that were common in the English colonies now met in daily use for the first time, and it is not surprising that an error was made in fixing the relative value of the former. Apparently they were rated too low, for they began to disappear. Thereupon Gage raised the rating of the French crown of six livres *tournois* from eight shillings to eight shillings and fivepence. Murray must have made the corresponding change from five shillings Halifax to five shillings and threepence, for Burton referred to it when he followed Gage's example a fortnight later.[82]

The orders issued for the support and protection of the occupying army weighed lightly upon the people. It was no hardship for them to be forbidden to sell liquor to the soldiers, to buy any of their accouterments, or to harbor deserters; nor could they complain of the penalties of fines and corporal punishment imposed for breach of these regulations. The heaviest burden was billeting the troops and supplying them with straw and fuel. But the army chiefs used consideration when imposing these duties. In the spring of 1761, for example, Burton quartered most of his forces on the common of Three Rivers for the express purpose of relieving the inhabitants.[83] Likewise the obligation of providing fuel was distributed so that no parish would feel it unduly, and within each parish the burden was adjusted by the natural leader of the people, the militia captain. He chose the place where the wood was to be cut and he ordered the men necessary for the work. At least some proprietors were paid for the timber felled on their land.[84] Apart from housing and heating, the inhabitants gave nothing for which they were not paid. What a contrast to the old régime with its hard unremunerated corvées and its requisitions which profited nothing! Instead of light pockets, the Canadians had heavy pockets, for now they were paid, and paid in good jingling money.

As the military officers had their army pay, and the necessary administrative services carried on by others were either self-supporting or performed gratis, the three governments had little need for revenue. This was particularly true of the two upper governments, whose people had suffered much less from the blight of war than had the population of Quebec. The king's feudal rights, discovered by Murray and by him drawn to the attention of the other governors, provided the only income that all had alike — which was very little. The public domain in Three Rivers was limited to the forges of St. Maurice, which were still operated by the old employees, but the iron they manufactured was better than the profits brought by its sale. In Montreal, when General Gage felt the military necessity of repairing the ancient crumbling walls, he found that the fiscal necessity might be met by enforcing an old law of nearly fifty years' standing. This imposed upon the town a direct tax of six thousand livres, one-third of which was to be paid by the Seminary of St. Sulpice, the feudal lord, and the remainder by the rest of the inhabitants. Gage sought to raise only a portion of the sum, but Burton, when he succeeded to the government, demanded the whole of it. As might be expected, the collection was put in the hands of the militia officers.[85]

To meet his greater needs, Murray found greater resources. Though he unearthed an old tax on all houses in the city for the maintenance of the barracks, he could not use it. So many houses and so many people had been ruined by two sieges in one year that he felt the necessity of giving rather than of taking. On the advice of his military court or council, he taxed the country people to relieve the distress of the townsfolk, who had lost everything they had possessed and yet were obliged to lodge the British garrison. The tax was one dollar for each horse and was collected from the parishes "least burdened with troops or with supplying carriages for their use." It was levied but once and brought six hundred pounds, which was distributed among the more necessitous proprietors of the buildings Murray had appropriated for public use.[86] This transaction is interesting because it reflects a considerable prosperity in the rural district of Quebec. The amount raised represents twenty-four hundred horses, and horses were much of a luxury, the land being tilled by horned cattle. The incident is also worth noting because of the use to which it was afterwards put. In later days Murray's bitter enemies charged him with levying illegal taxes, and cited this as an example. There was certainly no precedent for the imposition, but his military council advised it, and, considering the circumstances, none but a legal pedant could condemn it.

Two other sources peculiar to Quebec which the head of that government uncovered provided a steady income based upon the authority of the past. One of these was the King's Posts. Ainslie's management brought sufficient promise of profit to inspire Murray to write home to the treasury urging the lease of this trade. On receiving a favorable reply he turned the posts over, in September, 1762, to Thomas Dunn and John Gray for one year certain and for a further period of fourteen years unless contrary orders arrived from Great Britain, in return for four hundred pounds a year.[87] Murray's enemies later said that this was a nice gift to his friends. But four hundred pounds a year was much more than the French government had ever got for these posts. Also it was essential that they be placed in trustworthy hands, as they were. Both the lessees were very respectable merchants, and one of them, Dunn, was to rise high in the service of the Canadian government.

The other source of revenue that Murray found was the customs duties. As these were the old king's rights, they became the new king's rights, and therefore the governor was entitled to demand them. He saw, however, that the old tariff would work many injuries, and consequently he whittled it down to one item. On November 22, 1760, he published an order [88] enforcing a duty of sixpence a gallon on all spirituous liquors. Early in the following summer, mercantile arguments in favor of British traders and British shipping moved him to exempt spirits manufactured in Britain,[89] which meant that rum from the old colonies was about the only drink to be taxed. To Murray's enemies this duty was a most flagrant violation of the law, but the only flaw the lawyers later found was that sixpence a gallon was slightly higher than the old rate on rum, though less than what had been charged on other alcoholic goods. On Murray's behalf it should also be observed that he had the tacit approval of the treasury, to which he reported the steps he was taking and to which he accounted annually for his collections and disbursements.[90]

On looking back over all the enactments of the military régime, one is struck by the fact that the governors did more than follow the forms of the old régime. They caught its best spirit. They speak not as conquerors to a subject race, but as fathers to their children; their words are less stern commands than paternal admonitions. Upon receiving the news of George II's death, Gage performed his duty by publishing general orders prescribing the regulation mourning to be worn by priests and ladies and gentlemen. But after his commands, which entered into even such details as shoes and gloves of undressed chamois and the absence of buttons from gentlemen's sleeves and pockets, he recalled the distressed condition of the country and added that he would not insist upon exact obedience.[91] In Three Rivers, when Burton learned that his proclamation against selling to hucksters was being ignored, he had his secretary write to all the militia captains. The letter explained that the proclamation had been designed to protect the country folk against the danger of selling what they might sorely need, and it requested the captains "if you please to refresh the memories of the inhabitants." [92] Was not this the utterance of a sympathetic parent to thoughtless children? The repetitions of orders were numerous, and all seem to say: "You have not obeyed as you should, but be sure to do better in the future." The same friendly attitude smiles through many commands which have an added suggestion that compliance will be easy. "It is an order which will take so little time from each individual to execute that I am persuaded they will obey as soon as the present is received without a murmur." [93] These words at the end of a circular issued by Burton when calling for firewood are only one of many passages that might be chosen to illustrate the kindly tone adopted by the military rulers in addressing the conquered people.

The lively concern the governors felt for the welfare of the Canadians may be deduced from the substance, as well as the wording, of many of the decrees already mentioned. It was also clearly revealed in their efforts to relieve the distress which was acute in Quebec in 1760 and 1761. In addition to the havoc wrought by the two sieges of the city and the systematic destruction practiced by the army in rural parts, the district generally was suffering from the interruption of agricultural life caused by the war. Despite the voluntary aid of the British soldiers, the inhabitants were able to gather only part of their crop in 1759, and the military operations of the following spring interfered so much with seeding that there was another meager crop in the fall of 1760. The resulting shortage of grain, both for food and for seed, produced great misery and the prospect of greater still. Fearing a famine, Murray lent peas and oatmeal, while the army officers and the English merchants subscribed five hundred pounds and the soldiers insisted on giving up one day's provisions a month.[94]

But this aid, without which many would have perished, was only a temporary measure. The economic sickness could be cured only by the application of seed, and this was lacking. To procure it,

Murray turned to Burton and to Gage. The governor of Three Rivers ordered the captains of militia to make an exact report of all the grain in each parish,[95] but the result must have been disappointing, because he made no arrangements for exporting a surplus, and he renewed his prohibition of inhabitants selling produce to traveling merchants. The governor of Montreal was more favorably situated, for he ruled over a district which was for a long time the granary of Canada. From every parish he required a list of all who would contribute, with a statement of their capacity and their actual offerings. This was to be signed by the British commander of the local district, by the militia officers, and by the curé. The grain was to be delivered at appointed places for shipment to the lower government, and was to be paid for through the militia captains in two installments totaling four livres a minot, Murray having undertaken that the Quebec parishes would be collectively responsible for the payment. This call brought some response but not enough to please Gage, who learned that many were still holding a surplus for a rise in the market. Thereupon he reprimanded them for their callous selfishness and summoned them to make immediate delivery.[96]

Toward the close of the military régime the governors were placed in a very awkward position by orders from New York. After the outbreak of Pontiac's Revolt, Gage, who was now commander-in-chief, conceived the brilliant idea of adding Canadians to the forces that were to suppress the rising. Would not the appearance of their old allies dispel the illusions of the red men and induce them to submit? Therefore, on February 12, 1764, he commanded that three hundred Canadians be assembled in Montreal for the opening of navigation. One company of sixty men was to be raised in Three Rivers, and two companies were to be levied in each of the other governments. He appears to have given little thought to the way in which the recruits were to be secured, and to have taken for granted that they would be drafted from the militia, as they would have been under the old régime.

The three governors at once saw legal and political difficulties in this method. They feared that it might cause the conscription of French citizens and the alienation of the Canadian people, but they had no time to remonstrate. They consulted together and agreed that they should take only volunteers who elected to be British citizens, but that they would have to supply any deficiency by drawing from the militia. In their proclamations calling for recruits they offered generous terms — six sous a day, rations, clothing, twelve dollars bounty, a priest to accompany them, and a free discharge at the end of the campaign.

But these inducements, though supported by the strongest personal efforts of the governors, had little attraction for the Canadians. Murray was obliged to draft ten men to complete his quota, and though Haldimand reported his full number of volunteers he did not get them until he had deprived a couple of parishes of the firearms allowed them for the chase. In Montreal, Burton's task was easier, probably because of unemployment, for the rising had led Gage, not long before his departure from Montreal, to place an embargo on all trade to the upper country. The backwardness of the Canadians did not arise from any hostile feelings toward their late conquerors, nor is there any evidence that they hung back out of friendship for their old allies. The great reason for their reluctance to join the British colors seems to have been that they had had their fill of fighting in the years gone by, while of late they had tasted the sweets of peace. The ears of the governors caught echoes of wild rumors that ran through the countryside, rumors that this call for soldiers was only a ruse to capture Canadians and carry them to fight unknown foes in distant lands for the rest of their lives, but it is doubtful if all who sped the tale believed it, for its only foundation lay in their own desire to avoid military service.[97] The revolution that the British conquest wrought in Canadian character was showing itself. The spirit of the people was unbroken, but no longer was it marked by that strong martial quality which had been the result of environment rather than of inheritance.

The records of this military régime make it stand out unique in the annals of occupied territories. From the very beginning of the period the inhabitants were astonished at the lenity of their new masters and were delighted that the war had stopped with the fighting. *"Ces nobles vainqueurs ne parvient-ils pas de lors oublier qu'ils avoient été nos ennemis, pour ne s'occuper que de nos besoins et des moyens efficaces d'y subvenir!"* These words to all the faithful under his charge, uttered by the vicar general of Quebec, Briand, are but one of the many expressions of gratitude which the Canadians poured out in glowing terms.

The reasons for this wonderful harmony between conquered and conqueror are not far to seek. One of the most important causes was the very completeness of the British victory. It banished from the minds of the British the fear which might have been the father of cruelty. It was also a powerful incentive to submission on the part of the Canadians. Their submission was made more whole-hearted by the thought that France had deserted them and by the realization of the blessings which the British bestowed. These blessings were liberty, prosperity, and peace, and the greatest of these was peace. For this they had been longing with all their hearts. Though many had been stricken by the scourge of war, prosperity now returned, and it was greater than any they had ever known. And the liberty they now breathed inspired new life in them. No more cramping monopolies! No more oppressive extortions by government servants! They even disputed the tithes with their clergy.

Highly fortunate it was that the final treaty did not come swift on the heels of the capitulation, for then civilians would have tried their hands at the task of governing Canada, and they would probably have made a sorry mess of it. Civilian minds steeped in the tradition of English law would have disturbed the even tenor of Canadian ways by attempting to change the laws and customs of the country, for this is what they did at the close of the military régime. Heaven was kind to Britain and to Canada in keeping the army there. The army healed the wounds it had inflicted, and this is the best healing. Its leaders were blinded by no legal prejudices and so did not interfere with the complex organism of Canadian society. They gave the Canadians the finest quality of liberty — the liberty to be themselves. They did it by rule of thumb; they did it out of the pity that was in their hearts; they did it consciously and unconsciously on the great principle enunciated by Egremont. In the interest of the British Empire and of Canada the Canadians were to be won, and they were won.

Of all the glorious victories that British armies have to their credit, none is more glorious, none is more honorable, than the moral conquest that crowned the military conquest of Canada. The years of this military régime are of supreme importance in the history of Canada, for they planted in Canadian hearts that trust in British justice which has preserved the country with its dual nationality from splitting asunder. These years are also a watershed in the history of the British Empire, for the French in Canada were the first considerable body of an alien race to taste that liberty which is larger than English liberty and is the secret of the modern British commonwealth of nations.

CHAPTER IV

PEACE AND WAR

THE fall of New France was only one event in a war that was waged in four continents and on "the seven seas," and in this titanic struggle both Britain and France were linked with important allies. The peace settlement was, therefore, a highly complicated business. Here, however, it is necessary to examine the Treaty of Paris only as it affected the fate of Canada.

Britain could not hope to retain all that she had conquered from France. Britain was too weak and France was too strong. On both sides of the Channel tongues and pens joined in high debate over what colonies should be restored. In Paris, some were for putting forth every effort of arms and of diplomacy to recover Canada. With a solid empire on the continent of America, would not Britain's wealth and naval power grow until she might overawe the continent of Europe? Others, on the other hand, maintained that the cession of Canada would strengthen France and weaken Britain. It would relieve the former of a heavy obligation, and it would inject a dissolvent into the empire of the latter. No longer would the fear of French power to the north of them keep the English colonies dependent upon their mother country, and consequently the British Empire would split in twain. Thus to many Frenchmen it was more blessed to give than to keep Canada. But there was one thing that all Frenchmen were determined to retain at any cost. This was the right to share in the fisheries of the Gulf of St. Lawrence, the great nursery of seamen.

British opinion was even more sharply divided over what to hold and what to leave. "Some are for keeping Canada, some Guadeloupe, who will tell me which I shall be hanged for not keeping?" said Pitt in the house of commons. This alternative,[1] the chief of many under discussion, seems strange today, but was most natural then. Those who opposed the retention of Canada urged the necessity of binding the old colonies to the mother country, the possibility

57

of taking the furs of America from the back door of New France, and the fortyfold greater wealth then produced by the little West Indian island. They also argued the general superiority, both economic and political, of tropical over continental colonies. The former supplemented the economic life of the parent state whereas the latter competed with it. The former would always remain dependent, but the latter were growing too powerful to remain long in that condition.

Another battery of reasons defended the retention of Canada instead of Guadeloupe. It would prevent a renewal of the old war and would give protection to the old colonies. It would not lead to their revolt. They loved Britain too much and one another too little. By increasing the supply of cheap land, it would discourage American manufactures and thereby would actually tend to preserve American dependence. It would be the best guarantee against a costly blunder, for the little island might fall an easy prey to British sea power while Canada could be recovered only by another bloody and expensive war. Certainly it would entail a great material loss in the immediate future, but the more distant future promised a greater gain.

The industrial revolution was beginning to shift the foundations of Britain's economic life from agriculture and commerce to manufactures, which raised the vision of a new need — markets. Only as they expanded could Britain continue to grow in wealth and strength. This consideration threw new light on the relative value of tropical and of continental colonies. The former could never hold many customers; the latter might support a teeming population who would buy British wares in ever increasing quantity. Thus the industrial revolution tended to bring about a revolution in colonial policy.

Exactly how these various arguments, which were bandied to and fro in public, weighed in the private councils of the two interested governments it is impossible to say. But it appears that Guadeloupe would have been abandoned even if there had been no question of Canada's future. The British West Indian planters, fearing the ruin of their London market by inundations of sugar from Guadeloupe, were determined that the island should be restored. Their political influence, which was still powerful, rather than that of the manufacturers, who had not yet risen to a position of dominance,

seems to have been the deciding factor. Thus the treaty of 1763
does not mark a reorientation of colonial policy.[2]

As for the arguments in favor of restoring Canada, neither government considered them of sufficient value to warrant an effort to
act upon them. Britain never offered and France never demanded
the return of the colony. From the very beginning of negotiations in
the spring of 1761, its retention was officially taken for granted.
Nor was there much greater difference between the two governments over the fisheries of the gulf. Pitt wanted to exclude the
French entirely, but he saw that this was impossible. Therefore he
agreed to cede St. Pierre and to concede the right to use a portion
of Newfoundland's shores. But this was only one part of a big
bargain that covered the globe, and elsewhere the great war minister refused to pay the necessary price of peace. Consequently he
failed and fell.

The upshot for Canada was fortunate. It protracted that courting
time of French and English known as the military régime without
making any substantial difference in the terms upon which the
colony was finally ceded. When the much-maligned Lord Bute
reopened negotiations in the following year, he made no serious
modifications in Pitt's proposals except what were necessary to procure peace. The preliminaries were signed on November 3, 1762,
and then carried through parliament by a vote of 319 to 65.

Many have attacked the treaty as another instance of Britishers
losing by their heads what they had won by their swords, and critics
have explained away this overwhelming majority by asserting that
the members' heads were turned by the arguments which the elder
Fox had put in their pockets. But the bribes distributed by the leader
of the house of commons have been exaggerated and they were
probably superfluous. The terms of peace might have been much
the same, except in popularity, if Bute had neither descended from
Scotland nor ascended the back stairs of the British court.[3]

By the fourth article of the Treaty of Paris, which was finally
signed on February 10, 1763, the king of France renounced all claim
to Canada and Acadia and their dependencies, including all but two
little islands in the Gulf of St. Lawrence. By the same article,
the British sovereign undertook two obligations, one temporary and
the other permanent. The first was that he would allow all who
had been French subjects in the ceded territories to sell their estates

and to retire with the proceeds within eighteen months. The second was the guarantee of "the liberty of the Catholic religion to the inhabitants of Canada," in pursuance of which he promised to "give the most precise and most effectual orders that his new Roman Catholic subjects may profess the worship of their religion according to the rites of the Romish church, as far as the laws of Great Britain permit."

In later days some have charged the British government with bad faith because the promise in the capitulation was now qualified by the words "as far as the laws of Great Britain permit." But international law does not recognize the right of military leaders, by their essentially temporary agreements, to tie the hands of their governments when they come to arrange a permanent settlement. When negotiating the treaty the French wished to strike out this clause, but the British replied that their king, being under the law, could grant toleration under no other condition and that the only possible effect of dropping it would be an unfortunate misunderstanding. They were also able to quote precedent, for the French had accepted almost the same words in the Treaty of Utrecht fifty years before. How far the implications of the disputed clause might eat into the guarantee it qualified the British did not explain because they could not, which was a further and private reason for their insistence. This is the only ground on which one may attack the honesty of the British government. On two questions that later became live issues, laws and language, the treaty was silent.

The only other terms that touched Canada were those dealing with the fisheries. The fifth article renewed the thirteenth of the Treaty of Utrecht, whereby French fishers could land and build huts and stages for drying fish on the coast of Newfoundland from Cape Bonavista on the east, around the northern end of the island, and down the west side to Point Riche, some little distance below the Strait of Belle Isle. The fifth article also recognized the right of French subjects to fish in the gulf at a distance of three leagues from all British coasts. Outside the gulf, however, French fishermen were not to ply their calling within fifteen leagues of Cape Breton nor within thirty leagues of the shores of Nova Scotia.[4] By the sixth article, two little islands off the southern coast of Newfoundland, St. Pierre and Miquelon, were ceded to France as a shelter for her fishermen. To prevent these islands from being used for any other purposes, the same article prohibited their fortification, the erection upon them of any buildings not necessary for the fishermen, and the maintenance of more than fifty guards for police purposes.

The fate of the Canada paper, referred to in the last chapter, was not settled by the treaty. Though the British government, from both domestic and imperial motives, had pressed for some agreement, the French government had resisted because many people in France were involved and because it was already slipping on the verge of the bankruptcy that was to engulf it in the great Revolution. All that could be secured at this time was a public declaration that these old obligations would be liquidated in time.

Since the surrender of the colony, some Canadians had been buoyed up by the hope that France would not forget her child but would insist upon its return when peace came to be signed. But their deep disappointment was not shared by the mass of the people when the news of the treaty reached the St. Lawrence in May. Indeed, there was a note of optimism in the *mandements* published by the vicars general in charge of the diocese. Had not God been good to the Canadians? He had granted them peace, and He had given them a new government that was tender of their welfare, both temporal and spiritual. They had already enjoyed many proofs of the surprising beneficence of British rule, and now gratitude combined with duty to make them loyal subjects of George III. Such was the voice of the church, and it seems to have been echoed in the hearts of the people.

§

While contentment with the peace was thus spreading on the shores of the St. Lawrence, the flames of war were bursting in the west. The story of Pontiac's Revolt [5] is an intimate part of the history of the United States rather than of the history of Canada. Its scene lay beyond the present boundaries of the Dominion, and its actions touched only remotely the Canada of that day. Yet this striking tragedy cannot be ignored, because the extremely difficult problem of handling the very natives who figured in it was an important background of Canada's history for half a century.

The immediate cause of this dramatic native rising was the defeat of the French in America and the surrender of the western posts. Some of these, Oswego, Niagara, Duquesne, and the three connecting the last with Lake Erie, Venango, Le Boeuf, and Presqu' Ile, the French had lost or had abandoned before the end of the war. The remainder were included in the capitulation of Canada. Five days after the fall of Montreal, Major Robert Rogers, the famous partisan, started up the St. Lawrence with two hundred provincial rangers. He bore Amherst's orders to take over these posts and a letter from Vaudreuil directing Captain Bellestre, the French commander at Detroit, to deliver them.

Eleven weeks later, on November 29, after an arduous journey in open boats, he took formal possession of Detroit. Thence he dispatched a small party southwest to assume command of Fort Miami on the Maumee River and Fort Ouatanon on the Wabash, which commanded the communications with Vincennes down the latter stream and with the lower reaches of the Ohio. No effort was made to reach Vincennes, for it belonged to Louisiana and was therefore not included in the surrender of Canada. Not until the Treaty of Paris was Vincennes, along with the rest of the territory east of the Mississippi, ceded to Britain. After securing Detroit, Rogers set out for Michilimackinac, but growing storms and gathering ice turned him back from Lake Huron. It was in the summer of 1761, after the arrival of more troops, that the British took over this post on the southern shore of the strait leading into Lake Michigan and its dependent posts, Green Bay and St. Joseph on the latter lake and Ste. Marie on the river flowing from Lake Superior. All the surrendered garrisons, including Bellestre, who would have been insulted had anyone prophesied his future rewards for loyalty to Britain, were sent down to Montreal as prisoners of war. The French traders and settlers who lived in or around each post were allowed to remain on taking the oath of allegiance — with their lips.

This substitution of Englishmen for Frenchmen in all these centers of Indian trade and influence created an explosive situation. The change spelled disaster to the denizens of the forest. To them the French had displayed a fundamentally Christian attitude while the English had not. French missionary zeal may or may not have had a great effect upon the Indians in the next world, but it undoubtedly had a great practical effect upon them in this world, for it was a constant reminder that they were included in the French idea of the brotherhood of man. The English, on the other hand, cared little for the souls of the natives and less for their bodies. Sir William Johnson and his assistant, George Croghan, were Irish exceptions.

This general contrast between the two white races, as they appeared to the red men, had been heightened by the war. The Indians had been engaged in hunting Englishmen, and this pursuit had stimulated the savage thirst for English blood. At the same time they had grown more and more dependent upon the French, who, in their struggle against desperate odds, had sought to win and to hold every possible red ally by scattering presents with a lavish hand. The English, though few of them knew it, were thus stepping into an almost impossible position. Only by the most careful humoring of the natives could the newcomers avoid trouble, but, with characteristic blindness, they showed not the slightest disposition to humor them. When the British government called upon the commander-in-chief to curtail expenditures, he should have used the utmost discretion in weaning the spoiled and embittered children of the wilds. But of discretion he had none. To Amherst's shortsighted vision the Indians appeared to be of no more use. He refused to allow them "any presents by way of *Bribes,* for," he said, "if they do not behave properly they are to be punished." Some have damned him for his infernal suggestion of spreading smallpox among them by means of infected blankets. It is only fair, however, to observe that this, like Colonel Bouquet's proposal to hunt the natives with bloodhounds and Major Gladwyn's to weaken them by the free sale of rum, was made after and not before the atrocities of the rising had been perpetrated. But the excuse of boiling blood cannot wash out all the stain upon minds that could advance such ideas. No better was the mentality of the backwoodsman who was hewing his way into the hunting fields of the Indians down in the Ohio country. The loss of some scalps from his family only made him more convinced that the redskins were wild beasts and should be exterminated. This type of Englishman had no counterpart among the French.

Nor was the native temper likely to be improved by the English traders, who now pushed into the heaven of furs where only the French had trod. Competition between whites in the presence of an inferior people is apt to be dangerous to both colors. Competition for the Indians' furs had been restrained among the French; among the English it was unconfined. With the exception of a few rare individuals like Alexander Henry, whose character saved his life, the English fur traders were of an inferior stamp. Their greed was held in check by neither courtesy nor honesty. Thus the English did little to reduce and much to increase the poison that the French had instilled and the war had increased in the hearts of all the tribes around the Great Lakes and in the country to the south.

The Indians were also exasperated by evil tidings that came in the spring of 1763 — news of the Treaty of Paris and its delivery of the whole country out to the Mississippi. As in a later day they resented the British surrender of their lands but vented their rage upon the Americans who came to take possession, so now they hated the English for what the French had done. Moreover, why were the English strengthening the old forts and building new ones? Why were they placing garrisons everywhere? All this could not be against the French, with whom peace was now made; it must be against the Indians. Would it not be well to strike while the feared and detested invaders were still only scattered handfuls of men isolated in the wilderness? And what plunder might they not reap in pillaging the posts!

The passions of the red men were inflamed by some, but not all, of the few French who had settled around the forts, principally Detroit, or who came up from the Illinois country to trade. They were all more or less engaged in the fur trade, and they viewed the intruders with jealous eyes. Hence many Indians called the outbreak a beaver war. Some also had weird notions that the French empire might be restored in the heart of America with its base in Louisiana. Many were the wild tales that French mouths poured into Indian ears. One of the commonest was that the king of France had fallen asleep and had lost Canada while he slumbered, but now he was awake and strong and was sending his armies to fight side by side with his red children. The Indians were deeply stirred by these "whistlings of evil birds," as they later called them, for the influence of these Frenchmen was as great as their interest. The extent of this influence is not surprising, seeing that almost all these Frenchmen, by blood and by spirit, were close cousins of the natives.

For two years before the fierce storm broke, war belts of red and black and hatchets stained the color of blood were circulating

among the various tribes from the Mississippi to the southern shores
of Lake Ontario, and from council fire to council fire embassies
passed with flaming messages. Although the Iroquois had been
traditional friends of the English, the largest and fiercest of the
Six Nations, the Senecas, were now their bitter foes. Their deputies,
whom they sent far and wide, might have instigated a concerted attack in the summer of 1761, had the plan not been discovered just in time. Later in the season Sir William Johnson traveled
from his home on the Mohawk to Detroit, where he temporarily
satisfied the natives' hunger for food but not their thirst for English
blood.

In the summer of 1762 another plot was nipped in the bud, but
the seething ferment continued. No individual caused it, and no
individual arose to direct it until the winter of 1762–63, when Pontiac, the war chief of the Ottawa confederacy, began to stand out
as a leader and inspirer of the native movement. Even then, though
his agents sped everywhere, his actual command was limited to his
own people, who were only some of the Indians in the neighborhood of Detroit. Thus the name which has been given to the great
native war is misleading. But it would be difficult to find another
to replace it at this late date, and it may well stand, because Pontiac
was the only chief with any wide influence among all the tribes
that took part in the explosion and because he commanded the
siege of Detroit, which was the central point of interest.

True to their character, the red men planned to catch the white
men off their guard and to destroy them before they could offer
any resistance. On the morning of May 7, 1763, Pontiac, at the
head of fifty or sixty chiefs, entered the gate of Detroit for a conference with the commander, Major Gladwyn. According to the
Indian plan, the interview was to have been concluded by the
presentation of a wampum belt, and this public evidence of friendship for the English was to have been a private signal for the slaughter of every one of them. Each chief had a sawed-off gun under his
blanket, and many warriors and squaws were to have wandered
into the fort wearing the mask of peace while bearing concealed
implements of war. But Gladwyn had been warned of the conspiracy, and his garrison of six score were all ready to do to the
red men what the red men had been going to do to them. Therefore nothing was done that day. On the morrow the great chief,

with three companions, returned to smoke the pipe of peace with the British officers, but on the next morning, when he advanced with a swarm of braves for a bigger smoke, he found the gate shut in his face. Gladwyn offered to admit him if he left his company outside. Pontiac turned on his heel, and he and all his followers rushed off to vent their baffled rage upon the few English people to be found in the vicinity.

The war had begun, and its circle widened with the spreading of the news. As the red men naturally got the information first, they were able to surprise their prey. On May 16, exactly a week after the first bloodshed at Detroit, Fort Sandusky fell. This block-house, recently built at Sir William Johnson's orders on the south-west of Lake Erie, was held by about a dozen men under Ensign Pauli. Unaware that anything untoward had happened to the north, he admitted seven Indians, some of whom he knew person-ally, for a conference in his room. As they passed a calumet from lip to lip, an Indian at the door raised his hand — a signal for bloody action. Pauli was pounced upon, and when his captors led him through the parade ground he saw the corpses of his garrison. He was carried to Detroit, where, after a preliminary torture, he was given his choice between death at the stake and life as the husband of an old squaw who had lately lost her spouse and now wanted this youth as a substitute. He chose life, and a few weeks later he escaped from his "wife" and found a refuge within the walls of the fort.

At the close of this fatal month of May, two other forts of similar size and garrison were seized. On the twenty-fifth, Ensign Schlosser, the commander at St. Joseph, was asked to receive some Indians who had just arrived from Detroit. A Canadian at once warned him of his danger and he rushed out of his quarters to muster his men and as many Canadians as possible. It was too late. The sentinel at the gate fell under a tomahawk and a savage swarm poured into the fort. In two minutes it was pillaged and eleven soldiers lay dead. The fort was handed over to a Canadian who snatched several British traders from the jaws of death. Schlosser and three other survivors of the garrison were borne to Detroit, where, three weeks later, they were exchanged for some red prisoners.

Two days after this tragedy on Lake Michigan, another was enacted on the Maumee River. Ensign Holmes, who had charge

of Fort Miami, had long known the peril in which he lived. His
head was on guard, but his heart was not, for he had lost it to an
Indian maiden. Pretending to lead him to an ailing squaw who
desired his assistance, this North American Delilah led him to his
doom. He was shot in his tracks as he walked on his errand of
mercy. Three of his men who happened to be outside the pickets
dashed for the gate. They never reached it; they were dispatched by
tomahawks. Nine leaderless survivors prepared to defend the place,
but this was a hopeless task, and they were soon persuaded to surrender. They too were carried to Detroit, where some of them were
tortured to death.

The opening day of June witnessed the loss of Ouatanon on the
Wabash, where Lieutenant Jenkins had heard rumors of an impending rising. But he was not aware that it had begun when he accepted an invitation to a conference with some natives outside his
fort. He and three of his soldiers were seized and bound. The rest
surrendered, preferring to buy their lives rather than sell them.
Little did they know that they were really giving them away, as far
as the Indians were concerned, for the savages had determined to
slay them all. They were saved by two French traders who plied
the natives with wampum and other arguments, and thenceforth the
prisoners were well treated. Even the red men here seem to have
repented.

On the king's birthday, three days after the loss of Ouatanon,
Captain Etherington came out of Fort Michilimackinac to watch
the most famous game of lacrosse that was ever played in America.
His ear had caught murmurings of trouble, but his head paid no
heed to them, particularly on this day when red men seemed to vie
with white men in honoring the king by enjoying themselves.
The game, which was between two tribes, was swift and furious.
It fascinated the English onlookers. Suddenly the ball went flying
through the air toward the fort and the crowd of players dashed
after it. In a trice their cries burst into the war whoop. They rushed
the gate and, snatching weapons from under the squaws' blankets,
slew sixteen of the garrison and took the rest prisoners before one
of them could seize his arms.

Alexander Henry, who had been attending to his correspondence
rather than the game, looked out of his window and, as he says,
"saw a crowd of Indians, within the fort, furiously cutting down

and scalping every Englishman they found; in particular, I witnessed the fate of Lieutenant Jamette." By retreating to the garret of a Canadian neighbor he saved his life but not his freedom, for every live man with an English tongue in his head became a prisoner. Some days later a number of them were butchered as they lay bound hand and foot. Others were subsequently released to make their way over the Ottawa route to Montreal.

The outlying posts of Ste. Marie and Green Bay had a less tragic fate. The former had been deserted during the previous winter after an accidental fire. But this did not save the garrison, commanded by Lieutenant Jamette, who went to Michilimackinac, where they shared in the massacre. Green Bay was abandoned by Lieutenant Gorell and his seventeen men in the middle of the month upon the receipt of instructions from the captive Etherington. Gorell's sagacity, and probably native politics, had secured them the friendship of neighboring Indians, many of whom now accompanied them to the outlet of the lake. There they were joined by the prisoners who were released, and together they made their way down to the St. Lawrence.

Just after the middle of the month the three forts controlling the communications between Lake Erie and Fort Pitt were lost. On the fifteenth, the very day that Etherington's letter reached Green Bay, two hundred warriors from Detroit assailed Presqu' Ile. Having received warning, Ensign Christie had prepared for this "visit from the hell-hounds." The blockhouse of his fort was so strong that it was considered impregnable unless the foe could set it ablaze. Therefore the garrison of twenty-seven men covered the angles of the roof with fresh turf and prepared bark troughs to direct a saving stream of water to any part of the roof from a lookout at the top. Unfortunately they could not give the bottom of the blockhouse similar protection. In two days the besiegers had so undermined it that they were about to burn it from below. Thereupon the besieged surrendered on condition that they be allowed to march unmolested to the nearest post. But the moment they emerged from their scorched and bullet-scarred fort they were seized by the faithless savages. They too were carried to Detroit, where Christie managed to make his escape.

On the day after Presqu' Ile fell, Ensign Price with a dozen men was cooped up in the little blockhouse of Le Boeuf, fifteen miles to the south, upon which the attackers rained blazing arrows. Three times the defenders extinguished the flames, but when the fire caught the roof they could not master it. However, they cheated the red demons without and within the fort. With the aid of axes they escaped through a narrow window at the back while the Indians in front rejoiced at the thought of the white men's torture in the hot prison. In two days some of them reached Venango, where, instead of shelter, they found smoldering ashes and the half-burned bodies of its garrison. Not a man had escaped to tell the tale, and only long afterward did Sir William Johnson learn from an Indian witness what had happened at Venango. A large company of Senecas, gaining entrance under the cloak of friendship, had seized the place and had butchered all the inmates but the commanding officer, Lieutenant Gordon. Him they roasted over a slow fire for several nights until death released him.

In all the region of the lakes west of Niagara, the British flag still flew only at Detroit. There Major Gladwyn and his men heroically sustained a memorable siege. Cut off from reinforcements and short of supplies, they were in a perilous plight. At the end of May, Lieutenant Cuyler, who had set out for Detroit from Niagara with provisions, ammunition, and nearly a hundred men in ten bateaux, first learned that there was blood flowing when he saw it at Point Pelée, where he was ambushed. Only two boats escaped across the lake to Sandusky, which they found in ruins, and then back to the Niagara River via Presqu' Ile. The rest were taken and brought to Detroit, the captured soldiers serving as galley slaves for their red masters.

The loss of this convoy might have been fatal to the beleaguered garrison had not Jacques Baby already come secretly to their rescue. Unlike most of the Canadians who lived in the hundred houses within the fort or in the settlement that straggled for several miles on either side the river, he had wealth and he had sympathy for the hard-pressed British. During the whole of one dark night, six canoes were busy smuggling into the fort large quantities of beef, pork, and meal which he had gathered in his establishment on the eastern bank. In the middle of June the schooner "Gladwyn," which the major after whom it was named had sent to Niagara, returned with more provisions and fifty men, but not until the end of July, when Captain Dalzell with nearly three hundred men in twenty-two barges arrived, was the garrison really safe. Then, on the last night of the month, a party of two hundred and fifty men sallied out to strike the redskins at Parent Creek, a little more than a mile upstream. But the only result was that they lost twenty-two killed and forty-two wounded, and the creek changed its name to Bloody Run. The siege continued until November with little unusual incident.

The last victory of the savages, or rather the last massacre perpetrated by them, occurred on the Niagara carrying-place in the middle of September. Having delivered their freight at Fort Schlosser above the Falls, a train of wagons and pack horses was returning to the landing below the rapids on the present site of Lewiston. As they were skirting the Devil's Hole, an abyss that breaks the line of cliff along the eastern side of the gorge, a hundred guns blazed out from the woods on their right, and a hundred and more Seneca warriors burst with war whoop and tomahawk. In a moment all but three of the twenty-eight soldiers accompanying the train lay dead on the road above or dying in the chasm below. Hearing the shooting, another small body of troops hastened up from the lower landing, only to fall into an ambush from which few escaped. Major Wilkins, who commanded Fort Niagara at the mouth of the river, now marched up with all his forces. He saw no redskins, but he found seventy white corpses, many of them mutilated beyond possibility of recognition.

Already the revolt had spent its force. The natives' stock of ammunition, which they had greatly increased by the seizure of the posts, was largely shot away, and they had no means of replenishing it. Their supplies of food were likewise running low, so low that they applied pressure to the Canadians at Detroit to provide them with sustenance. They gained a little, but it was at a great cost — the loss of many good friends. More important still was their loss of heart. Eagerly they had been expecting the king of France to send them great aid, but from Fort Chartres, his nearest outpost, they had received nothing except doubtful words until the last day of October, when a messenger from this fort on the Mississippi arrived in Detroit. He brought a final statement that no help was coming because France had made peace with Britain, and that the Indians had better bury the hatchet because the struggle was hopeless. The character of the North American Indian has never lent itself to concerted action for any length of time on any large scale, and the combination of tribes, even around Detroit under Pontiac, had shown signs of cracking. It now broke up under the weight of this crushing news. The besiegers of Detroit abandoned their hopes of taking that place and went off to their several hunting grounds. The crafty Pontiac sent a message to Gladwyn asking him to forget the past, and then he set out for the Maumee with plans to renew the past in the following spring. But the British commander could not forget nor the Indian chief repeat what had been.

Meanwhile the British military resources were being marshaled for the recovery of the bloodstained wilderness. Not till eight posts had been taken by treachery did Amherst awake from his slumbers in New York. Then he gave vigorous orders. It was he who dispatched Dalzell to Detroit, and at the same time he instructed Colonel Bouquet to collect a force for the relief of Fort Pitt, which had been fitfully assailed. Bouquet, a companion in arms of his fellow countryman Haldimand, was the right man for the task. During his few years in America he had mastered the wild art of bush fighting. Moreover, he knew every foot of the road that he was to travel, for he had built it himself just five years before. Through the stricken frontier area he and his five hundred and fifty men were spurred on by many a gruesome tale of burnt cottages and scalpless skulls.

At Bushy Run, or Edge Hill as he called it, about twenty-five miles from Fort Pitt, Bouquet fought the only real engagement of the war. Early in the afternoon of August 5 he was surrounded by a hostile horde, but the tragedy of Braddock was not to be repeated. When the men lay down on their arms that night, they had lost sixty of their number and they knew that the battle had only begun. At daybreak it was renewed more fiercely than ever. The Indians pressed everywhere and yet, like shadows of the forest, they seemed vulnerable nowhere. Seeing his men falling fast and his line weakening in spirit as well as in numbers, Bouquet decided that only by a daring stratagem could he save the day. Withdrawing two companies from the point where the attack was hottest, he thrust them out unobserved under cover of a depression in the ground. The savages, believing that the troops were beginning to break, concentrated with redoubled fury where the line was thus thinned, only to be caught between two fires. Cold steel completed the rout.

Though tomahawk and scalping knife still visited terror upon many outlying settlements of the old colonies, the back of the rebellion was broken. In the spring of 1764 Sir William Johnson induced the Senecas to sue for peace, which he granted in return for their delivery of all prisoners and the cession of a strip of land four miles wide on each side of the Niagara River. There in July he met a great concourse of tribes gathered from afar by his emissaries, and he persuaded his guests to enter into an alliance with the king of Britain. In this diplomacy Johnson was supported by the presence of one of the two armies which were now proceeding westward. It was led by Colonel Bradstreet and it included the three hundred Canadians mentioned in the last chapter. After the conference, the contingent proceeded up Lake Erie to relieve the worn-out garrison of Detroit, and a detachment went on to reoccupy Michilimackinac.

Meanwhile Colonel Bouquet, who had returned to the east, was retracing his steps of the previous summer. He was leading the other force, which was to push west from Fort Pitt into country which the red men thought no white men would enter. When he reached his destination in the autumn, his stern mien and strong army effectively cowed the natives. They brought in a couple of hundred captives and deposited several chiefs as hostages for the safe delivery of the other white people in the hands of more distant tribes.

In the following summer the French handed over all the territory east of the Mississippi, and George Croghan, after a memorable journey through the Indian territory to the south, arrived in Detroit, where he met the neighboring tribes in council. They agreed to surrender all prisoners still in their possession, to recognize the British as their fathers, and to allow them quiet possession of the posts throughout the country. In return they begged for the reopening of trade. Pontiac smoked the pipe of peace and delivered it to be sent to Sir William Johnson, "that he may know I have made peace, and taken the king of England for my father, in presence of all the nations now assembled." Broken in power and in spirit, he wandered restlessly up and down the land until the spring of 1769. Then an Illinois Indian, bribed by the whiskey of an English trader, stole into the woods after the once great chieftain and buried a tomahawk in his brain.

The cost of the uprising can never be known even approximately. In addition to enormous quantities of government stores and private trading goods, hundreds of lives were destroyed, many with unspeakable cruelty, by the fury of the savages. But this great sacrifice of blood and treasure in America bought great wisdom in Britain. Thenceforth the Indian policy of the home government was the very reverse of what it had been. It had been scornful and niggardly; now it was sympathetic and generous. This new attitude was to be a prominent factor in Canadian history until after the War of 1812.

CHAPTER V

THE ESTABLISHMENT OF CIVIL GOVERNMENT

THE cession of Canada created one of the greatest problems in the history of the British Empire. Hitherto the empire had grown chiefly by peaceful expansion and settlement, and had remained substantially English and Protestant. Then, by conquest, it acquired a large territory where a people neither English nor Protestant had already established themselves firmly. How was this new and strange block to be fitted into the imperial structure?

Except that they lived in America, the Canadians bore no resemblance to the inhabitants of the other British colonies, and they had nothing in common with the people of Britain except their new sovereign. They had a different religion; they spoke a different tongue; they sprang from a different race; they lived under different laws and institutions; they had a different outlook on life; they were the product of a different civilization. Under any circumstances, the difficulty of finding a form of government that would effectively incorporate this alien people into the British Empire would have been very great, and existing conditions conspired to make it greater still.

Britain's task would have been easier had France been a traditional friend, but in those days France was the hereditary foe. Britain won Canada in the midst of what has been called the modern Hundred Years' War. For a century and a quarter, from the English Revolution to the battle of Waterloo, Britain and France were fighting off and on. Another war might break out at any time. Would it not transform the Canadians into a hostile people? Until the early years of the nineteenth century this shadow darkened the problem of how Canada was to be governed. A second complication appeared on the morrow of the conquest when a small but important English-speaking minority settled in the towns of Quebec and Montreal. How could a constitution be fitted to the needs of all the people in Canada when they were divided by race, language, and religion? Must not the minority be squeezed or the majority

74

oppressed? This dilemma was even more persistent and trouble-some than the shadow already mentioned. It lasted until the forma-tion of the Dominion of Canada more than a century afterward. A third embarrassment lay in the juxtaposition of the old colonies. Relieved from the brooding fear of French power at their very doors, they no longer felt the need for dependence upon the mother country. Their new sensibility, combined with the wide divergence between their character and that of Canada, made it impossible for the British government to give justice to the people in the new colony without giving offense to the people in the old colonies. This further dilemma, which the home government did not see at this time, passed in the upheaval which rent the empire asunder, but the proximity of the old colonies, grown into an independent state, has continued to influence the constitutional development of Canada down to the present day. A fourth difficulty in the way of finding a satisfactory solution on the morrow of the peace was the gathering storm cloud in the west. In deciding what should be done with the new colony on the St. Lawrence, the home government was distracted by a vain desire to forestall the fierce native rising described in the last chapter.

In approaching the Canadian problem, the British government could find no help in looking back or in looking forward. All they could look back to was Acadia, conquered fifty years before. But Acadia in 1713 was very unlike Canada in 1763. The former con-tained only seventeen hundred inhabitants, a mere handful com-pared with the sixty-two thousand in Canada. They sprang from another part of France, and in America they lived another kind of life. They were almost as remote from the Canadians in character as they were in position. Finally, British experience in Acadia, instead of shedding a light, threw a shadow across the minds of all who contemplated it. The tragedy of the famous, or infamous, deportation was not to be repeated. In looking forward, the British government of this time was quite as helpless because it lacked the insight of genius. Just when the highest statesmanship became most imperative, it became least possible. In the days of the Whig oligarchy, Britain's political life was not very healthy, and now the accession of George III cast a blight upon it.

Even the elder Pitt failed to see the necessity for reorganizing the very unsatisfactory machinery for handling colonial affairs.

Responsibility for managing the overseas empire rested on the secretary of state for the southern department, who also directed Britain's foreign policy in southern Europe and shouldered the duties of the home office. In colonial matters he relied on the lords commissioners for trade and plantations, commonly known as the board of trade. This body, created by the king in 1696 and abolished by parliament in 1782, exercised a general supervision over the detailed administration of the colonies. Its only real authority was to appoint members of colonial councils. Otherwise, though it corresponded directly with governors, it was an advisory body acting through the secretary of state or the privy council.

On May 5, 1763, the Earl of Egremont, who had succeeded Pitt as secretary of state for the southern department in 1761, asked the board of trade to work out a policy for the territories conquered in the late war and ceded by the peace treaty.[1] He directed attention chiefly to North America. The Canadian problem was thus bulked with other problems, which had its advantages and disadvantages. Of the papers that Egremont supplied to the board, those which concerned Canada were copies of the treaty, of the two capitulations, and of three reports that Murray, Burton, and Gage had submitted on their respective governments in 1762.[2] Murray's report, which was twice the size of the other two put together, was a full and penetrating analysis. The solution which the board of trade evolved for Canada in 1763[3] is spread over three documents, the royal proclamation of October 7,[4] Murray's commission as governor, dated November 21,[5] and his instructions, issued on December 7.[6] The proclamation applied to all the new acquisitions and established the main outlines to be filled out separately for each new colony in the commission and instructions, which were framed with an eye to local conditions. All were digested together and might have appeared together had it not been for the unrest among the North American Indians. An effort to quiet their fears hastened the birth of the proclamation.

The royal proclamation of October 7, 1763, in establishing and delimitating the new governments of America[7] changed the name and reduced the size of Canada. Until the Constitutional Act effected another alteration, it was to be known officially as the province of Quebec. It covered much the same area as the modern province of Quebec, with which of course it must not be confused.

Its boundary from Ristigouche Bay to the River St. Lawrence almost coincided with the present provincial line. From the St. Lawrence it ran straight to the southeast corner of Lake Nipissing, thus including a narrow strip of modern Ontario. From Lake Nipissing it struck northeast through Lake St. John and five hundred miles beyond to the head of the St. John River, then followed the southwesterly course of that stream to its mouth opposite the western end of the island of Anticosti. The northern boundary was purely arbitrary. It caused little concern to officials in England and none to people in Canada. The other boundaries were different; there was a reason behind each.

The definition of the eastern boundary, the St. John River, may be traced to the terms of peace. By granting France the islands of St. Pierre and Miquelon, and by giving her subjects the right to fish in the gulf and to dry on the shores of Newfoundland, the treaty allowed France to retain in the region of the gulf a foothold that seemed dangerous, at least to official eyes in London. There were fears that it might encourage smuggling and possibly hostile encroachments in that quarter. Before the proclamation was issued, therefore, the Labrador coast as far west as the St. John River was severed from Canada and placed under the jurisdiction of the nearer and distinctly naval government of Newfoundland.[8] The hinterland, which was then of no consequence, went with the coast as a matter of course. Being an accomplished fact, the change was automatically inserted in the definition of Canada's boundaries in the proclamation. The southern boundary was drawn with the purpose of cutting off territory which the Canadians had not yet settled and from which they were to be excluded. It was thought that these lands, by being annexed to Nova Scotia and New England, might develop into a solid English colony.

The new western boundary was considered the most important of all. It was fixed after deep discussion and as part of a high policy. Canada's great hinterland was torn away to make possible the creation of a huge Indian reserve in the heart of the continent. This meant confining the old colonies to the Atlantic seaboard. Although some people regarded such a restriction as desirable for economic and political reasons of empire,[9] and although the board of trade wished the expansive force of American society to operate laterally, up and down the coast, there is no evidence of any official desire to cramp the old colonies. The object of the board and of the government was the independence of the red man rather than the dependence of the white. The motive was really very simple. By preserving the hunting grounds of the savages from the intrusion of settlers, Britain might destroy the causes of Indian unrest and thereby save herself and her colonies from a deal of trouble.

This policy was proposed by the board of trade in a report dated June 8. Five weeks later Egremont replied that the king agreed with the end but questioned the means. He pointed out the dangers of leaving such a large tract of land derelict. Without a government, it would attract fugitives from justice, it would lie open to the intrigues of foreign powers, and it would allow the development of disputes over property in the years to come. For these reasons he urged that it be included in the new government of Quebec. To this proposal the board raised three counter-objections in a report of August 5: it would imply a French origin to the title of these lands, and the implication might have awkward consequences, particularly upon the minds of the Indians; it would give the province of Quebec a commercial advantage over the other colonies; and it would endow its governor with too great a military power, for a large garrison would be necessary to hold such a vast region and the troops would have to be placed under the authority of the governor. The original objections, the report continued, could be obviated by commissioning the commander-in-chief to govern the territory for the time being. Other arrangements might be made later. These arguments prevailed and the boundary was drawn accordingly.

Throughout the whole discussion there was no thought of locking up this territory to shut out white men entirely. The proclamation forbade the private purchase or occupation of any of these lands and ordered all who "either wilfully or inadvertently" had seated themselves there to remove forthwith. Apparently this command was not intended for the Canadians whose homes were already in the west, nor was it taken as such. It was aimed at the men who were hewing their way into the western forest — the backwoodsmen of the old colonies. While these farmers were to be excluded because they threatened to destroy the Indians' means of livelihood, traders were to be encouraged because they united the interests of the natives, of the colonists, and of the mother country. Any trader was to be allowed to go into the interior if he procured a license and gave security that he would observe the regulations that might be imposed. Licenses were to be granted "without fee or reward" by the commander-in-chief or by any governor. Lest this freedom create a haven for outlaws, all military officers and officials intrusted with the management of Indian affairs were directed to seize fugitives from justice and to return them to the colonies where their crimes were committed. By an oversight, no provision was made for dealing with crimes committed in this territory.[10]

Two famous promises concerning the government of the new colonies were inserted in the proclamation. One was that they were to have general assemblies as soon as circumstances would permit. The other was that meanwhile all persons inhabiting or resorting to these new colonies "may confide in our royal protection for the enjoyment of the benefit of the laws of . . . England." These promises bedeviled the Canadian situation for several years, and therefore it is necessary to examine why they were made and why they were put in this document. Their primary motive was to draw immigrants into these new members of the empire by guaranteeing an attractive form of government, and the guarantee was inserted in the proclamation because this was the most solemn, binding, and public method of giving it to those for whom it was intended.

It is also interesting to observe that the proclamation, in making these promises, said something that was palpably untrue. It stated that the various governors, with the advice of their councils, were already empowered by instruments under the Great Seal to call assemblies and to erect courts "for hearing and determining all causes, as well criminal as civil, according to law and equity, as near as may be agreeable to the laws of England," from which appeals might be carried to the privy council. The tense which made the above statement false was no mere slip of the drafting pen. It should have been true, and it would have been true had not the Indian question thrust itself forward. The proclamation was to have appeared *after* and not *before* the commissions. Grave consequences flowed from this inversion of order.

The proclamation also held out the offer of vacant lands in the three new colonies having large quantities of them, Quebec, East Florida, and West Florida. Retired officers who had served in North America during the late war and private soldiers disbanded in America and resident there were, upon application, to receive lands "without fee or reward." The grants were to vary from fifty acres to five thousand, according to the rank of each recipient, and were to carry no obligation for ten years. After that period the owners were to observe the same conditions of cultivation and improvement and to pay the same quitrents as other proprietors. To nonmilitary settlers the governors were to allot public lands "upon such terms, and under such moderate quit rents, services and acknowledgments as have been appointed in our other colonies," and such other conditions as might be imposed in future.

The commission and the instructions issued to Murray followed the accustomed forms with variations and additions to suit local conditions. The commission, dated November 21, 1763, appointed him "Captain General and Governor in Chief" of the province of Quebec.[11] As stated in the proclamation, it empowered him, with the advice of his council, to call assemblies and to create law courts, and also "with the advice and consent" of council and assembly to make laws for the colony. The council was simply taken for granted, as were also lieutenant governors of Three Rivers and Montreal. The whole government was to be Protestant, for the governor, lieutenant governors, judges, councilors, and assemblymen were to take the statutory oaths of office and declaration against popery. The commission gave no power to pass legislation before an assembly was summoned — an unfortunate omission.

The instructions issued on December 7, 1763, directed the governor to establish a council composed of the two lieutenant governors, the chief justice of the colony, the surveyor general of the American customs, and eight others to be chosen "from amongst the most considerable" of the residents in the province. As the nominated members had to receive the approval of the board of trade, Murray was ordered to remit their names and also a list of eight others from whom substitutes might be chosen for rejected nominees. Similarly, whenever a council seat became vacant, the governor was to submit a list of three or more from which one might be selected. If for any reason the council ever shrank to less than seven members, the governor might increase it to that number, but the new appointees were to be subject to displacement by orders from home. The governor might suspend or remove councilors for "just cause." As this authority was actually used, though not by Murray, the conditions prescribed by the instructions should be noted.

Charges against members and their replies were to be examined in council. A majority vote was to decide. If it went against the accused, a full entry was to be made in the minutes. Copies of all papers bearing on the case were to be sent forthwith to the board of trade. The governor might act on his sole authority if he found reasons "not fit to be communicated to the council," but then he had to make a report at once to the board of trade.

More important still, because of its subsequent use, was a short passage inserted in a long section dealing with legislation by governor, council, and assembly. Until an assembly was practicable, the governor was directed "to make such rules and regulations, by the advice of our said council, as shall appear to be necessary for the peace, order and good government of our said province, taking care that nothing be passed or done that shall any ways tend to affect the life, limb or liberty of the subject, or to the imposing any duties or taxes." Such rules and regulations were to be sent home at once for approval or disallowance.

The council, of course, was to be an executive body. The instructions explicitly required its consent for such things as the granting of public lands and the passing of the public accounts. It was also to have a judicial function, though this was not expressly stated. That it was to be the final court of appeal in the colony was implied by a passage in the instructions which directed the governor to follow the precedent of Nova Scotia.

The treaty guarantee of toleration was mentioned in the instructions, which enjoined the governor to observe it — with qualifications. Already he had been officially warned to watch this liberty closely. In August, writing to tell him of his appointment to the government of the colony,[12] Egremont had cautioned Murray against the political danger of allowing any connection between the Canadian clergy and the church in France, and he had pointed out that the clause about the laws of Great Britain excluded "absolutely all popish hierarchy in any of the dominions belonging to the Crown of Great Britain." The instructions now forbade the admission "of any ecclesiastical jurisdiction of the See of Rome, or any other foreign ecclesiastical jurisdiction whatsoever," and required a full report on the constitution, the claims, and the property of the church in Canada. That there was an ominous suggestion in these words appears clearly from a passage that follows almost imme-

diately. "To the end that the Church of England may be established both in principles and practice, and that the said inhabitants
may by degrees be induced to embrace the Protestant religion, and
their children be brought up in the principles of it," lands were to
be set aside for the support of Protestant clergymen and schoolmas-
ters, and the governor was to report "by what other means the
Protestant religion may be promoted." The home government entertained no design of persecution; it rather nourished the hope that
Canadians might be brought to see the light.

Another prominent feature of the instructions was the elaborate
provision for planting settlers upon the soil of Canada. Some later
writers have neglected this part of the document, which is long and
very detailed, because nothing came of it, and in so doing have
missed one of the most important points in the British government's
policy for the colony. As soon as possible an accurate survey of the
province was to be made, and then townships were to be laid out.
Each was to cover about twenty thousand acres and to have a town
site, near which four hundred acres were to be reserved for a clergyman and two hundred for a schoolmaster. Applicants for lands
were to satisfy the governor and council that they could and would
improve the grants they might receive. The basic rate, which might
be increased under special circumstances, was a hundred acres for
every head of a family and fifty additional for each dependent.
To receive and to keep their titles, grantees were to pay quitrents
of at least two shillings per hundred acres and to improve their
lands in a minutely specified manner. As soon as he could, the
governor was to issue a proclamation advertising the conditions
governing grants, and he was to take such steps as he thought
proper for publishing it in all the colonies in North America. He
was advised to insert in this document a "description of the natural
advantages of the soil and climate" of the country and "its peculiar
conveniences for trade and navigation." All this has a clear and
unmistakable meaning. The home government was anticipating a
large influx of population from the congested colonies to the south.

The program set forth in the proclamation, the commission, and
the instructions may be summed up in one short sentence. An old
French colony was to be remade into an English colony. This may
seem strange in the light of certain statements made both before and
after the policy was framed. In his long report upon the condition

of the country, which he submitted in 1762, Murray said that nothing could contribute more to making the Canadians staunch subjects than the belief that their religion was absolutely secure; and two days later, in a letter to Egremont, he observed that the Canadians were not "ripe for such a government as prevails in our other colonies." [13] In its report of June 8, 1763, the board of trade proposed to govern Canada simply by governor and council — without mention of an assembly. The board also pointed out that the Canadians "must greatly exceed for a very long period of time" all other settlers in the country, and it advised drawing in Canada's boundaries to confine as closely as possible "the rights and usages already secured or that may be granted to the new French subjects." Five years afterward Lord Hillsborough, who succeeded Lord Shelburne as head of the board of trade while the proclamation was being prepared, affirmed "that it never entered into our idea to overturn the laws and customs of Canada with regard to property." [14]

Hillsborough's words have lent color to an ingenious theory that the shuffling of offices and the rush to meet the native problem occasioned a serious oversight in the framing of the proclamation.[15] The theory is supported by an omission in a report of the board of trade of August 5, 1763,[16] which urged an immediate proclamation to remove the Indian danger and added that it might include an offer of lands to settlers in the new colonies of East and West Florida and the old colony of Nova Scotia. Canada was omitted from the list. According to the theory, the proclamation was not intended to apply to Canada. This colony was to be dealt with in another document which Hillsborough, who now succeeded Shelburne, and the Earl of Halifax, who took over Egremont's duties, completely forgot.

This theory rests on very little evidence and, more important, it is quite unnecessary. Though modern eyes may see the proclamation as an egregious blunder, the eyes of that day saw differently. Murray, whose greatest motive was sympathy for the French, accepted the proclamation with joy. In January, 1764, he wrote that it "gives everybody great content and satisfaction." [17] Moreover, in spite of his own sound advice, his mind was ever revolving unsound schemes for weaning the Canadians from their old religion. If he saw no incongruity in this, should the home government be blamed, or

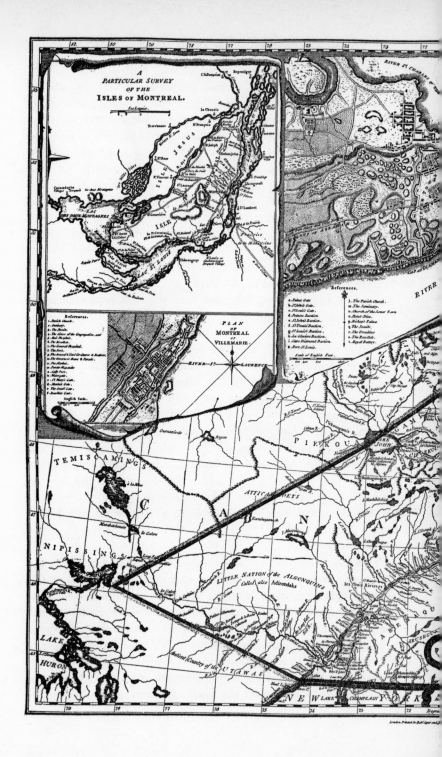

A
PARTICULAR SURVEY
OF THE
ISLES OF MONTREAL.

PLAN
OF
MONTREAL
OR
VILLEMARIE.

RIVER S.T LAURENCE

References.

1. Palais Gate.   1. The Parish Church.
2. S.T John's Gate.   m. The Seminary.
3. S.T Lewis's Gate.   n. Church of the Lower Town.
4. Poteaw Bastion.   o. Hotel-Dieu.
5. S.T John's Bastion.   p. Bishop's Palace.
6. S.T Ursula's Bastion. q. The Jesuits.
7. S.T Lewis's Bastion. r. The Ursulines.
8. La Glaciere Bastion. s. The Recollets.
9. Cape Diamond Bastion. t. The Recollets.
10. Fort S.T Louis.   u. Royal Battery.

Scale of English Feet.

References.

1. Parish Church.
2. Seminary.
3. The Recole.
4. The Sisters of the Congregation, and
5. Bowl Hospital.
6. The Recollets.
7. The General Hospital.
8. The Fort.
9. The General's Yard Residence & Battery.
10. The Governor House & Parish.
11. The Market.
12. Jesuits Monastère.
13. Gaily Fort.
14. Market gate.
15. S.T Mary's Gate.
16. The Jesuit's Gate.
17. Recollets Gate.
S. English Yards.

TEMISCAMINGS

C

NIPISSINGS

LAKE
HURON

PIEKOU

ATTICAMOUETS

C   A   N

LITTLE NATION of the ALGONQUINS
Called also Adirondaks

Ant.ient Country of the
UTAWAS

les Trois Rivieres

NEW   LAKE   COMPLAIN   YORK

London. Printed for Rob.t Sayer and J.

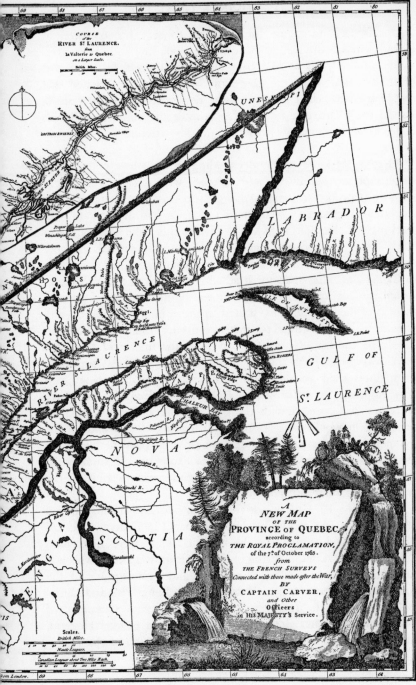

A
NEW MAP
OF THE
PROVINCE OF QUEBEC,
according to
THE ROYAL PROCLAMATION,
of the 7ᵗʰ of October 1763.
from
THE FRENCH SURVEYS
Connected with those made after the War,
BY
CAPTAIN CARVER,
and other
Officers
in HIS MAJESTY'S Service.

Course of the RIVER Sᵗ LAURENCE, from la Valterie to Quebec, on a Larger Scale.
British Miles.

LABRADOR

GULF OF Sᵗ LAURENCE

NOVA SCOTIA

RIVER Sᵗ LAURENCE

CHALEUR BAY

Scales.
British Miles.
Nautic Leagues.
Canadian Leagues about Two Miles Each.

should it need an excuse for the same thing? The omission of Canada's name on August 5, instead of pointing to a later oversight, is more likely to have been an oversight itself, for the report of June 8, drafted by the very same board of trade, asserted that one of the two "chief objects" of the new government for Canada should be "to increase as much as possible the number of British and other new Protestant settlers," and this assertion was not withdrawn.

Here is the key to an understanding of the whole policy. The surplus population in the old colonies was already worrying a number of people at home. Among them was John Pownall, who, as permanent secretary of the board of trade, had more to do with working out this policy than had anyone else. The offer of cheap lands and a "free" government might draw a solid English-speaking and Protestant population from the old colonies. Their migration to Canada, together with the gradual conversion of the Canadians, would provide a broad justification for the new system of government. As they had already started to move into Nova Scotia and were to pour into Canada a generation later, this calculation can hardly be condemned as wild. Even in the matter of the laws, there was probably much less oversight than has been supposed. In an unfinished sketch in the Shelburne Papers,[18] Pownall was very emphatic in insisting that "the laws of England shall take place and be observed with the greatest care and exactness," for, he added, "it would have been happier for this country and for the colonies themselves had this rule been close attended to." Only in the island colonies would he allow any exception. In short, what the home government proposed for Canada was, in view of the times, both natural and reasonable.

On August 10, 1764, when the military régime ended, Murray began to apply in Canada the system prepared in London. He had already picked his men for the council. They were Lieutenant Colonel Paulus Æmilius Irving of the Fifteenth Regiment, who was later commander-in-chief in the colony and administrator of the government between Murray's departure in June, 1766, and Carleton's arrival in the following September; Captain Cramahé, of whom something has already been said; Captain Samuel Holland, an engineer who had recently finished a great map of the colony and was to remain Canada's surveyor general for more than a generation; Walter Murray, a relative of the governor and at this time the heir of the Elibank family, who had lived long in the colonies; Adam Mabane, of whom much will be said later; Benjamin Price and Thomas Dunn, merchants from England; and François Mounier, a Huguenot merchant settled in Canada shortly before the conquest.[19]

This group of men deserves more than passing notice because it was to play a much more important rôle in the government of the colony than was anticipated. In the first place, it was virtually the whole council, though it was to have been only a part of it. Of the ex officio members, only the chief justice, William Gregory, attended regularly, and he might better have not come at all, for his only contribution was a bad judgment and an equally bad temper. The surveyor general of the American customs, because of his wide duties, was seldom in the colony and therefore was rarely able to take his seat at the board. The lieutenant governors of Montreal and Three Rivers never appeared. The responsibility for their absence rests upon the home government. While it stooped too low in picking the first chief justice, it aimed too high in choosing men to rule under Murray in Three Rivers and Montreal. It appointed men who would not serve — Burton and Gage. The former, though junior to Murray in military rank, had been his equal as military governor and had been his rival for the civil government. Gage had an even better excuse for his haughty refusal. He had been promoted over Murray's head in 1759 and now for several months had been his commander-in-chief. The new governor sent Irving and Cramahé to act as temporary substitutes, but shortly afterward he received a letter from the secretary of state announcing the discontinuance of both offices.[20] Thus by the virtual elimination of the official element, inserted to give tone and weight, the council assumed an unexpected character. In the second place, it was obliged to undertake an unexpected duty. The governor's refusal to call an assembly elevated it into the only legislative body in the colony. In the third place, this little knot of men, through whose hands passed everything of importance affecting the civil government transacted in the colony, were to have a more permanent influence than the two causes already detailed would imply. Being selected by Murray, they were marked by a strong sympathy for the Canadians and a firm belief that the government of the colony should be conducted in the interests of the "new subjects," an attitude which Murray's two successors came to share.

As others in the colony held very different principles, and as the council stayed while governors came and went, this group became the nucleus of a party, sometimes known as the "French party" and sometimes as the "king's party," which practically governed Canada until 1787. Irving and Mabane were its first leaders. Irving returned home in the spring of 1768, but Mabane never left the country, to which he was already becoming deeply attached and upon which he was to leave his mark. Having run away from his medical studies in the University of Edinburgh, he had continued them in the army as a surgeon's mate. In this humble capacity he had come to Canada in 1760,[21] when he was about twenty-seven years old. Since his arrival he had risen to commissioned rank, being now surgeon of the Quebec garrison, and had developed a valuable private practice as well. He was soon to become a judge also. It is characteristic of the man that as soon as he received a salary from the crown, though it was only a fraction of the income brought by his private practice, he gave up his fees but not his patients.[22] Possessing marked ability, a strong character, and a warm Scottish heart, he was an outstanding figure in the colony from his first civil appointments in 1764 until his death in January, 1792. Indeed, during most of this time few other individuals exercised anything like the influence he did over the actual administration of Canada.

The first meeting of the council was on August 13, 1764; on that day no business was transacted except the necessary formalities of installation. At the next session, a week later, its members at once approached the problem of erecting a judicial system. After hearing all the instructions to the governors of Quebec and of Nova Scotia bearing on the point, they ordered the chief justice and the attorney general to prepare a plan. Probably the attorney general, George Suckling,[23] did most of the work. He had greater energy and more legal acumen than had Gregory. Moreover, the home government had suggested that the courts be framed with an eye to what had been done in the other colonies, particularly Nova Scotia, and Suckling came from Nova Scotia, where he had had a stormy career in law and politics. On September 17, exactly four weeks after the chief justice and the attorney general had been asked to prepare a plan, the council approved an ordinance creating courts for the colony.[24]

The highest court was that of the king's bench, which was to sit in Quebec and hold two terms a year under the presidency of the chief justice. "All His Majesty's subjects" — a phrase used to cover Canadians — were to be admitted "without distinction" to juries in this court. It was to have both civil and criminal jurisdiction and was to apply the laws of England and the ordinances of the province. An appeal lay to the governor in council if the amount in dispute exceeded three hundred pounds, and thence to the privy council if the amount reached five hundred pounds. The chief justice was also to hold courts of assize and general jail delivery in the towns of Montreal and Three Rivers once a year soon after the winter term of the king's bench.

An inferior court for civil cases of more than ten pounds, called the court of common pleas, was to keep the same terms in Quebec as the superior court. As this was designed especially for the new subjects, it was allowed to apply French laws in suits originating before October 1, 1764, if both parties were native Canadians. Otherwise it was "to determine agreeable to equity, having regard nevertheless to the laws of England, as far as the circumstances and present situation of things will admit, until such time as proper ordinances for the information of the people can be established by the governor and council, agreeable to the laws of England," all of which was delightfully vague. Its decisions might be appealed to the king's bench if they involved twenty pounds, or directly to the governor in council if more than three hundred. In the common pleas either party could insist upon a trial by jury. Canadians were explicitly allowed to plead as advocates in this court, but they were implicitly excluded from its juries — which was clearly an oversight, for they were soon admitted without question.

In establishing inferior jurisdictions, the ordinance abolished the old threefold division of the colony, because there were not enough Protestants in Three Rivers to act as magistrates, and created two new and larger districts, those of Quebec and Montreal. Each was to have its own justices of the peace, three of whom could hold quarter sessions with the usual criminal jurisdiction and with a civil jurisdiction in cases of more than ten pounds but not over thirty. Their civil judgments might be appealed to the king's bench. Any two justices sitting together had final jurisdiction over civil causes involving not more than ten pounds, and a single justice had similar authority to determine disputes over property that did not involve more than five pounds.

For the policing and local administration of the towns of Quebec and Montreal, each was to have two justices of the peace sitting weekly in rotation — the only municipal government in the country for a long time to come. Throughout the province, every parish was annually to elect six men from whom the governor and council might select constables, or bailiffs and sub-bailiffs, as they were called. Their duties were to oversee the roads and bridges, to arrest criminals, to serve as coroners when a regular coroner was not available, and to settle by means of arbitration all disputes over the breaking and mending of fences.

Those who framed and passed this ordinance of September 17, 1764, wished to fit it into the life of the country, but they were conscious of being cramped by the proclamation, the instructions, and the "laws of England." In several particulars, however, they deliberately overstepped the narrow bounds they saw set for their feet. They did it because they could not help themselves, and the governor conveyed their excuses and apologies to the home government. They waived the law disqualifying Roman Catholics from serving on juries because it would have erected a handful of Protestants into "perpetual judges of the lives and property" not only of the new subjects but also of the military. This, however, was but "a temporary expedient to keep things as they are until His Majesty's pleasure is known on this critical and difficult point." They departed from a rigid adherence to English law in creating the court of common pleas especially for the Canadians, because to refuse them "such a court until they can be supposed to know something of our laws and methods of procuring justice in our courts would be like sending a ship to sea without a compass." Only because no English barrister or attorney in the colony understood the French language did they override the law against Roman Catholics practicing in British courts, and then they restricted the liberty to the court of common pleas. Very naturally, in this as in the clause opening juries, the ordinance avoided mentioning Roman Catholics, and thus, instead of flying in the face of British statutes, it skipped around them.

In selecting the personnel to put this ordinance in operation, Murray's hands were closely tied. The king's bench caused him no concern at the moment, for it was already filled, very inadequately as events revealed, by the chief justice. But where could he find judges for the common pleas? Of the few lawyers in the country, not one understood the language that would prevail in this court. Therefore he had to choose men who would get their legal training after instead of before their appointment to the bench. He looked about for some weeks, and then he pitched upon a merchant, a doctor, and a soldier.[25] The merchant was the Huguenot Mounier, who died five years later without making any particular name for himself. The doctor, of course, was Adam Mabane. The soldier was Captain John Fraser, a half-pay officer of the Twenty-seventh Regiment and uncle of the explorer Simon Fraser, who was not yet born. He was of an age with his fellow Scot and brother judge, whom he outlived by three years, and though he never attained quite the same prominence, he was an outstanding figure with many of the same striking qualities as Mabane.* Greatly as he liked these two personally, however, Murray was not happy in putting laymen on the bench, and he would have removed either or both of them, and would have had still less compunction about canceling Mounier's appointment, had he succeeded in his effort to procure proper judges from home.

In choosing the justices of the peace the governor had less time to deliberate over difficulties that were equally great or even greater. It was more urgent to fill the void created on August 10 by the disappearance of the established police jurisdiction over the civilian population than it was to provide for the trial of civil suits, which could wait if necessary. Therefore Murray appointed the magistrates weeks before he picked the judges of the common pleas — even before the council considered the outlines of the judicial ordinance. He did not have to wait for the passing of this measure, because it merely supplemented the authority already conferred by

* Fraser was reputed to have been educated by the Jesuits at Douay in Flanders and was suspected by some people of being secretly a Roman Catholic. He married the daughter of Deschambault, a Canadian seignior. Mabane never married, his sister Isabell keeping house for him. Murray seems to have hesitated between Fraser and John Marteilhe, an English merchant who was later appointed by Carleton in 1770. Though a good man, Marteilhe was inferior to Fraser, who also had the advantage of having lived in Montreal, where he had been paymaster of the forces from 1760. Both Mabane and Mounier resided in Quebec.[26]

British statutes upon those who might be included in the commission of the peace. Nor was it less important to find the right men
to serve as magistrates. They would function continuously and
would touch the life of the masses, whereas the judges would sit
only during term time and would have to deal with relatively few
people. Nor was it any easier to fill the commission of the peace,
for, though the magistrates would not have to know so much law,
there would have to be many more of them.

But the greatest difficulty in the way of selecting proper justices
of the peace was the legal obstacle mentioned earlier. Many were
excluded who should have been on the list, and some were included
who should have been left off — because Roman Catholics could
not sit on the bench. The number of Protestants in the colony was
so small that Murray was forced to take men [27] who had little
knowledge of what a justice of the peace was supposed to do, little or
no stake in the country, and no recognized position in its society.
The defect in intellect he tried to remedy by having the attorney
general draft instructions for the appointees; the defect in social
character he tried to overcome by mixing some half-pay officers with
the merchants who formed the main body of the bench. These
efforts doubtless had some good results, but heaven and the English
law determined that there should be black sheep in this Protestant
magisterial fold. For several years the colony suffered from their
inclusion, but for a much longer time and in a much more serious
way it suffered from the exclusion of the natural leaders of the
people, the captains of militia. As a body, they constituted an invaluable heritage from the days of French rule. This heritage, which
had been developed during the military régime to be the main prop
of the country's administration, was thus thrown utterly away, and
the vital contact between the people and the government was cut.
Had it been retained and improved, Canada would have had a very
different and a far happier history. Only the establishment of self-
government in the nineteenth century repaired the tragic loss of
1764.

In one important particular Murray did not complete the machinery of government according to the design prepared in England.
He refused to call an assembly. That London had nothing to do
with this decision appears in the first question which Hillsborough,
the president of the board of trade, put to Cramahé when the latter

arrived home in December, 1764. It was "whether the governor and council had as yet thought of summoning an assembly."[28] At this very time the governor of Grenada was giving Canada's West Indian sister an assembly, but he had gone out fresh to his job with his mind already made up, and he was to rue his rashness.[29] Murray, on the other hand, had lived long enough in Canada to love its people, and he would not deliver them into the hands of a few recently arrived English-speaking merchants by summoning an assembly.

A whole year had passed since the royal proclamation had promised representative government, English laws, and cheap lands to attract a population that might have supported such a legislature, but there was yet no sign of this promise drawing any immigrants from the south to settle on Canadian soil. Perhaps Murray thought that they would never come. In October, 1764, he sought a reduction of the quitrents stipulated in his instructions, because, as he said, the seigniors held every habitable part of the province and would let their lands for much less than the crown demanded.[30] But while these words imply a certain skepticism on his part, he loyally supported the purpose of the home government. Early in the following spring he issued a far from perfunctory proclamation advertising the country's lands and its other advantages. Indeed, this document has all the allurements of a modern immigration "poster." In a glowing account of the colony even the frost and snow were praised because "they not only contribute to fertilize the earth, but they certainly render land-carriage three-fourths cheaper here than in other countries." It closed with a fine flourish about the atmosphere, which it declared was "as healthy as any under the sun, for in no country do people live to a greater age with more uninterrupted good health."

This document was published broadcast in the old colonies, for the public accounts of the province show that twelve pounds in York currency was paid for inserting it in the newspapers of Virginia, Philadelphia, New York, New London, and Boston.[31] But Murray's proclamation, for all its flourishes, did not attract any more immigrants than did the king's. An assembly was, therefore, impossible. The miscalculation of the home government knocked the bottom out of its policy and caused a constitutional miscarriage in Canada. The natives of the country were shut out from every office except the burdensome one of bailiff, their laws were proscribed, and their religion was in jeopardy; and yet, as far as one could then see, they were to remain practically the whole population.

Murray's head and heart joined in revolt against this imposition of an English yoke upon a very un-English people. In the fall of 1764, even before he could know definitely whether a real English-speaking population would come or not, he sent Cramahé home to press for some readjustment in favor of the Canadians.[32] This mission, which lasted until the summer of 1766, the unhappy people's petitions which the governor forwarded, and the pleading dispatches he penned, drew the home government's attention to the injustice that was being done and started a reaction that was to culminate in the Quebec Act.

The first step was taken on June 10, 1765, when Attorney General Sir Fletcher Norton and Solicitor General William de Grey reported that the penal laws of England did not apply to Roman Catholics in Canada.[33] The law officers of the crown gave no reason for this opinion, perhaps because their only reason was common sense and not law.[34] Meanwhile the board of trade was busy, and on September 2, 1765, it submitted two reports on Canada. One,[35] addressed to the king, recommended the calling of an assembly and suggested that Roman Catholics, though they might not sit as members, might be allowed to vote. The other,[36] addressed to the privy council committee for plantation affairs, scored the judicial ordinance of the previous September, chiefly for refusing Canadians full equality with other British subjects in the courts and for sweeping away their laws and customs. It also urged the disallowance of the ordinance and outlined another system for administering justice in the colony.

In the middle of November the privy council committee ordered new instructions for Murray to remove all discrimination against Canadians in the jury box and at the bar. At the same time the committee referred [37] the broader question of a new judicial system to the attorney and solicitor general with directions to consult Cramahé and the agent of the English-speaking merchants in Canada, Fowler Walker.[38] Five months later the law officers presented a report that condemned the attempt to carry on the administration of justice "without the aid of the natives, not merely in new forms, but totally in an unknown tongue," and the interpretation of the proclamation as abolishing "all the usages and customs of Canada with the rough hand of a conqueror." [39]

On the government's orders the board of trade prepared new instructions based on this report.[40] The governor was to recast the whole judicial machinery. Though Roman Catholics were not to be permitted to mount the bench of the superior and the circuit courts that were to be established, they might become magistrates and, indeed, might hold any other office connected with the administration of justice. The courts were to apply English criminal law and French civil law governing real property and inheritance. "In all personal actions grounded upon debts, promises, contracts and agreements, whether of a mercantile or other nature, and also upon wrongs proper to be compensated in damages," they were to "adhere to those substantial maxims of law which invariably in all places govern and prevail in such cases," and thereby could not "materially err either against the laws of England or against the ancient customs of Canada." This reminder that English commercial law had not yet been differentiated from the law merchant of Europe is worth noting because it has an important bearing upon the Quebec Act, as will appear later.

The concessions that would thus be granted to the Canadians went much further than those the board of trade had itself suggested. The additions were the work of Charles Yorke, probably at Cramahé's suggestion. These wise instructions, which were completed in June, 1766, were never sent to Quebec. The cabinet meeting that should have passed them broke up without a decision because Lord Chancellor Northington, who had long neglected almost everything except the bottle, put in an appearance and broke out against the scheme. Shortly afterward, finding in this disagreement an occasion for which he had been waiting, he persuaded the king to dismiss the Rockingham ministry and to call in Pitt. The new government, absorbed in other questions, left its predecessor's reform in a pigeonhole, forgotten.[41] Meanwhile, to quiet Canadian fears, Murray and his council passed an ordinance continuing French laws of tenure and inheritance until August 10, 1765. The judges of the common pleas went further still, though they had no specific authority for doing so. Apparently without any effort to impose English law upon the Canadians in their court, they studied and applied the law of the colony as it stood on the eve of the conquest.

The more delicate question of the headship of the church was also solved while Murray was governor, but he can claim only part of the credit.[42] Much as he loved the Canadians, he did not wish them to have a bishop, for a bishop would consolidate the church, which he hoped to see undermined. After Pontbriand's death the chapter of Quebec had elected three vicars general to govern the diocese, Briand of Quebec, Perrault of Three Rivers, and Montgolfier of Montreal. They had done very well. Why could they not continue? Their impotence to create priests did not worry the shrewd Scot. The government, he suggested, could take men trained in the Quebec seminary and send them at public expense to a friendly Catholic country for ordination.[43] He was willing to go thus far because he realized that he must play his line to land his fish. Doubtless he was encouraged in his view by numbers of the Canadian clergy who were by no means anxious for a bishop. They could go their own gait more easily without an episcopal driver holding the reins of discipline. Murray, however, did not stoop to share their ignoble motive. His relations with Briand from the beginning of the military régime were more than honorable; they were cordial. Each frequently used his influence to support the other in managing the clergy and their flocks.

The desire for a bishop, necessary to preserve the church from present disorder and future death, was at first confined to a portion of the clergy. For some months after they learned of the definite cession of the country to a Protestant sovereign, they puzzled over the problem of how to proceed. Then, in September, 1763, the chapter assembled in Quebec and drew up an address to the king beseeching permission to have a bishop. Two days later, realizing the political impossibility of nomination by foreign authorities in Paris or Rome and the ecclesiastical impossibility of nomination by the Protestant government in Britain, the canons tried to cut the Gordian knot by reviving the ancient custom of election, which, incidentally, was still practiced in Germany. Briand was the natural choice. He had been secretary of the late bishop and was the senior cleric in the colony. But his excessive modesty, reinforced by economic considerations, led him to refuse. Thereupon the chapter elected Montgolfier, who, as superior of the Seminary of St. Sulpice at Montreal, was departing for Europe on business of his order.

The economic considerations were as real as Briand's modesty.

The bishop and chapter had derived most of their revenue from France. This source of supply was cut off by the conquest, but the Montreal seminary, being a large landowner, might easily support the head of the church. The election was to be kept secret until a favorable decision could be procured in London. If this were not forthcoming, and Montgolfier could not be bishop, the chapter trusted that Rome would commission him vicar apostolic with a title of bishop *in partibus* — the arrangement under which Laval had first come to Canada.

Murray could not see exactly what was happening under his nose, but he smelled something and he did not like it. He wrote home giving a very frank opinion upon the vicar general of Montreal, of whom he had received unfavorable reports. Meanwhile there was a marked awakening among the laity. From all parts of the country they began to cry for a bishop. The citizens of Quebec held a meeting after Mass on the Sunday following the selection of Montgolfier and decided to petition the king for a bishop and to send a representative to plead the people's cause in London. The citizens of Three Rivers and Montreal eagerly followed this lead. Each district drew up its own petition, but all combined in sharing the expenses of the deputy chosen in Quebec, Etienne Charest, lord of the broad seigniory of Lauzon. Murray could neither favor nor stop this popular movement, and therefore he compromised. He wrote Lord Halifax, the secretary of state, recommending Charest's person but not his object.[44] If the home government were to allow a bishop, Murray would have no one but Briand, who "has acted with a candour, moderation and a delicacy in such circumstances as deserve the highest commendation, such indeed as I little expected from one of his gown." [45]

The layman and the cleric, the former pressing the general and the latter the particular question, were both doomed to disappointment. Charest was turned back by a wall of politeness in the empire's capital, and he returned to Canada in disgust. Two insurmountable obstacles stood between Montgolfier and the episcopal throne, one in London and the other in Rome. The British government accepted Murray's words as an absolute veto. This was decisive. Had the bishop-elect been consecrated he would have been excluded from the colony and the whole scheme for securing a bishop in Canada would have been wrecked. But there was no chance of his being consecrated. Rome unwittingly backed the government in London and the governor in Quebec by declaring the election null and void and by condemning it as a dangerous revival of extinct power. Almost a year after the date of his election, Montgolfier, having returned to Canada, wrote the chapter resigning his pretensions in favor of Briand. In spite of the recent pronouncement of the papal court, the chapter at once "elected and presented" the vicar general of Quebec to be titular bishop, and the seminary of Quebec, though comparatively poverty-stricken, came forward with an offer to house and nourish him as head of the church.

Nearly two years elapsed between Briand's departure for England and his return as bishop with the consent of the British government and the blessing of Rome, for he encountered obstacles in the same quarters as Montgolfier had met them. In London the Protestant government naturally resisted the idea of solidifying the Roman Catholic church in Canada by allowing it to have a bishop. Three distinct influences stiffened this resistance. One was fear of France. Immediately after the signature of peace, the dean of the Quebec chapter, the Abbé de la Corne, had appeared in London to plead for a bishop. Because he came direct from Paris, where he had been residing for some years to watch over the interests of the Canadian church, and because he enlisted the influence of the French ambassador, he roused suspicion instead of sympathy for his cause. His comings and goings across the Channel — for he renewed the attack in 1764 and again in 1765 — did not allay suspicion. British eyes detected a political motive hidden under the cloak of religion.

A second influence was Père Roubaud, one of the most precious rascals in Canadian history. This renegade Jesuit had an insinuating way with low women and with high officials. He lived on both. By playing upon Murray's hope of a Protestant Canada he opened the heart and the pocket of the governor,[46] who sent him to England early in the summer of 1764. "This gentleman," said Murray's letter to Halifax, "is worthy of your notice. He is a man of extraordinary parts and great learning, and as eloquent as Cicero. He is possessed of a thorough knowledge of the views, sentiments and faculties of the popish clergy of this province and perfectly sensible of the errors of their doctrines. He proposed publicly renouncing the Roman Catholic religion here, but such a renunciation would

rather frustrate than promote my schemes for the reformation of
the inhabitants of this colony. For that reason I send him to London
where he may be useful and cooperate with me under the immediate direction of His Majesty's servants *in the great task I undertake of converting a great part of the Canadians."* [47] This introduction was an open sesame to the government offices on the banks
of the Thames, where Roubaud seemed like a Daniel come to judgment. Without a bishop, his insinuating argument ran, the clergy
would sooner or later fall into matrimony and the church would fall
to pieces. The third influence that hardened the government's heart
toward the prayers of the Canadians was the rise of the Whiteboys
in Ireland during the opening years of George III's reign. Though
the cause of the nocturnal raids in Munster and Leinster was economic desperation, Englishmen were sure that it was priestly inspiration.

Perplexed by the problem of the Canadian church, the government appears to have consulted the archbishop of York. In April,
1764, he submitted a number of suggestions [48] which the board of
trade adopted as the basis of a plan that they completed in May,
1765.[49] Although it was never applied and was to be forgotten for
over two years, it was revived and revised by a later administration,
which seriously considered applying it, and therefore it should not
be ignored. Its main features were as follows. The crown was to
license a superintendent of the Roman Catholic church, who could
fill no benefice nor make any ecclesiastical regulation without the
consent of the governor, and might even be suspended by him. The
dean and chapter were to be abolished. The seminaries of Quebec
and Montreal were to be consolidated at the capital, and from their
combined revenues the superintendent was to receive a fixed stipend
and the seminary was to be allowed an income just sufficient to
educate a limited number of priests. The Jesuits were to be abolished and the other religious houses were to be starved by forbidding
them to recruit. Out of the revenues of these establishments, the
existing members were to be subsisted until they died or were appointed to vacant cures. The harvest of property thus gathered was
to be applied to support Protestant churches and schools. Protestant-
ism was also to be encouraged by permitting the collection of tithes
only from Roman Catholics. In short, the Canadian church was to
be put in a strait-jacket and squeezed.

Though the obstacle in London thus rose to a dangerous height in the spring of 1765, it soon began to sink away. Murray relented from his stern attitude toward the episcopacy and actually urged Briand's appointment, not only by official dispatches but also by private communications to his brother Gideon, the dean of Durham, and even to the archbishop of York.[50] Cramahé[51] was also using his utmost influence on Briand's behalf. Various were the arguments advanced in the capital of the empire. Precedents were found and quoted. Roman Catholics in Montserrat enjoyed a number of privileges, and Roman Catholicism was the established religion in Minorca, then a British possession.

But precedent was not capable of deciding such an important matter. The issue seems to have been determined by a careful examination and balancing of possible evils. The refusal of the Canadians' desire might bring unfortunate and even dangerous consequences. It might lead many to emigrate from the colony and might leave a deep sense of grievance in the hearts of many who remained. Moreover, French priests might creep into Canada, and the "engines of popery" might operate in the dark. Nor, on further examination, was the danger attendant upon granting the Canadians' request so great after all. They were really modest in their demand, asking only for a "private" bishop who would share the simple life of the poor seminary in Quebec, and not for an ecclesiastical lord who would flaunt his power before the public. This argument derived its greatest support from the personality of Briand himself. He was as wise as a serpent and as harmless as a dove. He shrewdly escaped the snare into which De la Corne had fallen, by studiously avoiding the French embassy. A realist in politics and a saint in the church, he was clearly incapable of being a proud prelate. At last, some time toward the close of 1765, he was confidentially, but not officially, advised to get himself consecrated where he willed, and he was informed that, if he were discreet about the whole business, the British government would shut its eyes and let him return to Canada.

Meanwhile the strong representations of the dean of Quebec battered down the obstacle in Rome. Offended by the double election in Quebec, the papal court for some time insisted upon the appointment of a vicar apostolic. This was most displeasing to the Canadians. It would have reduced the dignity of their church below the position Laval had won. More important, it was utterly unacceptable to the British government, which would not dream of admitting into the colony any official whom Rome appointed and might recall. The Canadian church would remain without a head unless it could secure a titular bishop, who, once installed, would appear to derive his authority from his position as bishop of Quebec. To this bold reasoning of the Abbé de la Corne, Rome finally yielded, and the necessary bulls were issued on January 21, 1766.

On March 16, 1766, in a private chapel just outside Paris, Briand was quietly consecrated bishop of Quebec. He hastened back to London, whence he sailed for the land of his adoption, for like the other leading clerics of the colony he had been born in France. He arrived late on June 28, a few hours after his friend Murray, having entertained all the Quebec clergy at a farewell dinner, had sailed for England. Great was the rejoicing in the ancient capital. One cannot read the description in the *Quebec Gazette* without feeling the heart throb of the Canadian people. Bells rang, tears flowed, and to the parish church crowds flocked to catch a sight of their sainted bishop, the living guarantor that their religion would not die out in the land. Wherever people met, they congratulated one another, praised heaven, and blessed the king. All the leading old subjects, Protestants though they were, poured forth their hearty felicitations and thereby crowned the delight of the Canadians.

CHAPTER VI

THE TRIBULATIONS OF GOVERNOR MURRAY

THE history of Murray's civil administration of the province of Quebec is the story of a man overwhelmed by a sea of troubles. Probably no British governor has ever been thrust into a more impossible position than that in which he found himself. Being forced to oppress a people whom he admired and pitied was only one part of his embarrassment. He was involved in a most confused and exasperating three-cornered quarrel with the garrison of the colony and with the little community of English-speaking merchants who had come to seek their fortunes on the shores of the St. Lawrence. He had also to face a task which under any circumstances would have been far from easy — that of inaugurating the civil régime; and for this he was given means that were utterly inadequate. The upshot was that the home government recalled him in disgrace before he was able to accomplish much for his beloved Canadians.

The root of the quarrel between Murray and the garrison was a general principle laid down in London and applied in all the American colonies. This principle was that the military command was to be absolutely independent of the governor's control.[1] Down in West Florida, the only other continental colony that had a garrison comparable with that of Canada, this mistake of the home government so embroiled the governor with the military commander that they tried to arrest each other on high charges.[2] In Canada, which had by far the largest garrison in America,[3] the governor and the commander of the troops might have cooperated loyally had they been angels from heaven, but they were poor mortals between whom the tie of friendship was already snapped. On learning that all the forces within his government were placed under Burton, elevated to the rank of brigadier, Murray was naturally indignant, for the man who, though still his junior in the army, had been his rival for the governorship and had refused to serve under him as lieutenant governor was not likely to be a comfortable colleague. Had Burton established his headquarters in Quebec, the seat of the governor, the

102

friction between the two chiefs might have been more continuous. His residence in Montreal, however, by emphasizing his independence placed more than a geographical distance between them.

Murray's conflict with the English mercantile minority was even more serious than his trouble with the army. For this some have blamed his bad temper and others their bad character. Neither explanation can stand in the light of the fact that for many months he lived on excellent terms with a considerable number of them. What most poisoned their relations was the impossible promise of an assembly contained in the proclamation.

In addition to these two quarrels which the governor had on his hands, that with the commander of the troops and that with the mercantile minority, a third quarrel rent the peace of the colony. This was between the mercantile minority and the garrison. Each of these three quarrels aggravated the others. To understand the exasperatingly tangled situation which resulted, it is necessary to go back and trace the history of these merchants from their first appearance in the country.

They were really brought in by the army. There was no Army Service Corps in those days, and therefore merchants commonly accompanied military forces, to whom they ministered as sutlers. A hundred such, including their servants, were cooped up with Murray during the trying winter of 1759–60, and at their own request they were formed into an independent company of volunteers when the French forces closed in to retake the town.[4] Others must have appeared with the fresh troops that invaded the country in 1760, but it is impossible to give more than a vague idea of the numbers of these new arrivals. As the British army that came in this year was larger than that which had entered under Wolfe, the number of sutlers who followed it may have been even greater than the company that passed the previous winter in Quebec.

Still others came in the latter part of 1760 on the invitation of Amherst, as suggested in an earlier chapter. From Montreal, five days after its fall, the commander-in-chief sent a circular to the governors of New Hampshire, Massachusetts, and New York asking them "to invite the traders and adventurers of the province over which you preside to transport themselves hither and to Quebec, with quantities of molasses, salt, wines, teas, sugars and all kinds of grocery, as likewise sheep and every thing else that may occur to them to be useful" for the comfort of the troops and of a population that had been cut off from European sources of supplies for two years. He promised them "good markets and every encouragement they can in reason wish or desire." As he feared that the season was too advanced for them to venture the passage by water, he announced that he would leave orders with the officers on the Lake Champlain route to furnish the adventurers with boats and with hands to man them as far as Chambly, "whence to this town is only fifteen miles land carriage, which the inhabitants shall be obliged to furnish them at an easy rate." "The same route," he added, "may be taken by sleighs in the winter . . . and they may be assured the whole communication will be as safe and secure as any road in the other colonies." [5]

In a fortnight this invitation began to work. By sea as well as by land — for all did not share Amherst's fear that it was too late to sail up the gulf — the traders came.[6] On December 8, after he had returned to New York, the commander-in-chief reported to Pitt that goods to the value of sixty thousand pounds had been dispatched to Canada.[7] How long the "rush" lasted and how many merchants it brought is not definitely known, but they seem to have formed, along with those already in the country, the bulk of the English-speaking mercantile community.[8] In 1761 they were recruited by new arrivals, some of them direct from the mother country. After that they only trickled in. There may have been, as some have since thought, a considerable immigration at the time of the peace treaty, but this is doubtful. Apparently the only real increase in the numbers of the old subjects at this time was due to the reduction of the army. Few of the discharged soldiers, however, joined the merchant class even as clerks; most of them followed their old tastes, settling down as innkeepers.

As there were no Roman Catholics and only a handful of Jews among all the newcomers, one may gather a fair idea of their total number from three lists prepared in the early days of civil government. Two, which were sent home by Murray in October, 1764,[9] show that there were exactly two hundred "Protestant house-keepers" in the towns of Quebec and Montreal. According to a more detailed list [10] which he transmitted a year later, there were ninety-nine male Protestants, not necessarily householders, then resident in the town of Montreal, and thirty-four in all the rest of the upper half of the province. Of those living in the country, only two were entered as farmers; fifteen kept taverns. In the town, however, almost half were merchants. More than three-quarters of all the men on this third list had come as civilians, and about the same proportion of them were born in the British Isles. Unfortunately no such document for the Quebec district has yet been found. In the beginning there seem to have been more old subjects in the capital than in Montreal, but by the middle of the decade, after the crushing of Pontiac's Revolt and the revival of the fur trade, the balance was swinging the other way. Until about 1770 the total number in the colony increased slightly, and then it began to fall off.

Fully half of these English-speaking people, the innkeepers, the artisans, and the small tradesmen, took life as it came and have passed into oblivion, but a considerable section of the mercantile body did not. This minority of a minority made a noise and played a part in the history of the country out of all proportion to their numbers. The curses that the first three British governors of Canada heaped upon their heads have misled some into believing that they were a worthless crew. There may well have been some rascals among these adventurers on the outskirts of the empire, but the majority of the merchants seem to have been of respectable character and of no mean education. For the most part they were young men of spirit and enterprise, men on the make. Those who went to Quebec developed the fisheries of the gulf; those who settled in Montreal greatly extended the fur trade. As a body they controlled the export and import trade of the country, which was carried on almost entirely with the mother country. They had little capital of their own but they had great credit with solid business houses in London, and such firms do not deal thus with the scum of the earth.[11]

Before the establishment of civil government, lively quarrels between the military authorities and a number of merchants rent the towns of Quebec and Montreal. Three Rivers, having scarcely any representatives of the mercantile tribe, enjoyed peace. The trouble arose from the great gulf which in those days divided the business from the military world. It was still common for gentlemen to shrink from soiling their hands in trade and to regard military life as the noblest calling, and therefore the corps of officers looked down upon the traders as common trash. The latter, on the other hand, were proud that their hands were clean of the stain of human blood. To them the army was a barbarous profession. They deeply resented the conscious superiority of the officers, and they profoundly despised the ordinary soldiers as inferior beings. In consequence the rank and file of the army sided with the officers against the merchants. Politically the antipathy was just as great. As a class, the merchants were civilians to the core. They worshiped British liberty as much as their military rulers believed in British order. They insisted that they carried English laws "on their backs" and that neither French laws nor military orders could touch them.[12]

Several circumstances conspired to accentuate these differences. One was the preponderance of male society in the two chief towns. The gallant officers in their gay uniforms eclipsed the duller merchants in the bright eyes of the Canadian ladies who graced the social life of Quebec and Montreal. A second aggravation lay in the very nature of the times. This was the end of a great war period. The military men in Canada reflected the glory that British arms had won all over the globe and they had a particular pride in having conquered this fair land. Quite as natural was the feeling of the merchants than an era of peace had begun and that their day was now come. A third irritation had its origin in something deeper. Though only a minority of the merchants had been born on the American continent, so many of the others had lived in the old colonies that a distinctly American spirit infected the whole body. Thus the trouble in Canada was one of the rumblings of the coming American Revolution.

During the first part of the military régime the merchants and the army appear to have lived in tolerable harmony. This was natural, since the army brought the merchants and the future of the country was yet uncertain. But the elements of strife were too strong for this harmony to last indefinitely. So far as is known, the first notes of discord were struck in 1762 when Murray denounced Arnold Nesbit's monetary schemes [13] and a Montreal court-martial tried a group of merchants who had quarreled with a couple of officers.[14] The friction was not serious,[15] however, until the following year, when three events hastened the inevitable trouble. The first was the conclusion of the Peace of Paris. Now that Canada was definitely British, French laws and military rule were more questioned by those who were already disposed against them. Then came Pontiac's Revolt, causing enormous commercial losses. The merchants were naturally in an unpleasant mood, particularly in the fall of 1763, when they were unable to make their usual remittances to creditors in England. Finally the proclamation, with its promise of English laws and an assembly, made the continuance of the military and French régime seem like plain tyranny.

During the last autumn and winter of military rule the clash came. It was less bitter in Quebec than in Montreal, for two reasons. One is the smaller injury suffered by the commercial life of the town as a result of the native uprising. The other was Murray's early doubt, shared by no other military governor, of the jurisdiction that military courts possessed over British civilians. He sought to protect himself by persuading the merchants to use arbitration for their disputes,[16] and by relying on personal influence instead of on fines and imprisonments to keep them in order.[17] But his reliance on personal influence was not wholly successful. At least one merchant, George Allsopp, was wounded by the governor's sharp tongue. In September, 1763, when Quebec was disturbed by a mutiny [18] caused by a misunderstanding over the stoppage of some pay, a group of merchants upbraided a body of unruly soldiers and the latter replied with stones.[19] More serious was the friction that began in November, when the merchants were not included in invitations to their wives to attend a ball given by the officers. Some of the latter tried to extract the sting from the insult, but others "continued to speak of the merchants with great contempt and in a very improper manner," according to Dr. Brooke, the garrison chaplain.

In the growing feud one merchant stood out from his fellows as the most defiant of all. He was later to win considerable fame in the colony as the most consistent champion of English law during the first generation of British rule. This was George Allsopp, mentioned above, who came from Bristol, where he had respectable connections. He was a gay young bachelor who spent long evenings with good company and better wine.

One night early in 1764, after entertaining a party of twenty-odd people, he was escorting two ladies home, their husbands * walking

* One of them was Joseph Howard, who had already got into trouble in Montreal, as mentioned below, page 110.

close by. At two o'clock, when in the market place of the Lower Town, they encountered a corporal of the guard, who accosted them for violating a garrison order, issued in 1762 at the request of various civilians, requiring everyone abroad after ten o'clock to carry a lantern. Allsopp retorted that he had no light and that he might walk the streets without one whenever he pleased. The corporal insisted that the men come to the guardhouse, but allowed them first to see the ladies safely home.

When they reached the house the door opened, the ladies rushed in, there was a scuffle in the street, and Allsopp joined the ladies, leaving his coat in the corporal's hands. After some angry parleying, Allsopp left the house and donned his coat. On their way through the streets the merchant roundly abused his conductor and denounced all the soldiery in the town as "a parcel of rascals . . . from the highest to the lowest, thousands of whom he maintained daily" — presumably by the customs duties that he reluctantly paid. On being presented to the officer of the guard, he "talked very loud and in high terms of British liberty and the rights of a British subject." He also accused the corporal of attempting to steal his coat. Thereupon the poor corporal was placed in confinement while Allsopp was released.

All the while the other two merchants were mere onlookers, and back in Allsopp's house another of the guests, Dr. Brooke, was wondering what had happened to his host. When the latter at last returned, he confessed "that some rude expressions had dropped from him in the warmth of his resentment," and the parson preached forgiveness. Thereupon the two wrote notes to the officer of the guard requesting the release of the prisoner. Allsopp's cold pen forgave, but his hot head did not forget. This incident,[20] trivial in itself, illustrates how the English-speaking society in Quebec was splitting into two factions that hated each other.

The story of what was happening in Montreal was well told by the military governor of that place in a letter he wrote to the board of trade on February 1, 1764.[21] The chief trouble-maker was an Englishman who had lived in Boston, Thomas Walker. "By means of a tolerable cargo brought into this colony in 1763," said Burton, he had "given himself out for a man of great substance and larger credit, and by great facility of speech has endeavoured to persuade the other merchants here of his being thoroughly conversant with

the laws and privileges of Britons, and equal to convince any man
of the superiority of his abilities, therefore a most proper and unexceptionable leader for them." In the fall of this year, when sued by
one of his clerks, he and his wife insulted the court by their insolent
behavior. When judgment went against him, he defied the court
in very unpleasant language. Only a warrant for his arrest temporarily closed his mouth and opened his pocket. Thenceforth, continued the governor, "there has been among the British merchants
an appearance of dislike and disapprobation of the proceedings of
the courts established here," * and advertisements "sowing principles of sedition among His Majesty's subjects, giving to the new
ones a despicable idea of the present government, and to the old
British subjects strange notions of licentiousness under the mask
of liberty" appeared stealthily by night. Everything contributed to
the growing disturbance, even alcohol and gunpowder, as may be
gathered from further passages in the same letter. "In a late drunken
riot of a few merchants here, one of them entered forcibly, and
naked all to his shirt, the bed chamber of the widow of a creditable

---

* This resulted in at least one miscarriage of justice. Eleazar Levy, a Jew who
had settled in Quebec in 1760 and removed to Montreal in 1763, was delegated to
collect debts due to a bankrupt fellow merchant who had assigned to certain merchants in Quebec. Lieutenant Daniel Robertson, who had acquired a house along
with a Canadian wife, presented Levy with a big bill for rent owed and damages
done by the bankrupt who had occupied the house. Levy, who had not been able
to collect a penny and was moreover only an agent of the assignees, refused to pay.
The officer appealed to the court, whose jurisdiction Levy denied, and secured a
judgment by default for the amount of his claim to be paid out of the bankrupt's
goods in Levy's possession on the supposition that Levy was the assignee. The Jew,
sure of his ground, ignored the court's decree, and the officer appealed to Burton,
the governor, for an order of seizure, which he secured. Unfortunately this was
executed against Levy's goods while he was out of town. Discovering the mistake,
Burton reversed the judgment and ordered restitution. Levy refused to accept delivery because he wanted damages as well as his goods. After the establishment of civil
government, Levy successfully sued Burton, the town major and the provost marshal,
who were involved in the seizure, and Robertson. The defendants won on appeal to
the governor and council, whereupon Levy appealed to the privy council. After
many delays and two journeys to England, Levy rejoiced in 1771 when this court
restored the original judgment. But his rejoicing did not last long. On returning to
Canada he found that he was effectively stopped from procuring justice. On leaving Canada, the officers had deposited a bond to cover their obligations if the case
should finally go against them, but neither this document nor any official record of it
could be found. Chief Justice Hey had thoughtlessly returned the bond, which thereupon had been destroyed. The upshot was that Levy found himself out of pocket a
large sum — he said more than twenty-five hundred pounds. To add bitterness to his
gall, he discovered that the officers had been reimbursed for their legal expenses
because the case had arisen out of their actions in an official capacity.[22]

merchant of this town. The appearance of the man, and the appearance in which he had come in, so frightened the woman as to cause her to make her escape by dropping out of her window, naked as she came out of bed, leaving her room and two of her daughters in the adjacent closet, to the mercy of the drunken merchant. The uproar it occasioned soon spread, and at the desire of the woman, who took refuge in the house where a capt. of the 27th Regt. was quartered, the said capt. went with a file of men to quell the riot and seize the rioters. The said capt. was personally ill-treated, some merchants were confined, released upon bail, a general court martial was ordered, the whole body of merchants took fire at it. Upon a thorough examination, the court martial found some guilty and fined them. I mitigated the fine. Yet the most part exclaimed bitterly, talked strangely, and thought themselves so highly offended as to make it the subject of their consideration at one of their clubs, to know whether they should call upon the governor on the New Year's Day, or not. Some few who were for it were opprobriously attacked by the others; very indecent language was made use of, chiefly so by one Howard, a servant of the Crown, who held here a warrant as vendue master. Upon clear and undoubted proofs of his disrespect, I have thought it proper to dismiss him from that trust." The result of the debate was that the merchants publicly showed "their dislike to the established government by neglecting to pay the King's representative the compliments of the season, in a body, on the New Year's Day, as it has been practiced here since the reduction of the country."

Gunpowder played its part when an order was issued requiring all privately owned stocks of powder to be lodged in the military magazine, to prevent any possibility of its reaching and feeding the revolt in the interior. When the proclamation of October 7 arrived, it had not been posted an hour before the offending order about gunpowder was torn down.

One is tempted to wonder what the merchants in Canada would have done had they known what was passing in official correspondence across the Atlantic. In April, 1764, the commander-in-chief in New York received from the judge advocate's office in London a letter of February 11 which shook his equanimity. Inspired by recent events in Montreal, this letter challenged the right of military courts to exercise jurisdiction over civilians.[23] Half in anger and half in dismay, Gage threw back on the home government the responsibility for this serious flaw in the Canadian administration. The king, he pointed out, had sanctioned the system set up by Amherst, and the absence of any other jurisdiction over civilians had necessitated this illegal stretching of authority.[24] Both sides were right — a condition that makes the worst quarrel.

From the military régime Murray thus inherited an evil legacy for which he was not responsible. The merchants were nursing their spleen against the day when the establishment of civil government, by giving them control of the magistrates' bench and the legislature, would enable them to take revenge on the whole military tribe. Then came the division of authority which set the governor and the commander of the troops by the ears, and the refusal to call an assembly which embroiled the governor with the merchants. The combined result was a terrible three-cornered quarrel which rent the colony and wrecked the governor. Murray and his friends, Burton and his officers, and the mercantile body all hated one another. Each group was convinced that the other two were combined to destroy it. Of all the bitterness thus pent up in the little colony, the greatest by far was that of the merchants against the governor. He had balked them in their highest hope and had thereby roused their deepest rage. They were therefore determined, by fair means or by foul, to force him to call an assembly or to force the home government to recall him in disgrace.

In approaching the story of the confused triangular strife, one is not surprised to find Allsopp in the thick of the troubles that disturbed the capital. The lantern order had been continued and he disliked it more than ever. Early in October, 1764, he protested twice in his characteristic manner and at his favorite hour, about two o'clock in the morning. On the first occasion the sentry on duty at the Grand Battery stopped him and asked him for his light. Allsopp pointed to the moon. What the moon saw may never be known exactly, for each man swore that the other attacked him. The soldier lost part of his coat, and when the two men were disentangled Allsopp pulled from his pocket a lantern which he had "forgot to mention" on so bright a night. He was released in the guardhouse; but on the next occasion he spent the rest of the night in confinement. He quickly procured the arrest of both his "assailants," of whom one was acquitted and the other was fined a shilling.

These prosecutions caused much bad blood, for everyone in the army regarded them as "frivolous and vexatious."

Allsopp did not confine his efforts to nocturnal pranks and judicial prosecutions. At this very time his hidden hand was behind the famous presentments of the first grand jury impaneled in Quebec.[25] This document [26] was a thinly veiled attack upon the governor, the council, the justices of the peace, the army, and the Canadians. The whole judicial ordinance, it declared, was grievous and part of it was unconstitutional — for reasons the very opposite of those mentioned in the last chapter. To the injury of the inhabitants, public property was given away or allowed to fall into private hands. An interesting commentary on this passage is that the foreman of the jury had tried in vain to get part of that property.[27] The justices of the peace were pronounced ignorant — presumably because these jurymen were excluded from the magistrates' bench. The Sabbath was profaned by business and pleasure, and the city absolutely needed "a learned clergyman of a moral and exemplary life, qualified to preach the Gospel in its primitive purity in both languages." Amid various recommendations, good, bad, and indifferent, this body of men made an astounding proposal. The grand jury should be consulted before any ordinance was passed, and it should audit the public accounts of the province at least twice a year — because it was "the only body representative of the colony"! The authors of this document were not thinking of the preconquest council, the colonial counterpart of the parlement of Paris; they were thinking of a substitute for an assembly.

To all the above the seven Canadian members of the jury signed their names with the rest. Then the fourteen old subjects put their signatures to a further presentment denouncing the inclusion of army officers in the commission of the peace as unconstitutional and "an unwarrantable incroachment on the established maxims of a British government," and protesting against the admission of Roman Catholics to juries as "an open violation of our most sacred laws and liberties, and tending to the utter subversion of the Protestant religion and His Majesty's power." [28]

Ten days later the seven Canadians, among whom was Charest, drew up an indignant protest explaining how they had been hoodwinked by their colleagues. But meanwhile a public letter of thanks to the grand jurors "for their very spirited and laudable proceedings" was circulated and signed by about fifty people. The foreman and several of his co-deceivers soon repented [29] somewhat for their sins, moral and political; but Allsopp, who inspired at least the presentment against Roman Catholic jurors and wrote a good part of the congratulatory epistle, was unregenerate.

The whole incident has sometimes been used to illustrate the character of the British merchants generally. But the English-speaking members of this first grand jury were not a fair sample of the mercantile community. No mere chance assembled these fourteen old subjects. A rascally lawyer named Williams Conyngham, whose career in Canada was short and far from sweet, did the trick. He persuaded the official responsible for selecting the jury to turn the business over to him and he picked men who were "malcontents from not having been made magistrates and a few others whose want of understanding and whose situation in life rendered them the fit tools" of his own designs against the governor.[30] There was, however, a body of about half a hundred merchants in Quebec, as the public letter to the grand jurors reveals, who could be counted on as enemies of the governor. What better could they do than to strike him in the rear — in England? Accordingly they raised a subscription, and two of them who were departing for London, Daniel Bayne and William McKenzie, undertook to manage the business there. The former was one of the grand jury; the latter was the business partner of a second member of that famous body and bore the same surname as a third.

When sailing for England, Bayne and McKenzie represented more than the angry merchants of Quebec. They were also delegates of the corresponding group in Montreal, where, before the year was out, a great explosion occurred.[31] As might be expected, Walker was in the middle of it. He was one of the new justices of the peace. At once a question arises, Why should Murray do such a foolish thing as to appoint this man? The answer is not difficult to find. He felt a genuine sympathy for "the poor mercantile devils" of Montreal, as he called them. Most of them had incurred heavy losses from the Indian war and some had suffered fines and imprisonments inflicted by army officers. This feeling of the governor, heightened by his natural distrust of Burton, betrayed him into the error. Thus he thought that he was pouring oil on troubled waters [32] whereas he was really pouring it on a smoldering fire.

Being a more purely commercial city, Montreal differed from the capital in having no public buildings where the troops might be lodged, and therefore the army had there to be accommodated in private houses. When the authority to issue the necessary orders to civilians passed, with the passing of military rule, from the army officers to the new magistrates, the tables were turned in the feud between the army and the merchants. The result was natural. For four winters the soldiers had been accustomed to enjoy bedding, firewood, candles, and the use of kitchen utensils along with their billets, but as the fifth winter drew near the justices of the peace, appealing to the strict letter of the law, threatened to make their lives unbearable by withholding these necessary comforts. Pretexts were also found for turning some soldiers out of their quarters into the streets — an uncomfortable place to lie when the nights were growing cold. The most talked of incident in this campaign of annoyance was that affecting a captain of the Twenty-eighth Regiment named Payne, who stepped into a billet just vacated by another officer. A merchant and magistrate occupying quarters on the floor below claimed to have hired these rooms and at once called upon Payne, telling him to get out or he would have him put out. The magistrate was incensed by a cold dismissal followed by a cold shower — for Payne's ablutions were vigorous and the floor was not water-tight. In a few hours the officer was marched off to jail under a warrant signed by several magistrates, including Walker. This man was having the time of his life, leading his fellow merchants in paying off old scores. But the temper of the army was being dangerously strained, and Murray was so bombarded by complaints that he and the council ordered Walker and three of his fellows down to Quebec for an investigation. It was too late.

On the evening of December 6, 1764, two days before Walker was to leave Montreal, half a dozen armed and disguised men burst into his house and fell upon him. In three minutes Mrs. Walker returned from the cowshed, where she had taken refuge, and found the house quiet except for the groans of her spouse. He was lying on the floor, having received countless blows and having lost half his left ear and a slice off the adjoining cheek. His only internal injury was to his pride. A few minutes later two masked men surprised the adjutant of the Twenty-eighth Regiment by bursting into his room and throwing the missing piece of ear on his table "for his supper," as they muttered.

An alarm was immediately given, but in vain. The assailants had vanished into the night, and a search of all military quarters revealed no absentees. Montreal was thrown into a panic and Quebec was plunged into perplexity. In addition to three hundred pounds subscribed in Montreal, the government offered two hundred pounds reward. It also promised the informer, if a soldier, a free discharge and transportation to any other colony. The attorney general was rushed to the scene, and a few days later the governor and council followed. For nearly three weeks they remained in Montreal, doing everything possible, but already the crime was enveloped in an ever deepening mystery. The only man who was punished for it was Murray himself.

The rank and file of the army, and at least the junior officers, did their utmost to shield the rascals, who, it now appears, all belonged to the Twenty-eighth Regiment. Some of them were actually laid by the heels, and their friends twice rescued them from prison. On their final recapture the regiment retained the cleverest lawyer in the colony, Williams Conyngham, the rogue who had packed the grand jury in Quebec. Apparently he was in the secret of his clients' guilt and concluded that the only way to prevent their being punished was to prevent their being brought to trial. At once he set out to obstruct the even course of justice. He succeeded by worming himself into the confidence of Walker, whose temper was stronger than his intelligence. Taking advantage of an ordinance of March 9, 1765, fixing the trial of the prisoners at Quebec instead of Montreal, where an impartial jury could not be found, the wily lawyer worked the guileless merchant into a belief, which soon became a mania, that the governor himself was backing the army's effort to screen the culprits. The consequence was that Walker, the witnesses for the prosecution, and the jurors of the Montreal panel refused to appear in Quebec, and the trial could not take place. The exasperated governor then ordered a trial in Three Rivers three months later. This time Walker and his wife hid themselves to avoid a legal summons, and his principal witness, though properly summoned, refused to come. The case against the prisoners thus fell to the ground, and they were all discharged. In a few months they were out of the country, some having gone home and the rest having departed with their regiment for New York.

Apart from those who were in the secret, it is doubtful if anyone then saw what was really happening. People were thrown off the scent when Conyngham was disbarred before he could appear for the accused at Three Rivers, and then they were blinded by a cloud of legal dust thrown up by the pedantic attorney general, who tried, with considerable justification, to blame the chief justice for the failure to hold the trial in Quebec. The governor and the public were absolutely baffled, and the innocent members of the army had experienced a serious alarm. The atmosphere in the colony was almost unbearable for all the parties concerned in the three-cornered feud. The disaffected merchants in the two towns, having caught the contagion of Walker's mania, were bursting with righteous indignation against the governor and the army, while Murray was filled with equally righteous indignation against the Montreal garrison and the malcontent merchants in the whole colony for combining to defeat the ends of justice. At the same time those in the army who had had nothing to do with the miserable business hated the merchants more than ever and were confirmed in their suspicion that the governor was their vindictive enemy.

Meanwhile another difficulty in Montreal was feeding the quarrel between the civil government and the military command. With the suppression of Pontiac's Revolt and the re-establishment of the upper posts, Burton and his officers felt a lively concern for the communication on which these posts depended. During the military régime impress warrants had compelled Canadians to man the boats bearing supplies to the garrisons up country. Lieutenant Colonel Gabriel Christie, who as deputy quartermaster general was responsible for forwarding provisions, now followed the old procedure despite the establishment of civil government. Though the Canadians were paid for their labor they did not at all agree with the army authorities who affirmed that the rate of remuneration was fair. The habitants disliked the service because it was always performed under compulsion and it frequently interfered seriously with their agricultural operations.

When complaints poured down to the governor in Quebec, he saw three good objections to Christie's exercising this authority. It was illegal; it was maintained by terrorizing the Canadians; and it was used corruptly, the deputy quartermaster having private business interests as well as military duties. Murray therefore made two distinct efforts to provide the necessary transportation in a legal manner and under proper safeguards. He gave authority to the Montreal justices of the peace, and he issued a warrant to Judge Fraser of the common pleas. But Christie would not be beholden to civil authority on a matter of such vital importance to the army up country. He continued to wield his old power under the plea of absolute necessity and Burton came to his defense. This dispute,[33] which the home government settled in favor of the civil authority only at the end of Murray's government, together with the bitterness aroused by the Walker affair, precipitated a nasty crisis in the summer of 1765.

Murray sought to still the strife in Montreal, but only stirred it up in Quebec, by persuading Burton to send the troublesome Twenty-eighth Regiment down to the capital. Major Brown, who commanded this unit, shared the belief of his innocent officers and men that the governor, in seeking to prosecute the accused, was really trying to persecute the regiment, and he was only too glad to find an opportunity to hit the governor in a tender spot. The tender spot was Murray's belief that the garrison of the fortress of Quebec was under his authority because, though deprived of the control of the army in the colony, he still held his commission and drew his pay as military governor of the fortress. Brown's opportunity was his seniority over all the other officers who then happened to be in the garrison. The major quickly seized the command out of the hands of the general, who, to avoid unnecessary friction, thereupon took up his residence outside the city at Sans Bruit, which he had secured as a country house. But he could not escape from insult. He, the governor, was twice denied admission to his own capital! After the second repulse, he ordered the garrison under arms, had his commission as military governor read out, and insisted on giving the parole until contrary orders came from New York.

On top of this vendetta with the major, Murray was disturbed by the arrival of Burton to inspect the troops. The brigadier refused the governor's offer of his town house, preferring to lodge with Brown, and he gave a huge entertainment to all the principal malcontent traders, including the foreman of the famous grand jury. "I bore all this with the patience of a philosopher and the dignity of a veteran," said the fiery Scot in a letter to a friend in England.

In public he may have behaved this way, but in private it is fairly certain that he swore eloquently. Knowing how inflammable was the governor's temper, his enemies took keen delight in baiting him. Brown openly boasted that he was supported by the commander-in-chief in New York; Christie publicly wagered that Murray would soon be recalled; and several spread the rumor that Burton would have the refusal of the governorship. These and countless other incidents embittered the feud, which lasted as long as the two rivals were in the country. Some have blamed it all on Murray's pride and his perverse insistence on a command that was not his, but neither he nor his rival could help himself. After their departure the wretched wrangling would have continued with new principals had not the home government seen its error in clipping the military wings from the civil governor. Then were the wings restored and Carleton was given a chance to fly where Murray had been able only to crawl and squirm.[34]

The Highlander's temper undoubtedly intensified his quarrel with both army and merchants, but the chief inspiration which drove him to fight them was a noble vision compounded of patriotism and humanity. It comes out again and again in his letters. He saw the Canadians passing through a painful transition from citizenship in one empire to citizenship in another, and he felt a deep sense of responsibility for tiding them over the crisis. To fix them firmly in their new allegiance, he sought to impress their minds with the power and the dignity of their new government and to impress their hearts with the benignity of their new rulers. Such men as Burton, Brown, and Christie, by reducing his authority and by riding roughshod over Canadians, threatened to wreck the ship before he could bring it to port. So also did the merchants. Their defiant attitude toward the established government taught anything but obedience, and their clamor for an assembly through which they might legislate for and tax the Canadians could not but arouse their fears. The sympathy he displayed toward the ancient inhabitants gave such offense to the factious newcomers that the latter mobbed the former when, with the sanction of the council and in the presence of justices of the peace, they assembled in Quebec and also in Montreal early in 1766 to petition for equal rights.[35] Feeling ran so high that many of the malcontents were convinced that Murray was then actually creating an assembly from which not the new subjects but the old subjects were to be excluded, while the governor was equally convinced that the minority were determined to tyrannize over the majority, from whom they were divided by race, language, and religion.[36]

While Murray was becoming embroiled with the merchants and with the army, he was also wrestling with another impossible situation. He had to launch civil government and get it going, and yet he was denied the power and the assistance necessary for the proper performance of this task.

There was a serious lack of balance within the colony which he could not remedy. The home government fixed the seat of his government in Quebec, whereas the chief seat of disturbances in the country was Montreal. The troublesome character of the western city was due to several causes largely geographical at bottom. Being the capital of the fur trade and situated at the end of civilized settlement, it was in continuous contact with the untamed life to the west. This contact bred that bold and sometimes wild spirit that has marked the North American "frontier" throughout its long history. Also, because of its position at the northern end of the great water route of the Richelieu, Lake Champlain, and the Hudson, it was in constant communication with the old colonies to the south, and therefore its mercantile community was much infected by their growing restlessness. In this it presented a distinct contrast to the corresponding community in Quebec, which was more closely tied to the mother country. In short, Montreal was more "western" and more "American" in tone.

In Montreal, also, special military exigencies led many new subjects to play into the hands of the factious old subjects. The former felt the irritating burden of billeting even more than did the latter, and they alone were oppressed by impress warrants. The essentially commercial life of the place likewise contributed to attach a French tail to the discontented English mercantile body. The Montreal chamber of militia officers had been unlike any other chamber. It had been composed of merchants, and they were now disgruntled over being deprived of their consequence. This community of spirit between many of the old inhabitants and the recent arrivals was reinforced by material bonds. The newcomers who plunged into the fur trade had the necessary material resources, but they lacked the necessary experience with the Indians. Naturally they combined with those who had this experience, and many Canadians became economically dependent upon English-speaking merchants. Finally, Montreal was the headquarters of the governor's military rival, Burton.

For all these reasons the solid establishment of civil government was more needed in Montreal than in Quebec, and yet the only embodiment of civil government in Montreal was a bench of magistrates much weaker than that of Quebec. This was inevitable; the governor could not know the merchants who lived one hundred and eighty miles away as well as those who were settled under his own eyes. Either the capital should have been moved, a step which was not considered, probably because the support of a military stronghold was preferred, or a lieutenant governor should have been planted in Montreal. In October, 1764, Murray told the board of trade that such an official was absolutely necessary, but his advice was unavailing.

Even more serious were certain defects in the heart of the government. Those who framed the constitutional program in 1763 realized the necessity for a considerable legislative and taxing authority in the colony itself, and they trusted that an assembly would soon supply it. As a result of this miscalculation, the competence of the governor and his council was at a minimum at the very time when it should have been at a maximum. Also, it must be remembered, the governor was a military man with no legal training, and in the pioneer work of legislation he would have to lean heavily upon his legal advisers. There was thus greater need for care in selecting the first chief justice and the first attorney general than in choosing those who might succeed them; but Gregory and Suckling, instead of being stout supports to Murray, were only poor broken reeds. A total ignorance of the language of the country was the least of their defects. The attorney general knew some law, but not enough. Of human nature he knew nothing. His troubles in Nova Scotia, instead of teaching him wisdom, seem to have embittered his nature. About all that can be said for him is that he was honest. Chief Justice Gregory had no qualifications whatever for his responsible post. He had little legal knowledge and less character. He was taken from prison to be sent to Canada, where he was the boon companion and apparently the tool of the rascal Conyngham.

During the first year of civil government Murray and his council passed two dozen ordinances [37] — more than the total number enacted during all the other years before the Quebec Act. In this burst of legislative activity, necessary to lay the foundations of the new civil government, some measures were accepted without question. A number of them were borrowed from the military régime: the assize of bread, the control of butchers, the prohibition of forestalling markets, and the regulation of street traffic in the towns. The last ordinance, incidentally, contained a suggestive innovation. Offenders who refused to pay a fine of ten shillings were to be "put to hard labour for the space of four days in repairing the highways."

Other measures, however, stirred opposition in the colony and attracted criticism at home. One of the first things that the council had to do was to adopt a uniform currency rating for the whole colony. The Halifax and the York systems had their strong partisans in Quebec and Montreal, respectively, but a number of merchants in both places petitioned for the New England system, in which the dollar was worth six shillings, as superior to either of those that had been tried in the country. There were thus three parties divided by considerable feeling, and it was inevitable that two of them should be offended. But what was not inevitable was that the ordinance adopting the New England rating arbitrarily altered the value of every contract made without reference to any specific currency. This blunder, which the chief justice and the attorney general failed to catch, had to be corrected eight months later, but meanwhile it stirred the wrath of the mercantile community. The legal advisers of the government also overlooked the fact that this ordinance violated a currency statute of half a century before. On both counts the board of trade scored this enactment. But it was not disallowed, and the New England rating continued in force until after the Quebec Act. Then, in 1777, the Halifax system was restored.

Another urgent measure was one confirming the judgments of the courts during the military régime. It permitted appeals within two months for all cases involving over three hundred pounds, a regulation borrowed from the judicial ordinance. This limitation of time and of value stirred a violent agitation among the merchants, principally in Montreal, and also incurred the condemnation of the board of trade, but it likewise was permitted to stand. Some ordinances were disallowed by order-in-council because they exceeded the narrow limits prescribed for the governor and council. One was for discovering and suppressing unlicensed public houses, passed to prevent the debauchery of the troops. Two were to provide the army with billets.[38] Still another was revoked in the same manner because it would have imposed a stricter observance of the Sabbath than the laws of England required. Although this ordinance was contemplated before the famous grand jury deliberated, it may have been stiffened as a reply to one of its presentments.

Like the judicial ordinance, these enactments and others that it would be too tedious to mention stirred a great ferment among the English-speaking merchants. For the avoidable offense Gregory was chiefly to blame. The attorney general was only a draftsman occasionally consulted, while the chief justice was regularly deferred to even when absent from council meetings. Gregory betrayed the governor and council not only by his ignorance but also by his cowardice. Afraid to face the ugly music he heard rising around him, the chief justice privately persuaded the malcontents that he had opposed all the unpopular ordinances. Though he began this nefarious game in the first winter of civil government,[39] it was not fully exposed until the spring of 1766.[40] Meanwhile his duplicity inflamed the anger of the merchants.

Small wonder they openly said that the whole batch of ordinances, even including that establishing the courts, was not worth the paper on which it was printed! [41] They insisted that no law passed in the colony could have any validity without the sanction of an elected assembly. And why was there no assembly? Murray had broken the king's solemn word in order that he might rule as a military despot! The revolutionary fever which had already begun in the south was mounting to their brains, and in their heated imaginations the governor assumed more and more the aspect of a monster. "A Turkish bashaw," they called him. Thus, because he was given poor tools instead of able instruments, Murray came under critical fire from the home government, and the storm raging around him became wilder still. This, as will now appear, reacted to make the home government much more critical of the man who seemed to be misruling the colony, until at last he was ordered home.

The fury of the merchants in Canada was fed by hopeful news

from England, where they were moving heaven and earth to effect the recall of the governor and the summoning of an assembly — by blackening Murray's character. In approaching the home government they made great political capital out of the fact that they were finding an outlet for the manufactures of the mother country — a fine patriotic business. Even their own debts were turned to use. By persuading their London creditors that they would not be able to meet their bills and that the whole trade would die unless a "free" government were established on the shores of the St. Lawrence, they enlisted powerful business men in "the City" to fight for them. In April, 1765, through Bayne and McKenzie, they retained the services of an able lawyer, Fowler Walker of Lincoln's Inn,[42] to direct their campaign of slander, which had already begun. He did it vigorously.[43]

The attack began shortly after the arrival of the two delegates from Quebec in the latter part of 1764, when Lords Bute, Halifax, and Hillsborough each received a long private letter from William McKenzie.[44] In these letters, which were identical, every incident in Murray's Canadian career that an unscrupulous enemy could twist to his own ends appeared in a lurid light. One sample will sufficiently indicate the quality of this cargo of abuse. It was a reference to the governor's "ordering a merchant of eminence to be brought naked to the whipping post and there tied, condemning him to that infamous disgrace without any trial whatever." Neither name nor time nor reason was given, but months afterward, when he was allowed to see the various charges against him, Murray drew up a full and vigorous reply to them all.[45] This particular incident occurred during the trying winter of 1759-60, when a sutler named Hay was arrested for selling liquor to the troops contrary to orders. The governor's account of what happened is as follows: "Being a man much beloved by the officers," said he, "great importunity was employed in his favour. . . . I replied they were bad advocates, that punishments being inflicted to deter others from crimes the higher the example the better, and that Mr. Hay from their description seemed to be the only person of his profession I could not pardon. In short, the difficulty of saving Mr. Hay put a stop to the disease I wanted to cure. But to make the dose effectual, he was conducted to the parade, was stript and pardoned the punishment though not the disgrace due to his disobedience. . . . When I received the news of my being appointed civil governor, I assembled the merchants and, after several admonitions, I addressed myself to Mr. Hay, assured him of my entire satisfaction with regard to his conduct since the surrender of the country and that I had after regretted the necessity I was under to treat him as I had done in the winter 1759. The man generously replied he was obliged to me it was not worse, for he knew he deserved it, as the preservation of the place depended upon the sobriety of the troops."

Some of the charges in McKenzie's vicious communication were abandoned, but others were used again and again by the Canadian merchants, their London creditors, and Fowler Walker, in a regular bombardment of the home government. Very soon they procured new and more powerful ammunition with which to blast the governor's reputation. Wild accounts of the outrage on Thomas Walker and its exasperating sequel began to arrive in England. In April, 1765, a memorial signed by the lord mayor, four aldermen, four members of parliament, and the leading merchants in the North American trade, used the Montreal crime to prove to the board of trade that "a military government is entirely incompatible with the spirit and genius of commerce, and that a civil administration, with a regular house of representatives, is the only means to make this infant colony flourish and become useful to the mother country." [46]

Fowler Walker followed this with a strong representation against the first billeting ordinance passed in the colony. Then came two petitions to the king himself. One was from Quebec and the other from London.* Both demanded the governor's dismissal and the convocation of an assembly. Halifax, the secretary of state, referred the petitions to the board of trade, which body was already strongly prejudiced against Murray. This feeling arose partly because he was supposed to be the protégé of Bute and of Lord George Sackville, both of whom were then in ill odor with the administration. It was also induced by an apparently guilty silence on the part of the governor.

He had delayed making a report on the assault in Montreal until he had received what the victim had himself promised — a full statement of what had actually happened. Every day the governor

---

* Of the seventeen who signed the Quebec petition, nine had been members of the famous grand jury and at least two others were business partners of members of that body. Sixteen of the twenty-five who signed the London petition had signed the previous memorial about the assault, which had fifty-six signatures.

was expecting this important document, but it never came and he could not understand why. At last, on March 3, 1765, nearly three months after the event, he decided that he could wait no longer. Then, for some unknown reason, the dispatch he penned did not reach its destination until the end of June, more than six months after the crime. Meanwhile the government and the board of trade heard nothing except through hostile channels. By word of mouth, by letters signed and unsigned, and by petitions, a seemingly unanswerable case was being piled up against the governor. The result was an order-in-council of June 21, 1765, publicly rebuking him. Though his dispatch of March 3, which threw the chief blame on the army, arrived a few days after this order-in-council was issued, his enemies were still far ahead of him in their circumstantial version of the events following the outrage, and they insisted that he was the archvillain. Not until October did his explanations and counterchanges, which now extended to Thomas Walker and other merchants, catch up with the incriminations of his foes and induce the board of trade to take a neutral attitude.

But this did not save him. The three-cornered quarrel in Canada was blowing up a cloud of conflicting evidence that darkened counsel on the banks of the Thames. All that could now be seen by officials at home was that the colony was in an uproar as a consequence of the assault on that dark December night of 1764. Therefore a further order-in-council was passed on October 18, 1765, commanding the recall of Murray and Burton for an investigation into the state of affairs in the province. The merchants had conquered.

Except for the small circle of friends who surrounded him and the Canadians, who recognized him as their champion, the whole world seemed to have gone against Murray during his last year in Quebec. Scorned by his wife, who remained deaf to all his pleadings to join him in the colony, betrayed by the home government, which had tied his hands and had refused to support him in his mounting difficulties, defied by the mercantile and military factions, who were crowing over his impending disgrace, he drank deep of the cup of bitterness. He was forced even to drain the dregs. The secretary of state's letter ordering him to prepare to return to give an account of his government was slower in crossing the Atlantic than was the correspondence of the merchants, and consequently he received the crushing announcement from his jubilant foes.

On June 28, 1766, when he sailed for England, the tide there was beginning to run strongly in his favor. In September he had a long audience with the king, who promised the appointment of Canadian judges, admitted the error of separating the military command, and made him "blush by the many civil things he said." [47] The royal countenance cheered Murray's heart, but it could not smile away the black charges with which his enemies had clouded his character, both as a man and as a governor. Nor could his exhaustive reply to the detailed indictment lodged by Fowler Walker with the ministry give him any more than a private satisfaction.[48] He wanted a full investigation and a public vindication. He secured the latter but not the former.

Few, if any, of the accusations that had been leveled against him could stand the light of a fair trial. Their one purpose had been to effect his recall. Once the purpose was achieved, those who originated the charges had no more interest in them. Protected by the Atlantic Ocean, these men now deserted those whom they had used in London to convey and support their malicious assertions. When the privy council called on Fowler Walker and the London merchants to produce the proofs they had promised, they were helpless. Already the lawyer was suspicious that his principals dealt in exaggeration and at least one of the London merchants felt that he had been deceived.[49] The dénouement came in the Cockpit on April 2, 1767, the day set for the hearing to begin. There and then Fowler Walker admitted "that the papers sent over from Canada were never intended to come before the Council in a judicial way, and that he had no witnesses to support any of the charges." Eleven days later an order-in-council dismissed the "petitions and complaints against Governor Murray" as "groundless, scandalous and derogatory to the said governor."

Even before this public vindication, he had probably made his peace with his accusers in London. On April 8 he sent Fowler Walker his compliments and an invitation to join him on the tenth at the King's Arms Tavern, Cornhill, where he had arranged to meet the London merchants who had petitioned for his recall, that he might submit "his answers to the charges which were exhibited against him, as he had not an opportunity of doing it at the Cockpit." [50]

Though Murray remained governor of the colony for another

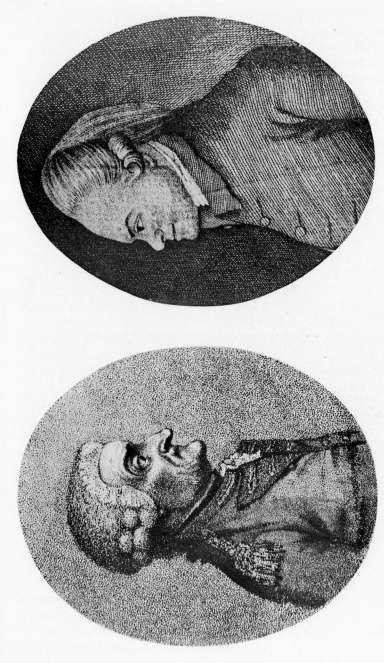

GENERAL JAMES MURRAY

[The portrait of General Murray is reproduced from an engraving published by R. Wilkinson in London on November 15, 1782, in the possession of the Public Archives of Canada. That of Adam Mabane is from a photograph taken some time in the middle of the nineteenth century by Livernois, a famous Quebec photographer, of an engraving which has since disappeared. The photograph is in the Archives of Quebec.]

ADAM MABANE

SIR GUY CARLETON, LORD DORCHESTER

[From a replica in the Public Archives of Canada of the original portrait in oils left by Dorchester in Quebec, later removed to Rideau Hall, and since burned]

year, he never saw the St. Lawrence again. He did not return because he did not wish to return, but why he so decided has not been discovered. His refusal may seem strange in the light of his strong affection for the Canadian people. Through all his tribulations he was borne up by the thought that he was suffering for them. This comforting reflection runs through his embittered correspondence until, in his last letter to the secretary of state, written on arriving home and giving an account of his government, he burst out with a fine flourish: "I glory in having been accused of warmth and firmness in protecting the King's Canadian subjects, and of doing the utmost in my power to gain to my royal master the affection of that brave, hardy people whose emigration, if ever it shall happen, will be an irreparable loss to this Empire, to prevent which I declare to your Lordship I would cheerfully submit to greater calumnies and indignities, if greater can be devised, than hitherto I have undergone."

His victory over his military and mercantile enemies also makes one wonder why he decided against return. Indeed, his biographer thinks it a great misfortune that he did not resume his duties at Quebec under happier auspices which would have enabled him to reap where he had sown instead of leaving Carleton to gather the harvest.[51] But one may well argue that Murray's decision was really fortunate both for himself and for the country. Though not vindictive, he had an explosive temper, and the mercantile minority were both vindictive and explosive. Could they ever have forgiven him now that he had added the crowning offense of being proved right? Murray had done his work, and it was a great work. To the French in Canada he had served as a buffer, softening the shock they might have received on the establishment of civil government. Without this protection the Canadian faith in British justice, born during the military régime, might not have survived.

CHAPTER VII

GUY CARLETON AND THE MALCONTENTS

EARLY in 1766 the British government determined to make a clean sweep in Canada. In addition to recalling Murray and Burton for an investigation, it summarily dismissed Gregory and Suckling. To administer the colony it now sent out a man with inferior rank but superior power. Though he was only lieutenant governor,[1] because Murray still held his commission, he exercised all the authority of the governor, which was now augmented by the union of the military command with the civil government. He was also supplied with legal advisers far superior to those that had been given to Murray.

Guy Carleton, with the appointment of brigadier in succession to Burton, was the lieutenant governor. He was born in County Tyrone of Anglo-Irish parentage on September 3, 1724; he entered the army at the age of seventeen and fifteen years later was lieutenant colonel commanding the Seventy-second Regiment. His quality as a man and as a soldier won the esteem of Wolfe, but his expressed disdain for Hanoverian troops earned the dislike of the Hanoverian King George II. As a result, when Wolfe was preparing to set out for his last and greatest victory he had first to conquer the royal prejudice before he could bring Carleton along as quartermaster general. During the siege of Quebec he also used him to supply the ability that was lacking among the engineers. While commanding the Grenadiers on the Plains of Abraham, Carleton was wounded, and six weeks later he retired from the country to recover. In 1761 he was again wounded, this time in the expedition against Belle Isle off the west coast of France. Promoted to be full colonel in 1762, he shared in the attack on Havana in the following year. There he received another wound and won more distinction. Thus the man who came to rule in Quebec was, like his predecessor, a soldier of experience and reputation. This was the type of governor that Canada needed as long as her back was to the wall — as it was until the close of the War of 1812.

As a man Carleton never inspired among those around him the warm attachment that existed between Murray and his friends. The Highlander would frequently unbend in a most engaging fashion; he always spoke his whole mind; and his explosive temper left no doubt about his feelings. The Anglo-Irishman was very different. Though never stiff, he was always on his dignity. He generally weighed his words to produce an effect, which was sometimes to mislead. His temper was treacherous. Instead of blazing out immediately, it smoldered like an underground fire and then caught its victims unaware. For a space of thirty years he seems to dominate the history of Canada, and yet on close examination he appears frequently to have been the tool of men under him. Though he has been known as one of the greatest proconsuls in the history of the British Empire, his judgment and his character were not always as sound as has been assumed. Still it cannot be denied that the interests of Canada and of the empire weighed heavily upon his heart and mind, and that he was something much more than a mere idol with feet of clay. No governor ever had a more searching eye for the dirty jobs that creep into the corners of an administration, and few have displayed a wider vision in matters of large policy.

The youngest of the trio who came out in the summer of 1766 to manage the affairs of Canada was the new chief justice, William Hey. Little is known of his career up to this time, but he was only thirty-three years old, a man of promise rather than of achievement. Now the promise began to be fulfilled. With one possible exception,[2] no fault has been found with his administration of justice, which lasted for seven years. In 1773 he returned to England, where he assisted the administration in preparing the Quebec Act and was elected a member of parliament for Sandwich. After spending a few months in Quebec in 1775 he returned to England and resigned his commission as chief justice in 1776. In 1777 he became commissioner of the customs in London, a post that he retained until his death twenty years afterward. His final departure from the colony was a distinct loss, for in some most important respects he had a sounder judgment of the Canadian situation than did Carleton.

Francis Maseres, the new attorney general, was two years older than Hey. After a brilliant Cambridge career, crowned by a fellowship and the publication of a dissertation on the negative sign in algebra, he had turned to the bar, where he achieved only a moderate success. After three years in Canada he returned to England, where he settled down in the sinecure post of cursitor baron of the exchequer to lead a quiet scholarly life, turning out volume after volume on mathematics, law, and history. It is doubtful if the home government ever sent a man with a more distinguished mind to share in the Canadian administration. Of pure French extraction, he was perfectly at home in the language of the country, but, as appeared shortly after his arrival, his Protestant bigotry was as great as the Roman Catholic bigotry that had driven his forbears from France. His religious obsession, however, neither tainted his fine legal mind nor wrought any injury to the country. He had too honest a character to permit the first, and others had too fine a judgment to allow the second. Though he was glad to leave Canada after his short stay, and though he lived for more than half a century afterward, he never lost his interest in the colony to whose history he made a considerable contribution during the eight years preceding the Quebec Act. He was the first to reveal the legal flaw that vitiated the whole constitutional settlement prepared in 1763 and to point with compelling logic to the necessity of replacing it by an act of parliament. He also won the confidence of the discontented mercantile minority and was thereby able to exercise a wholesome restraint over them.

Hey and Maseres arrived in Quebec on September 9, 1766, having come direct by the same ship, and Carleton appeared on the twenty-second, having landed in New York. All three, who were bound together by a high mutual regard, came with a prejudice against Murray and in favor of the malcontent mercantile minority. Before his departure from London the lieutenant governor had been shown the case against, but not the case for, the governor.[3] Both lawyers were close friends of Fowler Walker, with whom they carried on a confidential correspondence on their arrival in Canada. It has been suggested that the attorney general owed his appointment to the barrister of Lincoln's Inn,[4] and it is possible that the chief justice was under a similar obligation, for his letters to Fowler Walker contain profuse acknowledgments of unnamed favors. Perhaps Fowler Walker pressed their claims upon Charles Yorke, who, according to his brother, recommended both men in 1765.[5]

Coming with this political bias, Carleton, Hey, and Maseres were unable to hold aloof from the party strife that filled the little English-speaking society on the shores of the St. Lawrence. Of the three new officials, the lieutenant governor was particularly repelled by the group who were Murray's friends, although their patron, before his departure, had spoken to them in a very kindly way about Carleton. The commendation was fruitless because of circumstances and their own indiscretion. They were in continual correspondence with their patron in England, and they confidently prophesied his immediate vindication and his rapid return. No one can blame them for their eagerness to welcome back their old friend with honor fully restored, but unfortunately for their relations with the new administrator of the colony they were openly rejoicing in advance over an event which would mean his supersession.

Over against this group stood the party that, by dint of a bitter publicity campaign, had secured the governor's recall. Though they failed to support their principals in London in pushing home the charges they had raised, they now saw the possibility of Murray's return. This was their greatest dread. Their greatest hope therefore was to cry up Carleton. They were determined that the lieutenant governor should supersede the governor, and Carleton himself had to intervene to prevent their petitioning the home government on his behalf. Cramahé, recently back from London, had already turned from the setting to the rising sun and had been accepted by the latter as his secretary. Cramahé's change of allegiance is somewhat surprising because of his intimacy with Murray. Thomas Mills, another of the governor's old friends, who had arrived a few months previously to assume the duties of receiver general, also turned his coat. This is less surprising in view of the sorry figure that he cut in later years. Quite as natural was the outward transformation of the garrison chaplain, Dr. Brooke. As the intimate of Allsopp and the possessor of a loose tongue, he had barely escaped the condemnation of Murray. Now he trimmed no longer. In his sermons he proclaimed the praise of Carleton and in his prayers he took care, as Mabane wrote, "to particularise His Excellency now residing amongst us, for fear his audience should think he was so unfashionable as to pray for a recalled governor." [6] Neither the chief justice nor the attorney general resisted the embraces of their ready-made friends. Their submission, however, was not nearly so serious as that of the lieutenant governor, who found himself in the midst of a party eager to champion him. Though he suppressed petitions for his promotion, he soon let it be seen that the leading malcontents were high in his favor. Before he knew it he was caught in an ugly situation.

Allsopp was one of the foremost to rush into Carleton's arms, where he disburdened himself of two fresh grievances that distressed his pocket. In April he had secured from the patentee in England the appointment as deputy secretary of the province, only to find that Murray would not admit him to exercise the functions and to gather the emoluments of that office. His other complaint arose from an attempt which he and some other merchants, including Joseph Howard, had made to invade the King's Posts, of which Dunn and Gray had the lease. Appealing to the proclamation of October 7, 1763, which promised free trade among the Indians, they had defied the injunctions of the governor and council by erecting rough buildings in that preserve. In August, during the interim administration of Lieutenant Colonel Irving, the council had ordered the removal of the buildings by force if necessary.[7] Carleton hesitated to touch the first grievance until he received instructions from home, whither Murray had referred the matter, but he was careful to dissociate himself from the governor's attitude toward Allsopp.[8] The other grievance he sought to remedy immediately, and almost as immediately he got into serious trouble.

On October 9, 1766,[9] the lieutenant governor privately called together five members of the council, including only two of Murray's nominees, Irving and Cramahé, and with the consent of these five he suspended the order issued by the whole council in August. The minutes of this action were entered in the book as if a full and regularly summoned session had been held — the first for ordinary business after Carleton's arrival. The councilors who had not received an invitation to this select and private meeting were uneasy over their exclusion, and their uneasiness was increased to alarm by a rumor [10] that they were to be dropped permanently. At once they appealed to their friend Irving, who apparently had been innocent of the cause of their absence. As the senior councilor, and as the administrator of the government and commander of the troops who had recently "turned over" to Carleton, he felt it his duty to right the wrong committed by the new ruler, who was just finding his feet. He went straight to the lieutenant governor and had a friendly conversation with him over the matter. Being a man who would never admit that he had done wrong, Carleton hedged. He told Irving that his friends need have no alarm, because the meeting "was no council" — an allusion to the irregular way in which it had been called — and he proceeded to invite them all to dinner.

The mortified members were somewhat mollified by Irving's assurance that their exclusion had been "an accident," but they saw an important principle at stake. If a governor or a lieutenant governor could call to council just whom he pleased, he could reduce it to a mere echo of his will and could thus subvert the purpose of the home government in saddling him with such a body. Therefore they decided to present a remonstrance in which Irving joined. On October 13 Carleton received them and their document, which, apparently out of consideration for his feelings, they had worded so mildly that it needed interpretation to bring out its real meaning. Without any suggestion of hostility, the lieutenant governor promised a written reply. On the following evening he entertained them at dinner. During the conversation, which naturally turned to the recent incident, Carleton was brought to bay. Then he struck out wildly at his guests. He told Irving that he was a liar in reporting that it had been "an accident." He boldly asserted that it had been intentional, for he was determined to call to council "as few or as many members as he thought convenient" — a highly dangerous doctrine. There must have been a rather stormy time in "the Château."

Carleton was in a tight corner. He could not put on paper the words his mouth had uttered, nor, without danger of an explosion, could he meet his council, the majority of whose members he had now alienated by his own wrongdoing. He might indeed be recalled if the home government discovered what he had done and said. In his exposed position he was in desperate need of cover, and he found it in the obscure wording of the remonstrance. He discovered that he could interpret it as an effort to dictate what company he should keep! Pretending that this was its real meaning, he drafted an indignant answer, and he sent both documents home with covering letters vilifying the remonstrants. The absence of council meetings, which he could not conceal because he had to send home copies of the minutes, he explained by saying that it was to give the troublesome members "time to cool and reflect." Meanwhile the reply, which he led the home authorities to believe had been actually given as a just rebuke, he did not deliver, because, being no reply at all to the real charge, it would have given him away.

Though he had found temporary cover, Carleton could not escape from his perilous plight until he reduced the council to meek submission. Week after week he puzzled over his problem, and the council had a longer holiday than had yet been known. At last he found a chance to cut his way out of his difficulties. It arose out of the last phase of the Thomas Walker affair. Carleton had been specially instructed to clean up the mystery and to remove the blot it had left upon the administration of the colony. Six Montreal men were now arrested for the crime and brought to Quebec, where the chief justice refused bail because Walker would not consent, claiming that it would endanger his life. As the accused were highly respectable citizens, were commonly known to have had no connection with the crime, and were arrested on the bare statement of a criminal and army deserter who was only seeking the reward still offered, a wave of sympathy and indignation swept through the capital. On Sunday, November 23, almost everyone of consequence in the city signed a petition to Carleton urging that the prisoners be bailed or at least that the miserable condition of their confinement be improved. He received the petition immediately and gave an encouraging reply.

Here was his chance, but he did not recognize it at the moment, and he nearly let it slip. But on reflection he discovered that this popular movement for a just and humane end, upon which he had properly and publicly smiled, could be construed as a tumultuous attempt to interfere with the regular course of justice, which would give him a plausible excuse for expelling from the council Irving and Mabane, the leaders of the opposition, who had signed with the crowd. On Thursday, like a bolt from the blue, came a notice to these two that they were no longer council members. On Monday, December 1, as it was now safe, he met the council for the first time since the irregular session of October 9. He informed those present of what he had done, but he withheld his reasons. These, he said, he would "lay before His Majesty." In his letters to the secretary of state and to the board of trade he referred to the petition as "the first open attempt to disturb the peace and interrupt the free course of justice since my arrival in the province," and he added that he had dismissed Irving and Mabane as an example to others.*

His final blow seems to have been followed by a hush in the political life of the colony, because the example to others was really very different from what he led the home government to imagine. The man who would commit a greater fault to cover up the traces of a lesser fault was dangerous to cross. Carleton had demonstrated that he was determined to be master in his own government. This did not mean, however, that he was independent. Cramahé and Mills were suspected of pulling the wires behind the scene, and a few months later it was said in Quebec that they, along with Dunn,[11] were the lieutenant governor's "triumvirate."[12]

Carleton's high-handed action in the fall of 1766 broke the Murray party,[13] and early in the new year the hopes which they still nourished in secret were blighted by the news that their champion had no thought of returning. Irving and Mabane appealed to the board of trade for justice, but they found no satisfaction in that quarter. In 1770, after Irving had gone home, he and Mabane applied for redress to the secretary of state. He refused to go back upon the approbation which his predecessor had signified to Carleton, but he may have been impressed by their representations, for Irving was shortly afterward made lieutenant governor of Guernsey. Mabane was restored to his seat in the council and admitted to Carleton's favor when the Quebec Act was passed. This reconciliation, which may seem surprising, is easily explained. With Murray out of the picture, Carleton was gradually drawn to Mabane and his friends because of their views, and the old Murray party reemerged as the ruling French or king's party.

From the summer of 1766 the malcontent faction showed signs

---

* Mills, also a member of the council, was more prominent than either Mabane or Irving in the proceedings of the fatal Sunday, but Mills was Carleton's friend and therefore was not removed. Carleton did not dare dismiss Mabane from the bench, as he should have done if the explanation that he sent home had been true. The day after he notified Irving and Mabane of their removal from the council, he sent them copies of the reply which he had transmitted to London. On December 1 he ordered it entered in the council minutes, along with the remonstrance. As his reply bore the date of November 28, which might have betrayed him, he omitted it from the copy of the minutes which he sent home.

of breaking up. The disintegration was partly the result of the revolutionary spirit rising in the south. On Carleton's arrival in September a welcoming address was deposited for signature in a Quebec coffee house. There it occasioned "great disputes and very high words," [14] because it proudly referred to the acceptance of the Stamp Act in Canada [15] and loyally acknowledged the authority of parliament to legislate for Canada. Nearly seventy men, of whom a third were Canadians, subscribed.[16] Those who refused to sign this document prepared another address that pointedly omitted all reference to the rights of parliament. This secured forty-five signatures, the same proportion being Canadian.[17] A scrutiny of the names attached to these two papers reveals a division of those who had acted together on the first grand jury and in petitioning for Murray's recall.

Another disruptive force was the troublesome character of some of their number, particularly of Walker and Allsopp. The former now accused Joseph Howard, a fellow merchant and malcontent, with being one of his assailants. What the Don Quixote who tilted against the lantern order was up to now is not quite clear, but one of Hey's letters to Fowler Walker, a friend of Allsopp, leaves no doubt that the latter was rather prodigal in sowing seeds of discord.[18] A third influence was the retirement of the governor from the country. No longer welded together by common feelings of hate, they tended to fall apart. Their sting was also removed by the favor which Carleton showed them. He even recommended the foreman of the first grand jury for a seat in the council, which, for some unknown reason, was not granted. Much more important, however, was his interest in the economic troubles of the country.

One of the major causes of discontent was the unhealthy condition of the fur trade.[19] This was the colony's most important business, of which some account must now be given. The goods needed for traffic with the Indians were imported from England. As a rule they reached Quebec in the fall. During the winter they were brought to Montreal, where they were all unpacked. Some materials were then manufactured into articles, particularly clothes, to meet the native demand, and everything was done up in assorted packages, or packs as they were called, of about ninety pounds, a limit fixed by the necessity of frequent portages up country. In April these packs were carted to Lachine to avoid the rapids, and there they were loaded in birch bark canoes, each with a crew of six men, for transportation to the Indian country. Enough provisions were carried to last until the destination was reached, for time was too precious to be spent in gathering food on the way.

Before Pontiac took up the hatchet the Canadian trade was largely concentrated at three points, Niagara, Detroit, and Michilimackinac. To the two former places the natives could and would come to barter their furs, but the traffic that had been focused at the third place was very different. Michilimackinac was only the headquarters of a trade that was spread far and wide — out to the Mississippi, up to the Lake of the Woods, and beyond. Few of the red men whose furs passed through Michilimackinac ever visited it. They habitually dealt with traders who lived with them through the winter. This particular branch of the trade far surpassed that of Niagara and promised to outdo that of Detroit. All communication from Canada with Michilimackinac was over the Ottawa River, whereas that with the other two centers was over the upper St. Lawrence.

Those who were engaged in the fur trade were divided into three classes: voyageurs, traders, and merchants. The voyageurs who manned the canoes were all Canadians from in and around Montreal. They worked for wages. The traders were both old subjects and new subjects. Some worked for hire, some for a share in the profits, and some were independent. The merchants who supplied the goods and often engaged those who went into the interior were mostly old subjects, and of more substantial position than the traders. The loss occasioned by Pontiac's Revolt fell chiefly on these men who remained in Montreal. They had a large stock which now lay idle, and this stock continued to grow as a consequence of orders already sent to England.

When Murray heard from Gage that peace was restored, he immediately issued a proclamation, on January 31, 1765,[20] opening the doors of the western country. As this territory lay outside his government and was wholly under the control of the commander-in-chief, he was guided by advice from New York in making the announcement. Two conditions only were advertised. Each trader must give security that he would observe the regulations imposed by the commander-in-chief, the amount of the bond being double the value of the goods he carried out of the colony. Since many traders were unable to give this security, the merchants had commonly to supply it, which they did with considerable grumbling. More serious was the second condition: traffic was to be confined to garrisoned posts which were or might be established. Many apparently did not take this seriously, or perhaps they saw a loophole in the suggestion of new posts.

Traders rushed west only to find that they were confined to the three old centers. This was not particularly inconvenient to the trade at Niagara and Detroit, but it was disastrous in Michilimackinac. If the traders were to return to Canada in the autumn, they could not complete their business, because there were too few Indians coming in between the middle of June, the earliest time when canoes could arrive from Montreal, and the end of September, when they would have to set out on the return journey. If, on the other hand, they chose to winter here in the hope of effecting a complete exchange, they would physically eat up all their profits, because the cost of purchasing provisions in Michilimackinac or of bringing them from Canada was enormous. A few individuals were allowed to pass beyond, for the local commander realized the necessity of placating certain tribes who would be dangerously angry if they were cut off from all commerce. Hence arose charges of favoritism and corruption. Down in Quebec, Murray was pestered with exasperated complaints, and at the close of the year he agreed to write Gage. But the commander-in-chief was not to be moved. He thoroughly believed in this policy of restriction as a precaution against another bloody outbreak. The policy, as a matter of fact, was not Gage's. He had borrowed it from a plan prepared by the board of trade in 1764 for regulating the whole of the Indian traffic.

In 1766 the situation throughout the interior became much worse when Sir William Johnson, the Indian superintendent of the northern district, acting on instructions from England and in conjunction with the commander-in-chief, began to apply the board of trade's program of 1764 as far as was possible with the limited funds at his disposal. The essential feature of this scheme was the close supervision of all trade by the Indian department, acting through commissaries stationed at the various posts. The new regulations were designed to protect the natives, but they were badly conceived and badly imposed. Trading en route and advancing goods to Indians on credit, both common practices, were to be stopped. The commissary at each post was to establish a tariff every spring, and all had to abide by it in their transactions. To insure the observance of these and other rules, all traders had to submit their invoices and passes to the commissary on their arrival at any post and to disclose the state of their trade and their furs to this official whenever he demanded it. Very stupidly, these stringent conditions were imposed solely by instructions to the commissaries, who now took up their various stations. In the spring of 1767 Carleton said that he himself had not yet discovered what these conditions were. The traders seem to have received no warning whatever until they arrived with their canoes in the Indian country in 1766. Even then they did not know what new regulation might be forced upon them at any moment. They were at the mercy of any arbitrary or corrupt commissary, of whom there appear to have been more than one.

The blow thus inflicted in the interior was reflected in the decline of Canadian imports from England.[21] In 1767 they were scarcely more than half what they had been in the previous year. More serious was the appearance of French and Spanish traders in the region of the Upper Lakes. They were eating into the richest fur territory that had been discovered south of Hudson Bay. This territory had been tributary to Montreal, but now it looked as if New Orleans might steal it.[22] Then Canada would lose its chief value to Britain, for those were the days of the old colonial system.

The merchants appealed to the lieutenant governor, and he championed their cause vigorously. Johnson and Gage were alarmed by reports of unprincipled traders, but Carleton was more alarmed by the impending destruction of Canada's trade. On receiving complaints that Canadians had smuggled themselves into the west without passes and were intriguing with the Indians, he investigated the matter and found that the individuals referred to had been settled there for fifteen or twenty years. The following passage from a letter to Sir William Johnson, written on March 27, 1767, is a good sample of his spirited correspondence with the Indian department and with the home government on the whole business: "Ever since my arrival I have observed the Canadians with an attention bordering upon suspicion, but hitherto have not discovered in them either actions or sentiments which do not belong to good subjects. Whether they are right or wrong in their opinion of the Indian trade, I submit to those whom the king has appointed to direct and superintend the same, but the unanimous opinion of all here, Canadians and British, is that unless the present restraints are taken off, that trade must greatly suffer, this province be nearly ruined, Great Britain be a considerable loser and France the sole gainer, as they must turn the greatest part of the furs down the Mississippi instead of the St. Lawrence. . . . They say that their own interest will always be a sufficient reason and motive to treat these people well, and to use their utmost endeavours to keep them in peace, and the Canadians will engage to take some English in every canoe, to acquire a knowledge of these countries and the language, to shew they have no jealousy at their becoming acquainted with this trade. 'Tis imagined here that the other provinces, who are neither acquainted with these countries nor so advantageously situated for this trade, are the secret causes of their being so severely fettered." [23]

At the same time Carleton was championing another group of merchants who were encountering similar difficulties at the other extreme of the colony. These were the men engaged in the seal-fishing industry, which was conducted from Quebec.[24] The operations of this business, like those of the fur trade, lay beyond the boundaries of the colony, and they were therefore open to injury by outside authority. Indeed, this eastern trade was now in a worse plight than the western, for it was threatened with utter extinction.

The seal fishery was concentrated at about a dozen posts along the interior coast of Labrador, the northern shore of the Gulf of St. Lawrence from opposite the island of Anticosti to the Strait of Belle Isle. The seals were caught by large heavy nets. Each net was permanently fitted to block the whole of a water passage between the mainland and an island or small rock, and could be raised or lowered by means of a stout cable. The water passages selected were those through which, according to observation, schools of seals habitually passed two or three times a year. The favored season for catching the animals was December, when the seals ran for not more than a fortnight. After that a month was spent in extracting oil and preparing skins from the carcasses. Each post was continuously occupied and had a permanent equipment of nets, tackle, and buildings worth fifteen hundred pounds or more. The business was a delicate one because the animals, being extremely shy and endowed with an acute sense of smell, might desert the waters prepared for their reception if, in swimming along, they encountered offal, or if, when gamboling along the shore, they found refuse or even a footstep in the sand. Competition as in other fisheries was out of the question. The occupants of any one of the favored locations had to be secure from any intrusion for several seasons in order to avoid loss. From the whole coast the total annual produce amounted to somewhat more than two thousand hogsheads of oil and twenty thousand skins. The former fetched from three to five pounds each, and the latter, which were used for moccasins in the colony, brought about four shillings and sixpence apiece.

This industry had developed greatly during the last generation of French rule, when it seems to have been well regulated under a system of leases from the government. In addition to their obligations to the government, the lessees had to pay any proprietors of the mainland or islands that they used an amount equal to three per cent of the value of each year's catch, and also to purchase at a fair valuation from the previous lessees the equipment which they took over. The war caused the posts to be abandoned in 1758. On the surrender of the country several enterprising British merchants, purchasing the interest of Canadians and securing leases from the military governor of Quebec, reopened the business in 1761. The severance of this coast in 1763, when it was placed under the government of Newfoundland, roused some alarm, which was tempered by the confidence that the property rights of individuals would not be touched. In February, 1764, a number of merchants memorialized Murray on the question, and he submitted the memorial to the board of trade. That body viewed it with a favorable eye, and the fears in Quebec died away. The industry flourished until the spring of 1765. Then Hugh Palliser, the governor of Newfoundland, interfered rudely and without warning. He refused to recognize any permanent rights and he ordered the seal fishers to clear out immediately under pain of corporal punishment and the sale of their effects. One poor fellow was forced to set out for Quebec in a little open boat. He met others coming down to replenish the posts, and soon there was a panic among the Canadians, who, as in the fur trade, formed the main body of employees and numbered about six hundred. Nothing could persuade them to descend.[25]

In effecting this sudden disruption of the industry, Palliser was only doing his duty. The chief function of the Newfoundland government was to regulate the fisheries carried on by ships from the mother country according to statutes passed by the British parliament and regulations issued by the home government. One of these statutes gave the first fisher to reach any point on the coast the exclusive right to that location for the remainder of the season. In applying this law, Palliser had two ulterior objects. One was to prevent smuggling, of which there seemed a real danger, for at least one Quebec merchant connected with the seal industry tried this game.* The other was to clear the coast of all Canadians. For this also he had some justification. The British government, it will be recalled, had feared French encroachments in this important quarter. To the governor of Newfoundland these Canadians were Frenchmen. Indeed, he was actually fulfilling the two purposes for which this coast had been cut off from Canada and placed under his jurisdiction.

The home government was now deaf to Carleton's appeals on behalf of those interested in the seal industry. Some of the merchants managed to continue their operations by employing Englishmen and sending out ships from England to arrive at their stations early in the year, for Palliser had promised that he would not interfere if Canadians were not used. This, however, was an awkward way to conduct the business, and it is doubtful if it was successful.

* This was William Grant of St. Roch, who later became one of the richest and most respectable citizens of Quebec. At this time he was in partnership with John Gray, who, in addition to his interests in the King's Posts, had secured a lease of the Gros Mekatina seal-fishing station. Gray was also investigating the possibility of establishing a ship-building industry in Canada. In the fall of 1764, having constructed a vessel of about one hundred and ten tons, he commissioned his partner, who was then in England, to dispose of it for the best price possible and to apply the proceeds to pay for merchandise ordered from London. It happened that Grant was a speculator in the old paper currency, and his hope of realizing something on his speculation drew him across the Channel. While in Bordeaux, he fell in with some Irish merchants, who persuaded the young man that it would be easy to smuggle a cargo of wines into Canada through the Labrador coast. Thereupon Grant wrote Gray that he could find no purchaser for the vessel but would take it himself at a price which he fixed. He also informed his partner of the scheme for which he wanted the craft and offered him a share of the profits. Gray replied condemning the business, and when he heard that his partner was persisting in it he dispatched a vessel to Mekatina with orders to his overseer to prevent a landing of the illicit cargo or, if this was impossible, to stave in the casks and throw them in the sea. The guilty vessel was wrecked off the Strait of Belle Isle and what was salvaged was condemned in the vice-admiralty court of Newfoundland. Grant had to pay Gray eight hundred pounds in reparation for the property which he had appropriated and lost.

In Quebec it was commonly believed that Canadians, because of their skill and experience, were essential. A few years later, when the Quebec Act was being prepared, this grave injustice to an important Canadian industry was at last removed, probably at Carleton's instigation.

The western trade found earlier relief from the oppression under which it suffered, though not, it would appear, as a result of Carleton's efforts. The first respite was afforded by the famous ranger, Major Robert Rogers, shortly after he assumed command of Michilimackinac in 1766. The cries of the traders, the complaints of the Indians, and his own common sense moved him to defy his orders. From the time he threw down the bars and allowed the traders to winter among the natives, the traffic was free.[26] In 1768 this freedom received legal sanction because of financial considerations at home. The whole scheme outlined by the board of trade in 1764 was never applied because it was too expensive. The prospective cost mounted with further investigation until it became prohibitive. As a consequence the home government now threw up its hands and abandoned the plan. Johnson's commissaries and cramping regulations disappeared, and the various colonies were intrusted with the regulation of the trade in the interior.

A still further reason for the subsidence of ferment in the colony during the early part of Carleton's government was the breakdown of the principal source of revenue inherited from the French régime — the customs. The duties imposed by Murray appear to have been dropped by him when civil government was established because his instructions forbade him to levy any general taxes without the consent of an assembly.[27] Two series of suits were then commenced in Quebec, one by the merchants seeking to recover the duties which they had paid and the other by the government to collect the duties which the merchants had not paid but for which they had given their notes of hand. Attorney General Suckling seems to have succeeded in defending the first, but he lost in prosecuting the second. His failure was caused by a perversion of the jury system. The jurors simply shut their eyes to the evidence and declared for the defendants. Though probably friends of the defendants, the obstinate jurors appear to have been inspired by political rather than by personal motives. The English-speaking merchants as a body held strongly to the American doctrine that all taxes were illegal unless voted by their elected representatives.[28]

Meanwhile the government of the colony was launched without a revenue, except for the feudal dues and the rent of the King's Posts, which together brought less than eight hundred pounds, and was left to struggle along without one for a couple of years. This omission, which Murray supplied by drawing bills on the treasury, was due to several causes. At first it looked as if the home government might continue the old duties. On April 12, 1764, the attorney and solicitor general were asked for their opinion on the legality of the old duties, and four months later they replied that these could be collected "by proper authority." Nothing further was done for several months, probably because it was taken for granted that an assembly would soon be called and that it would pass legislation necessary for the financial support of the provincial government. When Cramahé arrived in London with the information that an assembly was out of the question and that some other provision would have to be made for a revenue, he made little impression for some time, for the government was then wrestling with the bigger problem of taxing all the American colonies. Six months after his arrival, however, the wheels of office began to grind. What they produced was far from satisfactory — a receiver general appointed on July 10, 1765, and instructions from the treasury dated March 10, 1766.

The receiver general was Thomas (later Sir Thomas) Mills. He was not unknown in Quebec, where he had served as town major during the military régime, and where he reappeared at the end of June, 1766, with the air of a great and powerfully connected man. He tried to dictate to Irving and the rest of the council, but he was quietly put in his place. His resentment was probably a secret influence behind Carleton's high-handed action in the autumn of that year. At first he showed signs of independence even toward the lieutenant governor, but he soon became subservient. He remained in the colony only a year, after which time his duties were performed by others until 1787, when personal financial difficulties drove him back to Canada. Then his private embarrassments led to public embarrassments, and his old friend Carleton, since raised to the peerage as Lord Dorchester, was forced to suspend him from office because he could not account for all the funds that were supposed to be in his hands.

The treasury instructions to the receiver general, issued under the authority of an order-in-council, directed the collection of all customs duties payable at the close of the French régime — much more than Murray had demanded. On July 7, 1766, a few days after the receiver general had presented the council with the commands of the home government, Irving conveyed them to the public by means of a proclamation. According to the old schedule now revived, rum was to pay one pound a hogshead, brandy sixpence a gallon, eau de vie liqueur fivepence a gallon, wine ten shillings a hogshead or, if bottled, either a halfpenny or a penny halfpenny according as it was ordinary or sweet, and all dry goods three per cent. The last duty was both export and import. Immediately, however, following further instructions from the treasury board, the tax on dry goods was waived [29] and that on British brandy reduced to fourpence.[30]

It was impossible to collect these duties. They were utterly abhorrent to the merchants in Canada, who were infected by the growing American spirit of resistance to taxation by parliament, and the duties had not even the authority of parliament. To the men who were called upon to pay, the British government seemed to be doing something like what Charles I had done when, in his effort to emancipate himself from parliament, he discovered moth-eaten laws to supply him with a revenue. Resistance was easy in Canada because the customs collector had no warehouse in which to lodge goods until the duty on them was paid. Imported merchandise was therefore delivered immediately to the consignees in return for their promise to pay what might be due, and this promise they might refuse to honor. On their refusal to pay, the only course open to the government was to sue them, and writs were issued at once. Several merchants were arrested: some gave bail immediately; others gave it after a few hours' reflection in jail.[31]

This was the situation when Hey and Maseres arrived in September, 1766. The first suit came to a hearing on November 8, Maseres prosecuting before Hey. The convincing legal arguments of the attorney general and the chief justice's injunction to the jury to return a special verdict were all in vain. The jurors took the law into their hands and brought in a general verdict of not guilty. This effectively stopped all further efforts to collect the duty for some time, and it inspired some of the merchants to pursue Murray in England, where, as he had accounted to the treasury for his collections, the government undertook the defense. The trial was commenced in January, 1768, under Chief Justice Sir Eardly Wilmot. He was confident that the legality of the old duties was unassailable, but he was denied the opportunity to pronounce upon it, for the case was compromised. The plaintiffs had been certain that the defense would not be able to prove that the duties had actually been collected before the conquest, and when the original French customs books were produced in court they were taken by surprise. But a modicum of legal right was found on the side of the merchants. During the trial it transpired that the military governor of Quebec had demanded slightly more than the old rate on rum — an understandable slip in finding British equivalents for French units of measure and French currency. As the exaction of this excess could not be defended in any court of law, the government straightway offered to refund it. The plaintiffs seized the offer and dropped their suit. For many months afterward, old receipts were presented in Quebec and many merchants pocketed a clear profit, for they had long ago recovered the whole duty in the prices they had charged. The collapse of the suit in London filled the treasury with new hope of success in Canada. Fresh orders were sent to Quebec for the collection of the duties, and in 1769 another trial was held in the colony. Needless to say it was only a repetition of the 1766 fiasco. Then the attempt to resurrect the old duties was finally abandoned.[32]

Naturally the mercantile community in the colony was happy over its victory. Little did its members realize that they were in a few years to pay a heavy price for this victory, or rather for the way in which it was won. When a new constitution was given to the country, the right of trial by jury in civil suits was stricken out because it had been abused to wreck the revenue. Some may think that the punishment was just, but others, having regard for the provocation, can argue that it was unduly severe.

Carleton's onslaught on the system of fees must have given further pleasure to many of the old malcontents, but it would be grossly unfair to suggest that this was his motive. Throughout his whole Canadian career he fought against the financial sordidness [33] that marked the public service of the eighteenth century. In this he stands out as superior to his predecessor, whose public morality was certainly not beneath the average.

In one respect the government of Canada during the first generation of British rule was purer than that of many other colonies. There was practically no "land grabbing" until the very last years of the century, for the simple reason that there was no demand for crown lands. But in another respect the Canadian administration was inferior, and that was in the method by which public officials were remunerated for their services. Few of these individuals had salaries, and all of them took fees. Though the prevailing custom, it bore more heavily on the society of Canada than on the society of almost any other colony, because the scale of fees was adopted *en bloc* from colonies where the standard of wealth was considerably higher. Some fees, like those of the attorney general, who was expressly allowed to charge according to the Leeward Islands schedule, were fixed by reference to a particular colony, others by reference to the nearest colony, and still others by reference to other colonies generally. As a rule, place-holders adopted the highest scales that they could find, and sometimes they even improved upon those scales.

Murray had complained about the system, but all he had done was, with the aid of the council, to draw up a list of fees, which he published in the *Quebec Gazette*.[34] This list, which includes over three hundred and fifty entries under twenty-seven separate heads, from the office of the governor down to that of the naval officer, was by no means exhaustive. Some offices, like the petty one of jailer and the important one of collector of the customs, do not appear at all, and some officials who were mentioned exacted fees that were not mentioned. A government clerk could not scratch a pen and the court crier could not open his mouth without pocketing a fee.

The whole system was rotten and Carleton rebelled against it.[35] From his arrival in 1766 until his final departure thirty years afterward, he never ceased to denounce it to the home government and to check its operations whenever possible. Unfortunately the system was deeply embedded in law and custom and he could not pull it up by the roots. All that he could accomplish at this time was to dismiss a couple of individuals who collected excessive fees [36] and to renounce his own perquisites. On November 7, 1766, he announced in the *Quebec Gazette* that he relinquished all his own fees except those for licensing public houses, and that these were to be turned over to the receiver general as part of the public revenue.* Ten days later he wrote to the chancellor of the exchequer explaining his action.[38] In this, the first of many letters on the general subject, he asserted that at least the representative of the crown should be above the suggestion of dirt and meanness in exacting fees on every occasion.

At the end of October, 1767, Carleton was presented with a problem which might have cost him the friendship of a considerable body of merchants. It arose from a quarrel among the creditors of a respectable Jewish merchant, Levi Solomons, who confessed his inability to meet his obligations. Most of his creditors were willing to compound for seven shillings on the pound, but others refused. The Jew consulted the attorney general about the best way to reach a settlement with all whom he owed. Maseres advised a bankruptcy commission, observing that the English bankruptcy law was as much introduced as were any other parts of the English law.† Thereupon Solomons petitioned for a commission, and Carleton, on securing Hey's approval, granted the request. A score of traders immediately signed a memorial objecting strongly to the introduction of a law which, they said, would work great havoc in the commercial community, and which, moreover, was not applied in Scotland, Ireland, or any British colony in America. Carleton at once recalled the commission to give the memorialists time to show why it should not be issued, but such strong differences of opinion developed that he declined to make any decision, referring the whole matter to the secretary of state, who commended his prudence

---

* This greatly annoyed Murray, who took it as a reflection upon himself. He replied in a letter to *Lloyd's Evening Post* in January, explaining that the governor's fees, except those for liquor licenses, were a mere bagatelle, and that the proceeds from issuing these licenses were, by an ordinance of November, 1764, to be applied to the public use as part of the general revenue. Murray's biographer, taking this statement at its face value, has accused Carleton of traducing his predecessor. This charge is unjust. Either Murray's memory or his relative deceived him when he penned this letter. The license fee (twenty-six shillings) was established by the above ordinance and was to have been applied as Murray said, but the ordinance was annulled by an order-in-council published in Canada in April, 1766. Though the money was collected, it was neither returned to those who had paid nor credited in the public accounts. Four days before the governor sailed, Richard Murray, a son of Walter, signed a receipt for £599 6s., the total amount collected, acknowledging that the money was received for the use of the governor. The fee was reimposed by a new ordinance in July, 1766.[37]

† His private opinion was that the whole introduction of English law was *ultra vires*.

and observed that there had been no thought of introducing "laws of that particular and municipal nature." [39] By holding his hand, Carleton avoided incurring the hostility of many merchants, for the commercial community was rent by a paper war over the question. But the Huguenot attorney general was not quite so canny. His controversial pen won him a number of enemies, including his predecessor in office, George Suckling, who had remained in the colony after his dismissal.[40]

The grievance of grievances, the mainspring of the movement which had driven Murray forth, caused Carleton little trouble. During his first winter in Quebec a few old subjects, having prepared a draft of a petition for an assembly, approached him and expressed the hope that he would not object to its receiving the signatures of all their fellows who would support it. The lieutenant governor shrewdly discouraged the project. He stated that he "had many objections to great numbers signing a request of any kind" — an assertion which came not ungracefully from one who had discountenanced addresses in his own favor. Of his "many objections" he advanced only two. A petition with numerous signatures "seldom conveyed the sincere desire of the subscribers" and "it had an appearance of an intention to take away the freedom of granting or refusing the request." He also disarmed his interviewers by assuring them that he had no objections to assemblies in general and would be obliged if they could find a satisfactory plan for an assembly, for he had been unable to hit upon any that would fit the peculiar conditions of the country.

A few weeks later, when these men returned with the same request, Carleton repeated his answer and followed it up by pressing them to disclose their ideas of who should be the electors and who the representatives. As the old subjects insisted that Roman Catholics could not be elected, though they might vote, the would-be petitioners felt the awkward point of Carleton's questions and the movement slumbered until the following winter. Then it awakened in a more determined form. Led by one John McCord, an Irish innkeeper, and George Suckling, some of the English-speaking minority essayed to proceed without Carleton's consent. But they won few supporters, and thereupon they abandoned the campaign.[41]

Thenceforth, until after Carleton went home on leave in 1770, there was no agitation in the colony for the establishment of an assembly. Quite possibly his far from honest finesse in smothering the demand for an assembly, against which, as will appear in the next chapter, his face was resolutely set, was reinforced by the influence of Hey and Maseres, both of whom condemned the idea of representative government in Canada. It is also possible that the merchants did not feel any impelling necessity to continue their agitation because they knew that the home government still clung to its policy of erecting an assembly on the shores of the St. Lawrence.

The absence of political ferment under Carleton is a striking contrast to the storm that had blown Murray out of the country. Some have taken the difference as a measure of the relative worth of the two men, but this is jumping to conclusions that are wide from the truth. Murray was not to blame for the storm that overwhelmed him, and Carleton was only partly responsible for the quiet sequel. Moreover, the methods by which he contributed to political peace in the colony, as set forth in this chapter, were not wholly to his credit.

CHAPTER VIII

TOWARD A NEW CONSTITUTION

THE reaction started by Murray against the constitution which he reluctantly imposed in 1764 halted in July, 1766, when the Rockingham administration fell. The instructions directing a reform of the judicial and legal system to be more in accord with Canadian needs lay unnoticed in their pigeonhole for nearly a year after their completion in June, 1766. The problem of the new colony was quite eclipsed by the problem of the old colonies until May, 1767. Then rumors that the Duke of Richmond meant to launch an attack upon the ministry for its neglect of Canada awakened Shelburne, the secretary of state for the southern department, to his forgotten responsibilities. At once he delved into the office files, devoured the papers relating to the province of Quebec, and poured out his thoughts in a letter to the board of trade.[1] He deplored the failure to dispatch the instructions of the previous year and he regretted that an assembly had not been called. "In every province which has been lately settled in America, there has been confusion and uneasiness until that form of government has been adopted by which the old colonies are governed; I mean by a governor, council and assembly. A governor and council being already appointed, as perfect tranquillity would be established in Quebec as in any of the other American colonies, could an assembly be called to reduce and assimilate such of the French laws as it may be necessary to retain to the standard of the English laws and to make others." Shelburne was not blindly following beaten paths, for in this letter he proposed a radical departure from tradition. He would open the assembly to Roman Catholics, and he would also admit them to the council. But he would not go so far as to grant equal rights. He wished to preserve a Protestant majority in each branch of the legislature. "A fourth part in each," he was sure, "would make the French inhabitants of Quebec very happy." It is fairly clear that he thought of this "fourth part" as being composed only of seigniors. To grant this privilege, he pointed out to the board of trade, the commission and the instructions to the governor would have to be changed. This, he observed, might be done by the privy council with or without the consent of parliament.

The attack which Shelburne feared began three days after he wrote the above letter, when Richmond persuaded the house of lords to order the submission of a long list of papers bearing upon Canada. A fortnight later, on June 2, the lords resolved "that the Province of Quebec for a considerable time past has wanted, and does now stand in need of, further regulations and provisions relating to its civil government and religious establishment." The affairs of Canada were thus thrust upon the attention of the cabinet, where a settlement by means of an act of parliament was now contemplated — the germ of the Quebec Act.

What was to be the scope of the enactment it is impossible to say. Shelburne's letter to Carleton on June 20, 1767,[2] may be interpreted as implying that the statute would be limited to the legal system. Though the secretary of state asked the lieutenant governor for any advice which might assist the deliberations upon the improvement of the colony's civil constitution, he was particularly anxious for any information which he could secure upon the possibility of blending English and French laws into a system which might be confirmed by parliament. To remodel the Canadian courts, Shelburne desired to revive the dormant instructions, but his colleagues feared to order such a sweeping change without further information. Therefore on August 28 an order-in-council[3] was issued commanding the governor and council, with the assistance of the chief justice and the attorney general, to report upon the judicial system of the province — what were its defects, what grievances the Canadians felt under this system, and how it could be improved. Their proposed alterations were to be drawn up in the form of an ordinance and sent home, without, however, being passed in the colony. To expedite the business and to enlighten the government, "a fit and proper person" was to bear these directions to the colony and to bring back the report. For this task, Shelburne selected his secretary, Maurice Morgann,[4] who reached Quebec in August, 1768.

While official interest in the civil affairs of the colony was thus being revived, the plan prepared by the board of trade to regulate its ecclesiastical affairs was resurrected. The privy council, shortly after receiving it in May, 1765, had referred it to the law officers of the crown for their examination. But instead of examining it they seem to have buried it. One of course suspects that this neglect was originally due to the delicate negotiations over the appointment of Briand. Finally, on January 18, 1768, the law officers replied to the communication of two years and a half before by presenting a report [5] which bears the earmarks of haste. Apparently pressure had been brought to bear upon them some time about the end of 1767, and probably this pressure was at least partly inspired by the appearance of a scheming renegade Récollet from Canada named Veyssière. In their belated report the legal advisers of the government recommended the appointment of a superintendent of the Roman church, though he had been unofficially appointed nearly two years before; they talked of advowsons as if they were common in Canada, which they were not; they declined giving any definite advice on the seminaries and the religious orders, because they were ignorant of their constitutions; but they did utter a word of caution against interfering with these bodies on the sole authority of the royal prerogative, and they asserted that Protestants could not be relieved from the tithe by a mere exercise of the royal prerogative if the obligation of the tithe rested upon the laws and usages of the country. Here the matter rested for some months until it was again referred to the board of trade, as will appear later.

Meanwhile another influence which was destined to dominate the settlement of Canadian affairs was beginning to make its weight felt in official circles at home. This was the advice tendered by Carleton. Though he concealed his inclinations from the old subjects, he had not been many weeks in the colony before the tide of his sympathies began to flow definitely in favor of the new subjects. As early as November, 1766, when penning the dispatch on fees mentioned in the last chapter, his chief thought was for the lately impoverished and recently annexed Canadians. Their new and tender loyalty might be blighted by the plague of fees, and therefore he determined that the plague must be abated. In the same letter he pleaded the cause of the poverty-stricken noblesse, who, in the old days, had been relieved by grants from the French king's purse. Carleton wished to revive the royal bounty and would apply the proceeds of the liquor licenses to this end.[6]

Carleton's plea for the noblesse was the first symptom of a fond illusion which colored his mind and warped his judgment for many years. The illusion might never have arisen had he lived through the military period when the captains of militia were the main pillars of society and government. But coming when he did, after this valuable inheritance of the French régime had been thrown away, he fell into the error of imagining that the clergy and the seigniors, whom he saw all around him, had been the only real leaders of the people. He never grasped the fundamental fact that frontier conditions had created in New France a freer and more democratic social structure than that of Old France, with which he was tolerably familiar. This familiarity, which was agreeable to him, his own disposition, which was aristocratic and autocratic, and the conversation of the upper classes of the Canadians, whose company he found congenial, all favored the delusion. The result was a tragedy. Lured by the mirage of a well-ordered Old-World feudalism which he imagined had existed in Canada and, if restored, would be an ideal solution for the Canadian problem, he strove to create what had never existed and could never exist on the shores of the St. Lawrence. This attempt was to give a painful twist to Canadian history.

Another important idea that was firmly fixed in Carleton's mind during the early months of his Canadian career was founded on reality, for it had to do with the military situation, and he was a soldier with a keen eye for strategy. In response to Gage's appeal for advice, Carleton wrote the commander-in-chief on February 15, 1767,[7] urging the erection of a strong place near New York, the construction of a citadel at Quebec, and the secure linking of these two *points d'appui* by repairing the crumbling fortifications at Crown Point, Ticonderoga, and Fort George. It was a masterly conception, which, if carried out, would have given British military power the key to North America and might easily have altered the outcome of the Revolutionary War. He was certainly thinking of cutting the old colonies in twain should their discontent ripen into rebellion. This letter has been used as the foundation of a strongly supported theory, which is as old as the American Revolution, that the dominant idea of Carleton's policy and therefore the main purpose of the Quebec Act was to forge in Canada a weapon which might be used to keep the old colonies in subjection.[8] But, as his later correspondence shows, he was also inspired by the fear of another French war. It was common for British soldiers then to consider a war with France likely to break out at any time, and no one could see better than Carleton that, should this happen, Canada would be the Achilles' heel of the empire. Therefore another theory has been cleverly advanced to prove that his controlling motive in driving toward the Quebec Act was to prevent the French character of the colony from drawing it back to France.[9] It is impossible, however, to speak with finality about all that was passing in his mind, and it may always remain so, for the very simple reason that his widow obeyed his injunction to burn all his papers after his death. Yet one may venture the conclusion that neither theory suffices; there is too much to be said for both. Moreover, in view of the chronic hostility between Britain and France in that age, Carleton could not envisage an American war from which France would long hold aloof, though he might conceive of a French war without a rebellion in the old colonies.

To return to the growth of Carleton's policy for the province of Quebec, he renewed his plea for the noblesse in September, 1767, when an outstanding Canadian, the Chevalier de Léry, presented him with a long petition telling how he had gone to France after the conquest, had appealed to the British embassy in Paris after being disgusted with vain promises of preferment in the French service, and had gone to England [10] and then back to Canada trusting in promises of a British pension, only to find that these were likewise vain and that he dared not set foot in France again after having so openly adhered to Britain. Carleton strongly urged the granting of this pension, not only in justice to De Léry, who was entirely worthy, but also "as a proof to the gentlemen of Canada that they are not forever to be excluded from the service of their present sovereign." He drove his point home by observing that several young Canadians, including the heirs of three of the first families in the colony, had entered the French service apparently out of despair of ever being employed by Britain. He concluded with the following significant proposal: "Should His Majesty think proper to raise a Canadian regiment, no doubt but these gentlemen would prepare to serve where duty and interest require them; 'till that scheme shall be adopted, the placing a few of the young gentlemen in the American battalions would make them turn their eyes from France, which undoubtedly will endeavour to preserve

an interest here for future events." [11] This was thenceforth a
favorite theme in Carleton's correspondence with the home government.

The church, Carleton believed, was another pivot upon which
the mass of the Canadians would turn to Britain or back to France.
Therefore he studied how to manage the clergy, which was not
quite such a simple problem as cultivating the noblesse. He had
not been long in the colony before he was met by two pressing
demands: the appointment of a coadjutor to the see of Quebec and
the filling of the vacancies in the chapter from which future bishops
might be chosen. Though empowered by Rome to nominate a
coadjutor *cum futura successione* in order to assure the continuance of the episcopacy, Briand realized the prudence, if not the
practical necessity, of procuring the government's consent and the
clergy's opinion before he made any nomination. Apparently in
all innocence, he began by writing Marchand, who had succeeded
Montgolfier as vicar general of Montreal, to push private inquiries
among his curés and to report who would be acceptable to them.
Someone was indiscreet and Carleton soon heard what was in the
air. He went straight to the bishop and insisted that this was a
matter which concerned the government.[12] In doing this, Carleton
was obviously inspired by the fear lest the head of the church
become independent of civil control. He was also moved by a
particular suspicion. At this very time his eye was on an able and
well-connected priest, the Abbé de Joncaire, whose behavior looked
as if he were aspiring after the miter. Though born in Canada, he
had lived for twenty-seven years in France, whence he had just
returned, and the lieutenant governor had visions of a nominal
Canadian but real Frenchman ruling the Canadian church. The
rebuff chagrined Briand but it taught him his tactical error in not
approaching Carleton first. The bishop corrected his mistake, but
the lieutenant governor replied that he would have to be well
informed of the merits of the candidate before he could recommend
the appointment at home. This unfortunate incident could not help
arousing apprehensions which may at least partly explain why
nothing further was done about the headship of the church until
the eve of Carleton's departure for England in 1770. The delay
was certainly not due to his opposition to the principle of selecting
a coadjutor in Canada, for he actually favored it as a means of

obviating the necessity of "sending to foreign dominions" for the consecration of a new bishop.

To the second demand, the completion of the chapter, Carleton returned the same answer as that with which he parried the first, but he did not regard this request with the same favor. Though the reasons for his attitude do not appear in his correspondence, they are not difficult to surmise. The chapter was not on a par with the episcopacy. It was neither essential to the church nor useful to the government. Indeed, had this body been rejuvenated, it might have turned out to be an embarrassing ecclesiastical authority. Therefore nothing was done to save it, and it expired with the last surviving canon in 1795.

Another aspect of the church problem which attracted Carleton's attention was the presence in Canada of priests from Old France. Before the conquest the colony had never been able to supply all the clergy that it needed, and therefore it had constantly drawn recruits from the mother country. The natural differences between the natives and the immigrants, reinforced by the preference consistently shown to the latter, led to the existence of two distinct parties in the priesthood. Carleton quickly sensed this division and the opportunity which it offered. By reversing the preference, he would attach the Canadian people to Britain and weaken their dangerous link with France. Another shrewd suggestion which he made to the home government arose from his nervousness about the Abbé de Joncaire. He was very anxious that every priest who desired to come to Canada should be required to procure a passport from the secretary of state's office. Such a regulation would check those who had no good reason for undertaking the voyage, and the restraint would be less obvious to Canadians than if it were applied in Quebec.[13]

Such were the thoughts which Canada's ruler had expressed when he received Shelburne's letter of June 20, 1767, informing him that the colony's constitution was being seriously considered and asking him for any light that he could throw upon the problem. With this encouragement, on November 25 he wrote a vigorous dispatch demolishing the assumption which had underlain all the plans of 1763, the assumption that the colony would be assimilated to the common English type. The burden of his argument was that the tremendous disparity in numbers between the ancient inhabitants and the newcomers would grow rather than diminish. Europeans who migrated would never prefer the long inhospitable winters of Canada to the more cheerful climates and more fruitful soil of the southern colonies. Few Britishers had come and most of them remained because they were stranded, the trade of the colony offering but small possibilities. Their numbers were more likely to decrease than to increase. On the other hand, the Canadians were multiplying daily, being favored by the climate which discouraged others. "Barring catastrophe shocking to think of, this country must, to the end of time, be peopled by the Canadian race, who already have taken such firm root, and got to so great a height, that any new stock transplanted will be totally hid and imperceptible amongst them, except in the towns of Quebec and Montreal." [14] Carleton was right, for the Canada of that day corresponds roughly in extent with the present province of Quebec.

In the letter just quoted, Carleton postulated three principles as guides for the settlement of the constitution. These were "the natural rights of men, the British interests on this continent, and the securing the king's dominions over this province." The last, he asserted, was "the foundation of all, without which other schemes can be little better than mere castles in the air." That this foundation was very shaky he had no difficulty in pointing out. The fifteen hundred troops in the country, together with the five hundred men who might be collected from among the old subjects, could not hold Quebec in its then defenseless state. The new subjects could put in the field eighteen thousand men, of whom more than half had already served with as much valor as the regulars from France, and with greater zeal and intelligence. On which side would they fight? His reply, though indirect, was unmistakable. "As the common people are greatly to be influenced by their seigneurs," he inclosed a return of the noblesse and of officers born in France whose military duties in America had given them an acquaintance with the country and "an influence over the people equal to natives of the same rank."

His conclusion was that France had one hundred officers all ready to be sent to Canada, where another seventy or so had held commissions of the French king. From the latter the most that he could hope was "a passive neutrality." "Should a French war surprise the province in its present situation, the Canadian officers sent from

France with troops might assemble such a body of people as would render the king's dominion over the province very precarious." Such considerations, he observed, had been partly responsible for his urging Gage to erect a citadel in Quebec, because this would enable the troops present in the colony to hold out until succor could arrive. He also followed up his proposal of two months previously by suggesting that "the Canadians could be interested to take a part in the defense of the king's government." His only reference, other than the doubtful one already cited,* to the possibility of a revolt in the old colonies, where Townshend's duties were reviving the opposition lulled by the repeal of the Stamp Act, was the following passage: "Time must bring forth events that will render it essentially necessary for the British interests on this continent to secure this port of communication with the mother country, as might easily be proved were they not too remote for the present purpose."

Carleton did not reply to Shelburne's particular request for information on the legal situation until a month later. The delay was probably due to his desire to consult fully with his legal advisers, for the letter which he wrote on December 24 [15] contains striking similarities of idea and even of phrase with Maseres' writings at this time. The parallel has been ignored until recently because the Huguenot lawyer, having changed his opinions, later refused to include in his voluminous publications the principal product of his pen during this winter.[16] Carleton's denunciation of the ordinance of September 17, 1764, was terrible. At a stroke it had overturned the country's entire legal system, upon which all the property of the people rested. It had introduced, without even promulgating them, laws which were not only unknown but were also entirely unsuited to the people, to the situation of the country, and to the interests of Great Britain. This, he said, was "a sort of severity, if I remember right, never before practised by any conqueror." Already there was confusion and discontent because the superior court, adhering rigidly to English law, reversed common pleas decisions based on French law. The trouble was bound to grow as long as English law was enforced, for the Canadians would not regulate their affairs by this law, and therefore most of their transactions were legally invalid.

Carleton also condemned the ordinance for making justice tardy and expensive, whereas it had been speedy and cheap. "Formerly

* "Barring catastrophe shocking to think of."

the king's courts sat once a week at Quebec, Montreal and Three
Rivers; from these lay an appeal to the council which also sat once
a week, where fees of all sorts were very low and the decisions
immediate. At present the courts sit three times a year at Quebec
and twice a year at Montreal, and have introduced all the chicanery
of Westminster Hall into this impoverished province, where few
fortunes can bear the expense and delay of a law suit." He would
sweep away the abominable measure as null and void, being a violation of the capitulation of the country and of the peace treaty, and
as beyond the competence of the governor and council who had
passed it. The old laws, of which he had had F. J. Cugnet prepare
an abridgment that he later sent home, he would leave in full force
except for such amendments as experience might suggest, or he
would amalgamate the old with the new laws judged necessary and
promulgate the whole as a Canadian code. He would establish
in each of the three towns a resident judge, who, with a Canadian
assistant, would hold court at least once a month. All this was
Maseres speaking with Carleton's vehemence. Two further ideas in
this letter, however, were the peculiar property of the man who
signed it. One was that there should be a thorough housecleaning
of administrative and judicial offices to get rid of all fees except
those of inferior officials, who should collect no more than what
had been authorized under the French government, and to replace
them by decent salaries. The other idea was that the old system of
laws had "established subordination from the first to the lowest . . .
and secured obedience to the supreme seat of government from a
very distant province." Here was Carleton's mirage floating before
his weary eyes.

The adoption of such fundamental proposals, being a matter of
broad policy, was something that lay within the sphere of the home
government, and therefore it could not be expected for some time.
But delay would allow the existing evils to grow, and the lieutenant
governor was anxious to impose some temporary check. The most
pressing question was the confusion in the laws of property. Therefore he had the attorney general prepare an ordinance for the continuance of the French laws governing the tenure, inheritance, and
alienation of lands; but he shrank from the responsibility of enacting
it, and therefore he inclosed the draft with his dispatch to Shelburne.

The next most pressing problem for which Carleton sought some interim solution was the slow movement of justice. Apparently he approached this also before he received the order-in-council of August 28, 1767, for Maseres was able to tell Fowler Walker the story in a letter written only a week after the order was submitted to the Quebec council in March, 1768. The suggested solution, which originated with the attorney general, was of course limited by the existing establishment. It was an ordinance providing for monthly sessions of the superior court, ten to be held in Quebec and two in Montreal, each to continue until the cases ready for decision were finished. The draft of this ordinance was neither sent home nor was it submitted to the council for adoption, because serious opposition appeared in two quarters, French and English. A Canadian notary and lawyer who had a large share of the business in the court of common pleas persuaded Cramahé that this development of the king's bench would alarm the Canadians by threatening the existence of their court, where they were allowed the use of their own language and their own laws. Maseres called this a ridiculous apprehension, and yet in the same letter he had already admitted that one of his objects was to undermine the common pleas, whose judges, he said, lacked ability and legal acumen. Nevertheless Hey presented the proposed measure to the grand jury, observing that it might be enacted if the public approved. Thereupon the English part of the jury, of which Allsopp was one, remonstrated because it would speed up actions for debt, and they feared such expedition "in the then low state of commercial credit in the province." Maseres added that these Englishmen did not acquaint their Canadian colleagues with the proposal.[17]

As Carleton's ideas developed, he continued to pour them out in dispatches to Shelburne without waiting for replies to the suggestions which he had already made. On January 20, 1768, after referring to the way in which a citadel at Quebec might lock Canada within the house of the British Empire, he wrote: "Still I shall think the interests of Great Britain but half advanced unless the Canadians are inspired with a cordial attachment and zeal for the king's government" — the very ideal which had inspired his predecessor. Treason laws and the oath of allegiance might "keep some quiet in case of a French expedition," but the mass could not be trusted "if brought to the test" unless they were bound by self-interest to their new sovereign. Therefore their pressing grievances must be redressed — the laws, the courts, the fees. Nor was this enough. "As long as the Canadians are deprived of all places of trust and profit," Carleton pleaded, "they never can forget they no longer are under the dominion of their natural sovereign; tho' this immediately concerns but few, yet it affects the minds of all, from a national spirit which ever interests itself at the general exclusion of their countrymen." He repeated his demand for a few military units raised from among the new subjects, and he urged the appointment of "three or four of their principal gentlemen" to the council. Such concessions "would divide the Canadians at least, and secure a part, in case of a French war, that would emulate the zeal of the king's national troops." [18]

On the form of legislature that ought to be established, Carleton, Hey, and Maseres were all agreed. Representative government was impossible. In the dispatch quoted above, after telling of McCord's agitation, Carleton delivered his opinion in no uncertain terms. The better sort of Canadians, he asserted, "fear nothing more than popular assemblies which, they conceive, tend only to render the people refractory and insolent." He had inquired what they thought of them and had received the reply that "they understood some of our colonies had fallen under the king's displeasure owing to the misconduct of their assemblies, and that they should think themselves unhappy if a like misfortune befell them." Carleton thoroughly agreed with them about "the misconduct," for, with a suspicious eye on the old colonies, he went on to say: "It may not be improper here to observe that the British form of government, transplanted into this continent, never will produce the same fruits as at home, chiefly because it is impossible for the dignity of the throne or peerage to be represented in the American forests." Here he anticipated the argument advanced by Charles James Fox during the debates on the Constitutional Act — that the virtue of the British constitution lay in a just balance of three principles, monarchy, aristocracy, and democracy. But Carleton's keener insight discovered a great truth which escaped the father of the modern liberal party — that this balance could not be reproduced in America, "where all men appear nearly upon a level." If allowed an assembly for its expression, he was convinced that the third principle would subvert the other two, and that it would encourage strong republican ideas. This, he pointed out, was something to be particularly avoided "in a province so lately conquered and circumstanced as this is." [19]

On April 11, 1768, Carleton again poured out his complaint about the curse of fees in a letter to Shelburne, winding up with a grand peroration which deserves quotation. "While they are restrained in the fur trade, cut off from the sedentary fisheries of the *loup marin,* deprived of the property they enjoyed for generations, are governed by laws they are ignorant of, and labour under such a weight of fees, how far we may reasonably expect the Canadians ever will relish their new government or not sigh after and heartily embrace the first opportunity that ever offers of returning under their ancient dominion, I humbly submit to superior judges." [20]

On the following day, in a further letter to Shelburne, Carleton set forth a clear-cut plan for securing "a proper subordination from this province to Great Britain" forever. It was the full and formal recognition of the feudal system, which could be achieved simply by summoning all who held of the king to pay faith and homage at the Castle of St. Louis as in the days of old. Such a step would insure the payment of the royal fines on alienation, which had largely fallen into abeyance since the conquest; it would bind the seigniors to appear in arms to defend the province whenever it might be attacked; and it would confirm the doubtful tenure of all property. To enlighten the government in Britain, he inclosed a list of grants made before the conquest and a statement of the conditions upon which they were held, and, to allay the suspicion which the seigniorial right of justice might arouse in London, he added that this right had been of little consequence in the colony. Indeed, at this very time Maseres was anxious to see this remnant of the old system restored. Apparently with the concurrence of both the chief justice and the attorney general, Carleton also sought permission to make new grants after the old forms, except in the Gaspé peninsula and around the Bay of Chaleur, "where the king's old subjects ought chiefly to be encouraged to settle." He recognized that Canadian tenures would differentiate the colony from the rest of the empire in America, but he believed that this could not be avoided "without entirely oversetting the properties of the people." [21]

What was the effect of these letters, to which Carleton's subsequent correspondence adds little except emphasis and expansion? Though addressed to Shelburne, they were delivered to Hillsborough, who was appointed secretary of state for the American department in January, 1768, when this office was carved out of the one that Shelburne filled. On March 6, 1768, Hillsborough penned his first reply, in which, referring to the fact that he had presided over the board of trade when the proclamation of October 7, 1763, was issued, he averred that there had never been any intention "to overturn the laws and customs of Canada with regard to property." He gave Carleton to understand that the Canadians were certainly to have these old laws, though the proposed ordinance to continue them, which the king approved, was to be shelved pending the government's deliberations upon the affairs of the colony.[22] The rest of Hillsborough's replies need not be examined in detail.[23] They promised an immediate general settlement, which was always being delayed, and they cordially commended Carleton's sentiments and motives. To only two suggestions did the secretary of state fail to return a favorable echo. The military employment of Canadians he merely observed was a very delicate matter which would have to be considered carefully. The denunciation of an assembly evoked no personal response, but the new instructions sent on August 12, 1768, following Carleton's promotion to be governor in the previous January, repeated the directions given to Murray for calling an assembly as soon as possible. This repetition was not accidental. Through Fowler Walker, Maseres knew in May, 1768, that Hillsborough planned the erection of an assembly, and, as will appear shortly, he stuck to his plan for some time.

Other influences were now brought to bear upon the discussions of the whole Canadian problem. On April 13, 1768, the Canada committee, an organization of interested London merchants something like the well-known West India committee, prayed Hillsborough for the establishment of an assembly as the best means to revive the languishing trade of the colony, and on September 20 another petition from the same source appealed to the precedent of Grenada and suggested that a limited number of Roman Catholics be admitted to both council and assembly. These documents, together with the law officers' report of January on the plan to regulate religious affairs in Canada, were referred by the privy council to the board of trade on September 28, 1768,[24] with a request to report what ought to be done in Canada under the heads of legislature, ecclesiastical affairs, and revenue.

The board of trade, though its personnel was to a certain extent continuous, now occupied a changed position. By a new commission issued in July, 1768, Hillsborough re-entered this body as president or first lord, and it became little more than an adjunct to his office. Consequently its report may be regarded as largely the work of the secretary of state and not, as it would have been in former days, the advice of a more or less independent body in whose deliberations no cabinet minister shared. This point is essential to an understanding of what happened in 1769.

According to its own statement, the board proceeded "with the greatest circumspection" and procured "the fullest information that could be collected as well from the correspondence of His Majesty's servants there as from the examination of persons here who have been resident in and are well acquainted with the affairs of Quebec." The report,[25] which was signed on July 10, 1769, found routine stupidity responsible for wrecking the constitutional settlement of the colony. "No provision has been made for establishing such a reasonable revenue as may be adequate to the necessary expenses of government, the whole of which is now a burthen upon His Majesty's Treasury here. The Roman Catholic religion, though barely tolerated by the treaty, remains without any regulation, reform, or control whatever, and that of the mother country without any provision or support. Besides these capital objects, there are many other constitutional establishments and necessary services for which no provision either has been or can be made in the present state of the colony; and it has even been found necessary to disallow several ordinances of the governor and council, in matters merely of local regulation and internal economy, from a considerable want of a due authority to enact them." All these ills could be traced to the insertion in the governor's commission, "without sufficiently adverting to the state of the colony," of the requirement that assembly members subscribe to "the Test." This had rendered an assembly impossible and thereby had emasculated the government of the country. Referring to the confusion which had ensued, the report continued: "There is no method of curing these disorders, and giving effect and stability to government, but by establishing a competent legislative authority conformable to the royal assurances contained in the commission and proclamation." Therefore the report urged that the Test be waived, as had been done already in the ceded islands, to admit new subjects into the council and the assembly. It would also admit them to the bench, as well as to other government offices. There is no evidence that the board considered or even saw any other solution than the erection of an assembly. As a beginning, the report proposed a body of twenty-seven members, fourteen elected by the three towns and thirteen by the country districts. Only seigniors were to be returned in the country districts and they were to be excused from the Test, but the town members and the speaker were all to subscribe. The assembly would thus be balanced between English commercial leaders and French feudal lords.

To reform the administration of justice and to regulate religious affairs, the board fell back upon its recommendations of previous years. It urged the dispatch of the instructions completed in 1766, with a few slight amendments, as a cure for the disorders prevailing in the courts. In reviving its ecclesiastical plan of 1765, the board acted on the caution of the law officers by proposing to extinguish the religious orders, to fuse the seminaries, and to vest their property in the crown for the support of a Protestant clergy, not by an exercise of the royal prerogative but by an act passed in Quebec. But no legislation, it pointed out, was necessary for preserving the royal supremacy by licensing "a proper person . . . to superintend the affairs of the Romish church" under the close supervision of the governor who might suspend him. This was to be effected by means of royal instructions, as was also the prohibition of the outward display of episcopal dignity and "public processions or other ceremonies of pomp or parade." Apparently by an oversight, nothing was said about Protestants paying or not paying tithes.

Under the third point of reference, the report proposed a detailed civil establishment which would cost about £10,000 a year. To abolish the system of fees, the schedule included definite salaries for some offices, and a considerable item for contingencies from which salaries could be paid to other officials. Instead of the mother country continuing to bear the cost of administering the colony, the governor was to get a permanent revenue bill through the assembly, as had been done in Jamaica forty years previously. This was to include a poll tax, an excise on liquors, licenses for retailing them, and customs duties [26] on their import, all of which were specified. It was calculated that this revenue bill would bring in £11,250 a year. All that was to be at the disposal of the assembly was what might be left after the deduction of the annual charges of the establishment and of any previous deficits.

The report concluded by urging the danger of longer delay and the necessity for immediate action without waiting for the return of the governor, who had written for leave that he might advise the government in person and that he might attend to some private affairs. Five days later Hillsborough wrote Carleton that he would postpone consulting His Majesty about leave until the privy council reached some decision upon the report, because the governor could not be spared from the colony "if the regulations and reforms recommended by the board of trade in respect to religion, judicature and revenue are approved and ordered to be carried into execution." [27] It will be observed that in writing Carleton, Hillsborough said nothing about the possibility of the government deciding for an assembly, though he referred specifically to all the other main points under discussion. Was this omission a slip? If it was not a slip but intentional, was it designed to conceal from Carleton the project of an assembly? Or was it inspired by an anticipation that this part of the scheme might be eliminated? In favor of the first suggestion it may be argued that the whole program was built upon the assumption of an elected legislature in the colony. But it must have been obvious to some that this foundation was not absolutely necessary, for the essential legislation could have been passed in London instead of Quebec — as was eventually done. Against the second suggestion stands the fact that Hillsborough had apparently made no secret of his intention to call an assembly, for Maseres learned of it through Fowler Walker. The third suggestion may be supported by what occurred when the report was actually considered.

In the above letter to Carleton, written on July 15, 1769, Hillsborough said that he hoped for some decision shortly, but he would not presume to anticipate what it might be. His caution may have been inspired by a consciousness that he had already presumed too much. By injecting into his report the proposal to revive the dormant instructions of 1766, which would have effected a reorganization of the courts and provided a definite solution of the legal tangle, he was forejudging the results of the investigation proceeding in the colony. He may have thought that he could do it because Shelburne, who had launched this investigation, was no longer in the government, having been squeezed out in the autumn of 1768. Still he had no business to touch this subject, for it was not included in the order of reference from the privy council to the board of trade.

Whatever may have been Hillsborough's ground for hopes of an early adoption of his proposals, he was doomed to disappointment. Shortly after the submission of his report, the members of the admin-istration scattered for their usual recess, apparently without giving any consideration to Canada, and not until November 4 did the father of this scheme secure the assurance of the lord president of the council that it would be immediately examined.[28] He still professed opti-mism, but in a further letter to Carleton, written on December 1, he had to confess that his colleagues refused to move until the return of Morgann, whose mission they regarded as the essential foundation for everything else.[29] Hillsborough had received a rebuff. He immediately sent Carleton the desired permission to return and also a copy of the shelved report. In inclosing the latter, the secretary of state observed: "I have little doubt that, considering it as a general outline, it will very nearly coincide with your own opinions." [30] Possibly he thought that the seigniorial element, being half of the proposed assembly, would neutralize the democratic tendency feared by the governor. He also enjoined Carleton not to divulge any of the contents of the document to anyone. This injunction has been interpreted as indicating a policy of secrecy about the future gov-ernment of the province, but there was nothing really unusual in the effort to keep strictly private something that was still under deliberation in the cabinet.

Meanwhile Morgann was bearing home the fruits of his mis-sion.[31] The three officials in Quebec were unanimous in finding that the principal grievances of the Canadians arising out of the administration of justice were the uncertainty of the laws, the delay and expense of legal proceedings, and imprisonment for debt. They partly agreed upon how the courts should be reconstituted and they wholly agreed that the French laws of real property and inheritance should be restored and that the English criminal laws, the Habeas Corpus Act, and trial by jury for cases of tort should be retained. But they were hopelessly divided over what should be the general groundwork of the laws. Carleton wanted it to be French; Hey wanted it to be English; and Maseres wanted it to be a code based on English law.

Maseres, however, developed this opinion only during his last year in the colony. Before that time he repeatedly urged the restoration of the French system as the only way of escape from the legal jungle in the colony. "We have done the reverse of what we should have done with respect to the Canadians in taking away their laws which did us no harm and the continuance of which was necessary to their happiness." These were the attorney general's words in July, 1767.[32] In May, 1768, two months after the order-in-council had arrived, he favored a declaration that the French laws had never been legally abrogated and that therefore they still subsisted. With only three amendments, the elimination of torture, the abolition of breaking on the wheel, and the introduction of the Habeas Corpus Act, he would allow the whole of the old law to remain, criminal as well as civil. A composite code he at this time dismissed as an impossible ideal.[33] In August, 1768, the thought of such a compilation was beginning to intrigue his mind, but he was still moving along in the old groove. "There would be no great advantage," he asserted, "in abolishing these laws and customs (if the Canadians could be imagined to be willing tamely to submit to it,) and introducing in their stead the laws of England. Nay perhaps it may be better for the interest of Great Britain that the inhabitants of this province should continue to be by laws and customs considerably different from those of the neighboring colonies, to the end that they may not join with those colonies in rejecting the supremacy of the mother country." [34]

Maseres undoubtedly convinced Carleton that the only solution was to revive the old laws with a few modifications, and, therefore, when a report was called for, the governor naturally employed the attorney general to prepare it. The work was finished in February, 1769, and when Carleton read it he must have felt that the Huguenot had betrayed him. The draft did not propose a restoration of the old laws as he had hoped, nor did it even point out what old laws should be retained and what new ones introduced, as the home authorities had desired, and it contained some passages about the church which must have appeared offensive. In this document Maseres' former ideas now appeared as only one of four alternatives. The first of the other three was an amalgam of French and English laws in a written code. The other two were the same in substance, being a general introduction of English laws except for parts of the old laws which might be allowed but which he did not specify. The difference lay in whether this exceptional body of old laws was to be codified or not. Though Maseres' draft discussed the merits and demerits of each alternative, it declined to "draw a final balance in favour of one of these methods" and threw back upon the ministry the whole responsibility for a decision. In enumerating the laws which were unquestionably in force in the colony, Maseres insisted on including the first statute of Elizabeth's reign, the Act of Supremacy. Therefore, according to Maseres, all ecclesiastical authority derived from Rome was prohibited in the colony as much as in the mother country; every clergyman, every official employed by the government, and every layman doing homage to the crown for lands must take the oath of supremacy; and anyone defending papal authority by word or pen was to forfeit all his goods and chattels. Some pages later he quoted the capitulation to prove that the tithes were either abolished or suspended, and that the Canadian laws and customs which gave the bishop a right "to establish new parishes, and to provide for the rebuilding of his cathedral and his episcopal palace, and to visit his diocese with the ordinary ceremonies, and to exercise the jurisdiction which had been exercised by his predecessors" were all abolished. Carleton rejected the draft "with resentment," and Morgann condemned it as useless and "improper."

The governor next applied to the chief justice. But the chief justice could not then draw up a report because he was just leaving to hold a court in Montreal. Thereupon Carleton and Hey persuaded Morgann to try his hand. Morgann succeeded in preparing a document which pleased the governor but not the chief justice. The latter, on his return from Montreal, found this draft so little to his liking that he sat down and wrote one of his own by the end of June. This contained no "specific mode of alteration," according to Morgann. Carleton's first inclination was to adopt Morgann's work, but he changed his mind and decided to combine it with what Hey had written. This he did himself, probably with the assistance of Cramahé.[35]

The report, which was signed in Quebec on September 15, 1769, advised the retention of English criminal laws, except those aimed at Roman Catholics, as generally satisfactory to French and English. It also advocated the Habeas Corpus Act and trial by jury for criminal prosecutions as a favor to the new subjects and the just privilege of the old subjects. To please the latter, juries were also to be called "in every case wherein pecuniary compensation is sought for personal wrongs," that is, for torts. "In all mercantile disputes, the custom of merchants" was taken for granted, as were also the British Acts of Trade and Navigation. Otherwise the old laws were to be restored as they had stood on the eve of the conquest. Both criminal and civil laws were to be revised as soon as possible in order to eliminate any undesirable features which they might contain, to give them greater certainty, and to stop recourse to French authorities for civil laws. With words of wisdom and of warning, this restorative policy was pressed. "We humbly conceive this on all accounts to be the wisest and most eligible measure, even tho' we should assume the opinion that it will be Your Majesty's intention, at some future period, to introduce the British laws into this province and to model its government in conformity to that of Great Britain, experience having sufficiently taught us that a thorough change of the laws and customs of a settled province can never be effected at once, but must be a work of great time, and can only be brought about by slow and gentle means." If, however, "Your Majesty should now resolve to crush them [the Canadians] with a strong hand into a similitude with the rest of Your Majesty's dominions, by compelling them to accept the same laws, we know not to what extremity a people so circumstanced would be reduced, or in what it might terminate. At best it would induce such despair and dejection of mind, and so alienate them from every good opinion of, or confidence in, the British government, as no time or circumstances would ever conciliate."

The other proposals in the report may be dismissed shortly. They aimed at copying as closely as possible the judicial and police organization of the old régime. Bailiffs were to disappear and the militia officers were to be "restored to the exercise of all the civil part of their former employments." The scope of the report precluded any reference to their military capacity. "To raise their characters and enlarge their civil authority," they were to be made coroners and conservators of the peace in their respective parishes. Even the seigniors might be allowed their modicum of jurisdiction and be invested with the functions of conservators of the peace in their respective seigniories. The intendant's *subdélégué* was to reappear as a police magistrate in each town, and each district was to have its weekly courts as of old. The only other suggestion worth noting here was the removal of the cramping restrictions upon the legislative competence of the governor and council.

Hey and Maseres objected strongly to the main point of the report, and each added his own criticism in a separate paper or supplementary report. They were willing to admit the old law of real property and of inheritance, but there they would stop. The general introduction of French law was to them a disastrous proposal. For one thing, it would give great offense to the English-speaking minority. It would also lead to an impossible situation in the courts. Englishmen would not be able to serve as judges if they had to master all the French law which would be introduced, and Canadians were not to be trusted on the bench. The chief justice would not have them because they were newly conquered subjects whose loyalty was as yet untried, and the attorney general abhorred them because they were Roman Catholics. In the third place, it would be going back upon the policy of bringing Canada gradually into conformity with the other colonies, a policy which these two officials deemed absolutely necessary. According to Hey, the blow already struck at Canadian laws was a great advantage which should not be thrown away. It had opened the door for "assimilating the Canadians to English sentiments and manners." Here, however, the agreement between the chief justice and the attorney general came to an end. Maseres, insisting that continual references to the custom of Paris and the parlement of Paris would nourish the Canadians' affection for their old sovereign, and, pointing out that certain parts of the English law would be quite unsuited to Canada, now came out whole-heartedly in favor of a code. He urged that the few French laws and all the English laws that were necessary should be welded into one compact system which might be amended as experience suggested. His supporting argument, so far as it referred to French law, was not quite fair, because the report itself anticipated the severance of the legal connection with France, though not at so early a date, and his proposal was curtly rejected by Hey because the times demanded an immediate settlement and could not wait upon such a work.

The differences of opinion which had developed over the report seem to have imposed no strain on Carleton's relations with Hey, who was a very discreet person. But with Maseres it was different. Never comfortable in the climate and the religious atmosphere of the colony, he was now more miserable than ever, for he found that the governor had become as cold as the winter. Therefore in October, 1769, he went home on leave, never to return.[36]

On January 18, 1770, Hillsborough reported to Carleton that Morgann had arrived and that his papers would pave the way for an early decision. But this was the perennial optimism of one who was not in the inner circle of the administration.[37] Five months later he wrote the governor that the settlement of the affairs of the colony waited only on his arrival.[38] Early in August, 1770, Carleton embarked, but even his presence was unavailing for a long time.

Before receiving permission to leave his post, Carleton's impatience with the judicial administration and his determination to remove Canadian grievances bore fruit in an important reform. In July, 1769, roused by complaints which characteristically came from Montreal, the governor and council wrote the magistrates of that district directing them to issue new regulations to meet the complaints.[39] When the justices of the peace, after a fortnight's delay, wrote a querulous reply instead of doing as they were bidden,[40] the council appointed a committee headed by Hey and assisted by Maseres to investigate the whole administration of the justices of the peace in the province.[41] In the middle of September they reported that the Canadian magistrates had more powers and fewer qualifications than had English justices of the peace, and that those in Montreal sometimes stretched their authority illegally and often used it harshly. Therefore they recommended [42] the repeal of that part of the "injudicious ordinance" [43] of September, 1764, which gave civil jurisdiction to the magistrates.

Acting on this report, the council passed an ordinance in February, 1770, which left the magistrates with only their criminal and police jurisdiction. The authority thus taken from them was added to that of the judges of the common pleas, who were now increased to four * and divided into two separate courts which were to sit continuously, except for short vacations, in the towns of Quebec and

* Mabane, Fraser, Cramahé, and Marteilhe (see note on page 91). Cramahé had succeeded Mounier on the death of the latter in 1769, and, when he took over the administration of the colony in 1770, he was succeeded by Dunn. Marteilhe was added to make four.

The vacations referred to were at seedtime, harvest, Christmas, Easter, and when the judges went on circuit through their respective districts twice a year.

Montreal. Friday was set apart for cases of small debts — those not exceeding twelve pounds — for the determination of which only one judge was necessary. The ordinance also contained a number of provisions to reduce costs and to give small debtors reasonable protection, so that habitants would not be sold up or lodged in prison for owing trifling sums.[44]

This reform stirred a great outcry among the English-speaking merchants. They asserted that continuous sessions of the common pleas would ruin trade by allowing traders to be called to account at any time by their creditors and by permitting delay in the sale of lands for small debts. They condemned the measure as "a very dangerous infringement of the liberty of the subject" and quite probably they feared it as a first step backward toward the old régime.[45] Carleton, however, stood firm. He rebuked the agitators for "their attempts to follow the conduct of a province which had incurred the displeasure of government at home and whose manner of demanding redress had proved the means of preventing it," and he told their delegation that he was ashamed of the way in which "many of the king's old subjects had behaved, sending about hand bills to invite the people to assemble in order to consult upon grievances, importuning, nay insulting, several of the Canadians because they would not join them." [46] If the governor in Quebec needed any further proof of the wholesome effect of the ordinance, the Montreal jailer supplied it a few months later. He applied for a salary, because his fees dropped with the number of his prisoners.[47]

Much more far-reaching was another step which Carleton's concern for Canadian feelings inspired him to take in July, 1770, just a few days before he sailed for England. It had to do with religion; and here it will be well to go back and pick up the story at the point where it was dropped in the beginning of this chapter. Instead of watching the church, he soon began to watch over it. He pressed upon the home government the wisdom of providing for the continuance of the episcopacy, without which the religion of the Canadians could not be secure, but Hillsborough, though he inclined a favorable ear in the spring of 1768, did not authorize the appointment of a coadjutor. At the same time things happened which made Carleton feel that he had to stand between the Catholic church in the colony and the Protestant government at home. Early in 1768 royal warrants were issued for the appointment of three French-speaking clergymen to preside over the Anglican congregations of Quebec, Three Rivers, and Montreal. This was following the revival of the board of trade's project for an ecclesiastical settlement, and this in turn came on top of the visit to England of the renegade Récollet, Veyssière. This fellow, whose character was less stable than his faith, now appeared back in Canada as the appointee to the living of Three Rivers. Very irritating also was the Quebec incumbent. He demanded that he be given possession of the Jesuits' church, and, appealing to the terms of his mandamus, claimed the right to collect and appropriate all the tithes in his parish. The governor of course refused, saying that it would be a violation of justice and a breach of treaty rights, only to be told by the grasping cleric that Britain need not keep faith with Roman Catholics because Louis XIV had kept none with Protestants.[48] Even the Jesuits were stoutly defended by Carleton against the home government's repeated orders to insist upon the payment of the annuity which the rascal Roubaud asserted was his by right. On Briand's behalf the governor likewise spoke out boldly when he learned that the bishop had been maligned in England.[49]

As he was about to leave the colony, to which he might not return, the governor decided to present the government in London with a *fait accompli* by having a coadjutor appointed. The priest whom he picked was of course a Canadian, the first native of the colony to become head of its church — L. P. M. Desglis, curé of St. Pierre on the island of Orleans. Briand was delighted not only with the recognition of the principle but also with Carleton's choice. Desglis was beloved by the people, respected by the clergy, and esteemed by the English. But the bishop's joy was not unalloyed. The governor demanded that the consecration take place immediately, and there was a little storm when Briand, who stood almost alone among his co-religionists on this matter, refused to act until he could procure the necessary bulls or at least the permission of some higher ecclesiastical authority. He was in an extremely delicate position, and he seems to have adopted a wise course. His own consecration as bishop of Quebec had been urged in England because it would make him independent of Rome. But this had raised suspicions in Rome which his resistance to the governor's importunity now dissipated. At the same time he tried to avoid awakening British suspicions of Rome by seeking to procure the bulls through an indirect channel, through two old members of the Quebec chapter who had settled in Paris, the head of the foreign missions and the Abbé de la Corne.

Nearly two years elapsed before the documents arrived, and then Briand consecrated Desglis bishop *in partibus* on July 12, 1772.[50] Cramahé, who had become administrator early in August, 1770, on Carleton's departure and had been appointed lieutenant governor in 1771, naturally reported the ceremony. Thereupon Dartmouth, who had just succeeded Hillsborough in office, pronounced it "a matter of the highest importance," and, as he could find no trace of any sanction having been sent from home, he scolded the innocent Cramahé for the results of Carleton's independent action.[51] However, the consecration was irrevocable and the principle of a coadjutor was established. Now it would be more difficult for the government to put a bridle and blinkers on the head of the church as the board of trade had planned.

CHAPTER IX

THE QUEBEC ACT

CANADA'S new constitution was born as the American Revolution was breaking. That there was a connection between the two events cannot be denied, but it must be remembered that for several years the new constitution had been in the womb of time. There it may be seen gradually taking shape, and an examination of the process strongly suggests that, until almost the moment of birth, fear of a colonial rebellion had little influence compared with apprehension of another French war or concern for the feelings and interests of the Canadians.

Many months before the Quebec Act was actually drafted, its principal features were clearly distinguishable. Already a large part of its legal face has been observed — English criminal law and French laws of real property and inheritance. True, there was a difference of opinion over the legislature, officials in Canada unanimously asserting that the colony was not ripe for an assembly and at least two members [1] of the administration at home favoring representative government. Still, one can forecast the outcome, because an alternative to an assembly does not seem to have occurred to the latter, while it appeared absolutely necessary to the former. The point was settled not long after the arrival of Carleton in England. On January 2, 1771, Hillsborough wrote Cramahé that legislation was proposed to endow the governor and council with definite powers for a limited time. [2] The assembly was dropped from the program! There is no evidence of any official recurrence to the idea during the interval of over three years which now elapsed before the passing of the Quebec Act.

About the same time as it abandoned the thought of establishing representative government in Canada — that is, around the end of 1770 or early in 1771 — the home government reached another important decision about the new constitution. It was to rest on a feudal footing. This was regarded as so important and so urgent that it could not wait until the material for the rest of the structure was gathered, and therefore it was embodied in an additional

177

instruction issued on July 2, 1771. This canceled all previous instructions regulating the granting of lands, including the provision that grants must be made in freehold, and ordered the governor to follow, except in one particular, the preconquest system of concessions *en fief et seigneurie*. The one particular that was to be eliminated was the seigniorial right of justice, a right which even in French days had largely fallen into abeyance.[3] In transmitting the additional instruction, Hillsborough expressed the hope that it would "convince His Majesty's new subjects of the king's gracious intentions to adopt and preserve in every case where it can be legally done the customs and usages that subsisted in the colony before the reduction of it and which His Majesty observes they are very desirous to retain."[4] The new subjects received it in this spirit, and the old subjects were just as delighted. The latter had no desire for lands under their traditional system, and in 1772, when they heard of the change, their petitions for new seigniories poured in upon the lieutenant governor and council. One is tempted to speculate upon what would have happened had not the outbreak of the American Revolution forestalled any action upon this swarm of appeals.[5]

The boundaries prescribed by the act of 1774 may also be anticipated from the discussions of several years before. The problem of the interior did not disappear in 1768, on the withdrawal of Johnson's commissaries and regulations and the transfer to the separate colonies of the responsibility for controlling the conduct of the Indian trade; it simply entered upon a new phase. The change of system robbed the heart of the continent of all civil jurisdiction. How were disputes which arose in the Indian country to be settled? How were the separate colonies to bear their new and mighty responsibility? How could they impose regulations in the interior? No colonial government could reach its hand beyond its own borders. Though each might pass regulations to be observed in the interior, it could enforce them only by confiscating the bond which had been deposited by an offending trader before he left for the west. But such a course would ruin its traders or would drive them to other colonies, unless the regulations of all were equally stringent, which was impossible. Competition between the colonies was thus placed upon a vicious foundation which threatened to destroy the traffic in furs.

Those who went into the interior in the summer of 1768 were alarmed at the prospect, and in the following spring English and Canadian merchants and traders of Montreal roused the governor and council in Quebec to the seriousness of the situation. Hey, Cramahé, and Dunn were appointed a committee to consider the memorials that had come from the fur-trading city. The committee's report, dated April 8, 1769, cut to the heart of the problem. It suggested a few palliatives, but pointed out that there was only one cure — annexation to an existing colony. It argued Canada's superior pretensions, geographical and economical. In those days when the rivers were the highroads, this territory was linked with Canada as with no other colony. The traders from Canada were more numerous than those from any other source. Moreover, they sold British manufactures, while the traders from New York, their strongest competitors, dealt more largely in rum. The report urged the governor to press these considerations upon the home government.[6]

At the same time the New York assembly advanced a purely American solution. This was concurrent legislation in the three colonies most concerned, Quebec, New York, and Pennsylvania. The proposal was sent to Carleton by Sir Henry Moore, the governor of New York, on June 11, 1769, but Quebec did not react at all until the summer of 1771. Then, on the receipt of an invitation to send commissioners to meet with like representatives of the other two colonies in New York on December 1 to regulate the trade with the Indians in the interior, the council decided to take this step. But no commissioners went from Quebec because Cramahé soon learned that the home government disapproved of congresses on Indian affairs at this time. Indeed, any American gathering at this time would look dangerous in London. But even if London had not interposed its veto, the plan was doomed. A committee of the Quebec council, after studying its details and consulting with a number of the Montreal fur barons, reported unanimously that it would injure rather than benefit the trade. Even more decisive was another fact brought out by this committee. The plan was to be operated by means of taxes imposed by the colonies on rum and dry goods sold in the interior; but the province of Quebec, unlike the provinces of New York and Pennsylvania, had absolutely no authority to impose any such duties.[7] Canadian cooperation was impossible, and without Canadian cooperation no colonial scheme would work.

Thus, by a process of elimination — first the prohibitive cost of a separate government for the heart of the continent, and then the practical impossibility of joint colonial control — the obvious solution was that urged by the Quebec council in 1769, annexation to some colony, preferably Canada. Here it may also be observed that the complaints of the Montreal merchants and traders revived the complaints of those in Quebec who were interested in the seal fisheries of the gulf, and both French and English inhabitants of the colony, long before the drafting of the Quebec Act, were of one mind in desiring the reannexation of the eastern as well as of the western territory which had been torn from Canada in 1763.

The correspondence that passed between London and Quebec during the years of Carleton's absence contains few references to the old colonies except the passages referring to the Indian congress which did not meet in New York. These letters, however, reveal a great concern over the possible danger from the Indians and from France, a connection which was not unnatural. Hillsborough had a distinct attack of nerves in the spring of 1772. It was occasioned by the receipt of a copy of a letter said to have been written to the secretary of the French ambassador in Madrid by a leading Canadian named Rouville, and the discovery that an officer in the French service then sailing from London for Canada was this Rouville's son. This coincidence, and rumors of a suspicious correspondence between Canada and France, moved the secretary of state to write Cramahé a secret dispatch in which he said: "As intelligence thro' different channels seems to indicate a particular attention at present in the court of France to what passes in Canada, it certainly becomes necessary that we should be very much upon our guard." [8]

Cramahé replied [9] defending the Rouvilles as honest men and justifying the intercourse with France as natural. The Canadians, he reported, certainly complained of the courts and the laws, "but they readily and indeed gratefully acknowledge the indulgence shewn to them in regard to religion and hope the same will be continued, altho' they have at times been likewise alarmed upon this head by the indiscreet talk of some individuals amongst us." He observed that the immigrant clergy, through jealousy of the preference now given to their native brethren, and the seigniors, through discontent over the impossibility of procuring employment for their children in His Majesty's service, might have an evil influence over the habitants if French assistance were at hand. He pointed out, however, that the Canadian clergy were ever stronger supporters of British power, and therefore he welcomed the consecration of Desglis, and he hoped that Charles de Lanaudière, a seignior who had accompanied Carleton to London to secure a commission for raising a Canadian regiment of two battalions,[10] would be successful in his mission.

A few weeks later, Cramahé reported an incident that might easily have confirmed British suspicions of France. An old militia officer named Dufy, one of the substantial bourgeoisie of Montreal, was notified that an honor promised him years before was now actually granted. It was the much-coveted Croix de St. Louis. He had only to repair to France for the investiture. Was this part of a deep design to draw leading Canadians back to their old allegiance, or was it only a shallow trick of relatives in France who hoped to inherit the wealth of a man approaching "three score years and ten"? Cramahé did not know, nor did he very much care. Dufy had declined with thanks and had told the lieutenant governor all about it. Again Cramahé repeated that French designs would be unavailing if only the confusion in the courts were cleaned up, the government were established upon a firm basis, and some employment were found for the noblesse.[11]

The hopes of an early and satisfactory settlement, which Cramahé frequently expressed for himself and for the Canadians, Hillsborough continued to feed as in the days when Carleton was champing the bit in Quebec. In December, 1771, the secretary of state lamented the delay but affirmed that it was unavoidable because the problem was one of such "delicacy and importance" and "almost every department of government" had to be consulted. Very probably the rising tide of troubles in the old colonies was also responsible. He now admitted the possibility of further delay, for, he said, "I am not without apprehension that it may at last be found necessary that the opinion of the king's servants should be submitted to parliament before any final settlement can take place." [12] Obviously the way was dark.

Already the government had appealed to its legal advisers for light, but the light was very slow in coming, and when at last it came it was far from clear. An order-in-council of June 14, 1771, required His Majesty's advocate, attorney, and solicitor general to consider "the several reports and papers relative to the laws and courts of judicature of Quebec, and the present defective mode of government in that province," and, with any further information which they could gather, "to prepare a general plan of civil and criminal law for the said province." This was asking the impossible. The three law officers of the crown could not come together on any plan. More than a year after the above order-in-council was passed, it was followed by another calling for three separate reports. The first appeared in December, 1772, and the other two were completed in 1773.

The greatest difference was between Advocate General James Marriott, subsequently judge of the high court of admiralty, and Attorney General Edward Thurlow, later lord chancellor. Marriott quoted Maseres copiously and adopted Hey's argument for going on and taking advantage of what had been already done, but he would not go quite so far as the chief justice of Quebec, for he admitted the policy of preserving the great distinction between the Canadians and the people of the other colonies. He would retain many positive enactments of the French régime which appeared well fitted to the nature of the country, and also its old laws of real property and inheritance, but he wished to inject the principles of primogeniture and socage tenure, and he advised the English law of personal property for English-speaking settlers. He would limit the right of habeas corpus, restrict arrests in civil cases, and reform the English criminal law, which he said was "dipt in blood," and he would never allow a jury to touch a revenue case. On matters of government he was somewhat vague, regarding an assembly as a future rather than as a present possibility. On religious affairs he was categorical. The toleration granted by the treaty included only the exercise of the rites of the Roman Catholic church and did not extend to its doctrines, organization, or government. He clung to the letter of the bond.[13]

Thurlow based his report on a principle which enabled him to avoid a discussion of details. His plan was to go back to the old laws and government and to allow no change without "actual and cogent necessity." He would not admit "the necessity of assimilating a conquered country in the article of laws and government to the metro-

politan state or to the older provinces which other accidents attached
to the empire for the sake of creating a harmony and uniformity,"
which he said was either unattainable or useless; nor "the necessity
of stripping from a lawyer's argument all resort to the learned decisions of the Parliament of Paris, for fear of keeping up the historical
idea of the origin of their laws"; nor "the necessity of gratifying the
unprincipled and impracticable expectations of those few amongst
Your Majesty's subjects who may accidentally resort thither, and
expect to find all the different laws of all the different places from
which they have come; nor according to my simple judgment, any
species of necessity which I have heard urged for abolishing the laws
and government of Canada." [14]

The report of Solicitor General Alexander Wedderburn, who,
as Lord Loughborough, was first to become chief justice of the common pleas and then was to mount the woolsack, stood between those
of his two colleagues, but much nearer to Marriott's than to Thurlow's. His fundamental principle was that "more attention is due
to the native Canadian than the British emigrant, not only because
that class is the most numerous, but because it is not the interest of
Britain that many of her natives should settle there." The second
reason, it may be remarked, was probably more innocent than it
seems, for emigration to the colonies was not officially encouraged
either in this or in the preceding age. He admitted the claim of the
Canadians to as much of their "ancient laws regarding private rights
as is not inconsistent with the principles of the new government,"
but he would permit individuals to transform feudal into freehold
tenure. He observed that considerable pruning was necessary before
planting English criminal law in the colony, and he too doubted the
wisdom of the unlimited right of habeas corpus in a recently conquered country. Arrest and imprisonment in civil cases he would
restrict, as in the old régime, to commercial actions. Though he
asserted that toleration had never overturned a state while the lack
of it had often endangered the public safety, he denounced all
ecclesiastical jurisdiction derived from Rome as a violation of the
royal supremacy. The bishop, whom he mentioned only inferentially, should do no more than ordain priests and give dispensations
for marriage. All the religious houses should disappear except the
convents, which were necessary "for the honourable retreat of un-
married women." The courts should be made to support the pay-

ment of the tithe — by Roman Catholics to their own clergy, and by Protestants to the receiver general. An assembly including Canadians he dismissed as "a dangerous experiment with new subjects" and "an inexhaustible source of dissension and opposition between them and the British subjects"; and an assembly without them he pronounced impossible. Therefore he proposed the elevation of the governor and council into a legislature with limited authority for a limited period of years. This, he remarked, would necessitate the provision of a revenue by act of parliament.[15]

These reports, which the members of the government had in their hands during the summer vacation of 1773, left the legal jungle in Canada as impenetrable as ever. Hence William Knox, the under secretary, was able to write: "Thus it fell out, that after all the pains which had been taken to procure the best and ablest advice, the Ministers were in a great measure left to act upon their own judgment." [16]

How far was their judgment swayed by the storm which at this very time was blowing up in America? Rhode Islanders captured and burned the government schooner "Gaspee" in June, committees of correspondence were formed to draw the colonies together, the Hutchinson letters were published and denounced, and the Boston Tea Party occurred in December — all in 1773. At the end of January, 1774, Wedderburn's tongue inflicted a mortal wound upon Benjamin Franklin's loyalty. In March, Lord North began to apply the whip to rebellious America with his four penal acts, closing Boston Harbor, revoking the charter of Massachusetts, removing trials for capital offenses from that colony to Nova Scotia or Great Britain, and providing for the quartering of troops. Then, on May 2, the Quebec Bill appeared in the house of lords, and at the end of the month it entered the commons, whence it emerged triumphant in little more than a fortnight. In a few weeks Carleton was sailing over the Atlantic to find, so he said on his arrival, a delighted Canadian race. Indeed, he trusted them so much that he at once sent half his garrison to the nervous Gage in Boston. Is the inference as true as it is obvious?

The old colonies naturally leaped to the conclusion that the Quebec Act was a blow aimed through Canada at them. By extending Canada's boundaries down the Ohio, did it not threaten to coop them up on the narrow Atlantic seaboard? Did it not re-establish

Roman Catholicism, the very antithesis of their religious faith? Did it not deny popular government, the very article of their political faith? What could be the meaning of all this unless it was intended to arm Canada to crush their economic, religious, and political liberties? Indeed, Britain seemed to have stepped into France's shoes in America, and the old menace, which they had thought forever banished in 1760, loomed up darker than ever.

The conclusions drawn by the Americans at the time have since been supported by an appeal to the way in which the measure was passed. The government rushed it through parliament at the fag end of the session and withheld all the official papers which had been connected with its preparation. The opposition called for the reports of the governor and of the law officers, but their motions were rejected by a two to one vote. The house of commons was allowed to examine Carleton, Maseres, Hey, who had returned in 1773 because of his health, Lotbinière, a leading seignior, and Marriott. Thurlow and Wedderburn, being members of the house, spoke from their seats. Carleton, Thurlow, and Wedderburn approved the bill as it stood. Maseres and Hey repeated their previous criticisms, though the chief justice was now willing to grant the Canadians a little more, their demands having risen during the long delay. Lotbinière disliked the provision for a nominated council, preferring an assembly half of the members of which would be seigniors. Marriott, with an agile wit that refreshed the weary members, parried every effort to extract his real opinions. All this was very unsatisfactory to those who fought the measure, and they threw out insinuations of dark designs behind the bill.[17]

Against these arguments of the Americans then and of others later there is a good deal to be said. The imagination of the old colonists was already so disordered by their own resistance and the home government's retaliation that they were sure to see wild visions in anything that Britain did short of yielding to their every demand. Their nervousness might have been less had they known that, after the passage of the Quebec Act, Carleton was sent back to the colony without permission to raise one Canadian regiment, the object of his prayers for seven long years. Moreover, the main character of the act was mostly determined before people in England heard of the tea party that suddenly brought on the American crisis. The new boundary line, foreshadowed in a letter which Dartmouth wrote

Cramahé on December 1, 1773, had long been an obvious necessity. An assembly seems to have been out of the question from the beginning of 1771, and any doubts lingering in Maseres' mind were removed by a statement which he received from Lord North in the summer of 1773.[18] The feudal system was restored to its full vigor in 1771 as an earnest of legal concessions repeatedly promised. The only major questions that had not been settled were the extent of the legal restoration and what should be the regulations for the church. On the second question the government's hands were already somewhat tied by the consecration of a coadjutor, and for several years it had been taken for granted that Roman Catholics would be admitted to office and that the tithe would be continued. On the other question the government's decision was materially altered after the news of the Boston Tea Party arrived, but the change had no relation to that startling intelligence. It was due to the arguments of Hey and Wedderburn and was in favor of English law, as will appear later.

The way in which the bill was railroaded through parliament is no proof of any evil motive on the part of its sponsors. It simply proves beyond all shadow of doubt that the coming of the Revolution merely precipitated the birth of the Quebec Act. The foundations of the British Empire in America were shaking. Canada might be swallowed up in an earthquake unless her constitution were immediately established on a firm basis. When not a moment was to be lost, can the government be blamed for withholding the preliminary papers that would have enabled the opposition to prolong the debate indefinitely? This was reason enough for the majority to defeat the motions for the production of the reports, and it was reinforced by the fatigue which they were suffering at the close of an exhausting session. There is no justification for saying that they voted under orders. The opposition's taunts that the government had some concealed purpose in framing the bill need not be taken seriously. Parliament had eagerly passed four penal statutes against the old colonies, and if the government designed this as a fifth, its supporters could have advanced no stronger argument for hurrying it through the house.

That the Quebec Act was not designed as a blow at the old colonies is the conclusion one draws from a careful examination of the act itself and of the new instructions that followed it.[19] The two documents must be read together, for the latter lights up the dark corners of the former.[20] This comparison, however, is not necessary for an understanding of the first section of the act, that which reunited to Canada all the territories cut off in 1763. This change, which might have been effected by the royal prerogative instead of by parliamentary legislation, was inserted in the act to make Canada's new boundary less impeachable and more public. The addition of Labrador on the east caused no criticism and therefore may be dismissed as a mere reparation for the wrong done eleven years before.

But the extension of Canada's boundary up the St. Lawrence, through Lake Ontario and the Niagara River to Lake Erie, along the western edge of Pennsylvania to the Ohio, and down the Ohio to the Mississippi, stirred a great outcry and therefore merits closer scrutiny. The old colonies had no ground for complaining that the enlargement of the province of Quebec invaded their territories. The act was carefully worded to avoid any encroachment upon Pennsylvania in particular and it stipulated "that nothing herein contained relative to the boundary of the province of Quebec shall in anywise affect the boundaries of any other colony." But the old colonies were alarmed for other reasons. New York traders feared that they would be excluded by their Canadian rivals from the Niagara and the Detroit trade which they had shared. Furthermore, the half-forgotten British policy of 1763, the preservation of the heart of the continent as a great native reserve and the restriction of settlement to the narrow territory on the east, stared the old colonies in the face. Hillsborough, out of office but still consulted by the government, wished to have this stipulated in the act, but it was felt to be unnecessary, the polity established in Canada and extended to these lands being deemed a sufficient deterrent to migration into this reserve. There may well have been some thought of restricting the old colonies, which were getting out of hand, but had they been as meek as lambs the new boundary would probably have followed much the same line. French traders coming up the Mississippi were taking advantage of the growing confusion to insinuate themselves into this derelict territory. Some provision for its government was an urgent necessity. The only practicable solution was annexation to an existing colony, and there was only one choice. This country belonged to Canada historically, geographically, economically, and even ethnically. Its only inhabitants were a few Canadians and the

Indians, who were foster children of New France. The red men could be more effectively managed through the governor of Quebec than through any other, for he alone was unchecked by an assembly. If Britain made any great mistake in the disposition of this territory, it was in 1763 rather than in 1774. Had not Canada's boundaries been clipped so close after the Seven Years' War, they might have been more extended at the close of the Revolutionary War.

The section of the act dealing with religion gave a wider latitude and a parliamentary sanction to the treaty guarantee of toleration. For the Elizabethan oath of supremacy and other tests framed to exclude Roman Catholics from office it substituted a simple oath of allegiance specifically designed to admit them. This important reform of the law, by which Canada got Catholic emancipation more than half a century before Britain, was passed without debate.[21] The act also recognized the continuance of the tithe but allowed the Roman Catholic clergy to collect only from their own people. The right to collect from others was reserved for the support of a Protestant clergy.[22] The Huguenot attorney general of Quebec was the only official adviser of the government to oppose this provision, which was necessary to preserve unimpaired the religion of the Canadians. According to William Knox, the under secretary of state for the American department, there was "very good authority" for believing that the legality of the tithe had not been impaired by the conquest or by the establishment of civil government — probably on the ground that the old laws still subsisted in full force, never having been abrogated or superseded by competent authority. Therefore, as far as the tithe was concerned, the Quebec Act restricted rather than extended the rights of the Roman Catholic church, the only change in the law being the exemption of Protestants from the obligation to support the Roman church.[23]

The practical effect of parliament's recognizing the rights of the Roman Catholic clergy is very hard if not absolutely impossible to estimate. Tithes were still collected by spiritual authority, the only difference being that before the act the courts might or might not have enforced payment, whereas after the act there could be no doubt whatever. The clergy were so grateful to Britain for the act that they exerted every effort to hold their people loyal during the trying days of the American Revolution. Was this influence quite outweighed, as some maintain, by the feeling of resentment which the legal recognition of the tithe stirred among the mass of the Canadians? No positive answer can be given to this question. That the church's demands met with resistance greater than had been common during the French régime is supported by Murray's statement in 1762 and by Maseres' later assertions; but no other direct evidence has yet come to light, and Maseres was a prejudiced witness. Of indirect evidence there is only the clergy's profound gratitude to the British government for the act, and the exact value of this is doubtful because they had been worried by something else that seemed at this time to have been settled in their favor.

For several years there had been talk of restriction and confiscation, and now the burden of these fears was rolled away, for the act contained no such provision. The clergy may never have known to what an extent the board of trade's policy was officially adopted, for it was embedded in a confidential document, the instructions, and was largely neglected by the governor. He successfully opposed the suppression of any religious communities, except the Jesuits, whose order was already dissolved by the pope and whose property was not actually appropriated by the crown. But the government continued to prohibit the only other male order, the Récollets, from admitting novices, which would mean its ultimate extinction. On the other hand, the communities of women and the two seminaries were at last permitted to recruit. Carleton also pleaded for a free hand to deal with the "very delicate business" of ecclesiastical regulations, and he exercised it in spite of the government's formal refusal to grant it. Had the governor obeyed his instructions, the bishop could have done nothing except under the authority of a license bearing the seal of the province and revocable at pleasure; he could have ordained no priest without special permission; each curé would have been appointed by the government and have been removable only by the same power; every clergyman holding a benefice or ecclesiastical office would have been forced to take the new oath before the council; any cleric might have married without being subject to any penalty prescribed by the church; and all Roman Catholic missionaries among the Indians would have been gradually recalled and replaced by Protestants. These regulations were ignored until a generation later, when an agitation to enforce them helped precipitate the racial strife which destroyed the peace of Lower Canada for many years.

The neglect of these instructions, coming on top of the Quebec Act, may have riveted Roman Catholicism upon the Canadian people, but one may also argue that a strict observance of the instructions would have produced the same effect in a more injurious way, for pressure may harden rather than crush. It is likewise impossible to determine how far the settlement as a whole really strengthened the church in Canada, or even if it strengthened it at all. If, however, it could be established that the religion of the Canadians was definitely reinforced, there would always be differences of opinion over the wisdom of what had been accomplished.

To make way for a legislature which was not elected, the royal promise of an assembly had to be revoked. The king could not do it because, according to the principle recognized by Lord Mansfield's famous judgment in Campbell v. Hall delivered at this time, he had renounced his legislative prerogative by issuing the proclamation of 1763. Only the supreme power of parliament could remove the obstacle, and therefore the act did it. The governor and council were given what they had not really possessed — authority to legislate for the colony. The act gave them more power than they had exercised under the invalid authority of the instructions. On the other hand, it was less than that conferred upon, but never used by, governor, council, and assembly under the commission. The restrictions which parliament imposed to compensate for the absence of any popular check upon the legislature were a prohibition to levy taxes except for local improvements, a suspension of all ordinances touching religion or authorizing punishments greater than fine or three months' imprisonment until they received the royal approbation, and a limitation of the legislative season to the first four months of the year — that is, to the period immediately preceding the opening of navigation. The last restriction reduced to a minimum the interval between the passage and the disallowance of an objectionable measure. In other words, it brought the new legislature under the more effective control of the home government. The new council was to be nearly twice the size of the old one, for it was to have not less than seventeen nor more than twenty-three members. They were named in the instructions — twenty-two in all — and appear to have been Carleton's nominees. Except one who had been temporarily added to make a quorum, all the old councilors who had continued to attend were retained, and Adam

Mabane was restored. George Allsopp, who had been deputy secretary since 1768, was also given a seat at the board. Eight of the twenty-two were Canadians, one being a Protestant and an old member, the other seven being Roman Catholics admitted under the new oath.

The act has been severely criticized for violating the most fundamental principle of British government. An assembly had been forced upon the governor of Nova Scotia in 1758 and the result had been good. If an assembly was to be introduced by the act of 1791, why not by the act of 1774? True, the Canadians neither wanted nor understood an assembly, but they would have to begin governing themselves some day. As for the English-speaking minority, did not the denial of an assembly wound their loyalty? When the vigorous renewal of their old agitation in the closing months of 1773 only hardened Dartmouth's heart and increased his anxiety to destroy the hopes aroused ten years before, was there not some canker in the vitals of the home government? It has been maintained that the British government committed a fatal blunder in abandoning the plan of 1769. But should it be blamed for acting on the advice of the governor, the chief justice, and the attorney general, who, much as they differed on other points, were unanimously against the board of trade's proposal of representative government? The two groups in Quebec and Montreal which cooperated in producing the petitions of December, 1773, looked suspiciously like the committees of correspondence in the old colonies. To official London of that day they naturally smelled of sedition. It must also be remembered that Canada in 1774 was not Nova Scotia in 1758. There were great differences of place and time. The Acadians were ignored when an assembly was called in Halifax, but the Canadians could not be ignored. Had an assembly been created without them, as the English-speaking minority really wanted, their hearts would most probably have turned back to France. On the other hand, had these newly conquered people been admitted to an assembly, the risk would have been tremendous. Under any circumstances such an experiment would have been very bold, and the circumstances of the time were far from being auspicious. One may well question whether any British government, seeing chronic French hostility in the background and American troubles looming up ahead, would have felt justified in running such great and unknown risks as

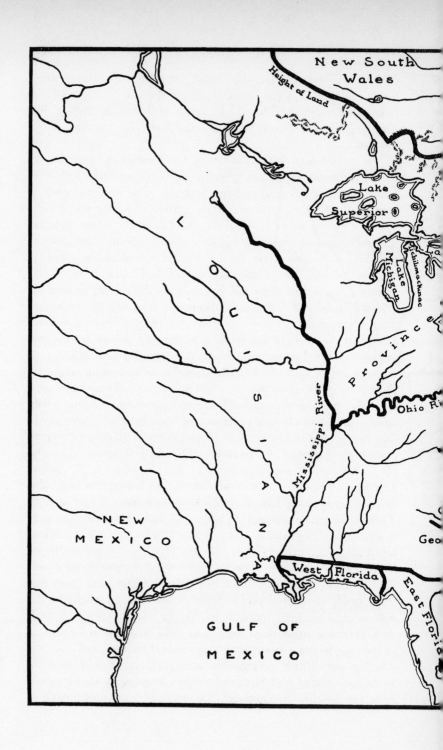

New South
Wales

Height of Land

Lake
Superior

Lake
Michigan

Michilimackinac

L

O

U

I

S

I

A

Province

Mississippi River

Ohio R.

NEW
MEXICO

Geo

West Florida

East Florida

GULF OF

MEXICO

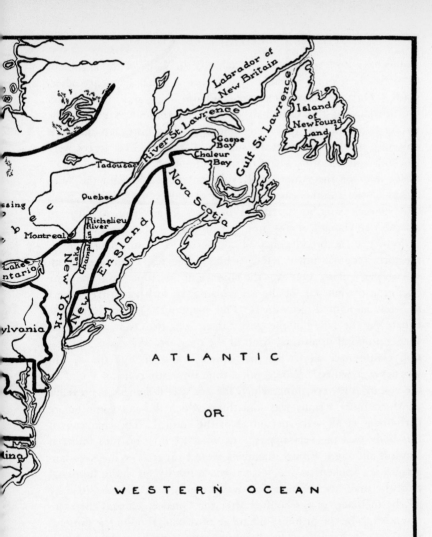

Labrador of
New Britain

River St. Lawrence

Island
of
New Found
Land

Gulf St. Lawrence

Gaspe
Bay
Chaleur
Bay

Tadousac

Nova Scotia

Quebec

Richelieu
River

New England

Montreal

New York

Lake
Champlain

Lake
Ontario

ylvania

ing

A T L A N T I C

OR

W E S T E R N   O C E A N

THE BRITISH COLONIES IN NORTH AMERICA SHOWING THE
BOUNDARIES OF THE PROVINCE OF QUEBEC
AS DEFINED BY THE QUEBEC ACT

Drawn from a map engraved by William Faden in 1777

would have been involved. And what is the value of the argument of 1791? Is it not weakened by a glance at what happened afterward? Did not Lord Durham condemn the Constitutional Act for introducing the Canadians to self-government at exactly the wrong end? But all this leaves one with the impression that it is only talk playing about on the surface of things. Great forces were working underneath. The British conquest of Canada was inevitable; it made the American Revolution inevitable; and the rumblings of the coming earthquake just as inevitably created a mentality which was so distrustful of popular government that an assembly in Canada at this time was simply out of the question.

Whether the broad policy of the act be condemned or upheld, the form of government which it established was open to criticism in two particulars. One was the absence of any time limit upon the operation of that part of the act which gave such extensive powers to a few appointed individuals. This point was pressed during the debate on the bill, but the government was firm, having rejected such a proposal in an early draft of the measure. Why was a limitation clause necessary when parliament could change the system whenever it willed? Would not a time limit stir political unrest in the colony, the very thing which the act was designed to prevent?

Much more serious was something which did not come before parliament at all — the personnel of the council. The character of this body was the very opposite of what its division into fourteen English and eight French members would suggest. When two languages are spoken in any society, the minority are more bilingual than the majority. French was thus the only tongue understood by all the members of the council after the Quebec Act and therefore it tended to be the ordinary language of debate, though the minutes were kept in English. The change of tongue seems startling, but it was only superficial, for the council remained what it had been, preponderantly French Canadian in tone. This fact now acquired a new importance from the enlarged powers conferred by the act. The English-speaking merchants in the colony were thus placed at the mercy of a council the majority of which was decidedly unsympathetic toward them, and as a result they got very much less than justice. Another grave defect was the aristocratic flavor of the council. It included nine seigniors — the seven Canadians just added and two of the old subjects. The rest of the English-speaking members of the French, or king's, party shared their out-look on life. Thus the council, like the governor, failed to un-derstand the habitant, who had quite a democratic spirit. In the crisis through which the colony was about to pass, the lack of harmony between its government and the vast bulk of its people was little short of tragic.

Because it refused to establish an assembly, the British govern-ment had to adopt some other method of providing the provincial government with what it had lacked since the conquest — a revenue. There was no longer any thought of supplying the defect by means of legal quibbles. It was done boldly by a separate parliamentary statute, the Quebec Revenue Act,* which repealed the defunct duties and imposed new ones. These were confined to spirits, rum, and molasses, the last article being already imported for the domestic production of rum as well as for more innocent purposes. The rate on brandy or other spirits was threepence a gallon if manufactured in Great Britain. Rum was charged a shilling if it came from non-British possessions, ninepence if from British colonies on the con-tinent of America, and sixpence if from the British West Indies. No duty was imposed on rum from Britain. This intra-imperial discrimination was designed to benefit British shipping by encourag-ing the import of rum from the British West Indies via the mother country, and to protect Canada from a drain of specie by discourag-ing import from New England. There is no evidence of any politi-cal motive behind the discrimination against the continental colonies. For years the merchants in Canada had been complaining of the injury wrought by the importation of rum from New England because New England, unlike the West Indies, refused to take the colony's produce in return. The duty on molasses was threepence a gallon if imported in ships of the British Isles or of Canada and sixpence if brought in other vessels — another encouragement of direct trade with the West Indies. The Quebec Revenue Act also did what the governor and council had been condemned for attempt-ing: it required every publican to pay a license fee of one pound sixteen shillings and imposed a penalty of ten pounds for retailing alcohol without a license.

Finally it reserved the rights of the crown to the casual and terri-

---

* This act was to come into force on April 5, 1775, to prevent any evasion by an early opening of navigation. The Quebec Act came into force on May 1, 1775.

torial revenue inherited from the French régime. This covered the old feudal payments. As sovereign, the crown could exact a mutation fine, the *quint,* equal to one-fifth of the purchase price when a seigniory was sold, and as seignior in the town of Quebec it could demand a corresponding fine of one-twelfth, known as *lods et ventes,* and the small annual dues owed by tenants *en roture* to their feudal lords. For prompt payment, one-third of each fine was customarily remitted. As there had been reasonable doubts of the continuance of the old laws which prescribed these obligations, the receiver general's office had not pressed collection and few had paid. It was now thought that the removal of these doubts by the Quebec Revenue Act would transform what had been a sickly revenue into a healthy income. But, as will be explained in a later chapter, the laxity of the receiver general's office, the interested inertia of private individuals, and the apprehensions of the government defeated this hope and thereby increased, if they did not create, the chronic deficit in the budget of the provincial government.

The solution of the problem arising from the confusion of the laws has often been misunderstood and therefore merits close examination. The Quebec Act prescribed English criminal law and the old civil law of Canada. But it did this with qualifications, both particular and general, that were intended to be important. The particular qualifications were three in number. The restoration of the old civil law was not to restrict the freedom of bequest; it was not to prevent the execution of wills by English law when so desired; nor was it to apply to lands which were already or might in future be granted in common socage. This third qualification could have only a narrow application, because few freehold grants had been made and the additional instruction of 1771 directing that all future concessions be made in the old way was incorporated in the new instruction. Until the eve of its submission to parliament, the bill contained a clause permitting individuals to convert feudal into freehold tenures. This provision, which ran counter to the purpose of the recent additional instruction, was deleted on the advice of Hillsborough and Carleton. The latter's objection was that it was not desired by the Canadians and would have no effect except to undermine the "great power" which the feudal system gave over any evilly disposed seignior. The general qualification was that English criminal and Canadian civil laws were to hold "until they shall be varied" by provincial legislation. As Lord North pointed out on the first day of the debate in the commons, the act established only a foundation upon which the Quebec legislature could build a legal system suited to the conditions of the colony. "In a general plan of government," he said, "it is not possible to enter into a detail of what is proper, or what is improper, in Canada: it must be left to the legislature on the spot to consider all their wants and difficulties." [24]

There was no thought of transporting English criminal law "in the lump," for those were the days before reform made "the punishment fit the crime." No one wanted to establish in Canada such things as benefit of clergy, burning in the hand, and death for small crimes. Indeed, early in 1768 Maseres ascribed to national prejudice the common belief that the criminal law of England was superior to that of France. The latter, he argued, had distinct advantages, in addition to being free of many of the defects of the former. Some time after his return to England, Carleton appears to have swung back to this view. The seigniors upheld it out of social, as well as racial, prejudice because they objected to being squeezed into a jury box along with habitants. Thurlow also favored the revival of French criminal law with amendments. As drafted in January, 1774, the bill provided for the revival of the old criminal law except for treason and the trial of capital offenses. Supported by Wedderburn, Hey objected strongly. He believed that the Canadians as a whole did not dislike English criminal law, while the old subjects would be so mightily offended by the restoration of French criminal law that they would leave the colony as soon as possible. He urged that the objectionable features of the English law might be eliminated by the governor and council.[25] After some weeks this reasoning prevailed, and the result was questioned only by Carleton when the people of Canada did not stand the strain of the American Revolution as well as he had expected.

The general approval accorded the establishment of English criminal law did not extend to the continuance of the old civil law, which has survived to the present day and still arouses dislike in various quarters. But many of the attacks on the Quebec Act and on the government which passed it have been wide of the mark because the responsibility for the serious grievances which arose from the enforcement of French civil law lies elsewhere. The

English-speaking minority did not challenge the wisdom of allowing the old laws of real property and inheritance with the particular
qualifications noted above, but they complained violently because
the restoration did not stop at this point, and their laments have
been echoed ever since. They had developed and they continued
to control the commerce of the country. The Canadians had little
interest in it, their chief concern being for their lands. Why was not
this division of interest reflected in the legal settlement? Why did
not the act establish English civil law except for real property?
It must be remembered, however, that when the act was passed
the number of English-speaking people in the colony was very
small and was growing steadily smaller. Would it have been just
to introduce the general body of English civil law when the ancient
inhabitants outnumbered the newcomers by thirty to one, and when
they might outnumber them still more in the years to come? Nor
must it be forgotten that both elements of the population had taken
offense at certain features of this law. The new subjects had cried
out against arrest and imprisonment for debt, and many of the old
subjects had successfully fought the English law of bankruptcy.
Another difficulty lay in the fact that laws are not lifeless things.
They grow together so organically that it is impossible to tear a
limb from one body and attach it to another dismembered body
without incurring a grave risk. The unforeseen consequences would
have been great and might have been disastrous, had this rough
surgery been attempted.

The British government, however, had no idea of sacrificing the
minority. Indeed, it made careful provision to protect them. Though
the civil law of New France was adopted as the general rule, the
act empowered the governor and council to modify it, and the
instructions specifically directed them to use this power in favor
of the old subjects. The instructions strongly recommended the
provincial legislature to introduce the right of habeas corpus and
to allow English law for "personal actions grounded upon debts,
promises, contracts and agreements, whether of a mercantile or
other nature, and also of wrongs proper to be compensated in
damages." The government has been severely criticized for leaving
these holes in the act and expecting them to be patched up in the
colony, but there were good reasons for this arrangement.

The omission of the Habeas Corpus Act, contrary to Carleton's formal report, was supported by the advice of the law officers at home. If based upon a British statute, the right might be dangerous in Canada, where it could not be suspended if necessary. That it might be necessary was a simple deduction from the fact that the vast bulk of the people in the colony were newly conquered and still cherished fond memories of their old mother country, Britain's ancient foe. Moreover, they were quite unused to such a privilege. Yet the British government did not wish to rob the English-speaking minority of their birthright. Here was a nice dilemma. Was there any escape other than by trusting the governor and council, who were on the spot, to discover some safe way of introducing the law? For the elimination of jury trials in civil suits the old subjects themselves were responsible. Almost a fortnight after he had introduced the bill into the house of lords, Dartmouth persuaded Lord Chancellor Apsley to agree to a clause allowing causes between merchants to go to a jury if either party desired it. But on the following day the chancellor remembered how the mercantile minority had perverted the jury system to avoid paying the old duties. Immediately he dashed off a note withdrawing his consent, observing that it would be "more advisable to stand the harangue of the day than to yield to the request which certainly squints at the revenue." [26] Still the government did not wish to penalize the merchants. Here was another dilemma of granting too much or too little. Was there any better way out than by trusting to the local legislature?

There remains the question of English mercantile law, about which there has been a great illusion in the minds of some critics of the act. They have blamed it for robbing the merchants of something which they had not yet acquired! In 1774, by his judgments in the court of king's bench, Lord Mansfield was only beginning to give definite shape to English mercantile law as something distinct from the law merchant of Europe. Through the discussions prior to the act ran the supposition that this law would govern the settlement of commercial disputes. Though the new law was so inchoate that the instructions did not mention it by name, they provided for its gradual substitution in place of the older system. Had the instructions been carried out, the settlement of the laws

would have worked no hardship upon the English-speaking minority. They suffered grievously because the instructions remained
a dead letter. For this tragedy Carleton was to blame. The story
of his disobedience will be told in a later chapter, but it is necessary
to mention it here because he was the author of much of the iniquity
which has been erroneously ascribed to the Quebec Act and to the
government that passed it.

French Canadians have praised the Quebec Act as the charter
of liberties which saved their race in its time of trial; others who
deplore the existence of French Canadian self-consciousness have
denounced the act for having made a real national unity impossible
in Canada. Both exaggerate. Just as the chief value of the Magna
Charta was posthumous — a rallying cry for later generations — so
perhaps the greatest effect of the Quebec Act has been psychological.
It is idle to imagine that the French of Canada could have been
assimilated. Races have been merged in others, but only when the
assimilated did not possess an old and fixed civilization, or when
they were in a minority. Neither of these fundamental conditions
existed in the colony. The French possessed a civilization as ancient
and as fixed as that of the English, and they vastly outnumbered
them. Not until the middle of the nineteenth century were there as
many English as French in Canada. If the policy of 1763 had been
developed and enforced, instead of being abandoned, it might have
driven Canada out of the British Empire and into the American
union. For all its denial of an assembly, the Quebec Act embodied
a new sovereign principle of the British Empire: the liberty of non-
English peoples to be themselves. During the military régime it
had appeared for a while, but then it was not a carefully thought
out policy of state, as it was in the Quebec Act. Given a government that was Canadian in character, a government that would
leave no grievance to rankle in their breasts, the Canadians would
be weaned from their old allegiance and thus, though they might
never become English, they would become true Britishers — a
strength rather than a weakness to the empire. Some may be tempted
to go into raptures over this transcendent vision of the empire of
the future, but an analysis of the feelings which inspired this vision
induces a cooler judgment. They were good, bad, and indifferent —
sympathy for the Canadians, distrust of the old colonies, and fear of

France. Unfortunately the sympathy for the Canadians was entirely
misplaced. The British ministry saw Canada through Carleton's
eyes, and Carleton's eyes were blind to the real nature of the great
mass of the population, the habitants. Their sturdy independence
could not be bridled by the noblesse and the clergy, as the governor
had fondly imagined. The consequence was that the Quebec Act
failed to achieve its purpose. The Canadians as a people were not
won; they could not be used to keep the old colonies in order; and
the entry of France into the war sapped the loyalty of the only
Canadians who were really pleased with the act — the noblesse and
the clergy.

CHAPTER X

THE INVASION OF CANADA [1]

ON SEPTEMBER 18, 1774, Carleton landed in Quebec with the young family which he had acquired during his four years' residence in England — a wife who was half his own age, and two infants. The wife was Lady Maria, daughter of his great personal friend the Earl of Effingham. She had been reared in Versailles and, as a consequence, she shared and may even have strengthened her husband's predilections for a well-ordered society after the pattern of the Old World. That he was now about to achieve this ideal on the shores of the St. Lawrence and thereby to solve the problem of fitting Canada securely into the British Empire, not a doubt seems to have crossed his mind. The noblesse and the clergy burst forth in a chorus of praise to their new constitution and their old governor, and with this sweet music in his ears he settled more comfortably than ever in his false heaven.

Down in Boston Gage felt very far from heaven, for his attempt to apply the recent penal legislation provoked popular defiance that he had not the power to crush. Thereupon he wrote to Quebec asking the governor for two of his four regiments and inquiring if he could raise a body of Canadians and Indians to be used against the old colonies if necessary. Carleton received this letter on the day after his arrival, and at once he hurried off half his garrison to help the commander-in-chief nip rebellion in the bud.[2] As the remaining half of the garrison, numbering less than eight hundred effectives, was disposed in scattered detachments stretching all the way from Quebec to Michilimackinac, he was virtually denuding the colony of troops. But he had not the slightest idea that he was sending away what he would soon need most desperately. He felt absolutely secure. The Canadians, he told Gage, would be delighted to form a regiment if they were allowed to do so. He also reported that the Indians were in good humor and would be encouraged by the appearance of a Canadian unit. "But," he added by way of caution, "you know what sort of people they are."

Not until the shots fired at Concord and Lexington on April 19, 1775, were heard across the Atlantic did the home government authorize the governor to levy any Canadians. Then, on July 1, Dartmouth wrote directing him to raise a force of three thousand, and three weeks later he commanded him to make it six thousand. But long before these orders reached Quebec Carleton's house tumbled about his ears and he awoke from his dream. Instead of drawing an army from Canada to assist in conquering the old colonies, Britain had to send an army to Canada to prevent its being conquered by them.

When the empire began to break asunder because its geography had outgrown its constitution, Canada was shaken to its foundations and seemed about to be engulfed. Because the colony on the St. Lawrence commanded the back doors of the colonies on the Atlantic seaboard, it was bound sooner or later to be involved in their hostilities with the mother country. That this happened sooner rather than later was directly due to Carleton and the Quebec Act. They caused the revolting colonies to strike at Canada in the very beginning, and they were likewise responsible for this blow cutting deeply into the country.

Since the English-speaking population of Canada was an offshoot from that of the old colonies, there was right in the heart of the country a body of people whose traditions and connections drew them to sympathize with the colonial cause. In the fall of 1774, when the merchants of Quebec sent a thousand bushels of wheat and the merchants of Montreal sent a big bill of exchange to help feed the poor of Boston, the givers were undoubtedly thinking of poor Boston. The punitive measures of the British government against Boston had quickened their American patriotism.

But their own predicament was also pushing them toward rebellion. It must not be forgotten that Canada's Americans, on whichever side of the ocean they happened to have been born, had greater justification for denouncing Britain's tyranny than had any people in the old colonies outside the capital of Massachusetts. When they looked forward, what did they see? They were condemned to lose certain precious things that they had inherited from their forbears. On May 1, 1775, the day when the Quebec Act was to come into force, their ancient rights of habeas corpus and of trial by jury for civil suits would be swept away. Though Maseres wrote them in

August, 1774, expressing the hope that the new legislative council would continue these liberties,[3] the governor was ominously silent and they had well-grounded fears. By letting them think that the British government intended to rob them of this birthright, Carleton administered a serious shock to the loyalty of the mercantile minority.

They were likewise plunged into despair because parliament had revoked the solemn promise of their sovereign that they would have an elected assembly. They had shrewd suspicions that they would get neither justice nor mercy from the government of the colony. All that would be left them was English criminal law, and even this seemed far from safe. The power given to governor and council to remove its bad features seemed like a license to destroy its good features. They felt that they were undone if the abominable act were allowed to stand, and the only hope they could see was in an appeal to the new parliament elected in the fall of 1774.

Encouraged by the news of the opposition which the bill had aroused in parliament and also in "the City," * and likewise encouraged by the resentment which the act, along with the other measures popularly coupled with it, had evoked in the old colonies, the English-speaking residents renewed their agitation. A committee was formed in Montreal and another in Quebec, and in November, 1774, nearly two hundred names were signed to petitions to the king, lords, and commons for the repeal or amendment of the Quebec Act.

Carleton instantly wrote Dartmouth about these "town meetings" and "nocturnal cabals," as he called them. He reported that they were causing the Canadians uneasiness and were "calculated to throw this province into the same disorders that reign in other parts of this continent." The governor also informed the secretary of state that he had assured the Canadians "that such proceedings could never affect the late measures taken in their favour, nor did I believe they ever would succeed with Government upon any occasion." [4] The hint betrays some misgivings in Carleton's mind but was probably unnecessary. In May both houses of parliament rejected motions for the repeal of the Quebec Act, thereby killing the only

---

* The lord mayor of London, accompanied by several aldermen and more than one hundred and fifty of the common council, had prayed the king to exercise his veto upon it.

hope of redress by constitutional means. By the summer of 1775, therefore, there was serious disaffection among the English-speaking dwellers on the banks of the St. Lawrence.

No less serious was the disaffection among the French-speaking population. In proportion as the Quebec Act pleased the clergy and the noblesse, it displeased the rest of the Canadians. The clergy, who were in closer contact with the people, seem to have been more discreet than the noblesse. The latter were now jubilant at the prospect of being what they had never been before, the real lords of the land, and they had considerable justification for this feeling. Every Canadian added to the council was drawn from their midst. No bourgeois, no captain of militia, was to be admitted to the inner circle of the government. To the people, whose real representatives were thus excluded, the character of the council was made even more objectionable by the fact that most of the new Canadian councilors belonged to the haughtiest section of the noblesse, the wearers of the Croix de St. Louis. The nature of the new government was stirring uneasiness in town and country. Already Carleton's aristocratic policy was beginning to bear evil fruit.

The uneasiness abroad in the country was much more dangerous than that in the towns because the habitants formed the great bulk of the population. They simply would not fit into the governor's scheme of things. They were not hewers of wood and drawers of water for their feudal superiors, nor were they abject slaves of the church. The voyage across the Atlantic had emancipated their ancestors, and for generations the freedom of the forest had been breathing a spirit of liberty into Canadian society. The habitant's attitude toward the seignior was also affected by subtle changes which the British conquest had wrought in rural Canada. By terminating the war, which had checked the expansion of agriculture, the conquest had given full vent to the demand of the growing population for land. This gave an advantage to those who controlled the available supply — the seigniors — and they were able to make the most of it because the conquest did something else. It removed the wholesome restraint which French officials, particularly the intendants, had exercised upon the seigniors in their relations with their tenants, for the new government, unlike the old one, had not grown up with the feudal system and was therefore not attuned to it. The consequence was that the British régime saw the development of an unfortunate strain and stress in the working of the feudal system in the colony; the habitants were more than ever distrustful of their seigniors.

Some writers have also maintained that the conquest leavened the Canadian lump with ideas of British liberty. But it is impossible to estimate the effect of these ideas, if indeed they had any appreciable effect, because it is so easily confused with the pioneer spirit carried over from the days of French rule and with the feelings engendered by the improved position of the seigniors. Equally difficult to determine is the extent to which resentment against parliament's recognition of the tithe contributed to the disaffection of the mass of the Canadians, which was very evident in 1775.

To the old colonies the Quebec Act was like a charge of electricity. Maseres asserted that it "contributed more perhaps than any other measure whatsoever to drive them into rebellion against their sovereign." But he was likely to be hysterical over this piece of legislation, and from his seclusion in the Inner Temple he could not see what is apparent today — that the American upheaval would in all probability have come quite independently of the act. However, it did cause the revolution at the very outset to thrust a fiery arm up into Canada. The establishment of popery and of arbitrary government in the north revived the terror of bygone days in the south and may even have magnified it, for France had been able to strike only in the rear while Britain could attack both front and rear. Many Americans at once feared that their cause would be hopeless unless they could prevent Britain from using Canada against them. This was why they invaded the country in 1775. But before they used arms to accomplish their end, they tried the effect of words.

The continental congress which assembled in Philadelphia in September, 1774, addressed the Canadians in a long letter of October 24. It proclaimed the rights of British subjects to government by their own elected representatives, to trial by jury, to habeas corpus, to free tenures, and to liberty of the press; it pointed out how the mother country had violated these fundamental principles by imposing a government composed of tools of the governor, who, in turn, was the tool of the British government; it invited them to join in an eternal brotherhood of liberty, and, as a first step, it advised them to form a provincial congress which would send delegates to the next continental congress in the following May. One significant passage in this document suggested that Canada would be treated as a foe if it would not be a friend.

About the same time that this formidable message was sent, the provincial congress of Massachusetts, under the influence of Samuel Adams, began to feel about for some way of getting in touch with the people on the St. Lawrence. In December it appointed a committee "to correspond with the inhabitants of Canada," and in February, 1775, John Brown, a graduate of Yale and a promising young lawyer, set out for Canada as the agent of the Boston committee of correspondence. He went armed with official letters and a stock of revolutionary pamphlets. In addition to these public approaches, there were also numerous private and semiprivate appeals, for Montreal's communication with the south was broken only during the spring and autumn, when Lake Champlain was impassable. Brown, incidentally, was delayed several weeks by the breaking of the ice on this body of water.

The door of Canada was wide open for the Revolution to enter. In the English-speaking minority was a band of missionaries all ready to spread the new gospel, and through the countryside were many people waiting to be converted. Though the *Quebec Gazette,* the only organ then in Canada, was alone among American papers in refusing to publish the congressional appeal, the silence of this semi-official sheet made little difference. Copies of the original and of a translation were plentiful. Thomas Walker and other merchants had sheaves of them, and they had many connections with Canadians, even with the habitants, for they regularly traveled through the rural parishes buying up the surplus grain. The message from the south, improved by local comments, was soon echoing up and down the valleys of the St. Lawrence and the Richelieu, awakening in the hearts of the Canadians hopes and fears which drew them to the old colonies. The habitants were reminded that they had taken an oath not to fight against the English, and "English" was now interpreted to mean their American brethren. These credulous people also learned that the Bostonians were "as numerous as the stars" [5] and would lay their country waste if they ventured to appear in arms against them. No less effective with a race that had been sickened by perennial wars in days gone by was the assertion that Britain meant to draft them off to fight her battles under distant skies. These were only some of the wild rumors which went flying through the land during the winter and spring. Although they were designed to hold the Canadians neutral in the coming struggle, a further vision began to arise. Brown was delighted with what he saw and heard, and messages from him and from many others began to pour south announcing that the dreaded Canadians were all friendly and would even join in revolt against the mother country.

Carleton caught fleeting echoes of the sedition that was eating through the colony, for here and there a priest laid his hands on an incriminating document and reported his find to Quebec. But the governor did not know how to stop the mischief, and he seems to have been like a man in a trance. In February, 1775, he wrote Gage a letter which betrays a certain consciousness that the ground was slipping from underneath his feet. Even the gentry, he found, had not forgotten what had happened when the regiment raised in 1764 to fight Pontiac had been disbanded. The officers had been dismissed without the half pay on which they had counted, and their services had been forgotten. He was still less sure of the peasantry. The nerveless government of the colony had allowed them to emancipate themselves, and only "time and discreet management" could "recall them to their ancient habits of obedience and discipline." He was averse to embodying the militia because the noblesse much preferred commanding regular units. It would also, he said, "give an appearance of truth to the language of our sons of sedition at this very moment busily employed instilling into their minds that the act was passed merely to serve the present purposes of government, and in the full intention of ruling over them with all the despotism of their ancient masters." [6]

Though there was considerable ferment in the town of Quebec, Montreal was, as might be expected, the main center from which the propaganda spread. Of what was going on there Carleton heard more than mere echoes, for a number of correspondents were anxious to keep him posted. Probably the most assiduous of these informants was Hertel de Rouville, who haunted the post-office to pick up crumbs of news, some of which were maliciously manufactured on the spot for his special benefit,[7] and was soon rewarded for his services by a seat upon the bench. Thus the governor quickly learned of a meeting of merchants in the Montreal coffee house on

April 3, 1775, where Brown presented himself and his credentials
and where Thomas Walker, "a great republican," gave full rein to
his eloquence in favor of electing delegates to Philadelphia.[8] Carleton was probably relieved to hear that no decision had been reached,
but he would have been less pleased had he known the reason.
The merchants in Canada, being utterly dependent upon trade with
England, saw ruin staring them in the face if they were to be bound
by the non-importation agreement already adopted by the continental congress, for the French operating up the Mississippi would
immediately capture the fur traffic of the upper country.

Very naturally the tense feeling in Montreal grew more tense
as May 1 drew near. On the morning when the detested act came
into force, the citizens of the town awoke to find that during the
night some unknown hands had taken insulting liberties with the
king's bust on the Place d'Armes. The face was blackened, and
around the neck hung a rosary of potatoes bearing a wooden cross
with the inscription: *Voilà le Pape du Canada ou le sot Anglois.*
The guilty were never discovered, though a reward of fifty guineas
was promised by the officers of the Twenty-sixth Regiment, then
in Montreal, and another of two hundred dollars by the governor.

Needless to say the insult to His Majesty raised many tempers
to the boiling point. One of the new councilors, Picotté de Bellestre,
who was present on May 2 when the officers' reward was published,
cried out that he would like to see "the detestable wretches whipped
by the hands of the hangman and then turned out of the province,"
and he added that this penalty "would be too lenient, for they deserved to be hanged." His words were caught up by a young man
named Franks. He was the son of a Quebec merchant and had just
completed his education in Philadelphia. To his retort, "Hanged!
What, for such a trifle!" Bellestre burst out, "What! Do you look
upon the transaction as a trifle? You are a giddy-headed insolent
spark." Bellestre seized him by the nose, and the young fellow
"returned the compliment by a blow with his fist over the right eye
which deprived the old gentleman of his senses for some time and
was the occasion of the loss of some blood." About the same time
a Jewish merchant named Solomon loudly professed his belief that
"some Canadian scoundrel was the author of the insult," and
knocked down a Canadian named Le Pailleur for replying that a
Jew might as well have done it.[9]

A fortnight later came the first irruption of arms into the colony. Beyond the borders of Canada, at the southern end of Lake Champlain, lay two forts garrisoned by detachments of the Twenty-sixth Regiment. Ticonderoga, at the very extremity of the lake, had two score men under an officer, and Crown Point, fifteen miles to the north, had a dozen soldiers under a noncommissioned officer. Here was a spear point aimed at the back of the old colonies, and it was regarded with suspicious eyes by the nearest settlers. These were the squatters in the future state of Vermont. Because of their location they were known as the Green Mountain Boys. When passing through this country on his way to Canada, Brown took in the situation at a glance — the weak state of the forts and the strong feeling of the pioneers. He reported to his principals that these places should be seized directly hostilities broke out and that these settlers were the proper people to do the job.

But they were not to do it alone. Gage was besieged in Boston by the angry multitude which sprang to arms when blood was spilled at Concord and Lexington. With only muskets, the Americans could not reach the British commander and his forces, and an urgent call for cannon went forth. Benedict Arnold, a druggist, bookseller, and shipowner of New Haven, was before Boston at the head of some Connecticut volunteers, and he announced that there was a plentiful supply guarded by only a handful of soldiers in these two forts on Lake Champlain. At once he received a Massachusetts commission to lead an expedition to seize the necessary articles.

After appointing a few captains to gather recruits who would follow, Arnold dashed off to the Green Mountains, where he knew that there were many men eager to take the forts. There he found that another impulse and material assistance from Connecticut had already led them to organize to perform the task under their own commander, Ethan Allen. For a moment there was a tussle between the two men, and then they agreed to share the leadership. At dawn on May 10, with about eighty-five farmers suddenly turned soldiers, they surprised the sleeping garrison of Ticonderoga, and on the following day Crown Point surrendered without a blow. The spearpoint was reversed, and in a few days it gave the first prick.

Though the patriots from the south had secured more than a hundred cannon, they had missed something with which their work might be undone. The possession of the forts depended upon water communications, and the control of the lake was still potentially in British hands, for the solitary armed sloop that plied these waters had sailed down to the end of navigation at St. John on the Richelieu within the borders of Canada. Arnold now determined to seize this necessary prize as soon as possible. With about thirty of his own recruits who soon arrived he embarked in Major Skene's schooner, which had been seized up at Skenesborough. On the morning of May 17 he burst upon the guard of ten men posted at St. John and overpowered them. Hastily loading all the ammunition and provisions he could find, he sailed away with the sloop and every bateau that was immediately serviceable. The other boats he of course destroyed.

After covering a few miles Arnold met his rival Allen with about ninety men in a little fleet of bateaux. The Green Mountain Boys had determined to take and hold St. John. Their leader, now that he was within reach of his goal, would not listen to Arnold's advice to return but insisted on pushing on into what might have been a fatal trap. Unknown to any of them, a force of about one hundred men of the Twenty-sixth Regiment under Major Preston was rushing over the few miles from Montreal, where the alarm had been given.

That Allen and his men were not surprised was owing to the warning of a merchant named Bindon. He crossed the St. Lawrence with these troops, having secured permission to look after a shipment of goods which he had sent south on the previous day. On landing at Longueuil, he leaped on a horse and left his military companions behind. In the evening he galloped into St. John just after the arrival of Allen and his party. Early next morning, after a brush with the advancing contingent, the Americans tumbled into their boats and scuttled away. The British soldiers, having met Bindon returning from St. John only a few hours before, had a shrewd suspicion that he had betrayed them, and when they arrived back in Montreal two days later they broke loose on a mad hunt. The merchant was caught and might have been hanged had not some officers arrived in the nick of time.[10] He confessed indiscretion, but nothing more could be proved against him. The incident greatly inflamed party feeling. Some citizens held an indignation meeting to demand the punishment of the riotous soldiers, but others, who believed Bindon a traitor, easily persuaded the commander of the regiment to wink at the natural conduct of his men.

On the evening of May 19, when Allen was retreating up Lake Champlain, urgent orders from Gage reached the governor in Quebec. These announced the beginning of hostilities in Massachusetts and directed Carleton to send the Seventh Regiment and several companies of Canadians and Indians to Crown Point as a diversion to relieve the pressure on Boston. On the very next morning a half-pay captain who had settled on the Richelieu, Moses Hazen,* arrived express with the startling news that colonial insurgents had captured Ticonderoga and Crown Point and had seized the sloop which gave them control of the lake. Thus, overnight, the governor's thoughts were turned from offense to defense. He rushed up to Montreal to direct operations for the protection of the colony.

St. John was the bottle neck through which the Americans threatened to pour, and he sought to cork it tightly. He had all summer to do it, for the forces on Lake Champlain, being small in number, hastily assembled, ill organized, and at first disowned by the continental congress, were not prepared to deal another effective blow for several months. During this respite a fort arose at the strategic point — two redoubts, a hundred feet square and two hundred yards apart, connected by a strong palisade; the construction of a little fleet was commenced; and as many men as possible were concentrated.

As Carleton's available troops were very few, he tried to draw on the man power of the colony. The result was disheartening to him but natural withal. Though most of the English-speaking merchants drew back when their agitation brought them to the brink of rebellion, as a whole they would do no more than form militia companies to defend the two towns in which they dwelt. Nor would the habitants march under the British flag. The mandement which Briand hastily composed at the request of the governor when the latter was setting out for Montreal, and the efforts of the parish clergy, may have checked disloyalty but they failed to stir

---

* Not long afterward this New Englander's loyalty cooled and he tried to protect himself and his extensive property by appearing friendly to both sides. He gained nothing by his trimming; neither side trusted him. From this awkward position he escaped by throwing himself whole-heartedly on the American side, raising a contingent of Canadians to fight the British.

an active loyalty. The peasantry asserted that the quarrel between the colonies and the mother country was none of their business and therefore they would remain neutral.

Carleton had been drifting and now he floundered. Observers of both races condemned him for having made no effort to prevent the "sons of sedition" from spreading their poison through the country. During the critical months following his return to Canada, his rigid mind had been set on what he could not do — raising regular units — and he had neglected what he might have done — preparing the militia. When at last he had to act, and the militia was his only possible resource, it was apparent that his brooding had brought no enlightenment. After a fortnight of futile efforts in Montreal, he fell back upon the plan of reviving the old militia under the officers commissioned by Gage, Murray, Burton, and Haldimand, and he issued a proclamation accordingly. But he foolishly continued, as he had already begun, to use seigniors and old French army officers to rouse the habitants. Chief Justice Hey called this "the first unlucky step," and it was certainly taken against his advice.[11] By their commands and their threats — for the proclamation declared the execution of martial law * — these emissaries of the government inspired defiance instead of obedience. In a number of parishes the peasantry appeared bearing agricultural implements, clubs, and even muskets to fight their would-be leaders if necessary.

Had he been so minded, Carleton could have employed a couple of thousand Indians, despite many efforts to win them for the colonial cause. On May 24 Ethan Allen wrote the Caughnawaga braves urging them to "ambush the regulars" and promising them money, blankets, tomahawks, knives, and paint. After smoking many pipes, the recipients of this letter delivered it up and offered to prove their loyalty by invading New England. In July, Colonel Guy Johnson, who had succeeded his uncle, Sir William, as superintendent of Indian affairs, met nearly fifteen hundred warriors of the Six Nations in council at Oswego, and they agreed to aid the British in the war that had opened. Thereupon Johnson descended to Montreal and urged the governor to launch the savages against the back

* This alarmed many English-speaking residents. Carleton at this time repented having recommended the Habeas Corpus Act and English criminal law. Shortt and Doughty, *Constitutional Documents*, p. 665.

settlements of the old colonies. Some whose patriotism was of the vengeful type were eager to subdue the rebels with this red nightmare, but Carleton, be it remembered to his honor, refused flatly. He would use a party of natives as scouts at St. John, but he would allow no natives to cross the boundary line of the province. Thus restrained, most of the denizens of the forest made their peace; "the rest," said the governor, "will not act unless they see the Canadians exert themselves also." [12]

When the invasion began in earnest, Canada's southern gate was held by a pitifully small contingent under Major Preston. In addition to the above-mentioned party of scouts there were less than six hundred and fifty men at St. John, and no more could be drawn from the colony. The two regiments accounted for four hundred and seventy-four of this garrison. The rest was composed of thirty-eight of the Royal Artillery, twenty of the Royal Highland Emigrants, a regiment then being raised by Lieutenant Colonel Allan McLean in different American colonies, and about ninety Canadian volunteers, most of them gentry and bourgeoisie, under Bellestre.[13]

Meanwhile a force several times this number was gathering on the lake, for the Philadelphia congress, reversing its earlier attitude, had declared for the invasion of Canada and its conquest if possible. This decision was partly the result of the battle of Bunker Hill and partly the effect of public opinion in the colonies within reach of Canada. They feared what Britain might do if she were allowed to concentrate her strength there, and they hoped to be able to take the country quickly, for they knew that it had only a handful of troops and a disaffected population.

The command of the gathering host was in the hands of Philip Schuyler, who held the rank of major general conferred by congress. He had some of the best Dutch blood and owned some of the best lands in New York. But he had also seen the best of life, for he had reached seventy years, and was therefore not the best man to organize and drive an impromptu army of turbulent recruits. Fortunately for those he was supposed to lead, his health obliged him to remain behind. Just as his army was about to launch its attack, he retired to his mansion in Albany, where he maintained a general supervision over the expedition. The leadership thus devolved upon the brigadier general, Richard Montgomery, who was also a man of position, being the son of an Irish baronet, a product of Trinity College, Dublin, and married into the Livingston family, then one of the wealthiest and most influential in New York. In other respects Montgomery was superior to Schuyler. He was little more than half his age; he was a trained soldier; and he knew the theater of war. As a young British officer he had shared in the capture of Ticonderoga and Crown Point from the French, and he had marched into Montreal under Amherst.

On September 4 the Americans advanced to the foot of the lake and established a camp on Ile aux Noix in the river only twelve miles from St. John. Twice within the next week they were defeated in their efforts to advance from this base. On the sixteenth they moved again, and this time they were successful. Montgomery's forces swarmed around the fort, some passing beyond to occupy the country as far as the shore opposite Montreal, others pushing on to the mouth of the Richelieu. The habitants living within the triangle formed by the two rivers treated the invaders like visitors, and several hundred of them turned out as their companions in arms to fight for American liberty — whatever they may have thought was the meaning of this term.

When the Americans appeared at La Prairie on the twentieth, some craven hearts in Montreal, where there were only three score soldiers, wanted to yield the town to save their property. But the only attempt to take this place before the fall of St. John was made by Ethan Allen, who was once more a free lance and was still burning to cover himself with glory. It was only a foray, and it ended in the Green Mountain hero's defeat and capture on September 25 at the hands of a nondescript force composed chiefly of French and English militia from the town. A few days later the prisoner was joined by his friend Thomas Walker, who had been seized at L'Assomption, where he possessed potash works and a farm and had been engaged principally in levying Canadians to fight the British. Many marveled that he had enjoyed liberty so long, but perhaps Carleton had been afraid to touch him before.

Meanwhile the fate of the upper and more developed part of Canada was hanging in the balance at St. John. Reinforcements pouring up from the south raised the besiegers' numbers gradually from about two thousand to about four thousand, and would have raised them very much higher had not disease, bred by the wet, low-lying ground, caused a great wastage. During the first four weeks of the blockade nearly a thousand men were sent back as unfit for further service. Living in a swamp did more than weaken the bodies of the besiegers; it dampened their ardor. But even if the atmosphere had been salubrious, their morale would have been unhealthy, for they were strangers to military discipline and they had larger appetites than their crude commissariat could satisfy. Their *matériel* was also defective, for they were short of ammunition and their guns were too light to breach the walls of the fort. The siege, thus become a struggle of endurance, dragged on for over seven weeks, and it might have lasted until winter brought what Carleton could not send — relief to the beleaguered garrison — had there been no Chambly.

Twelve miles down the river, just below the rapids, stood this square stone fort occupied by four score men under the Honorable J. Stopford, who held the rank of major. Until after the middle of October the invaders only looked at this place, and that only occasionally, for they thought it impregnable. Then one of the Americans who had settled in Canada * proposed the experiment of bombarding the stone walls. Chambly was now besieged by about three hundred Canadians and a much smaller number of colonials, who dragged down a few nine-pounders. These little pieces blew holes right through the thin masonry, and without waiting for any of his men to receive a real wound, Stopford yielded on the eighteenth. Very excusable and humane was his immediate surrender of a fort that was only an imposing sham, but very inexcusable and inane was his delivery of everything in the place. With the water flowing beneath one of the walls, he need not have handed over to the victors two hundred-odd barrels of provisions and considerably more than a hundred barrels of gunpowder. One wonders also why this food and ammunition had not been lodged in St. John. The effect of the surrender was so obvious that many blamed him for not holding out and believed that his aristocratic relations shielded him from censure. By failing to distinguish between his yielding the place and his delivering the stores it contained, they confused the issue. Carleton must have seen the real point, but he refused to cast any blame upon Stopford. To have done so would have

---

* Livingston or Duggan, probably the latter, who was soon described as "formerly a hairdresser, now a major in America." He had lived in Sorel.[14]

raised the awkward question of why these valuable stores lay where they did.

The moral and material gains at Chambly greatly strengthened the discouraged besiegers at St. John. Now they had more heart, fuller stomachs, and a greater supply of precious ammunition. Still, in spite of their brisker fire, which did considerable damage to the fort, they could not breach the works. But those who were behind the works were depressed by the news of Chambly's fall. Their rations were cut down; their stock of gunpowder was running low; and sickness forced them to reduce their guards. A despairing appeal to Carleton for assistance was worse than useless, for it was intercepted. The only attempt to send succor failed at the end of the month. McLean was laboring up the Richelieu with some of his own men and a party of Canadians whom he managed to pick up on the way. He hoped to effect a junction with Carleton coming from Montreal with a body likewise composed mostly of Canadians. On the thirtieth the governor embarked with about eight hundred, including a number of Indians, but the fire of three hundred Green Mountain Boys dissuaded him from attempting to land. He repeated his failure on the following day.* Then his disheartened party dissolved. Word of this repulse reached McLean at St. Denis and robbed him of his habitant followers. Thus he had to retire also. On November 2, with only three days' provisions and hardly any ammunition left, the gallant garrison under Major Preston capitulated on being accorded the honors of war.[15]

The fall of St. John entailed the immediate evacuation of Montreal. Its walls could withstand nothing stronger than musketry. In some places they were falling and in most places they could be enfiladed from the rising ground beyond. The population contained a large doubtful element. One night every English-speaking militiaman on guard lost the flint from his musket without knowing how it happened.[16] Carleton could not have held Montreal at all, but even if he could have held it he was too good a soldier to think of making a stand there, because his position was turned. He had just learned that Arnold was descending the Chaudière with another army to lay siege to Quebec, and he saw that Montgomery might ignore Montreal and pass down the Richelieu and the St. Lawrence

* A few landed and were taken prisoners. Two of them were brought to St. John to give an account of the fiasco that should persuade the garrison to surrender.

to join in the siege. Quebec was the natural objective of the Americans. Having broken in the back gate, they were beginning to overrun the country, but they might be chased out unless they could take and hold the much stronger front gate.

The governor's immediate duty was to rush down to his capital with every resource that he could command. Having foreseen this crisis, he had already embarked most of the military stores and provisions in Montreal. He quickly finished the business and transferred every soldier and gun from the town to the waiting vessels — three armed ships and eight smaller craft. Contrary winds delayed his departure until the evening of November 11, after the enemy had begun to cross the river from La Prairie to take possession of Montreal. On the following day one of the armed ships ran aground, causing considerable delay, and that evening the wind fell as the little squadron drew near Sorel. On the morning of the fifteenth Carleton found that more than the wind was contrary. His vessels were bombarded and they had to shift their anchorage upstream. For more than a week the Americans had been at the mouth of the Richelieu erecting shore batteries and constructing floating batteries to take the retreating vessels with all that was in them. On the night of the sixteenth the governor persuaded the master of one of his vessels, a Canadian named Bouchette, to pilot him in a whaleboat past the enemy's guns. In passing the sentries, the crew shipped their muffled oars and paddled with their hands. On the nineteenth Carleton landed in Quebec and the fleet from which he had escaped surrendered.*

For the defense of Quebec, Carleton had almost no regulars left. With the exception of a few detachments locked up in the western posts, practically all his troops of the line were now prisoners of war in the old colonies, having capitulated in Chambly, in St. John, and on the St. Lawrence. Fearing lest he be reduced to this strait, he had written to England and to Boston begging for reinforce-

* There is ground for believing that the Americans bluffed Brigadier General Prescott, whom Carleton left in command of the vessels, into surrender. The wind veered to a favorable quarter after Carleton's departure, and might have carried the vessels, which were armed with nine-pounders, past the batteries, which had nothing heavier than twelve-pounders. But the Americans pretended that they had a "grand battery" at the mouth of the Richelieu. There was also the danger of a stray shot exploding the powder stored on the vessels. The capture of the little fleet ended the imprisonment of Thomas Walker, who was on board, but not that of Ethan Allen, who had been sent to England.

ments as soon as possible. It was all in vain. The letter to Gage was delivered to Sir William Howe on October 10, just a few hours after he had succeeded to the chief command in America. At once he ordered two transports to take a battalion to Quebec, but Admiral Graves reported that his captains would not venture the voyage up the St. Lawrence at such a late season. This discouraging news was awaiting the governor when he landed back in his capital. In England several regiments were actually embarked for Canada but they failed to arrive. The end of navigation was at hand, and hope of succor had now to be deferred until the following May.

The retention of Quebec thus depended on an improvised garrison which was already on the alert when the governor stepped ashore on November 19, for Arnold had been in the vicinity for eleven days. The responsibility for preparing the capital to stand a siege had fallen upon Cramahé, and Carleton was well pleased with what his lieutenant governor had done.[17] In September the walls had had many breaches and few cannon. By the middle of November the breaches were repaired and many cannon were mounted. They had been tested and were manned by companies of artillery formed from the militia. As there had been no ships of the navy at Quebec, Cramahé had hired and armed four craft to control the navigation of the river. To man them, and to increase his meager garrison, he had placed an embargo on all shipping. On the subsequent arrival of three of His Majesty's vessels, he had twice called a council of war with their officers, his own officers, and the two judges and councilors in Quebec, Mabane and Dunn. The council of war had continued the embargo and had decided that the naval vessels should be laid up in Quebec that their crews might assist in holding the place. It had also determined the destruction of all houses, particularly those in the St. John's Suburb, that might offer shelter to the enemy, and had examined returns of the provisions and of the garrison in the town. The provisions were enough to last until the middle of the following May.

The garrison, commanded by McLean, numbered about twelve hundred. There were three hundred Canadian militia headed by Noel Voyer, an old captain of militia to whom the governor had given a temporary commission as colonel. The English militia, two hundred strong, was organized under Henry Caldwell. This former favorite of Wolfe had recently retired from the army with the rank of major and had settled down as a seignior, having leased the estates which Murray had acquired, including the great fief of Lauzon or Pointe Lévis. The rest of the garrison was made up of about two hundred Royal Highland Emigrants, double this number of seamen and marines, and nearly a hundred carpenters and other artificers. Though McLean's regiment contained many retired officers and old soldiers, it also included eighty recruits, just arrived from Newfoundland, who were described by Cramahé as "Irish fishermen unacquainted with the use of arms." Nor was the lieutenant governor very complimentary about the militia, which, he said, was "with difficulty brought to mount guard and consequently not much to be depended on."

Just a few hours before Carleton arrived, and quite in ignorance of his approach, Cramahé had written home warning the government of the very precarious condition of the colony and urging the dispatch of a large land and naval armament in the spring. Its arrival early in May, he pointed out, was necessary "to reconquer the country and seize a proper hold of it," whether Quebec stood or fell.[18] This letter followed one written two months before by Carleton in Montreal advising the government at home that "whatever is our fate, I think that this war cannot be carried on more advantageously than from hence, and that a body of ten or twelve thousand men here, early next spring, completely equipped, with some frigates, might greatly change the face of things on this continent." [19]

The weakness of Quebec was more than physical. Back in September, according to the chief justice, the governor had written "in a very desponding style, which he is not used to do where any hope remains, and has ordered Lady Maria C. to embark as fast as she can and proceed to England," which was not very encouraging to the officials or to the people in the capital.[20] Indeed, there was a spirit of distrust abroad, and much bad feeling was festering. Cramahé angrily told Zachary Macaulay, one of the merchants of the place, that it was their "damned committees that had thrown the province into its present state and prevented the Canadians from taking arms." [21] The merchants explained everything by going back one step further. "Most people on this side," wrote one Quebec firm to a commercial house in London, "owe their present misfortunes to our G–v–r, the Quebec Bill and its promoters." [22] Caldwell, whose tenants had risen against him when he tried to form them in militia companies, blamed the governor's tardiness and timidity in calling the people to arms.[23] Allan McLean insisted that holding back the Indians from attacking the rebel colonies had done more mischief than anything else,[24] and he poured forth his own fury in a multitude of curses upon the heads of the Canadians and the English-speaking inhabitants.

But for all its strength, McLean's profanity could not galvanize the population of Quebec. Some citizens talked openly of surrendering the city and a number were suspected of being ready to betray it. A group of old subjects had positively refused to join the militia, and not a few who had taken up arms had laid them down again. The same was true of the new subjects. From September to November the militia had shrunk by several hundred. Cramahé had extracted from the original English-speaking recalcitrants "their obligations in writing not to do anything that may hurt the King's service." Though some zealous patriots thought this a puerile proceeding, the lieutenant governor may have been wise in refraining from bolder measures before the arrival of the governor.

Carleton did not hesitate to purge the town, and he would have been foolish if he had, for the siege was now about to commence. On November 22, just three days after his arrival, he issued a proclamation to rid the place of "useless, disloyal and treacherous persons." All who persisted in their refusal to bear arms were, with their wives and children, to quit the town within four days and to be out of the district by the end of the month, "under pain of being treated as rebels or spies."

Now departed John McCord, the political publican, Zachary Macaulay, a member of several "damned committees" and the first to sign the petition for the repeal of the Quebec Act, Edward Antill, a lawyer from New Jersey who became chief engineer of the besiegers, and various other malcontents, including four or five who had been appointed militia officers. There is no evidence extant to indicate how many Canadians withdrew. Nor is the number of the English-speaking exiles known, though it does not appear to have been large. Some merchants evaded the issue by managing to reside outside the town during this winter. One of them who attained prominence in later years insisted that he withdrew because of his health.

That all who remained within the walls did not enjoy the best political health appears from a few letters which, having been intercepted, have been preserved among the state papers.[25] They tell how the firm of John and Aclam Bondfield deposited their goods in vaults in the capital, where one member of the family remained in charge while the other members went out, one of them traveling down to Philadelphia to procure contracts from the continental congress. Though there may have been others who stayed to take out political insurance against commercial loss, the exodus following the governor's proclamation was admitted to have had a wholesome effect. "Cabals then ceased," wrote Caldwell. The numbers of the garrison rose, reaching eighteen hundred by the end of the month, according to Ainslie. The mere arrival of the governor was also a tonic. Any misgivings he may have had he kept to himself, and his calm demeanor inspired confidence.

The forces which closed in to take Quebec were actually much weaker in number than those which were mustered to defend it! This curious fact has often been overlooked, and therefore it is necessary to examine what had happened to the followers of Arnold and of Montgomery. On reaching the St. Lawrence, Arnold had only six hundred and seventy-five men — about half the army that had set out from Cambridge eight weeks before to surprise the capital of Canada when it was denuded of troops. His idea was brilliant, but his attempt to realize it by leading this expedition up the Kennebec over the height of land and down the Chaudière was mad. All who did not turn back, conquered in spirit by the perils of the wild way, might have died in their tracks had not friendly Canadians sent up droves of cattle and other food to revive the famished heroes, who had been trying to sustain life on such things as candle ends and leather pouches.

The survivors were in no condition to take Quebec when they set eyes upon it from Pointe Lévis on November 9. Rugged rocks, plunging mountain streams, tangled forests, and bottomless swamps had robbed them of almost everything except the rags they wore. For four days they could not cross the river because Cramahé had ordered the removal of all boats from the south shore and the guns of the frigate "Lizard" and the sloop "Hunter" commanded the passage. Then on a dark night, in canoes and dugouts they had gathered, they slipped across. In the morning they paraded before the walls and gave three loud huzzas, but Quebec was not Jericho. On November 18, hearing that the garrison was to make a sally on the following day, they looked to their arms and ammunition — they had no guns — and found that nearly a hundred of their muskets were useless and that they had no more than five rounds for each man. They decamped during the night, marking the path of their retreat with the blood of their "shattered hoofs." They retired to Pointe aux Trembles to wait for their brethren from Montreal.

Montgomery was able to bring to Quebec no more than half as many men as Arnold had there. Indeed, he was not going to come down at all, but was planning to spend the winter at home or in Montreal. He changed his mind on the very day he entered Montreal, when he received the first news that the force from the Kennebec had actually penetrated to its destination. This committed him, but it did not commit his men. Their term of service was expiring and they were loath to renew it. St. John had resisted so long that many of them, anxious to get home before the changing season barred the route over Lake Champlain for several weeks, had been persuaded to go to Montreal only on the promise of release as soon as that town surrendered. It was impossible to hold them any longer. Having signed up for only a few months, they had to get back to attend to their own affairs. The spirit of adventure had sickened and died in the marshes of the Richelieu, and the prospect of a Canadian winter did not revive it. Moreover, these men had "done their do." With the Declaration of Independence and official war against Britain still in the future, the appeal to arms was as yet designed only to repel immediate danger and to teach wisdom to a stupid government in London. The great object of this campaign was accomplished. Canada was no longer a sword of Damocles. The victorious army dissolved and the Philadelphia congress was not prepared to replace it. Montgomery's appeals moved only eight hundred men to re-enlist until the spring, when they would have to leave to reach home for seeding time, and out of these he had to provide garrisons for Montreal, St. John, and Chambly.

To furnish even this number, as well as to feed and to re-equip Arnold's tattered contingent, was a difficult problem for Montgomery. The stores and provisions captured with the fleet in the river were not enough for his needs, and he had to borrow several thousand pounds from James Price, Walker's partner. The friendship of the Canadians was so vital that the American general feared to let the weight of his army rest upon the population. The weather turned very cold and ice was running in the river before he embarked on November 28 in the vessels taken nine days before. But heaven smiled and blew upon him. The temperature rose and a southwest wind struck up, carrying the expedition down and preventing the British vessels from coming up from Quebec to destroy it. On December 2 Colonel Arnold saluted General Montgomery, and the latter, after reviewing the corps of the former, pronounced its discipline superior to what he had been accustomed to during the campaign.

On December 6 the combined forces sat down before the town. Arnold's men occupied the region of the St. Charles and the others the Plains of Abraham. Montgomery planted his headquarters in Holland House. When the roads from Quebec were thus barred, the American general wrote a letter summoning the British governor to surrender. Carleton ordered a drummer to seize it with a pair of tongs and throw it in the fire. Then he told the messenger to report to Montgomery how his communication had been received.

The five months' siege of Quebec opened with the odds decidedly against the Americans. With the exception of their leader they were all amateur soldiers, and they were inferior in numbers, being only a thousand against at least fifteen hundred and possibly eighteen hundred. They could not dig trenches, nor could they mine. The frost had made the earth as hard as the rock that came close to its surface. Their artillery was little better than a few popguns would have been. Five mortars in the suburb of St. Roch threw small shells into the town with but slight effect. Their only other battery was on the Heights about eight hundred yards from St. John's Gate. It was composed of five six-pounders and twelve-pounders and a single howitzer and was protected by ice gabions made of snow drenched with water, for earthworks were impossible. This defense was soon shattered and the guns were quickly put out of commission by thirty-two-pounders from the walls.

A blockade was equally hopeless. Before the besiegers could starve Quebec into surrender, it was sure to be relieved by a British fleet, and their own term of service would expire. Arnold's con-

tingent had enlisted only until the end of the year and Montgomery's men were promised their freedom by the middle of April.
While waiting they were bound to suffer much more than the
garrison. They had no walls to protect them from the hot fire of
the British guns and no warm houses to shelter them from the cold
blasts of winter. Moreover, the besieged seemed to have remained
fairly healthy while the besiegers were smitten by various diseases.
The worst was smallpox,* which broke out a few days after they
took up their position before the town. The only advantages they
possessed were a bold spirit and the friendship of the Canadians,
two hundred of whom joined them in arms, and the second advantage was bound to decline as the invaders were forced to resort
to paper money to procure necessities. The marvel is not that Quebec withstood the siege but that there was a siege at all.

Realizing the futility of bombardment and of blockade, Montgomery and his officers decided to try surprise. They planned two
simultaneous attacks, one on the Lower Town, which they might
enter from the mouth of the St. Charles, and the other on Cape
Diamond bastion, which they might enter by escalade on a dark
night, preferably in a storm. They hoped that their attempt would
be aided by treachery within the town, but the only treachery that
occurred at this time was in their own camp. At least one of the
besiegers betrayed the plan to the garrison, which was therefore
ready to invert the surprise. At two o'clock on the morning of December 31, in a blizzard blowing from the northeast, between eight
and nine hundred Americans turned out. The main blow was to
be delivered by six hundred men under Arnold, who was to strike
from St. Roch and get into the Lower Town at its northern end.
Montgomery, with less than three hundred men, instead of scaling the bastion at the top of the cliff was to proceed along its foot
and penetrate the southern extremity of the Lower Town. The
garrison was to be drawn to the main works by a blaze of gunfire
and by the Canadian contingent advancing to burn the St. John's
Gate.

Between four and five o'clock, two rockets shot up from Cape
Diamond. This signal to those waiting outside the walls warned
those who were within. Soon all was noise and confusion. Except
at one point the attackers failed immediately. Some Canadians ran

* It had been in the town also, but had ceased to be serious there.

away and the rest could not burn a hole into the Upper Town. Montgomery, under the shelter of the cliff, pushed past a couple of undefended barriers. Leading his long thin line, he rounded Cape Diamond and halted fifty paces before a house straight ahead at Près de Ville, the entrance of the Lower Town. Then, with sword in hand, he charged. But four small fieldpieces, loaded with grape-shot and bags of bullets, were mounted in this house of Simon Fraser and were trained on the road. In a moment the American general, his two aides-de-camp, and ten others lay dead in the snow. Those who were following quickly deserted this road of death.

On the north side of the town Arnold had plunged east through swirling snow and high-piled drifts. When the main body passed the Palace Gate, the watchers on the crest above began to rain a deadly fire upon them. Before the vanguard reached the Sault au Matelot, where the Upper Town thrust out a spur as if to reach the river brink, they encountered a barricade across the narrow way. The six-pounder that was to have battered it down had been abandoned on its sleigh in the drifts, but, nothing daunted, they hurled themselves on and over it. Around the corner, some two hundred yards beyond, they ran into a second barricade. Here their impetuous assault was checked. The main body was very slow in coming up to support them. There was no road until near the first barrier, and the wind wiped out the tracks of the advance party. Through the dark night and the deep snow, the soldiers of the main force stumbled into irregularly placed storehouses and over ships' hausers, pieces of timber, and blocks of ice. Day dawned before they arrived where they were desperately needed, and then most of their muskets were reduced to clubs by the snow that had got into the priming.

Meanwhile the defenders mustered in greater strength, and from the windows of the houses within the barrier they picked off many an assailant. Scaling ladders were brought up and raised, but a Canadian Hercules named Charles Charland wrested them from the hands below and pulled them up and over. From the storm of bullets that swept the street, the assailants took refuge in the houses and continued the fight from the windows. If only they could hold their position until Montgomery caught the defenders in the rear! Little did they know that they themselves were about to be caught like rats in a trap by an attack from the rear. Carleton had ordered five hundred men with several cannon to sally out of the Palace

Gate. There was no escape for the Americans and they had to surrender.

As a result of these few hours' work in the last morning of the year, about four hundred and thirty officers and men were now captives in the town which they had hoped to capture. Over one hundred more were killed. Some bodies were not found until spring uncovered them. Montgomery's, however, was brought in on New Year's Day and, being recognized, was given a decent burial. Neither death nor prison claimed Arnold, for a painful wound in his left leg, received before his men took the first barrier, had carried him back to the General Hospital, where he lay groaning. The garrison lost about ten killed and twenty wounded.

The importance of this event has sometimes been overestimated. The ultimate fate of Canada was not at stake. The armament that Britain sent in the spring was strong enough to blow out of Quebec any force that the Americans could have placed in it had they captured it during the winter. The nearest they ever came to capturing it was on December 31, and then they were very far from reaching their goal. Even if Montgomery and Arnold had penetrated the barriers which stopped them, where would they have been? They were not striking at the military strength of Quebec; they were attacking only its commercial part, the Lower Town. The Upper Town, the real fortress, could not be taken from the Lower Town, and Montgomery, at least, seems to have known it. His only hope was that those above, seeing the enemy seize their property below, would force Carleton to surrender.

The most astonishing thing about the American invasion is the continuance of the siege of Quebec after the terrible repulse on the last morning of the year. That disaster had robbed the blockading force of considerably more than half its numbers, and disease was eating into the remainder. To make matters still worse, not a few of the survivors left the scene of their misery and made for home. Their time was up and the game was up. Those who stayed to continue the hopeless task did so partly out of bravado, encouraged by Arnold from his bed of pain, and partly out of fear of what the Canadians might do to them if they retired, for the attitude of the country people was now far from friendly. By a vigorous sortie, Carleton could have utterly ruined the pitiful fragment of an army that lay outside the walls. But he remained steadily on the defensive, and after a few weeks the besiegers began to receive recruits, first from Montreal and then from the old colonies.

In little better plight was the occupying army in the upper part of the province under Brigadier General David Wooster, who became the senior American officer in Canada on the death of Montgomery. When Edward Antill galloped into Montreal on January 2, 1776, to beg him to repair the disaster before Quebec by rushing down with all the troops and guns he could gather, Wooster replied that he could do nothing because he had now to secure his own retreat. Before the end of the month he did send a couple of hundred men and some guns and at the end of two months he himself appeared at the capital, but when Antill arrived he was in a state of alarm bordering on panic.

Wooster can hardly be blamed for being nervous. He had only about five hundred soldiers of doubtful reliability to hold Montreal, St. John, and Chambly, and the hostility of the population was rising. But he was a good deal to blame for the threatening attitude of the people. Being a very stupid fellow, this American commander had inclosed himself in a vicious circle. The precautions he had taken and was still taking to make his position more secure only made it less secure. By stopping all communication with the west he had paralyzed trade and alienated the mercantile class, who actually appealed to Philadelphia against him. Only a few like Walker and Price, who feared that canoes going up country might carry arms and ammunition for hostile parties to bring down, supported his policy. He also had Judge Fraser [26] and many other citizens sent south as prisoners because he suspected them of designs which he could not prove. By such methods he roused more enemies than he removed. Even more stupid, if that be possible, was his attitude toward the Canadians and his failure to disguise it. He despised them and they knew it. They saw it in his behavior and they heard it from their priests. He wrote a letter in which he said that they were only one remove from the savages; and the letter, being intercepted, found its way into the hands of Montgolfier, who of course made good use of it. Indeed, if report be true, Wooster was insane enough to prohibit Mass on Christmas Eve! But even if this general had been endowed with iron nerves and a commanding intelligence, he would still have found himself in a very difficult position.

For three broad reasons quite beyond the control of any individual, the mass of the population turned against the Americans. The invaders were weak in numbers; their material resources had given out; and they were Protestants in a Roman Catholic land. In the early days of the invasion, the little loyalty of the Canadians to the British connection had ebbed and flowed with the apparent tide of victory. The capture of Ethan Allen, for example, temporarily swelled the numbers who rallied to support the governor in Montreal. Relatively few took up arms at all, but of these few, more were on the American than on the British side,[27] and as a whole the Canadian people favored the invaders and assisted them in countless other ways, especially when they were overrunning the country. Then the big battalions from the south vanished and the Canadians saw that the Americans were not almighty. Their newfound friendship had been quite fortuitous, for there had been little or no mutual understanding, and it quickly dissolved when the habitants discovered that the invaders could not win salvation for them. They realized that the difference between revolution and rebellion was the difference between success and failure, and they wished to avoid the sad fate of rebels.

Equally powerful as a dissolvent was the way in which the Americans supported themselves. On first entering the country they had won golden opinions by paying for everything in good sound metal. When they spent all that they had brought, the Americans got more by borrowing in Montreal. The biggest lender was James Price, who advanced twenty thousand pounds. But these resources also gave out. Then the occupying army had nothing but paper for a people who had been sickened of paper only a few years before. As of old, the Canadians were reluctant to give their goods and their services for this stuff. But officers and men had to live and therefore they insisted, sometimes pointing their argument with a bayonet. Many a certificate was illegible or even without a signature, and sometimes kicks and curses took the place of the less offensive paper. More and more the weight of the occupying army ground down the peasantry. One cannot but pity these poor forlorn people.

A third factor was the influence of the clergy, which makes one wonder what might have happened if parliament, by adopting the board of trade's anti-Catholic scheme, had driven the clergy to throw all their weight into the American scale. But Britain had won them by the religious provisions of the Quebec Act, and the Philadelphia congress had alienated them by denouncing these provisions. In consequence they strained every effort to make their people loyal, even going to the extreme of withholding absolution from those who aided the invaders.

The reaction produced by Wooster's folly and these general causes became very noticeable by the close of 1775, and of course it continued. Its positive aspect appears to have been restrained by lack of scope, Quebec being the only place in the settled parts of the colony where the British colors were still flying, and it must not be imagined that the revulsion of popular opinion was complete. Before the end of the siege there was only one movement of the natives in favor of the British cause, and that was toward the end of March, when an old colonial officer named De Beaujeu, who lived thirty miles below Quebec, gathered three or four hundred habitants to relieve the capital. It came to nothing, however, for the expedition broke up when its advance party was surprised and destroyed by an American detachment aided by other Canadians. The latter were probably influenced by a new development in the general situation: the invaders were gaining in numbers.

Antill's wild ride did not end in Montreal nor even in Albany, where he found Schuyler helpless and the town trembling because seven hundred Highland settlers of the Mohawk Valley had risen in arms under Sir John Johnson. The desperate messenger rushed on to Philadelphia, which he reached on January 17. He electrified many members of congress, but they could not electrify the people. Congress was not yet a government and the people were not yet a nation. After an infinity of orders there was a trickle of reinforcements flowing north, and then the trickle swelled into a stream. It was only well started when it was interrupted by the coming of spring, which cut the communications over Lake Champlain. At the same time, in order to make sure of the colony on the St. Lawrence, the revolutionary leaders felt the necessity of sending more than soldiers. As Canada had not acted on the invitation to send representatives to congress, congress decided to send representatives to Canada. This was on February 15, but another month was spent in deciding who should go and what they should do. Not until April 2 did the three delegates, Benjamin Franklin, Samuel Chase, and Charles Carroll, leave New York, and they too were held up by the melting ice on the lake. On April 29 they reached Montreal, and reinforcements were again pouring north.

But it was all in vain. The three wise men from the south wasted their wisdom in the north. To speak to the Canadians through the mouth of their own church, the delegates had brought along the Jesuit who was to be the first archbishop of Baltimore, John Carroll, the elder brother of Charles, but the Canadian clergy would have nothing to do with him. Likewise the French printer Fleury Mesplet and his press, brought all the way from Philadelphia by Franklin, proved utterly useless. They were established in the cellar of the Château de Ramezay without any effect whatever upon the people. Another sad surprise was that no one in Montreal would cash the personal bills of Charles Carroll, though he was perhaps the wealthiest man in America. The Philadelphian trio reversed Wooster's policy of repression, but the results of their own lenience frightened them into reviving it. They issued orders to and received appeals from the army with the results that usually follow civilian interference with military commanders in the field. About the only good thing they accomplished was to persuade congress to recall Wooster — but not until he had displayed his incompetence before Quebec, as will shortly appear.

The Americans were incapable of holding Canada. For all the reinforcements that came over Lake Champlain, their army in the colony gained little strength. Those who had re-enlisted until the middle of April insisted on going home and thereby caused a serious upheaval. Their places were taken by recruits whose bad discipline was not improved by the continual shortage of necessities. To the very end of the occupation the American leaders could not find enough food for their numbers, and they were absolutely destitute of cash. The smallpox raged more than ever, for the men inoculated themselves, believing that they would have only a mild attack and gain subsequent immunity. Some did it to escape duty. All did it in defiance of orders, until at last the practice had to be officially countenanced. At the end of March the force investing Quebec numbered twenty-five hundred, of whom nearly one-third were unfit for duty. On the morning of May 1 they numbered nineteen hundred, of whom nine hundred were sick. Of the remainder, three hundred were importunate for their discharge and two hundred had inoculated themselves. The well were occupied more by nursing than by fighting. Then came a new general, John Thomas, more reinforcements, and — the end of the siege.

Quebec was impregnable to the Americans. During the three months after the fall of Montgomery, all that they could do to the garrison was to alarm them out of a little sleep and to reduce their supply of firewood by burning broken and deserted houses in the suburbs. On April 3 they unmasked a battery on Pointe Lévis. Three weeks later they started a bombardment from across the St. Charles and renewed their firing from the Heights. Their guns were now a little heavier, but still they could not compare in weight and number with the artillery on the walls, and they had only a few days' supply of powder.

One other method of attack remained to be tried, and it became possible only when the ice went out of the river. This was a fire ship, to which the besiegers now pinned their little faith. They hoped that it would not only destroy the shipping still laid up in the Cul-de-sac but would also, by the spreading of the conflagration, weaken the watch on the walls and even open a breach in the palisade. As few men were needed to prepare the craft, the secret could have been better kept than it had been before the assault — if Wooster had not come down from Montreal. In a public address to some of his troops he told them about it, and it was soon a favorite topic of conversation in the town. As days passed and nothing happened, many thought it a false rumor, and after sunset on May 3, when a brigantine rounded the Island of Orleans, a large number were deceived into thinking it the object of their heart's desire — a ship from England. But the warning had not been in vain. Guns were trained on the stranger, and when she did not answer with the signal appointed by Cramahé before the siege began, they were touched off. A small boat [28] pulled hurriedly away and she burst into flames. Only a hundred yards from the shipping the ebb tide caught the blazing mass and bore it away, spluttering shells and hand grenades. The besiegers could do no more. In three days they were running away as fast as their legs could carry them.

A big British fleet with over ten thousand regulars, including a regiment sent by Howe from Halifax, a powerful battering train, and abundant supplies of ammunition, provisions, and money, was on the way to relieve Quebec. Mysterious columns of smoke rising

from point to point warned the besiegers that something unpleasant
was coming but gave them no idea of the strength of the approaching armament. They did not dream that it had come from across
the sea; they thought that it was only a body of reinforcements sent
by Howe and therefore very much weaker than it actually was. As
the Americans before Quebec then numbered three thousand, their
false belief might have encouraged them to stay and be caught, if
they had been a real army. But this they were not, and, therefore,
on May 5 a council of war decided that the retreat should commence next morning so that it might be completed in an orderly
manner before the arrival of the new British forces, which, it was
supposed, were still some days off.

At dawn, however, a frigate well named "Surprise" poked her
nose around the island, and shortly afterward another frigate, the
"Isis," and the sloop "Martin" hove in sight. This vanguard of the
fleet bore one hundred marines and two companies of the Twenty-
ninth Regiment, who were hastily landed. The delight within the
town was balanced by the panic without. The Canadians immediately deserted the Americans, who thus found themselves "like
Pharaoh's chariots, without wheels." At noon the governor led
eight hundred men out of the St. John's and the St. Louis gates,
and shortly afterward the "Surprise" and the "Martin" sailed up the
river to fire upon the fugitives' flank.

Carleton could not reach the enemy, who "ran as if the Devil
was after them." General Thomas lost his dinner, which was devoured by some of McLean's hungry Highlanders, and his men
lost their heads and a great deal else besides. In their panic they
abandoned loaded guns without firing them, and many threw away
their muskets and even their coats and waistcoats to speed their
flight. The detachments posted at Charlesbourg and Pointe Lévis
escaped into the woods, and not until several days later were they
able to join their comrades in distress. By midnight the main body
covered the thirty miles to Pointe aux Trembles, and before daybreak on the seventh they were off again to Deschambault, fifteen
miles further on. There the ignominious flight stopped. How ignominious it was may be gathered from their continued belief that
only reinforcements from Howe were coming up the river, and
from the fact that Carleton had long since given up the wild chase.
He was busy collecting the spoils, which included important mili-

tary papers, and preparing to resume the pursuit with the aid of a real army.

At the other end of the colony minor operations now gave a further illustration of how precarious was the American hold upon the country. On the very day that Thomas' men took to their heels, Colonel Bedel of New Hampshire, with smallpox in his veins and fear in his heart, took command of a stockade recently constructed at Cedars, forty-three miles above Montreal, to bar the gateway of the west. Two cannon were mounted to control the shore and the river, and half a regiment held the place. Meanwhile a British force was gathering up at Oswegatchie, now Ogdensburg, under the command of Captain George Forster of the Eighth Regiment. He had forty of his own unit drawn from Niagara, about a hundred Canadians, mostly employees of fur traders, and four or five hundred Indians. The irregulars had been collected by Lorimier, an old French officer whose life had been filled with thrilling adventures. He had flitted in and out of St. John, doing valiant service for the beleaguered garrison, and in March he had slipped through the fingers of the American sentries at Montreal and disappeared up country. This motley host set out on May 12, armed with nothing heavier than muskets.

As soon as he heard that they were coming, Bedel went to Montreal, but Major Butterfield, who was left in charge, resembled his senior officer in body and in spirit. He too was coming down with smallpox, and Indians were a nightmare to him. When Forster appeared on the eighteenth and summoned the fort, adding that the Indians would give no quarter should they take it by storm, Butterfield asked permission to retire with his men. Forster refused and the attack began. On the next morning, when the American commander woke to see a breastwork in front of the fort, his terror was greater than ever, and he capitulated on receiving a new summons. He and his four hundred men, only one of whom had been wounded, became prisoners of war. They were promised only their lives and the clothes on their backs.

On the previous morning a reinforcement of nearly a hundred and fifty men with a stock of provisions had crossed the Ottawa from Ste. Anne on the Island of Montreal, but hearing that the woods were full of hostile Indians they had retired in the evening. On the twentieth a hundred of them crossed again and made for

Cedars. Embarrassed by the large number of his captives, Forster detailed Lorimier with a party of Indians and Canadians to meet the advancing party, who likewise surrendered after a skirmish in which they lost five or six men.

The road to Montreal now seemed open, and on the twenty-fourth Forster advanced as far as Lachine. Then he retired, having heard from friends in Montreal that Arnold had dug entrenchments and had filled them with stout fighters. Thereupon Arnold advanced to rescue the captives. They might all have been massacred by the Indians had he crossed the Ottawa. Fortunately he could not, because Forster's muskets and the two guns that had been taken at Cedars checked him. Meanwhile the prisoners agreed to a cartel, which Arnold had to accept and congress later repudiated, along with a truce of six days to allow the delivery of the unfortunate captives. "It had been demonstrated to the satisfaction of many in Canada that the British lion, opening his mouth even a very little, could eat up five hundred American soldiers and retire unsinged."

Though the numbers of the Americans in Canada were increasing, so was their confusion. They were faced with the alternative of abandoning the country or of making a stand at some place where they might have a chance of success. They rejected the former but could not decide upon the latter. The ideal spot was Deschambault, where a commanding crest of land jutted out into the river and where rapids, since removed by dredging, impeded navigation. Though Thomas and the congressional commissioners had independently of each other thought of fortifying this pass, nothing had been done. Therefore a council of war, over which the American general presided, at noon on May 7 voted for a stand at Sorel, and the retreat was renewed. On the eighth Thomas changed his mind, for he was no longer pursued and he had learned that troops, provisions, and guns were coming down, and he issued new orders accordingly. On the twelfth, moved by a false report that Carleton had started up from Quebec two days before, the American general again reversed his commands. Three Rivers was to be his advance position, while he went back to the mouth of the Richelieu, where the stream of reinforcements was halted. On the twentieth he told the commissioners that lack of provisions necessitated the abandonment of Three Rivers, and on the following day it was evacuated.

The Americans at this time numbered five thousand, but their confusion was indescribable. From Montreal the commissioners wrote the president of congress: "You will have a faint idea of our situation if you figure to yourself an army, broken, disheartened, half of it under inoculation and other diseases, soldiers without pay, without discipline, and altogether reduced to live from hand to mouth, depending on the scanty and precarious supplies of a few half starved cattle and trifling quantities of corn, which have hitherto been picked up in different parts of the country." There was also a shortage of shoes and stockings.

On May 31 Samuel Chase and Charles Carroll started for home, Benjamin Franklin and John Carroll having preceded them by three weeks. On June 2 the effectives at Sorel mustered eleven hundred, three times as many were unfit for duty, and their general died of smallpox. A further retreat had already begun, but it was stopped by the approach of a fresh army of about twenty-five hundred under Major General John Sullivan. He was determined to reverse the disgraceful situation, all the more disgraceful since the retreating Americans had seen no foe after the first push out of Quebec, and even yet they appear to have been ignorant of the arrival of any forces from England so early in the year. Their new leader, therefore, seemed to personify restored reason when he dispatched two thousand fresh men under Brigadier General Thompson, who had come only a fortnight before, to seize Three Rivers. They left Sorel on June 6, imagining that they had to drive only a handful of British troops out of the town.

It was exactly a month since Carleton had lost contact with the foe. This breach of one of the most fundamental principles in the art of war was not serious, because the campaign here was limited to one dimension. Nor was Carleton in any way to blame. The Americans ran too fast and he had too few men at hand to follow. His reinforcements were slow in coming up. On May 22 he sailed up the river with the only two regiments that had yet arrived, but steady head winds stopped him a short distance below Three Rivers. There he posted a Canadian guard to watch the enemy, and then, after a few days' absence, returned to his capital, where the harbor was becoming crowded with ships. Only a few stragglers had yet to come when sixteen vessels dropped anchor at sunset on June 1. Instead of unloading there, which would have caused delay, the transports, victualers, and storeships were ordered by the governor to push upstream with Three Rivers as their objective. Thus both armies were moving on the same objective and neither knew what the other was doing.

Thompson reached Nicolet at the east end of Lake St. Peter on June 6 toward midnight. It was too late for an attack at dawn on the seventh, as he had planned, and therefore he lay low until the next evening. He knew that there were several vessels anchored above Three Rivers, but he was unaware of the presence of Brigadier General Simon Fraser * with a thousand men and some artillery in the town, and of the approach of twenty-five more ships, which anchored just as he was setting out to surprise the place. To give a wide berth to the vessels which had arrived earlier, Thompson's fifty bateaux merely crossed the end of the lake and beached at Pointe du Lac about two in the morning on the eighth. His men then started their march to fall upon a sleeping town. But Antoine Gautier, a local habitant whom they pressed into their service as a guide, buried them in a swamp. Half water-logged, they extricated themselves and resumed their advance. Daylight came upon them still far from their goal.

Meanwhile, warned by the Pointe du Lac captain of militia, Fraser had procured more guns and more men from the ships, and the latter had prepared their deadly broadsides. Still the Americans pressed on until the cross-fire shattered them. Their retreat was cut off by a detachment that chased away their boats and another under Major Grant that held the bridge at Rivière du Loup. During the rest of the eighth and the whole of the ninth, the scattered fragments of the army floundered hither and thither in the trackless swamp. Nearly two hundred and fifty, including Thompson and his second in command, gave themselves up. None of the rest could have escaped had not Carleton, who had just come up from Quebec, opened the trap by recalling Grant. On the evening of the eleventh the wretched remnant reached the mouth of the Richelieu. The British loss was eight killed and nine wounded; the number of the American casualties is unknown.

Carleton had three score vessels and ten thousand men at Three Rivers, and by a vigorous forward movement he might have taken

* Not to be confused with the owner of the house at Près de Ville, mentioned above, page 226.

practically all the Americans who remained in the country. Ignorant of the British strength and inspired by his own pride * and a recent resolution of congress that the retention of Canada was absolutely necessary, Sullivan was determined to stem the tide at Sorel, though he had only twenty-five hundred effectives and a large army of sick. On the thirteenth a strong column under Fraser, marching up the north shore of the St. Lawrence, was seen in Sorel, and that evening nearly all the field officers in the American camp urged their general to retire. Reluctantly he yielded. In the morning, as sixty British vessels approached the beach, his force started up the Richelieu, some in bateaux and the rest along the shore.

About an hour after they left their camp, some redcoats were in it. But no pursuit began until the next day, Saturday the fifteenth, when Major General John Burgoyne, who had come out in charge of the army of reinforcements, started with four thousand men and six pieces of field artillery. He never gained contact with the enemy, for he was not to press hard until the main body reached its position. The main body under Carleton sailed for Longueuil, hoping to reach it Saturday evening and to cut off the Americans on the Richelieu Sunday morning. Not until nightfall on Monday the seventeenth did Sullivan get all his army and boats above the rapids at Chambly and set fire to the fort and storehouses there. Tuesday morning Burgoyne surveyed the embers.

Meanwhile, on the Saturday morning before, Arnold in Montreal had sent Captain James Wilkinson (the general in the War of 1812) with dispatches for Sullivan, thinking that the latter was still in Sorel. About three o'clock in the afternoon of that day, as the messenger drew near Varennes, fourteen miles downstream, he heard guns and straightway landed. He found the village full of soldiers from Carleton's windbound fleet, which he now sighted anchored in the river. Stealing a horse, he galloped back to Longueuil, and at five P.M. he astounded Arnold in the Château de Ramezay with his news. Four hours later the whole garrison of Montreal, about three hundred men, left Longueuil for La Prairie on the road to St. John. Fearing to be caught, Arnold had ordered Wilkinson to post to Sullivan for reinforcements, and, having stolen

---

* Having risen through the stages of stable boy, hostler, innkeeper, lawyer, and politician, Sullivan was conscious of his eminence and inclined to credit himself rather than heaven for his success in the world.

another horse, Wilkinson was in Chambly about the time that Arnold was leaving Longueuil. Sullivan, of course, was still many miles from Chambly, and the troops at this point were so demoralized that the messenger saw no chance of getting what he had come for until the next morning, Sunday. Then "mad Anthony" Wayne, who had received his baptism of fire at Three Rivers, volunteered to round up a contingent.

But the precaution proved to be unnecessary. Arnold reached St. John on Sunday, to find that Sullivan was still struggling somewhere away down the river and that the boats which Chase had warned Schuyler to have ready for an emergency at St. John had been detained up the lake to bring reinforcements north. Late Monday evening Sullivan's mob covered the twelve miles from Chambly. On Tuesday, the boats having at last arrived, they embarked after destroying everything that they left behind. In the evening, when the last of the Americans had just rowed out of musket range, Burgoyne's men dashed into St. John. Carleton and his forces arrived next morning. Wednesday! They should have been there and they could have been there on Sunday! Had they come then, or on Monday, or even on Tuesday, they could have captured the whole American army!

Carleton's conduct of the campaign from the moment he arrived in Three Rivers on the evening of June 9 was most extraordinary. First he unsprung the trap when the enemy were caught in it — the recall of Grant from Rivière du Loup. Then he set the trap again, but this time he refused to spring it until his prey had all passed through it. From everything else that is known of him as a soldier, it is impossible to avoid the conclusion that his strange behavior was deliberate, that he wished the Americans to escape. This was a truly astonishing desire for a man in his position to harbor, but an explanation for it may be found in his attitude toward those already caught.

Four days after the besiegers vanished from before Quebec, Carleton issued a decree the words of which are significant. "Informed that many of His Majesty's deluded subjects of the neighbouring provinces, labouring under wounds and divers disorders, are dispersed in the adjacent woods and parishes, and are in great danger of perishing for want of proper assistance," he ordered the militia officers "to make diligent search for all such distressed persons, and afford them all necessary relief and convey them to the General Hospital, where proper care shall be taken of them." To encourage the rescuers he promised to pay all reasonable expenses, and to allay the fears of the sufferers in hiding he announced "that as soon as their health is restored they shall have free liberty to return to their respective provinces." On June 13 he ordered all the prisoners in Quebec to be sent home by ship, requiring only that the men "engage not to serve any more against the king," and the officers "to surrender themselves at any time when called upon by any commander-in-chief of His Majesty's forces." [29]

Having done this solely on his own authority, he stayed his hand, saying that he felt obliged to wait until the sanction of the home government or the good effect of his action "among the deluded people of the colonies" justified him in proceeding further. Meanwhile he expressed the desire that the confinement of those taken after his departure from the capital should be "as light and as short as possible." [30] It was shorter than they anticipated, for he changed his mind about waiting. On August 4 he issued orders that all who wished to return were to be sent home as prisoners on parole.[31] "This surprised them not a little," he wrote the secretary of state, and he added with a touch of shrewdness: "If they fulfill their engagements they will become good subjects, if not these can never turn the scale." [32]

Carleton felt that he was dealing with men who were not ordinary belligerents, nor even common rebels. They were fellow subjects who had been led astray. Pity rather than punishment was the uppermost thought in his mind. By proving, as he said, that "the way to mercy is not yet shut," he hoped to undermine the influence of the revolutionary leaders in Philadelphia and thereby to restore peace to troubled America. In a letter to Howe written on August 8, after referring to the repudiation of Forster's cartel, he remarked: "It appears that this congress is intent only upon exciting the people of America to acts of blood, and industrious even with every falsehood best calculated for their purpose, to divert them from all hopes of reconciliation. Probably the sending back their prisoners, notwithstanding this, loaded with every favour which was in my power to confer upon them, will be such testimonies to the thinking people among them, of the humanity and forbearance with which His Majesty's just resentment towards his revolted subjects is tempered as may serve effectually to counteract the dangerous designs of those desperate people whose fatal ascendency over them has already conducted them to the brink of ruin." [33] In conclusion, Carleton's action in recalling Grant from the bridge at Rivière du Loup and his own inaction at Varennes seem to have sprung from a fear of pushing the colonies over the brink. The statesman had overruled the soldier.

Carleton's inaction when the Americans were scrambling to get out of the country ruined the campaign of 1776 and possibly altered the outcome of the war. It will be recalled that he had written home in September for an army of ten or twelve thousand, urging that the war "cannot be carried on more advantageously than from hence." The government sent him the desired army but he threw away the means of using it, for he did more than let the American soldiers escape from his grasp. He had only to reach out his hand to seize their boats and the control of Lake Champlain. Then he might have succeeded in 1776, where Burgoyne was to fail in 1777, in breaking the back of colonial resistance to the British government. As it was, the large army in Canada was forced to lie idle, unable to stir over Lake Champlain until a fleet was created — fighting vessels to clear the way and transports to use it. This preparation took so long that the great blow had to be postponed for a year.

Not until October 4 did Carleton sail from Ile aux Noix, keeping a sharp lookout for the armament which Arnold had been constructing at the upper end of the lake. On the eleventh, when the British vessels had just passed Valcour Island, which lies nearly halfway between Ile aux Noix and Crown Point, they sighted the enemy anchored between that island and the western shore of the lake. Beating back against the wind, they attacked from the south. The Americans got a severe drubbing, but, under cover of darkness and fog, they slipped past the British and escaped the destruction that was awaiting them in the morning. On the thirteenth the British squadron completed its victory a few leagues short of Crown Point. The garrison of that place burned it and retired to Ticonderoga. On the following morning redcoats took possession of the ruins. Carleton had no thought of striking at Ticonderoga, where there were now nine thousand men under General Gates, and he soon gave up all thought of trying to build winter quarters for his men at Crown Point. On November 2 he and his force turned north to spend the winter in Canada. This movement, which was perhaps inevitable, relieved the pressure on Gates and released a considerable portion of his force to move south. Howe felt the result — successful attacks by Washington.

As a reward for holding Quebec, the cabinet on June 20 thought that "even if some parts of his conduct were doubtful," Carleton ought to be given the red ribbon,[34] and accordingly he became a Knight of the Bath on July 6, 1776. This honor, however, could not cure a wound which he had received not long before. He may have been piqued by the appointment of William Howe to command the main army in America, for though they were both major generals Carleton was the senior, and he was certainly "much hurt"[35] by not being included with this officer and his brother, Admiral Lord Howe, when they were appointed to be commissioners for the pacification of America in the spring of that year. General Howe was correspondingly embarrassed by the thought of a junction with the army under Carleton, his senior officer, and he wrote home about it.[36] Military etiquette had been overlooked. To correct the error that might have led to an awkward situation, the secretary of state for American affairs wrote Carleton on August 22 to remain behind after he had cleared the enemy out of the country. He was then to concentrate upon his proper task of "establishing good order and legal government in Canada," while he detached Burgoyne or some other officer with all the troops that could be spared to move on New York, there to "put himself as soon as possible under the command of General Howe."[37] The ship bearing this letter failed to reach its destination, though it entered the Gulf of St. Lawrence three times before it finally turned back. Thus Burgoyne's command did not begin until 1777.

The news of Carleton's retirement from Lake Champlain, when it reached London, naturally created disappointment and stirred criticism that he had not accomplished more with the strong army that had been sent him at his own request. Indeed, the king, who had displayed a tenderness for Carleton's feelings,[38] entertained the fear that the cabinet might decide upon recalling the governor in disgrace. This he was anxious to avoid as "cruel and uncalled for," and he suggested to Lord North on December 13, 1776, that he postpone the whole discussion if the proposal were actually made. The question of who should command the army that was to march from Canada to join Howe was again being considered, but it was a foregone conclusion that Carleton would not lead it. Even George III admitted that he was perhaps "too cold and not so active as might be wished," [39] and then there was the obstacle of military etiquette still standing in the way of his marching south. The natural choice was Burgoyne, who at this time seemed more promising and was certainly better known than Carleton. The decision was bound to go hard with the governor of Quebec, the senior major general in America.

As any stick is good enough to beat a dog, so are unjust accusations hurled against unpopular characters. Such a character was Lord George Germain,[40] who had succeeded Dartmouth as secretary of state for American affairs in the fall of 1775, and such an accusation is the oft-repeated statement that he superseded Carleton because of some unexplained private grudge. But there is no proof of any animus on the part of this minister before he had ample reason for it. Moreover, he was not a man who could turn the king's head and swing the cabinet simply because he harbored a personal spite. A careful examination of the correspondence that passed between Quebec and London shows that most of the quarreling was on Carleton's side and most of the right on Germain's side.

Probably the root of the trouble was Carleton's professional disdain for Germain because of his behavior in 1759 on the battlefield of Minden, where, as Lord George Sackville, he had repeatedly refused to let the cavalry charge to turn into a smashing victory the success gained by the infantry. Why Sackville refused now appears to be a mystery, the key to which may lie in tortuous politics, but contemporaries unhesitatingly damned him as a coward. He was court-martialed, and at the command of George II the sentence was read out to the British army everywhere with the comment that it was worse than death. Not until May, 1776, did the governor know that he had to take orders from this man, and the information seems to have galled him.

The minister's letters were studiously correct, but Carleton's were not. They began by being querulous and soon they became insolent. More and more they read like those of an overgrown governor. Everything had been going wrong with him. He had promised that Canada would be a tower of strength but it had turned out to be a broken reed. He had held out hopes of striking

a vital blow at the rebellious colonies if only he were given a sufficient force, but when given this force he threw away the chance of
using it; and as the political mirage which inspired his otherwise
strange inaction soon vanished, he must have been tortured by fear
lest the real reason for the escape of the American army be detected.
He hoped to repair his fault and to play a leading rôle on the
American stage in 1777, only to learn in the spring of this year that
his chance had passed away. Also, as will appear in the next chapter, he was getting into trouble in the field of civil government.
All the bitterness thus engendered in his surly nature he seems to
have vented in his letters to Germain.

The result is not surprising. In the words of the king himself,
who was by no means favorable to the minister, "Carleton was
highly wrong in permitting his pen to convey such asperity to a
Secretary of State and therefore has been removed from the government of Canada." The removal took the form of a prompt acceptance of his resignation, which was inspired by the news that he was
not to command the expedition led by Burgoyne. The resignation
was received by Lord North about July 1, 1777, and would have
taken effect that year had not heaven intervened to turn back the
vessel in which his successor embarked. There is one thing, however, which must be said on Carleton's behalf at this time. He gave
every possible assistance to Burgoyne, who later testified that the
governor could not have displayed more zeal "had he been acting
for himself or for his brother."

The campaign of 1777 was designed to effect what had been
hoped for in the previous year. The main idea thus originated with
Carleton, but the actual plans were the work of Burgoyne himself,
who spent the winter of 1776–77 in England. With very little variation, the secretary of state adopted the proposals which this combined soldier, politician, playwright, and social leader submitted
on February 28, 1777 — even to the detail of the particular units
to be left in Canada. A month later, Germain wrote his instructions to Carleton. The governor was to keep 3,700 men, and to
place 7,100 under Burgoyne for the main expedition and 675 under
Lieutenant Colonel St. Leger for a "diversion" from Oswego down
the Mohawk. Each of these two leaders was to make for Albany
and there "put himself under the command of Sir William Howe,"
the main purpose of the campaign being "the most speedy junction

of the two armies" then in Canada and in New York. Nothing was said about Howe moving north. He was merely to be informed from London and from Quebec of these operations, and until they received orders from him, Burgoyne and St. Leger were to "act as exigencies may require." Meanwhile Howe was planning an expedition to the south which received Germain's sanction.

Tradition has held these two expeditions to have been incompatible and has blamed the secretary of state for the disaster which ensued. But neither Howe nor Burgoyne nor Carleton observed any incompatibility. On April 5 Howe wrote Carleton a letter in which he said that he could not "detach a corps in the beginning of the campaign" to act up the Hudson, and, as he would probably be in Pennsylvania at the time the army descended from the north, he would not be able "to communicate with the officer commanding it so soon as I could wish." He added that Albany could be taken by the army from the north, and that further progress of this army would be assisted by the numerous friends of the British government in that part of the country, so that it would "prove no difficult task to reduce the more rebellious parts" of the colony of New York. All that he undertook to do was to have a corps on the lower reaches of the river to open the communication obstructed by some recently constructed forts. In spite of this highly important intelligence, which Carleton received in due course and which he delivered to Burgoyne in Montreal on June 10, neither of them seems to have had any misgivings. The reason is obvious. The idea of Burgoyne conducting only half a campaign sprang from Saratoga and had no official existence prior to that fatal event.[41]

Though he received less support from the Canadians than he had anticipated, Burgoyne was full of confidence when he reached Skenesborough just before the middle of July. He had chased the Americans off Lake Champlain, and he was looking forward to enlisting hundreds of settlers in his army.[42] But his troubles soon began. Instead of friends he found foes; and instead of plentiful provisions he found a countryside laid waste. St. Leger's men were too few and his guns too light to take Fort Stanwix. In the latter part of August he retired, abandoning his stores and artillery.* This retreat, however, made little difference to the main body. It

---

* The Indians under Joseph Brant who accompanied the expedition did not retire with the white troops but pushed down the Mohawk and joined Burgoyne in a few days.

was already entangled in a hostile country and was commanded by an officer who was more than ever obsessed with the idea of doing what he could not do. Having more bravery than brains, he waited around on the upper Hudson until he was surrounded by vastly superior numbers and forced to surrender at Saratoga on October 17, 1777.

Though the course of Burgoyne's campaign does not really belong to the story of Canada, its outcome does. Measured by its results, the capitulation of Saratoga is one of the most important events in Canadian history. It precipitated the entry of France into the war, and the entry of France determined that the Americans were to be successful and all that that has meant for Canada. The immediate effect of the French declaration of war was twofold and contradictory. It rendered the colony on the St. Lawrence much more vulnerable, but at the same time it made it less likely to be attacked. The first is quite obvious, but the second requires explanation.

In the fall of 1778 congress adopted an elaborate plan, which had originated with Lafayette, for conquering Canada in the spring of 1779. American forces from various points were to advance on Detroit, Niagara, Oswego, and Montreal, while a French army was to sail up the St. Lawrence to take Quebec. A few days after this decision of congress, the French admiral in American waters, D'Estaing, printed an address designed to stir French feelings in Canadian hearts. Sedition was seething on the shores of the St. Lawrence and the end of Canada as a British colony seemed in sight. But Washington intervened, condemning the scheme before the French government passed any judgment upon it. In a letter to congress he heaped up all kinds of material objections, from the impossibility of subsisting the troops to the difficulty of coordinating forces operating from widely separated bases and the necessity of first clearing the old colonies of British forces. It was, he said, "not only too extensive and beyond our abilities, but too complex." To the president of congress he spoke his mind more fully. Would French troops surrender the key of Canada once they had secure possession of it? France, re-established on the St. Lawrence, and Spain, her ally controlling the mouth of the Mississippi, could throttle the United States. In the beginning of January, 1779, congress shelved the whole business.

But the American desire for Canada was not so easily killed, and Washington changed his mind about the designs of France. In the spring of 1780, and again in 1781 after Cornwallis' surrender at Yorktown, he revived the idea of a northern campaign. Then the French vetoed it, the first time on the ground that the proper objective was the British headquarters in New York, and the second time with the excuse that Louis XVI had joined the Americans in arms to help them win independence and not conquests. But behind these words lay a deeper reason. The French government calculated that Canada in the hands of Britain would make the Americans dependent on France, just as it had kept them dependent on Britain so long as it had remained in the hands of France. Neither of the allies wished the other to get Canada. They preferred Britain to keep it, and therefore she did.

CHAPTER XI

A REACTIONARY GOVERNMENT

THE outbreak of the American Revolution caught Canada at an awkward moment of transition from one form of government to another. On May 1, 1775, all previous provision for the civil administration of the colony, including the ordinances passed by governor and council and the commissions issued to judges and other officials, were annulled by the Quebec Act. Nearly two years elapsed before new arrangements replaced what had thus been destroyed.

To prevent a gap between the new and the old constitutions, or at least to bridge it as quickly and as completely as possible, the home government directed the governor to call the new council together on April 1, or as soon after as was convenient, to frame the necessary ordinances. For some unknown reason, Carleton did not obey this order. He had made no sign of summoning the legislature when the hostile activity of the insurgents on Lake Champlain and the Richelieu distracted his attention to the problem of military defense and led him to proclaim martial law on June 9. Not until this alarm passed and the summer wore on without any repetition of the attack on St. John did he approach the problem of civil reconstruction. He did not have to wait until the opening of the next regular legislative period in January, 1776, for the act allowed him and his council to pass ordinances at other seasons of the year if there were "some urgent occasion." He proposed to exercise this exceptional authority in the summer of 1775, for the disappearance of the courts of justice and of the law against selling intoxicants to the Indians had certainly provided an "urgent occasion."

Accordingly he inaugurated the new legislature on August 17, when all the twenty-two members named in the instructions assembled in the council chamber of the Castle of St. Louis. The opening session was almost entirely devoted to the taking of oaths and the reading of commissions. The only other business transacted on this day was the appointment of a committee to prepare two bills, one to create law courts and the other to stop the sale of liquor to red men.[1] Twice again the council sat before the serious invasion of the province suspended its session indefinitely, and the minutes of these meetings, held on September 2 and 5, record only the preparation and first two readings of the second measure.[2] What had happened to the other? Why, indeed, had it been referred to a committee? Chief Justice Hey had remained over the winter in England consulting with the home government upon the judicial system to be established, and he had the draft of an ordinance all ready for presentation to the council! [3]

The mystery is explained by the attitude of the majority of the members and of the governor. Led apparently by La Corne St. Luc, one of the new councilors, the legislature would not hear of jury trials in civil cases, which Hey's draft proposed. The clash is echoed in a letter written by the chief justice on August 28 after two meetings of the committee. Referring to the Canadians, he said: "The little I have seen of them in council gives me no idea of their abilities or moderation inflexible to any arguments either of expediency or justice. They will admit no alteration in their ancient laws, particularly in the article of commerce which I insist upon and believe shall carry in favour of the English merchants." [4]

Hey might have encountered no serious opposition if Carleton had obeyed his instructions, one clause of which commanded him "forthwith" to impart to the council the other clauses "wherein their advice and consent are mentioned to be requisite." Then the council would have seen that the home government had urged what the chief justice was proposing. As it was, Hey could not convert his colleagues, and the strange impression got abroad that it was he who had prevented the council from doing anything.

Although the first ordinance under the Quebec Act was not passed until 1777, the colony meanwhile was not left utterly devoid of judicial machinery. Anticipating some delay before the new courts could be erected, the governor had issued a proclamation on April 26, 1775, announcing that, under the authority granted by his commission, he had appointed six conservators of the peace with authority "to render all offenders against the law, and absconding debtors, amenable to justice, by obliging them to appear before such courts when the same shall be established," and as "commissioners for suing out civil process and causing the same to be executed." [5]

The conservators of the peace were Adam Mabane, Thomas Dunn, John Fraser, John Marteilhe, Jean Claude Panet, and Hertel de Rouville. The first four were the judges of the old courts of common pleas; the fifth was the outstanding Canadian lawyer in the capital; and the sixth, who had an estate at Chambly and resided in Montreal, had exercised a minor judicial office during the French régime. There is little doubt that Carleton had already selected these two new subjects to sit on the bench along with the previous four as soon as the new courts were set up.

The resumption of civil government occurred in the summer of 1776, although, so far as is known, the proclamation of martial law was not revoked. The province was then clear of "rebels," and the governor had made all his arrangements for building a fleet to pursue them over Lake Champlain. He was thus free to return to Quebec, as he said, "for the purpose of establishing courts of justice and other civil arrangements which were indeed much wanted." [6] In the latter part of July he issued a commission to the three conservators of the peace resident in Quebec, Mabane, Dunn, and Panet, appointing them "judges of a court of civil jurisdiction within the district of Quebec," [7] and he issued a similar commission for Montreal to Peter Livius, William Owen, and Gabriel Elzéar Taschereau. Livius and Owen were judges sent out from England, and Taschereau was a member of the well-known Canadian family. They replaced the three conservators of the peace who resided in Montreal. Marteilhe was incapacitated by illness [8] and the other two were prisoners in the old colonies. In August the governor also appointed justices of the peace.[9]

Why did not Carleton summon the council to do this and other necessary work in the summer of 1776? He should have done it and he knew it. The only excuse he gave to the secretary of state was very lame — that "neither the season or circumstances of the province" would permit him to call that body together.[10] His real reason was possibly a fear of what might happen in the council. Various circumstances had reduced its size and thereby altered its character.[11] Four members had been carried off prisoners, three had died, two were in England, and one was so old and infirm that he was unable to attend. Of the seven Canadians admitted by the new oath, six were excluded in one or other of these ways. Moreover, of the remaining twelve members who could appear, about half were willing, so it soon transpired, to placate the English-speaking minority in the colony by allowing them English law and trial by jury for civil suits. That the governor was uneasy over the personnel of the council is suggested by a letter to Germain in which he intimated that he was going to appoint four councilors to replace the three deceased and to fill the one original vacancy [12] — which would have been usurping an authority that he did not possess, his instructions empowering him only to nominate for the home government to appoint.

The same suggestion is conveyed by his creation at this very time of an inner or "privy" council. In addition to passing ordinances, for which the Quebec Act prescribed a quorum of a majority of the members, the consent of the council was necessary for various kinds of business, such as the passing of the public accounts and the granting of lands, for which the instructions prescribed a quorum of five. On August 8, 1776, taking advantage of loose wording in this document, the governor appointed Cramahé and four others whom he thought he could trust — Hugh Finlay, who had charge of the post office, Thomas Dunn, John Collins, the deputy surveyor general, and Adam Mabane — to be a "board of privy council," and he empowered the lieutenant governor to summon any other member or members of the council whenever he thought necessary.[13] The truncated council of 1766 died in its cradle, but this "privy" council lived for several years before the home government, discovering its nature, killed it. During the interval the administration of the colony was in the hands of a select group of councilors. Of course there was grumbling among those who were excluded, but all save one kept very quiet about it, and the only one who dared challenge Carleton on the issue paid heavily for his temerity. He became a broken man, as will be explained below.

Legislation by proclamation was practiced sparingly during the abnormal suspension of the council from September, 1775. On June 25, 1776, to prevent the abuses against which the abortive ordinance of the previous September had been aimed, the governor issued a proclamation against selling rum and other spirituous liquors to Indians. This was before he returned to Quebec. He was also concerned over the supply of provisions in the country, but he did not venture to tackle this problem by himself. He referred it to his privy councilors at their first meeting. The old

council had commonly been consulted in the preparation of proclamations, except those of a routine nature, but Carleton thenceforth
consulted only the smaller body, though his proclamations sometimes stated that they were issued "by and with the consent of His
Majesty's council."

Having investigated the immediate resources of the province with
an eye to the needs of the population and of the army, the privy
councilors brought in a report on August 24, which, incidentally,
shows that the invasion had not greatly disturbed the agricultural
life of the country. The report stated that a large surplus of the
previous year's wheat was still on hand, that an abundant harvest
had already been gathered in the district of Montreal, and that the
crop in the Quebec district promised to be "fine and plentiful." It
also found that "the province does not superabound with live stock
and some persons are already buying up a number of oxen with a
view to export." It concluded by recommending a proclamation,
which the governor published six days later, placing an embargo
on cattle, flour, and biscuit except to the fisheries, Nova Scotia, and
the West Indies, and allowing the free export of wheat. When
navigation opened in 1777 the prohibition was extended to wheat,
but later in the season the embargo was lifted.[14]

The export of cattle seems to have been unusual, but a thriving
trade in the other articles had sprung up. The export of wheat had
risen to a maximum of 460,000 bushels in 1774, which must have
been fully as much as was consumed in the country. The drop to
175,000 bushels in the following year was due, at least in part, to
the invasion. The bulk of this grain had been shipped to the West
Indies and a considerable amount may have been sent to southern
Europe. The export of flour and biscuits was very much smaller,
the greatest quantity being 2,400 barrels of flour and 4,600 quintals
of biscuits in 1775. Most of the flour and biscuits went to the old
colonies until this proclamation stopped it. Though this would
appear to have been a subject for legislation by the full council, it
was dealt with by proclamation rather than ordinance until 1780.

The new constitution came into full operation in 1777, when
the provincial legislature at last began to function. Then it produced the greatest batch of ordinances in its history, sixteen in all.
On January 21, in obedience to a proclamation of seven weeks
before, twelve councilors gathered in the Castle of St. Louis. These

were all who could attend, the governor on second thought having wisely refrained from making any appointment on his own authority.[15] He opened the session of the legislative council, as it was now called to avoid confusion with the smaller group, with an address in which he commented upon "the interruption of all public business" and outlined the measures that ought to be considered.

This suggestion of a speech from the throne was something new in Quebec, but it now became an annual custom. This was in keeping with a change which came over the government of the colony at this time. Under the new constitution the governor inclined to be a viceroy and the council tended to imitate parliament. Though he had presided over the old council and had been an active member of it, he now stood aloof. The new legislature always deliberated apart from him [16] and soon it began to meet under a separate roof. From 1780 it sat regularly in a council chamber prepared across the way in the Bishop's Palace. It saw the governor only on ceremonial occasions, when he opened or closed its sessions or passed ordinances under his signature and the great seal of the province, for which formalities it continued to repair at his summons to the council chamber in the Castle of St. Louis.

The governor's old place at the head of the board was taken by the senior member, who was known officially as the president of the council. The lieutenant governor was of course the senior member and the chief justice ranked next. As before the Quebec Act, each bill was usually prepared by a committee, but in 1777 for the first time the council followed the parliamentary rule of reading each bill three times before submitting it to the governor for his assent. This was rarely withheld. Carleton never refused,[17] because he did not need to. He kept such a close rein upon the legislature that it never produced a bill which he disliked. Under Haldimand there was some independence, but with a single exception, he bowed to the will of the majority on the few occasions when it differed from his own. Only two ordinances passed by the new council were disallowed by the home government.[18] This constitutes a marked contrast with the heavy mortality among the legislative children of the old council. The difference is largely explained by the much wider lawmaking powers conferred by the Quebec Act.

The establishment of law courts was the first item on the program submitted by the governor on January 21, and the first business

undertaken by the council when it assembled two days later to commence its regular work. After a month of discussion it passed its
first two ordinances, one establishing civil courts [19] and the other
regulating their procedure.[20] Then a bill to provide for the administration of criminal justice was introduced and rushed through in
two sittings.[21] The new judicial machinery was much the same as
that which had existed after the reform of 1770 — a court of king's
bench, a commission of the peace, and two courts of common pleas,
one in Quebec and the other in Montreal, from which appeals lay to
the council and from the council to the king.* Two old subjects
who had become seigniors, James Cuthbert of Berthier and Conrad
Gugy of Machiche, desired a return to the days when seigniors
appointed local judges and the intendant summarily decided disputes touching seigniorial rights, but their proposals were shelved
and never heard of again.[22]

There is little to criticize in the machinery the council created
but there is much to criticize in the legal system it allowed to come
into operation. It accepted the criminal law of England and the
civil law of New France without making the adjustments intended
by the home government to satisfy the people in the colony. The
minutes record no effort to humanize and modernize the barbarous
and antiquated criminal law of that day, though Hey's draft ordinance had proposed a beginning by substituting fine and imprisonment for the penalty of burning in the hand. Nor does there appear
to have been any consideration given to the principle of the Habeas
Corpus Act. Perhaps the psychology born of the Revolution explains
the silence on these two points. But the two major issues raised by
Hey in August, 1775, were not passed over in silence, though he
was no longer present, for he had retired to England and resigned
his commission. In spite of an announcement by Cramahé that
"the governor would not pass any ordinance in which mention is
made of juries," a motion was introduced requiring judges to follow the "laws and customs of England" in determining commercial
disputes and providing for optional juries for commercial cases

---

* The new king's bench lacked the civil jurisdiction which the old court possessed concurrently with the common pleas, and also its right to hear appeals from
the common pleas. The dividing line between civil suits which required two judges
and were subject to appeal and those which could be settled summarily by one judge
was reduced from twelve pounds to ten pounds. Captains of militia were empowered to serve locally as coroners and as justices of the peace. They replaced the
bailiffs.

involving more than ten pounds. It should have passed, for it proposed merely to continue the English-speaking minority in the enjoyment of rights which conflicted with neither the interests of the Canadians nor the safety of the state, and probably it would have passed had it not been for Carleton's ultimatum, for it was lost by a vote of only seven to five. Moreover, the bill denying the two things postulated by the motion was not enacted, as were the other two judicial bills, for an indefinite period. It was to expire in two years' time,* when, said the lieutenant governor, a fuller board would consider the matter. This limiting clause appears in two other measures of the session and was the brand of an "unpleasing ordinance." The only concession allowed the racial minority was the English law of evidence in commercial suits.

The defeat of the motion was an important event in Canadian history. Though a majority of the members, on whichever side they voted, hoped for a change at the end of two years, they became a minority before that time arrived, and for years the council refused to alter what it had accepted in 1777, regarding as final what had been intended merely as the imperfect beginning of a Canadian jurisprudence. In addition to being more lasting than anticipated, the result of that vote was more far-reaching than appears upon the surface. If ever civil juries were needed, they were needed in Canada at this time because of the nature of the bench. It was occupied by members of the French party who were filled with strong prejudices against the British-born merchants as a class. Thus the latter now saw the determination of the facts in all their civil cases taken out of the hands of their fellows — the jurymen — and placed in the hands of their political foes — the judges. Nor was this the extent of their suffering. The old subjects were also robbed of the law merchant of Europe, which had governed all their business transactions.

This strange result, not at all contemplated in 1774 when the new constitution was prepared, followed because the law merchant, though codified in Colbert's day for application in the towns of France, had never been formally introduced into New France, where commercial life had remained relatively limited and simple. Not until after the conquest, when this life was expanded by the

* The instructions forbade the enactment of any legislation for any period shorter than two years.

old subjects who settled there, does the law merchant of Europe seem to have entered Canada. Then it came as an adjunct of English law, having been adopted by the courts in England. It was swept aside by the rejection of the motion, and its substitute was intolerable. The courts were forced to fall back upon the laws and customs of the colony as they existed at the close of the French régime. It is therefore necessary to examine what were these laws and customs. The *coutume de Paris* was the foundation and main body of the law of New France, but it was so antiquated and inapplicable that it had long since been abandoned in France, if indeed it had ever been used, for the determination of commercial suits. The only French law of commerce was the compilation referred to above and known as the *code marchand*. Because it had never been registered in the *conseil supérieur* of Quebec, the colonial counterpart of the French parlement, legal theory could deny its extension to Canada. On the other hand the practice of the preconquest courts had violated this constitutional principle, for at times they had enforced unregistered edicts. In other words, the only law that was undoubtedly in force did not apply, and the only law that might possibly apply was of doubtful validity. No better were the preconquest customs, save in a few particulars connected with the operations of the fur trade. The general consequence was that when English-speaking merchants brought their affairs into the courts under the Quebec Act they were at the mercy of their enemies, the judges, who were able to exercise an arbitrary power which has seldom been paralleled in the courts of western civilization.

Thus were the British-born merchants forced to drain the dregs of the cup of bitterness. Their first draughts, downed in Murray's day, may have reduced some swollen pride, but the medicine had become a poison. The denial of an assembly had turned the heads of some, and, coming on top of this, the denial of their rights under the civil law turned the hearts of more. They abominated the unjust rule of Frenchmen and of Englishmen who were, if anything, more French than the French, and their pent-up feelings contributed not a little to the racial strife which tore Lower Canada in the first half of the nineteenth century.

The fatal turn in 1777 was due to Carleton. He had been ordered to tell the council that the home government expected it to pass certain legislation to protect the rights of the racial minority. Not only did he withhold this information, but, through his "fidus Achates," he actually threatened the council when it contemplated doing one of the very things which he was instructed to have done. Perhaps he had an uneasy conscience over the abolition of civil juries. At the very session in which he signed this "unpleasing ordinance," a committee was named and ordered, in consultation with merchants outside the council, to prepare a plan for a chamber of commerce.[23] Four weeks later the committee submitted such a scheme for the city and district of Quebec. All merchants who cared to subscribe were to elect a board of directors, who, in addition to passing by-laws, were to serve as a jury in commercial disputes submitted by the interested parties.[24] In his correspondence home, the governor distinctly referred to the proposal as a substitute for juries in the civil courts,[25] but nothing came of it, though the council continued in session for a month after the committee made its report.[26]

If Carleton ever gave an excuse for his delinquency, which was not discovered until after he ceased to be governor, it has not yet been found. But one may easily surmise why he defeated the home government's purpose of preserving a just balance between the rights of the English-speaking minority and those of the French-speaking majority. His predilection in favor of a well-ordered society encouraged the upper-class Canadians in their natural belief that the country really belonged to them and their people, and the revival of their old laws seemed to prove it. Why should they weaken the proof by making any concession to intruding merchants whose only interest in the country was the profit that they could make out of it? This appears to have been the attitude of the Canadian noblesse and of the few old subjects, like Adam Mabane, who completed the circle within which the governor moved. His prejudice coincided with their prejudice, and they were the only people in Canada whom he really knew and trusted * at a time when the foundations of the empire were shaking. His failure to inform the home government that he had not obeyed his instructions probably sprang from a fear that officials in London would not see conditions on the St. Lawrence as he saw them. One is tempted to find an excuse in his distrust of Germain, but his quarrel with that minister

* The clergy were an exception to the above statement, but they seem to have exercised no influence in this connection.

had nothing to do with the beginning of his fault. It began in 1775 before Dartmouth was succeeded by the "coward" of Minden.

Another and pleasanter feature of the government of the colony, though not unconnected with the one just described, is suggested by a provision in the first article of the ordinance regulating the procedure of the civil courts. It required every writ of summons to be in the language of the defendant. Although this was its only legal recognition, bilingualism had been growing ever since the official use of French disappeared at the end of the military régime. In practice the new courts were completely bilingual. They had dual clerks and records, and no one seems to have questioned the right of the French language to be on an equal footing with the English in the administration of justice. Indeed, on one occasion in the Montreal court of common pleas, according to the evidence produced at the investigation in 1787, Hertel de Rouville, pretending ignorance of English, insisted on an English barrister addressing the court in French. When the barrister turned to repeat his speech in his own tongue for the benefit of the other occupant of the bench, who really knew no French, Rouville stopped him, saying that this was quite unnecessary because he himself would interpret it to his brother judge, and straightway he displayed a knowledge that he had just denied. After the Quebec Act, as before it, all proclamations were published in French and English, and ordinances were passed in the same manner.[27] Though the minutes of the legislative council and of the "privy" council, like the records of their single predecessor, were kept only in English, French was now spoken at the council board. Indeed, it tended to supplant English as the language of debate, because it was the only medium with which all members were familiar.

Until 1785 little was added to the legislation of 1777, most of which was a re-enactment, with a few amendments, of the ordinances that had expired with the old constitution. Some of these measures, together with the register of the Montreal court of quarter sessions, which has been preserved, lift the curtain of time that has fallen over the everyday life of the people of that age. Habitants flocked regularly [28] into the two populous centers of Quebec and Montreal, bringing livestock, grain, hay, garden produce, and other articles for sale in the markets, which opened at six A. M. in summer and at eight A. M. in winter. Butchers and hucksters tried to forestall the purchasing public, but the law imposed a fine of five pounds for buying during the first three or four hours of the market if the goods were to be resold. Even an ordinary citizen in search of supplies for his own household was fined twenty shillings if he purchased them before they reached the market place, where all country produce, whether brought by cart or canoe, had to be exposed before sale. The one exception to this rule was designed to encourage dwellers on the south shore and in the more distant parts of the province who brought their goods in "schooners, sloops and other such like craft." They could sell on board if they gave previous notice to the townsfolk by means of the bellman. Even then, butchers and other middlemen had to wait three hours before making their purchases. All the penalties were for buying and none for selling, because their purpose was to protect the producer as well as the consumer.

In addition to the above regulations imposed by ordinance, the justices of the peace established many others. Butchers were a common sight in the Montreal market and a common worry to the authorities. They had to be prevented from slaughtering in the market place, and they had to be forced "to keep three feet round, behind and before, their stalls always clean from filth and dirt." [29] The ordinary rate for a stand in the market was twopence a day in 1766 and one shilling and threepence in 1780. Butchers with permanent stalls were each charged twelve shillings a year in 1766 and twenty in 1780, and a number of them lived up to their reputation for being troublesome by refusing to pay. The fees were collected by the clerk of the market, who kept the place clean and was in regular attendance to preserve order and to inspect the weights and measures used. [30]

On the first Monday of each month, in Quebec and Montreal, the commissioners of the peace, or any three of them, were required to meet and fix the assize of bread, [31] and the regulations which they then drew up they had to publish in the *Quebec Gazette*. To prevent evasion of the assize, the clerks of the market were empowered to inspect bakeries and other places where bread was sold, [32] and every loaf manufactured for sale had to bear the mark of the baker's initials. Unsigned bread was to be confiscated for the use of the poor or of the prisoners in jail, and any baker found guilty of turning out underweight loaves was to be fined forty shillings.

Another important regulation, which originated in 1769, was framed to meet a serious difficulty which had arisen in Quebec and Montreal twice a year. In the spring and fall, when the roads were very bad, the country people could not bring in their supplies of grain and other provisions, and there was a consequent temporary shortage of food and rise of prices. Many bakers made matters worse by shutting up their shops at these times when their profits were reduced. Their customers then flocked to the other bakers, who were often unable to meet this exceptional demand because they had laid in a stock sufficient only for their own regular trade. There ensued "a great and unnecessary scarcity and dearness of bread" which was "very grievous to the poorer sort of inhabitants." The council therefore required every baker to find two bondsmen, each of whom would deposit a security of ten pounds to guarantee that he would continue to ply his trade continuously for at least a year without any intermission longer than three days, and ruled that anyone baking and selling without having entered into such a recognizance was to be fined five pounds each time he was caught. Montreal had two dozen bakers in 1780.[33] Quebec seems to have had fewer.

The above ordinance on markets and bakers applied also to Three Rivers before the Quebec Act, but not afterward. As far as its food supply was concerned, this place was still in the happy position of a rural village. In the way its few houses were crowded together, however, it resembled the larger centers of Quebec and Montreal, and therefore was not excluded from the application of the legislation to reduce fire risks when this was re-enacted in 1777. The old law [34] had been twice altered and now there was further amendment because fires were a frequent occurrence and everyone knew how disastrous they might be. In Montreal on May 18, 1765, over one hundred houses, containing double that number of families, were destroyed with a loss in buildings, merchandise, furniture, and apparel amounting to nearly ninety thousand pounds, and about three years later ninety houses, two churches, and a charity school went up in flames. The former conflagration started from hot ashes carried into a garret to make soap, and the latter began in an outhouse. Needless to say, legislation prohibited people from putting hot ashes on wooden floors or in wooden vessels and from lighting any fire in an outhouse.

Much commoner was the danger that lurked in the chimneys. Quebec, Three Rivers, and Montreal each had an official, appointed by the governor, who was first called the overseer of chimneys; but he had more than chimneys to look after, and therefore, from 1777, he was termed overseer to prevent accidents by fire. He was responsible for having every chimney used in town or suburb swept and scraped once a month.* He employed his own sweeps, paying them out of what he collected from the occupants of the houses at a rate of sixpence a chimney each time it was cleaned. He was fined five shillings for each neglected flue and an additional forty shillings if one took fire. The same fines were imposed on occupants who refused to have their chimneys swept. Each house had to be supplied with two buckets, a hatchet, two fire poles, and ladders. The fire poles were ten feet long and five inches thick and had crossbars at intervals of six inches. They were used for knocking off roofs of houses that were on fire or in danger of catching fire. The ladders had to be attached to the house with iron hooks or bolts, and so arranged that one could run up to the top of any chimney. A householder was fined five shillings if his dwelling lacked any of the prescribed articles and an additional forty shillings if it took fire. Unless he was the owner, however, he did not need to pay for these things, for he could deduct their cost from his rent.

The ordinance also contained a number of building regulations designed to reduce the fire hazard. The erection of wooden houses was absolutely prohibited. All new houses had to have their gable-end walls raised three feet above the roof, for the houses were commonly built in terraces with their gables parallel to the street, and though fire could not penetrate the stone walls which separated them, it might run along the roofs. The use of shingles, which had become common since the conquest, was closely restricted because they took dangerous wings in the event of a fire. Boards or other more substantial materials had to be used except over garret windows, around chimneys, at angles where two roofs joined, and where the roof boards joined the walls.

Another recent innovation, which reflects an expanding population, was the division of old houses into tenements. This necessi-

* In September, 1778, Quebec had 628 houses and 1,002 chimneys in use, according to the report of the overseer Franks, the father of the "giddy-headed insolent spark."

tated new fireplaces, which were connected with the old chimneys by oblique and twisted flues.[35] Such flues were doubly dangerous, for they could not be cleaned and they might collapse if the building burned. They therefore had to be removed or stopped up permanently.[36]

In Montreal, where the greatest losses had occurred, there was also a voluntary organization known as the Union Fire Society, which undertook the construction of a public reservoir with conduits leading to basins in other parts of the town. In February, 1771, this organization appealed to the council for assistance and procured a vote of one hundred pounds to complete the work.[37]

For the local government of Quebec and Montreal, including the suburbs, the council contemplated some permanent regulations in 1777, but it did not frame them because it approached the problem too late in the busy session. It applied, therefore, a "temporary remedy," which became a permanent provision by a regular re-enactment.[38] The "temporary remedy" was the old one of throwing the responsibility for the local government of these places upon the justices of the peace. At their general quarter sessions they were authorized "to make such rules and orders" as they deemed necessary and to decree fines up to forty shillings to enforce obedience. These orders were always published through the mouth of the town bellman and sometimes also in the pages of the *Quebec Gazette*. Anyone charged with breaking one of these regulations could be tried summarily by a single justice.

The records of the Montreal court of quarter sessions show that butchers in the market were no greater problem than publicans in their taverns. These friends and enemies of mankind debauched the servants of others and the soldiers of the king. One of their favorite devices, which was stopped with difficulty, was to keep billiard tables on which their guests decided "who pays?" It was stopped by an order to the proprietors to remove the tables if they wished to keep their licenses.[39] The game must have been quite popular, for the existence of other and more innocent billiard rooms is attested by a court order that they shut their doors on the Sabbath.[40] Genuine beggars armed with clergymen's licenses were tolerated by law. But adult imposters and juvenile imitators were not. To save the latter from a life of idleness, the magistrates ordered people to chase them away and at the same time threatened the gamins with chastisement.[41] Among other undesirables roaming the streets were horses, cattle, mastiffs, and, on one occasion, a herd of goats.[42]

The speed mania still attacked drivers, who still attacked pedestrians, just as in the days of the military régime. The ordinance passed in 1764, imposing the appropriate punishment of four days' hard labor on the roads on all reckless drivers who refused to pay fines, was not revived in 1777. But this made little difference. Thenceforth the justices of the peace had to tackle the problems as best they could, and they did it by new regulations much like the old ones.[43]

In Quebec and Montreal the commissioners of the peace were required by law to fix a tariff for the carriage of goods by cart, truck, or sled, and at least in Montreal they obliged each carter to take out a license and to have a tin plate with his number attached to his conveyance.[44] The magistrates of Montreal also wrestled with the old nuisance of people dumping filth on the streets and over the walls, and with what may have been a new nuisance — sinks and gutters discharging in the streets.[45] In 1766 they ordered every householder to "pave, flag and repair the foot path" in front of his premises, and fourteen years later they specified that the sidewalk must be four feet broad "in the big streets of St. Paul and Notre Dame" and two feet and a half in the cross streets.[46]

The repair of roads and bridges in the country was regulated by ordinance and managed after the fashion of the French régime when a *grand voyer,* or surveyor general of the highways, issued necessary orders to the inhabitants through militia captains and reported to the intendant. Now instead of a single *grand voyer* there were two, one for the district of Quebec and the other for the district of Montreal. Before the Quebec Act they operated through the bailiffs and under the eyes of the justices of the peace; from 1777 they used militia officers as officials and were under the more immediate supervision of the governor and council and of the judges of the common pleas on circuit.

As of old, each owner or occupier was responsible for maintaining the roads, bridges, and ditches adjoining his land, except when the burden was so great that it had to be spread over others as well. The ordinance laid down that the highroads were to be thirty feet wide and the byroads twenty feet, with ditches and fences on either side. The *grand voyer* was to command the fences to be removed in winter wherever they might cause drifts of snow to block the way. In the fall, before the ground was frozen, the sides of each road had to be marked every twenty-four feet by poles eight feet long, commonly little pine trees bound to stakes driven into the soil; and throughout the winter, after every snowfall or drifting, the people had to get out and beat a smooth passage wide enough for two sleighs. No horses or hogs were to be allowed to run loose on the roads. Occasionally, however, some hogs played havoc with the surface of the highways, to the great annoyance of the traveling public.[47] The law was also very explicit about bridges. They were to be eighteen feet wide, with sleepers of cedar, floors of ash or red spruce logs well squared, and side rails three feet high continued at each end out to the ditches. Wherever they were in danger of being flooded, bridges had to be loaded with large stones. During the first ten years or so of British rule there were complaints that the highways had degenerated since the conquest, but afterward there seems to have occurred an improvement in the tempers of travelers, if not an improvement in the roads.

The only measure passed by the council in 1777 that was not designed to restore something destroyed by the Quebec Act was the militia ordinance. This declared that with a few general exceptions [48] all inhabitants of the colony between the ages of sixteen and sixty were bound to serve in the militia of their respective parishes. The captain of each parish had to assemble all the men of his company "to inspect their arms, fire at marks, and instruct them in their duties," on the last two Sundays of June and the first two of July and at other times when ordered by militia inspectors or other senior officers. From the various companies, officers and men could be drafted for special service with the regular troops wherever and whenever the governor commanded. Furthermore, all tenants *en roture* had to furnish carts, sleighs, or other vehicles for the public service when summoned through their militia captains, for which duty the inhabitants of each parish were to be detailed in rotation and paid at rates fixed by the commander-in-chief. Another clause made every militia officer responsible for arresting all deserters, stragglers, suspected emissaries of the "rebellious" colonies, or "persons spreading false reports to the detriment

of government and persons leaving the province without a pass,"
and forbade anyone's harboring such miscreants.

As might be expected, the ordinance bristled with penalties. For
refusing to enroll or to perform carriage duties there was a fine of
five pounds; for a second refusal, the fine was repeated and the culprit was forbidden to keep any firearm under pain of still another
five pound fine and a month in jail. These penalties were doubled
for those who refused to go on draft. The obligation to perform
double carriage duties at half price was added to the above punishments as a matter of course, but was the sole penalty attached to
expulsion from the militia for other improper conduct. A fine of
ten shillings was prescribed for each unexcused absence from a
regular muster.

During the debates on this measure, the chief criticism came
from Hugh Finlay. He had dozens of Canadians scattered through
the province to forward the mails, and through these individuals
he could feel the pulse of the people better perhaps than any other
British-born subject in the country. In addition to seeking exemption for post-office employees, which was refused, he sought some
provision to favor those who had remained faithful in the presence
of the enemy. He admitted that most of the habitants merited punishment. "Yet," he said, "it may be an impolitic step to chastise
them at present, and perhaps it may be the wisest measure to forgive them at last." Therefore he suggested two amendments to
lighten the burden on all. One was to adopt the practice of the
ancien régime of clothing and equipping the militia when ordered
on service, and the other was to remove the existing complaints of
the peasants "that under pretence of being on the king's service
people have forced their horses from them without payment." Finlay's words of wisdom did not move his colleagues, who insisted
on a measure that alienated the habitants.[49] This was another "objectionable" measure which was re-enacted before it expired.

The militia ordinance made little difference to the Canadians
except in the way they were punished. It was now relatively precise
and specific. It had been quite clumsy and general; for example,
in the fall of 1776, Carleton had ordered the rawest troops to be
cantoned in mutinous parishes and had had their officers remain
to take care of them. For nearly two years the governor had been
trying with indifferent success to force the people to perform militia

service and corvée duty, and he continued to insist while they continued to resist and to suffer for it.[50] Now, as the tide of war had rolled back from the province, he laid more emphasis upon the corvée, or forced labor for the government, of which the carriage duties mentioned in the ordinance were only one aspect raised into prominence by the necessity of transporting Burgoyne's army south. In spite of the implied promise in the ordinance, only a few who were called out on corvée — "artificers employed in their professions"—seem to have been paid regular wages;[51] some may have been supplied with blankets and shoes;[52] many toiled for nothing, unless kicks and curses be counted.[53]

The governor admitted the "great inconveniences" [54] of this inequality, which apparently he did not know how to avoid, and he made some effort to adjust the burden. He ordered a smaller proportion of men to be drawn from those parts of the country which had borne the weight of the invasion.[55] He also took into account the differences between urban and rural life. On the one hand, because town-dwellers could not be spared from their daily tasks so easily as habitants from their holdings, he directed the former to be used as little as possible and then to be given some allowance.[56] On the other hand, he commanded the corvée to cease at harvest time, except for deserters who were caught.[57]

But such consideration as was shown could not make any impression upon Canadian resistance. At least half the men sent to help move Burgoyne's army never reached Ticonderoga, which was their destination,[58] and in the following year Haldimand asked the Montreal colonel of the militia to supply a list of all who had refused to go on corvée that he might prohibit their employment by the merchants in the up-country trade.[59] A perusal of the records of that day leaves the impression that the habitants, when called out for such service, regarded themselves as public slaves. This was very natural. Since the conquest they had known no corvée, save what was necessary to repair their own roads, and the revival of this objectionable feature of the *ancien régime* inspired a sullen resentment against British authority in England and in Canada.

No happier than the habitants or the mercantile minority was the governor himself. He had seen his fond illusions shattered, and he was obliged to take orders from a man whom he abominated. The peevish tone of his letters to Germain has been already referred to in the discussion of military arrangements. He was just as ill tempered and wrong-headed in his correspondence over civil appointments.[60] He told Germain that he had refrained from filling the vacancies in the council with his own nominees "as the delay could not prove so offensive to them or hurtful to the king's service, as after some time enjoying the office to find themselves turned out of their seats by your lordship, and others set up whom they might with some reason deem deserving of little favour from the crown." [61] Not a word did he breathe of his own legal incapacity to fill these vacancies. In his desire to pick a quarrel he unjustly accused the secretary of state of foisting placemen upon the Canadian establishment to the injury of worthy individuals who were thus robbed of their offices. He even blamed him for stirring up factious intrigues against the government in Canada!

To this monstrous and absolutely unsupported charge the minister replied with a well-merited rebuke. But taking their correspondence as a whole, Germain appears to have been as anxious to avoid taking offense as Carleton was to give it. Indeed, an examination of the governor's dispatches suggests that he was trying to dare the minister into recalling him. His own brother gave him away when he wrote to a friend in England that his "correspondence with *Cain* will not dispose the latter to continue him in his government." It was perhaps fortunate for him that he sent his resignation when he did, but he was certainly unfortunate in not being able to leave the province until the following summer. Early in August, 1777, a month after Carleton's resignation reached the prime minister, Germain summoned Frederick Haldimand from a holiday at his home in Switzerland, informing him that he was appointed governor of Quebec and should repair to his post as soon as possible. Hurrying back to England, the new governor sailed late in September in a frigate which was to bring home the old governor, but contrary winds forced the vessel to put back in October. The embittered Carleton was thus obliged to spend another winter in Canada, and before he could turn over the reins of government to his successor things were to happen that have done his memory no good.

Of the three judges sent out from the mother country after the passage of the Quebec Act, two were weak and colorless individuals, but the third was not.[62] That was why Peter Livius came to

Canada. The son of a German father [63] who seems to have been in English employ in Lisbon, he had become a member of the English bar, a fellow of the Royal Society, and a doctor of laws of Harvard, and he had risen to uncomfortable prominence in New Hampshire. There he practiced law for some years until he was promoted to the bench and admitted to the council. Being one of those persons who annoy by being always in the right, he was soon embroiled with the governor, whose administration was not "simon pure." He was dropped from the bench and gagged in the council. He appealed to the privy council in London, who upheld him but administered only a reprimand to the governor. The latter was allowed to remain at his post because he had some good qualities and may have had some influence. Though vindicated, Livius feared to return to New Hampshire, where his political enemies were still in power and full of malice. From this intolerable prospect he appealed to Dartmouth, who sent him out to Canada with the understanding that he might succeed Hey as chief justice. The secretary of state recommended him highly to the governor. Dartmouth said that he would appoint Livius to the council as soon as Carleton agreed, and he suggested that meanwhile the newcomer be granted a seigniory. Though the governor obeyed neither suggestion,[64] his relations with Livius seem to have been unclouded for about two years.

Cramahé was the first to cross the path of Livius. In the late summer and early autumn of 1777, when the latter had become chief justice and the former was in charge of the government during the absence of Carleton in the upper part of the province, they clashed in the court of appeals. Livius knew more law than all the rest of the members put together, and he and Cramahé fought over the confinement of a tanner and his wife who were arrested for babbling sedition. At Cramahé's orders they had been lodged in the military prison to prevent any possibility of their being bailed.

This use of military authority to tie the hands of civil authority roused the old champion of righteousness in government. Livius rated the provost marshal for asserting that he would not release the prisoners without an order from Cramahé, and he scolded the lieutenant governor for flouting the law. "As chief justice," he said, "I and I only in this province, while civil law prevails, have lawful authority to commit without expressing a cause . . . and it is my duty to take care that so extraordinary a power shall not be usurped." Livius was not seeking to release the prisoners if any good cause for their detention could be shown, but rather to substitute legality for illegality. Both disputants appealed to the governor, who upheld Livius but shielded Cramahé by making the provost marshal a scapegoat.

Not until about the close of 1777 did any friction arise between Livius and Carleton, and then, as usual, the former was right. Having discovered in some way now unknown that the governor had defeated the purpose of the home government by secreting his instructions on the question of the laws and by creating the "privy" council, the chief justice tendered him some "private advice" on these two points. As this approach had no result, except perhaps to convert Carleton into a sullen foe, Livius then waited until the meeting of the legislative council provided him with an opportunity for more effective action.

Several important issues came up at the session of the legislative council in 1778. The first was raised by Carleton in his opening address on March 23, in which he urged the council to examine the whole system of fees and to enact a reasonable scale. He confined his attention to this one point and obviously intended it to be the principal business discussed.[65] On the following day the council resolved itself into two committees to explore the matter. After a month's labor they had their reports ready for legislative action on April 25, when, as will presently appear, something very unexpected happened.

Meanwhile the council met from time to time for the discussion of other questions. One was brought forward by William Grant of St. Roch. Sir Thomas Mills, still receiver general and still an absentee, had made him his deputy, and as such the home government had thought wise to place him in one of the vacant council seats. Grant was naturally concerned over the neglected casual and territorial revenue, and he desired a bill to enforce its collection. Twice he proposed it and twice it was rejected.[66] Possibly the seigniorial members were not eager to pay their mutation fines, but this problem will be discussed in a later chapter.

Another measure was sought by Finlay, who was wrestling with a difficult problem in his management of the post-office. The *maîtres de poste,* whom he had engaged to forward the mails from stage to stage through the country, were used and sometimes abused by the traveling public. Many of them complained that they would have to throw up their contracts unless they were organized in a regulated system for the conveyance of the traveling public as well as the mail bags. Finlay therefore proposed what appears to have been a very sensible bill to establish posthouses, which, in return for a monopoly, would be obliged to keep sufficient horses and vehicles to perform their dual function, to maintain a regular service, and to abide by a fixed tariff of charges.[67]

Back in the fall of 1776, understanding that Carleton desired such a measure, he had sent him a plan and had given Cramahé the draft of an ordinance to be passed in the session of 1777. The draft was returned to its author and then placed on the table. But when Finlay desired the clerk of the council to read it, the lieutenant governor announced that the governor would pass no ordinance regulating posthouses. This strange turn may have been the postmaster's reward for criticizing the militia ordinance and for supporting the motion in favor of English law and of juries in commercial cases. He bowed to authority and withdrew the bill.

When presenting his motion in 1778, Finlay expressed regret for this withdrawal, asserting his belief that the governor would not have vetoed the bill had it been supported by a majority.[68] Though the motion was lost, it was by a majority of only one.[69] On April 23, when the fees committees reported and the council was therefore readier to consider other business, Finlay renewed his proposal, and this time he secured a vote of two to one to proceed with the measure at the next meeting [70] — the memorable one of April 25.

A fourth subject debated during the session was the temper of the people. This was raised by Henry Caldwell, who, like Grant, had recently secured a seat at the board. He introduced a series of motions, the first of which was for the amendment of the militia ordinance. Though all these motions were voted down,[71] the matter did not rest here, for Finlay, who had supported Caldwell, revived the question on April 23. He referred to "the discontent reigning in the country" and observed that the peasants had reason for complaint, because they were forced to perform services and to supply various things for little or nothing, and they were illegally oppressed by the militia captains. He urged three reforms. One was that every habitant who performed a corvée or was commanded to provide anything, such as firewood for the troops, should receive a reasonable price for his labor and the value of whatever he furnished. To insure this he proposed that certificates specifying what he did or gave should be issued by his militia captain. To stop the prevailing abuses of power by the militia captains, Finlay proposed that each parish priest, according to the ancient custom, be required to read the ordinances to his people on the first Sunday of every month. The trouble, he said, was due to ignorance. Nine-tenths of the militia officers and a very much larger proportion of the people being illiterate, the former imagined that they had much more authority than the law allowed and the latter believed that they had to obey every order delivered with a tone of authority.

"Let us endeavour," he pleaded, "to avert the fatal consequences that may attend that spirit of disgust which is but too general and rankles in the hearts of our fellow subjects of this country. This is a critical juncture. The Canadians, in sound policy, ought not to be irritated, let us strive to conciliate their affections. The first proper step towards regaining their confidence would be to shew them that the late ordinances were not intended to scourge but to protect them." The ears of Finlay's colleagues were no longer stopped and it was agreed that the whole business should be considered at the next meeting [72] — on the fateful April 25.

Livius did not broach the problem that was worrying him until a fortnight after the session had begun. Then he moved that the governor "be humbly requested" to communicate his instructions bearing on legislation "in order that this legislative council may dutifully endeavour to conform themselves to His Majesty's intentions." The motion was ordered to be translated for consideration at the next meeting, when it was lost by a vote of eleven to five.[73] After this defeat, the chief justice waited until April 23, which seems to have been a sort of "field day" in the council, before he raised his second point in a lengthy motion. After a preamble which explained how a select knot of councilors had been passing the public accounts and doing other public business as if they were the whole council, and observed "that these proceedings are irregular and illegal, tend to introduce confusion, uncertainty and discontent, and if not timely remedied will give opportunity and means of collusion and impunity to future peculation and perversion of public money under any future governor," the motion called for "an humble address" to the governor stating these premises and praying for "convenient remedy." This too was ordered to be translated and considered at the next meeting, when it might have secured the support of the majority, for, unlike his earlier motion, this made a personal appeal to every member who had been excluded from the select circle.

Carleton was being cornered. When the council reassembled on Saturday morning, April 25, the decks all cleared for legislative action to begin, there was no action at all. The lieutenant governor produced an order from the governor proroguing the legislative council until further notice.[74] Thus did Carleton, to save his own skin, blow up the important work of the session, including the measure on which his mind was set — an ordinance to establish fees on a satisfactory basis.

The spirit of independence had sprouted in this session, and Carleton, not content to nip it in the bud, determined to pluck it up by the roots. The majority had begun to follow after Finlay, and apparently they were about to support Livius in his dangerous motion. Therefore, like Irving and Mabane in 1766, these two individuals had to be punished. Finlay found that he was dropped from the "privy" council, which now met frequently,[75] and he saw other signs that he had fallen from grace. Having small means and a large family, he could take no chances with fate. The blossoming or blighting of his career seemed to depend on whether the favor of the governor was extended or withheld. But it would be unfair to him, one of the most worthy and even lovable men in the colony, to imply that he was moved by economic motives only. He had a fine nature and he was painfully wounded by the slights cast upon him.

Seeking counsel with his friends, he learned that his offense lay in the motions he had made. Thereupon he wrote Carleton a most pathetic letter in which he said: "I have not been called to council since the prorogation of the legislative body, and this hurts me, because I conceive that your Excellency intends it as a mark of your disapprobation of my conduct, and to be punished without being heard sits hard on me. I have ever studied to merit your good opinion." He then reviewed his own conduct in the last two sessions, explaining that he had never canvassed the opinions of other members, that he had always detested the spirit of faction, and that everything he had done had been solely to advance the welfare of the country. "If I have erred," he confessed, "I regret that my mistake has offended you." [76] He retracted nothing, for he was too honest; he simply pleaded for a hearing that he might clear his character of evil imputations. What else passed between the haughty governor and the humble councilor is unknown, but there is reason for believing that the poor postmaster was not forgiven.[77]

Livius was not so easy to handle. The home government had placed him in an exalted position and nature had made him of tougher fiber than the sensitive Finlay. It was characteristic of both the governor and the chief justice that the latter observed no cloud on the brow of the former when they met during the last week of April. As Livius filled an ex officio seat at the board, Carleton could not remove him from the council without also dismissing him from his office of chief justice, and he had yet found no flaw in the head of the judicial administration. But, just as twelve years before, he lay in wait for an opportunity, and he thought that he had found it on the last day of April, when the council sat as a court of appeal on a case that had stirred live interest and livelier gossip for many a month. In 1776 a Montreal merchant named Dobie transacted some business with another named Carignan on a Sunday evening, and on the next morning "Carignan broke." Soon the rumor flew that Dobie had cheated Carignan's creditors. The rumor was true, but no one save Livius seems to have realized that Dobie had kept within the letter of the law. Therefore the public, including the governor, desired to see the merchant receive exemplary punishment. Dobie was sued, and when the judgment went against him he appealed.

Feeling was still strong when the case came up for hearing in Quebec. On the eve of the trial, Dobie's attorney, James Monk,[78] who happened to be a friend of Livius, went to the chief justice and advised him to remain away from court, saying that he knew what his opinion must be but that it could not swing the rest of the court and might do himself much harm after the offense given by his recent motions in council. But Livius was no man to be frightened from the path of duty. He went to court and made such a penetrating analysis of the law governing the case that a unanimous judgment was given for Dobie. The next morning the chief justice was "fired."

Thenceforth Livius knew nothing but trouble. Dumbfounded, he wrote the governor praying to be informed of the accusation against him, but all he received in return was an oral message "that there was no answer." Indeed, there could be no answer. Carleton had struck rashly and now he must have seen his blunder. Apparently he was puzzling over how he could put his action in the proper light to be reviewed in England. In his correspondence home he made no mention of what he had done until eight weeks had passed and he could delay no longer. His successor was coming up the river and expected to land on the following day. The letter which he then wrote the secretary of state painted a picture of the chief justice trying to step into the vacant shoes of the French intendant. From misrepresentation he sank into falsehood, stating that he prorogued the council only when the factious opposition of Livius, Finlay, Grant, and Allsopp, stupidly supported by Caldwell, destroyed all hope of arriving at a settlement of the important business of fees. The dismissal of the chief offender had caused his associates immediately "to sink into a proper sense of their duty," and was necessary to protect Haldimand from "great embarrassment and difficulties."

Returning to England, Livius appealed to the king, and his case was investigated by the board of trade and the privy council. Characteristically, Carleton refused to put in an appearance to justify what he had done. He had been wrong and he knew it. An order-in-council of March 29, 1779, vindicated the chief justice and commanded his return. Because Livius never saw Canada again, some have leaped to the conclusion that Carleton was morally right though legally wrong. But Germain repeatedly urged the chief justice to return to his post, and he would have been back in Quebec had not a storm off the Banks of Newfoundland dismasted his ship and forced it to return to England in the fall of 1780. A long illness and financial difficulties arising from the detention of his salary also held him. In 1782, when about to sail again, he appealed to the secretary of state for some "preventive measures" against a repetition of his suffering. Then, for the first time, officials at home decided that it was better for him to stay in England. But he remained chief justice until 1786, when a successor was appointed and sent out to Canada.

The whole affair has more than a personal interest. In his fall,

Livius dragged down Carleton's "privy" council with him, for he revealed to the home government the existence of this illegal body. He also revealed that Carleton had secreted his instructions, and consequently Haldimand, who had followed in his predecessor's footsteps, was ordered back into the straight and narrow path. The colony suffered, however, from being deprived of a chief justice for eight years. Manned by amateurs left without anyone competent to guide them, the courts dealt out such a poor quality of justice that a desperate feeling arose in the business communities of Quebec and Montreal. This was the real tragedy of Chief Justice Livius.

CHAPTER XII

A WAR OF RAIDS AND SURPRISES

ON THE evening of Friday, June 26, 1778, the ship bearing Lieutenant General Frederick Haldimand [1] anchored before the capital of Canada. At noon on the following day he came ashore amid booming salutes from the ships in the river and the garrison of the town. From the landing place to the Castle of St. Louis the streets were lined by regulars and militia, and between their files the new governor passed up to the council chamber. There Carleton introduced him to the members, his commission was read, and he was duly installed by taking the oaths of office.

Few native Britons have served their king and country more faithfully than this adopted son from Switzerland who, after an absence of thirteen years, now returned to the shores of the St. Lawrence. During the interval he had commanded in West Florida for six years until, in 1773, he went to New York to relieve the commander-in-chief of the British forces in North America. In this capacity he received from Governor Tryon an appeal for troops to suppress riots that had broken out, but he refused to interfere. At the time of the Boston Tea Party he again applied the principle that the sword should not be unsheathed until all the resources of civil authority have been exhausted. When Gage returned to America, Haldimand remained as second in authority until the home government, fearing the effect upon the turbulent colonies should any accident cause the chief command to devolve upon a foreign-born officer, recalled him in 1775. As compensation he was advanced in rank [2] and given the sinecure post of inspector general of the troops in the West Indies.

Having risen to such an eminence by his own merit in an age when many were pushed or pulled up by others, Haldimand was too valuable a man to be left without active employment. For this and for various other reasons — his wide knowledge of America, his five years' experience in Canada, and his community of language with the people of the colony — he was the logical successor of

Carleton, to whom, moreover, he was senior in age, rank, and service. He was also superior in character. Carleton would stop at nothing to cover up his mistakes, but Haldimand was a man of scrupulous honesty. Even in little courtesies the difference between the two was striking. The retiring governor persuaded his successor to purchase all his furniture and equipage and to take over all his servants, but when he came back in 1786 he hurt the gallant Swiss by refusing to return the compliment.[3] A perusal of the voluminous records of the day leaves the impression that the new governor was a fine, courtly gentleman endowed with considerable ability and inspired by lofty ideals of public service and of private conduct.

Haldimand was sent out to do more than govern Canada. The prime purpose of his coming was to defend it. His task weighed all the more heavily upon him because France declared war as he was sailing up the St. Lawrence. Though the combination of Britain's new and ancient foes actually reduced the external danger to the colony, it seemed at the time to have quite the opposite effect. The illusion was fed by the enemy on both sides of the water, because it was worth many battalions to them. The constant fear of an attack in the north naturally tended to weaken Britain in the south, where the issue was to be decided. And at the same time that the external danger loomed larger, the internal weakness of the colony grew.

Only fifteen years had passed since the Treaty of Paris had dashed the hopes of the Canadians that their country might be restored to France. The British yoke, which had first sat lightly upon them, now bore heavily. This aided time in dimming the faults and in brightening the virtues of the old régime. As if on the wings of the wind, the tidings flew from village to village that France was once more at war with Britain. Old memories and new hopes sprang up within Canadian hearts. Before Admiral d'Estaing's manifesto, published in October, 1778, mysteriously appeared on the doors of the parish churches telling the people, *"Vous êtes nés François, vous n'avez pu cesser de l'être,"* they felt the call of their own blood. Even those whom Carleton had not ceased to trust, the clergy and the noblesse, were being drawn back to their old allegiance. How long could Canada have remained British had it been assailed in front and rear by a French fleet sailing up the St. Lawrence and an American army pouring down the Richelieu? Had there been a rush to arms, it would probably have been to those of the invaders.[4] Carleton came through only one crisis in Canada; Haldimand lived through an almost continual crisis. As long as the war lasted, which was more than four years after he landed in Quebec, he was faced by the prospect of losing the colony as a consequence of a simultaneous external attack and internal collapse. From officials in London, in New York, and in Halifax he received repeated warnings of the impending blow; and dark rumors were forever starting up all around him. Moses Hazen and other "rebel" emissaries flitted in and out, invisible only to those who sought to catch them, and many Canadians betrayed an uncanny interest in vessels down the river and even in the gulf.

Haldimand complained again and again that the forces at his disposal were hopelessly inadequate to hold the country against an attack, and he pleaded for reinforcements. But the only answer to his prayers came from New York — an English regiment and some Germans in 1780, and some more Germans in 1781. In the summer of 1778 there were sixty-seven hundred names on the muster rolls of the troops in the colony. But, the governor reported, six hundred men were ill or on leave or in captivity, nine hundred were away off in the upper posts, and a thousand would be tied up in Quebec, Montreal, Chambly, St. John, and Ile aux Noix, leaving scarcely more than four thousand to take the field in an emergency. His later dispatches reduced the last figure. His effectives were less effective than he could have wished. Most of his Germans were there because they had not been good enough to go with Burgoyne. Nor did the later arrivals please him more. These soldiers from Europe, he observed, were fit only for garrison duty, being "heavy troops unused to snow shoes, to handling the axe and the hatchet." He also condemned them as lazy and inclined to desert.[5] The English forces he conceded to be better. But they had spent only two winters in the country and were consequently inferior to the Americans, who, to quote his own words, "are trained to the woods from their infancy, know well how to shelter themselves from the cold, and are excellent marksmen."

Not all of this class of resourceful men, however, were on the American side, for the number of loyalists was growing. In 1776, on the day after Montreal was recovered, Carleton had been joined

by Sir John Johnson, a refugee from the broad estates recently
inherited from his more famous father, Sir William. With Sir John
had come a couple of hundred volunteers. Most of them had been
his own tenants, and many of them had been born in the Scottish
Highlands. They formed the nucleus of the King's Royal Regiment
of New York, of which he was made colonel. This unit numbered
nearly four hundred when Haldimand arrived. At this time there
were also between one and two hundred Butler's Rangers, organized in the previous year from among fugitives from the Mohawk
Valley who had gathered in Niagara around their natural leader,
John Butler. He was deputy superintendent of the Six Nations,
and his loyalty, like Johnson's, had lost him broad lands in the
colony of New York. In addition to these two bodies there were
loyalist corps raised by Ebenezer Jessup, John Peters, and others
commissioned by Burgoyne. They had survived that general's disaster and found their way to Canada. In the summer of 1778 they
included nearly six hundred men. From this time on, destitute and
desperate recruits continued to arrive from the south of the province
line until, at the close of the war, there were some fifty loyalist
companies, comprising about three thousand fighters.

The location of Sorel attracted the governor as the best pivot for
his military plans. Montreal was indefensible, and though he
ordered the strengthening of the fortifications on the Richelieu that
had temporarily checked the Americans in 1775, he could not count
on these defenses to hold back another invasion. Moreover, it was
no longer certain that the Americans, if they returned, would follow the Richelieu. They might descend the St. François, to which
their attention had been drawn of late. It offered a shorter route
from their nearest settlements, and upon it lived a tribe of Indians
who were suspected in Canada of being attached to the Revolutionary cause. Sorel watched both avenues and also the road to
Montreal. In addition, it was the highest point that ships of burden
could always reach.[6] In the eyes of Haldimand it possessed a
"singular advantage either for advancing or retreating," and was
indeed the strategic center of the colony. Here, under the shelter of
permanent defensive works, the governor determined to plant his
main magazine and to concentrate the principal part of his troops.
Accordingly, shortly after his arrival in the colony, he began the
construction of storehouses, barracks, and fortifications, and, with

an eye to business as well as to defense, he at once wrote the home government to purchase the seigniory from the firm of London merchants who had acquired it.[7]

Of course he realized that he could never make Sorel what nature had made Quebec — the proper center for a last resistance. The military strength of the capital had been too great for the weak force that had invested it in 1775 and 1776, but Haldimand saw that it was not prepared to withstand an attack by a regular army with a real siege train. He pronounced its fortifications "utterly rotten," and straightway he began the slow and difficult task of transforming it into a genuine fortress. The other works which he undertook in order to increase the security of the country were in the west and will be mentioned in connection with the war in that quarter.

From 1778 the character of the war was completely changed so far as Canada was concerned. Because Britain abandoned Carleton's idea of cutting the old colonies in two by a great blow delivered over Lake Champlain, and France's entry into the war prevented a renewal of the drive against Canada, large operations designed to conquer were succeeded by many small ones calculated to harass, and hostilities were dispersed over an immense area instead of being concentrated at one point. Though such a war of raids and surprises defies the descriptive pen, an outline of its broad features may show how it rested like a heavy cloud upon the country for more than four years.

The fisheries down the river and in the gulf, an important part of Canada's life, and the communications with the outside world, vital to the colony's trade and defense, had been safe so long as Carleton was governor, for then the war had been confined to the land. But now they were in jeopardy because the war had spread to the sea directly France plunged into the struggle. Louis XVI presented the Americans with what they needed most desperately — a navy. The assistance given by French sea power, together with the shelter offered by French ports, tempted increasing numbers of American privateers to venture out on the high seas. For five summers, from 1778 to 1782, they infested the Gulf of St. Lawrence, pillaging fishing posts and preying upon merchant shipping.

In the fall of 1778, hearing of their first depredations and fearing an invasion by sea in the spring, the governor sought to detain one

of the two men-of-war then lying in Quebec. The senior naval officer, however, replied that the admiralty had ordered both ships
to convoy the trade fleet, which sailed as a rule on October 25.
Equally vain was the letter that Haldimand wrote Lord Sandwich,
the head of the admiralty, a few weeks later. The invasion did not
come, but the privateers did. One of them would have plundered
Tadousac, only forty leagues below Quebec, had not contrary winds
turned back the marauder.

On June 18, 1779, the governor again appealed to the admiralty.
Not a sail had yet arrived from Europe, and he had only a little
sloop of ten guns, the "Viper." In August, Sandwich replied that
he could send only a 24-gun frigate, the "Hind," because there were
"calls from all parts of this extensive Empire," and England herself
was threatened by a French invasion. A month later, Haldimand
reported that the fisheries on both shores were "almost utterly annihilated." [8]

The American privateers were most active in the spring before
warships arrived from England and in the fall after their departure.
Had a few vessels of the Royal Navy wintered in Quebec, they
might have patrolled the gulf as early and as late as the rebels.
Haldimand repeatedly urged this solution, but the authorities at
home would not lock up fighting ships that might be needed elsewhere. Thus left to do the best he could, the governor in 1780 had
two armed brigs of the provincial navy, the "Polly" and the "Liberty," fitted out to join the "Hind" and the "Viper," which was
wrecked shortly afterward,[9] and when a 22-gun British privateer
arrived from Liverpool he purchased her and sent her on the same
service under the new name of the "Wolfe." Prying into all the
creeks and bays, the little fleet did good work, capturing three
American craft and taking seventy-six prisoners during this season,[10] but the plague continued until the close of the war.

Canada's trade of course suffered. Many vessels bound to or
from the colony were snapped up by the privateers. Even those that
went in convoys could not avoid the risk. In 1780, for example,
the spring trade fleet from the Old Country was scattered by heavy
weather and many ships were taken prizes. By the middle of September only fourteen had reached Quebec, and the governor feared
that no more would come. "The rebel papers," he wrote, "are
crowded with reports of their being carried in by their privateers." [11]

London merchants calculated that the loss on this occasion amounted to four hundred thousand pounds.[12]

The injury to commerce was not so alarming as the danger to the military force that was holding the country. This force depended upon the periodical appearance of storeships and victualers, and sometimes the margin of safety was very narrow. Throughout Haldimand's correspondence with the secretary of state, the problem of supplies runs like a constant refrain. His advice that he should be sent enough to keep a year's stock on hand[13] was a counsel of perfection, and his repeated request that the spring fleet be dispatched in March was no better. All the vessels of a convoy could never be assembled on time, and the passage across the Atlantic was painfully slow, the speed being determined by that of the slowest sailer. In 1779 the departure of the spring convoy from Britain was delayed until April 30, and the voyage lasted until the middle of July. On June 18 the governor was so desperate that he wrote direct to the head of the ministry, Lord North. His desperation must have grown during the succeeding weeks, for his troops were reduced to a very few days' rations before the victualers arrived.[14] In the following year only two small vessels of the autumn provision fleet reached Quebec, and he had to bring down from Sorel and Montreal provisions that had been stored for shipment to the posts on the lakes as soon as spring opened the way.[15]

On land the war assumed the form of numerous forays. They had started when Haldimand arrived and they continued well into the summer of 1782, when he stopped them in obedience to orders from home to cease offensive operations. The sphere of their activity stretched from the back settlements of New England to the shores of the Mississippi. Their general effect was to thrust the Americans back, except in the southwest. Regulars, loyalists, and Indians went on these raids. Of the natives, who were used as scouts and auxiliaries, the Six Nations were the most prominent. They were the most pressed by the advance of white civilization, and they were the most warlike. One red leader towered over all the others: the Mohawk chief Thayendanegea, better known as Joseph Brant. He became a hero to the British and a devil incarnate to the Americans. Officials of the Indian department generally kept the savages in hand, but once, toward the close of the war, the latter practiced refined cruelty on some prisoners and the commandant of Detroit threatened to deny them the support of the rangers if they did it again. This warning sufficed.

The men of the loyalist units were not used in the southwest, but elsewhere they played the principal rôle in this fierce drama, and they were peculiarly fitted for it. Having been driven from their homes, robbed of their little property, and often subjected to cruel personal treatment, they were consumed with a desire to wreak vengeance for all the wrongs they and their families had suffered. The flame within them was not their only qualification for this work. They were not effete city folk. They were sturdy pioneers who had lived on the edge of civilization, and many of those whom they attacked believed that they had lived beyond the edge. Like their dusky allies, they knew the ways of the wilds. They needed no lessons from red men on how to surprise a sleeping post or village. Eight years after peace was signed, a retired British officer visited Niagara and the Mohawk Valley. In the former place he met many of Butler's Rangers, and in the latter he conversed with numerous people who had experienced the onslaughts of these men. Drawing upon the memories of both communities, he wrote most enthusiastically about the exploits of the loyalists in these stirring years. "This chosen corps, this band of brothers, was rarely worsted in any skirmish or action, though often obliged to retire and betake themselves to the wilderness when a superior force came against them. Sir John's corps and Butler's Rangers were very distressing to the back settlers; their advances and retreats were equally sudden and astonishing, and to this day the Americans say they might have as easily found out a parcel of wolves in the woods as them if they once entered; that the first notice they had of their approach was them in sight, and of their retreat their being out of reach. . . . I have known many of them, both officers and soldiers, and the account they gave of the fatigue and suffering they underwent is hardly credible were it not confirmed by one and all of them." [16]

Cold reason directed the predatory expeditions launched from Canada, though hot passion commonly inspired those who went upon them. Sitting in the Castle of St. Louis, the governor ordered a thrust here and a thrust there — not just at random but for some very definite purposes. One was to assist the British forces fighting in the old colonies by weakening the Americans there. Continual alarms on the frontiers had the effect of a military diversion, and the wholesale destruction of crops and cattle robbed the congressional troops of much-needed supplies. Another object was to protect Canada by forestalling any invasion of the main part of the colony or attack upon the communications with the upper country. To this end American advance posts were seized and demolished, and settlements that might support a hostile expedition were wiped out. Sometimes, also, an irruption into the old colonies was designed to release loyalists who were still detained.

A good example of the border warfare conducted along the southern boundary of Canada was a double blow delivered in the autumn of 1780. One force of about six hundred men, comprising detachments of regulars and loyalists quartered in the Montreal district and a few score Indians from Caughnawaga and the Lake of the Two Mountains, gathered at Ile aux Noix under the command of Major Christopher Carleton.[17] This motley company sailed up Lake Champlain to Crown Point and thence moved swiftly and silently overland to Wood Creek. There they surrounded Fort Anne, which surrendered at the first summons. After a night's rest they headed west for Fort George, and they surprised the greater part of its garrison on the way to relieve Fort Anne. The remainder capitulated without a blow. The two forts went up in smoke, as did many houses, barns, and mills in that part of the country. Thus the protecting wilderness between Canada and her foes was widened.

The other party, which was of about the same size, was composed of Six Nation Indians, regulars drawn from Niagara and Carleton Island, a new post at the head of the St. Lawrence, and loyalists of Johnson's regiment and Butler's Rangers. Under the leadership of Johnson it assembled at the site of Oswego and crept east. In a fortnight it burst upon the head of Scoharie Creek and like a fiery hurricane swept down this valley and up the Mohawk, burning thirteen gristmills, several sawmills, a thousand houses, and as many barns, containing over half a million bushels of grain. This human storm lasted for three days. Then superior forces threatened to block the retreat of the invaders, but they cut their way through with little loss — except to their foes. Washington loudly lamented the havoc, for he was crippled by the destruction of supplies on which he had counted. The scourge from the north repeatedly hit the upper Mohawk country and led to the evacuation of Fort Stanwix by the Americans in 1781.

The other area of settlement which lay over against Canada was hardly affected at all. This was the district between Lake Champlain and the Connecticut River. There dwelt the Green Mountain Boys, who had begun the war on their own account in 1775 and who might have been particularly unpleasant foes had they not withdrawn from the strife. Their neutrality arose from an intercolonial quarrel that had begun some years before, when they settled on lands granted by New Hampshire but claimed by New York. After securing a favorable decision from the privy council in 1764, New York had ordered the pioneers to surrender their titles, which were then legally worthless, and to repurchase their lands from officials in Albany. Having little kinship with the meek who shall inherit the earth, these people defied New York and appealed to arms.[18]

This local state of war was only temporarily overshadowed by the outbreak of the American Revolution. Then the Declaration of Independence of the thirteen colonies inspired the Green Mountain inhabitants to publish their own declaration of independence, and they followed it up by organizing as a separate state to be called Vermont. As New York still asserted her authority and the continental congress refused to recognize the new government, the Vermonters naturally turned to play Britain off against America. One of the Allens was reported to have said "that there was a north pole and a south pole, and should a thunder gust come from the south they would shut the door opposite that point and open the door facing the north." Whether the words came out of his mouth or were put into it, they exactly expressed the attitude of these political outcasts.

Germain thought that they might be redeemed, and in the spring of 1779 he ordered the commander-in-chief in New York and the governor of Quebec to draw them back into the British Empire. The chief responsibility for the negotiations fell upon Haldimand, who proceeded cautiously. Everything that he could learn about the Vermonters led him to regard them as "profligate banditti," and he soon developed a shrewd suspicion of their double game. No one, however, can accuse him of missing a chance to recover this fragment of the lost empire, because, as it now appears, no such chance existed. The long and intricate story of the conversations, which were opened in 1780 under cover of an exchange of prisoners and were closed by Haldimand after the peace treaty, when their continuance would have meant interference in the internal affairs of the independent United States, belongs to the history of the American republic rather than to the history of Canada. Canada was concerned only in the temporary effect of the negotiations — the local cessation of hostilities.

The war in the southwest was marked by a disaster which, according to the belief of some, affected the whole future of Canada. To see it in its proper setting, it will be well to consider first the whole problem of the west, which was throughout the war a veritable nightmare to Haldimand. From the time he assumed responsibility for the defense of the colony, he saw the vast hinterland depending upon a few far-flung posts, and these posts depending for their existence upon a precarious communication with their base on the lower St. Lawrence River. How was he to strengthen these posts and to link them more securely with the main part of the colony?

To accomplish this second object he built more vessels on the lakes, he founded a great depot at Carleton Island, he reoccupied Oswego, and he dug the first Canadian canals. The depot at Carleton Island was founded to prevent a possible break in the line of communication where lake and river navigation meet. From Lachine to the head of the St. Lawrence the ordinary means of transport was the bateau, a stout flat-bottomed boat with pointed ends which was poled or tracked up the rapids and propelled over smoother waters by five rowers assisted by a square sail when the wind favored. At the foot of Lake Ontario the cargoes of these smaller craft were transferred to sailing vessels that unloaded them at Niagara for cartage above the Falls, where they were loaded on other vessels bound for Detroit or Michilimackinac. The weakness of the line at the Niagara portage was offset by the presence of a garrison, the existence of some fortifications, and the distance from the foe. But Americans could easily penetrate from the upper reaches of the Mohawk to the place of trans-shipment at the head of the St. Lawrence, where there was neither garrison nor fort in the summer of 1778. There large quantities of military supplies, Indian presents, and traders' merchandise often lay a long time before they could be moved on, there being only two snows * and a sloop on the lake.

To protect this valuable prize, the seizure of which would have been disastrous, Haldimand at once sent Lieutenant William Twiss, an engineer, with several companies of soldiers and a body of artificers to find a good spot for a depot and to fortify it.[19] Twiss examined Cataraqui, but twelve miles down the river he found a site that pleased him more. It was on an island, to which he gave the name of the last governor, and there he erected a fort which he called after the new governor. Carleton Island at once became one of the most important places in Canada. Today it is more than half forgotten, for the works were dismantled and the place was abandoned at the close of the war, when the boundary drawn by the treaty gave the island to the United States. Oswego had been destroyed as useless at the end of the Seven Years' War, but Haldimand was very nervous lest the Americans seize and refortify it. They would then have a secure base from which they might cut off all the British garrisons lying to the west. Therefore he revived the old fort in 1781. He had wanted to do so earlier, but he could not for the simple reason that he lacked the necessary men and supplies.

The canals were not dug to allow vessels to pass between Montreal and Lake Ontario, which would have meant too great a work, but to avoid the risk to bateaux with their precious freight navigating the boiling waters of the upper St. Lawrence. Haldimand knew their perils well, having seen the rapids take their toll of human life when he descended the river in 1760 as a member of Amherst's army. The operations, which were directed by Twiss, began in 1779 at Couteau du Lac, just below Lake St. Francis, and by the end of the following year a canal nine hundred feet long and seven feet wide was completed. It had three locks with two feet and a half of water at the sills. As this improvement would incidentally benefit commerce, Haldimand had Twiss call a meeting of Montreal merchants in February, 1781, to see if they would share the expense of maintenance, and they agreed to pay ten shillings for each bateau.

Already this engineering lieutenant, who became a captain before he was through with this work, had begun to conquer the

* A snow is a small sailing vessel resembling a brig.

rapids at Cedars and the Cascades, later circumvented by the Beauharnois Canal. He employed Cornish miners to cut through the rock, and by the close of 1783, when he dismissed his workmen, he had constructed three channels. One was just above Cascades Point and was four hundred feet long. The other two, at Trou du Moulin and at Split Rock, were each half that length. The channel at Trou du Moulin was a mere cutting, but each of the other two was equipped with a single lock. On the completion of these improvements the charge for a private bateau passing through the whole system was raised to twenty-five shillings. Since two hundred and sixty such craft were already going through the canals each year, Twiss calculated that they would pay for maintenance and repair. Government bateaux of course passed free.

Though Haldimand improved the communications with the posts in the west, he could do little to strengthen the posts themselves. They were widely scattered, weakly garrisoned, poorly fortified, and utterly dependent upon the fickle friendship of the surrounding savages. He could not augment the meager garrisons because he had no men to spare, and even if he had been able to send more troops he could not have fed them in these distant places. It was all that he could do to subsist those who were already there. To strengthen their defenses, about all that he could send were orders to the commanders to do what they could, and they were reduced to such expedients as removing guns from the vessels that plied the lakes. To counteract the enemy agents who were trying to seduce the tribes of red men he had to rely upon the distribution of presents, which were ever short, and upon the personal influence of those who commanded in the interior. They were not all that they should have been, and their resources were pitifully inadequate.

When the Quebec Act carried Canada's boundaries into the heart of the continent, the home government recognized the impossibility of making the governor at Quebec directly responsible for the control of the vast interior. The new establishment provided for four subsidiary governments centered at Michilimackinac, Detroit, Vincennes on the Wabash, and Kaskaskia in the Illinois country on the Mississippi,[20] with Patrick Sinclair, Henry Hamilton, Edward Abbott, and Mathew Johnson as lieutenant governors,[21] but the outbreak of the Revolution interfered with these officials' taking over their duties. Johnson never appeared in the Illinois country, which was left under Philippe François Rastel, Chevalier de Rocheblave, an old French officer of great energy who had been temporaily put in charge of Kaskaskia. Sinclair was taken prisoner in New York in the summer of 1775 and did not turn up at Michilimackinac until the autumn of 1779, and then he caused no end of trouble.* Abbott arrived at Vincennes in May, 1777, until which time this little settlement seems to have been left to itself. Hamilton was the only one to reach his post in 1775, and he just escaped falling into the hands of the revolutionaries when on his way to Detroit.

Hamilton held the key of the west.[22] All the communications through Canada's great hinterland radiated from Detroit. Having been an army officer for over twenty years, Hamilton was not unprepared to face the responsibilities of his position, and, having warm Irish blood in his veins, he threw himself into his task with true Celtic fervor. He discovered that the Shawnees had received speeches and belts from some Virginians, and he demonstrated the worth of the senders by tearing up the speeches and by cutting the belts to pieces in the presence of some two hundred Indian deputies. In consequence of orders from Quebec and from London, he prepared the Indian warriors for any expedition that might be commanded, and, like them, he strained at the leash when months slipped by and the expected orders did not come. Early in 1778, hearing that Fort Pitt was held by a rather weak garrison, he offered to capture it. Carleton referred the proposal to Haldimand, who discouraged it, saying that nothing would be gained by a temporary occupation of the forks of the Ohio but that much might be accomplished by the destruction of frontier settlements. He advised the lieutenant governor of Detroit to support Butler's operations from Niagara. But the attention of the zealous Hamilton was soon concentrated upon another quarter.

Vincennes and Kaskaskia were more weakly held than the posts on the lakes. Neither nature nor the government had given Edward Abbott adequate resources for his task, and he gave himself over to despair. In February, 1778, fearing to face the Indians when they returned from their winter hunt, he abandoned Vincennes,

* Meanwhile the responsibility which he should have borne fell upon the abler Major A. S. de Peyster, who commanded the garrison. He was moved to Detroit to replace Hamilton when the latter was taken prisoner.

leaving several of the inhabitants in authority until the place could be reoccupied properly, and with his family he reached Detroit a month later.

Down at Kaskaskia, Rocheblave had much more spirit, but he had little else with which to hold the Illinois country should any Americans come, and they came like a thief in the night. On July 4, after his scouts had returned without finding a trace of any foe, Rocheblave was surprised and captured by one hundred and seventy-five American backwoodsmen under George Rogers Clark, who thereupon occupied the settlement. Early in August the news reached Detroit, Clark's ultimate objective, and Hamilton began to be seriously alarmed. The only remaining barrier between his command and Clark's forces was on the Wabash — Vincennes, which had been deserted, and the dependent tribes, who had been neglected. At the end of the month, before he could do anything to strengthen this barrier, an Indian arrived with the startling intelligence that Vincennes too had fallen.

It must be recovered at any cost and at the earliest opportunity. This was Hamilton's immediate decision. After five weeks of feverish preparations, he set out on his six hundred mile journey with a party of about two hundred. It included a few soldiers from Niagara, some militiamen of Detroit, and all the Indians he could gather at the time. As he pressed along he rallied more natives until his force numbered five hundred. On December 17 he took Vincennes as quickly and as quietly as Clark had seized Kaskaskia. Organizing the inhabitants to defend the place, he allowed the militia from Detroit and most of his regulars to return. For over two months he remained at Vincennes preparing the natives to root the Americans out of the country, while Clark, a hundred and eighty miles away at Kaskaskia, was planning a surprise for the Britisher. Suddenly, on February 23, 1779, the American swooped down on Vincennes. The British Indians fled, the French villagers refused to fight, and Hamilton was forced to surrender unconditionally. He was led off to Williamsburg, Virginia, where he lay in irons for many months.

Though the stars in their courses determined that the thirteen colonies should become an independent country, it was not so inevitable that the whole territory between the Ohio and the Great Lakes should be torn from Canada and added to the new republic. Was it decided by these few rapid blows in the western wilderness, struck by only a handful of men on either side? Some admirers of George Rogers Clark have said that it was,[23] but there is little ground for such a conclusion. It is not supported by the military sequel. Though the British were too weak to retrieve the disaster that had swallowed up Hamilton, their position on the Great Lakes remained unassailable, and Clark himself was so weak that, far from being able to follow up his conquests, he had to abandon them in 1780 and 1781. Moreover, there is no evidence that his exploits had any influence upon the peace negotiations, and, as will appear later, there is good reason for believing that the new international boundary would have been drawn precisely where it lies even if he had remained quietly at home.

CHAPTER XIII

THE SHADOW OF THE WAR

THE war cast a deep shadow over Haldimand's régime in Canada, and as a consequence his memory has been unjustly blackened. For a long time it was the fashion to depict the Swiss governor as a suspicious tyrant who filled the jails with innocent people. This tradition sprang chiefly from the voluminous writings of his principal "victim," Pierre du Calvet. It was nourished by the known facts that the governor was distrustful and that the prisons were packed. It was able to take deep root because Haldimand never courted public opinion and because Du Calvet died too soon. His death at sea in the spring of 1786 stopped the lawsuit he had instituted against his "persecutor" and prevented the truth from coming out in the courts. Haldimand was suspicious because he was no fool. He knew that the French blood that coursed through the veins of the Canadian people could not be counted as British blood at a time when Britain was at war with their old mother country, and he can hardly be blamed for regarding French-born residents as alien enemies. He was also aware that many of the English-speaking inhabitants sympathized as much as they dared with their brethren who had risen in arms against Britain.

With traitors and half-traitors swarming in the colony, and with enemies at its very gates, it would not have been surprising had Haldimand practiced a policy of wholesale arrest. But he did not. His nerves were too steady and his judgment was too sound. The printer of the *Quebec Gazette,* who was an American, went further than he soberly dared when he had "a cup too much," which was not seldom, but all that his indiscretion on these inspired occasions earned him was a word of caution. The governor neither wished nor ordered the arrest of Du Calvet. When the officer commanding in Montreal, Brigadier General Speth, reported the arrest of three Canadians, Haldimand forbade him to act on his own authority again lest he invade "the liberty of the subject," which was "very sacred." [1] This is only one illustration of the restraint he imposed upon the zeal of his subordinates. Whence, then, came the prisoners who were so numerous that they overflowed into the holds of vessels anchored in the river? They came from the outskirts of the neighboring colonies, where they had been captured by raiding parties. Discarding the fulminations of Du Calvet, whose hysteria had destroyed his little sense of truth, one can find evidence for scarcely more than a score of political arrests in Canada during the years that Haldimand was governor.[2] Of those who were taken up, only a dozen or so were detained, and half of these were not British subjects.[3]

Pierre de Sales Laterrière was apparently the first to be caught. He was legally a citizen of France, whence he came to Canada in 1766. At first he was associated with another Frenchman, Pélissier, who was in charge of the St. Maurice forges, and in 1776 he succeeded Pélissier when the latter, thoroughly compromised with the Americans, withdrew from the country.* Laterrière was suspected of having had a hand in providing the invaders with the many articles they procured from the works at St. Maurice, but he was not molested until the end of February, 1779, when evidence was collected that he had encouraged Canadians to desert to the Americans and was preparing for the reception of an invading army.

The next to get into trouble were Fleury Mesplet and Valentin Jautard. Their legal status was the same as that of Laterrière. Mesplet came to Montreal with Benjamin Franklin to broadcast American propaganda for Canadian consumption and remained to print for his own profit, there being only one other press in the colony, that of the *Quebec Gazette*. He seems to have had too few wits, and his editor undoubtedly had too many. This was Jautard, a lawyer who had more than a flicker of Voltairean genius, which was frequently lighted up over the bottle. Mesplet was left in peace until he began to ply his trade in 1778. On June 3 of that year he produced the first number of a weekly paper, the *Montreal Gazette*. Quite legally and most naturally, considering the times and his most inauspicious introduction into the country, he and his associates were ordered to leave the province. Thereupon a number of leading

---

* This was not the only way in which he succeeded him. Mme. Pélissier remained and without any legal authority changed her name to Mme. Laterrière. The domestic difference between the two men may have obscured their political harmony, thereby postponing Laterrière's arrest.

citizens of the town, anxious to have a local organ, appealed to the governor, who suspended the order under certain conditions. One was that as long as the war lasted Mesplet and those working with him should print only what had been previously submitted to, and sanctioned by, an official appointed by the governor.[4] They flagrantly violated this condition by publishing an onslaught against the bench, and then they pointed their insult by going to the court and taking seats there. Judge Rouville complained [5] to Haldimand in June, 1779, and the two foreigners were locked up. With one possible exception [6] there appears to have been not another political arrest in 1779.

The incarceration of this trio failed to reach the heart of the treason in the colony. The mysterious comings and goings across the border continued as before. The man who did most to trace them to their Canadian end and to discover their meaning was the Major Christopher Carleton who led the expedition of 1780 already described. He was posted at St. John,[7] perhaps the best location for this purpose, and he was so zealous that he sometimes pushed those whom he employed into being *agents provocateurs*.

All his efforts were in vain until the summer of 1780, when he reported that he was coming upon "the head of the snake" — the leaders of a conspiracy to deliver the country into the hands of the enemy. They were encouraging an invasion by betraying the weakness of the colony's defenses and by conveying the intelligence that large numbers of its population were collecting supplies for an invading army and would join the Americans when they came. In spite of their cautious methods — writing with invisible ink between the lines of a song inscribed in ordinary ink, the detachment of signatures to be conveyed separately in leaden bullets, and the concealment of papers in a hollow walking stick — a considerable quantity of their treasonable correspondence was intercepted and forwarded to the governor. A number of arrests followed in the autumn of 1780.

One was that of a prominent Scottish resident of Quebec, Charles Hay. Sometimes referred to as a cooper, he was a substantial merchant who imported rum and wines and exported timber, principally barrel staves. This branch of his business gave him many contacts through the rural parishes. South of the border he had another important contact — his brother, with whom he appears to have communicated frequently. Charles and Udney Hay had managed to remain out of the capital during the siege. Charles returned in 1776, but Udney joined the American army as a colonel and was now quartermaster general in Albany. With this exception, the chief confederates discovered were Frenchmen, the few Canadians caught in the government's net apparently being only their tools.

The natives of France who appear as principal plotters were three, all residents of Montreal. One was a merchant named Cazeau, a friend of Thomas Walker and of Charles Hay. He had made a good fortune out of trade with the Indians and had exercised a bad influence over some of them, persuading them that a British victory would be against their interests. Another of the Montreal group was Boyer Pillon, a physician living in the Quebec Suburb. He corresponded with his son, who was with the congressional troops at Albany, and he also wrote letters to Washington and to Lafayette.

The third was Pierre du Calvet, who, like Cazeau, was a merchant of considerable wealth. Being a Protestant, he had procured a commission as justice of the peace shortly after his arrival in 1766, and being a victim of megalomania he had taken violent offense at the reform of 1770, which clipped the wings of the magistrates. Among the papers left by the Americans when they fled from Quebec in May, 1776, was a receipt for his pay as an ensign in the invading army. To escape from the suspicion that enveloped him, he presented Governor Carleton with an anonymous letter he had received — probably from himself.[8] He was frequently in trouble in the courts, where Jautard represented him, and he consequently conceived a bitter hatred of the judges, which he aired through Mesplet's press.

In the summer of 1780 Du Calvet went down to Quebec. Major Carleton reported that he had gone to get, along with other papers, a plan of the new fortifications, and that the physician's schemes were merely waiting upon his return. In September, when ordering Pillon's arrest, Haldimand deliberately refrained from taking any steps against the Huguenot merchant, hoping to discover other principals of the plot by allowing this one to remain at large a little longer. But Allan McLean, who then commanded in Montreal, fearing what Du Calvet might do when he heard of Pillon's seizure, dispatched an officer who took him into custody as he was passing through Three Rivers. The governor was chagrined by this precipitate action but he did not dare undo it.

None of the political prisoners was brought to trial, yet Haldimand seems to have been justified in detaining them. The two cases that stirred the greatest outcry were those of Hay and of Du Calvet. The former's able wife and the latter's facile pen made a great fuss, maintaining the absolute innocence of their masters and the rank injustice of their detention without a hearing. The governor, however, had little difficulty in satisfying the secretary of state that they should not be allowed their liberty. The evidence against them may not have been as strong as that against Pillon,[9] but it was supported by word from New York. Their names appeared in a list of traitors sent to Haldimand by Clinton, who was gathering some interesting information from Benedict Arnold.

The confinement of the prisoners lasted no longer than was necessary and appears to have been as light as possible. All who had not been previously released, such as Laterrière, who was freed in the summer of 1780 on condition that he leave the province, were set at liberty in May, 1783. Meanwhile at least the better known prisoners were treated more like gentlemen in difficulties than like criminals in jail. They were given commodious quarters and the best of food.* Their friends were allowed to visit them and their wives to stay with them. Nor were these their only liberties. Jautard made love to Madame Laterrière until her husband rudely stopped him, and the two fathers of the *Montreal Gazette* were frequently able to enjoy themselves by getting drunk. Du Calvet was allowed to carry on his business correspondence, and when he offered to sell some goods to the government, Haldimand directed the acceptance of his proposal if the terms were reasonable. Indeed, the governor expressly stated that he did not wish the Huguenot to suffer financially because he had to be kept away from his counting-house. Such consideration, far in excess of what would be shown today under similar circumstances, was due solely to the governor. The secretary of state had advised him that political prisoners against

---

* Laterrière, Hay, Jautard, and Mesplet had a room thirty feet square all to themselves. Laterrière and Hay each curtained off a corner. After his release Du Calvet complained bitterly about the quarters and the food that had been allowed him, whereupon those who had been in charge of him as a prisoner repudiated his allegations most indignantly and pretty well proved that he was a liar.

whom there was insufficient evidence for a conviction should be shipped to Halifax, where they might be detained with less trouble and in greater safety; but Haldimand, out of consideration for their private interests, decided against deportation.[10]

In addition to arresting a few leading conspirators and their agents, the governor took what appears to have been a very sane precaution against seditious designs among the masses. The intelligence gleaned in the country that inhabitants were preparing for the coming of the Americans was confirmed by news that filtered up from the south. In the last days of 1780 he received an alarming letter from Sir Henry Clinton in New York. Clinton stated that according to information he had recently obtained, the Americans were probably planning a drive on Canada as soon as the winter set in, and added that he had heard of a combination of inhabitants to join them. He advised Haldimand to prepare for the crisis by commandeering all flour and other provisions scattered through the country, leaving the people sufficient only for their subsistence.[11] But Haldimand believed that the same end could be achieved in a less drastic way. He decided to order the people to have all their grain threshed and ready for transportation to places of safety on the first alarm. He was prepared to destroy the supplies of those who disobeyed should the Americans actually come.

Cramahé, whose mind was feeling the effects of advancing years and declining health, showed signs of panic. Fearing that the proposed order would only alarm the countryside and defeat its own purpose, he urged cautious buying through private agents and the proclamation of martial law immediately the hostile movement against the colony was known to have begun. The governor replied that he would never proclaim martial law until the Americans had actually entered the country and he doubted if, even then, it would be of any real advantage. Secret purchases he condemned as a dangerously slow method.[12] On January 15, 1781, he signed and sealed a proclamation embodying his decision. The militia officers were to supervise its execution and to make complete returns of the livestock, grain, and flour in each parish. Though the peasants scouted the idea of a winter invasion, and though they threshed their grain with reluctance and concealed their resources under false returns,[13] the proclamation was not regarded as a complete failure, for it was repeated in the beginning of 1782 and again in 1783.

Thus did Haldimand prepare for the danger without inflicting any hardship upon the habitants. None of their property was seized, because the Americans did not try to take the country.

Being no mere soldier, Haldimand was not content with these superficial precautions. He wanted to go deeper. Seeing that his difficulties sprang chiefly from the unreliable temper of the Canadian people, he sought to correct it by working upon its causes. One cause that struck him forcibly during his first few months in Quebec was the prevailing ignorance. His reaction is interesting. Before the winter was out he launched a subscription for a public library. It was to be half English and half French, for it was to draw the two races together. The project proved more popular than he had hoped. Many priests, some Canadian laymen, and most of the English-speaking residents undertook to pay five pounds down and two pounds a year. The subscribers chose a board of directors to take charge of the library. The board decided to ask the playwright, Richard Cumberland, who held the sinecure post of agent for the colony, to select and order the volumes, and Haldimand wrote him accordingly. Even in this business the war seems to have played tricks upon the governor, by making it difficult to procure French literature. He was deeply disappointed in the fall of 1780 when he received the first books and they turned out to be all English. At once he decided to hold them back until the others arrived, for he was most anxious to prevent any jealousy from arising in sensitive Canadian minds. One cannot help feeling a warm regard for the man who, with such noble purpose, established the first public library in Canada.*

The clergy also attracted Haldimand's attention as being at the root of his problem. His scrutiny was not that of a Protestant bigot, for he had nothing but sympathy for the church *qua* church. He had not the slightest desire to weaken the spiritual authority of those who guided the consciences of the people. His great desire was that their personal influence, which could not be separated from their priestly power, should be exercised to strengthen rather than to weaken Canada as a British colony. This was the point of his criticism when he observed that the clergy tended to be either inferior in quality or dangerous in character. He attributed the trouble pri-

---

* After a separate existence of nearly ninety years, it was merged in the collection of the Literary and Historical Society of Quebec in 1869.

marily to a social tradition of the colony. The better classes of
Canadians had always shown a distaste for an ecclesiastical life.
War and its profitable substitute, trade with the Indians, had been
their favorite pursuits. Hence the priesthood was recruited from
France and from the lower order of Canadians. The conquest had
made matters worse. The years when ordination was stopped and
the education of young men for the church was interrupted had left
a mark which the restoration of the episcopacy in 1766 could not
obliterate. Death had created so many vacancies that Briand had to
confer orders on many students who were not fully qualified. Nor
was the evil likely to stop there. The ban on French-born priests
obliged the seminary to replace the deceased members of its own
staff with Canadians, who, not possessing a good education themselves, could never bestow it upon others. Finally, the superior
quality of the priests from France, who would not die out for many
a long year, gave them an undue influence over their Canadian
brethren, which they naturally exerted against the interests of
Britain.[14]

One of these sons of France who mixed political tares with the
seed of the gospel, De la Valinière by name, was actually deported
in 1779. It was a most delicate business, but the governor handled
it carefully. Taking advantage of a quarrel between the trouble-
maker and the bishop, he procured the latter's consent to the former's enforced voyage to England, and thus made the blow appear
to come from the proper ecclesiastical authority.[15] Though quite
successful on this occasion, Haldimand was too much of a realist to
dream of expelling the whole of De la Valinière's tribe. And even
if it had been possible to get rid of the canker in this manner, there
would still be the sickness in the heart of the native clergy. This
impressed the governor as being of far greater importance because it
was deep-seated and permanent. He feared that the body ecclesiastical would never be really healthy until some new life had been
injected into it.

To inject this new life he conceived the idea of importing a handful of carefully picked priests from Savoy. Natives of this state
would be friendly to Britain and yet have distinct affinities with the
French-speaking people of Canada. Planted in the seminary at
Quebec, where they would surely be admitted because the heads
of this institution were sensible of their need for good professors,

they might gradually influence the whole church, counteracting the poison spread by Britain's foes. Those who could not be adopted in the seminary could easily find parishes with incomes of at least two hundred pounds a year. They would all be so happy in Canada that they would draw more of their kind to settle on the shores of the St. Lawrence, and the political regeneration of the colony's clergy would be accelerated. Haldimand easily persuaded the home government to give his scheme a trial. Thereupon the British minister at Turin was instructed to procure the individuals to work the magic, and in September, 1781, four of them arrived in London after the last ships had departed for Canada. In the spring of 1782 the quartet sailed for Quebec, but they never reached it. The vessel that carried them was captured on the high seas and they were all brought back to Europe. The governor, though disappointed, was not discouraged. He urged the secretary of state to find substitutes, if he could not lay hold of the originals, to embark in the spring of 1783.[16]

As the war died out, the home government appears to have lost interest in Haldimand's scheme, and instead of Savoyards two priests from St. Sulpice in Paris landed at Quebec in the spring of 1783. Being clad in lay garb, the Frenchmen escaped the notice of civil and military authorities and the governor knew nothing of their existence until he received a letter from Montgolfier stating that he had admitted them into the Montreal seminary and begging permission to retain them. Haldimand was startled. He saw the specter of French political influence creeping into this British colony under the cover of priestly robes, and he dispatched his English aide-de-camp, Major Brehm, to bring the smuggled pair down to Quebec for shipment to Europe as soon as possible.

The governor anticipated no difficulty, but the extraction was not painless. The bishop pleaded; Montgolfier protested through the seminary's *homme d'affaires,* who traveled down to Quebec for the purpose; the citizens of Montreal assembled and sent two representatives to persuade the governor to relent; and the countryside was stirred by circular letters to the captains of militia.[17] The superior of the Montreal seminary was partly responsible for the general outcry gaining such strength. Contrary to a promise in his original letter to Haldimand, he had permitted the newcomers to appear in public processions and to mount the pulpit. There they had announced a further supply of laborers in the vineyard of the Lord from the Seminary of St. Sulpice in the French capital. The sight of the strangers had captured the imagination of the people and their promise had carried them away. But there were other forces at work among both clergy and laity. Britain's prestige had been greatly lowered by the outcome of the war and consequently many Canadians felt that their demand could not be refused if they pressed it boldly. Some old subjects, actuated by ulterior motives, played upon this feeling by telling the people that the Americans would have let them have all the priests from France that they desired. Montgolfier's agent actually repeated this argument to Haldimand's face. Finally, the Canadians were driven by new and vague fears for their religion. They were disturbed by the prospect of the loyalists already in the country, and an unknown number yet to come, settling down in their midst.

This popular movement for the retention of the two Parisians only strengthened Haldimand's determination to get rid of them immediately. At the same time he realized that his firmness might be interpreted as hostility to the religion of the people, and he explained to his petitioners what was already known at least to Montgolfier and the Montreal seminary. He told them that, while he was opposed to priests coming from France, he was so much in favor of priests from other parts of Catholic Europe that he had done his very best to bring them. The episode closed with a characteristic incident. One of the Frenchmen appearing to be ill, the sympathetic governor allowed Major Brehm to bring them ashore at Murray Bay, where the major permitted one of them to say Mass. The fellow took advantage of this indulgence to engage some of the habitants to help him escape. To prevent an unpleasant noise, Haldimand hurried his Canadian aide-de-camp, M. St. Ours, to Montreal with a letter to Montgolfier requesting the delivery of the fugitive. He was handed over accordingly and in a few days was away down the St. Lawrence. Naturally the governor used the whole of this unpleasant affair to prove to the home government the urgency of his request for Savoyard clerics, but his pleading was of no avail.[18]

The keynote of Haldimand's policy was to placate the Canadians. Like other Britishers who had governed before him, he saw this as the only way to hold the colony within the British fold. As the French war, which they had merely contemplated as a possibility, had become a grim reality, it was more imperative than ever that no offense be given to Canadian sensibilities, however absurd they might be, except of course when the security of the colony dictated otherwise, as in the return of the French priests.

Though the interest and feelings of the racial minority were of secondary importance to the governor, he was genuinely anxious to deal justly by them. Before leaving England he had had several conversations with the secretary of state about the affairs of the colony, and he had promised Germain that he would eschew the prejudices of Carleton. On his arrival in Canada he began well, making a very fine impression upon the members of the mercantile body.* The merchants sang his praises in letters home and their eulogies came echoing back through official dispatches addressed to the Castle of St. Louis. But soon a different note was heard, as friction developed between the governor and the commercial community. For this the war was broadly responsible.

Much of the trouble arose out of a fundamental clash of interests in the west between the government and those engaged in the fur business. The upper posts were retained for the sake of the valuable trade conducted from these centers; but the trade made it more difficult to secure the posts, and precautions designed to secure the posts hurt the trade. The trade had led to the building and operation of private shipping upon the Great Lakes,[19] but private shipping on the lakes, because it might fall into the hands of the Americans, by collusion or otherwise, was a danger to the British possession of the western posts. In 1777 Carleton had therefore prohibited all save government vessels from navigating these waters. Haldimand naturally continued his predecessor's orders and just as naturally they stirred resentment, for they cramped the fur trade sorely. Though Michilimackinac could still be served by private canoes over the Ottawa River route, it received a considerable quantity of supplies and merchandise over Lake Huron, and it had not yet supplanted Detroit as the chief point for the collection of furs. Thus the great bulk of the trade was affected. For transporta-

---

* His courtesy was unfailing and his desire to further the material welfare of the merchants was obvious. They knew that he did his utmost to protect their seaborne trade and he won their gratitude by changing the piloting regulations which had hampered navigation between Quebec and Montreal.

tion it had to rely on the vacant space offered by the commanders of the "king's" ships, who had orders to accept private freight in so far as it did not interfere with the "king's service." The traders had to bear all the risk; they had to give certificates to cover the carriage charges, which were left unsettled;[20] and their goods had to wait their turn, which sometimes meant a year's delay. Those in charge of the vessels were instructed to observe the strictest impartiality, but occasionally a preference was shown to a merchant who was of particular service at one or other of the posts, and more than occasionally the traders believed that they were the victims of favoritism.

Transportation was only one phase of the complicated conflict. Out in the west some traders tried to turn a dishonest penny by trafficking with others than Indians. Hamilton caught several who were attempting to correspond from Detroit with Americans, and a number were suspected of opening a guilty channel through Michilimackinac, which Sinclair said would not be difficult.[21] In consequence a close watch was kept on all men and cargoes destined for the west. Through the system of licenses by which this trade was regulated, the governor checked what appeared to be a suspicious growth of the quantity of arms, ammunition, and spirits shipped into the interior, and he exercised a control over who should be allowed to go up country. Joseph Howard once slipped away without the requisite license, with the result that he paid a heavy fine and Haldimand detained him the next time he wanted to go west. Howard's influential correspondents in London interceded on his behalf and theirs, but the governor was politely firm. Few men seem to have found themselves in Howard's predicament, but the restraint imposed on the amount of commercial goods sent to the west was sufficient for the governor to forewarn the secretary of state of the complaints that were bound to arise.

This interference with the operations of commerce was probably based on a misunderstanding. Instead of being proof of an extensive illicit trade with Americans through hidden paths in the interior, the increase in western shipments that occurred during this period seems to have been largely due to two other causes. One was a genuine expansion of the trade in the direction of the northwest, which is reflected in the larger fur exports of these years. Early in 1780 the North West Company appears by name in the correspondence from Michilimackinac, and in justice to the governor it must be observed that the men who formed it were open to suspicion because they had sent an embassy to the continental congress in 1776. Indeed, Sinclair recommended that they be given no passes unless they forwarded government stores to his post.[22]

At first the trade that centered around the posts was apparently injured by the competition of the commanders responsible for holding them. As the friendship of the natives had to be cultivated at all costs, presents were distributed with an increasingly lavish hand. Similarly the practice of using red men as scouts and raiders, or of holding them in readiness for such service, distracted them from the hunt. But the traders soon came out on top. The native appetite for presents grew by what it fed on, and the traders stimulated this voracious demand until it far surpassed the government's ability to meet it directly. The local commanders were then compelled to purchase an increasing quantity of goods on the spot at monopoly prices. Thus more and more merchandise, particularly rum, was imported into the interior to be exchanged for orders on the government instead of pelts gathered by Indians. Here was the other reason for the mounting imports.

The cost of maintaining the western posts was astounding, and it leaped up and up. For merchandise, provisions, and rum purchased at Detroit during the ten months following November, 1779, the bills presented at Quebec totaled nearly a hundred thousand pounds, of which nearly four-fifths was claimed by the single firm of Macomb, Edgar, and Macomb, who then enjoyed a practical monopoly at Detroit.[23] In 1779 Sinclair went to Michilimackinac with orders and determination to reduce its expenses, but in two years' time they were trebled. The home government became alarmed at such wild spending of the public funds and sent Haldimand peremptory orders to stop it. He had already tried in vain to do so. He forbade the officers in charge of the posts to make local purchases, but he could not compel strict obedience when they replied that it would kill the vital friendship of the natives. While he scolded in his letters west, he apologized in his letters east. Repeatedly he complained to the secretary of state that the presents he had requisitioned from England were so short in quantity, so inferior in quality, and so late in arriving that the post commanders were at the mercy of the merchants.

Haldimand's helplessness recalls the situation before the conquest, when the government in Quebec could not control the officers who were scattered over the interior and who were responsible for holding the red men loyal to the French cause. Indeed, the same conditions were producing much the same results. Even the corruption of the French régime was reappearing under the British, though it does not seem to have mounted quite so high, there being at this time no evidence of official collusion at Quebec. In the west the distribution of presents was actually allowed to fall into the hands of interested parties. Sinclair's bills covered gifts made by the traders to the Indians on their wintering grounds. At Niagara the situation was worse. There the whole business, even including the keeping of the Indian accounts, was intrusted to the firm of Taylor and Forsyth.[24]

The responsibility for the criminal negligence at this post lay upon the shoulders of Colonel Guy Johnson, superintendent of the Six Nations, who lacked both ability and integrity.* He simply drew bills for the amounts which Taylor and Forsyth said the government owed them for goods they had advanced out of their own stores. In March, 1781, they presented one of his bills for thirty-five thousand pounds, and only when the demand was paid did Haldimand discover by mere accident that they had not supplied merchandise to the value represented. Not until then did he know of the loose methods in vogue at Niagara. He wrestled with the evil as best he could. At last he refused to honor Sinclair's bills, and he summoned the Michilimackinac commander to come down to Quebec; he sued Taylor and Forsyth, recovering fifteen thousand pounds New York currency; and he persuaded the home government to get rid of Colonel Guy and to appoint his cousin, Sir John, as superintendent general of Indian affairs.

Still corruption continued to eat into the business of buying native support. Sir John ordered a consignment of presents through Pollard, a merchant who had sold extensively to the government in the interior, and a number of "gentlemen" presumably familiar

---

* Peeved at Carleton's refusal to launch the savage hordes against the old colonies in the summer of 1775, he had deserted his post, sailing for England in November of that year. Though back in America in 1776, he was down in New York and his deputy, John Butler, did not hear from him for two years. In the summer of 1779 he at last wandered back to Quebec with lame excuses for his long absence and a lively desire to return to his duties. Haldimand would have preferred to leave Butler in charge, but he had no authority to dismiss or to detain Johnson.[25]

with such matters were asked to compare this consignment with one sent from England on the direct order of the government. These commercial jurors decided in favor of Pollard, who was then given Sir John's and Haldimand's blessings and sent across the Atlantic with a recommendation for his employment by the home government. Arrived in London, Pollard approached the under secretary of state, William Knox, with the interesting proposition that six thousand pounds be added to the cost of the goods to be bought for the Indians, three thousand for each of them. This brazen offer, which was of course indignantly rejected, may suggest what had been going on in Canada.[26]

Turning from the problem of the west to the economic affairs of the main part of the colony, one sees another conflict between the governor and the merchants. The immediate cause of the friction was the disappearance of the country's agricultural surplus and the appearance at times of a shortage. Here is something strange that demands investigation. The production of wheat in Canada had risen steadily until 1774, when it was double the consumption. Then conditions were reversed. The embargo of 1777 was reimposed in 1778, and it was continued until the close of the war.[27] What had happened?

A leakage to the colonies in arms is entirely out of the question, because the only practicable route for transport was over Lake Champlain, and that was closely guarded. The dislocation of agriculture occasioned by the American invasion is likewise a false assumption, for the damage was much less than might be imagined. When the enemy were all out of the country, there was still a large stock on hand from 1775, and the crop of 1776 was bountiful. Nor is the mystery explained by the colony's abnormally large consumption resulting from the maintenance of a bigger garrison after 1776 and the coming of the loyalists with their dependents. These extra mouths could not begin to eat up an amount equal to the average export for the previous five years. Moreover, they had other sources of food, for the government imported large quantities of meat and flour.* Another possibility that suggests itself is that of a general falling off of production arising from natural conditions.

On this point there is conflicting evidence. In September, 1779,

---

* The upper posts had to be supplied entirely with English flour because the Canadian article, on account of inferior milling and packing, would not keep.[28]

the governor reported that the previous year's crop had proved shorter than anticipated, and he predicted an even shorter one in the current year. He spoke of dry hot weather in the Montreal district,[29] and at the end of December the *Quebec Gazette* printed a Montreal letter stating that a six months' drought had just ended. At a later date Haldimand wrote that the harvest was a failure in the Quebec district but was quite "tolerable" in the other, which meant that the colony could not have been badly off, because the Quebec district normally accounted for only a small fraction of the whole country's production. This conclusion is borne out by the behavior of prices. Wheat was worth four shillings a bushel in the spring of 1779. By the beginning of the winter the price had risen to ten shillings.[30] Then it stopped climbing and seems to have settled back to about eight shillings. Relief could not have come from outside at that season of the year. In 1781 there was a plague of caterpillars that destroyed much of the grain, but no economic crisis seems to have followed. Finally, in June, 1783, before anyone could be sure of the coming harvest, but as soon as it was definitely known that peace had come, there appeared such pressure to export that the embargo imposed in 1776 was suddenly lifted.[31] Throughout the period of the war, moreover, there was such a distinct movement onto the land that labor was very scarce and wages were unusually high,[32] which implies an extension of agricultural operations. In conclusion, one is left with a suspicion that the margin between production and consumption could not have been wiped out.

Assuming that the shortage that embroiled the governor and the merchants was fictitious, it is not difficult to explain what happened. The peasants who inhabited the "granary of Canada," the district lying south of Sorel, were notoriously sympathetic with the Americans, and there were many rumors current that they were hoarding supplies against the return of their friends from the south. This was physically possible. The habitant seldom sold before March, and until then he housed all he possessed. He could easily manage to stow away several times the amount that his family would consume in a year. Furthermore, it would not be difficult for a few speculators to corner a market like that of Canada at this time, and it looks as if they did.

The first price disturbance, which occurred in the spring of 1779, followed immediately upon the arrival of an express from Halifax bringing the first news of "the amazing price of wheat and flour in other parts of America." [33] As the embargo, not yet made permanent, was due to expire on August 1, the merchants had visions of great profit and they began to buy feverishly. Allsopp was undoubtedly in the game, and so were several other members of the council. John Drummond, who was well connected at home and had been allowed to inherit his late father's seat at the board,[34] was probably the worst sinner, for he enjoyed a peculiar advantage. He and his partner, Jacob Jordan, were army commissaries and also the Canadian representatives of Harley and Drummond, who had secured the contract for remitting cash to colonial governments. In their former capacity Drummond and Jordan were familiar with the business of purchasing grain and in their latter capacity they were frequently intrusted with large sums of money. They were the recipients of the express mentioned above, and soon it was stated in Quebec that they had invested fifteen thousand pounds of public funds in wheat on their own account, concealing the transaction under the names of two Canadian merchants. Drummond was also reported as boasting that he could do as he liked because of his intimacy with the governor.[35] At the same time the Montreal justices of the peace, most of whom were engaged in commerce, asserted that the disturbance of the market, which incidentally forced the bakers to threaten that they would shut up their shops, was caused solely by orders given to various individuals to buy at prices hitherto unheard of in the colony. They denied that there was any scarcity at all.[36]

In May, 1779, the governor consulted the "privy" council, which, including only one representative of the mercantile element, agreed at once to a prolongation of the embargo in order "to reduce the present exorbitant prices of wheat and flour." A month later, conditions being no better and the attorney general having advised the governor that the laws of England provided severe penalties for "forestalling, regrating and ingrossing," the "privy" council backed Haldimand in issuing a further proclamation that defined these offenses and set forth the punishments prescribed — confiscation, imprisonment, and the pillory. But it was uncertain whether these laws, which were very old and at least half forgotten, applied to purchasing for export, and there were doubts whether the embargo by proclamation was legal. Cramahé intimated to Haldimand that it was not.[37] Under such circumstances of course the speculation would not stop. Then it was encouraged by the bad crop in the Quebec district and by a bad financial practice of the government, which will be explained shortly. This stimulation may well have caused the doubling of prices already observed.

The restraint on export had stirred grumbling among the merchants, but now it was the governor's turn to complain. He saw habitants of the Quebec district traveling up to the Richelieu to buy seed grain and returning empty handed, having been unable or unwilling to pay the price demanded; he saw the townsfolk's food supply threatened; and he saw all the needy ones looking to the government to rescue them from the clutches of private greed. Proclamations having proved a broken reed, he summoned the legislative council in January, 1780, to forge a more powerful weapon — an ordinance to compel sale at fixed prices. Though the home government, on the advice of its law officers, later asserted the competence of the legislature of the colony to pass such a measure and expressed astonishment that anyone could believe otherwise, there was a long and angry debate around the board on this very point.

The mercantile members were solidly opposed to the governor's plan as *ultra vires,* and they found two valuable allies. One may have been a surprise to them, for he was none other than Lieutenant Governor Cramahé, president of the council. In private discussions with Haldimand Cramahé had already roused the gubernatorial ire by his strenuous objections to the proposal. He condemned it as illegal and impolitic — illegal because it would be "taxing" wheat and flour and the Quebec Act forbade the imposition of any tax, and impolitic because it might cost Britain the whole province. The least spark, he said, might set the colony ablaze from one end to the other, and he feared that any price-fixing measure would strike a big spark from the peasantry in the Richelieu Valley, by far the richest and the most disaffected in the country. The seigniors were all for the bill, but Cramahé affirmed that they did not appreciate the change that had come over the people since the conquest. He also reminded his chief that the revolt of the old colonies had been provoked by a miserable tax.[37] The other ally was outside the council but none the less valuable because he was the attorney general, James Monk, whose legal opinion the board naturally demanded. Already a thorn in the flesh to the governor because he consistently supported the merchants as a class, he gave the advice that the opposition desired. Thus reinforced, they carried the day by a narrow majority.

All that the council would do was to substitute ordinances for the existing proclamations. One prohibited the export of foodstuffs for two years. The other enlarged the offenses of forestalling, regrating, and ingrossing to cover purveyors of milk and manufacturers of flour. This, like the instrument it superseded, was based upon a statute of Edward VI that Monk said was still the law. No one present on March 9, when the governor signed and sealed the ordinances of the session and prorogued the council, knew that the fundamental statute had been repealed in 1772 and that the penalties which had been copied from it were severer than those allowed at the time in Britain. The discovery was made by a young loyalist lawyer who had recently come to the country and who was later to be chief justice of Upper Canada, William Dummer Powell, and it obliged Haldimand to recall the council to re-enact the bill with the pillory and other illegal penalties removed.[38]

The governor attributed his defeat, which stands alone in the history of the council under the Quebec Act, to the perversity of the lieutenant governor, of the attorney general, and of the merchants in the council. Though impatient with Cramahé, he did not question his good faith, but he viewed the others with different eyes. He had already come to suspect Monk as a politician and now he thought even less of him as a lawyer, first because of his stand and secondly because of his slip on this occasion. In the mercantile section of the council, upon whom he cast the chief blame, he saw men who were abusing the trust reposed in them on their appointment. Were they not taking advantage of their public position to promote their private ends? Fortunately no great damage ensued. In 1781 Haldimand had the satisfaction of seeing the categorical opinion of the attorney and solicitor general of Britain upholding his own contention about the competence of the council inserted in its minutes by order of the secretary of state.[39] But there is no evidence that he then betrayed any feeling of triumph, for his was not a vindictive nature. Nor did he renew his effort to have the bill enacted. It was not necessary. The price of food did not

resume its upward trend even though the ordinance against fore-
stallers and regrators, under which there appear to have been no
prosecutions, was disallowed at home.*

Toward the close of the Revolutionary War the governor and
the merchants found themselves involved in a serious financial
tangle, not unconnected with the troubles already mentioned, which
caused a further estrangement and left a legacy of hate that was to
have far-reaching consequences.[40] The tangle began in the fall of
1779, immediately after the Honorable John Cochrane, a young
scion of an ancient noble house, landed in Quebec. He came as the
remitters' agent to replace Drummond and Jordan, who were dismissed because of their dishonest speculations, but he was no improvement upon them. He was either a knave or a dupe. It is hard
to say which, but it makes little difference. He was undoubtedly
clever; he was endowed with a forceful character; he had high
connections, and he held a most responsible position. With this formidable combination he at once impressed the innocent Haldimand
as a financial wizard and had little difficulty in persuading him that
he, the governor, would become responsible for an enormous loss on
exchange unless the merchants were immediately permitted to give
their notes as well as cash in return for bills drawn on the remitters
in London. This method of selling on partial credit had been
practiced in North America during the Seven Years' War and had
led to losses which the remitters of that day disputed with the government.[41] There is no evidence, however, that either Cochrane or
Haldimand was familiar with this experience of twenty years before,
and no one seems to have warned the old soldier that the system
was pernicious. He simply gave his consent to what he was told was
inevitable. Thenceforth the government "pegged" exchange at par
by lending money to the merchants. Each loan was free of interest
for a variable period, which seems to have been about two months,
and then it bore the usual rate of six per cent.

Why did Cochrane plunge Haldimand into this financial morass?
Sooner or later, one would imagine, the heavy war expenses of the
government in the colony would knock the bottom out of exchange
with London. Had this crisis arrived, or was it impending? An

* The tide of opinion in England was running against the laws upon which it
was based, and the board of trade advised that the embargo would suffice to keep
prices of wheat and flour down to reasonable levels.

examination of how the government of the province was financed until this time suggests that there was no reason for any panic and that the governor was the dupe of the agent, who, in turn, was either the dupe or the accomplice of scheming merchants. Murray had regularly procured cash for his public needs by selling bills on the treasury, and the merchants had been glad to give this accommodation because they secured in return a convenient means of paying their creditors in London.

This method of finding funds, altered only by the substitution of the remitters for the treasury, had survived the coming into force of the Quebec Revenue Act because the new revenue fell far short of the public expenses, which were piled high by the war, and very little specie was sent out. It worked well until Cochrane arrived. Sometimes the government gained and sometimes it lost, but never very much. Exchange fluctuated around par until 1772, when it reached an unprecedented variation, six and four-tenths per cent below. Then it rose until the disturbance of the invasion forced it down to ten per cent below. It returned to par in 1776 — probably because of heavy imports of specie with the army — and in the two following years it was slightly above par. In 1779 it fell to five and a half per cent below, from which point it climbed to three and a half per cent above, falling off again to one and seven-tenths per cent above. In the accounts of the civil government this was the rate at which were negotiated the last bills to be sold wholly for cash.[42] Unfortunately the corresponding transactions to fill the military chest have not yet come to light, but it is unlikely that they were governed by a different rate.

Though Haldimand immediately wrote the treasury telling what he had done, no note of warning reached Quebec until the spring of 1781, and then it came from Harley and Drummond — a peremptory order to Cochrane to stop granting credit. Instead of doing what he was told, the agent approached the governor with the assertion that it would be impossible to supply his requisitions unless the practice were continued. He explained that what his principals really desired was protection against loss and he intimated that Haldimand might satisfy them by officially assuming responsibility for the debts contracted by the merchants. This time, instead of simply accepting Cochrane's word, the governor turned to those who appeared most competent to give advice on such matters. Judging from his description of them,[43] they probably included William Grant, the wealthy Quebec merchant who had become deputy receiver general, and his predecessor in this office, Thomas Dunn, whose interest in trade continued after his elevation to the bench, and possibly Cramahé, who had likewise acted in Mills' absence. Whoever they were, they confirmed the agent's statement that the continued granting of credit was absolutely necessary unless large quantities of specie were sent out from England. This advice may have been partly due to interested motives, but, being tendered in June, 1781, it had greater justification than Cochrane's arguments in the fall of 1779. Had it been rejected now, the disastrous results that followed the abandonment of the system on the return of peace might have been precipitated, though to a lesser degree, during the crisis of the war. Aware of the dangers involved in the practice, these men drew up half a dozen safeguarding regulations. Haldimand adopted them and directed Cochrane to continue, assuring him that the crown would accept responsibility if they were observed.

If he had not done it before, the agent now certainly betrayed the governor, who still believed in his integrity. The young man saw to it that the regulations were not observed and that the old soldier should not learn what was passing under his nose. Credit was granted on an ever more lavish scale, occasionally to four times the amount received in cash, and bills were drawn far in excess of the governor's requisitions. In the pyramiding of debts one firm alone, Shaw and Fraser, came to owe the government more than £134,000 by the spring of 1783.[44] From the start Haldimand had felt some uneasiness, but he had accepted Cochrane's assurances until the early months of 1782. Then, beginning to suspect that his confidence had been abused, he demanded a full statement of accounts. The agent refused to give any information without a further guarantee that the crown would assume all the risks that had been incurred. The governor naturally refused to comply with this condition and a deadlock ensued. In June definite orders from the astonished treasury at last reached the Castle of St. Louis, and the practice of selling bills on partial credit was officially ended. But in defiance of these orders Cochrane granted further credit. He did it on the same principle on which a modern bank "carries" an embarrassed customer. In the spring of 1783 came more orders from the home government to exact an immediate payment of all outstanding debts. The engines were suddenly reversed and, relatively speaking, Canada experienced the worst financial wreck in its history; but the story of this wreck belongs to the period following the peace and will be told later.

Meanwhile the merchants had been making merry at the expense of the government. The "easy money" that began in the fall of 1779 gave wings to the usual war-time speculation. The last fillip in wheat prices referred to above appears to have been the first result. It was nothing to what followed. In 1780 the rum market was cornered.[45] In June, 1781, the governor reported that most of the business done in the colony was "transacted by the aid of public money." [46] This was bad enough in itself. It was made much worse by the fact that the supply houses then performed the function of banker for their customers. Thus the Canadian merchants were enjoying the dangerous luxury of two bankers. With bills bought on credit in Quebec, they were able to meet obligations in London more promptly and thereby to purchase still further credit there. Business in the colony was blowing itself up into a gigantic bubble. The inflation was reflected in an enormous increase of brandy and tobacco imports and in the trebling of the revenue from customs duties collected at Quebec.[47]

At first the merchants were pleased with the governor for doubling their resources and he returned their smile, glad to know that he was of assistance to them. But a cloud settled upon his brow as he detected a political danger in the commercial intoxication. What if a rebel army should come? Would it not be welcomed as a sponge to wipe out the mounting debts owed to the government? Fortunately his suspicions were never put to the test. Except indirectly through the speculation it stimulated, the vicious system did not antagonize the governor and the merchants until 1782, when he split with Cochrane and tried, though in vain, to stop the credit machine. Their relations became infinitely worse in the following year, when, in obedience to the home government, he insisted upon immediate payment, which was utterly impossible. Then they thought that he was trying to ruin them, and he was convinced that they were determined to cheat the government.

These years were likewise marked by a serious constitutional struggle, to which the friction between governor and merchants over economic affairs contributed. The issue was whether the twist that Carleton had given to the new constitution should be straightened out. Haldimand early set his face against any change. His determination had its roots in his tender regard for the feelings of the dominant race in the colony, in his not unnatural suspicion of the mercantile minority's political inclinations, and in his belief that it was dangerous to tamper with the constitution in time of war.

The governor tried to stand erect and on his own feet, but he found it difficult because of the forces brought to bear upon him to alter what had been established, and hence he leaned more and more upon the French party, the circle of friends inherited from his predecessor. Apparently he was not so intrigued as Carleton had been by the mirage of a society ruled by noblesse. The difference may be accounted for by Haldimand's different background and by his observation of the effect of the French war upon the upper class of Canadians. He was, however, much drawn to the group of English-speaking officials. He saw them as men who had made their homes in the country instead of trying to make profit out of it, as men who had cooperated in governing the colony instead of making it more difficult to govern, as men who believed that Canada would belong to Britain so long as it belonged to the Canadians and had therefore swallowed all their English prejudices, and, above all, as men who had never been tainted by any sympathy for the rebel cause.

The man most after his own heart was the one whose strong character made him the outstanding member of the group, Adam Mabane. As time passed, people observed how often these two, the governor and the doctor judge, both bachelors, dined at each other's table, how frequently they were closeted together, and how Mabane, even more than Cramahé, voiced Haldimand's opinion in the council and out of it. Then the rumor grew that almost everything proposed by the governor emanated from "the doctor." Indeed, the day came when Haldimand supported Mabane's claim to be made chief justice in the place of the absent Livius. Unlike Cochrane, Mabane would never have dreamed of deceiving his chief, but it is a nice question whether he did not mislead him, for his judgment was not so unimpeachable as his honesty. The English-speaking merchants hated this judge as they hated no one else, for he was the implacable foe of any change in the law, and next to the governor he was the most powerful man in the colony. It is quite possible and even probable that he retaliated by closing Haldimand's mind to the wrong his predecessor had wrought and by hardening his heart against every effort to undo it.

From two different quarters pressure was brought to bear upon the governor to pull the colony's constitution back into proper shape. One was the home government, which, as soon as the Livius investigation revealed how the system of laws and the form of government had been warped, decided that the original design should be followed. Accordingly, in March, 1779, two additional instructions were issued.[48] The first condemned the "privy" council and forbade the governor to summon only a select knot of councilors to perform the function of the whole body. The second enjoined prompt obedience to the original instructions, which required the governor to communicate to the council every article that concerned legislation. The first meant that Haldimand was to throw open the "government" of the country to men whom he distrusted. The second meant that he was to urge the legislature of the colony to pass measures that he and his trusted advisers condemned as dangerous — ordinances introducing English commercial law, trial by jury for torts and mercantile disputes, and the principle of the Habeas Corpus Act.

The other quarter was the mercantile interest in Canada, which strove to effect a change through its representation in the council. Here the pressure was not applied equally to secure the abolition of the "privy" council and the amelioration of the laws. It was furtively applied to effect the former but openly to achieve the latter. And even in the matter of the laws there was discrimination born of war conditions. The desire to introduce the principle of the Habeas Corpus Act was qualified by a willingness to postpone its application until hostilities were over; the demand for the other legal reforms would admit of no such delay.

The personal equation did not enter into the governor's conflict with the home authorities, but it dominated the struggle in the colony. George Allsopp, who had played a minor part in Livius' day, now stood head and shoulders above all others in the attack. Perhaps he had been tutored by the absent chief justice, and certainly he was one of the ablest men in the colony. He thoroughly believed in the righteousness of the cause, and he was a born fighter. But with all his cleverness and courage, Allsopp had serious defects which prevented him from winning much confidence outside his own circle. His private character, even in that unpuritanical age, aroused frequent and unfavorable comment, and his political character was profoundly suspected. He never lived down the reputation he had gained in the days when he prowled about the streets of Quebec by night without a lantern and when he quietly prompted the famous first grand jury to bring in an insulting presentment. These incidents, instead of fading from memory, were actually touched up by perennial gossip, so that many people came to know more than had happened.

It was also believed, and with good reason, that his political agitation was spurred on by a private grievance. Carleton, who had admitted him to the office of deputy secretary, had led him to believe that he would become secretary of the province, with an official seat at the board, when the Quebec Act was passed; but when the new government was established he found, without any warning, that he was to be only an ordinary councilor. The disappointment, which seems to have been due at least in part to the distrust he stirred in Carleton's mind,[49] rankled deeply within him.

Much more serious was the belief, commonly held in official Quebec, that Allsopp was a rebel in his heart. Many things contributed to this belief — his language, his general attitude, and his personal connections. He sympathized with the Americans as much as anyone then at large in Canada dared. He had been the consistent opponent of the government of the colony, and even yet he continued to advocate an assembly. He was married to a sister of the Bondfield brothers, who had tried to take out political insurance against commercial loss when the Americans closed in on Quebec; and his business partner, John Welles, had openly joined the invaders in 1775. In justice to Allsopp's memory it should be observed that, judging by what evidence has survived, this stormy petrel of Quebec was a fundamentally loyal citizen of the British Empire. Still one can see how, in the war-heated atmosphere of the time, the official mind in Canada naturally recoiled from him and his principles as highly dangerous to British authority on the shores of the St. Lawrence.

In the background, outside the council, stood two other interesting figures. One was that of the attorney general, James Monk, likewise a disciple of Livius, with whom he had been on familiar terms. For half a century Monk was a prominent character in the life of Canada. After many years of service as attorney general he was appointed chief justice of Montreal, and shortly before his death he was knighted. But he was ever discontented because he never attained the goal of his ambition, which was to be chief justice of the province. It was not that his ambition overreached his ability. His want of legal knowledge on the subject of price regulation was an exception.

There can be little doubt that the real cause of Monk's failure was a weakness of character. There was something disingenuous about him which may have been accentuated by various accidents of his career. On coming to Quebec in 1776 he found himself under a cloud, for he was Germain's nominee and Carleton therefore resented his appointment. His consequent discomfort, together with his previous experience as solicitor general in Nova Scotia, where the French were comparatively ignored, inclined him to side with the mercantile opposition. Though careful to avoid Carleton's displeasure, he quickly aroused the distrust of Haldimand. The latter may have looked askance at him because he had been born in Boston, but the new governor was more particularly disturbed by his political attitude, which had become more pronounced. The attorney general gave his superior dark hints of impending changes in the laws, and at the same time he egged Allsopp on to demand these changes. Haldimand intimated to Monk that it was the attorney general's duty to support the policy of the government that employed him. But these mutual suggestions, far from drawing the two men together, drove them apart.

The lawyer also offended by his self-seeking. This trait appeared distinctly in 1780, when the council passed the fee ordinance that would have been enacted in 1778 had not Carleton torpedoed the work of that session. Monk was affected not only as attorney general but also as Livius' surrogate in the vice-admiralty court. The bill allowed him all that he could justly claim,* yet he was determined to get more, and he bombarded the council with written statements and oral arguments. Indeed, he became so obstreperous that his right to address the board was challenged and his mouth was shut by a vote of twenty to one. The one vote, of course,

* He was allowed to charge one-third more than what other lawyers could demand for services in the courts.

was Allsopp's.[50] Though silenced, the attorney general would not admit defeat, particularly because the council would not even allow the payment of some claims that seem to have been just. Year after year he continued to submit charges, some of which were founded only upon the law in his own mind. It is not surprising that Haldimand placed less and less reliance upon this official and at last, in the final winter of the war, deprived him of some of his lucrative duties by reviving the long dormant office of solicitor general,[51] to which he appointed Jenkin Williams, a Welsh lawyer who had been practicing in the colony since 1767 and had been serving as clerk of the council from 1777.

The other figure that troubled the political peace of Quebec was the ghost of Livius. His vindication was a great encouragement to his old friends to continue the fight in which he had fallen, and at the same time it stiffened the reactionary spirit of the majority in the council. Mabane and his kind were now emboldened to resist reform, even though commanded by the home government in new instructions, because they knew that these orders were inspired by the absent chief justice, against whom they harbored violent prejudices. They felt a deep responsibility for upholding true principles in Quebec when Livius had persuaded the authorities in London to urge false doctrines.

Haldimand was obliged to face the issue of reform when he called his legislative council together for the first time on January 11, 1779. The ordinance regulating procedure in the civil courts, the measure that should have granted English commercial law and jury trials for torts and commercial disputes, was, along with the other two pieces of temporary legislation of 1777, about to expire. In his opening address the governor threw out a strong hint to the councilors. He announced that there would have been no session at all had it not been necessary to renew the expiring ordinances, and he expressed the hope that the requisite business would be completed with all possible dispatch, for his supreme duty of caring for the defense of the province might soon draw him away from Quebec.[52]

Allsopp refused to take the hint. He had been waiting for this opportunity to reopen the whole question according to the promise given by Cramahé two years before. When the lieutenant governor broke his promise by moving that the offending ordinance be renewed without amendment for another period of two years, the old agitator at once demanded that it be read and considered article by article. The motion from the chair was accorded precedence and the vote was taken according to custom — for no rules had been formally adopted — by roll call in the ascending order of seniority. When Cramahé's turn came at the end, the vote stood nine to eight against him. He made it a tie. Then the tie was broken, not by the casting vote of the president, for he was not recognized as having any such right, but by the peculiar method of striking out the negative vote of Allsopp.[53] This blow beneath the belt appears to have knocked the breath out of the champion of the merchants. The minutes record no further motion from him during the remainder of the short six-day session.

In the following September Haldimand was embarrassed by the receipt of the two additional instructions already mentioned — his first communication from the home government on this question. What troubled him was not a feeling that he had done wrong, for his conscience was clear, but the difficulty of knowing what was the right thing to do then. His doubts are suggested by his letter acknowledging these orders. He promised to obey as far as he could "consistently with that duty I owe to the royal interest in this part of the world." [54] How far would that duty permit him to go? On September 27, a fortnight after he had written the above words, he met all the councilors who could assemble in answer to his summons, and he had the first of the additional instructions read in their presence. But this burial service was pronounced over a body that was not yet dead. The "privy" council lived on, enjoying a sort of subterranean existence for another three years, during which time the legal executive council remained only a legal fiction. Its minutes, kept in what is called the State Book, are almost a blank for the whole of this period. Even the semiannual passing of the public accounts does not appear, for this business was handled by the members of the old select group, appointed by special warrant for the purpose, a procedure against which Allsopp protested in a letter to the secretary of state.[55]

Was Haldimand sinning as Carleton had sinned? Was his formal obedience in September, 1779, designed to cover his actual disobedience in the three years that followed? This is possible but not probable. A knowledge of the whole man leads one to conclude that he intended to do what he was ordered by the home government, but, having taken the first step, he studied the reaction and judged that it would be unsafe to go further until the end of the war was in sight. It must also be remembered that the original sin was Carleton's. Haldimand did not create the "privy" council; he inherited it. The same was true of the warped legal system. Here the new governor's position was much more difficult than that of his predecessor. By withholding the concessions that should have been granted to the English-speaking community, Carleton stiffened the attitude of the Canadians, confirming them in their mistaken belief that these concessions clashed with their own interests. This belief, which quickly became almost an article of religion with them, was an obstacle in the way of repairing the injustice done to the racial minority; and, it need hardly be added, there was the additional obstacle created by the French declaration of war.

In October, 1779, while puzzling over what he should do with the second additional instruction, Haldimand received a third,[56] likewise a by-product of the Livius affair, directing a reform of the judicial machinery. The discovery that the chief justice had no jurisdiction in civil cases, except as a member of the council sitting in appeal, revealed to the board of trade an obvious waste of the best judicial ability in the colony. The board was also impressed by the argument, which Livius presented in a memorial on the defects of the judicial administration, that the fusion of the legislative and judicial powers in one body was wrong in principle and bad in practice. Therefore this third additional instruction, issued in July, ordered the governor and council to pass an ordinance making the chief justice the presiding judge in both courts of common pleas, which were thenceforth to hold more restricted terms, and creating a new court of appeals to be composed of four judges, including the chief justice and four laymen named from the council. The lieutenant governor, who had presided over the court of appeals, was not to be of this number.

Haldimand now appears to have made up his mind to compromise by obeying the third but not the second instruction. Accordingly he replied to Germain that he would submit this document to the council, although he expressed the fear that it would not meet with approval in the colony, and he intimated, without actually stating, that he would defer action on the other instruction.

He spoke of hints accidentally dropped by Monk that "other alterations are upon the carpet," and he repeated what he had already
told the secretary of state by word of mouth and in various dispatches — that all changes in these ticklish times were highly dangerous, "especially when taken up from the suggestion of lawyers
attending more to mere matters of form than to substantial justice"
and without any regard being paid to the "disposition of the people
at large." [57]

In the next legislative session, which opened on January 27, 1780,
the submission of the third additional instruction gave Allsopp an
opportunity to renew the strife. In desperation he broke loose and
for nearly four weeks the council had rather a wild time. When
Colonel Caldwell opened the debate with a motion against the proposed ordinance, Allsopp at once pressed a question which he said
should be considered first. "For the better understanding of the
business we are met upon" he moved that the governor be requested
to lay before the board every instruction he had received having to
do with legislation. Then, he added, the council could "prepare
themselves humbly and dutifully" to meet the intentions of the
home government. The council refused to consider Allsopp's motion before the colonel's and the latter was carried by a vote of
twelve to six. The minority then began what soon became a common practice. They insisted that the reasons for their dissent from
the majority be entered in the minutes. Their purpose in thus
registering their protests was to appeal to the home government
through the attested copies of the minutes that had to be transmitted regularly. Their device, however, was unsuccessful. The
records of the council's proceedings do not seem to have been read
by those in authority across the water. The majority, who likewise
realized what a serious step they had taken, decided to justify
themselves in a more effective but less honest way. On Mabane's
suggestion they prepared an address to the governor explaining
why the additional instruction should not be obeyed, and they
railroaded it through the council to make it appear an expression
of the opinion of the whole body.[58] Haldimand of course would
inclose the document in a letter home. There it would be read, and
by the secretary of state.

The address is a revealing document.[59] First, it contained a
thinly veiled attack on the absent chief justice, who was more than

suspected of stirring up this business, and criticized the instruction for proposing to allow him to sit in appeal on his own judgments. Secondly, it defended the existing arrangements for the administration of justice. It condemned the idea of fewer terms for the courts of common pleas as a bad practice that had been abandoned; it asserted, without giving any reasons, that the suggested change in the court of appeals, far from being of any advantage, would only lessen the dignity of the highest court in the colony; and it commended the personnel of the courts of common pleas.

The last point requires a little explanation. The three amateur judges who were members of the council, Mabane, Dunn, and Fraser, believed that over in London Livius had been decrying their judicial capacity — as indeed he had, and with some justification — and they had taken this instruction as a direct personal reflection upon themselves, though it was not so intended. Their resentment was bitter and their friends around the board shared their feelings. On the day the address was submitted to the council, one of these friends called for a return of all cases that had been adjudicated in the court of appeals. On the morrow, when it was presented, Fraser gloated. There were only twenty-one judgments reviewed; five came from the Quebec court and were all sustained, though the two English judges of that court were not bred to the law; and of the fourteen appealed from Montreal six were wholly or in part reversed, though delivered by his own legally trained colleagues. Immediately it was agreed that the list should be appended to the address.[60]

The third point in the address worth noting is that it proclaimed the political faith of the French party. The laws of the country might be improved, but alterations "should be made with moderation and be more the effects of experience than of any preconceived theory or opinion." Very deplorable were the rumors circulated every summer, when communication with London was open, that the form of government was to be changed — a reference which, like the preceding one about theory, Allsopp was to elucidate. When the empire was passing through a great crisis, such rumors "disquiet the minds of the people and furnish plausible pretences to the emissaries of the revolted colonies and the other enemies of the state to insinuate that nothing is permanent under a British government, and [that] the Quebec Act, the result of the generous and tolerating spirit which distinguishes an enlightened age and nation, was the effect of a narrow and interested policy and would be repealed as soon as the ends for which it was made were effected." In conclusion the address defended the general course pursued by the council, asserting that it was aimed to preserve Canada for the empire.[61] The Quebec Act as already applied was the ark of the covenant and the French party were the high priests of patriotism!

Even more illuminating is the counterblast that Allsopp prepared and inserted in the minutes.[62] After naming those who had voted for the address and referring to them as the majority "styling themselves the legislative council," he proceeded to more serious matters. The judges of the common pleas, "not being versed in the science of the law or the usages of courts of judicature, consequently cannot be supposed capable to form or keep up proper regulations . . . nor do they confine themselves to rules of law but occasionally decide on the equity of the case, contrary to the letter of the law." They were sadly in need of the guidance of the chief justice, particularly since they had become sole judges of the facts and the interpreters of laws and customs "which form the most imperfect system in the world for a commercial people." "In matters of trade," the system had "been long since exploded in France and the *code marchand* introduced in all their towns in its stead," but this code was not adopted in Canada, there having been no "great occasion" for it. The decisions of the judges were "too arbitrary and their powers too unbounded to tally with the principles of the British constitution." They had even handed over Protestant orphans to be educated by Roman Catholics. The existing court of appeals, being also the legislative council and the executive council, violated the fundamental principle of the separation of powers enunciated by Montesquieu, whom he quoted. He also cited the learned Scottish judge, Lord Kames, who had uttered a dictum against courts with a fluctuating personnel, to condemn this court which "does not consist of the same members at each sitting."

Allsopp ridiculed the inferences drawn from the return of appeals submitted with the address. The list suggested that appeals were few, whereas they were many. It said nothing of the larger number of cases that were still undetermined. The upholding of inferior judgments meant nothing when few of the decisions on appeal were unanimous. He reminded Cramahé of the only occasion on which he did not preside in the court of appeals — "when upon a division of voices it was determined he should not give two votes, though contended for by him and therein supported by two judges of the common pleas." He turned Fraser inside out. "It is admitted that the decisions of all causes removed from the court of common pleas at Quebec that are yet tried in appeal have been confirmed, but does not this tend to prove too much?" And as for the upsetting of Montreal judgments, did not this reflect upon the court of appeals rather than upon the "law judges"?

He taunted the majority for defying the royal will by voting the continuance of their own authority as appeal judges, and he boldly referred to the disobedience of the governor and his predecessor in holding back the instructions directing the restoration of juries and the commercial laws applied in England. If Carleton had summoned the council in the spring of 1775 to pass these ameliorative measures, or if he had only published the intentions of the home government, leaving them to be carried out later, he might have killed the ferment which spread from the old to the new subjects and crippled the colony when the Revolution turned north. This, Allsopp affirmed, was no "preconceived theory or opinion" but a sound judgment based on a knowledge of the feelings and passions of men who were deeply wounded. The rumors that flew about when summer came were hatched by the Quebec Act itself. Did not its phrase, "whereas it is at present inexpedient to call an assembly," suggest a time when it might be expedient? The mere thought, even if it had not been encouraged by the act, was bound to have a wholesome rather than a deleterious effect.

Allsopp's words let loose an angry storm around the board. He was accused of insulting the governor, the council, and the judges. Caldwell wanted to have the protest torn from the minutes, and he talked of "arraigning, trying, convicting, censuring and suspending" the offending member, who was unintentionally rescued from a most uncomfortable situation by a message from the governor commanding the attendance of the council at the Castle of St. Louis for the bills of the session to receive his signature and to be passed under the seal of the province.[63]

This session of 1780 saw the high tide of the battle. Though the ordinance regulating proceedings in the civil courts came up for renewal when the legislative council met again on January 16, 1781,

Allsopp contented himself with a few simple motions which were overwhelmingly defeated.[64] The most pointed of his proposals was couched in the very language of the original instructions and contained a rider to the effect that cases between Canadians might, if they desired, be determined without the intervention of a jury. This motion appears most reasonable, and yet not a single member would vote with Allsopp in support of it. The reason for his modesty and his loneliness was twofold. His boldness in the previous year had greatly offended his colleagues at the board, and he himself seems to have felt that he had overshot the mark.[65] Moreover, Haldimand had just imparted to the councilors the information, received from Clinton, that an invasion of Canada was to be expected at any moment. As a consequence the session of 1781 ended only four days after it began, all the necessary business having been completed in this record time.

Meanwhile Haldimand had unburdened himself in several dispatches written toward the end of October, 1780,[66] when no reply was possible until the following summer. In these he reviewed the career of the old agitator to give a significant background to the account of the stormy session, and to hint that he should be removed from the council. He also stated clearly for the first time that he could not present his instructions directing a change in the laws of the country. He told Germain quite frankly that he thoroughly agreed with the attitude and the policy of the majority of the council. "The Quebec Act is a sacred charter granted by the king in parliament to the Canadians as a security for their religion, laws and property." These were the real people of the colony, and it should be governed accordingly. Their interests and their feelings should override those of the English-speaking inhabitants. The latter were only three per cent of the population; few of them could "with propriety be considered as residents of the province"; and many of them were more American than British. "The clamor about the trial by juries in civil causes is calculated for the meridian of London." However well the institution might work in England, it was not applicable in Canada, where it would be abused by the small trading community, would offend the Canadians, and would expose the foreign troops to insult. The principle underlying the Habeas Corpus Act was excellent, but it might cause ruin in a country surrounded by enemies and infested with spies.

Stern was the rebuke administered by the secretary of state. On April 12, 1781, Germain replied to Haldimand: "Your withholding from the council the instructions which you were originally commanded by the king to communicate to them, and that command repeated by an additional and special instruction from His Majesty, is considered by His Majesty, as well as the lords of trade [67] and myself, as such an instance of disobedience to the royal authority as ought not to be passed over, if longer persisted in." At the same time it is quite apparent that the secretary of state sympathized with the governor, for he softened the blow by assuring him that the purity of his motives was not questioned and that his administration of the colony was in every other respect most commendable. He also agreed with him in his adverse judgment of Allsopp, but only half caught the hint about his removal. However, his words suggested that Haldimand might have suspended him or that the board of trade might have recommended his permanent exclusion from the council had Haldimand requested it. [68]

On receiving this definite command, Haldimand yielded a prompt obedience. He did not even wait until the next legislative session after the new year, but called the council together on August 30, 1781, and had the cogent articles of his original instructions read and entered in the minutes. [69] No action of course was legally possible at this season, but Allsopp was sure to demand it when the council again met for legislation after the new year, unless some restraint were applied. Therefore the governor opened the next legislative session on February 2, 1782, with a curt statement, which had the undoubted approval of the great majority of the council, that the state of affairs in Canada and in the neighboring colonies demanded expedition and unanimity, and that to avoid any loss of time he had directed the attorney general to draft the ordinances necessary to renew those that were about to expire. [70]

During the debates * it became evident that Allsopp had fully recovered his confidence and his breath. The minutes reveal that he twitted his fellow councilors for their past opinions on more than one subject. True to form, he again overshot the mark. In a

* Thomas Dunn presided during this session, Cramahé having been called home on Sir Thomas Mills' request to help settle the tangled accounts of the province, and Finlay, the only other member senior to Dunn, having also crossed the water on business.

motion on the laws he inserted the remark that his protest of two years before had evidently inspired the order from England which had occasioned the meeting of August 30. After this malicious dig at his colleagues and at the governor, he moved for leave to introduce three bills. The first was to secure what he had vainly demanded in the previous year — English commercial law and compulsory jury trials for civil causes except when both parties were Canadians. The second was for the introduction of the right of habeas corpus as it existed in England; and the third was for the suspension of this right until the end of the 1783 session. He got the leave that he desired, but nothing more. When he moved to proceed with his proposed ordinances, one of the Canadian members, De Longueuil, intervened with a motion for a year's hoist. The first bill was then shelved by a vote of fourteen to three, but the other two mustered eight supporters against nine.[71]

In the session of 1783 the cause of reform was weaker because its bold leader was excluded from the board. On summoning the council the governor had ordered the clerk to notify Allsopp that he was suspended, particularly for his protest in 1780.[72] Apparently Haldimand and his advisers feared that the troublesome merchant might create another scene, for the ordinance regulating procedure in the civil courts was coming up again. Now it was renewed without any motion for civil juries. But the right of habeas corpus was obviously considered in a different light. It found a military champion. Though violently opposed to Allsopp personally and politically, Colonel Caldwell had voted with him on the question of habeas corpus, and now he moved for the legal adoption of the right and its suspension "during the time of the present unnatural rebellion." On this occasion only seven votes supported the proposal against a motion to postpone its consideration for another year.[73] Thus, as long as the war lasted, the reactionary forces triumphed against the double pressure exerted by the home government and by the mercantile community in the colony.

CHAPTER XIV

THE SHADOW OF THE PEACE [1]

BRITAIN'S empire in America could not be rent in twain without leaving raw edges. One of these was in the Gulf of St. Lawrence, where New Englanders, as British subjects, had played a leading part in developing the fisheries, which constituted one of the most treasured resources of the empire. Were they, because they ceased to be British subjects, to be excluded from the waters and shores that they had come to regard as their own and upon which their prosperity depended? The idea was intolerable. Therefore the American commissioners negotiating over in France were instructed to insist "that in no case, by any treaty of peace, the common right of fishing be given up," and they did insist. Consequently, in the third article of the treaty signed in Paris on September 3, 1783, Britain granted all citizens of the United States equal rights with British subjects to fish in all British North American waters, and also allowed them to land and dry their fish in the unsettled bays, harbors, and creeks of Nova Scotia, the Magdalen Islands, and Labrador, but not of Newfoundland. Until recent years this sharing of the fisheries produced serious recurrent friction, but the trouble need only be mentioned here. As it did not develop until the early years of the nineteenth century and as it concerned the maritime provinces more than what was then Canada, its discussion lies beyond the scope of the present volume.*

Much more important is the second article of the treaty, which fixed the new international boundary.[2] This left its mark on Canada for all time, and almost immediately the complications it produced injected a bitter poison into Anglo-American relations. To understand this boundary, it is necessary to divide it into three parts, each of which had an independent origin: (1) the middle of the St.

---

* By the Treaty of Versailles the rights enjoyed by French fishermen under the treaty of 1763 were also slightly altered. They lost the right to land and cure on the east coast of Newfoundland between Cape Bonavista and Cape St. John, but on the western coast their right was extended over the much longer line from Cape Riche to Cape Ray.

Croix River to its source and thence straight north to the height of land that divides the rivers flowing into the St. Lawrence from those emptying into the Atlantic; (2) the height of land to the Connecticut River, down that river to the forty-fifth parallel of latitude and thence straight west to the St. Lawrence; and (3) through the middle of the St. Lawrence and the Great Lakes system, up the chain of waterways to the northwest corner of the Lake of the Woods, and thence straight west to the Mississippi.

The first section was what was supposed to have been the boundary of the older Nova Scotia, which then comprised what is now New Brunswick. Its definition has been responsible for the loss of many tempers and the spilling of much ink because of the subsequent difficulty of determining which was the St. Croix River, but the painful story need not be repeated here, because it belongs to the history of the maritime provinces. The second part raises no difficulty because it was taken from the Quebec Act, which in turn had taken it from the famous proclamation of 1763. The definition of the third section stopped at the Mississippi because the United States then claimed no land beyond. The supposition that the line would reach the Mississippi was an error which gave rise to further negotiations and has left its trace upon the map in the little detached portion of American territory to the west of the Lake of the Woods. As the adoption of the forty-ninth parallel belongs to a later period and to the history of the Canadian Northwest, the only question left for examination here is why the boundary was run as it now lies, through the middle of the St. Lawrence River and the Great Lakes and up to the northwest corner of the Lake of the Woods.

We have long since come to regard this line as natural, but it was not natural in the beginning. Several important considerations suggest that the boundary should have followed another course, which would have greatly enlarged the scope of Canada's development and restricted that of the United States. Of all the country lying north of the Ohio, the Americans had seized only the southwest corner, and this they had not been able to hold. Though the British had not reoccupied this quarter, their position on the Great Lakes had remained unassailable and at the end of the war they were in virtual possession of the whole of the "Old Northwest" of the United States. Moreover, this territory was then valuable only for the furs it produced, and of these the Americans were getting practically none. Except for a trickle of peltries down the Mississippi, the trade was focused at Montreal. True, the war had given Montreal a monopoly which peace was bound to break, but peace could not rob this Canadian town of its natural advantage over any rival on the east side of the continent. The part of the continent lying north of the Ohio was then and for years to come much more accessible from Canada than from the thirteen colonies that had established their independence.

Why did Britain agree to surrender this great land which she still held, and which belonged historically, economically, and geographically to Canada? The mystery deepens when one considers what followed. In spite of the stipulation in the treaty for a speedy evacuation of American soil, Britain refused to surrender the keys of this territory for another thirteen years. Why did she refuse? Persecuted loyalists and repudiated debts can no longer be pleaded, though British persistence may still lead an odd individual to repeat these old excuses. Did the British government suddenly realize that it had committed a great blunder, and, having realized this, determine to put forth every effort to undo it? If so, what was the nature of the blunder? Was it in surrendering the seat of the fur trade, as Americans then and since have contended, or was it something else?

One explanation of the boundary of 1783 that leaps to mind is that the Americans coveted the fur trade and demanded a boundary that would give it to them. But there were deeper causes than this. The royal proclamation of 1763 and the Quebec Act of eleven years later constituted a strong predetermining influence. Had not the former instrument cut off the whole of Canada's natural hinterland, she might have got more of it in 1783. The restoration effected by the second instrument was too recent and too intimately associated with the beginning of the American quarrel to pass unchallenged in the day of reckoning. The proclamation gave the Americans a solid ground for the claim that their intense hatred of the Quebec Act drove them to make.

A passage in a letter from Lord North to George III on March 25, 1778, suggests that Franklin was then demanding the repeal of the Quebec Act as an essential condition for peace.[3] Three weeks later, a great friend of the colonial cause, Sir George Savile, rose in

the house of commons and moved for the repeal of the act "upon
the ground of its being odious and inimical to the Americans, and
consequently an obstacle to our attempts to make an accommodation with them." This motion was supported by fifty-four members
against ninety-six.[4] In the summer of 1779, when defining the
boundaries claimed by the confederated states, the continental congress simply took the line drawn in 1763 and continued it westward
from Lake Nipissing to the Mississippi. In the spring of 1782, when
negotiations were opened with Benjamin Franklin in Paris, this
astute bargainer went further. He demanded the cession of the
whole of Canada as a pledge of peace. Then, on learning that the
British government would not listen to such a proposal, he took
his stand on the line laid down by congress three years earlier,
demanding the restriction of Canada to the limits existing before
the Quebec Act.

On August 29 the British cabinet decided to accept the terms that
Franklin had offered.[5] This meant severing from Canada all of
what is now the older part of Ontario except a narrow strip along
the Ottawa. In the middle of October the cabinet grew a little
bolder. Britain's right to the "back country" was to be asserted as a
means of indemnifying the loyalists. But the Americans were to be
told that this claim would not be pressed if these sufferers were
otherwise justly provided for in any part of the peace settlement —
with the United States or France or Spain.[6] Thereupon the American commissioners offered the British a little more, presenting an
option between the continuation of the line along the forty-fifth
parallel of latitude from the St. Lawrence to the Mississippi, which
would have given southern Ontario to the United States and the
northern tip of Michigan and most of Minnesota to Canada, or the
present boundary to the Lake of the Woods and thence straight
west to the Mississippi. The second alternative was accepted and
inserted in the preliminary articles of peace signed in Paris on November 30, 1782.

Every post on the Great Lakes was thus promised to the Americans, the chief of them being the fortified and garrisoned centers of
Carleton Island, Oswego, Niagara, Detroit, and Michilimackinac,
and the rendezvous of the trade to the far northwest, Grand Portage.
That Carleton Island lay south of the line was probably unknown,
and there may have been some uncertainty about the location of

Grand Portage, but there could have been no doubt that the other four places would be on American territory, which Britain agreed to evacuate "with all convenient speed." One factor in this settlement, the American demand, is quite intelligible; but the other, the British surrender, cries out for explanation.

At first glance it looks as if Britain were carelessly presenting the Americans with the keys of the fur trade. The merchants who were interested were not consulted at all, and when they learned what had happened they raised a loud cry. At the close of January, 1783, they memorialized Lord Shelburne, the head of the ministry, and a week later they interviewed Richard Oswald, who had been intrusted by that statesman with the management of the negotiation. Then the merchants learned to their chagrin that their remonstrances were too late; and, according to the story told years afterward, the negotiator of the treaty, on hearing what he had done, burst into tears and confessed his complete ignorance of the value of the country yielded and even of the existence of the posts he had signed away. The story is undoubtedly apocryphal, and yet the truth of what he had agreed to is startling enough. In the previous August, Franklin had actually persuaded him to advise the British government to cede the whole of Canada. This was only one example of a conciliatory disposition which led the Duke of Richmond to tell the king early in December that he could not understand why Oswald had not been replaced, since every member of the cabinet except Shelburne "had long seen he pled the cause of America, not of Britain." [7] Modern writers also have condemned the imbecility of the British agent and have asserted that he was the dupe of the wily old American.

But Oswald was no fool. He was a Scottish merchant resident in London. He had acquired a large fortune, partly through army contracts; and through his wife he had become possessed of great estates in the American colonies and in the West Indies. He was an old personal friend of Shelburne, to whom he had been introduced by Adam Smith, and on more than one occasion he had been consulted by the ministry on the subject of American affairs. A cynic might suggest that he was looking after his American interests by currying favor with Franklin and his associates, but no one then or since has really suspected him of harboring such a motive. Not in Oswald lies the explanation of Britain's surrender, for the simple reason that he did not have a free hand in Paris. He was closely bound by instructions, and he signed only what the cabinet in London had already accepted. He was a mere agent.

Parliament itself was responsible for the bargain arranged in the French capital. On March 4, 1782, General Conway had moved in the house of commons that all who should advise or attempt the further prosecution of the war in America would be enemies of their country, and the resolution had been carried without a division. This decision, leading to the fall of the North administration, tied the hands of the new government. When one country publicly announces that it will fight no longer, the other may get almost any terms it desires. Nearly a year afterward, when the document signed on November 30 was submitted to parliament, there was much talk of a ruinous war being concluded by an equally ruinous peace; and of the various articles which came in for bitter criticism that defining the boundary was one. Though Shelburne declared that the preliminary terms were only provisional and need not be regarded as binding, the opposition formally accepted them as final and then carried a resolution condemning the government for having made unnecessary concessions. Obviously, as Pitt said, the house voted to turn out Shelburne rather than to bring in a better peace.

That Britain was sick of the war was one great reason why the Americans got what they demanded, but it was not the whole explanation. From the beginning of the negotiation Franklin urged, and Shelburne believed, that the defeated mother country should grant really generous terms to the victorious colonies as a means of permanently severing them from their European allies and of binding America to Britain in a lasting friendship.

Still other and more particular calculations lay behind the absence of any haggling over the boundary. The profits of the fur trade had been as dust in the balance when compared with the cost of preserving that trade in the late war, and Shelburne knew it. He realized that a line on the map would make no difference to the natives. They would carry their skins to the traders who attracted them most. He also saw that the mere restoration of peace was bound to break Montreal's monopoly by opening other channels into the interior from the new republic, and he regarded the prospect with complacency. Through whatever paths the furs came out, they would still be brought to London, the world's fur market;

and English manufactures would still be required for the Indian trade, since the Americans had no competing industries. Like Oswald, his agent, Shelburne was a disciple of Adam Smith and was thoroughly opposed to commercial restrictions. Indeed, the idea of free trade presided over the whole of the negotiations, and it was agreed that the British and the Americans should have equally free access to the interior irrespective of any boundary line. This was to have been stipulated in the treaty along with the provision for the free navigation of the Mississippi by citizens of both countries. Incidentally, the American commissioners proposed to extend this provision to the St. Lawrence,[8] but as it then meant little to them, they refrained from pressing the point. They openly said that the inhabitants north and west of the Alleghenies could be more easily supplied with European goods through the two great waterways of the continent than overland from the ports on the Atlantic seaboard, and therefore Britain might enjoy a sort of commercial empire over the vast interior.

There is every reason for believing that the American commissioners meant what they said and that the treaty would have been drawn as intended had not difficulties appeared on Britain's side which prevented her from seizing the prize within her grasp. The commercial arrangements were to be general, and this meant overhauling British legislation on the subject. Therefore, at Britain's request, everything pertaining to commerce, except the provision for the free navigation of the Mississippi, which became the eighth article of the peace, was deleted in order to be settled by a separate treaty. Then the shipping interests raised such a clamor against tampering with the sacred navigation laws in the interests of a late enemy that the commercial negotiation was stillborn. Thus, like a passage the meaning of which is changed by being lifted out of its context, was the border between Canada and the United States fixed.[9]

Though the boundary was then defined on paper, years passed before Britain would recognize it in practice. She refused to hand over the posts on what was now the American side of the line, and for eleven years would not even agree to any specific time when she would deliver these keys to the west. For all the Americans knew until 1794, she was determined to retain them indefinitely. To use plain English, Britain violated the treaty. Why did she do it?

Many American writers have insisted that she was simply trying to keep the fur trade in her own hands,[10] and another American historian has recently advanced the plausible suggestion that the violation was a natural outgrowth of the incomplete nature of the treaty.[11] British writers, on the other hand, have defended the retention of the posts as a justifiable reprisal for two American violations of the treaty: obstacles placed in the way of the recovery of British debts, and the treatment meted out to loyalists. A close examination of the documents shows that none of these explanations accounts for the beginning of the British violation of the treaty.

The responsibility for starting this violation can be traced to Haldimand in Quebec. On April 26, 1783, he received from New York a printed copy of the peace preliminaries. This was his first intimation of what the new boundary was to be, and it came as a great shock. Immediately he saw what the merchants saw, the commercial loss foreshadowed by the surrender of the western posts. But this was not his chief concern, as he himself said. What most alarmed him was the possible reaction of the Indians. What would they do when they discovered that Britain had betrayed them by agreeing to deliver their lands to their "implacable" foes? [12] By the letter of the bond, this was exactly what she had done. By formal treaty with the red men at Fort Stanwix in 1768, she had established the boundary between possible white settlement and the great native reserve contemplated in the proclamation of 1763, and now she had washed her hands of this old obligation.

Shortly after he had received this disturbing news, the governor was embarrassed by a visit from Joseph Brant and another chief named John. They came as delegates of the Six Nations, who had heard evil rumors, to demand an explanation of the terms of the treaty. He put his visitors off with soft words and he dispatched Sir John Johnson to Niagara to allay the forebodings of the savages, but his own mind was sorely troubled.[13] Not twenty years had elapsed since the suppression of Pontiac's Revolt, whose horrors still caused many a shudder. But the memory of that nightmare might, by comparison, appear as a sweet dream if the doom now hanging over the whole of the west were not averted. He knew not how the awful blunder had come to be committed, but he saw the demons it was conjuring up and he realized that the urgent task of exorcising them rested upon the shoulders of one man — himself.

Two objects he at once set before his eyes. One was to reconcile the Indians with the Americans; and from this time forth, through the troubled years that followed, there was a fairly consistent effort, directed from Quebec, to restrain the red men and to persuade them that their real interest lay in coming to terms with the victors in the late war. Haldimand's other object was to restore the confidence of the Indians in the British. Whether it would be possible to repair the damage he was not quite sure. "It will be a difficult task," he wrote Lord North, "after what has happened to convince them of our good faith." But he was determined to do all in his power to prove to Britain's red allies that she had not forsaken them. To this end he undertook immediately to provide lands under the British flag for all Indians who were expelled from their old homes by American forces. This part of his policy may here be dismissed since it has an important bearing on the settlement of the loyalists and will be discussed in the next chapter. A second method he adopted was to persuade the suspicious savages that Britain had not really done what they thought she had done.[14] From now on through many years the tortuous argument was pressed by different agents in various councils with the Indians, but it is doubtful if they were much impressed by the marshaling of words in syllogisms. To their untutored minds, words had little power compared with actions, and Haldimand saw to it that these were not omitted. Presents were distributed as liberally as possible, and — the crowning point of the practical argument — the western posts were not delivered.

Meanwhile congress had instructed General Washington to make proper arrangements for securing possession of the places on American soil still occupied by the British, and he sent Major General Baron von Steuben up to Canada to see about the western posts. Steuben, who appeared in Chambly early in August, 1783, did not come to demand the surrender of the posts. That would have been premature, for the definitive treaty of peace was not signed for another month. His mission, which was quite natural and proper, was to negotiate with Haldimand an agreement on how the posts should be delivered when the time came, and to visit them that he might report how they should be garrisoned and supported when they were taken over.[15] On learning of the arrival of this rather distinguished professional soldier who had been imported from

Prussia to put stiffening into the Revolutionary army, the governor appointed Sorel their place of meeting. He said that he was just going up on other business,[16] but one suspects that his real reason was the fear of prying eyes in Quebec, for the visitor was accompanied by "three aides-de-camp and a French engineer, all of whom had French domestics in their suite." [17]

In a few days Haldimand bowed Steuben and his company out of the province. He did it so graciously that the disappointed emissary wrote back from Crown Point thanking the governor in the warmest terms and expressing his lively appreciation of all the officers with whom he had come in contact.[18] The baron had nothing to show for his mission save two letters from his late host. One was addressed to Washington. In it the head of the Canadian government professed his anxiety to do all in his power to meet the wishes of the American commander-in-chief, but professed his utter inability to do anything just yet because the only instructions that had reached him were for a cessation of hostilities. He greatly regretted having to disappoint Steuben but was delighted to have made his acquaintance.[19] The other letter was addressed to Steuben himself and said much the same thing in much the same way.[20]

Haldimand's polished manners and captivating hospitality were on this delicate occasion something more than the expression of his own fine nature. They were inspired by duty, for he had been instructed "to do all in his power to conciliate the affections and confidence of the United States of America." [21] Why, then, did he not accommodate himself to the wishes of the American government in a matter that was purely preliminary and provisional? The excuse he gave in the two letters just mentioned was a good one, but it was only an excuse, as he implied in his subsequent dispatch to Lord North on August 20. In reporting the incident he frankly admitted that he was playing for time. "Many bad and no good consequences," he wrote, "might have arisen from such premature discussion. The longer the evacuation is delayed, the more time is given to our traders to remove their merchandise, or to convert it into furs, and the greater opportunity is given to the officers under my command to reconcile the Indians to a measure for which they entertain the greatest abhorrence." [22]

Curiously enough, the merchants instead of contracting their business in the interior were expanding it. The goods they shipped west from Montreal in this season were worth more than a quarter of a million pounds, an increase of twenty-odd per cent over the previous year. This of course was only part of their commitment, two or three years being necessary to complete the cycle of trade. Their boldness was based on the hope that their London correspondents would be able to retard the delivery of the posts. Perhaps, also, they were inspired by the sympathy of the governor. He would not have been worthy of his position had he not been solicitous for the preservation of the principal commerce of the colony. At the very time when he was entertaining Steuben, he blessed Brigadier General Allan McLean, then commanding at Niagara, for turning back three bateaux from Schenectady laden with rum for traffic with the Indians.[23]

Some have maintained that the governor's desire to exclude the Americans from the fur trade moved him to refuse the surrender of the posts and to urge this policy upon the home government. But he had not yet reached this decision, and when he did reach it he was moved by other considerations. When he penned his dispatch of August 20 he was contemplating making delivery and he advised how it should be done. He cautioned Lord North against accepting the proposal of congress, which Washington's agent had presented, to purchase the military stores and provisions in the different forts. "I hope no such idea is entertained in England, for such a measure would be considered by the Indians as selling them to their enemies and will, in all probability, be the signal for an attack against our garrisons and people. I wish that the orders in consequence of the definitive treaty may be to withdraw the stores and troops from the forts, leaving it to the Indians to make their own conditions with the Americans. This appears to me the measure the best calculated for the safety of His Majesty's troops and subjects who are too much dispersed to be able to resist an attack from the Indians, who are forming a general confederacy for their own security and which may be directed equally against us as the Americans." [24]

Not until November, 1783, did the governor reach the conclusion that Britain ought to hold on to the posts, and then he was brought to it by the consideration of something much more precious than furs. It was blood. Notwithstanding all the striving of the officers under his command to cultivate peace between the Indians and the Americans, ominous reports had been coming in from the west. On October 14 he wrote to Lord North: "The Indians are still impatient for the communication of the conditions of the definitive treaty and of His Majesty's gracious intentions for their future welfare, which I promised them as soon as my dispatches should arrive. They have completed the general confederation from one extremity of North America to the other. They keep a watchful eye over the conduct of the Americans settled on the frontiers of this country. I hope the American States will exert themselves to prevent their subjects from making encroachments upon the Indian lands, to which some of them have had the imprudence to assert a claim in consequence of the provisional treaty. In case things are carried to extremities, the Indians seem determined to defend themselves and to make the Americans feel the difference of a war carried on in their own manner from the late one, which was subject to the restraints imposed upon it by His Majesty's officers." [25] Six weeks after he wrote this letter and some days after the last ship of the season had left Quebec for London, the governor dispatched a messenger down to Halifax and intrusted him with a more important letter to Lord North.

This letter bears the date of November 27, 1783, and contains the final reasoned judgment of the shrewd watcher in the Castle of St. Louis. The Indians, he said, "entertain no idea (though the Americans have not been wanting to insinuate it) that the king either has ceded or had a right to cede their territories or hunting grounds to the United States of America. These people, my Lord, have as enlightened ideas of the nature and obligations of treaties as the most civilized nations have, and know that no infringement of the treaty in 1768 which fixed the limits between their country and that of the different provinces in North America can be binding upon them without their express concurrence and consent. Your Lordship will observe that the object of their general confederacy is to defend their country against all invaders. In case things should proceed to extremities, the event no doubt will be the destruction of the Indians, but during the contest not only the Americans but perhaps many of His Majesty's subjects will be exposed to great distresses. To prevent such a disastrous event as an Indian war, is a consideration worthy the attention of both nations, and cannot be prevented so effectually as by allowing the posts in the upper country to remain as they are for some time." [26]

In proposing the retention of the posts, Haldimand did not even mention the fur trade as a supporting argument. In this crucial dispatch his only reference to the trade of the interior occurs incidentally in a further suggestion of what should be done, and in this passage he was so far from hoping for a continuance of the British monopoly that he proposed an equal sharing of what was then the great bulk of the trade. The governor's further suggestion, which anticipated what was to become a prominent feature of Britain's American policy until the signature of Jay's Treaty in 1794, may be best put in his own words: "It would certainly be better for both nations and the most likely means to prevent jealousies and quarrels that the intermediate country between the limits assigned to Canada by the provisional treaty and those established as formerly mentioned by that in the year 1768 should be considered entirely as belonging to the Indians, and that the subjects neither of Great Britain nor of the American States should be allowed to settle within them, but that the subjects of each should have liberty to trade where they please." [27]

Haldimand's words struck a responsive chord in London. The British government had been worried by the latent danger in the interior of America. Early in June, 1783, the negotiator of the definitive treaty, David Hartley, had proposed that the British garrisons should remain in the western posts for three years to secure the lives and the property that were at the mercy of the natives. The American commissioners had immediately replied that the occupation should continue only until congress had ordered the evacuation of these places and American garrisons had arrived to hold them. There the matter stood until August, when the American commissioners were presented with the draft of a definitive treaty, which Hartley was ordered to sign forthwith if they accepted it. The phrase "with all convenient speed," which had been used in the provisional articles of peace, was repeated in the draft. What did these words mean? Already a wide divergence of interpretation had developed. Nevertheless the Americans accepted the treaty with the ambiguous phrase, and what they then apprehended came to pass.

Carleton observed the strict letter of the treaty by withdrawing from New York in a few weeks, but there was no suggestion of any British move from the western posts. Some line of policy for these places may have been settled by the coalition of Fox and North, but they fell on December 18, 1783, without giving any indication of it, and the first evidence that the new ministry headed by Pitt had as much as considered the problem is in a letter of April 8, 1784. It was written by Lord Sydney, the secretary of state responsible for colonial affairs, in reply to Haldimand's letters of the preceding summer and autumn. He commended the governor for his handling of Steuben and assured him that His Majesty's ministers would never sanction the sale of military provisions and stores in the western posts. He fell in with the suggestion that these places should not be delivered, and he advanced two reasons in support of this policy. One was an echo of an argument used more than once by Haldimand that it would benefit rather than injure the real interest of the Americans. The other, which was not inspired by Haldimand, was as follows: "The seventh article stipulates that they shall be evacuated with all convenient speed, but no certain time is fixed, and as America has not on her part complied with even one article of the treaty I think we may reconcile it in the present instance to delay the evacuation of those posts, at least until we are enabled to secure the traders in the interior country and withdraw their property." [28]

Before this letter reached Quebec the governor had again to face the awkward question of evacuation. On May 7, 1784, a certain Lieutenant Colonel Fish arrived with a letter from Governor Clinton of the state of New York requesting Haldimand's assurance that as soon as he had received orders for the surrender of the posts, if such had not already arrived, he would notify the state authorities of the time when the transfer could take place. But the only assurance Haldimand would give was that he would scrupulously obey his orders — when they came. Meanwhile, he pleaded, he could do nothing. Of course he was full of regrets. In his reply to Clinton he wrote: "Some accident which has befallen the packet or messenger has hitherto prevented me from receiving from England any notification of the definitive treaty." He ventured further in verbal replies to Fish, to whom he confessed, as his own private opinion, that the evacuation should be delayed until the Americans had executed the treaty articles in favor of the loyalists. He remarked that he had allowed many to return to recover their property and they had come back empty handed after suffering much abuse.

Fish replied that the persecution of loyalists was condemned by the leading men in the various states, and he cited the example of Governor Clinton rescuing a British captain from the insolence of the New York mob. Like Steuben, Fish retired with a pleasant personal impression. At the time of the above-mentioned visit Haldimand also received a letter from Governor Chittenden asking when a small Lake Champlain fort known as the Loyal Block House would be surrendered to Vermont. How this missive came the governor could not discover, and apparently he did not reply to it. His silence was probably due to the fact that the existence of this state had not yet been recognized in the new republic.[29]

Haldimand immediately reported to London what had taken place, and he added two suggestions. One was that, since Britain had contracted the definitive treaty with the United States and not with any one of them, he was bound to treat only with accredited representatives of congress. The other was "that evacuation of the posts might be delayed as the means of obliging the congress to prolong the term of one year granted by the treaty for the loyalists to solicit the recovery of their estates, for from the want of government and good order in the different states it has not hitherto been safe for the loyalists to go amongst them for that purpose."[30] This passage accords with the traditional British position, but it must be remembered that the man who wrote it had already urged the retention of the posts to avoid an Indian war, and though he had not yet received it, the government's reply was on the way informing him that the evacuation might be indefinitely postponed.

The last American effort to secure the posts by applying in Quebec was made in July, 1784, when Lieutenant Colonel Hull arrived armed with a letter from Major General Knox, the republican secretary of war. By this time Haldimand had received Sydney's letter, but it did not help him very much. Though fortified by the intimation that he should evade the issue again, he was provided with no new weapons to do it. He wanted to give the Americans a good home thrust by inserting the argument of the loyalists in his formal reply, but this would have been committing his government beyond what was authorized by the general words of the British secretary of state. Therefore he had to content himself with talking to Hull in much the same way as he had spoken to Fish.[31] After this rebuff it was quite apparent to the government of the republic that the real obstacle was in London, and thenceforth the pressure to secure the withdrawal of the British garrisons was applied through diplomatic channels.

Though the British violation of the treaty was thus initiated out of fear of a great Indian war, this motive was soon tangled up with others. During the next ten years, to repeated demands that the Americans made for the return of the posts, the reply ever came pat — loyalists and debts. There can be no question that the treatment meted out to the loyalists and the obstacles placed in the way of recovering British debts in America constituted two real grievances. Nor, in the game of diplomacy, can the government in London be very much blamed for playing the western posts to force a redress of these grievances. But her excuses lacked the full flavor of honesty. Her position might have appeared faultless if she had made a move to deliver the posts and then had held back when these grievances developed, but she had not made the slightest gesture to observe this part of the treaty.

British writers have dealt too cavalierly with the traditional American contention that the fur trade supplied the real motive for the retention of the posts. In the British archives there are reams of documents that may be used to support the charge. From the moment the public discovered where the new boundary was to run, the mercantile interests of London besieged the government with appeals sent from Montreal and inspired by their own fears. If ever "big business" brought pressure to bear on public policy it was to make the British government unmake the treaty in so far as it affected the interior of America. The fur trade lived by the friendship of the natives, and the friendship of the natives would not be worth a day's purchase if the posts were surrendered. They must be held for two or three years at least to enable the withdrawal of the capital already ventured in the country beyond; and, if at all possible, they should be retained indefinitely. Such was the argument that was dinned into the ears and piled upon the desks of the king's ministers. Then came the reassuring intimation, quickly spread among the interested parties in England and in Canada, that the British garrisons would remain; and thenceforth, in the official correspondence between London and Quebec, there were frequent references to the connection between the retention of the posts and the protection of the trade. The revival of confidence in London had an immediate and vigorous reaction in the heart of this continent. With goods procured in Montreal, traders pushed down into the Illinois country, out to the Mississippi, and even across this river into Spanish territory. Still further afield they penetrated in the northwest. Away up on Lake Athabaska the fur-trading fort of Chipewyan was built in 1788. So great and sudden was the expansion that one might almost call it an explosion.

During these years of phenomenal activity the British monopoly of the trade was supported by an embargo on intercourse between Canada and the United States, now a foreign country. The embargo was legal but it was illegally extended. It sprang from the failure to stretch the peace settlement to cover commercial relations. It was extended to keep Americans out of American territory — a direct consequence of the retention of the posts. Envious and exasperated traders from the south approached but never passed Oswego, Niagara, and Detroit. The British officers who barred the gates of the west had no legal right to do so, but they were not responsible for this infringement upon the sovereignty of another country. They simply obeyed their orders, and their authority was never put to the test. Incidentally, British traders sometimes suffered by the enforcement of the ban. In 1785 one of them was advised by the commander at Oswego to turn back with his cargo of merchandise from New York if he wished to keep it. But, being a daring fellow, he ran the risk — and he rued the loss of all his goods, which were promptly seized. The fur market in the United States, starved by the exclusion of American traders, also tempted some Britishers to evade the prohibition on the export of peltries, for the ban worked both ways, and when the validity of this part of the embargo was questioned it was reinforced by a provincial ordinance of 1788.[32] Smugglers were still caught, but apparently a growing number got their skins out safely by forbidden routes. But this illicit traffic, aided by Monk as the local judge of the admiralty,[33] was only a little leak in the stream of wealth that flowed down the St. Lawrence.

Further support for the traditional American contention that Britain's main motive was the preservation of this monopoly may be extracted from a study of the evolution of the trade during the period following the war, to which attention must now be drawn. Lack of capital and an excess of competition had already driven traders and merchants into loose and temporary organizations. The movement continued with the appearance of such combinations as the General Company of Lake Superior and the South, known also as the General Society or the General Store, which operated from Michilimackinac from 1785 to 1787,[34] and the Miami Company of Detroit, which existed from about 1786 to 1789. But these and others like them are not to be compared with an organization founded in the winter of 1783–84, when the Frobisher brothers, Benjamin and Joseph, Simon McTavish, and several others of lesser note entered into partnership. This was the beginning of the mighty North West Company, which in a few years swallowed up the bulk of the trade and for many years threatened to put the great Hudson's Bay Company out of business. In sheer efficiency and relentless driving power it is doubtful if any corporation created on this continent of gigantic corporations has ever surpassed this one. Its headquarters were in Montreal and its rendezvous was first at Grand Portage and then, from 1803, at Fort William.[35]

The contrast between the rise of this company, which gathered its harvest from regions extending far beyond Lake Superior, and the eclipse of the companies that drew their furs to Michilimackinac and to Detroit arose from several causes. One was the necessity for greater capital to bear the heavier transportation charges and to support the longer business cycle of the more distant trade. Here was a field where independent individuals or small concerns with limited resources could not survive. A second reason for the astounding success of the North West Company was the superior quality of the pelts to be found in more northerly latitudes. Thirdly, just as the best crops are grown on virgin soil, so in the history of the fur trade the richest returns have come from new ground, and the northwest territory was new ground, whereas the district from the Great Lakes out to the Mississippi and down to the Ohio had been worked for years. Finally, chaos reigned in much of this territory, for the relations between the Indians and the Americans grew worse instead of better, and war broke such a troubled peace that the only difference was the substitution of wholesale slaughter for individual bloodshed. During these disturbed years, red vengeance was not very discriminating, and more British traders felt its effect than survived to tell the tale. The last cause only hastened what was a natural development, but by how much it is impossible to say.

What was taking place was something more than the rise of a powerful company. The whole fur trade was shifting in a north-westerly direction. The trade of Niagara had long been at a low ebb, so low as to be negligible, and now the tide was receding fast at Detroit, while at Michilimackinac it was still at the flood and in the northwest it was rising rapidly. From 1784 to 1790 the annual value of the Detroit trade fell from sixty-five thousand pounds to forty thousand, that of Michilimackinac stood fairly steady at something over sixty thousand pounds, and that of the northwest increased from twenty-five thousand to forty thousand pounds. In the next four years the greatest change was in the northwest trade, which leaped to a hundred thousand pounds.[36] It is also interesting to note that as a direct consequence of the implicit promise in the treaty to present the Americans with Grand Portage and the canoe route thence, two explorers * sent out by Benjamin and Joseph Frobisher discovered in 1784 an all-British canoe route over Lake Nipigon to the northwest.

The economic importance of the western posts was being undermined. In addition to the shifting of the field of trade from American to British soil and the discovery of a British pathway to the west, there was a growing feeling that the traffic still conducted in the area between the Great Lakes and the Mississippi would continue to be focused at Montreal even if the western garrisons were withdrawn. Geography favored Canada, and the trade could look after itself if only it were freed of two annoying restrictions. One was the prohibition of private vessels on the Great Lakes, imposed for military reasons during war time and continued after the peace to check any possible drain of furs to the south. As early as 1785 it was apparent that the confinement of the trade to government vessels did more harm than good, and there was some relaxation of the old order.[37] In 1788 it was entirely abolished. The second was the time-honored regulation that government passes or licenses were necessary for every man and all goods going up from Montreal. For like reasons this too was swept away in 1791. The increasing confidence that heaven and not man had made Montreal

---

* Edward Umfreville and Venance St. Germain. The route which they discovered was rather difficult. It was never used, the North West Company being able to follow that from Grand Portage until a better substitute was found in the Kaministikwia route. This, the old route of pre-conquest days, was rediscovered just before the close of the century.

the capital of the fur trade was justified by the event. The execution of Jay's Treaty in 1796 gave no shock to the commerce of the St. Lawrence. Now what does all this mean? That Britain simply clung to the posts until she saw that they were of no real value to the fur trade?

Strong though it seems, the American argument about the fur trade and the western posts breaks down when pushed to its logical conclusion. American writers have overlooked an important calculation that was made in Britain during the peace negotiations and that can scarcely have been ignored in the years that followed — a balancing of the cost of keeping the posts over against the loss of the fur trade that might follow their abandonment.

The interested merchants never maintained that anything more would be lost than the trade on the American side of the line and the capital already intrusted there. In 1784 they estimated that this trade brought to London furs worth a hundred and forty thousand pounds a year — two-thirds of the furs imported from Canada — and, as they set the total debt owed by the interior to Montreal at three hundred thousand, the capital in jeopardy was about two hundred thousand pounds. It was by no means certain that all this capital would disappear, but even if it did this would be equivalent to no more than twelve thousand pounds a year, six per cent being then good interest. Of the trade, what was at stake was not a hundred and forty thousand pounds a year, the selling price of the furs, but only a fraction of it, the annual profit. Nor would all this be sacrificed. Some of the trade might have been destroyed, but in mercantile circles it was commonly asserted that the surrender of the posts would simply deliver the trade into the hands of the Americans, for they would then have effective control of the country. But, as we know, Shelburne and others associated with the government in London saw that Montreal, by reason of its natural advantages, would probably continue to draw a goodly portion of the furs gathered on the American side of the line; that almost all the furs, whether they passed through Canadian or American channels, would still find their way to the London market; and that British manufacturers would still have their Indian market, for there were then no American manufacturers to supplant them. The profit made in Britain would be little affected. The only British sufferers would be the merchants and traders of Canada, who would no longer collect their share of the profit on the trade that would cease to pass through Montreal.

To sum up, the total possible annual loss would be twelve thousand pounds, representing the capital mentioned above, plus a part of the profit on a part of the trade — at best a very small fraction of one hundred and forty thousand pounds. Perhaps twenty thousand pounds would cover both items. Whatever it was, it could not begin to approach the annual cost of keeping the posts, for the government had not only to maintain garrisons far removed from their source of supplies but also to send out shiploads of Indian presents to win and hold the support of a red population whose appetite was almost as large as the area over which it roamed. Though no one could predict in 1784 how long the garrisons were to be kept on American soil, it could not have been difficult to foresee that the public loss would soon outweigh all possible private gain in the fur trade. From a purely business standpoint it was to Britain's interest to abandon the posts, if only the fur trade were taken into account. Therefore we must seek other reasons for such a serious violation of the treaty.

It is quite possible that the London government's procrastinating policy was partly influenced by a vision of something of greater permanence and of wider scope than the fur trade — a British commercial empire over the heart of the continent. The vision, first conjured up during the peace negotiations, was transformed and magnified by the conditions prevailing during the following decade.

This was the "critical period" of the young republic, when its whole future was darkly clouded. The loose union born of war began to dissolve on the advent of peace. The thirteen colonies having thrown off the yoke of one superior power were reluctant to place their necks under another, even though of their own making. When their independence was recognized they had only the shadow of a government, and the shadow faded away in the fall of 1788, when the continental congress expired of inanition. For nearly six months there was not even a shadow of a government, and when the Constitution, ratified by only nine of the thirteen states, gave birth to the government of the United States in 1789, there were grave doubts about the life of the new infant.

During these years, also, the young republic, if such it can be called before it achieved any unity, was rapidly growing over the

Alleghenies, and the mountain barrier threatened to break it in two. The older communities looked out on the Atlantic and the newer ones, of which Kentucky was the chief, faced the Mississippi. They were back to back and they were pulling apart. The strain was felt in many ways but only the most serious need here be mentioned.

This arose from the position of Spain. She sat astride the mouths of the Mississippi, the only route by which the people west of the Alleghenies could get rid of their rapidly increasing surplus produce. By closing this door Spain could strangle them; and they had no wish to live by the grace of the Spanish government or by the corruption of Spanish officials. Moreover, Spain possessed all the continent west of the Mississippi, and covetous eyes were already being cast across the river. The feeling of Americans west of the Allegheny Mountains was rendered almost explosive by the not ungrounded fear that their brethren to the east would betray them. The people living on or near the seaboard, deprived of the valuable commercial advantages they had enjoyed as part of the British Empire, were in such desperate need of finding substitutes that they were inclined to purchase admission to the ports of the Spanish Empire by surrendering to Spain the American claim to free navigation of the Mississippi. It is not surprising, therefore, that leading Americans on "the western waters" contemplated secession from the Atlantic states, and looked for some outside power to come to their rescue by pulling Spain out of New Orleans. The invitation was actually extended to France and repeated to Britain with the suggestion that whoever seized the gate would be richly repaid by securing a monopoly of the commerce of the whole Mississippi Valley.[38] Nor did temptation cease here. From the commander of an American Revolutionary regiment who was now anxious to establish a colony by the Missouri the government in London received a proposal that it should order the seizure of the territory west of the Mississippi, thereby greatly extending the British Empire.[39]

There is no evidence that George III's ministers went so far as to consider any positive move on the confused American chessboard, but surely they were shrewd enough to see the advantage of playing a waiting game. A premature surrender of Britain's strategic position on the Great Lakes might throw away the opportunity of winning an enormous prize.

Finally, the motive that seems to have initiated the policy of procrastination has been unduly ignored by those who have insisted that the British gaze was fixed upon furs. The fear of a great Indian war engulfing the vast country between the Mississippi and the Ohio did not diminish; it increased. It fills masses of documents that passed between Quebec and London. Peace might have been preserved had the 1768 boundary treaty been observed, but the obligation imposed by that instrument had been incurred by Britain and not by the Americans. They neither would nor could abide by it. They would not, because it would cramp their growth. They could not, because the pressure of the sturdy race of frontiersmen would have defied any government, and they had no real government at all. The continental congress did issue orders against the illegal occupation of Indian lands, and officers at Pittsburg tried to enforce these orders. But it was all in vain. The pioneers pushed on, armed against all opposition, white or red.

At Fort Stanwix in 1784, at Fort McIntosh in 1785, and at Fort Harmar in 1789, attempts were made to solve the ugly problem by negotiating new boundary treaties that would allow room for the expansion of white settlement beyond the old line, but the political organization of the Indians had much less solidity than the political organization of the Americans and the new treaties remained only scraps of paper. American agents were negotiating everywhere and all the time, but to no avail. The trickle of blood along the frontier grew into an angry stream. After the failure of the old congress and the establishment of the new government under President Washington it was decided to cut the Gordian knot by sending a military force into the heart of the native country. In the fall of 1790, with a composite force of regulars and militia, General Harmar set out for the Maumee villages to impress the might of the republic upon the minds of the savages. The impression he left was the very opposite. He was not able to control his own men, much less the natives. The latter surprised him near the source of the Maumee and drove his whole force back in disorder. To wipe out the disgrace of this failure, General St. Clair, who had been appointed governor of the northwest territories of the United States, conducted a more carefully planned invasion in the following year. But the disgrace was only piled higher by the smashing defeat which the Indians administered to him.

Meanwhile the rising tide of war was being closely watched by British eyes. Officials of Sir John Johnson's department were scurrying hither and thither from council fire to council fire. Their long reports were studied in Quebec and then sent to London for study there. Except that it was ever more critical, the situation was exactly the same as when it had first aroused Haldimand's alarm, and the policy that was pursued, now under direction from England, was simply what Haldimand had struck out on the spur of the moment — to reconcile the Indians with the Americans and to recover the confidence of the natives. Both objects seemed necessary, and yet the relation between them made their attainment a task so delicate that it was almost, if not quite, impossible. Too great an effort to bring about a native reconciliation with the Americans would defeat itself by destroying what little confidence the red men still had in the British. On the other hand, too great an effort to recover the lost confidence would encourage the savages to fight rather than to make peace. The first eventuality would drive Britain from the interior of the continent; the second might drag her into war with the United States; and either would drench the whole of the west with blood.

The surrender of the posts seemed more than ever out of the question. Indeed, the government in London was contemplating something more than the mere retention of the garrisons. To make them secure, Britain must hold the friendship of the natives. But how far should she go? Here was the practical question. Joseph Brant spent the winter of 1785–86 in England seeking compensation for his losses and striving to commit the government to support his people should the worst come to the worst. But it was only too obvious that a promise of military aid would make the worst come to the worst, and consequently, though he achieved his first purpose, he failed to accomplish his second. The secretary of state assured him that the king would never forget his Indian allies and would always be anxious to further their interests and happiness. To this was added the advice that they remain united and seek peace.[40] Equally vague were the instructions issued at the same time to the administrator of the colony, Lieutenant Governor Hope. "Open and avowed assistance, should hostilities commence, must at all events in the present state of this country be avoided; but His Majesty's ministers at the same time do not think it either consistent with justice or good policy entirely to abandon them, and leave them to the mercy of the Americans, as from motives of resentment it is not unlikely that they might hereafter be led to interrupt the peace and prosperity of the Province of Quebec. It is utterly impracticable for His Majesty's ministers to prescribe any direct line for your conduct should matters be driven to the extremity, and much will depend upon your judgment and discretion in the management of a business so delicate and interesting." [41] In other words, if the Indians were hard pressed, Quebec was to lend secret aid which could be repudiated in London.

The hesitating tone of the above dispatch was the natural expression of a government groping in the dark. If the administration had formulated any clear-cut idea of what was to be done with the posts, surely it would have been imparted to Lord Dorchester when he sailed for Quebec in 1786. Yet the government sent him out with scarcely any clearer notion of its purpose than his predecessors had been able to gather through correspondence. There is a note of certainty suggested by two letters that the new governor wrote to Sir John Johnson within a few weeks of his arrival in Canada. In one he insisted that the natives should know that he had no power to commence a war "which might involve half the globe with all the seas in blood and destruction," and that every effort should be put forth to persuade them to make peace with the Americans.[42] In the other he directed the head of the Indian department to sound out the Six Nations upon the retention of the posts, especially Oswego and Niagara, because if they were indifferent there would be no reason for anxiety to keep these places. At the same time he declared that any American attempt to seize them would be the opening of hostilities, and "war must be repelled by war." [43]

A month later, however, his mind was full of doubts and his spirit was consumed with impatience. Writing to the secretary of state, he roundly condemned the government's policy of "no resolution," and he urged some definite decision. Were the posts to be retained? If so, their garrisons would have to be increased and much money would have to be spent in putting them in a proper state of defense. Or were they to be surrendered? This would help the Americans to conquer the Indians, would "draw on us many reproaches," would entail the loss of much of the fur trade, and would open the door for smuggling. Or were the posts to be abandoned and destroyed? Then the evil consequences would be greatly retarded. He concluded with a prayer for advice about what to do should the Americans attack and capture the posts.[44]

In spite of his appeal, London threw little light upon the dark path that Dorchester had explored after his arrival. He was told that he could spend money to put the forts into "a temporary state of defence," and if they were seized and he thought himself strong enough to recover them it would be his duty to use every endeavor to accomplish this end. As for the Indians, all their reasonable wants were to be satisfied. To afford them active assistance, said the secretary of state, would be extremely imprudent, and yet "it would not become us to refuse them such supplies of ammunition as might enable them to defend themselves." This, however, was "to be done in a way the least likely to alarm the Americans" or to incite the Indians "to any hostile proceedings." Exactly how this ammunition was to be reserved for purely defensive purposes was not mentioned. Along with this uncertain advice came a more certain statement of the government's motives. The war cloud was evidently spreading north. The safety of the posts, "the protection of the fur trade and perhaps the general security of the Province of Quebec" might depend upon the attitude of the red men. "Were we to be governed only by the expectation of further advantage from the friendly disposition of these people, it might even in such case be prudent to attend to their reasonable wants. But considering their former services, and the sacrifices many of them have made, there cannot remain a doubt of the conduct we ought to observe towards them." [45]

In addition to the broad features of the whole ugly situation, there were many lesser features that caused perpetual worry. The handling of Indian presents was marked by corruption, much the same as during the war. No one questioned the honesty of Sir John Johnson, but it was whispered that he was too easy-going, he was too eager for popularity, and his relatives, mostly red, were far too numerous.[46] Goods bearing the king's mark stamped upon all Indian presents were sold in the private store of Butler's son at Niagara, and Colonel Butler himself, though deputy superintendent of Indian affairs, was a principal in a transaction, as shady as it was huge, in lands lying on the American side of Lake Ontario. When these and other similar dealings were discovered, lame excuses were offered. Young Butler had lent goods to the government and later had secured the equivalent from a stock of Indian presents deposited with him. The father was trying to procure a large estate for his relatives in New England.[47] Brant was involved with the colonel in real estate speculation, but it was not possible to bring him to account. Indeed, his general conduct throughout this period does not accord with the tradition which lauds him as a staunch British hero. No one quite knew what he was doing in all his restless movements to and fro across the country, but enough was known to make him suspected and feared in Quebec. Nevertheless he should not be judged too harshly. Endowed with more wits than his fellows, he could see more clearly that they all had their backs to the wall. Therefore he charged the British with being stingy, the Americans with being greedy, and his own people with being sluggards, and he was ever on the alert to seize any advantage from all three.[48]

One trembles to think what might have happened had the Americans tried to seize by force what was theirs by right. Though some were itching to try the desperate game, wiser councils prevailed among the leaders of the new republic, and Britain has to thank them for saving her from another war at this time. Through devious channels their sane decision became more or less clearly known in Quebec even before President Washington had Governor St. Clair write the commandant of Detroit that the military preparations afoot in 1790 were not at all aimed at the British garrisons but solely at the repression of the savages. The reassuring knowledge relieved the strain on British nerves, which sometimes got on edge, but could not reduce the perplexity in British minds, for the plight of the red men was becoming more critical.

With the apparent passing of the crisis, due to Indian victories, British policy lost some of its cautious uncertainty and entered upon a new phase. Though at last deprived of the excuse of obstacles in the way of recovering British debts in America — for the United States Supreme Court decided that the treaty was part of the law of the land — the authorities in London seemed more determined than ever to hang on to the posts. They entertained the hope that Dorchester might mediate between the Indians and the Americans to establish a peace which would protect the former in such hunting grounds as they needed, and the idea enunciated by Haldimand of a new boundary treaty which would establish a neutral Indian reserve between the back parts of Canada and those of the United States began to float within the bounds of seeming possibility.[49] Thus might Britain at last tie up the loose end of the treaty which had compromised her with the children of the forest and, as a consequence, with her own independent sons. This was the mirage that British eyes saw in the heart of the American continent when the old province of Quebec passed out of existence.

CHAPTER XV

THE LOYALISTS

ANOTHER shadow of the peace was the fate of the loyalists.[1] British feeling was deeply stirred at the time because, as Lecky has pointed out, this treaty was an exception to a common practice in civilized countries — that of closing civil strife by generous acts of amnesty and restitution. The American Revolutionary War was largely a civil struggle, but in the terms of the treaty ending it the defeated faction found little real provision for justice and less for mercy.

In the fifth article congress promised that it would "earnestly recommend" to the legislatures of the various states that they restore the confiscated property and rights of "real British subjects" and of those people who were within the British lines in America but had never borne arms against the United States. Others — that is, those Americans who had fought to preserve the British connection — were to be free to return and remain for a twelvemonth unmolested while they employed their own efforts to procure restoration. To assist them congress promised to send the state legislatures two further "earnest recommendations." One was to the effect that they should reconsider and revise their legislation affecting these unfortunates to make it "perfectly consistent, not only with justice and equity, but with that spirit of conciliation, which, on the return of the blessings of peace, should universally prevail." The second was to the effect that property and rights were to be restored, the loyalists, however, repurchasing at the price paid whatever had fallen into other private hands. The sixth article of the treaty stipulated that there were to be no further prosecutions or confiscations arising out of anyone's participation in the war.

The fifth article was a farce, and the sixth was a nullity. The "earnest recommendations" were sent, but except in South Carolina, where considerable justice was done, they might as well have come from George III. Far from there being any repentant restoration, confiscation went gleefully on, and the loyalists who returned to their old homes to get their own property only too often got something very different. Some were murdered; more were tarred and feathered; and many were glad to escape with their lives. Who was to blame?

When the terms of peace were debated in Westminster, the opposition accused the government of deserting the loyalists, and asserted that the acceptance of the treaty, "unless marked by the just indignation of parliament, would blast forever the honour of this country." But a candid survey of the situation absolves the British government. From the beginning of the negotiations Shelburne had urged Oswald, and the latter had pressed his utmost, to make the protection of the loyalists a corner stone of the treaty. It is hard to see how this could have been accomplished unless Britain had been prepared to renew the war. Rather than commit herself to such a course she preferred to compensate her own suffering children.

Some have ascribed the ensuing tragedy to the bad faith of the American peace commissioners and the American congress. But this charge, still repeated in Canada, is likewise unfair. Having only a limited power delegated by the thirteen states, congress had no authority to bind them; and the commissioners, instead of trying to hide this fact, emphasized it in their Paris discussions. Here lies the root of the difficulty. The peculiar conditions under which the treaty was negotiated precluded the insertion of any effective guarantee of justice for the loyalists. Of the two parties to the agreement, only one possessed the attributes of sovereignty. America could bind Britain, but Britain could not bind America. In America responsibility resided in each of the thirteen states, and not one of them incurred a single legal obligation under the Peace of Paris.

A few outstanding American statesmen of the time, men like John Jay and Alexander Hamilton, scorned this legal argument and maintained that their country was violating the treaty. Many modern American historians have also condemned the treatment meted out to loyalists, not merely because it deprived the new republic of a valuable element in its population but also because it was essentially unjust. On the other hand, a Britisher who similarly purges himself of national bias must ask a pertinent question. Did the loyalists get less than they would have given to "rebels" had the war gone the other way? It is highly doubtful.

What happened to the loyalists can be told in only a general way.

England was their favorite resort, and many were able to find a relatively comfortable existence in the mother country by reason of the property they had saved, the compensation they procured, or the personal connections they possessed. The others were scattered up and down America. Many returned to their old homes or found new ones in the United States. A considerable number of southerners went to Florida and to the British West Indies. The rest, who were only a minority of the whole exiled body, settled in what is now the Dominion of Canada. They laid the foundations of the English-speaking part of the country; and their anti-American bias, together with the racial fears of the older Canadians, has been a strong influence in preserving British North America from being drawn into the great neighboring republic.

A sharp distinction must be drawn between the loyalist migration to old Canada and the corresponding settlement in old Nova Scotia. The treatment of these two movements as if they were really one, distinguished only by geography, has been an error as misleading as it has been common. It has obscured the interpretation of the history of Upper Canada. The loyalists of the maritime provinces numbered some thirty thousand. They were mostly, though by no means entirely, civilian refugees who had been gathered in New York under the protection of the retiring British forces. They were shipped en masse in 1783. They swamped the much smaller number of English-speaking settlers who had been moving in from the time of the Seven Years' War, and they remained a dominant element in the population. To a great extent they seem to have been people of property, education, and superior social standing in the more populous and highly developed part of America along the Atlantic seaboard. They were forced to face rough pioneer conditions for which their previous manner of living ill fitted them, and they had to adjust themselves with an effort that was as painful as it was heroic.

Very different is the tale of the Upper Canadian loyalists. Their numbers were nothing so large, nor did they come as a body. Except for a few hundred shipped from New York in 1783, they had been drifting in from the early days of the war. Most of them had followed the Lake Champlain route; a few had gone as directly as possible to Carleton Island, Oswego, Niagara, or Detroit. The men went chiefly to join the British colors, and in their anxiety to fight, many arrived without their women-folk and children, who followed or were fetched both during the war and at its close. These were the first white people to found permanent settlements in what was to be Upper Canada, but they were not destined to enjoy the same position there as did the loyalists in the provinces down by the sea, for they soon became a minority of the population. In contrast to the migratory movement from the United States into the maritime provinces, which stopped when the refugees were all evacuated from New York, this human stream from south of the new international line continued to flow, gathering volume with the years, for more than a quarter of a century. This difference is linked with another and a greater one.

The loyalists who began to clear the forests of Upper Canada were, taken as a whole, an entirely different kind of people from those who settled in the maritime provinces. When the Revolutionary War broke out, the more cultivated society in the old colonies was almost entirely confined to the seaboard, whence it was practically impossible to reach Canada overland so long as the war lasted. With the exception of the few hundred refugees shipped from New York to Quebec, of whom at least a large part belonged to the artisan class,[2] one would expect to find the loyalists gathered in Canada to be people who had been living up country away from the centers of culture.

This is exactly what one finds on examining the documents of that day, particularly the correspondence and the record of the British commissioners who came to America to examine claims for compensation. These commissioners did not intend to visit Canada. Instead they advised the government in Quebec to send the loyalists to submit their claims in Nova Scotia. Lieutenant Governor Hope, who was then administering the colony, replied in January, 1786, that few loyalists in Canada were "persons of great property or consequence." Indeed, he doubted whether any had lost enough to make the journey worth while.[3] "They are chiefly landholders, farmers and others from the inland parts of the continent. . . . Their claims to compensation cannot singly be considerable. . . . A small compensation for their losses would restore to the greater part of them all the comforts and conveniences they have lost." To extend them this favor, he added, the commissioners would have to come to Canada.[4] They came in the spring of 1787 and traveled

as far as Niagara. In the fall of that year one of them, Colonel
Dundas, reported that the claims were individually very small, the
claimants "being mostly farmers from the back parts of New York
Province." [5]

The records of some six hundred cases examined in Canada,
representing of course a much larger number of persons, have been
preserved and published,[6] and they bear out what Dundas wrote.
They are interesting reading at first, but they soon become mo-
notonous, for they tell the same tale over and over again. The list
contains not a single lawyer and only two doctors, one of whom
came from Crown Point and the other from Fort Edward. A fair
average claimant was a man who had abandoned a hundred-acre
farm, often only leased, of which he had cleared no more than ten
acres. While some claimed more, many lost less. Five-sixths of
all the cases came from New York, the rest chiefly from the interior
settlements of Vermont, New Jersey, and Pennsylvania.

As a body, the loyalists were of the very type needed to open a
new country, for they were sturdy backwoods farmers from the
frontier between civilization and the wilds which had begun to roll
westward across the continent. The racial mixture that has marked
this frontier movement is clearly reflected in the entries of the
claimants. Exclusive of dependents, whose birthplace is usually not
given, nearly half were born in America, one-fourth in Scotland,
one-ninth in Germany, one-twelfth in Ireland, and one-sixteenth in
England. The names of the American-born show that they were of
diverse racial origin, including a large admixture of Dutch.

Another well-known feature of the frontier in America has been
the absence of educational facilities, and hence it would be surprising
to find a high percentage of literacy among the pioneers who hewed
their way into the woods of Upper Canada. The minutes of the
commissioners are silent on the subject, but other records are most
revealing. All who received grants of land were required to take
the oath of allegiance, and officials were sent around to swear the
new settlers and to take their signatures as evidence. Some of the
books used for this purpose are still extant and they show that a
large proportion signed with a cross and that many others had
great difficulty in tracing their names.[7] There were some, of course,
who had a real education, and they were reinforced a few years after
the war by a small secondary migration from the maritime provinces.

Bearing in mind the nature of the original Upper Canadian set-tlement, one can readily understand why the stream continued to flow from south of the line. The frontier movement was pulled north. The first comers left many friends and relatives behind, and these had other friends and relatives. All were interested in getting good land as cheaply as possible, and here was the best of land to be had for nothing. Almost as soon as the war was over, inquiries from Vermont, New York, and Pennsylvania were forwarded to Quebec, and a number of individuals traveled up to spy out the land for themselves and their fellows. Of course those who were anxious to remove in order that they might live under the British flag asserted that they were really loyalists who for various reasons had not been able to fight, or if they had fought on the American side, had done so against their will. Often they could prove their assertions, and many were actually suffering for their faithfulness to their sover-eign. Naturally the government at Quebec was glad to welcome those who had adhered to their British allegiance, and promised them free land, though it would not undertake to supply them with provisions. Even this indulgence, however, was granted to those who obviously needed it in the early days after the war.[8] Far from resenting any intrusion, the original loyalists were delighted at the coming of their own people, and like the government they rejoiced at the prospect of a more rapid development of the country. Thus the migratory movement went on, and while the motive of loyalty was replaced by the pioneering urge,* the same kind of people continued to pour into Upper Canada until the outbreak of war dammed the stream in 1812.

The number of the Upper Canadian loyalists has been set by tradition at ten thousand, but this would appear to be much too high. It ought to have been easy to give a fairly accurate figure, for it was ordered, on November 9, 1789, that an official record of all the loyalists be kept. On that day Lord Dorchester intimated to the council "that it was his wish to put a mark of honour upon the families who had adhered to the unity of the Empire and joined the Royal Standard in America before" the peace in 1783. With hearty concurrence the council immediately "ordered that the several land

---

* The American who executed Major André appeared in Kingston and procured land and provisions as a loyalist! He was recognized by chance and was whipped out of the community.[9]

boards * take course for preserving a registry of the names of all persons falling under the description aforementioned, to the end that their posterity may be discriminated from future settlers." [10] Unfortunately the land boards neglected this task. In 1796 Simcoe issued a proclamation calling upon the magistrates to do it. From these sources and from others, such as muster rolls and provisioning lists, the honor roll was compiled.[11] It ought to have been authoritative, but it was not, as a perusal of the minutes of the Upper Canadian council shows. At various stages of the process many names were improperly inserted by carelessness or collusion, and after the compilation was supposed to be completed there were further additions and erasures. The looseness with which the whole business was handled suggests the absence of a clear-cut distinction between genuine loyalists and others in the society of Upper Canada at the only time when it might have been possible to draw such a distinction. Indeed, one wonders how possible it was then, with original loyalists shading off into "late loyalists," as they were called, and "late loyalists" shading off into simple land-seekers.

As the honor roll stands, more than eight hundred of the fifty-four hundred names appearing on its two lists, the original and the supplemental, have no business to be there at all. The evidence for this deduction is in the lists themselves. Four hundred represent disbanded British regulars. The rest cover German troops, duplicate entries, and settlers who obviously were not present in 1784, such as a group of immigrants who came straight from Scotland. On the other hand, one must add the twelve hundred women and children mentioned, though not named, in the lists. This is a generous addition, for there is reason to suspect that some of these children were not born until several years after the original settlement. However that may be, we are left with a total of less than fifty-eight hundred. Apparently the errors on both sides canceled each other, for this is approximately the figure derived from the muster rolls made in August, September, and October, 1785. These rolls show sixty-eight hundred loyalists, men, women, and children, living within the confines of the old province of Quebec. Five hundred of them were settled on the Bay of Chaleur or at Gaspé and about the same number at various places in the older parts of the colony, chiefly Sorel, leaving fifty-eight hundred in the newer districts to the west.[12]

* See below, page 395.

To Haldimand fell the responsibility of caring for the loyalists, and from the beginning he undertook to supply their necessities. As early as 1778 he appointed his old friend Conrad Gugy to look after the helpless refugees — women and children and some men — who had come in from the south, and he ordered the neighboring captains of militia to assist Gugy in erecting huts for them on his seigniory of Machiche. There the poor creatures lived, being provided for out of the government stores.[13] With the progress of the war the number of destitute refugees increased, and they constituted an increasingly difficult problem. They overflowed the limited quarters at Machiche and had to be accommodated wherever room could be found for them, until at last they seemed to be swarming everywhere between Sorel and the upper end of the Island of Montreal.

Some were rather difficult to handle, being more eager to live on the royal bounty than to fight for the royal cause. A few disappeared, having recrossed the line, and not a few who remained were suspected of being spies. In the fall of 1779, when commanding in Montreal, the choleric Allan McLean wrote to Quebec that he was plagued by "royalists real and pretended." "I wish to God," he said, that these people "now straggling through the country were ordered to join some corps or other and then they would be missed at least within the 24 hours."[14] Later in the winter he ordered three dozen able-bodied refugees at Varennes to join a unit at St. Ours. They objected that they could not pay for the transportation of their families and belongings, and he removed their excuse by sending cart trains to their very doors. When they still refused to budge, he cut off their supply of firewood and provisions.[15] Haldimand commended McLean's judgment in this instance, but he refused, a few months later, to let the Highlander imprison forty recent arrivals who resisted all efforts to recruit them and insisted on wandering at large. That, said the governor, would be "a harshness very discouraging to men who profess loyalty."[16] Wayward as some of the loyalists were, and there were many complaints on this score, the old Swiss soldier proved himself throughout a kind and considerate guardian to them all.

The first of these uprooted people to resume the tilling of the soil were a few families whom Haldimand planted at each of the upper posts in 1780. His primary motive was to relieve the strain upon the commissariat by creating a local food supply for the garrisons.[17] This war-time settlement, it is interesting to note, fore-shadows one of his leading ideas in the permanent settlement after the peace.

In the fall of 1782, when the end of the war was in sight, he discussed the whole problem in a letter to the home government.[18] The evacuation of New York would mean the emptying of the main reservoir into which loyalists had been pouring, and it was predicted that large numbers would rush into Canada as well as into Nova Scotia. This possibility worried him. Indeed, he was anxious to prevent their seeking an asylum under his government. The place for them was not Canada but Cape Breton. "The unconceded lands in this country are unfortunately of little value, not improvable in themselves and at a great distance from the River St. Lawrence. . . . In conversation with Major Holland, who surveyed Cape Breton in the year 1776, it has occurred to me that an establishment might be procured for the unfortunate people on that island, which in a few years would become comfortable to themselves as well as beneficial to the mother country." It contained "a great quantity of improvable land as well as many valuable harbours and stations for fisheries." Nor were these the only advantages of that island. "Its proximity to Newfoundland, the Island of St. John's and Gulf of St. Lawrence is such that the fleet or cruisers necessary for its defence will be equally useful for the protection of the trade carried on at these places." Finally, he intimated that the people who were driven from the seacoast of the old northern colonies should be planted by the sea. Although he was not given to hiding his motives, there was probably another which he did not mention in this letter. He believed that Canada should be preserved for the Canadians, and therefore he could scarcely relish the prospect of a large immigration from the port of New York.

Nevertheless the governor did not seek to disburden himself of the loyalists already on his hands and still coming in "from the frontiers of New England and New York." They were inland folk and they could be planted in the interior far away from the main body of the Canadians. He contemplated establishing them under a sort of military government — they were accustomed to military life — at or near Detroit, which he did not dream was soon to be signed away. Such a colony, composed of men whose loyalty had been tried by fire, would cement the alliance of the western natives and, after a few years, would be capable of feeding "the garrisons which it will be necessary to keep in the upper countries."

The prophecy of a general migration from the port of New York to Canada was not fulfilled, and it would be interesting to know if Haldimand's advice was responsible for deflecting to Cape Breton a movement that might otherwise have gone to Canada. The Detroit part of his scheme collapsed because the land he had in view lay on the wrong side of the line. Yet he did not abandon the underlying idea — the use of the loyalists as a prop to the Indian alliance and as a support for British interests in the west. It appears prominently in the actual settlement.

For some months after the conclusion of the war, Haldimand did not know where he was going to plant the loyalists under his care. He would have preferred a location by the sea, had it been possible, for the sake of the fisheries, which in those days were of much more than economic value. Sea power then rested largely upon an ample supply of trained sailors, and fisheries were nurseries of seamen. Therefore in the summer of 1783 he sent a party to explore the country by the Bay of Chaleur,[19] and until the autumn he entertained hopes of a large number going down to live in Cape Breton. The exodus was being arranged by Abraham Cuyler. This former mayor of Albany, after much moving about among the refugees, believed, or at least professed to believe, that he had persuaded some of their leaders to bring three thousand of them down to Cape Breton if he could procure enough land in that island to accommodate them.[20] With a letter of introduction from Haldimand to Lord North[21] he embarked at Quebec in November. But when the news came in the following year that Cuyler had got his grant, his people were already settled elsewhere. Only a hundred or so rallied to escort Mrs. Cuyler to join her husband in Cape Breton.[22] The expedition to the Bay of Chaleur was a little more successful. The summer of 1784 saw the beginning of loyalist settlements on the shores of the Bay of Chaleur and the Bay of Gaspé under the charge of Lieutenant Governor Nicholas Cox. But the new communities ruled by Cox accounted for no more than a small fraction of the refugees in the old province of Quebec. As has been remarked, their population in 1785 was only about five hundred. An equally small number found homes in the old part of the colony, half of them fitting into the life of the two towns and the other half, in accordance with instructions from London, being established in 1784 on the recently purchased seigniory of Sorel.[23]

It may seem strange that Haldimand did not place the main body of loyalists in the district now known as the Eastern Townships of Quebec. There was ample room for all on these rich and yet vacant lands lying between the existing Canadian settlements and the southern border, and there were several obvious reasons for establishing them there. They would be greatly assisted by having a market near at hand, and the colony might be strengthened by the consolidation of its population and the creation of a barrier against possible American aggression. Lord North wrote Haldimand directing him to locate them there, and numerous loyalists in Canada and professed loyalists in Vermont besieged him with requests for land in the vicinity of Lake Champlain. But the governor would not countenance any such settlement in this part of the colony. So determined was he in his opposition that when some squatted near the new international line and defied orders to remove, he deprived them of the provisions which he regularly allowed to loyalists, and he even threatened to burn their buildings over their heads.[24] It may here be added that he also discouraged, though he did not utterly oppose, the settlement of loyalists on any of the old seigniories except that of Sorel,[25] which now belonged to the government.

The explanation of Haldimand's stern attitude is threefold. He was apprehensive lest a door to illicit trade with the Americans be opened. Indeed, it was commonly suspected that those who sought grants near the border were inspired by the hope of engaging in smuggling rather than in agriculture.[26] Secondly, the governor argued that it would be dangerous to let the loyalists live so close to their late foes. He feared lest proximity engender friction that might reopen the strife, and he doubted whether it would be worth while going to war to preserve the colony, whose chief value, the fur trade, would be greatly diminished by the cession of the western posts. Thirdly, he insisted that these lands should be reserved for the Canadians, who were increasing so rapidly that they would soon need this territory and who would provide a more effective barrier because they differed from the Americans in race, language, religion, and culture.[27]

Haldimand converted Lord North to his views, and it would

have been well had he imparted his wisdom to others who were to come after him. He was a farseeing statesman in laying down the principle that these lands should be reserved. In a few years it was forgotten or rejected, and what has been the result? Before the French were prepared to enter into the possession of what they regarded as their natural heritage, an English-speaking population, first from across the line and later from across the sea, was allowed to occupy the Eastern Townships, only to be squeezed out in the fullness of time. Had the counsel of the old Swiss been followed, the end to which he looked forward, and which today is being approached, would have been reached long ago, and one important cause of racial animosity might have been avoided.

Haldimand was also reluctant to establish the main body of loyalists in what was soon to be Upper Canada. That was then Indian territory, and he was highly sensitive to the danger arising from the encroachment of white settlement upon the lands of the natives.[28] Not until almost the very day on which he bade farewell to Cuyler did he decide that he could and should do it, and the natives themselves played a not inconsiderable part in bringing him to this conclusion. His initial step was taken in the spring of 1783, when he received his first copy of the provisional treaty and was shocked to discover that the negotiators in Europe had apparently forgotten the red men in America. The governor was quick to see that he must provide immediately for the Indians who had been driven from the land of their forefathers — the whole Mohawk tribe reinforced by a few Senecas and Cayugas. The only place where he could provide for them was in the remaining British Indian territory to the west. Therefore at the end of May he ordered Major Holland up the St. Lawrence to examine Cataraqui — the modern Kingston — and the adjoining country to see if the dispossessed natives could be established there.[29] His choice was probably dictated by the location of the old French fort. This he hoped to rebuild to take the place of Carleton Island and Oswego when they would be handed over to the Americans. The surveyor general was accompanied by the two chiefs who had embarrassed Haldimand by their visit. They liked the proffered land and said that their people would be happy to live on it. Thereupon the governor arranged for their settlement. To this end he had the Indian superintendent, Sir John Johnson, purchase the land from the Missisaugas.

Meanwhile, directed by the governor, Holland and his staff were quietly looking about for lands that might be occupied by white loyalists, a few of whom soon joined in the search. At the same time, down in New York, Carleton came into contact with a German saddler and harness-maker of that city.[30] This fellow, Michael Grass, had been a prisoner of the French in Cataraqui years before, and he asserted that this was a fine location for loyalists. The upshot was that Grass received a militia captain's commission, a few hundred nondescript refugees were organized in six militia companies under his command, and they all sailed for Quebec en route to their promised land. In the middle of July, just as Haldimand began to receive encouraging replies to his own inquiries about the nature of the country for which they were destined, he learned that they were coming. They reached Quebec in August, and in September the governor directed John Collins, Holland's deputy, to go up to Cataraqui and lay out townships for them and any others who wished to go with them. A few of the recent arrivals, including Grass, went with the deputy surveyor general to assist him and to start clearing the land; the rest remained below until the following spring. Though Haldimand thus forwarded the project he continued for some time to regard it with an unfavorable eye. In the middle of October he reported what he had done for those who "will persist" in taking up land at Cataraqui. He was still talking of large numbers going to Cape Breton.[31]

In three weeks the governor changed his mind completely. Instead of being reluctant to allow a few hundred loyalists to deposit themselves near Cataraqui, he had become eager to send as many there as he could. Grass, who imagined himself a sort of modern Moses, claimed all the credit; but the governor had a justly low opinion of him and does not seem to have been influenced by him at all. Various expeditions, under orders from the Castle of St. Louis, had been scouring the country up the St. Lawrence, up the Ottawa, and over the Rideau route between the modern cities of Kingston and Ottawa, and had discovered plenty of good land for all the loyalists who were then in Canada or might yet arrive from the south. Other news wiped out Haldimand's fears of thrusting white settlers into Indian territory. Instead of seeking isolation in the wilderness, the Six Nations who had agreed to take up their abode by the Bay of Quinté were now positively anxious for their white brethren in arms to live near them. The Missisaugas also welcomed the coming of white settlers.

The governor's problem was solved, and the solution pleased him. It pleased him because, in addition to ending his difficulties, it offered the prospect of several positive advantages. In this fertile country with its more favorable climate he saw the development of "a granary for the lower parts of Canada where the crops are precarious and liable to be engrossed by a few designing and interested traders." The interior, he said, would be more securely British, and even the fur trade of the colony might profit by the settlement of loyalists at Cataraqui. Exactly what he meant by this reference is not clear. Presumably he was thinking of the reduction of provisioning costs and the chance of preserving a larger proportion of the trade for Canada. Of one thing, however, there is no doubt. In a letter to Lord North written on November 6 and containing the above arguments he was enthusiastic in his anticipation of a general settlement of white as well as red loyalists supporting and supported by the rebuilt fort of Cataraqui.[32]

This project of Haldimand's was to be only half realized. On December 1, 1783, Sir John Johnson, who was living in Montreal, wrote to Quebec asking that his regiment be allotted lands along the upper St. Lawrence from the last seigniory, that of Longueuil.[33] The request carried weight because the man who made it was the outstanding loyalist in the colony and the men for whom it was made constituted the senior provincial unit. The governor complied with Johnson's wish for the first battalion, which was cantoned in Montreal, but not for the second, which was doing garrison duty above. He also agreed to place Jessup's corps beside Johnson's first battalion. This meant dividing the main body of white loyalists into two fairly equal halves separated by the stretch of rough and uninviting country which he already knew lay to the east of Cataraqui.[34] He may have contemplated this division when he wrote Lord North in November, but his words on that occasion suggest that he was at this time consciously departing from his policy of concentration in the vicinity of the modern Kingston. In doing this he could see certain countervailing advantages. The dwellers on the upper St. Lawrence would be in contact with the older part of the colony without threatening to cramp its growth — for the Eastern Townships were reserved for French expansion — and there would be fewer loyalists who would be obliged to live back from the water-front.

Another important change of plan was occasioned by a split in the ranks of the red refugees in the spring of 1784. Only a minority, a few Mohawk villages then encamped in the woods near Lachine, took up their abode by the Bay of Quinté, the majority having decided to go elsewhere. All might have gone together had not the chiefs of the minority hoped to enjoy a greater consequence in a separate settlement. The majority preferred a location on the Grand River, which flows into Lake Erie.[35] They wished to be nearer the main council fires of the Six Nations at Niagara, for they had been appealed to by their cousins the Senecas, who lived just east of that river and who were now nervous about their position on what was to be American soil.

The homeless Iroquois had only to express their will to have Haldimand carry it out. He dared not run the risk of losing their precarious friendship. Consequently he ordered a second purchase from the peaceful Missisaugas, and in May, 1784, the crown became possessed of a large area in the peninsula of southwest Ontario. Of this the governor set aside a tract six miles wide on either side of the Grand River from its mouth to its source as a reserve * for the Mohawks and any others of the Six Nations who wished to join them. There in the spring of 1785 he established the main body, about a thousand in all, under their famous warrior whose memory is perpetuated by the name of the modern city of Brantford. For their further benefit he at once provided them with a school and a church. These were the first of such buildings to be erected in Upper Canada.† It was in this church that, after many wanderings, the set of communion silver that good Queen Anne had pre-sented to the mission on the Mohawk River at last found a resting place.[36]

The year 1784 is memorable in the annals of Ontario as that of the great settlement. Early in the spring Collins and his staff re-sumed their labors above Cataraqui, and others began to survey from the western boundary of Longueuil. Before the season closed the

* It has left its mark on the modern map where it may be traced in county and township lines.

† With the exception of the mission chapels built by the French before the conquest.

front portions of fourteen townships were laid out, nine on the St. Lawrence and five higher up. Each series had a name, the former being called Royal and the latter Cataraqui, and the townships of each were distinguished by being numbered from the east. The present Lancaster, however, does not fit into this scheme. Though ninety people were mustered there in October, 1784,[37] the ground was considered too low and too wet for any considerable settlement. This explains why the numbering began with the next township, the modern Charlottenburgh. In this, Number 1 Royal Township, were planted the Roman Catholic Highlanders of Johnson's first battalion, for at their own request the men of this unit were sorted out for settlement according to race and religion. The Scottish Presbyterians were established in Number 2 Royal Township, where a little town sprang up on the site chosen by Johnson early in the year to serve as a center for his settlement.[38] It was known as New Johnstown until, some years later, it was rechristened Cornwall, the name then given to the township. Above the Scots came the German Calvinists, the German Lutherans, and the Anglicans in Numbers 3, 4, and 5, the modern Osnabruck, Williamsburg, and Matilda, respectively. Numbers 6, 7, and 8 Royal Townships, later Edwardsburgh, Augusta, and Elizabethtown, received the larger part of Major Jessup's corps.

Township Number 1 Cataraqui, the modern Kingston, was of course allotted to the pilgrims led by Grass. In Number 2 Cataraqui, or Earnestown, were located the rest of Jessup's corps and some who had served in McLean's Royal Highland Emigrants, the Eighty-fourth Regiment. Johnson's second battalion was divided between Numbers 3 and 4, Fredericksburg and Adolphustown, in the former being joined by Major Rogers' corps and in the latter by a party that had come in the wake of Grass from New York under the leadership of Major Van Alstine. To the southwest, across the Bay of Quinté in Number 5 Cataraqui, Marysburg, were deposited detachments of disbanded regulars, including some Germans under Baron Reitzenstein. Land in the Cataraqui area was also offered by Haldimand to Butler's Rangers. But they preferred to remain where they were and he acquiesced in their settlement at Niagara.[39] The only other loyalist settlement was that of a mere handful, including Alexander McKee, the active Indian agent, who moved across the river from Detroit. In the fall of 1785 there were eighteen hundred

ENCAMPMENT OF THE LOYALISTS AT JOHNSTOWN

[From a water color by James Peachey, dated June 6, 1784, in the possession of the Public Archives of Canada]

SIR FREDERICK HALDIMAND

[From a replica in the Public Archives of Canada of the original portrait in oils by
Francis Lemuel Abbott]

families in the two series of townships and something under three hundred families at Niagara.[40]

The planting of all this population was no child's play. It was a great task beset by numerous difficulties. Yet it was ably performed, so ably that it inspires the admiration of one who pores over the records of that day. The responsibility for directing the work at Niagara was shared by the commandant, Major De Peyster, and Colonel John Butler. It was relatively light because the Rangers were not numerous, they were already on the spot, and they had the nucleus of a settlement in the colony started in 1780. Much more onerous was the work of supervising operations in the fourteen townships. This task was intrusted to Sir John Johnson, whose paternal position, inherited in times of peace and worthily sustained in times of war, seemed to Haldimand to mark him out as the father of the colony to be. He was placed over Stephen De Lancey, who had already been appointed inspector of loyalists. In the actual distribution of the land Johnson was associated with Major Samuel Holland, the surveyor general. Another individual to whom the loyalists were greatly beholden, though it is doubtful if they knew it, was a quiet, unassuming man who remained in Quebec. He wore a major's uniform and wielded a pen — the governor's secretary, Robert Mathews. Judging by his voluminous correspondence he must have toiled night and day straightening out all manner of annoying details as well as securing and transmitting his chief's advice on matters of greater importance. There is still another man to whom the loyalists owed much, and to him they owed more than to any of these. It was the governor himself.

Haldimand should ever be honored as the founder of Upper Canada. He fixed the main outlines of its original settlement, and he did it in a masterly fashion, for in addition to a high sense of duty and a deep feeling of compassion he possessed imagination and organizing ability. Very simple and yet highly important was his decision that the loyalists should be mustered, moved, and settled in their old units. It was the easiest and most natural way to handle them, and it prevented what appears to have been a very serious danger. The release of the provincials from military discipline on the disbandment of their corps, and the desire of most men and many women to secure the best location, might easily have produced hopeless confusion with individuals running hither and thither and scurrying everywhere. Haldimand's plan had also a positive and a more permanent advantage. The human ties essential to a community were already formed. And how were they formed! The mutual loyalties of comrades in war were too fine an asset to be thrown away in the days of peace. What better neighbors could there be than men who had been true to one another when face to face with death?

A second wise regulation laid down by Haldimand governed the distribution of the land. Instructions issued by the home government on July 16 and August 7, 1783, prescribed the scale of grants. Fifty acres were to be given to a single civilian, one hundred to the head of a family, the same number to a reduced private, and two hundred to a former noncommissioned officer. To these amounts, fifty acres were to be added for each member of the recipient's family. Those who had held commissions were entitled to larger grants, an ex-subaltern to five hundred, an ex-captain to seven hundred, and an ex-field officer to a thousand acres. In addition to their more generous allowance, many officers of the provincial corps claimed the right to pick their lands before the rank and file were satisfied. This presumption, which was but an expression of the mental habit of superiority that clung to more than one individual for several years, caused friction between "officers" and "men" in some of the infant settlements. There was thus a danger that the new communities would be blighted at their birth by a continuation of army distinctions.

The governor saw it clearly and determined to avoid it as far as possible. Though he did not question the principle of unequal grants, he tried to apply it in such a way that its economic and social consequences would be reduced to an almost negligible minimum. To establish this equality, and also to provide for solid settlement, he issued a few simple rules. The townships were to be divided into lots of uniform size between parallel concession roads running at regular intervals. Beginning at the front of each township, the surveyors were to mark off a sufficient number of lots to meet the immediate necessities of those who were ready to occupy the land they might claim. Each man, whatever his previous rank had been, was to draw for a lot. The decision of chance might be modified by choice, exchanges being allowed between those who had drawn. Those who had the right to a surplus were to select it later from the land that was left. Under this system the first settlers did not have to take up farms farther back than the third concession in most townships. Cornwall was an exception because of the large number of the Scottish Presbyterians to whom it was allotted. According to a map of 1786, it was then occupied in part as far back as the eighth concession.[41] The only other exception seems to have been Fredericksburg, where, judging by its slightly larger original population, settlement must have penetrated as deep as in Cornwall. The system worked out well, though it was not always rigidly applied. Sir John Johnson and Major Holland occasionally allowed ex-officers a preference. When he heard of this, Haldimand was naturally annoyed, and he reprimanded the disobedient pair, but he did not dare order them to undo what they had done.

Here it may also be observed that the governor, military man that he was, appreciated the desire of the ordinary loyalists to escape from even the appearance of military control. The more the business of settlement was conducted under the civil power, he said, the more would it be relished by the people. Therefore, in the summer of 1784, he began to appoint justices of the peace in the new districts.

Of prime importance was the material assistance Haldimand gave the loyalists to start their lives afresh.[42] The land would otherwise have been a vain gift to most, for they were destitute, and there would have been little new settlement away from the older part of the colony had he not cared for them as a wise father cares for his children. He clothed them and fed them until they could support themselves, and he supplied them with the means of becoming self-sufficing if they exerted themselves. The authority for doing all this he either assumed himself or persuaded the home government to grant. The part he played is well illustrated by his refusal to obey an order from the treasury to reduce the issue of provisions to the loyalists. Well-fed and unimaginative officials in London thought a full ration no longer necessary now that peace was signed, whereas it was more necessary than ever. The people were just moving onto their lands and could not be expected to conduct clearing operations on half-empty stomachs. Hence the governor ordered the commissaries to go on delivering the usual provisions. He faced the possibility of having to pay the extra expense out of his own pocket, until he succeeded in persuading the home government that the full issue should be continued until the summer of 1786. Fortunately he had a surplus stock at his disposal, for he no longer had a large army to feed, and the upper posts had lost some of their voracious appetite.

Haldimand sometimes found it more difficult to cover the backs than to fill the mouths of the new settlers. Many an army blanket had to do service as a coat, and a few people who did not receive their proportion of clothing were given pots and kettles as compensation! [43] He did his utmost to arm the pioneers for their attack upon the wilderness, providing them with implements and materials, including iron and steel. Here and there hammers and saws were soon busy, but many a cabin was built with the aid of only one tool — the axe that was given to every settler. With the axe went the hoe and the spade. Many had nothing else with which to cultivate the soil during the first year in their new homes. The government also built a few sawmills and gristmills for the use of the new population. The stones and the ironwork were shipped up the St. Lawrence in bateaux. The first mill was constructed by Lieutenant Brass of Butler's Rangers at Niagara before the general settlement, and as soon as he had finished it he was brought to Cataraqui to erect the second. Another boon was the allotment to each township of some of the bateaux that had transported the settlers upward and had earlier plied to and fro between Lachine and Carleton Island to preserve the upper posts. Nor did the thoughtful governor forget to distribute arms and ammunition that the people might enjoy the fruits of the chase in a land that abounded with game.

Of course seed was provided, but the season of 1784 was so far advanced before most people received their land that few were able to raise anything for themselves that year except a shelter against the winds of winter. The few managed to grow some patches of potatoes, turnips, and Indian corn. The first seed wheat, procured from Vermont, the Mohawk Valley, and the older part of Canada, reached Cataraqui in October, 1784. One request Haldimand did refuse. This was the demand of the insatiable Michael Grass that the government supply cattle. But this refusal did not mean that the new settlements were deprived of livestock. Several herds of cattle were driven up from the old colonies in the summer of 1784. They belonged to some loyalists who managed to salvage at least part of their property back in their old homes.

Before proceeding with this story of beginnings, it will be well to glance at the dwellings that were springing up in the wilderness.[44] The cabin, which replaced the tent of canvas or of heaven, varied in its proportions with the size of the family it was to accommodate, but seldom was it larger than fifteen by twenty feet inside measurement. The walls, which were seven or eight feet high, were made of logs laid horizontally and notched at the ends to fit into one another. Splinters were fitted into the chinks and then the surface, inside and out, was plastered with clay. The roof, which had a single slope, was made of slabs of bark, commonly elm, four feet long and two or three feet wide tied to and supported by poles resting on the end walls. A blanket hung on the inside commonly took the place of a door until logs could be ripped up with a whip-saw, and the solitary little opening left for a window was not glazed for some time. The earliest floors, after the turf, were of split logs. The fireplace was constructed of stones gathered near by and the chimney was of reinforced mud, having been built up around a framework of poles. Almost all the furniture in most of these "shanties" was likewise improvised. Such was the home of the ordinary loyalist who with his axe slowly ate his way into the hardwood forest and with the aid of his hoe planted his first meager crops. He and his equally indomitable family were the real heroes of the conquest of the wilderness. In them lies the principal secret of the success of the work that was directed from the Castle of St. Louis.

By the fall of 1786 the new settlements had taken firm root. With the gathering of that year's harvest the issue of government rations ceased to be necessary and was stopped.[45] The transition to an independent economy was painful to those who, deaf to repeated warning, believed that "Old George," as they familiarly called their sovereign, would continue indefinitely to play the part of Providence; but the number of these trusting souls seems to have been very small. Detailed returns of the township of Matilda, which may be taken as typical, paint a picture of prosperity. In the fall of 1784 this township had a population of one hundred and seventy-seven, and fifty-six and a half acres of cleared land.[46] By September, 1787, it had a population of two hundred and forty-seven, one-third of whom were children under fourteen, and four hundred and thirty-nine acres of cleared land. Although this was scarcely more than four per cent of the amount granted, it was more than enough to meet the needs of the people. A harvest of forty-five hundred bushels had been gathered from something over five hundred bushels of seed, and the community possessed considerable live-stock — forty-four horses, twenty-four colts, fifteen oxen, twelve bulls, sixty-seven cows, forty-seven heifers, five sheep, and two hundred and seven hogs. One family of three men and a woman living on an ordinary holding of a hundred acres, twenty of which were cleared, had reaped a crop of two hundred and forty bushels, and owned a horse, a yoke of oxen, a cow, a heifer, and eighteen hogs. A number of other settlers were nearly as well off.[47] In estimating the material condition of the loyalists it should not be forgotten that fish and game were plentiful. Many a deer was shot near the pioneer's cabin; wild pigeons were so unwary that they were sometimes killed with a pole; and the streams contained such an abundance of salmon or trout that they were caught by thrusting down a forked stick upon their backs.

But there came a year when food was short and the shadow of famine rested over the land. This was 1789, "the hungry year," of which many tales have been handed down.[48] According to tradition, which varied from locality to locality, beef bones were boiled and boiled again, and were carried from house to house for the tantalizing process to be repeated; only the eyes of potatoes were planted for seed; to fill empty stomachs, roots were dug up, bark was stripped from trees, swelling buds and also common weeds were gathered and cooked; a little salt allayed some pangs of hunger; lands were sold for a bushel of potatoes or a few pounds of flour; and many people died of starvation. Tradition ascribes the misery to a burning heat that dried up wells and springs and blasted the crops in the fields. But these stories are not wholly reliable. They were not written down until long years afterward, and it is well known that old people's memories often play tricks even upon themselves.

We get a somewhat different, though still miserable, picture if we gather up and piece together the scraps of contemporary evidence. The shadows are not quite so deep, but the canvas is much broader. The documents tell of no one who perished of hunger, and they suggest that there was much more suffering below the mouth of the Ottawa than above it. Therefore in relating this trying experience we must see the colony as a whole.

Bread was scarce throughout Canada for about six months, from the late winter until the harvest of 1789. The causes lie back in 1788, when there was a heavy export and a light crop. Ten thousand barrels of flour, half as much again of biscuit, and more than two hundred thousand bushels of wheat were shipped out of the country at low prices.[49] The crop shortage, which extended throughout the adjoining territory of the republic, cannot be explained with certainty. According to a Quebec traveler who passed through the state of New York in the spring of 1789, a wet season and the Hessian fly had wrought the damage south of the boundary line.[50] But no one mentioned the presence of the insect in Canada, though the *Quebec Herald* reported its appearance in New Brunswick as well as in the United States.[51] One suspects that something else had been at work here — smut. As seeding time drew near in 1789, both Quebec papers reflected a public interest in fighting this pest, which suggests that the fault of the weather had been that there was too much rather than too little rain.

However that may be, there is reason for believing that the main loyalist settlements had a considerably better harvest in 1788 than did the district of Montreal, the old granary of Canada. Lord Dorchester visited the loyalists in the late summer of that year, leaving Quebec at the end of July and returning to Montreal in the beginning of September, and in reporting to the home government upon his journey he commented on the prosperity of the new settlements. Not one word did he say of any distress or fear of distress among them.[52] On February 23, 1789, a loyalist wrote from Montreal that "many hundred Canadians" had been "among the new settlers this winter to purchase grain for the support of their truly miserable families in this season," and he proudly added that the loyalists had been able "to alleviate Canadian distress with many hundred bushels of wheat at a much lower rate than it could have been bought from their more fortunate countrymen below."[53] In the Montreal district, where some habitants reaped no more than they had sown, a half crop was gathered. The country around Quebec was a little more fortunate, whereas Niagara seems to have been badly hit.

Perhaps the greatest suffering was in the towns of Montreal and Quebec, where the price of bread soared above the reach of the poor. Their plight moved the staid *Quebec Gazette* to remark on May 21,

1789, that they "in such a year of scarcity as the present are exposed to the extremity of want and liable to perish if the benevolence of their fellow subjects in better circumstances should overlook or neglect them." Charity was already coming to their rescue. On that very day the Merchants' Club of Quebec provided an ox and a hundred loaves "that the wretched might in some degree participate in that pleasure felt from the happy information of His Majesty's recovery" from illness.[54] A fortnight later the Barons' Society of the same city celebrated the king's birthday by distributing seven hundred pounds of beef and six hundred loaves.[55] Toward the end of June the freemasons of the capital ordered four hundred and fifty loaves to be delivered to the poor.[56] Late in July a member of the Quebec seminary contributed an old French recipe for jelly from boiled ground bones. He gave it to the public through the *Gazette*,[57] remarking that he would hold himself "guilty of the sufferings of the poor of this province" if he kept it secret.

In Montreal, where the need was greater, there was a public subscription for the destitute. The result, as reported in the middle of June, was as follows: "For eight weeks an average number of more than six hundred rations of provisions consisting of ½ lb. bread [and] ½ lb. beef per diem, besides a few peas for the three first weeks, have been issued to the poor, which has contributed to support or relieve from distress above 1400 people daily." This had cost about £385. Scarcely any of the money collected now remained, and the council was informed that "God only knows what those poor families will suffer when that is finished." [58] Something more must have been done, though we know not what, for the price of bread continued to mount, reaching a high point of fourteen pence for the four-pound white loaf and sixteen pence for the six-pound brown loaf at the beginning of July,[59] and even those who had the money were frequently unable to buy.

In the rural parishes conditions were described as inconceivable. Habitants who generally had an abundance to sell were begging about the country to escape starvation. Not a few were devouring the carcasses of such dead animals as were to be found. Some even killed their horses to save their families, and "many had little else to give their children than broth of boiled peas straw." Between Longueuil and St. John the consumption of wild roots was common, and it was reported to the council that at least one-third of the Rivière du Loup parishioners had deserted their homes for the shores of Lake St. Peter in an endeavor to support their families upon fish.

Up at Niagara conditions were equally bad. A letter from there, cited by the *Quebec Herald* on April 13, 1789, stated that a bushel of wheat was hard to get for one pound York currency, and that "cats etc." had been substituted for "beef etc." The writer stated that potatoes and salt pork "got by great entreaty from the soldiers" were almost his constant diet, and he did not know how he and his neighbors would "be able to spin out life until the next harvest." In the beginning of June, Philip Stedman of Niagara appeared before the council in Quebec with a further tale of woe. According to him, the population of that settlement amounted to three thousand, and of these not more than twenty families had had bread for nearly three months, their wants having been chiefly supplied by boiled basswood bark and Indian potatoes. On his way down he had observed that the people in the main loyalist settlements were "in nearly the same situation." At Kingston he had seen a guinea offered for a bushel of potatoes.[60] If his cursory impression of hardships on the upper St. Lawrence be accepted as sound, it is difficult to escape the conclusion that the people in this region were suffering for their excessive passion for money or their excessive compassion for the Canadians.

The crisis passed with the gathering of the harvest in 1789, and the reduction of the economic pressure may be read on a reliable gauge. The Montreal magistrates, meeting for the monthly assize on August 3, lowered the price of the white loaf from fourteen pence to ninepence, the rate of the previous January, and two months later they cut off another twopence. But it would be a mistake to imagine that all the relief came from heaven or the soil of Canada. The governor first looked to the United States. The door of trade with that country, shut tight by the Revolution, which placed it outside the empire's colonial system, had been unlatched by a provincial ordinance of 1787,* and in 1789 he opened it wide for the admission of foodstuffs. Some help did come from south of the international line,[61] but not much, for the adjoining territory of the republic was likewise stricken.

* See below, pages 450–51.

As there were well-grounded fears that the crop of 1789 would bring only temporary relief, since too many people had eaten what they should have sown and the weather spoiled part of the crop,[62] Dorchester importuned the home government to rescue the province by sending out supplies. The answer to his appeal came in November, 1789 — a thousand tons of flour, twenty-three thousand bushels of wheat, and twenty-four thousand bushels of peas. These provisions were more than sufficient to prevent a return of the crisis. Half the stock was still on hand when the following summer came.[63] In the spring of 1790, however, there were fears that the fall of prices, though they had not yet reached the low level of 1788, might lead to a repetition of that year's folly, and the council passed an ordinance placing an embargo on the export of foodstuffs. This was lifted by proclamation on August 25, a bountiful harvest having banished all nervousness.

Returning from this digression into the general agricultural life of the colony, and concentrating once more upon the life of the new settlements in the west, we may observe that, though the crisis was really over in the fall of 1789, Haldimand's hope of transforming the wilderness into a granary was not realized until long after Upper Canada was erected into a separate government. Meanwhile the crudest pioneer conditions prevailed. Some slight mitigation appeared along "the front," partly the consequence of favored location and partly the result of the half pay that ex-officers received. Their families, thanks to this small income, found life a little easier than it was for the great majority, who were typical settlers of the North American frontier. The average man and his family were largely self-sufficing, pretty well consuming all that they produced and producing all that they consumed. They bought little because they could sell little. The first salable commodities they produced were by-products of their clearing operations. Getting rid of most of the trees by burning them, they had considerable quantities of wood ashes. These, and the potash that was sometimes extracted, they sold to the few shopkeepers, often innkeepers also, who were soon found along "the front." Only two varieties of trees did they spare from the consuming fire, because they and they alone had value as timber. Pine for masts and oak for lumber had a market down in Quebec, and this induced many a settler to spend the whole winter out in the woods with his sons cutting logs, which they rafted down the river in the spring. Occasionally the lumbering business injured agriculture by usurping the place of first importance. Generally speaking, however, the ashes and the timber only enabled these people in the backwoods to purchase the few articles they could neither make themselves nor do without.

What these resourceful pioneers did not need, and how they contrived to satisfy their real wants, would astonish their descendants, who have become the slaves of a mechanized society, for they belonged to a type of English-speaking people that has passed away and is now being forgotten. Most of them lived happily and healthily without schools or books, without churches and parsons, and without doctors [64] and patent medicines. It is impossible to say definitely how well they were supplied with other medicines. There is a record of nearly one hundred and fifty pounds worth being purchased for them in Quebec by the government.[65] Still one may suspect that their chief medicine was procured by the settlers themselves to improve the spirits of the hearty rather than to heal the bodies of the sick. They were also unable to bring in any agricultural implements to supplement the spade and the hoe, but they knew how to use a brush-harrow and how to construct wooden rakes and ploughs. The latter were shod with iron and steel supplied by the government.

At first the backs of these people were covered by issues from the army stores, but it was not long before practically all their clothing was made at home of materials that were not imported. Deerskin coats, shirts, trousers, dresses, and even petticoats were soft and warm and well-nigh everlasting. The same stuff made wonderful bed covers. Soon the hides of domestic cattle were available, and every man, assisted by his wife and children, was his own tanner, cobbler, and harness-maker. Flax was grown and sheep were kept that the women-folk might spin and weave linen and cloth. The product was coarse and stout, but substance rather than style was desired.

As suggested by the figures of the return for Matilda Township in 1787, pork was the standard meat — except when the wolves carried it off from the place where it was hung up to dry. One of the few articles of food that had to be bought — and it was rather expensive — was salt. Sugar was easy to procure, being extracted from the maple. Potatoes and turnips the settlers had from their first sowing, and milk, butter, and eggs were soon plentiful. Though wheat tended to become the principal grain crop, the Scots could not be expected to live without oats, and most of the settlers relied greatly upon Indian corn in the earliest years. A much-relished dish, often prepared to reward the weary harvesters, was the "pumpkin loaf," compounded of pumpkin and cornmeal. The prevalence of this native cereal is recalled by the name "hominy block." The mills constructed by the government were too few to serve most of the scattered pioneers, who therefore had to grind their grain by hand. Some along the St. Lawrence ground it in little steel contraptions like coffee mills, but there is no memory of any such machines being distributed in the region of the Bay of Quinté. There are stories of men and women using the head of an axe on a flat stone, but the common method was to pound the grain with a wooden pestle, called a "stamper," in a hardwood stump hollowed out with heated iron to form a mortar or "hominy block." The bran was separated from the flour by a horsehair sieve which commonly did service for a whole community.

That "man shall not live by bread alone" was believed by these pioneers, as appears by some items in account books of those days. Robert Clark, who built the Napanee mills, entered "2 gallons and 3 pints of Rum, 17s 6d" for raising the sawmill on March 23, 1786, and two months later he charged four gallons and a quart against the raising of the gristmill.[66] Nor was strenuous manual labor necessary to earn such refreshment. In September, 1790, down on the St. Lawrence just one mile below the present limits of Dundas, a law court was sitting in the tavern of one Richard Loucks, and long afterward the record was read in his handwriting — sundry entries of "Licker for the gentlemen of the grant gury," and of "decanters broken." [67] Such circumstantial evidence supports the charge leveled by the early missionaries against the people that they were "woefully addicted to carousing and dancing," a charge that might have been very true if the word "merrily" had been substituted.

Before they actually settled on the land in 1784, many loyalists grumbled because they were to live in a colony where there was no assembly, where English law did not prevail, and where the only form of land tenure was feudal. The first point does not appear to have concerned them nearly so much as the last, which, because it has sometimes been overlooked, is worth stressing. Each township was legally a seigniory and all who received land in it became feudal tenants, for the royal instructions issued to the governor did not allow him to make freehold grants. The contrast with Nova Scotia, where the loyalists lost none of their British birthright, increased the discontent of the newcomers in Canada; and very naturally a number of them pressed Haldimand for a promise that the discrimination would be removed. To all such demands he returned short answers. Ever since he had taken up his residence in the Castle of St. Louis, talk of assemblies and English laws had sounded in his ears like the murmurings of sedition, and he was still worried by the great problem of how a conquered French colony could be permanently fitted into the British Empire. But the exiles did not despair, for their leaders fed their hopes of obtaining justice sooner or later.

Their greatest champion was the chief among them, Sir John Johnson. At Haldimand's special request he had put off going to England, where his interests called him, that he might direct the business of settlement in the summer of 1784; but in the autumn of that year he crossed the water to plead in London for those who were opening up the back parts of the old province of Quebec. In April, 1785, he presented to the home government a strong petition signed by himself and a number of other leading officers. They prayed that the refugees might be relieved of the strange burden of seigniorial tenure and be governed by the laws that were familiar to them. To achieve these ends they proposed that all the country west of Point au Baudet be organized as a sort of sub-colony, with its own lieutenant governor and council subordinate to the government in Quebec, as was the administration of Cape Breton to that of Nova Scotia. The petitioners supported their case by developing the argument of justice suggested above, and by pointing out the political advantages of such an arrangement. If consideration were to be shown the new settlers they would draw numerous people from the lost colonies, and the new country would develop greatly. Otherwise there would be emigration rather than immigration, the British influence over the Indians would be undermined by the Americans, and the ultimate result, implied though not stated, would be the loss of the west.[68]

One serious practical grievance mentioned in the petition submitted in London had already been brought to the attention of the council in Quebec. This was the want of law courts in the new settlements. Though justices of the peace resided here and there, their criminal jurisdiction was confined to petty cases and they had no civil jurisdiction whatever — a consequence of the reform of 1770 which survived the Quebec Act. To require the new settlers to repair to Montreal, or to Quebec if they lived down at Gaspé, for the sake of procuring justice was simply to deny them justice. Consequently, in March, 1785, Lieutenant Governor Hamilton, whom Haldimand had left in charge of the government when he returned to England in the previous November, urged the legislature of the colony to pass a remedial measure. Thereupon the president, Finlay, introduced a bill to confer a limited civil jurisdiction upon justices of the peace in the remote parts of the province until regular law courts could be established where they would be needed. The bill was passed only after a struggle and by a narrow majority, for most of the French party were loath to admit that Canada might become a country with a dual nationality, and they feared this as the thin end of the wedge. They had cherished vain hopes of enlarging French Canada by forcing the people in the new settlements to conform to the system of the old settlements, and this ordinance seemed to augur the cramping of French Canada by the establishment of an English system on both sides of it.[69] This explains why there was such hot opposition to such a mild bill, for it was very mild. All that it gave was power to determine civil suits involving personal property up to five pounds. If the amount in dispute was no more than two pounds, one magistrate sufficed; two were necessary if the amount was larger. There was no provision for causes involving real property, presumably because there was as yet no private real property, strictly speaking, in the new settlements. No one had received more than a certificate of occupation. This "location ticket," as it was called, merely entitled the individual named to occupy and improve a specified parcel of land, and promised him a deed after he had been settled on this land for twelve months. The promise was not fulfilled until many years afterwards.

In 1786 the feudal specter began seriously to trouble the minds of the freeborn Britishers living west of Point au Baudet. This was a totally unexpected result of their own agitation for more mills. The

small number already erected by the government served only a few
people, and complaints pouring down the St. Lawrence convinced
Lieutenant Governor Hope, Hamilton's successor, and the council
that every township should be provided with a mill. Undoubtedly
the people who were crying out for mills expected the king to pay
for them, but the government in Quebec thought differently. Why
should the lieutenant governor and council incur such a heavy
public expenditure when it was not really necessary and when the
habitant had received no such royal gift? According to the law
and custom of the colony, the seignior might build a mill and
thereby acquire the right of *banalité* attached to it, but if he neglected his opportunity someone else might build the desired mill
and acquire the right of *banalité* for ten years, at the end of which
time it reverted to the seignior. Thus the habitant really paid for
the mill. Why should not the inhabitants above do likewise? Every
new township was legally a seigniory of which the king was
seignior. If he chose to neglect his feudal opportunity, why should
not others be allowed to seize it? Accordingly, in February, 1786,
the provincial government advertised the conditions under which
mills could be built and operated. The cost was to be borne locally
by private individuals who, in return, were to possess the rights
of seignior in everything pertaining to each mill "according to the
laws and customs of the province." After fifteen years — a lengthen-
ing of the period to inspire prompt action — each mill and its right
of *banalité* would revert to the king without compensation.[70] The
publication of these conditions came as a great shock to the new
settlers. They had asked for bread and they were given a stone,
and this at the very time that the government issue of provisions
was being stopped.

The feeling of distrust that this shock spread in the loyalist districts was fanned into an almost hysterical flame by the breath of
wild rumors that circulated in the autumn of that year. Those who
had not been honored with His Majesty's commission observed great
comings and goings among the half-pay officers, and they knew that
these mysterious actions had some connection with the arrival of a
new and powerful governor down in Quebec. What could this secret
and important business be? So far as is known today, it was only
a complimentary address to the new head of the government, the
old commander-in-chief in America, but outside the little privileged

circle the whisper ran that the officers were scheming to perpetuate the feudal system and to seat themselves in the saddle. On into the new year the ugly rumor ran, and the atmosphere of the country grew dangerously heated before a special commission of investigation, coming up from Quebec in the summer of 1787, opened the windows and let in some fresh air.

Though they little knew it, the ordinary people living west of the Ottawa had new and solid ground for hope at the very time that they began to give way to despair. Though their greatest pleader, Sir John Johnson, had accomplished little in London, he was back in the colony, where, as adviser of the new governor, he was to accomplish much. The new governor was of course the old governor, Sir Guy Carleton, raised to the peerage as Baron Dorchester, but the government of Dorchester was to be very different from the government of Carleton. The change in his political outlook, and the possible reasons for it, will be examined later. Here it may suffice to observe that he who had championed the loyalists in New York now championed them in Canada, and in so doing he seems to have followed implicitly the advice of Sir John Johnson.

On November 6, just a fortnight after he had landed in Quebec, Dorchester divided the council into four committees, each of which was to report upon some broad subject or group of subjects concerning the general welfare of the province. Only one of these committees need be noted here. Its field covered population, agriculture, and the settlement of the crown lands, and its personnel included Johnson, who was that day sworn in as a councilor. There is little doubt that the new member soon made an unpleasant discovery. The majority of his colleagues in the committee were stoutly opposed to the natural desire of the new English-speaking communities to escape as far as possible from the control of a French government in Quebec.

This discovery may have been at least one reason why, about the end of the month, he wrote to the magistrates in these communities telling them of the governor's concern for their interests, explaining the business upon which he himself was engaged, and advising a general petition in which the demand for free tenures should be stressed. The result, on paper, was all that could be desired — a strongly worded demand for freehold tenure and a request for regular law courts and English laws. Unfortunately the magistrates, who were ex-officers, acted without taking the people into their confidence, and thereby inflamed the popular suspicion. Shortly afterward, somewhere about the close of the year, another and clearer call was sent up from the east. This was a circular letter from Stephen De Lancey, inspector of loyalists, directing the heads of townships to assemble the inhabitants to elect representatives who would report their wants. The elections, which were held early in 1787, saw the climax of the movement against the officers. A captain formally elected in Lancaster was frightened into resigning, and for a month afterwards he went about armed. In Cornwall feeling was bitter against a captain who had abused his trust as a magistrate and was believed to be a principal in the supposed conspiracy to rivet feudalism upon the country. As head of the township he summoned and presided over the meeting, but for some reason best known to himself he left early. Then the people cried out that the officers had ruled long enough and straightway they selected three of their own number. In the upper townships, apparently, there was less turbulence accompanying the elections. These being finished, it took several weeks for the chosen representatives of communities stretching all the way from Lake St. Francis to the Bay of Quinté and of the distant settlement at Niagara to transact their business, so that it was not until April 15 that they signed a petition in which the whole of these communities spoke with one voice.[71]

First and foremost, they wanted "the blessings of the British constitution" and freehold tenure. Contrasting their own position with that of their fellow sufferers in Nova Scotia, they asked to be put on the same footing, and to this end they begged for the arrangement outlined in Johnson's London petition of two years before. They prayed "for some assistance in establishing the Church of England and Scotland, in this infant settlement, and that a glebe of four hundred acres of land in each township may be set apart for a clergyman," and also "for some assistance towards establishing a school in each district, vizt. New Johnstown, New Oswegatchie, Cataraqui and Niagara, for the purpose of teaching English, Latin, Arithmetic and Mathematics." Nor were material blessings omitted from their prayer. They besought a prohibition of the import of ashes and lumber from Vermont and a bounty on the same articles. They also asked for a bounty on hemp produced in the colony.

Among other things they begged for three months' provisions of pork, for a post road between Montreal and Cataraqui with post-houses at New Johnstown, New Oswegatchie, and Cataraqui, and for the continuance of the privilege of using the canals — apparently free of toll. This petition was the first outcome of the popular movement in the country west of Montreal.

The second outcome was the investigation referred to above. The ex-officers brought it on their own heads by accusing Patrick McNiff, an official of Samuel Holland's department, of stirring up sedition among the rank and file. To examine this charge, to find out what was wrong in the restless loyalist communities, and to select worthy instruments for the government to employ in the local administration that was soon to be set up, Dorchester sent John Collins and William Dummer Powell. Their report,[72] dated at Kingston on August 18, 1787, praised McNiff and castigated the officers. Some had used their magisterial authority in an irresponsible and oppressive manner, and all had tended to keep themselves aloof as a superior class. The result was "a very dangerous jealousy" and an "alarming situation" requiring "a delicate and tender treatment." "No task," said the report, "can be more difficult than properly to direct that premature puberty which may be said to characterise this infant settlement," and there was only one way to do it. That was for the magistrates to consult the people, whose illiteracy and "general sense of just political subordination" came in for special comment. Then they would "be led warmly to second every plan of government as the child of their own desires."

Two other recommendations of the report concerned education and religion. The inhabitants of Earnestown, unaided, had already started a village school, and there was hope that other townships would soon follow this example. To continue the good work, the report urged the government to grant assistance "to establish a seminary in Kingston, where the youth may receive improvement and information" beyond what might be given in a village school. "After making provision for the first elements of education," continued the report, "the object most obvious to promote a decency of manners and consequent happiness among the people appears to us to be the establishment of some minister for public worship in each town or in small districts, and this we are led more particularly to observe by having remarked that a licentiousness of manners and conversation appears already to be no longer the subject of shame or reproach, which in so young a country we attribute to the want of a standard and a marked example for sober manners only to be expected in so mixed a body of people from characters set apart and looked up to for that purpose."

Meanwhile, down in Quebec, Johnson was ably advancing the loyalist cause. In spite of all that he could say and in spite of the magistrates' appeal which he produced, the committee of which he was a member curtly dismissed the demand for free tenure in the new settlements. But he insisted on presenting along with their report on February 6 a reasoned statement to the contrary over his own signature, and on Dorchester's referring back these contradictory papers to the committee they replied a week later that Johnson's dissent was intended to be part of the report. His immediate object, of course, was to move the provincial government to advise the home government to change the royal instructions so as to allow freehold grants. Though he had failed to carry the committee with him and though it is possible that he might also have been overborne in council had the report come up for adoption or rejection, he had not lost the day. The governor was with him. Perhaps this was why the adverse report was never submitted to a vote in the council. However that may be, Dorchester wrote home on June 13, 1787, inclosing the petition of April 15, which he had received in the interval, and pressing for an immediate alteration in his instructions. Mere prudence, he said, dictated that the new settlers should be placed in as advantageous a position as would be the Americans who were bound, sooner or later, to live in great numbers just across the narrow waterway dividing the two countries.[73]

The home government inclined a favorable ear. In the autumn an additional instruction containing the desired change was drafted and an order-in-council to launch it was prepared.[74] But George Chalmers, the learned chief clerk of the privy council committee on trade and a former resident in America, raised strenuous objections. He insisted that "a free and common socage tenure necessarily produces independence of mind, independence of action, and independence of government."[75] His intervention caused the whole business to be held up. In the spring of 1788 the governor again wrote urging the change,[76] but the first real satisfaction he received was in a letter written by the secretary of state in the following September. It contained the assurance that the occupants of lands in the new settlements were to hold them in free and common socage.[77] The legal provision for this reform was finally made at the time of the Constitutional Act.

Though the dwellers in the new settlements had also to wait until after this act for the adoption of English civil law in place of the French system, they were given courts of their own at an earlier date, for this accommodation did not require the consent of the home government. Gaspé was part of the judicial district of Quebec and the newly opened western country was in the judicial district of Montreal, by reason of an old provincial ordinance which a new one might undo. During the legislative session of 1787 provision was made for the creation of new districts, each of which was to have a sheriff, a court of quarter sessions, and a court of common pleas. The actual creation of the new districts was delayed, however, by the difficulty of finding men fit to fill the new offices.[78] This was partly the result of the bitter feelings born of the social cleavage revealed by Collins and Powell. They feared that either party would distrust almost anyone selected from the other. But even if brotherly love had reigned instead of suspicion and hate, it would have been hard to pick suitable officials. The difficulty had another and deeper cause. It lay in the very nature of Canada's refugee population, which was very unlike that of Nova Scotia, where educated people were common and the professional classes were well represented. In all the new Canadian settlements men of education were rare, and there was not a single lawyer. For the courts of common pleas Dorchester might have chosen judges from the gentlemen of the bar in Montreal and Quebec if he had been able to pay them good salaries, but he was not able to offer any salaries, there being no provision for such in the establishment which had been sanctioned at home. After hesitating for a year, the governor pitched upon the best local laymen he could discover, and he provided for their remuneration by means of fees.

The new judicial districts, which were decreed on July 24, 1788, were five in number and were bounded by north and south lines drawn through specified points. The territory lying south of the St. Lawrence to the east of Cape Cat became the district of Gaspé.

Luneburg,* extending from Point au Baudet to the mouth of the Ganonoque River, covered the nine townships on the upper St. Lawrence. The next was Mecklenburg, whose western limit was the mouth of the Trent at the head of the Bay of Quinté. It included the original Cataraqui townships and some others recently laid out. Then came Nassau, in which was Niagara, reaching as far as Long Point on Lake Erie. All that lay beyond became the district of Hesse.

In each of the four western districts three judges were commissioned to compose the court of common pleas. Of the whole dozen appointments, only three appear to have been particularly acceptable — those of Colonel Butler and William Hamilton of Niagara and Richard Cartwright of Kingston. Unlike Butler, who had already made his name, Cartwright and Hamilton were coming men. They were merchants who had been partners during the war, when they did an extensive business with the government at Niagara. The first clergyman of Upper Canada, the Reverend John Stuart,[79] who settled in Kingston in 1785, refused a seat on the bench of Mecklenburg, and after a very few years one of the ex-captains who was made a judge in Luneburg departed rather suddenly to live in the United States, against whose independence he had recently fought. The difficulty was greatest in Hesse. There the situation was more complicated, the old French population outnumbering the English newcomers and Detroit having a considerable commerce. In this settlement a loud outcry arose when the personnel of the new court was announced. There was little objection to one of the appointees, Captain Alexander McKee, the astute Indian agent, but there was great objection to the other two. These were Duperon Baby, eldest son of the savior of Gladwyn's post from Pontiac's fury, and William Robertson. They were the two big business men of that part of the country, and it was pointed out that one or the other was bound to be somehow interested in almost every case that would come before them. Therefore Dorchester removed all three and appointed a lawyer, William Dummer Powell. To induce him to go into the western wilds the governor had to assume the responsibility of promising him a salary

* Some have thought this a misprint for Lunenburg. Luneburg was a fair city of Hanover and this, like the other names, was selected as a compliment to the king. Mecklenburg was named in honor of his father-in-law.

of five hundred pounds. The home government later sanctioned the arrangement, at the same time cautioning Dorchester not to do the like again until he received special permission.[80]

Another modicum of autonomy granted to the country above Montreal followed closely upon the establishment of a separate judicial administration. It concerned something in which an even larger proportion of the population was vitally interested — the granting of land. Far from being completed, this business only began in 1784, and it pressed more and more heavily upon the governor and council, forcing them to develop a special organization to handle it. The first move was made on February 17, 1787, when Dorchester named a committee headed by Chief Justice William Smith, whom he had brought out with him a few months previously. This committee was to examine certain specified petitions already submitted and all other applications that might require speedy decision, and to report upon them to the whole council. Under the above date, also, is to be found the first entry in Land Book A.[81] This marks the beginning of another division of the council's records, the first differentiation having occurred after the Quebec Act when a separate book was started for the minutes of legislative meetings. The second step in the development of a special organization was taken on November 19, 1787, when the land committee became a permanent body meeting weekly. Its personnel was somewhat altered, other councilors were allowed to sit and vote in it, and Finlay was appointed to serve as chairman in the absence of the chief justice. The subsequent records show that the chair was regularly occupied by Finlay. His assumption of this responsibility, which was by no means light, opened an important chapter in his career. Until Canada was divided, this faithful old servant of the crown presided over the land-granting business in the whole country; after the division he filled a similar position in Lower Canada and was kept even busier by the land rush that developed there.

The third and final step was taken in the latter half of 1788 as a consequence of the visit that Dorchester paid the newly created western districts, where representations were made to him "of delay and expense being occasioned to many loyalists desirous of forming settlements in the upper country from the want of authority on the spot for allotting lands for them." On December 29 he announced in council that to remedy the inconvenience he had appointed four local land boards, the members of which he named. Each board was to take over the business of making all ordinary grants within its own district. It was to examine into the loyalty and the character of all applicants and, on being satisfied, it was to see that the oath of allegiance was administered to each applicant. Then it was to furnish him with an order upon the deputy surveyor of the district for a lot. Further detailed regulations were framed by a special committee of the council during the next few weeks. One board was located in Montreal and placed under the presidency of Sir John Johnson, who had taken up his residence there. The other three were for Luneburg, Mecklenburg, and Nassau, and each was composed principally of the common pleas judges. A land board for Gaspé was named on March 12 and one for Hesse on April 11, 1789, but the last, unlike the others, never really got down to business before the Constitutional Act came into force.

Though these land boards were limited to routine operations and had to make regular and full reports to the governor's secretary, and though the council with the assistance of its land committee had to scrutinize these reports and also to deal with every application or trouble that was in the least way out of the ordinary,[82] yet the burden at Quebec was lightened and, what was of much greater importance, the delegation of authority was a blessing to the new districts.

Several causes conspired to augment the government's land business from 1784. In that year many people received only a portion of the land to which they were then entitled, and they soon began to seek the remainder. The officers were not the only ones who had to be satisfied, for the "family lands" promised to all were rarely covered by the original allotment. The demand was also increased by the many new settlers who were appearing in the country west of Montreal. In September, 1786, a ship with the appropriate name of "McDonald" or "Macdonell," dropped anchor before Quebec, having borne some five hundred Highlanders from Greenock.[83] With the exception of ninety-six immigrants from Arisaig and Egg who came four years later,[84] this was the only body of immigrants to arrive from the mother country until after the turn of the century. It comprised nearly the whole population of a Glengarry parish under the leadership of their priest, Alexander Macdonell. He and his flock were on their way to join their clansmen and kinsfolk in the new Glengarry. Some, however, were settled at the head of the St. Lawrence, where confusion arose because they were given lands already allotted to loyalists.[85] In 1787 a number of Canadians who had demonstrated their loyalty by bearing arms and who refused to be forgotten were established on the south side of Lake St. Francis just west, of Lotbinière's Beauharnois seigniory. In the early summer of 1788, orders were issued for the survey of a township, later Chatham, on the north side of the Ottawa next to the seigniory of Argenteuil for the officers and men of the Eighty-fourth Regiment, the Royal Highland Emigrants, who had not received the lands promised them in Cataraqui in 1784. But, as already observed, the great bulk of the immigrants came from the United States, "late loyalists" and land-seekers who brought their effects with them and were immediately at home. Publicly and privately they were encouraged to come, for they contributed greatly to the development of the new country and there were few fears on the score of their loyalty. Indeed, their coming was regarded as a sort of "prodigal's return."

With the swelling of the demand for land, the government grew more generous in giving it. The first increase in scale was ordered by the home government in the instructions issued to Dorchester on his appointment in 1786. It was to keep an old promise made to the officers of the Royal Highland Emigrants when their regiment was organized. Lieutenants were to receive two thousand acres, captains three, and field officers five. When it became known in Canada that the reduced officers of this unit were to be given between four and five times as much as had been allowed to other ex-officers, the latter became jealous and petitioned the governor for equally liberal treatment. Dorchester could not turn his back on this request, and on October 22, 1788, the council concurred in his proposal to remove the inequality. This was the second increase decided by the authority in Quebec, for on June 2, 1787, the governor, with the advice of the council, had ordered an additional two hundred acres to be given each head of a family who had improved his lands. This was known as the additional, or Lord Dorchester's, bounty. The encouragement offered to incoming settlers was likewise increased by doubling the initial grant, making it now a whole lot of two hundred acres. A further increase was decreed by the governor and council on November 9, 1789. Thenceforth the land boards were to give two hundred acres to every son of a loyalist on his coming of age and the same amount to every daughter of a loyalist on her marriage, provided the lands already assigned to the head of the family to which he or she belonged had not been neglected.

The growing demand for land and the government's generosity in meeting it swelled the numbers of Samuel Holland's staff and kept them all very busy with their chains and maps. By the time of the Constitutional Act there was a series of townships along the north bank of the Ottawa; and the whole country to the south, as far west as the line of the Rideau carried on to the head of the Bay of Quinté, was pretty well covered with townships. There settlers followed close on the heels of the surveyors. From the head of the Bay of Quinté westward to the site of Toronto, the "fronts" of townships were laid out ready to receive a population. Already there were pioneers in the townships surveyed all along the south shore of the lake from Niagara to the head of Burlington Bay, and more people lived in the two townships fronting the Niagara River below Chippewa Creek.

Though there had been confusion in this region because some settlers anticipated the surveyors, it was nothing compared with the troubles in what is now the southwest corner of Ontario. In the autumn of 1791 the land board of Hesse had issued not one location certificate though it had received over three hundred applications. It had first been held up by difficulties over Indian titles to the land and by the absence of properly qualified surveyors. About a hundred young men of Butler's Rangers and many who had come from the south after the peace, even as late as 1790, had gone back to the United States in disgust. Others had procured land from individuals who had secured it from the Indians, and still others had satisfied themselves by direct negotiation with the natives. Thus, in addition to the old and solid French settlement on the east side of the Detroit River, to which it had spread from the west side during the French régime, and on the southeast shore of Lake St. Clair, new and scattered settlements had appeared on Lake Erie and on the River Thames before proper surveys were begun in 1790. Though these were pushed in 1791, the land board was then tied up by the conflicting claims of those who had applied and waited for particular lots and those who had occupied and improved them, and by the reluctance of landless applicants to settle in the rear concessions of the townships being laid out.[86]

Though it is possible to indicate the area over which settlement was scattered in Upper Canada when it became a separate colony, only the vaguest notion of the size of its population at this time can be given. The total figure has been placed as low as ten thousand and as high as twenty-five thousand. Whatever the number may have been, it was spread very thinly except in the line of townships stretching along the waterfront from Point au Baudet to the head of the Bay of Quinté and in the angle between the Niagara River and Lake Ontario. Almost everywhere else the amount of land cleared was the merest fraction of what had been granted. This suggests that the government might be blamed for being too liberal. But a more restrictive policy might have produced worse results, since it would probably have failed to restrain these sturdy and independent frontiersmen. On the whole, the ex-officers were the only individuals who got much more than they might have taken for themselves, and this was relatively little, because they were a small group. It should also be remembered that the land-grabbing orgy that sowed the seeds of future political trouble did not begin until after the Constitutional Act, when the inrush of immigrants was greater and the business of granting land was no longer controlled from Quebec.

In concluding this story of Upper Canada before it became Upper Canada, only a word about politics need be added. The one dominant interest of all the people there was land, free land and, if possible, freehold land. Their desire for English laws was secondary. In replying to Sir John Johnson, the magistrates assembled in Kingston in December, 1786, said that the application of "the Laws of England is a matter much to be wished," but they went on to imply a willingness to accept other laws if compiled and printed so that they might know them. Three years later the judges of Mecklenburg, Richard Cartwright, Neil McLean, and James Clark, said much the same thing.[87]

Even less was the concern for an assembly. It is a striking fact that the original settlers, the loyalists, turned their backs on the opportunity to go to Nova Scotia, where an assembly existed, and were eager to take up land in a colony whose governor frowned on any suggestion of popular government. No less striking is the fact that those who followed on the heels of the loyalists and soon formed the bulk of the population abandoned the self-governing United States to live in a land that had no self-government. True, there was talk of a separate government for the country that was being opened up, but there is no evidence that the people who settled there were anxious to control it. Nor is this surprising. Their background explains their political apathy. As pioneers on the very edge of civilization in the old colonies, about the only laws by which they had been consciously affected were those touching land. Government had meant next to nothing to these independent backwoodsmen until they found it a benevolent agent in Canada, and an assembly was something which had meant little, if anything, to them.

CHAPTER XVI

A RISING STORM

THE ending of the war let loose a political storm in the older part of Canada. The mercantile minority — no longer confined to Quebec and Montreal, for there were now a score or so of old subjects in Three Rivers — had been bound and gagged. The peace removed the gag but left the bonds. The natural result was a great outcry for deliverance. These freeborn Britishers were denied the right of habeas corpus, they were deprived of juries in the trial of civil suits, and they were unprotected by any known mercantile law, all of which meant that they were at the mercy of their political foes, the judges. And why were these people in this evil plight? They knew that the British government had not willed it. They knew that London had instructed Quebec to pass legislation to remove their grievances. They knew that the wrong had been done right in the provincial capital by a little knot of men who controlled the council.

The nature of this control was no secret in Canada. How could the council contain independent men when Allsopp, and Livius before him, had been driven out for speaking out? Independence meant expulsion and the loss of a hundred pounds a year, the salary given to each member since the Quebec Act. To whom were the councilors responsible? To the governor! He made them and he could break them. Theoretically he had been controlled by his superiors in the heart of the empire; practically he had been guided by a small oligarchy of his inferiors in the colony, an oligarchy that included the hated judges. The system had been bad and now it was worse.

Of the little group that had wielded unconstitutional power, one member had grown to overshadow the rest so completely that, in the field of civil government, the rule of the few was becoming something that looked very much like the rule of one. That man was Adam Mabane,* the Scot who had been transformed into an upper-class French Canadian. With all the zeal of the convert he became the implacable foe of the whole tribe of English-speaking merchants. Small wonder that the racial minority burst forth in denunciation of the act of parliament under which such a perversion of government had developed! Small wonder that their agitation for an assembly flamed forth more fiercely than ever!

Circumstances of the moment heightened the storm. Financial ruin was hanging over most of the countinghouses of Quebec and Montreal. The bubble of speculation, blown to prodigious size by Cochrane's operations, had been punctured. Peace had caught the merchants with enormous stocks which they could not sell and for which they could not pay their principals in London. At the same time, they were faced with the demand for a full and immediate settlement of the heavy debts they had contracted through the agent of Harley and Drummond. Of course they could not satisfy that demand. Thereupon the governor, impelled by peremptory orders from the treasury to collect, appealed to the law in the spring of 1783. As almost every merchant was more or less involved in the tangle, one suit gave rise to another and a welter of litigation followed. In the struggle to keep their heads above water, not a few of them were submerged.

The bitterness of the strugglers was intensified by an ugly twist given the whole business at the very start. Cochrane refused to be joint plaintiff with the crown except on terms that would have covered all his irregularities. The crown then sought to recover by suing him and by simultaneously attaching the effects of his principal debtors. This method was adopted against the advice of the attorney general, who doubted whether the courts could uphold the crown. But Haldimand had already suspected Monk on several counts, and at this moment he suspected him more than ever, for he saw him as the friend of the parties who were being pursued. Needless to say, he was not employed as counsel for the crown, a lucrative commission that was given to his rival, Solicitor General Williams.

* After Haldimand's departure Finlay wrote: "The doctor was considered here as premier, nay more, that all civil propositions from the Chateau originated with the doctor; that it was he who planned, and his plans were adopted as no doubt highly proper coming from a man of law."[1]

Cochrane was at last openly hand in glove with the merchants, and they were encouraged by Monk to believe that the government could not do what it was trying to do. But the dice were loaded against them. As Haldimand's confidant, Mabane had suggested how the government should proceed and he was sure to support on the bench what he had advised in private. The defense challenged his right to sit, justly claiming that he was prejudiced, but he rudely brushed aside the challenge. With his colleagues whom he usually dominated, Dunn and Panet, he delivered the desired judgment. There is no need to follow the miserable business from this first judgment handed down in Quebec in August, 1783, to its final conclusion, at considerable loss to the crown, by a commission five years later. The important fact is this. To the whole mercantile community in Canada, the fountain of justice was poisoned! [2]

Besides being spurred on by desperation, the agitators were inspired by hope. From London they received new letters from Maseres urging them to new efforts.[3] They were also encouraged by the fact that the war was over. It had been used as a conclusive argument against any innovations and now this argument was gone. Then there were the loyalists. Though these newcomers refused to support the agitation in the older part of the province, their mere presence in the country above stimulated the movement in the country below. Surely, thought the merchants, the British government must now recognize that there was a considerable English-speaking population in the colony and arrange its government accordingly!

The storm began to gather in a petition to the king dated September 30, 1783. After lying at Cochrane's to collect signatures it was carried to London by his lawyer, William Dummer Powell. It fervently pleaded for the repeal of the Quebec Act, for the establishment of an assembly, for the endowment of the assembly with power to impose taxes and customs duties necessary to defray the expenses of civil government, for the repeal of all existing laws authorizing the collection of any such revenue in the colony, for the creation of a larger and unpaid council, for the appointment of trained judges, for the provision against arbitrary dismissal or suspension from office, for the inclusion of the Habeas Corpus Act as part of the colony's constitution, for the introduction of English commercial laws and the right to have juries in the trial of civil suits, and, in general, for the treatment of Canada as a genuine British colony inhabited by British subjects entitled to British rights, the rights that had been solemnly promised in 1763.[4]

Haldimand could not understand the goings on around him. One glimpse, and one glimpse only, did he have into the forces at work. He perceived a lively apprehension lest the commercial treaty, then spoken of on the shores of the St. Lawrence as a reality, should betray the interests of the colony. This feeling was a natural consequence of the peace treaty, in which Britain seemed to be quite willing to sacrifice Canada's principal trade. How could the danger be averted except by a local legislature empowered to impose protective duties, which of course meant an elected assembly? This reasoning, said the governor, led "a few men of good conduct and moderation" into the bad company of the main body of petitioners. Indeed, it somewhat unsettled his own mind, for he wrote home that he could not give a positive opinion on the argument until the commercial treaty was published.

From every other point of view Haldimand unhesitatingly condemned the idea of a popular legislature. Twelve thousand pounds a year, the average deficit of the civil budget of the colony,* was a small price for the British government to pay to keep such a troublesome and dangerous institution out of Canada. Some who advocated it were really republicans working for annexation to the United States. Many were simply seeking "to vent their resentment against those who have either prevented or brought to light their abuse of public money" — a reference to the nasty Cochrane business. As for the loyalists, he had "great reason to believe these unfortunate people have suffered too much by committees and houses of assembly to have retained any prepossession in favour of that mode of government and that they have no reluctance to live under the constitution established by law for this country." More than ever he was convinced that the Quebec Act had saved Canada for Britain in 1775 and was absolutely necessary to preserve it in the future. For two great reasons the act must stand unshaken. To the Canadians it was a sacred charter; the hands that would touch it were impious. To the government it gave much-needed power; those who would reduce this authority were traitors. The colony was not yet safe and it would not be secure until the Cana-

* This estimate was too low. See the note on page 481 below.

dians were brought back "to a regular subordination" and organized in a "well disciplined militia." [5]

But Haldimand was not opposed to all change. He saw that it might be well to adjust the civil law to meet the needs of commerce and even to amend the criminal law. Nevertheless, he said, such "alterations ought to be made with prudence and discretion, and no doubt the legislative council will do it at a proper time." That the proper time had not yet come he was quite certain. But he believed that peace had brought the time for the adoption of the Habeas Corpus Act or an equivalent, and when opening the legislative session of 1784 on March 22, he placed in the very forefront of his speech a recommendation for such an ordinance.

The session of 1784 produced little legislation and much excitement.[6] The council passed only three ordinances, of which two were simple renewals of expiring laws, those governing fees and posthouses, and the third was almost a copy of the Habeas Corpus Act. This meager achievement fell far short of what was promised at the beginning. During the first week, various other measures of a more or less urgent nature, such as the reform of fees, the registration of deeds, and the regulation of the medical, the notarial, and the land-surveying professions, were introduced; and it was agreed that committees should examine and report upon the navigation of the St. Lawrence, the conduct of the fisheries, and the state of the fur trade. This large program was shelved for two reasons — lack of time and a greater interest in other things. Time was short because the governor had postponed the opening of the session in the vain expectation of dispatches based upon the definitive treaty which he knew had been signed in the previous September. There is no ground for suspecting that he harbored any ulterior motive. The distractions were the habeas corpus ordinance and an address to the governor upholding the Quebec Act.

Long and angry was the debate over the ordinance to introduce the right of habeas corpus. The trouble began when a committee headed by Mabane produced the original draft. According to Finlay, it was such a mutilation of the model pointed out by the royal instructions that had it passed into law "it would have alienated the affections of this people from Great Britain." [7] Fortunately it was amended to restore what had been cut away until it became, as already remarked, almost a copy of the British statute.

Even in this form the measure raised strenuous objections from two quarters. Mabane and some of his Roman Catholic friends persuaded their colleagues that the new law should not interfere with those who had taken the vows of any religious house in the province, and a provisory clause was added accordingly. This addition produced an unexpected result. The religious communities, apparently thinking the clause unnecessary, considered it invidious. They appealed direct to the council to remove it, and secured their end by a vote of nine to eight. Mabane and his friends protested loudly. They feared what might happen should an inmate of one of these institutions apply for a writ of habeas corpus. By a large majority the protesters succeeded in having the matter referred to the aged bishop through whom, they said, the representation should have come. Briand replied in a polite and noncommittal note that gave no opening for a reconsideration of the question.

Another group in the council fought stubbornly to enlarge the terms of the ordinance. These members feared that a mere transcript of the Habeas Corpus Act would not be adequate because in Canada it would be divorced from English civil law. Exactly what might be lost they could not tell; but their suspicions had been roused and they were determined to avoid all risk. Repeatedly they pressed for the inclusion of some general statement that would guarantee to residents in the colony the full measure of personal liberty enjoyed in the mother country. The strong opposition they encountered exaggerated their fears and intensified their struggle. Only by a narrow majority were they defeated.

The session had run for scarcely a fortnight when the public began to knock at the door of the council chamber. Several gentlemen requested admission to hear the debates. Their message, conveyed by the doorkeeper, started another debate across the board. Some members wished to let the strangers in, but they were overborne by the argument that the oaths they had all taken as councilors enjoined secrecy. The strangers were turned away and the council adjourned for three days. When it reassembled, Lieutenant Governor Hamilton began the day's business by announcing that his vote against opening the door had been given simply because there were no rules to govern the occasion. To supply the defect he proposed that the door be opened on the president's taking the chair, that each member be allowed to admit two strangers, a limit set by the size of the room, that a space be marked off for strangers, and that the room be cleared at any time upon the motion of any member. The suggestions were tabled.

More spirited was the action of Grant, who presented a written protest against the vote taken at the last sitting. He riddled the argument of the oaths. These did not bind the members of the council when they sat as a legislative body, for they were precisely those taken by members of the two houses of parliament in Westminster. By admitting the public the council might win its confidence. Mabane at once demanded that the doorkeeper disclose the names of those who had been turned away. He was anxious to know who the public were, and he doubtless felt at least an inward glow of satisfaction when the doorkeeper announced that the public had been composed of Cochrane, Adam Lymburner, who was one of Cochrane's sureties in his appeal, and two other merchants, one of them a Grant.

The council was on the point of resuming its discussion of the habeas corpus ordinance when the doorkeeper brought in a note to the lieutenant governor signed by the above-mentioned quartet and seven others — their respects to the president of the council and a request to be admitted. The public was growing, but again its request was voted down. After these interruptions the council succeeded in reading one article of the habeas corpus ordinance before the doorkeeper entered with another note. The eleven gentlemen waiting without were sorry that the business of the legislative council would not permit them to be admitted that day, but they prayed to be informed if they could be admitted at some other time. Then Fraser moved and the council decided by a vote of eleven to six that the answer already given was to serve on all future occasions. Hamilton consoled himself by inserting a short protest in the minutes and Finlay by entering a long one.

The climax of this tumultuous session came in the last week. It began with a motion by St. Luc. After referring to the petition of the previous September, he proposed a formal address from the council to the governor to be forwarded to His Majesty praising the Quebec Act and praying for its indefinite continuance unaltered by so much as a jot or a tittle. On the following day Grant carried the war into the enemy's camp by moving the preparation of an address for an elected assembly and the insertion in the address of a whole battery of arguments which would blow up the existing régime.

Grant's arguments may be summarized as follows. An assembly had been solemnly promised by royal proclamation twenty years before, was still confidently expected, and was absolutely necessary. Since the government of the colony had no authority to levy taxes, public buildings had been maintained at the expense of the crown or had been left to fall into ruin. He might have added, as Finlay did later, that the Montreal sheriff refused to accept any prisoners for debt because he had no place where he could keep them in safe custody. By the Declaratory Act of 1778 parliament had debarred itself from raising any further revenue in the colony for the colony, except what might arise incidentally from legislation passed for the sole purpose of regulating commerce. The revenue problem alone made an assembly imperative, unless the burden were to be borne by the taxpayer at home. It is quite obvious that the deputy receiver general was speaking.

As a Britisher, he pointed out that the power of raising a revenue for the support of government and the encouragement of the general interests of the community "was as essential to every free government as personal liberty and security, and equally the right of every British subject," and he referred to the many in the United States who were suffering for their loyalty to the crown and might be tempted to settle in Canada by the establishment of representative government.

As a Britisher and a merchant, Grant demanded that His Majesty be entreated to direct that all actions for tort or of a mercantile nature be tried with the aid of a jury if either party desired it. Finally, he wanted it to be "warmly and humbly urged" as an additional motive for granting an assembly that the people in the colony were "exceedingly alarmed" and felt "much uneasiness" when they contemplated the nature of the council and the astonishingly wide powers it possessed. Its members were "amovable at the will of the crown" — a subtle reference to the fate of Livius and Allsopp. There were then seventeen councilors resident in the colony, the minimum allowed by the Quebec Act. Nine formed a quorum and five might play fast and loose with the laws of the country, criminal as well as civil.

All this Grant would put in the address to startle the ministers in London. But his motion was too startling for his colleagues. He soon learned, if he did not know already, that he had advanced to a point where none would support him. St. Luc also seems to have had some suspicion that perhaps he himself had gone too far, for he withdrew a little from his position, rewording his address to make it appear less bold. Grant fell back to try new tactics, moving that St. Luc's motion be split in two. All would gladly lend their names to the first part expressing gratitude to His Majesty for his paternal care during the late troubles, but some could not support a petition for the continuance of the Quebec Act as the best means of attaching the people of the colony to the mother country. Grant's new attack was defeated by a vote of twelve to five. Straightway St. Luc completed his victory, his address being carried by the same majority. Again the minority insisted that their protests, and the reasons for them, be inserted in the minutes of the council. Immediately after the address was signed, the members adjourned to the Castle of St. Louis, where the governor terminated the session.

Haldimand's day was done. For some time he had been anxious to retire from the government of the colony. He was feeling not only the weight of years and of public cares, but also the pressure of private disappointments. Having no family of his own, he had taken three nephews under his wing, and all had disappointed him. Two of them were by this time dead, and all three, though nice boys, had embarrassed both themselves and him by their decided inclination to sink into debt. Though he had served his royal master with unremitting faithfulness, he had been hurt by the treatment accorded him on more than one occasion. His foreign birth had prevented him from being commander-in-chief at the outbreak of the war, and toward its close he had been informed that he might be superseded by his junior in the service. Carleton, then in New York as commander-in-chief, was to go up to Canada if necessary to save the colony. So far as is known, Haldimand did not utter a murmur when he was removed from Boston because of his alien blood, but when he learned that the government contemplated supplanting him in the colony he had administered through a protracted crisis, he wrote home asking to be relieved. In this instance, it is but just to remark that Carleton, realizing how he would humiliate Haldimand by going to Quebec, immediately wrote him that he had no intention of returning to the shores of the St. Lawrence. This courtesy pleased the governor, but it could not banish the thought of retirement, for he was old and weary, and in the summer of 1784 he was at last satisfied by receiving permission to depart on leave of absence for an indefinite period. Of course he would retain his commission till a successor was selected.

It was time that Haldimand went. Though his general policy received the sanction of the secretary of state, Lord Sydney, who agreed that the habeas corpus ordinance was the utmost "relaxation of the powers of government" that ought to be allowed "in the present state of the province" and that those who wished to go further were "designing men" of doubtful patriotism,[8] yet there is evidence that Haldimand's policy for the colony did not inspire a whole-hearted confidence on the part of official London. The permanent under secretary, Evan Nepean, was developing a private correspondence on public affairs with Hugh Finlay and other responsible individuals in Canada who did not see eye to eye with the governor. Whether or not this had anything to do with the granting of Haldimand's desire it is impossible to say, but there can be no doubt that he had ceased to be the man to rule the province. He had fallen too much under the influence of Adam Mabane, who, though thoroughly upright, was thoroughly prejudiced — a fine example of the important truth, too often ignored, that a clear conscience is frequently a bad one.

So completely did the governor share the prejudices of "the doctor" that he was led, at the close of his Canadian career, to behave rather shabbily toward the lieutenant governor, Henry Hamilton. As a reward for his services and a compensation for his sufferings, the former lieutenant governor of Detroit had been appointed to succeed the decrepit Cramahé in 1782.[8a] He succeeded him in a way that he did not expect, for Cramahé had latterly been excluded from the governor's confidence and Hamilton was never admitted to it. When the advent of peace shifted attention from military to civil affairs and released the agitation for constitutional change, a wide breach opened between the governor and the lieutenant governor. The former could not forgive the latter for his independent though moderate attitude, particularly during the legislative session of 1784. The man who presided over the council should uphold the politics of the government and, above all else, he should not traffic with disloyalty. Such was the old soldier's attitude, and he showed it in a stern and forbidding mien.

The rift between the two men became very serious for Hamilton in July, when he learned that he would soon have to assume the reins of government. He lived in daily expectation that his chief would relent and give him some insight into the affairs of the province, but he waited in vain. As week after week passed by and he was still left in outer darkness, he grew nervous at the prospect of having to bear a responsibility for which he was not prepared. In September and again in October he wrote to his superior pleading for his confidence, each time getting only a curt note in reply. He was given no instruction of any kind until three or four hours before the governor's ship weighed anchor on November 16, and then all he received was a trunkful of papers that he could not begin to read before he had to give a receipt for them.[9]

Hamilton's administration of the province, which lasted for nearly a year, was a striking contrast to all that had gone before. To the English party it was like a warm springtime after a long and severe winter. There would have been a different story to tell if Hamilton had been true to type. All the governors and lieutenant governors intrusted with the management of the colony from the conquest until more than two generations later were military men, and with one exception they had military minds. That one exception was Hamilton, who, after thirteen years' service as a captain, had disposed of his commission on his appointment to Detroit. He had a thoroughly civilian mind, a thoroughly civilian conception of government.[10] He sympathized with the aggrieved merchants, though not with all their aspirations. His views on the question of an assembly probably coincided with those of Finlay, who shrewdly foresaw that the agitators for representative government were crying for something that would work their own undoing. Their hope of controlling an elected legislature through the representation of the towns was a delusion.

Still Hamilton had put off the soldier so completely that he would not lift his little finger to crush the movement. He believed in the expression, not the repression, of public opinion. With the desire for a reform of the legal system he heartily agreed, and he hoped to see it satisfied when the legislative council met. His sympathy went out likewise to the rank and file of the Canadians who

had suffered under the corvée during the war and were still suffering under it in the district of Montreal, where the hated custom
was continued for the purpose of forwarding supplies to the garrisons in the interior. This grievance too he hoped to see removed
at the coming session by a revision of the militia ordinance. He
was not in the least deterred by the written instructions left by
Haldimand to avoid all "innovations." He felt that his duty to the
people of the province and to the home government was higher
than his duty to the absent governor.

The change of tenant in the Castle of St. Louis caused the storm
to blow more violently. Hardly was Haldimand's back turned when
those eager for reform held public meetings in Quebec and Montreal, where they chose committees to manage their campaign.[11]
In a few days a monster petition was under way.[12] There is no
need to analyze its contents here, for it was substantially the petition
of the previous autumn — with one striking difference. The appeal
of September, 1783, came from ancient subjects only; this November
petition purported to be the united voice of both races. The mercantile minority had at last come to realize that their cause was hopeless so long as they stood by themselves. Their only chance of
impressing the home government was to discard their old religious
bigotry and racial arrogance and to blow themselves up to look like
the whole population of Canada. Hence this petition had almost
two French signatures for every English one.

Some of this inflation may be accounted for by the genuine
attraction of English legal and political principles; much may be
explained by economic dependence in the field of trade; and at
least a little was due to English cunning. Protestant merchants in
Montreal actually encouraged the frustrated Roman Catholic desire
for more priests from France, a machiavellian game started during
the war. In their hope of stirring things up, the discontented old
subjects also played upon the suspicion with which the ordinary
Canadians regarded the so-called upper classes. The suspicion had
been quickened in 1775 and had not since been allayed. There was
also an effort to capitalize the burdens of the corvée, though it does
not seem to have been very successful in spite of a rumor, as-
siduously circulated, that the military authorities were exercising a
power that the law did not allow. But it must not be imagined that
all the dupes who signed were French. An English schoolmaster,

hearing that it would please those in authority, added his name and had all his boys do likewise.[13] By scouring the highways and byways, the committees managed to collect about twenty-three hundred signatures.[14] On January 9, 1785, the day after he received the petition, the lieutenant governor sent it to London, and when it reached its destination the merchants there, at the instigation of the committees in Canada, gave it their strong backing.

Meanwhile the members of the seigniorial or French party, an even smaller minority than the mercantile faction, were thoroughly alarmed. They knew full well that their aristocratic world would be turned topsy-turvy by a democratic assembly, and this flaring up of the agitation for an assembly seemed doubly dangerous since Hamilton ruled in Haldimand's stead and the English minority were winning Canadian support. Consequently a strong counter-agitation was started immediately. Six days after the big November petition for an assembly was launched and nearly six weeks before it was presented to the lieutenant governor, it came under fire at a meeting held in the house of the Récollets in Montreal.[15] The criticisms there set forth were printed by Mesplet and circulated. This document came to be known as "the objections." It denounced an assembly as a taxing machine that would lay upon Canadians a burden such as they had never borne and were incapable of bearing; it curtly dismissed the idea of any tinkering with the laws; it denounced civil juries as benefiting the rich at the expense of the poor because special juries, being remunerated, would favor those who could pay for them and other civil juries would take men away from their work without giving them compensation; and it justified the corvée as a means of escaping taxation. These arguments were all for consumption by Canadians — to fortify them against English wiles.

To neutralize the influence of the mercantile minority upon the imperial government, the enemies of the November petition engineered a petition of their own in December. It repudiated the assumption of the other petition to speak for the Canadian people; it asserted that they did not want an assembly and that it was against their interest to have one because they were too poor to pay taxes. Should there be any inclination to yield to the desires of the ancient subjects, it begged for a suspension of judgment until the inhabitants of the country had been called together and had expressed their wishes in unmistakable fashion. It also contained two positive requests which had no apparent relation to the question of an assembly. The first was for permission to import priests from Europe, meaning France, on the ground that this was essential to the unimpeded continuance of the religion of the Canadians. Here the sponsors of the petition were taking the wind out of one of their enemy's sails. The other request was for increased representation in the council and was advanced as a specific application of the general principle that there should be no discrimination against new subjects in the matter of government patronage. The petition pointedly referred to the fact that they comprised "nineteen-twentieths" of the population and left it to be inferred that this had been overlooked in the filling of public offices.[16]

The contrivers of this December petition were as wise as serpents but not as harmless as doves. Of course the seigniors wished to keep their estates free from taxes — like the nobles of France. And what was to be the position of the habitant? He was to oppose an elected chamber that he might escape the opportunity to levy taxes on himself — to say nothing of seigniors — and to achieve this desirable end he must willingly bear the full weight of the corvée, from which all seigniors were exempt. And on the backs of their humble compatriots more seigniors were to ride into the council. But the best bait of all was the appeal of the church. This petition mustered nearly four thousand supporters.[17]

Intense though it was, the strife did not cut into the vitals of the country. The appearance of French and English on both sides prevented each from launching a wild appeal to racial prejudice. Equally fortunate was the fact that the division cut across religious differences. It is also worthy of note that the whole agitation scarcely touched the great mass of the people. Though both of the opposing factions pretended to represent the large majority of the population, neither did so. Finlay gave Nepean an excellent analysis of the situation in a letter of January 10, 1785. Against the "placemen and Canadian noblesse whose sway would be affected [and] power annihilated if any change should be made in the present form of government," were arrayed "the mercantile body, some of the noblesse and the better sort of bourgeois, new as well as old subjects." The habitants who had signed one or other of the petitions had "been wheedled by their English friends or intimidated by orders" from their militia commanders. They were incapable of deciding for or against an assembly because they knew nothing about it. To instruct them on the question "would be a work of time," and, because of their illiteracy, would have to "be done from the pulpit." Meanwhile, he said, "exempt a Canadian peasant from taxes, corvées and from billeting soldiers, let him go to mass, and little will he care who governs or what form of government he lives under." [18]

While fighting for the favor of the home government, the combatants did not forget that crucial changes might be decided in Quebec, and with mingled hope and fear they looked forward to the legislative session of 1785, the only one that Hamilton was to call. It lasted from February 10 to April 30, during which period the strife centered in the council chamber of the Bishop's Palace. There the parties were evenly balanced. Though the friends of reform had lost two votes, Hamilton withdrawing because he was acting in Haldimand's place and Grant being over in London, whither he had gone to settle his accounts as deputy receiver general, two absentees had returned, Caldwell and Pownall, both of whom were settling down as members of the English party, and Mabane was losing his hold over some who had followed him.

The session of 1785 [19] was more productive of legislation than any preceding session except the famous one of 1777, when the new constitution was got under way. Most of the time, however, and all of the rising temper of the members, were spent upon two issues presented by the lieutenant governor in his opening speech. The ordinance governing the administration of justice in the civil courts and that regulating the militia were about to expire, and he intimated that they should be altered before being re-enacted. Finlay, who occupied the chair as senior councilor, made a general motion for the amendment of the former measure to make it accord with the royal instructions and he carried his point by a majority of one. In this division Mabane's biggest surprise was the desertion of Dunn, his fellow judge, whom he had already sounded out. Dunn's vote was probably influenced by the fact that he was a merchant as well as an occupant of the bench.

Dunn headed the committee appointed to prepare a new bill, which he produced in a few days. The ninth article provided for the application of English commercial and common law to all mercantile causes. The tenth introduced juries into the civil courts, the courts of common pleas. A commercial dispute or a case of tort was to be tried with the aid of a jury if either party demanded it. The jury was to be composed of old subjects or new subjects or both in accordance with the native origin of the principals. The agreement of nine of the twelve jurors was to suffice for a legal verdict. The eleventh article extended the application of the English law of evidence, hitherto confined to mercantile cases, to all suits tried by jury. Among other things, this provision meant that the testimony of relatives to the third degree and of servants, excluded by the Canadian civil law, was to be admitted for damage suits when a jury had been demanded. The twelfth article required the judges to write out and sign all their charges to juries, that these charges might be reviewed on appeal. Even this draft did not go far enough to please the chairman of the committee. He moved, as a further change, to abolish the "writ of saisie and arrêt" for "attaching monies in the hands of third persons," and the "writ of saisie conservatoire" for "seizing the goods and property of a debtor," because the use of these writs, which were issued before any trial had taken place, was "frequently attended with very dangerous consequences" and was "very detrimental to the commerce of this province." The reforming fever had certainly touched Dunn.

The arguments that flew back and forth across the council board grew very hot. The reactionaries brought a Daniel to judgment in the person of Shepherd, the sheriff of Quebec, who declared that the jury would not be a safe institution because there were too few who were really qualified to serve. Thereupon the reformers produced long lists to prove the contrary, and they pointed out that the sheriff was talking not of legal qualifications but of mental qualifications and of his own private estimate of these. They pointedly asked why jurors might be intrusted to decide upon the life but not upon the property of citizens. Two of the seigniorial members asserted "that the trial by jury would be extremely ill received by the Canadians in general and that several respectable families, to their knowledge, had already taken the resolve to quit the province if such a law should pass." Both parties swelled the minutes by inserting long protests arising out of the many divisions, for the majority swung back and forth, often by a single vote.

By this narrow margin the ninth article, applying English law to all commercial cases, the eleventh, extending the English law of evidence to all civil suits tried by jury, and Dunn's motion to abolish the writs of *saisie* were rejected. By a larger majority the twelfth article, requiring judges to commit themselves on paper, was thrown out, and the tenth, granting optional juries, was retained, though in a modified form. Mabane fought in vain to give a Canadian litigant the right to override an English litigant's demand for a jury, but he had the satisfaction of seeing the scope of the provision reduced so that it would not apply to commercial cases unless both parties were merchants or traders.

The mutilation of Dunn's bill occasioned some plain speaking on the part of the president. Referring to the lost eleventh article, Finlay remarked that "a jury must acquit on a civil where they had condemned on a criminal prosecution," and, alluding to the ferment in the province, he told his fellow councilors that they, and not the Quebec Act, were to blame. Yet something of great importance had been gained. Jury trials for civil suits were at last introduced, and for this boon the leading merchants of Quebec and Montreal publicly expressed their gratitude to Lieutenant Governor Hamilton.[20]

On the other great issue of the session the reformers were defeated. Quite early it was decided that the militia ordinance should be renewed without amendment, but only for a year. The minority attacked the legality of this extension on the ground that the royal instructions forbade, unless really necessary, the enactment of any measure for less than two years; and with the further support of a popular appeal addressed to the whole council, they continued the fight.

The point, of course, was the corvée. The French party claimed that there was no grievance and quoted the quartermaster general's department to prove that the habitants still engaged in the transport of supplies worked voluntarily and had always been paid liberally. Finlay, whose contacts had been very wide, could not allow this claim to pass unchallenged. He told his colleagues who were upholding the corvée that they did not know what they were talking about. He knew the people. He knew that there was much discontent, not only in the district of Montreal, but throughout the country. Memories of the late war still rankled. "It is the duty of this council to remove every cause of discontentment in the province. It is owing to the fatal spirit of procrastination which has hitherto prevailed at this honourable board that objection has been made to the constitution granted by parliament." Caldwell, referring to the continuance of the corvée in the neighborhood of Montreal, roundly asserted that it was illegal, and he seems to have been right. This home thrust he followed up with a high appeal, declaring that the king "should reign in the hearts as well as over the persons of his subjects." But the ears of the majority were stopped, for they were very angry.

Their anger was roused by the popular appeal referred to above. This was a poorly framed representation against the abuses of the corvée. It came from Montreal and purported to be signed by many who had suffered, but the French party claimed that it had been sent up from Quebec and signed in Montreal by the riffraff of the town and by only a few respectable people who did not realize what they were doing.

This paper and the mild answer it drew from Hamilton enraged the reactionaries. To them it was a libelous and rebellious document which he should have blasted with righteous indignation. Brigadier General Henry Hope felt that he and his predecessors in the office of quartermaster general had been viciously attacked and weakly betrayed. He took up the cudgels; in the columns of the *Quebec Gazette* he belabored the authors and signatories of the representation. His outburst drew a retraction from a handful and a bold reply from the others. Feeling became terribly bitter, and violent words were bandied about. Mabane summed up the results of the affair by saying that Hope had "gained great credit with the friends of government and order" but had "raised against himself the resentment of the wasps and vipers which abound in the province"; [21] and in the executive council, where the whole business was discussed both before and after the legislative session closed, one of the Canadian members exploded with the remark that all of his race would welcome a return to French allegiance.[22]

Hamilton was sailing through difficult seas, and it was not long before he struck a reef. What is not a little puzzling is that he seems to have done it with his eyes open. After having run for many years, the lease of the King's Posts down the St. Lawrence had expired in 1781, but the lessees had not been disturbed. Hamilton had been warned by Haldimand to do nothing about these posts until he heard from London, because the home government had the matter under advisement. On March 15, 1785, Lord Sydney wrote directing a transfer to new lessees whom he named, but on May 18, three days before he received this dispatch, the lieutenant governor renewed the old lease. As the town was already filled with gossip of the impending change, a vessel having arrived on the fifteenth with letters for a number of private individuals telling them all about it, Hamilton's action appears in a particularly bad light. Yet everything else that is known about him repels the suggestion that he had a dishonorable motive. Nor is it impossible to find an explanation in keeping with his fine character. He was aware that a battle over the lease had been fought in London, where William Grant, one of the old lessees, had been opposed by George Davison, another merchant of the colony and member of the council. He also knew that Haldimand, who was in close touch with the home government, was prejudiced against Grant and in favor of Davison because the latter had been as zealous for reaction as his rival had been for reform. Very naturally the lieutenant governor would regard the transfer of the lease as a gross injustice.[23]

Even if Hamilton had avoided this reef, which wrecked his Canadian career, it is doubtful if he could have continued his course much longer. Sydney had grown uneasy about the situation in the colony. He saw it through Haldimand's eyes, and Haldimand's eyes had been more and more troubled as he read his voluminous mail from Canada. His old friends there had no illusions about Hamilton ushering in the spring. To military men like Brigadier General Barry St. Leger, whom he had left in command of the troops, and Henry Hope, who had succeeded Thomas Carleton as quartermaster general, and to the placemen, of whom Mabane was king, the political unrest was downright sedition. They could not agree on whether the lieutenant governor was actuated by perversity or by stupidity or by weakness for his friends, chief of whom were Finlay and Monk, or by demagogic craving for popularity. But they were all convinced that he was opening the floodgates of revolution, and they wrote home about it. Sydney was coming to the same conclusion when, in August, he heard what had happened

to the lease.[24] Thereupon he recalled Hamilton and gave his place
to Hope. To the latter he intimated in no uncertain manner that
the strife must cease.

There was rumor in London, echoed in Quebec, that Haldimand
was about to return, but the government decided that he was to
retire. As a consolation, he was made a Knight of the Bath in
September, 1785. Thus two very fine though very different admin-
istrators passed out of Canadian history at the same time. Only a
few years of life were left to each of them. In the British capital the
elder man had already settled down to the rather delightful existence which is mirrored in his diary.[25] He was honored by his
sovereign, at whose court he appeared from time to time, and by a
wide circle of friends, with whom he dined and danced and played
cards. But age soon kept his feet from the dancing floor and drew
his heart to his native land. There, in the home of his brother, the
courtly old gentleman died in 1791. Though Hamilton returned to
England under a cloud, he did not remain under it. The discovery
that he had suffered unjustly was followed by his appointment to
govern Bermuda, on whose map his name has thenceforth been
written, for the capital, founded at the time he went out, was named
after him. Not there, however, but in Antigua, he breathed his last
in 1796.

Hope took over the government of the colony on November 2,
1785, a fortnight after he had received word of the change. His
administration was as long as his predecessor's, but its record is so
short that it may be dismissed in a few words. In contrast to Hamilton, who had achieved one positive result — trial by jury for commercial causes and torts when desired by either party — and who,
through the political ferment that his mild policy encouraged rather
than created, had thrust the Canadian problem forward in London,
Hope contributed nothing. His hands were tied by the secretary
of state, who directed him to maintain order and the status quo
until the administration at home could determine what, if any,
changes should be made in the arrangements for the province.

Even if the new lieutenant governor's hands had been free he
would have accomplished little or nothing that was positive, for he
was not at all afflicted with the reforming itch. Indeed, he would
have liked to freeze Canadian society and government to preserve

them. He was prepared to sacrifice the loyalists in order to cultivate loyalty among the Canadians. The newcomers, he wrote Sydney, could not be given a different kind of government without
creating jealousies among the ancient inhabitants; and he backed
up his preference by observing that the loyalists' numbers were "not
so considerable nor their desire for change so firmly rooted" as to
render such a measure necessary, at least immediately. The only
change he proposed was what his seigniorial friends were longing
for, an enlarged Canadian representation in the council, and he had
the satisfaction of being officially informed that his "sentiments
upon matters in general relating to the province" were "directly
correspondent with the opinion entertained" by the ministers in
Britain.[26]

Meanwhile the Quebec and Montreal committees had lost no
time in enlisting the London merchants. The latter had promptly
approached Lord Sydney and then reported back to their correspondents on May 26, 1785, that the government would not act
until "the sense of the whole people should be taken on the substance" of the petitions. They also advised the committees to gather
more signatures and, in particular, to tie up the loyalists with their
agitation. This the Montreal committee undertook to do, but the
loyalists, having submitted a petition of their own, would not lend
their names to swell the agitation of the mercantile community
below. Indeed, the attempt to unite actually served to divide. It
brought out a fundamental conflict between the people in the new
settlements and those in the older parts of the colony. To realize
their desires the former wished to be cut loose from the latter,
whereas the latter were stoutly opposed to any such separation because it might undermine their position. The Quebec committee
did nothing, excusing themselves on the ground that the people
were sure to rally to the cause of reform as soon as the government
carried out its intention of consulting them. Then came the startling news of Hamilton's dismissal and Hope's appointment. It
spread a hush through the colony, for it struck a chill of fear into
the heart of the English party. To the friends of reform it seemed
as if the winter had returned, blighting all their hopes. They
expected the colony's constitution to be "absolutely fixed" in the
capital of the empire before navigation opened again, and they

feared for the worst unless their London friends could do more than they had been able to do in the past.[27]

But the future was not quite so dark as it appeared to the disheartened ones on the St. Lawrence. For all the imperial government's sympathy with Hope's reactionary views, his appointment was intended merely as a temporary remedy to reduce the fever of the province while the mother country went in search of a doctor. A vague knowledge of this soon began to spread in the colony and the hush gradually changed from one of despair to one of expectancy. Thus peace reigned while Hope ruled.

CHAPTER XVII

CHIEF JUSTICE SMITH AND LORD DORCHESTER

THE American Revolution is one of the most important events in Canadian history; its influence has permeated the whole of British North America's subsequent development. Among its many results was the planting of the seed that another great crisis in American history, the Civil War, was to bring to sudden fruition in the formation of the Dominion. The man who seems to have found the seed and put it in the soil, from which it sent up a promising but premature shoot, was William Smith. For this reason, and because he was the most powerful single influence in the conduct of Canadian affairs during the closing years of the old province of Quebec, he deserves more attention than has usually been accorded him.

Smith was born in New York in 1728, the son of a judge, and educated at Yale. He practiced at the bar in his own city for many years and in 1769 was appointed to the council of his native province. When the Revolution came he was sadly torn. There is a doubtful tradition, which accords with his timidity of character and his philosophical cast of mind, that he could not decide whether to support the British or the American cause until about 1778.[1] Two years later he became chief justice of New York, a position his father had once filled. Another fact about the father, which may throw light upon the son, is that when the latter was twenty-six years old the former was a delegate to the Albany congress, where he voted for the union of the American colonies.[2]

Though Smith could not help being interested in the affairs of the neighboring province of Quebec — he discussed them with Maseres when the latter was on his way home in 1769 — he might never have had anything to do with them had not Carleton been sent out in the spring of 1782 to liquidate the war in America. They were then thrown together because the new commander-in-chief needed advice on matters of law and government, and no one in New York was better able to give it than the chief justice and councilor. Moreover, Carleton's chief task was to protect the loyalists, and Smith, being perhaps the leading loyalist in the place, was equally solicitous for their future. The services rendered by the lawyer to the soldier are suggested by two documents preserved in the Smith Papers. One is a memorandum on the restoration of civil government in New York. The other is a charter for the loyalist town of Guysborough in Nova Scotia. The similarities between the two men thus thrown together were calculated to draw them together. Both were aristocrats,* both were strong imperialists who had experienced intellectual difficulties at the beginning of the Revolution. But the friendships formed when people thrown together find that they have important interests in common become deep and permanent only when they are bound together by their differences. Carleton and Smith each supplied something the other needed. As a clever wife may seek the fulfillment of her own aspirations by inspiring her unimaginative husband, while he enters heartily into the game because she stimulates his mind, enlarges his vision, and caters to his pride, so did Smith establish himself as Carleton's mentor. Therein seems to lie the secret of the intimacy that sprang up between them and lasted until death parted them.

During their sojourn together in New York they must have discussed the imperial tragedy, and the lawyer must then have imparted to the soldier his theories of how it came to pass, how the damage might be repaired at least in part, and how the remaining colonies might be saved.[3] These questions forced themselves upon the minds of thinking Britishers of that day. Most were inclined to find the causes of the tragedy in the attempt to tax colonies in which democracy had been allowed to grow unchecked. Few saw hope of recovering anything that had been lost. The problem was rather how to preserve what was left, and the obvious method was that advocated by Under Secretary William Knox in 1783, a policy of *divide et impera*.[4]

Smith went deeper into the past and soared higher into the future. He agreed with the common diagnosis of democracy running wild. In this he confirmed Carleton's opinion at the time of the Quebec Act that the British form of government could not be transplanted to America without suffering a change. At the same time he blamed Britain for not having placed a bridle upon Ameri-

* Smith left a considerable estate on his death.

can democracy while that was still possible. As the old colonies grew up and became capable of sharing the imperial responsibility, they should have had a common government through which they would have willingly taxed themselves to pay for their own defense. Shameful neglect allowed them to increase materially and intellectually without a corresponding development of their polity. On this ground, and on this ground alone, the justice of the late war could be arraigned. If what had been neglected once were to be neglected again, he said, "we shall not only repeat the error of infusing a disproportionate leaven of republicanism into the administration" of the remaining colonies, but "be the more criminal, for their risk of the contagious principles and practices of their neighbours, independent of whose seductions a jealous spirit will keep pace with their population and prosperity, and at last break out into claims which at this juncture may be obviated by a settlement of wisdom, justice and liberality, to which in process of time every thing dear to them should be tacked."

In addition to saving what was left of the wreck, Smith believed that his plan might bring about the recovery of at least some part of what had been lost. If Britain put her American house in good order, it would be an attraction to those who had broken away. In short, the chief justice of New York had a glorious vision of the regeneration of the empire on this continent, and he saw beside him the man who might accomplish it.[5] Small wonder Carleton was attracted to a man who would raise him up to so dizzy a height. Savior of the empire and lord of America!

Together the two friends returned to England at the close of 1783. There they found the government wrestling with the problem of the old undivided Nova Scotia, where some readjustment was necessary because the recent arrival of thirty thousand loyalists had suddenly changed the character and trebled the size of the population. During the first half of 1784 a solution was worked out. Nova Scotia was cut into three unequal parts. The largest became the colony of New Brunswick with Colonel Thomas Carleton as governor. The smallest, Cape Breton, was given a separate administration over which a lieutenant governor was placed. This division suggests that the policy advocated by Knox was in the ascendant, but other arrangements made at this time imply that it was not.

The status of Prince Edward Island, then known as the Island of St. John, was reduced to that of Cape Breton, and both became sub-colonies, their lieutenant governors being put under the governor of the truncated Nova Scotia. In all this business it was only natural that the administration should lean on the advice of the proconsul who had just returned from America, and any doubt that it did so is removed by the words of an official memorandum drawn up in the following year. It states that these governments were "officered pretty generally by his recommendation." [6] Nor was this the only way in which Sir Guy entered into the changing picture. When explaining the new arrangements to Governor Parr in Halifax at the end of May, 1784, Sydney observed that the few remaining provinces had gained in importance and it was "intended to place a person on the spot to settle matters without the delay of referring everything to Britain." [7] That Carleton was the person then contemplated was clearly stated in a letter by Nepean two years later.[8] These new arrangements for the maritime provinces in 1784 look like the first fruit of the marriage contracted in New York. They embody Smith's ideas; they were made in consultation with Carleton, who leaned on Smith; and there is reason for believing that the latter had direct as well as indirect access to those in authority.[9]

Smith's influence becomes clearer when we turn to the province of Quebec. There is abundant evidence in his own handwriting that he worked hard on the Canadian problem when it was thrust forward early in 1785 by the arrival of the November and the December petitions. He studied these contrary petitions and drew up a detailed report upon them; he prepared two different drafts of an act of parliament to regulate the Canadian government; he sketched, revised, and supported with reasoned arguments the powers that should be given to Carleton when he went out to undertake the work of imperial regeneration.

Smith's report on the petitions from Canada dismissed the demand for the repeal of the Quebec Act as absurd because the act "grants what is asked for in the third and fourth articles" of the petition for repeal — English criminal and commercial laws. Nor, as will be explained presently, was the repeal necessary for the creation of an assembly, to which the author looked forward. The establishment of an elected chamber would "prevent such of the Canadians as are discontented without an assembly from confederating with congress" and would also "satisfy the friends of Great Britain in the United States who being disgusted there wish to remove into Canada but" would not go "till there is greater certainty respecting the future condition of that country." The enlarging of the council could wait upon the governor, who, moreover, would "not refuse his assent to any act for introducing conformity to the British administration of justice" in the matter of jury trials. Everything could be arranged without further recourse to parliament if only it restored the crown's prerogative to remodel the provincial government. Then the governor could go out empowered to convene an assembly.

In proceeding to outline a bill for this purpose, Smith was impressed by the conflict of opinion in Canada. For this reason, he observed, a further investigation of conditions in the colony would have to be undertaken before the governor could decide to call for elections. One of the two drafts, dated June 11, 1785, was entitled "An act for the regulation of the Province of Quebec" and provided simply for the restoration of the royal prerogative referred to above. The other is not dated. As originally composed, it was called "An act to repeal part of an act entitled 'An act for making more effectual provision for the government of the Province of Quebec in North America' and for the better regulating of the British colonies on that continent." The preamble stated that "the late changes in the condition of the continent of North America may require alterations and arrangements not only in the Province of Quebec but in the neighbouring Provinces of Nova Scotia and New Brunswick and the other islands, territories and dominions belonging to the crown of Great Britain in North America which on occasions not now foreseen may be very necessary and not admit of delay." To this end its single enacting clause revived the royal prerogative over all the remaining American colonies. That this draft was written first is evident on the face of it, for Smith scratched out every passage inspired by the larger idea and otherwise amended it to make it substantially the same as the one dated June 11.[10]

These documents, at least one of which Smith gave to Carleton,[11] are the only direct evidence yet discovered that anyone in England was then toiling over the Canadian problem. The November and December petitions were circulated among the ministers, but none of them called for any papers dealing with the colony until early in

August, 1785. Then Sydney awoke and dashed off a strong memorandum for Pitt.[12] This memorandum brought things to a head.

Immediate action was necessary, said the secretary of state. "The
Province of Quebec in its present situation is a dominion of a very
precarious tenure to Great Britain. . . . I cannot help dreading . . .
that the cabinet will separate without a decision . . . upon which
in my humble opinion depends whether Canada shall remain ours
a twelve months longer or not." After discussing various details of
the Quebec administration [13] he said: "If a Governor General of all
that remains of British possessions in North America can be now
appointed,[14] Sir Guy Carleton is in my opinion for many reasons
infinitely preferable to any other person," but he was not sure "if
Sir Guy can be prevailed upon." Apparently Carleton had been
playing coy.

Within three weeks or so the matter was settled. On September
3 Nepean wrote to Hope that "some arrangements have taken place
which I think it right to communicate to you for your private
information. The first and principal one is that of Sir Guy Carleton's appointment: he is to be placed in the situation of Governor
General, his powers to be very extensive in all respects, so as to give
him a full control over all our possessions in America, excluding
only the West India Islands. Sir Guy is just come to town to be
consulted upon the extensive business he is to carry into execution,
and I conclude we shall be ready to dispatch him in the course of
this month by the way of New York, as the season will be too far
advanced before his departure to make it prudent to attempt a
passage by the River St. Lawrence. . . . Livius, the chief justice of
Quebec, is to be succeeded by Mr. Smith, who served in the same
capacity at New York, in compliance with the desire of Sir Guy
Carleton." [15]

A whole year elapsed before Carleton and Smith set sail together
for America. Many things had to be settled before Britain could
send a governor general to take charge of the empire in America.[16]
The determination to unite the governments of the North American
colonies meant reducing the consequence of the two individuals
who had charge of Nova Scotia and New Brunswick. From being
governors who took their orders direct from the seat of empire, they
were to become lieutenant governors under the control of the governor general in Quebec. The readjustment was a delicate business.

Also the cabinet had to decide what was to be the exact nature of the new and great office which the proconsul would fill.

Smith was soon ready with an answer, which he gave to Carleton.[17] Though dated September 19, 1785, there is internal evidence that the main part of it was composed some time before the cabinet's decision. The document begins with a sweeping view. "Whatever the present object of Great Britain in the internal arrangements of the provinces she holds on the continent of America,— whether to save these as essential to her insular dependencies in the West Indies — or to regain her dominion over the thirteen severed States — or to set a new king at the head of the whole or a part of that country,* it will be of use to recollect that the defective system of colony administration was the *remote* cause of the late rent in the Empire."

Then comes the enumeration of powers that Smith deemed necessary for imperial regeneration. This part was obviously written before the ministry determined to place a governor general over British North America. It builds everything upon the rôle that Carleton had filled in New York from the spring of 1782 until the end of the following year. Commencing with the proposition that "there will be doubtless a commander-in-chief of the army," it continues with the suggestion that "the same person may be the governor of each province" and commander of its militia, "who by acts of assembly may serve unitedly with the king's troops." "The naval power in those seas may be also subjected to the general's direction," and "the king can give him authority for all national negotiations and treaties with any people or power upon that continent." He should be "the reservoir of all information and the sole conduit of communication" between British North America and the mother country. He should fill "all the great offices usually appointed in England" and have power to create any new ones that he might deem expedient. "He may also be authorized to confer with the inhabitants of those countries upon an arrangement to be made for taking their *united aids* in future towards the general defence of the Empire" and for this purpose to form two chambers, one composed of members appointed for life and the other of "delegates elected by the assemblies of the several provinces." Then

* During the "critical years" there was not a little talk of the United States becoming a monarchy under a cadet of the Hanoverian house.[18]

he would "declare to what objects their powers as a *common* legislature shall extend, and under what conditions, reservations and
limitations, that the same, when established with the concurrence of
parliament, may stand as a permanent bond of union between these
countries and the rest of the British Empire." Without such a
legislature, the author added, "the population of those immense
territories will be discouraged and the security for their dependence
weakened," and there could be no "hope of attracting the confidence
and affection of the old provinces." To sum up, Smith wanted his
friend to be a viceroy.

But the ministry, after a winter's reflection, would not make him
anything more than commander-in-chief and multiple governor.
On April 15, 1786, Carleton was gazetted governor of Quebec,
governor of Nova Scotia and its dependencies, governor of New
Brunswick, and commander-in-chief in all these provinces and
Newfoundland. He simply held all these offices together, receiving
no commission as governor general. Not until toward the end of
August did the official mill grind out the instructions for each of
his gubernatorial offices, though their departure from the traditional
forms was very slight. At the same time he received a short "set of
particular instructions in some measure applicable to the government of the whole but more immediately founded upon some local
circumstances of the Province of Quebec." His capital was to be
the city of Quebec, whence he was "occasionally" to visit the maritime provinces, and to take upon himself "the command and government thereof" whenever he judged it expedient. With this in
view he was to direct their lieutenant governors to correspond with
him "by every opportunity," informing him of the actual state of
the territories under their charge.[19] The wording clearly reveals
that he was not expected to exercise all his offices in person all the
time. Though he and his *alter ego* might dream of pulling together
what was left of the American wreck, the government in London
had a shrewd suspicion that geography might prove an insuperable
obstacle, as indeed it continued to be for more than two generations.

The chief task of the new governor was to diagnose the complicated ills of Canada and to prescribe for them. London was puzzled
by the discord that had broken loose in the older part of the province. Should the constitution as established by the Quebec Act be
allowed to stand? Or should it be altered, and if so, how? These

were questions he was to answer as soon as he could after obtaining on the spot "the most full and authentic information of the real sentiments of the inhabitants."

It is interesting to observe that these instructions did not ask him to advise the ministry on whether it should grant or reject the loyalists' prayer for emancipation from Quebec. Apparently the government had already decided to divide the colony, at least "for the present." He was merely to report on matters of detail. Where was the line to be drawn? What should be the constitution of the new province? Should it resemble that which was or might be established in Quebec? Or should it follow the traditional pattern, which had been copied down by the sea? Rather searching questions relating to the colony's trade, which will be discussed in the next chapter, were also pressed upon the governor's attention.

It should not be forgotten that along with all these responsibilities the ministry placed upon the governor's shoulders practically the whole burden of the empire in the unsettled interior of America. Without any light from London, as already explained in a previous chapter, he had to face the exasperating problem of the west — the retention of the interior posts, the apparently insoluble dilemma of Britain's relations with the Indians, and the possible alternative of the collapse of the empire or its unlimited extension in the heart of the continent.

Never did a Britisher leave the shores of England bearing a heavier load than this man, and he seems to have been all eagerness to depart. He was raised to the peerage as Baron Dorchester on August 21, that he might possess a rank more commensurate with his exalted position.* On the twenty-sixth Sydney sent him his instructions.[20] Three days later he was in Portsmouth, and the following day he was on board.[21] On October 23, after a passage of fifty-two days, he landed in Quebec.[22] The lieutenant governor and council welcomed him at the waterside and escorted him up to the Castle of St. Louis, where he was once more installed as governor of the province of Quebec.

Failure is written across the whole story of his career in Canada's ancient capital. As Carleton he had disappointed himself and the home government, and as Dorchester he did the same. His handling

---

* It is also possible that the honor was granted as a solace for his not receiving a *more* exalted position.

of the tangled western situation, having been treated in a previous chapter, may here be dismissed with the remark that he did no better than his immediate predecessors. For this no blame need be attached to him.

Nor can he be held responsible for the defeat of his high hopes of pulling British North America together. He never assumed the government of the maritime provinces, though immediately after landing in Quebec he opened a correspondence with Halifax and expressed his intention of going down during the following summer to visit even the islands of St. John and Cape Breton. Only one journey was he to make before he returned home on leave in 1791, and that was in 1788, when, as already mentioned, he ascended the St. Lawrence to see the new loyalist settlements. True, he continued to correspond with the other provinces, and their affairs were not infrequently discussed in the letters he exchanged with London. But practically none of these affairs were settled in Quebec. The lieutenant governors down by the sea continued to act as governors, reporting directly to the seat of empire whence their orders still came. Dorchester stood at one side, occasionally consulted and generally aloof. Great as he might appear to be, geography was much greater still. It prevented the hand of his authority from reaching over the other provinces and confined the exercise of his power to the province of Quebec.

Even as governor of Quebec he failed. The ministry relied upon him to find a solution for the tangled constitutional problem of the colony, but he could not do it and he was forced to confess his inability.[23] This throwing up of his hands is in striking contrast to his cocksure attitude of some years before. Nor does the contrast end here. Totally unlike the Carleton who was so enamored of power that he played the autocrat, Dorchester let the reins of the civil administration fall from his nerveless grasp. A shrewd observer on the spot compared his régime with the rule of King Log, who, according to Æsop's fable, appeared with a splash that inspired only a temporary awe.[24] Before many months had passed, the secret was out, and it soon became common knowledge in Canada that the governor only reigned while the chief justice ruled. Even in trusting the advice of Sir John Johnson on all things touching the loyalists, Dorchester seems to have been guided by Smith, who counted their leader as one of his main followers.[25] One wonders what the gossips of the day would have said and what the home government would have done had they lit upon the fact, which now stands revealed to anyone who examines the papers in Smith's own handwriting preserved in the New York Public Library,[26] that the chief justice corrected and even drafted some of the more important dispatches that the governor signed and sent to the secretary of state.

The difference between Carleton and Dorchester is easier to see than to explain. His whole political outlook had suffered a revolution. Pondering over his earlier experience, he may have come to realize that he had completely misunderstood the nature of the French Canadian people and that in imagining he could control them through the clergy and the noblesse he had been following a mirage. He may also have come to see what an injustice he had done to the racial minority and how this injustice had weakened the colony in the hour of trial. Of course he would never admit that he had been wrong, for in this he was unchanged, and he did not need to do so. The mere passing of the war and the coming of the loyalists provided sufficient reason for his reorientation. The protection of the interests and the feelings of these people was a matter of pride to him.

Moreover, their coming altered the whole future of Canada. Being the first body of English-speaking people to take root in the soil of the country, their settlement was the real beginning of Canada's dual nationality. No longer did he view things through a narrow French eye. Though not unmindful of the sensibilities of the ancient inhabitants, his vision was now English, or, to be more exact, English with a strong American tinge. Smith fitted him with a new pair of spectacles. This American, who knew his own people as Dorchester could never know them, was confident that, if properly encouraged, they would flock to Canada and become staunch Britishers. He looked forward to the day when this flood from the south would submerge the French Canadians, and from his own wide knowledge of what had happened in the old colonies he advanced proofs that he was right. New York, New Jersey, and Pennsylvania had possessed solid settlements of people "addicted to foreign laws and usages and understanding none but a foreign language," yet these elements had been gradually and quietly absorbed.[27] The English had great powers of digestion.

This transformation in the outlook of one who was such a lover of consistency probably had a good deal to do with Dorchester's appearance as King Log. He must have felt considerable embarrassment in returning to the land where the French party, his own creation, were waiting for him with open arms, and his embarrassment was doubtless increased by a knowledge that his old friend Mabane had suffered a crushing disappointment. The aging Scot had hoped to crown his career by becoming chief justice, only to find a stranger in the place he coveted. Incidentally, there was thus injected a strong flavor of personal bitterness into the struggle that followed, the bitterness being chiefly if not wholly on Mabane's side.

But, to keep to the point, the governor seems to have sought an escape from his embarrassment by assuming an aloof attitude while giving free rein to the chief justice. This resignation was the more natural because the man who was to be the driving power had mapped out the course to be followed. Health and age may also have contributed. The vigor of youth had departed from the soldier. On one occasion reports of his illness carried from Quebec to London alarmed the secretary of state.[28] Though the chief justice was only four years younger than the governor and was to die fifteen years before him, yet the impression one gathers from the records of the time is very different from what this comparison might suggest. Smith appears to have been full of energy and optimism, whereas Dorchester seems to have been a sadly disillusioned and impotent old man, indeed an almost pathetic figure.

The new chief justice had not been many weeks in the country before he released the storm that Hope's appointment had suppressed, and it raged more fiercely than ever. The trouble began in one of the committees into which Dorchester divided the council, a fortnight after his arrival, to report upon various immediate problems of the colony for his own enlightenment and for possible legislative action during the session which he announced would begin on January 15.[29] Though the committee in question was merely to deal with "the courts of justice" — the words were obviously chosen by or for the governor to exclude the highly controversial issue of English laws — its meetings witnessed a clash between Smith and Mabane. The latter set his face against all the reforms the former suggested, including new judicial districts for the loyalists and jury trials for any personal action. Here it is worthy of note that Smith apparently adopted the procedure that was to become habitual with him as a presiding officer in the council and its committees. He prepared the report beforehand. To carry it on this occasion, however, he had to insert all the opposite views that Mabane presented.[30]

While the chief justice was thus playing with the reactionaries in the committee, he was preparing to deliver in another quarter a shock that would paralyze them. The other quarter was the court of appeals, where he had them at his mercy. There he dominated, the other judges not being able to appear,[31] and his hands were free to touch what had been placed beyond the reach of his committee. There he short-circuited the legal system, causing the old storm to break loose with a vivid display of lightning and thunder. He did it on almost the last day of the year, when, in reversing a judgment of Mabane's court, he gave to the Quebec Act a new and startling interpretation. The section prescribing the ancient law, he declared, must be read in the light of its opening clause, which set forth the purpose of the entire section. The clause merely stated that all His Majesty's Canadian subjects, except the religious orders and communities, were to hold their property and other civil rights according to their old customs. As "express words" were necessary to grant Canadian laws to Canadians, so also were they necessary "to take away English law from Englishmen," and there were no such words in the act. Therefore, Smith concluded, no British-born subject in the country had lost his birthright of English law. The modification foreshadowed in the act and enjoined in the instructions, which might have been quoted against him, was not intended, he said, to satisfy the racial minority. There was no need for that. The object was to give to Canadians the advantages of English laws concerning commerce and torts.[32] To sum up, there were two systems of civil law in force in the colony, one for new subjects and one for old. Thus did the chief justice suddenly accomplish by a judicial decision what the racial minority had for years been agitating to get by legislative action.

Smith's pronouncement filled the English party with rejoicing [33] and the French party with consternation. The common pleas judges replied through the mouth of Mabane, who from his place on the bench publicly denounced the novel doctrine; [34] and a number of leading Canadians, professing to fear that this revolution in the colony's jurisprudence would shake the foundations of all their people's property, petitioned the governor to prevent any innovation. Dorchester does not seem to have been surprised by the startling opinion of the chief justice. He probably knew that it was coming and he may have secretly welcomed it as a salve for his sore conscience. When the matter was presented to him by his old friends, however, it came as a burning question and he would not touch it. In leaving the onus on Smith he was quite right. Legal authorities should decide questions of legal casuistry until the legislature intervenes. In reporting the incident home he was equally cautious. He simply wrote a covering letter to Sydney[35] inclosing one from Smith to Nepean explaining the judgment in the court of appeals.[36] Naturally this was referred to the law officers of the government in London, who replied on August 3, 1787. Though much impressed by the argument of the chief justice, they were obviously skeptical. They advised an appeal to the privy council for a final decision.[37] The idea seems to have been dropped, however, probably because a revision of the constitution was in the offing, which was expected to include a readjustment of the legal system.

Meanwhile the storm raged in Quebec, where for a while it was focused in the meetings of the legislative council. There the two parties closed in a mighty struggle that is more important than it seems at first, for it was a great turning point in the history of the country. The French party, which had ruled so long, won its last victory and thereby precipitated its own defeat. In this crisis one can see the tragedy of future years beginning to take shape — the bitter racial strife that rent Lower Canada in the first half of the nineteenth century.

Ostensibly the central issue of the session of 1787 was the form in which the biennially contentious ordinance governing the civil courts, then about to expire, should be renewed. As might be expected, the chief justice introduced a bill for its continuance with certain amendments. The court of appeals was to be made a more effective bridle upon the courts of common pleas by requiring the latter to keep and to send up fuller records, by depriving them of various technical means for blocking appeals, and by preventing any of their judges from sitting in the higher court under any circumstance.[38] The writs of *saisie*, whereby property was impounded before trial, were to be safeguarded in their application and restricted in their scope. The trial of civil suits between natural-born subjects was to follow exactly the pattern of Westminster Hall — a legislative confirmation of his judicial decision that was being flouted by the common pleas judges. For the fullest protection of the new subjects, however, any such trial might be stopped by the defendant's plea that he was "one of His Majesty's Canadian subjects or descended from any person that was so at the conquest, in the paternal or maternal line," and could not be resumed unless the court found to the contrary. New judicial districts were to be set up for the loyalists, but there likewise the new subjects were to be guaranteed their own laws of real property and inheritance.[39] At the very next meeting, Paul Roc St. Ours, perhaps the most truculent of the Canadian members, countered Smith's move by introducing a bill to renew the 1785 ordinance in a very different shape.[40] His bill would have cut away the reforms that the minority were already enjoying — trial by jury for mercantile causes and English rules of evidence.[41] This was reaction with a vengeance.

At the beginning of the session, more than three weeks before Smith launched his bill, the public had again knocked at the door of the council chamber and had been turned away by a straight party vote in which the reactionaries had a majority of two.[42] But the day was at hand when the public would no longer be excluded. The conflict within the chamber soon reverberated outside. The English party honestly believed in publicity and would not be bound by the majority. The French party were not so consistent. They violated their own principle of the secrecy of debates to blow up an agitation against the chief justice's bill, which was then published by the English party in the belief that a knowledge of its safeguards for Canadians would allay the fears aroused. Thereupon the French party denounced their opponents for doing openly what they themselves had done furtively. They were consistent, however, in rejecting the petition of a group of English-speaking merchants for a copy of St. Ours' bill,* for they knew that it would be like a red rag to a bull. But this refusal only served to irritate, for the English party in the council gave to their friends outside the substance of the

---

* Hope voted last, according to rule. When his turn came, there was a majority of one in favor of granting the request. He made it a tie, and this was interpreted as a rejection.[43]

proposed measure. These two bills threw the politically conscious part of the colony into a panic, which raises an interesting question. Why should a few amendments of an ordinance that had never lived more than two years produce such a disturbance? The answer is that there was something much more at stake and they all knew it.

The real issue was a fundamental one. It was racial. Neither side believed that the dual nationality that the country had come to possess should or could continue indefinitely. Either the majority must be Anglicized or the minority must be Gallicized. On this alone were they agreed, and hence, though both sides talked of the union and harmony of the races, their every move bred discord. The long years of their Egyptian bondage had hardened the hearts of the English party and had fortified their determination to press on toward their goal once the way was opened, as now it seemed to be.

Of course they saw that rapid progress was impossible. Only step by step could they proceed, until at last they impressed their character upon the whole people. Smith's bill they saw as an important step that would lead to others. A dark passage in one of its final clauses is lit up by a marginal note apparently added by Finlay when he sent a copy to Nepean. The note reads: "Canadians to ask ye English Common Law." Contrary to the impression left by Messrs. Shortt and Doughty in their admirable compilation of documents,[44] this comment was not on the printed copy circulated in Quebec at the time. It would have destroyed the whole purpose of publishing the chief justice's handiwork. It would have betrayed to the Canadians the ulterior motive that the backers of the bill were most anxious to conceal. They thought they kept it a secret. Hence their utter astonishment at the uproar against Smith's bill and their blind faith that its publication, by proving how perfectly innocent it was, would hush all opposition. They hoped to deceive the Canadians but they only deceived themselves.

The leaders of the French party did not know that Finlay was writing to Nepean "to cherish a predilection for every thing that is French is not, in my opinion, the most likely means to make Englishmen of the Canadians,"[45] but they did not need to know it to feel certain that there was a conspiracy against French Canadian nationality. It was in the air they breathed.

That very winter the Quebec merchants, in replying to a council committee's request for advice on how the colony's commerce might be developed, had made three threatening proposals. One, of course, was that French law, except for real property and inheritance, should be swept away. A second was that American loyalists and other immigrants should be encouraged to settle on the ungranted crown lands behind the seigniories, as well as in other parts of the country, by granting them these lands in freehold tenure. Such measures, said the merchants, would "soon give this province the form and figure of a British colony." By "British" they meant "English." Thirdly, they urged the establishment of a system of free schools to teach the inhabitants English and other useful knowledge "on an approved liberal plan." [46]

The French party had smelt the coming danger when the loyalists were planted on Canadian soil and their alarm had grown as the migration continued. They saw what Smith saw and it filled them with fear. The British-born members of this party were convinced that Britain's hold on the country was in jeopardy. Only by the most careful fostering of French Canadian nationality could the colony be kept from being swallowed up by the United States. They had a political abhorrence of all "Yankees." Those who were uncomfortable in the United States should go to the maritime provinces and not come pouring into Canada to destroy it. Such was the attitude of men like Mabane and Hope. The attitude of their Canadian colleagues was much the same except that they cared little or nothing for the empire. This was quite natural. They were wholly inspired by the instinct of self-preservation; their concern was for themselves as seigniors and as Canadians.

Thus the members of the French party, whatever their racial origin, were of one mind in their insistence that all who chose to reside in Canada, having placed themselves under the laws of the country, should conform to its life. They must become Canadians. [47] St. Ours' bill pointedly made no reference to either new or old subjects. He was avowedly aiming to abolish the distinctions which he said had caused so much discontent in the province. [48] He would abolish them by making everything French.

The battle of the bills began on March 3, when St. Ours moved that his measure be considered before the other as soon as the chief justice, who was up in Montreal, had returned. The motion was carried by a majority of one. By the same majority, Hope, Mabane, and Fraser voting with a solid French phalanx, the chief justice was defeated when he returned and moved to have his bill given its rightful precedence. This was on the twenty-second. When the council reassembled four days later, Smith read a formal protest in which he delivered some good home thrusts. He told the Canadians that the surest way to keep the privileges granted by the Quebec Act was to manifest a corresponding liberality toward the British-born. He reminded the common pleas judges that, being empowered to find both fact and law and also to declare what had been custom, they needed protection against hostile clamors. The rejected bill was designed to quiet the murmurs against the administration of justice that had been current for years and "to heal the divisions and animosities which have so long subsisted in the colony to its disgrace and detriment." The vote had been a blow to the loyalists and to the commerce of the colony. He even took the lieutenant governor to task for his timid truckling to Canadian opinion out of doors.[49] But the majority had taken the bit in their teeth and it was plain that something more drastic was needed to stop them. One of Smith's closest friends did it — James Monk.

Never was there a more dramatic sitting of a Canadian legislature than that on Saturday, April 14, 1787. Determined at all costs to prevent St. Ours' bill from becoming law, the merchants had successfully petitioned to be heard against it, and this was the day set. To present their case they engaged the best pleader in the colony, the one lawyer who had always supported them — the attorney general himself. Of course he did not appear in his public capacity. He had a right to practice as an ordinary lawyer whenever he secured the government's consent, and from both Dorchester and Hope he got permission to become the merchants' counsel.[50] At the appointed hour the petitioners were called in, the door of the council chamber was left open for the crowd of interested listeners who followed, the petition was read, and Monk advanced to deliver one of the most remarkable speeches ever uttered in Canada.

For six hours Monk spoke, and it is most tantalizing that we can find only scattered fragments of what he said. Nevertheless, it is easy to follow the drift of his argument. Apparently he spoke extempore, studying his audience, as he proceeded, to see how far he dared go. He dared to the utmost. Instead of confining his attack to the bill lying on the table, he blew up the whole administration of justice. He told the common pleas judges to their faces that they were thoroughly incompetent, that they were inconsistent, arbitrary, and ignorant. When a client came to him he was unable to give advice because there was no way of telling beforehand what law the court would apply. "I must," he said, "watch the bias, prejudice or caprice I may discover in the judges to insure justice for my client." Other lawyers were in the same predicament and for guidance had to "catch at the caprice and benefit by the prejudices they discover actuating the judges at an early stage" of a hearing. Under such circumstances it was possible for counsel to win decisions against the law. He himself had done it. Nor had the court of appeals been any better, for the simple reason that it had comprised only laymen, none of whom had ever had any real legal training. Thus did he arraign the whole council as well as the courts of common pleas.[51]

Days of angry debate followed. The judges wanted the attorney general's head for vilifying the administration of justice. They were not trying to shield themselves. No consciousness of wrongdoing shadowed their innocent minds. Just as Lord Chancellor Bacon a century and a half before had interpreted the first attacks of the house of commons as pure faction, so did these lesser men see nothing but malice in Monk, a malice that would undermine the foundations of government. Smith and his friends, on the other hand, fought for an investigation by the council into the conduct of the courts, against which "high charges" had been raised, and for the withdrawal of the vicious bill. Hope, who at first stood with the judges against the attorney general, ended the impasse, possibly after a hint from the Castle of St. Louis. From his seat at the head of the board he pointed out that the council, being itself implicated, could not with propriety conduct any examination into the courts, and he proposed the dissolution of the committee presided over by St. Ours which had prepared the offending measure. Thereupon the council requested the governor to direct an investigation in such manner as he might think fit and it passed a compromise bill.

The compromise leaned in favor of reform, for the new ordinance was not a mere renewal of that which was about to expire. Though it contained no reference, explicit or implicit, to the introduction of English law and though it left the composition of the court of appeals unaltered, it embodied a number of reforms sponsored by the chief justice. It strengthened the jurisdiction of the court of appeals, it confined the use of writs of *saisie* and provided against their abuse, and it authorized the erection of new judicial districts for the loyalists.[52] The momentary triumph of St. Ours over Smith had been a Pyrrhic victory.

On May 18, a fortnight after the close of the session, the governor ordered the investigation [53] to be undertaken by the only man in the colony capable of doing it — the chief justice himself. It was a bitter pill for the judges of the common pleas and they were loath to swallow it. They had long been the main support of government in the colony, whereas he was a newcomer who would wreck everything for which they stood. He was their most powerful political foe, the friend of their principal accuser and of all the malcontents.

But Mabane and his colleagues put on a good face. They appeared at the hearings, which opened on June 11, not to defend themselves but to prove their case against Monk. When they had done this to their own satisfaction, which required only a few days, they insisted that the chief justice should close the investigation and submit his report on the evidence presented. In other words, they still sought to secure what they had been fighting for in council, a limitation of the whole business to an investigation of the attorney general. Smith overruled their contention and proceeded. Thenceforth they were represented by counsel, who commonly waived the right of cross-examination and occasionally protested against the manner in which the affair was being conducted. Monk, on the other hand, was more assiduous than ever, and no one who harbored a grievance was denied a hearing. The chief justice accepted every scrap of evidence that was offered, contenting himself with registering objections raised against admitting particular pieces of evidence. The judges' counsel tried to shut out as interested parties all who had signed the petition against St. Ours' bill and attempted to show that all complaints against the bench originated with Cochrane and his creditors. Some witnesses were asked the embarrassing question, "Where were you during the winter of 1775–76?" and they had to confess that they had withdrawn from Quebec — for their health or other good reasons.

The attitude of the chief justice throughout the investigation is a little puzzling. The minutes show that he was partial to the attorney general. But they also betray an anxiety to be fair to the judges. The total impression, however, is one of weakness and timidity. Perhaps the explanation is Smith's consciousness of the extremely delicate position in which he was placed. When the hearings were closed on November 6, that the results might be sent home by the last ship of the season, he presented long excuses for presenting no findings whatever. The whole mass of undigested material that he had accumulated he unloaded on Dorchester, and he helped the latter to get rid of it by drafting a cautious covering dispatch to the secretary of state.[53]

The records of the investigation fill thirteen folio volumes.[54] Being unenlightened by any finding, they are as annoying to the modern student who examines them as they were to the secretary of state who received them and the chancellor to whom he turned them over.[55] Little of the evidence can be taken at its face value because most of it was *ex parte*. Nevertheless, it is impossible to avoid some broad conclusions about the unsatisfactory state of the courts.

The Quebec Act had not brought order out of the chaos of the law. As Monk had said, no one could tell what law would be applied to any case. In the court of appeals, each member voted according to his prejudice, English or French. With the exception of Southouse, an ineffectual Montreal judge who had come out from England,[56] both courts of common pleas were strongly prejudiced against English jurisprudence, and yet they were inconsistent. Rarely making any ruling on what law should govern and habitually delivering their decisions without any supporting reasons, the judges had been pulled hither and thither by the lawyers, whom they had allowed, with seldom a reproof, to concoct every conceivable mixture of law in presenting their briefs. The consequence may easily be imagined. In addition to the custom of Paris, French royal edicts applicable to New France, and the provincial enactments of both French and British régimes, the judges had drawn from what they conceived to be the custom of the country and had followed the *code marchand*, Roman law, and even English law and equity. They had no rule for awarding costs. They gave no direction to juries, who therefore brought in illegal verdicts which were straightway accepted as valid. The confusion of the law was confounded by the disorder of the court records, the judges having neglected their duty of directing and inspecting the work of the clerks. Judgments on the books did not tally with the judgments delivered and executed. Evidence was received and used without any minute being taken. Many papers that had been submitted were missing. Appeals were sent up with incomplete files, causing sound judgments to be overthrown. The Montreal court was at times like a coffee house, so it was said, where everyone was speaking at once.

None of the judges seems to have been consciously corrupt, yet the professional conduct of some of them was open to strong censure. Little exception was taken to the behavior of Dunn and Panet in Quebec or of Southouse * in Montreal, but the charges against their colleagues were many and bitter. According to common gossip in Quebec, it was a simple matter to load the dice in the game of litigation. All that was necessary was to retain a young Scottish lawyer by the name of Alexander Gray. He commonly dined with Mabane and discussed with the judge the cases he was to bring before him on the morrow. Mabane was the judge to "get" because he dominated those who sat beside him. His arbitrariness was matched by that of Fraser and Rouville. The Montreal bench refused evidence offered in court, preferring to follow information privately gained, and otherwise dealt in a summary fashion with lawyers and litigants who were out of favor. Much as the commercial fraternity hated Fraser, he does not seem to have been so high-handed as his Canadian colleague. One of the stories widely circulated against the latter was to the following effect. A certain McKenzie hired a horse to drive to Sault au Récollet. While he was dining there, another traveler took the horse and drove to the Isle Jesus, pressing the beast so hard that the poor creature died soon after. The owner of the horse sued the innkeeper at the Sault au Récollet, and McKenzie, hearing of the case, went to court out of curiosity. When Rouville spied him, he declared that the man who had hired the horse was answerable, and straightway he dismissed the suit against the innkeeper and ordered judgment to be entered against McKenzie. From this there was no appeal, the amount involved being too small. Rouville's chief faults seem to have been an ungovernable temper, which might explode in court at any time, and an unquenchable thirst. Whenever one of his decisions was mentioned in Montreal, as like as not someone would ask, "Was it a morning or an afternoon judgment?"

This investigation was like an earthquake. It did a lot of damage

* But there were many complaints about his ignorance of the law.

and no good. Though Smith and his followers were confident that it would move the home government to effect a thoroughgoing reform in the administration of justice, and the judges were so nervous about their position that they retained an able lawyer in London to protect them,[57] these hopes and fears were vain. Nothing happened for a year and a half and then the axe fell in a surprising manner. In April, 1789, Sydney informed Dorchester that Monk was dismissed and that Gray, Mabane's friend, was to be attorney general.[58] There is no indication that the tory secretary of state even contemplated the removal of anybody from the Canadian bench. But the judges did not come through unscathed, for they had been dragged in the mud and had not been given a bath. Much as they might rejoice over Monk's fall, they missed the public and official vindication they so much desired. The chief justice was injured through having been put in an impossible position, and even the governor seems to have suffered in prestige. A shrewd observer condemned the whole inquiry as one of the most mischievous jobs he had seen in Canada. "Great men did little things," he said, "good men nothing at all, and Nero fiddled while Rome burned." [59]

The investigation caused no real improvement in the administration of justice. The only possible exception is that there may have been less slovenliness in the keeping of court records. Though it was observed that after the explosive speech of April 14 "the Code Marchand and French laws were given in charge in all cases," [60] this change appears to have come before the investigation got under way and to have been effected by the new ordinance which, for the first time, required the occupants of the bench to state the laws and customs that were to apply to each case. With the old judges in the common pleas and the new chief justice in the court of appeals, the clash of laws and decisions continued. During the winter of 1787–88, nine judgments were reviewed by the court of appeals, of which eight were reversed.[61] In January, 1790, the sheriff of Montreal called the situation "truly alarming"; nine-tenths of the Montreal judgments carried to Quebec had been upset in the past two or three years.[62] In the previous November, two years after the investigation closed, Dorchester sent home a memorial from merchants and other citizens of Quebec and Montreal who stated that "the inefficiency and uncertainty of the laws, the contra-

A View of Montreal in 1784

[From a water color by James Peachey, dated October 15, 1784, in the possession of the Public Archives of Canada]

CHIEF JUSTICE WILLIAM SMITH

[From an engraving by W. B. Hall in the possession of the
Public Archives of Canada]

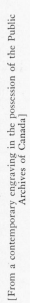

CHIEF JUSTICE PETER LIVIUS

[From a contemporary engraving in the possession of the Public
Archives of Canada]

dictory decisions of the courts of justice thereon and the confusion which prevails in the forms of judicial proceedings have become more and more manifest and destructive to the interests of His Majesty's subjects." [63]

Why did the home government leave things as they were? In the first place, no action was possible for some time simply because of the enormous bulk of the papers that had to be studied. Then the conclusion reached seems to have been much the same as that of the shrewd observer quoted above. "It was necessary," he remarked, "to have a dash at something, and here lay their mistake; the battle was not fought with *a thing, as it ought to have been,* but it was maliciously fought with *men,* which it ought *not to have been.*" In other words, the judges were largely the victims of circumstance. On the whole, this opinion was right. Much of the trouble arose from the long absence of a chief justice who might have checked the exasperating confusion that grew up in the courts under well-meaning but unguided men. In removing Livius, Carleton had injured much more than the man. He had injured the colony.

More important still was the system of jurisprudence and the system of politics that the governor riveted upon the country on the morrow of the Quebec Act. The system of jurisprudence did not fit the needs of the community and the system of politics precluded any readjustment. His responsibility for what had happened may have escaped the attention of the home government at this time, but the fundamental difficulty did not. It sprang from the conquest itself and was inherent in the very nature of the population. The plan of 1763 had failed completely and the plan of 1774 had not been applied. French civil law could not be swept out nor, without grave injustice, could English law be kept out. The problem thrown by London to Quebec in 1774 and now tossed back again had to be solved and in no uncertain manner before the Canadian bench, whatever its personnel, could deal out satisfactory justice. Therefore the government put off doing anything with the courts until this fundamental question was settled; and, as it was a task for expert rather than lay minds, the law officers were set to work upon it. The plan was to incorporate their solution in the new constitution which, it was becoming more and more evident, parliament would have to give to the colony.

CHAPTER XVIII

TRADE, EDUCATION, TENURES, AND FINANCE

BEFORE proceeding to an examination of the origin and character of the new constitution, which is the natural conclusion of this volume, it will be necessary to consider several other matters that attracted public attention during the closing years of the old province of Quebec. One of these was the colony's trade. Its several branches were the subject of considerable discussion both in and out of the council.

On the eve of his departure from London in August, 1786, Dorchester's attention was drawn to a problem that had arisen in connection with the fur trade. The men of the North West Company had been agitating for a ten-year monopoly of the trade beyond Lake Superior. They gave three reasons for their request. One was the very nature of the business conducted in the distant wilds with the red men. Competition among whites for the peltries gathered by Indians demoralized the natives and damaged the trade. The second reason was the expense to which they had been driven by the peace treaty. Faced with the alarming prospect of Grand Portage and its route to the west being turned over to the Americans, they had sent out an exploring expedition that had found an all-British route to the west. The third was a promise of something that might be highly important to the empire. They would explore all the west between the fifty-fifth and sixty-fifth parallels of latitude as far as the Pacific Ocean, where, as they pointedly remarked, the Russians had already established a trading post and the Americans threatened to do likewise. Haldimand, to whom the Montreal fur barons had submitted their petition a month before he left Quebec, had told Sydney that the project of discovery merited favorable consideration; and Hamilton, whose intercession was later sought, had written home suggesting that if all "greedy and needy adventurers" were allowed to penetrate the west, the returns of the trade might leap up for a short while, "but the Indians would be drowned in rum." [1] The government did not know how to regard this request, and therefore Sydney asked Dorchester to investigate the whole problem and to advise what policy should be adopted.

The suggestion that the government might hand over the northwest fur trade to a monopoly came to nothing. By the time the governor arrived in Quebec, the necessity for a monopoly was no longer felt and the idea seems to have died. The North West Company had got into its stride and was about to absorb its only remaining Canadian rival. By the amalgamation of 1787 it acquired a practical monopoly of all the northwest trade that was focused at Montreal.

A more sweeping proposal, however, was advanced by a leading Montreal merchant during the winter of 1786-87, when the whole of the fur traffic came under review. One of the committees into which Dorchester divided the council a fortnight after his arrival was to explore the possibilities of the country's commerce, and this committee naturally appealed to the trading communities of the two towns, each of which then appointed a committee of merchants to do what was asked of them. The chief concern of the Montreal committee was furs, and it was to this committee that Joseph Howard, who had been engaged in the fur trade for over twenty years, made his proposal. Competition, he said, was ruining Indian and trader alike. Rum and blood were flowing far too freely in the interior, and the fifteen hundred men whom the business drew from the agricultural life of the colony were five hundred too many. Moreover, the government was missing an opportunity to save both Indian and trader and to make some money to boot. The right to engage in the fur trade he would divide into a hundred shares, to be sold singly at public auction in Montreal for a period of seven years. The highest bidders would then form themselves into one company which would control the whole traffic beyond the Long Sault on the Ottawa.[2]

But Howard was a voice crying in the wilderness. The merchants' committee brushed aside his ingenious scheme and the council committee likewise would have none of it. The trade was clamoring for freedom. Indeed, it demanded more freedom than the provincial government would yet allow, for official opinion in Quebec was no mere echo of commercial opinion in Montreal on questions of the fur trade, even though this was the biggest business of the country and a more liberal spirit was beginning to reign in the provincial capital. The Montreal committee strongly criticized the license system and the regulation that all shipments over the lakes must be carried by government vessels. The council committee ignored the former criticism and replied to the latter by reporting in favor of continuing the shipping regulation.[3] It was not long, however, before Quebec yielded on both points. Though the fur barons had no seat in the council, they had an argument that was bound to conquer. The Spaniards were stealing up the Mississippi and its tributaries, and American traders would push into the territory which the treaty of 1783 recognized as American. Artificial restrictions formerly designed to protect the Canadian fur trade were now calculated to destroy it. To meet this foreign competition successfully, it had to get rid of these shackles. Therefore, as mentioned in a previous chapter, 1788 saw the opening of the lakes to private vessels and 1791 marked the close of the licensing system.

Until 1787 there was no regular commercial intercourse between Canada and the United States. It could not be allowed under the old colonial system. But the people of Vermont, who during the war had been flirting with the idea of political reunion with the empire, began to press for commercial reunion as soon as peace was signed.[4] These North American Ishmaelites were in a desperate position. Excluded from the United States until 1791 by the hostility of New York and from the British Empire by the treaty of 1783, they were cooped up in the interior and threatened with economic suffocation. Dwelling by the shore of Lake Champlain, they saw that their natural outlet was over the Richelieu and the St. Lawrence, and they were determined to open this door. What they had to offer was considerable — masts, spars, and timber for the navy, an expanding market for manufactures, and the possibility of commercial annexation ripening into political annexation.

The offer of naval stores was particularly tempting because of a recent experience. In 1780 the Armed Neutrality of the North had threatened to shut Britain out of the Baltic, whence she drew the naval stores without which she could not maintain her sea power. Nor was the market for British goods in Vermont something to be lightly thrown away. Despite their isolation, the inhabitants of that state were increasing rapidly. In 1780 they numbered forty thousand, and before ten years had passed they were twice as numerous. With free trade the population would multiply even faster and would consume only British manufactures. Here it should be remembered that British industry was rising to become an appreciable factor in the calculations of British policy. The suggestion of ultimate political annexation — the eastern counterpart of the vision of empire inspiring the continued retention of the western posts — appears to have been of lesser value in the eyes of those who received it as well as in the eyes of those who made it. Indeed, the British were told that by the commercial annexation of Vermont they might enjoy all the material advantages of possessing a thriving colony without any of the liabilities.

That the old colonial system should be abandoned in the interior of America was also suggested by the contemplated division of the province of Quebec. It would create something that Britain had never possessed, a colony cut off from access to the sea. Upper Canada would be in a position somewhat analogous to that of Vermont. With a population drawn from the United States and still being attracted from that source, having little in common with French Lower Canada, from which it wished to cut loose, and being mostly surrounded by the United States, would not its natural economic affiliation be with the republic? This question arose in Sydney's mind, and hence, when dispatching Dorchester in August, 1786, he asked him to report upon whether "the inhabitants of the province so to be erected may not be supplied with European and other produce and manufactures with greater facility and upon easier terms by the subjects and through the territories of the United States of America than by our subjects and through our province of Quebec, and thereby a connection and intercourse between the subjects of the two countries be unavoidably promoted and encouraged." [5] This may seem a startling thing for the tory secretary of state to say, but he may have suspected that geography would there break down the sacrosanct system, and certainly he saw that its enforcement might cramp the growth of Upper Canada. Apparently, also, he contemplated using that colony as an economic magnet to recover something of what had been lost.

In lifting the latch of the empire's back door, the governor and council seem not to have been influenced at all by the problem of the projected new colony. Indeed, Dorchester apparently ignored Sydney's interesting query, possibly because he was hoping against hope that the home government would abandon the idea of dividing the province and because American settlement was yet too remote from the future Upper Canada for its possible commercial relations with the United States to be a practical issue. But the possibility of trade with Vermont was a burning question that had been much discussed on both sides of the Atlantic. Ever since the peace the merchants of Montreal and Quebec had felt like Tantalus. A rich trade was offered them but was held just out of their reach.[6] Their London correspondents were also impatient.[7] From Quebec, where the agents of Vermont first applied, the matter had been referred to London. There it had been discussed by the government,[8] but nothing had been settled. One very pertinent point, however, had been suggested. Did the statutory restrictions of the navigation laws, which had only maritime intercourse in view, apply with equal force to land communication and to inland navigation? Here was a possible loophole for the exercise of the prerogative. Still there was apparently no clear understanding between Sydney and Dorchester, when the latter left England, on what he might do when he reached Quebec. What he ought to do, in the opinion of the mercantile people in the colony, he was not long in discovering.

The council committee on commerce and the assisting merchants' committees of the two towns urged the wisdom of opening wide the door of Vermont except for the export of peltries, which had been expressly forbidden by the home government. Though an imperial order-in-council of March 8, 1785, prohibiting the import of any goods of the United States into Quebec by sea had created in Quebec a certain opinion that all intercourse was outlawed, the council committee pointed out that this order did not apply to Vermont because it was no part of the United States, and the governor observed that it extended only to navigation by sea. Moreover, he thought it illogical that British ships should not be allowed to carry from the St. Lawrence goods that could be imported into Britain in ships of the United States.[9]

After consulting the chief justice and getting the support of his legal opinion, the governor permitted a limited commercial intercourse with the "neighboring states" by way of Lake Champlain. He did it by a simple order to the collector of customs on April 18, 1787, requiring him to admit the free import of lumber, naval stores, hemp, flax, grain, provisions, and livestock, the produce of those states, and the free export of British products except furs. Five days later he recommended to the council the passing of an ordinance to allow the import of leaf tobacco and of pot and pearl ashes, and the council complied with alacrity.[10]

His falling back upon an ordinance to enlarge his order suggests a suspicion in his mind that he had started off on the wrong foot. The confirmation of this suspicion was conveyed to him in a delicate manner. What he had done was referred to the privy council committee on trade and plantations, who reported that the regulation of intercourse by land or by inland navigation between the province of Quebec and the adjoining states should be left to the governor with the advice of the legislative council. Sydney sent Dorchester a copy of the report,[11] and in the session of 1788 the order was transformed into an ordinance.

In conceding this liberty to the provincial government, the home government imposed certain restrictions. In addition to giving a general warning against contravening British laws, the privy council committee insisted that the governor and council should on no account permit the export of peltries or the import of foreign spirits or foreign European manufactures — an interesting comment on Sydney's earlier speculation about the complete emancipation of Upper Canada from the old colonial system.

During 1789 the food shortage in the colony occasioned a temporary change in the regulations of 1787 and 1788. The alarming rise in the price of bread moved the governor at the end of January to take the law into his own hands by ordering the naval officer at St. John on the Richelieu, the port of entry for all this trade, to admit bread, biscuit, and flour of any grain,[12] and at the beginning of April to issue for the relief of the new settlements a proclamation authorizing the free import of foodstuffs by any inland waterway west of St. John, provided they were brought in British craft.[13] The order and the proclamation were to be effective only until August, but in July a further proclamation extended the time to the end of the year. Even bolder was his action in June, when, on the advice of the council, he authorized importation of American foodstuffs by sea until the close of navigation.[14] He did it knowing that he was violating an imperial statute,[15] but he felt that it was necessary and he trusted the home government to provide him with the necessary legal cloak. Indeed, this exercise of the prerogative was already covered, though he did not know it, by an imperial order-in-council of May 20.[16]

In 1790 an effort was made to extend the regular trade with the south over Lake Champlain, for the hopes of 1787 and 1788 had been followed by disappointment. It had been expected that large quantities of timber in its various forms would pass through Canada to Britain, but the cost of marketing the products of Vermont's forests proved too heavy. This was apparent by the summer of 1789, when two enterprising Vermonters presented an ingenious proposal to the government in Quebec. They would reduce the financial burden by imposing a physical burden. They would use the rafts to bear down iron which they would extract from "the crags of Vermont," if iron were now added to the list of articles admitted. Their petition was referred to a council committee, which welcomed the idea and drafted a bill to carry it out. The submission of this measure to permit the free import of Vermont pig iron raised strong objections from Caldwell, Mabane, and Dunn. The colony's one real manufactory, the forges of St. Maurice, should not be injured for the benefit of two unknown foreigners. To win their point the trio insisted that the legislative council was legally incompetent to pass the bill. Their strenuous protests were successful. To save the bill from being thrown out, its sponsors added a suspending clause which, while it made possible the passage of the ordinance in April, 1790, prevented its coming into force until it received the royal approval.[17] This does not seem to have been granted, though the governor urged the policy of going much further. He did it in a letter to the secretary of state on July 21, 1790.[18]

"Three considerable advantages" he saw in throwing this inland door wide open for all American produce to be exported from Quebec on the same terms as Canadian produce. "Canada must gain by the passage of all commodities through the country, Great Britain by an increase of her carrying trade, and both by interesting our neighbours to preserve in the hands of Great Britain this outlet to the sea and to the most profitable markets for all their produce." It might not be wise, he observed, to extend the full indulgence immediately. Caution might be advisable in order "that our settlers on the north side of the lakes may acquire strength and get the start of those on the opposite shore in population, improvement of their settlements, and the navigation of the upper lakes." Britain's immediate interest was neither "to encourage the settlements of our neighbours south of those lakes and the river Saint Lawrence, nor yet to check them by .ny violent measures." It was rather "to let them take their own course." "We ought nevertheless to pay a vigilant attention to their progress, and act as the change of things may require, taking great care firmly to establish in those parts the national character for justice, moderation and liberality." Because it would be a gradual process requiring constant care, full power to act should be left with the governor "as at present."

It will be observed that the governor's thoughts were not confined to Vermont but ranged over a much wider area. Inspired by Smith's vision and by his own perception of Britain's strategic advantage in her control of the outlet of the great St. Lawrence drainage system, he saw Britain's influence spreading over the northern part of the territory that she had deeded away. He implied that there was everything to gain and nothing to lose by forming "alliances with our neighbours as soon as things are well matured for that purpose." "Their own interest alone can render them zealously attached to us and give duration to any of their engagements." But these shrewd suggestions seem to have fallen upon deaf ears in London.

Another interesting subject of debate during these years was the regulation of the country's grain trade. In their reports to the council committee on commerce in the beginning of 1787, the merchants' committees of Quebec and Montreal drew attention to the prevailing unsatisfactory conditions and made recommendations that anticipated the legislation of later generations. The Quebec committee observed that "the present mode of buying and collecting wheat and other grain by going to the inhabitants' houses tends to enhance the price, to create unnecessary trouble and expense to the purchasers and to prevent an improvement in the quality of it." The same committee scored the dealers severely. In spite of "the strongest remonstrances," they continued to indulge in evil practices. They mixed bad or smutty wheat with good wheat. They kept grain "in low, damp or confined places, and in a few instances" were suspected "of sprinkling it with water in the store or on board vessels in order to increase the measure." The remedy recommended was the establishment at convenient places in different parts of the colony of public markets and granaries through which all wheat for export would have to pass. The Montreal committee was less explicit about abuses and more detailed in its suggestions. No damp or dirty wheat should be received. There should be separate compartments for different grades, and a system of covering certificates. Twelve to fifteen granaries, each with a capacity of from ten to twenty thousand bushels, would be required for the district of Montreal.[19]

Despite these revelations and recommendations, nothing was done or even attempted at this time, presumably because of the expense involved. Then followed the grain shortage, discussed earlier; and when this had passed, the council approached the problem in the mills. Using bad wheat, they were turning out bad flour, to the injury of the country's commerce and to the danger of its citizens' health; and the bad grain they kept as toll was being used for seed, to the detriment of agriculture. During the legislative session of 1790 the council thought that these evils might be checked by requiring every gristmill to install wind and screen cribbles and by imposing heavy penalties for the sale of flour or meal made of uncleaned wheat. A bill for this purpose was considered, but along with other accumulated business it was put off until the following year. In the session of 1791, the last before the new constitution was inaugurated, the bill was resubmitted in printed form, but again it was postponed,[20] and the unsolved problem of damp and dirty grain was bequeathed to the new province of Lower Canada.

The sea-borne traffic of the old province of Quebec was likewise much discussed to little effect during these years.[21] This discussion also is worth recording because of the light it throws upon the colony's trade with the Newfoundland fisheries, with the West Indies, with southern Europe, and with the mother country. The great question was whether Canada, along with the maritime provinces, should supplant the lost colonies as the main source of supplies for the Newfoundland fisheries and the British West Indies. The Canadian merchants had been exporting some biscuit and flour to the fisheries, but they had been too far away to enjoy any such share of the West Indian market for fish, flour, and lumber. On the morrow of the peace it was obvious that British North America was totally unprepared to take over the whole business of supplying the fishermen and the island planters. It was equally obvious that the fisheries, as the nursery of seamen, and the West Indies, as the source of tropical produce, were far too important to sacrifice on the altar of the navigation laws.

Consequently, a temporary expedient was adopted in 1783. Parliament gave the crown power to regulate trade with the United States, and this power was used to permit both the fishermen and the planters to be supplied from the United States in British bottoms. In 1784 and 1785 the government in London hoped that the influx of loyalists, by rapidly developing British North America, would soon render this expedient unnecessary. But the hope proved vain, and the enabling act of 1783 was renewed year after year until 1797. Meanwhile the disappointed merchants in Canada continued their trade with the fisheries in competition with the Americans, but their efforts to break into the West Indian market were well-nigh fruitless.

The failure seems striking in view of the fact that Canada, including the thirsty fur-bearing interior, drank about half a million gallons of rum a year,[22] and the island plantations consumed large quantities of fish, flour, and lumber. Why could not a profitable exchange be set up? The greatest obstacle in the way was the colony's geographical position. All-year ports and closer proximity to the West Indies gave the Americans an enormous advantage. When the Canadian merchants tried to struggle against it, they were further handicapped by certain provisions of the Quebec Revenue Act — the duty of sixpence a gallon on rum brought direct from the British West Indies, the absence of any duty on the same article if imported via Britain, and the threepenny duty on molasses brought in British ships. In practice this meant molasses from the French and Dutch settlements and a duty of fourpence, the additional penny being the old imperial customs.[23] Here it should also be explained that a gallon of molasses produced a gallon of rum. These rates had failed to achieve their purpose of establishing a just balance between the British shipping interest, the West Indian planters, and the Canadian distillers. It was cheaper to import rum duty free from London than to pay the duty on rum brought direct from the British West Indies, and it was even cheaper to distill it in Canada from dutiable foreign molasses.

The difference in cost being slight, the basis of the Canadian supply shifted only gradually. By the end of 1786, however, the Quebec merchants regarded it as a serious problem. During that year only 138,000 gallons of rum came direct from the British West Indies, whereas 168,000 gallons of foreign molasses were imported.[24] "If the law remains as it now stands," said the Quebec committee, "the consumption of rum in Canada will inevitably be supplied from distilled foreign molasses, without a saving to the consumers" — the difference in cost being too small — to the detriment of British shipping, of the British planters, and even of the colony, for cash instead of goods had to be paid for the foreign molasses. The British West Indian planters would have liked to see the prohibition of the import of foreign molasses into Canada, and they wished to secure control of the Canadian market, where they could get more for their rum than in London. Naturally the Quebec merchants rejected the idea of making the colony so dependent upon the British planters, but they would give them a decided preference, by halving the duty on rum and by imposing a threepenny excise on the Canadian product "whenever we have a legislature competent thereto." Such a readjustment, they said, would be doubly beneficial to the colony. Its revenue would be increased and its trade enlarged.[25]

The members of the council committee, to whom this report was submitted, did not mention these specific recommendations, but they brought out another aspect of the question which the merchants had strangely ignored. If the importation of foreign molasses were "prohibited by equalizing duties, or otherwise" — there had been talk, and there was soon to be more talk, of suppressing distilleries in British North America — then the distillers of the United States "would supply their Indian traders and fishermen with that most essential article *rum* at *one half* less at least than the British trader and fisherman could be supplied by the British West India planter, British American merchant or distiller," to the great injury of the British fisheries and the British fur trade. The council committee also pointed out the danger of smuggling rum into British North America from the United States.[26]

Before the governor sent home these reports, which he did without comment, the standing committee of West Indian planters and merchants in England pressed the problem upon the British government. At a meeting in the London Tavern on April 5, 1787, this committee resolved that the sixpenny duty on rum should be abolished or at least reduced, that the duty on foreign molasses should be increased, and that the distilleries in Canada should be suppressed and prohibited.[27] On May 28 Sydney sent Dorchester a copy of these resolutions and, referring also to the possibility of smuggling from the United States, asked for a general report including recommendations of what should be done. On receiving this letter and its inclosure, the governor turned them over to the council, and in November he received from it a long and specific report, which he immediately transmitted to the secretary of state.[28]

According to this council report of November 7, 1787, the province had four distilleries, three in Quebec * and one in Montreal, with a total annual capacity of 420,000 gallons. "Owing to the difficulty of procuring molasses, shipping and other local and temporary inconveniences," they had never handled more than 200,000 gallons in any one year, and there was little likelihood of more distilleries being erected in the near future. The cost of domestic manufacture, including a penny a gallon for casks, was sixpence or sevenpence a gallon — threepence more than the corresponding American figure; and the total cost of the finished product was two shillings and two- or threepence a gallon, about one shilling more than the price of American distilled rum in New York, Boston, and Albany. The Canadian importer had to pay about two shillings and ninepence for rum from the Leeward and Windward Islands and three shillings for Jamaica rum, but when he watered them down to the same strength as the Canadian product, the three articles were much more nearly equal in value. The imported varieties had a superior flavor, but this was generally ignored both by the Canadian inhabitants and the Indians.

There was then relatively little smuggling of rum from the United States into the colony, the price of the Canadian article not being quite high enough to induce much illicit trade. But the danger would be great if the distilleries were suppressed. On all the above statements the council was unanimous. The final recommendations, however, were carried only after some warm debating and by close voting. To check the danger of cheap American rum eating into the British fisheries and the British fur trade, and to encourage a direct trade with the British West Indies, the majority of the council advised the elimination of both the sixpenny and the fourpenny duty, and the revival of the old law which would force British planters to get all their provisions and lumber from Britain

* William Grant owned two with a combined capacity of 200,000 gallons.

or her colonies. The revival was urged as compensation for giving the island planter an advantage over the Canadian distiller.[29]

Canada's retort was more than spirited; it might be called reckless. These proposals struck at the West Indian planter, who could not carry on without American supplies; they struck at the British shipper, who would transport rum direct to Quebec instead of over to London and then out to the St. Lawrence; they struck also at the revenue of the province of Quebec, the major portion of which was derived from the customs on rum and molasses. Though Dorchester observed none of these things in his covering dispatch, they could not escape attention at home, where the demands of Canada probably appeared more unreasonable than those of the West Indies.

To resolve the clash between Canada and the West Indies, without doing too much injury to British shipping or the Quebec revenue, the government passed an act through parliament in June, 1788. This amended the Quebec Revenue Act to allow a certain reciprocity. Vessels taking lumber and provisions to the British West Indies could bring back and land, free of duty, rum to an equal value.[30]

The concession was illusory. A couple of vessels were loaded in October, 1788, to take advantage of the new arrangement, and they brought back rum in the spring of 1789. But during 1789 only one of all the vessels that cleared for the West Indies, a little schooner of fifty or sixty tons, left with the intention of returning. What was the matter? The shortage of food and the consequent embargo was not the only cause of disappointment. Canadian lumber was ill assorted, and Canadian flour was not so fair as its American rival. The colony possessed no ships fit for the West Indian trade and could attract none to engage in the projected exchange, for the simple reason that it did not pay. A full cargo of lumber and provisions could, at the very best, purchase exemption for only half a return cargo of rum. It was still cheaper to import that article via London.

In December, 1789, more than three score merchants, millers, bakers, and coopers of Quebec came forward with a proposed amendment which, they said, would make the act of 1788 operative. Any exporter should be allowed to import rum, duty free, to the amount of lumber and provisions he had sent to the British West Indies, without regard to any particular ship. The council, to whom

Dorchester referred it, unanimously supported the suggestion,[31] but it was shelved in England.[32] Many important things concerning the colony were then being put off until after the passage of the bill giving the colony a new constitution. As a consequence Canada's direct trade with the West Indies continued to languish. Incidentally the revenue also suffered because of the growing importation of duty-free rum from London.

Another interesting branch of Canada's trade was with southern Europe, chiefly with the port of Barcelona. There was the market for the colony's surplus wheat, next to furs the most important of its exports. This trade also took off some codfish, though in much smaller quantities. Most of the codfishing in the gulf was carried on by ships from Jersey and Guernsey, the only provincial catch being that of the settlers at Gaspé and the Bay of Chaleur. Some flour was also sent to southern Europe. The vessels laden in Canada for that part of the world there exchanged their cargoes for wines, fruit, and cash, and proceeded to Britain. Only a portion of these wines — some of the cheaper varieties — and only a little of the fruit were then imported into the colony, the balance of these articles and the cash being used to establish credits in London. This balance was relatively large because twenty-five or thirty thousand bushels of wheat could purchase all the wines and fruit the colony consumed. Therefore this trade was regarded favorably.

But it had one feature that caused considerable complaint in Quebec. Under the navigation laws these imports into the colony could not come direct from their place of origin. They had first to be landed in Britain, where they paid duty. The Quebec merchants, in their report of January, 1787, objected to this regulation because it injured them greatly while it benefited British shipping only slightly. "Those common wines," they said, "are liable to grow sour in two long summer voyages, they arrive so late at market as frequently to render the sale and distribution of them impracticable, and are generally much the worse for keeping over the winter." Nor is it likely that the fruit was improved by the extra journey and handling. When many British vessels were being licensed to supply the West Indies from the United States, why could not a few vessels leave England with licenses to carry wine and fruit direct to Canada? Why could not the duty then retained in Britain on re-export be collected in Quebec? [33]

These questions may have been inspired, at least in part, by an ulterior motive. The merchants said that the trade as a whole was not very profitable and they as much as said that it would be reduced to the value of the wines procured in exchange "if we have a market to take off our flour." The report of the council committee made no reference to the above questions but developed the meaning of the words just quoted. "Until the West Indians agree to take our flour in preference to that of the States, and until Newfoundland is restrained from supplying its fisheries with the bread and flour of New York and Philadelphia, surely every encouragement ought to be given to our export intercourse with Spain and Portugal and such of the Italian states as take off the great permanent staple productions of our country — wheat, flour and cod fish." [34]

But the demands of the merchants and the hints of the councilors were made in vain, and the whole subject seems to have been dropped after this discussion in the winter of 1786–87. In 1789 the colony had no wheat to export. This of course did not mean that wine importations ceased. But the licensing of vessels to carry southern European produce direct to Quebec was neither so urgent nor so simple as the licensing of the American trade to the West Indies. A little sour wine would not ruin Canada, and the transfer of customs collections from London to Quebec involved complicated legal questions.

§

The problem of education was thrust forward in the spring of 1787 by the receipt of an official communication from London on another subject: the Jesuit estates. During the French régime the Jesuits had acquired considerable property in the colony, and they used it for two objects, to support missionaries among the Indians and to educate the youth of the country. The order was doomed in Canada ten years before it was dissolved by the pope in 1773. It was doomed by the cession of the colony to Britain, whose government at once decided to suppress the organization and to confiscate its property, of course making some provision for the surviving members. Then began the long and troubled story of the disposition of these estates, lasting for more than a century.

Over in London Amherst persuaded the king that the Jesuit property in Canada would be a fitting reward for his services in conquering the country, and on November 9, 1770, an order-in-council was passed requiring the attorney and solicitor general to prepare the necessary instrument. Amherst was to get everything except "the colleges and chapels" in Quebec, Montreal, and Three Rivers, but was to compensate the dispossessed fathers. The law officers reported that they could not obey the order because they had no authentic account of the estates in question. The disappointed general immediately petitioned for a renewal of the order and for the submission to the law officers of Governor Murray's description of the property. This prayer was granted but the property was not. The desired instrument was not forthcoming, legal scruples and procrastination standing in the way. In March, 1779, Amherst tried to bring matters to a head by presenting a further petition. Still was he disappointed and then, as he later said, out of consideration for Britain's troubles in America, he ceased to press for action until the war was over. On the return of peace he started the official wheels revolving again. The result was an order-in-council of August 18, 1786. It stated that a full and "up-to-date" description was necessary to effect the grant, and it called for an inquiry to be held in the province. Now it was laid down that all was to be given except such parts as the governor might report necessary to reserve for public uses. This order-in-council, sent to Dorchester on February 7, 1787, was the communication referred to above.[35]

While Amherst was angling for their property, the Jesuits in Canada were allowed to drift along.[36] Their activities were curtailed and their numbers reduced by death, but they were permitted to retain control of most of their property. Their missionary work survived into the period of the Revolutionary War, though it would have been stopped earlier had the successive governors strictly obeyed orders from London. Their college in Quebec ceased to function in 1763, when the government refused permission to continue it. But the school, which was attached to the college, they somehow managed to maintain until 1776, when it was crowded out of existence by the intrusion of the archives of the province. In this year, also, troops were lodged in the greater part of the college building, and there they remained, "the fetid atmosphere" of the garrison offending the neighborhood. Another part of the structure was occupied by the court of common pleas on week days and by the congregation of the Church of Scotland on the Sabbath. Part of the buildings in Montreal became the common jail of the district, and an adjoining unfinished chapel was a magazine until the close of the Revolutionary War, when it was fitted up for the Church of England. The surviving priests retained the rest of the buildings in both towns and the whole of their lands — ten seigniories, with sixteen hundred inhabitants, bringing in eleven or twelve hundred pounds a year.[37] They were no longer able to apply their revenue to the ends for which the property had been given to their predecessors; they were using it for poor relief. This situation could not long continue, for in 1787 there were only four fathers left and they were well advanced in years.

On May 31, 1787, Dorchester submitted to his council the order he had received from London, and at the same meeting he appointed the chief justice and eight other councilors, four old subjects and four new,[38] to report on education in the colony.[39] In creating this committee the governor was only anticipating the popular outcry of English as well as French against the object of the investigation into the estates which was now launched. The French felt very strongly that the property really belonged to the colony, that the Jesuits had been trustees rather than owners, and that the endowment should be employed for the benefit of the people by the revival of the college under new trustees to be elected by the inhabitants. The English residents joined in this demand, hoping to see their children share the advantages to be derived from giving the Jesuit estates to education instead of to Amherst.

It was commonly admitted that the country was sadly deficient in educational facilities. In 1789 there were none outside the towns except a few small schools run by priests in the more populous rural parishes. The seminary in Quebec and that in Montreal, each with about one hundred non-theological students, were the only collegiate institutions. The former admitted English youths on the same terms as French, except that Protestants were excused from religious exercises. To enter, students had to be able to read French and Latin. Twelve was the average age of the lowest class and twenty-one the average of the highest. The Montreal institution was housed in the Hôtel de Vaudreuil, once the residence of the French governor general, which had been bought in 1774 by the churchwardens of the parish because the old building was too small. This seminary also conducted two schools, an upper and a lower, with a combined registration of about one hundred and fifty boys. Roman Catholic girls were taught in the religious houses of the three towns.

Quebec had six Protestant schools with ten teachers, two of whom received stipends from the government, and about two hundred pupils, mostly boys. Montreal had four such schools with five teachers, one of whom received public assistance, and about one hundred and thirty pupils, including perhaps a score of French. Lachine, L'Assomption, and Sorel each had a Protestant school, and there were two English schools in Three Rivers. These five had a total enrollment of about eighty-five.

The schools were supported by fees, which ranged up to two guineas a quarter for day pupils and to thirty pounds a year for boarders. The Montreal seminary schools made the lowest charge, five shillings a year, and collected it only from the few parents who could afford to pay. The salaries the government gave to Protestant teachers — the three mentioned in Quebec and Montreal and one down in Gaspé — together amounted to only two hundred pounds and covered a select number of pupils taught gratis. The best English school in Montreal was soon in such financial straits that a public subscription had to be raised to prevent its dissolution.[40]

It will be observed that the English were well served compared with the French. Broadly speaking, the old subjects were an educated people and were determined that their children should be, whereas the children of the new subjects were going to resemble their parents in lacking any formal schooling. The illiteracy of the French was the subject of frequent and disparaging comments on the part of the English. It was said that not more than half a dozen persons in a parish could read and write, and that the priests had kept the people ignorant in order to dominate them.

Bishop Hubert [41] denounced such statements as vile calumnies. He proudly asserted that at least two dozen in each parish could read and write, and that the clergy had always taken the greatest pains to secure for the people all the instruction of which they were capable. If his people were backward, neither they nor their church were in any way to blame. Climatic and pioneering conditions were responsible — and the government. The policy of filling public offices with old subjects, often strangers to the country, discouraged the Canadians from seeking an education.[42]

Though Smith deplored the educational defects of the colony, he did not call his committee together for two years and a half. There was no need for haste, and there were good reasons for delay. The inquiry into the Jesuit estates proceeded very slowly, perhaps with a purpose; and the chief justice wisely waited until the upheaval over his investigation into the courts had subsided, and until he had canvassed the whole situation carefully. His caution had its reward. On November 26, 1789, the committee held its first meeting and unanimously approved the rather elaborate plan the chairman had prepared. A month later it was submitted to the whole council, and on the advice of that body the governor ordered the report to be printed in both languages and circulated through the country by means of the magistrates and the parish clergy.[43]

The plan of the chief justice called for a system of free parish schools, one in every village, for the teaching of the three R's. Elementary instruction, he remarked, was necessary in all countries to lift the lower classes out of "a state of base barbarism." He also proposed a system of county or secondary schools. These too were to be free and their curriculum was to include such practical subjects as bookkeeping and surveying. Each school should be supported by a local assessment under the authority of a provincial enactment for that purpose. Nowhere would the burden be heavy except perhaps in the new settlements, and there the people would be encouraged by the fact that the governor had set aside a glebe of two hundred acres in each township for the support of a free school. Also, as soon as their wants were properly revealed, they could count on aid from some of the numerous charitable foundations and societies of the mother country.

To crown the whole, the author of the scheme wanted a university. This was what he had most at heart. That it might draw the two races together, its curriculum should exclude theology and its governing body should include the leading citizens of the colony irrespective of their religion. He would begin with the judges and the Roman Catholic bishop. The visitation should be vested in the king or his representative. There would be little difficulty in collecting able men to form the original staff. A rector and four professors would suffice in the early days. The institution could have a library and a building immediately — the public library founded by Haldimand, and the Jesuit college. The problem of an initial endowment was simple. The solution was suggested by the words of the imperial order-in-council which anticipated the governor's reserving from the grant to Amherst such portions of the Jesuit estates as might be needed for public purposes. From waste crown lands lying close to existing settlements, this endowment might receive a valuable addition. Private benefactions could also be expected. If properly started, the university would be "like a reservoir for watering the surrounding fields" — providing teachers for the schools — and Quebec would be the intellectual capital of British North America. Indeed, it might be more than this, for the opportunity "of acquiring one of the most universal languages of Europe" would draw students from an even wider circle. In making this suggestion, Smith probably had his eye on the lost colonies.

The project of a secular university caused considerable fluttering in the clerical dovecots. Bishop Hubert and others of his cloth were set on a revival of the defunct college, which of course would be controlled by the church, and they told the governor that the remaining Jesuits were willing to surrender their estates to provide the necessary revenue. Though Dorchester put them off, they proceeded with their scheme and had almost completed their arrangements for a clandestine transfer of the estates to a group of lay trustees before he heard what was afoot. He stopped it at once.[44]

Another effort to preserve the ecclesiastical control of higher education was made in 1790 by the members of the Seminary of St. Sulpice. Backed by a number of laymen, they petitioned for a charter to create a college in Montreal for the teaching of the humanities, mathematics, engineering, civil law, "and the other sciences judged most useful to the needs of the province." A certificate from its principal would suffice to admit its graduating students to degrees of the university should it be established. To win official sanction the petitioners proposed that the college should be under the inspection of the crown and should be called Dorchester College, and when the governor declined this honor they substituted the name of the Duke of Clarence. The governor referred the petition to the council, who decided that it should be submitted to the home government.[45]

The only Roman Catholic cleric who came out in favor of a nonsectarian university was the coadjutor, Bailly.[46] In the spring of 1790 he wrote the council a letter in which he heaped sarcasm upon the objections of Hubert,[47] with whom he was on very bad terms.

Among the French laity, however, the idea won more support. A Montreal lawyer named Simon Sanguinet, an adherent of the French party who had recently been elevated to the bench, died in this year leaving his seigniory of La Salle and other property, worth four or five hundred pounds a year, for the endowment of a university. Though challenged by his heirs, this bequest gave encouragement to others. Later in the year a goodly number of new subjects in Quebec joined with old subjects in petitioning for a university such as the chief justice had proposed, and they cited Sanguinet's will as an augury of success.[48]

The investigation into the extent and nature of the Jesuit properties was completed by November, 1790. In sending the results home, the governor turned over to the authorities in London the whole problem of education in the province. He advised the retention of the Jesuit buildings in Montreal to serve as the residence of the governor general of British North America. The communication with the United States over Lake Champlain and the immensity of the country lying to the west made this, he said, the best location. For the support of Protestant worship he would appropriate the Jesuits' churches and chapels in Quebec and Montreal and part of their land in Three Rivers. The rest of the land in the three towns, he advised, should be kept by the crown. The revenue from the Jesuit seigniories he would charge with the support of the surviving fathers, now reduced to three, and with the maintenance of missionaries among the Indians.

The governor also reported the general condemnation of the diversion of the estates from public uses and the desire of the most enlightened people in the country "to see all such parts as are not wanted by the government appropriated to the support of a university for teaching the liberal arts and sciences on a plan avoiding every occasion for religious disputes by the exclusion of all theological tuition." With this desire he concurred heartily. "It will be very material so to organize and endow this institution that the inferior schools pointed out by the committee, throughout the country of Upper as well as Lower Canada, may be subordinate to its government and in some measure dependent upon it for support, so that the whole system may be animated by one common principle under the eye and control of the crown." A royal charter, as the chief justice had observed, was necessary and, the governor added, parliamentary action might be needed to establish the whole unified educational system.[49]

Lord Amherst, Chief Justice Smith, Bishop Hubert, the Montreal seminarists, and all who backed any of these, were building castles in Spain. On March 7, 1791, the secretary of state wrote the governor that the disposal of the property and the founding of the university could not be considered until the Constitutional Act was passed.[50] Then the only outcome of all this discussion in Canada was the failure of Amherst to get what his sovereign had long promised him. Some may lament the fact that the plans of the chief justice were pigeonholed in London, and they may assert that a grand opportunity was neglected, an opportunity to educate the people and at the same time to draw the two races and religions together. But others, remembering what happened to the similar plan of a few years later, known as the Royal Institution, may argue that differences of creed and tongue would have wrecked the schemes of the New York dreamer.

§

Another step that the sanguine chief justice thought French Canada might take along the path of progress was the conversion of seigniorial tenure. Though Mabane and his circle fought to preserve the feudal system over the whole extent of the colony, it became apparent soon after Dorchester took the reins of government from Hope that the freehold system was destined to prevail in the new settlements. It then occurred to one of the Canadian councilors, Charles de Launaudière, that he might profit by the conversion of his own property, and in January, 1788, he petitioned to have his lands regranted to him in freehold tenure. His petition was submitted to the council,[51] where the matter slept for a while.

In the following year, when the first draft of the Constitutional Act was prepared in London, a clause was inserted to permit anyone holding lands *en fief et seigneurie* to surrender the same and receive them back in free and common socage.[52] Dorchester, who had begun by pressing the necessity for this tenure in the upper country, had already come round to the view that the introduction of the same system would be advisable in the older parts of the colony. He therefore welcomed the idea. But in a letter of February 8, 1790, he pointed out that the clause would operate unfairly because it would relieve the seigniors of feudal obligations without passing on the benefit to their tenants. Smith corrected the fault by adding a passage to extinguish all feudal obligations within every tract surrendered for regrant.[53] It was then the secretary of state's turn to accept the principle and to criticize its working.

On June 5 he replied that the seigniors would suffer if, as he correctly surmised, they would lose from their tenants more than they would gain from the crown. Therefore some arrangements for compensation would have to be made.[54] In answer to this suggestion, the governor wrote home on September 25 saying that he saw no practical method for an immediate and universal change, but that the amended clause would work by throwing on the seignior the onus of coming to some agreement with his tenants. If, he added, the crown set an example in the seigniory of Sorel and the Jesuit estates, the process in the other seigniories might be speeded up.[55] Meanwhile other developments had taken place which made the problem appear more urgent and which suggested that the solution should be worked out in Canada rather than in London.

These developments were on the international border. In the summer of 1788 Hugh Finlay smelt a danger from the south, and he wrote to Evan Nepean about it. Families from Vermont were reported to be clearing land and building huts on the Canadian side of the forty-fifth parallel. These American squatters would attract others from across the line and there would soon be trouble unless that empty Canadian region were promptly and solidly settled by good people. Finlay had no doubts about how it should be done. He was positive that from twenty to thirty thousand real Britishers still in the United States would be attracted immediately if they could get freehold grants. "The tenure in free and common socage encourages population; the feudal system checks commerce and damps industry." That was his explanation of the fact that New England, though younger, had four or five times the population of Canada.[56]

The irregular encroachment that Finlay feared in 1788 became so serious by 1790 that a council committee composed of new and old subjects unanimously urged his solution — rapid settlement by freehold grants. The immensity of the problem, as well as its urgency, was brought out in the committee's report. It stated that, according to the surveyor general's office, there were nearly eleven million acres of improvable land in Canada south of the St. Lawrence capable of supporting a population of over six hundred thousand. On August 25, 1790, when this report was presented, the governor appointed the whole council to be a committee to investigate the comparative advantages of the two kinds of tenure, and, if it should appear advisable to adopt the English system in place of the French, to report how the transformation might be effected, and to draft any necessary legislation.[57] Apparently there was considerable alarm in the air.

As might be expected, the chief justice dictated almost the whole of the findings and recommendations, which were submitted on October 20. The only advantage the report found in the feudal system was that it had produced a small revenue. The receiver general's accounts showed that from May 1, 1775, until May 1, 1788, the crown had received a little over three thousand pounds in mutation fines from seigniors and about twice that amount from tenants *en roture.*

The disadvantages of the system were summed up in one result — the slow progress of population and settlement, "the cultivated parts, even in the central districts of Quebec, Three Rivers and Montreal, being to this day confined to the banks of the St. Lawrence and the mouths of the navigable streams that fall into it." "The grant of the waste lands of the crown in free and common socage is essential to the growth, strength, defence and safety of the province." If the system were continued in the old French seigniories, largely uninhabited, "their land market must be at a stand, to the detriment of the proprietors, until the cultivation of the waste lands of the crown is damped by their remoteness from all water carriage and the conveniences and benefits of commerce." But if the seigniors abandoned the feudal system, their estates, being more favorably located, would be the first to fill up. They would benefit materially. So would the tenants *en roture,* who ought to be placed in as favorable a position as those who would be seated on the waste lands of the crown.

The prerogative was competent to establish the English system over all the lands still in the possession of the crown, but legislation was necessary to make that system universal. At this point Smith hesitated, for he saw the folly of attempting to give a great and sudden jolt to an old society. "An absolute and universal commutation of the ancient tenures, though for a better, would be a measure of doubtful policy." The only compulsion that should be applied was that which would operate automatically — self-interest. He concluded by submitting a draft ordinance that followed almost word for word his revised version of the clause in the bill which the governor had sent back to England. It also provided for the immediate conversion of all lands held *en roture* of the crown, and a provision that the whole should not come into force until it had received the royal assent.[58]

True to form, Mabane entered a protest on the minutes. He denied that the feudal system had cramped the growth of population and settlement. Indian and English wars and the lure of the interior had done it during the French régime. Under British rule there had been a "rapid and almost unexampled progress of population." He was right in saying that the Canadians had doubled in numbers since the conquest, but he was wrong in implying that this rate of increase was appreciably greater than that of the preceding generations. Also he shut his eyes to the argument about immigration because he did not want to see any immigration. He admitted that the public revenue derived from the system had been small, but he urged that it should not be thrown away. It would increase greatly with the expansion of settlement.

Mabane's crowning argument was that the abolition of feudalism would destroy a fine principle. As the law stood, seigniors could be forced to concede their lands at the customary rates. If it were changed, "the children of the present inhabitants of the country and all others desirous to settle thereon would be left entirely subject to the arbitrary exactions of the seigneurs." He conveniently ignored the fact that the part of the law to which he referred had become a dead letter, and he blindly ignored the effect of the competition of cheap crown lands.[59] His real appeal was to prejudice. He feared the steam roller which the chief justice would drive over Canada.

Because the council was not in session as a legislative body, the chief justice's reform had to wait. The whole report, including the draft ordinance and Mabane's dissent, was printed in both languages for circulation among the members of the council. Then differences sprang up. Though Smith had carried the majority of the council with him, he could not convert the public. His proposed measure stirred up such a tempest out of doors that on March 22,

1791, just a week after Dorchester had opened the last legislative session of the old province of Quebec, the council unanimously abandoned the bill for the conversion of tenures.[60] Meanwhile the government in London had washed its hands of the business the government in Quebec had undertaken. The provision for the conversion of tenures in Lower Canada had been dropped from the bill which became the Constitutional Act.* Two generations were to pass before the reform was finally enacted.

§

Another matter of serious concern in these years was the unsatisfactory state of the provincial government's finances. They were in an almost hopeless jumble. One thing that was wrong was the notorious laxity with which the casual and territorial revenues were collected.[61] Indeed they were rather received than collected. There was no effective check upon casual payments made to various officials. For example, officers of the several courts collected fines but were not held to a strict account for their receipts. Of the payments due to the crown as landlord, the only part which was regularly remitted was the rent of the King's Posts, which brought in a few hundred pounds a year.

The trouble with the rest was partly a heritage of the decade before the Quebec Act, when it was uncertain whether the mutation fines, the *quint* from seigniors and the *lods et ventes* from holders of town lots on the royal domain in Quebec and Three Rivers, were legally payable. During those years the receiver general's office made no effort to collect; it merely accepted the few fines offered by those whose conscience or caution inspired them to pay. When the Quebec Act settled the legal question, the American Revolution raised a practical question. Was it politic to insist?

There were objections both within and without the council chamber. Public resistance began to manifest itself when William Grant, the deputy receiver general, moved Carleton to take an initial step toward collection by appointing F. J. Cugnet clerk of the terrar of the royal domain and by issuing a proclamation.[62] The proclamation, dated August 28, 1777, summoned all who held land of the crown to appear at Quebec before December 1, 1778. Seigniors were to perform fealty and homage and to surrender

* But it provided that future grants in Lower Canada might be made in freehold tenure.

their title deeds and rent rolls in exchange for authenticated copies. Tenants *en roture* were merely to exhibit their titles and to declare the rents and duties which they owed for their lands. The time was twice extended by further proclamations before seigniorial obedience was even partly secured in 1780. Then Haldimand granted a year's credit, and even at the end of the time he did not insist upon payment. The *censitaires,* apparently, remained obdurate. Meanwhile, within the council, the deputy receiver general tried to secure legislation compelling notaries to inform his office of every transfer of real property. But the selfish interest of some of his fellow councilors and the lack of interest on the part of the governor defeated the attempt. Therefore the old situation continued. There were small receipts but no collections.

After the war the effort to enforce payment was renewed, with equally disappointing results. On being commissioned acting receiver general in 1784, Henry Caldwell began to investigate. He consulted F. J. Cugnet, the local pundit of the ancient laws,* he wrote the treasury, he sought the advice of Lieutenant Governor Hamilton, and in 1785 he acted. In April he secured the legislative aid which Grant had wanted, and in the summer he put an advertisement in the *Quebec Gazette* warning all who owed *quints* or *lods et ventes* to pay within a given time or they might be sued. Though disappointed by the result, Caldwell was encouraged by the treasury to persist. His next step was to procure a plan of the town of Quebec showing the part from which *lods et ventes* were due, and with this to guide him he sent to the recalcitrant individuals a summons to pay. At first a few complied but soon he heard that the resisters were holding meetings and making subscriptions to defend themselves at law. To break this movement he sued some of its leaders. When they found that judgment was likely to go against them, a petition to the king for remission of all mutation fines was presented to Lieutenant Governor Hope.

This document, dated February 18, 1786, set forth a strong case. For over a quarter of a century property had been bought and sold in confidence that no fines would be demanded. Many lots had changed hands so often that the arrears exceeded the market price, and present holders could not recover from their predecessors who

---

* He held the official position of *avocat consultant aux lois françaises* in addition to the posts of official translator and French clerk of the council.

were dead or bankrupt or gone from the colony. An insistence upon collection would start endless lawsuits between individuals, would ruin many families, and would cause more distress than the siege by the Americans, when many of the houses against which alienation fines were charged had been demolished or considerably damaged.

Moved by this appeal, Hope directed Caldwell to defer execution on the judgments he had secured and to commence no new actions until further orders.[63] The lieutenant governor expected a delay of only a few months before the home government would return some final answer to the petition, but the months became years and Hope's order was not revoked. As before, the receiver general's office had to be content with accepting what was offered, which, on account of the recent circumstances, now meant almost nothing.[64]

The arrival of Dorchester and Smith made no change because the members of the council, though contemplating a renewal of action, could not agree upon a method. The chief justice maintained that neither the common pleas nor the king's bench was competent to collect any part of the revenue and that a court of exchequer should be erected, while Mabane insisted that his court had full power to enforce payment of what was due to the king. The dispute simmered till March, 1789, when Mabane's contention was defeated in a committee of the whole council by the casting vote of the chairman, and by the same narrow margin Smith's demand for legislation to create a new court was put off until the home government had considered the question.[65] Then the movement in favor of commuting seigniorial into freehold tenure suggested an easy solution for the troublesome problem of feudal arrears.

Most of the revenue gathered in the province was derived from the Quebec Revenue Act — customs duties and taxes on public houses. The provincial secretary issued the licenses to public houses in return for the statutory payments, which totaled £800 or £900 a year. He turned the whole amount over to the receiver general. This branch of the revenue occasioned no criticism. But there were many complaints about the methods of the collector of customs. He turned over only a portion of his receipts, which averaged nearly £6,000 annually, though more than once the governor and council pressed him to make full payment. The story of his recalcitrance, if such it may be called, is a good illustration of the loose management of public finances in the eighteenth century.

Thomas Ainslie was collector of customs throughout the whole existence of the old province of Quebec, and during most of this period he pocketed a double emolument because he really held a dual position. In the beginning Murray appointed him to collect the duties continued from the old régime to support the new government, allowing him to retain a certain percentage for his trouble. This arrangement was confirmed by the treasury. In addition to being a provincial officer, Ainslie became an imperial officer when Canada definitely became part of the British Empire and came under the imperial laws governing colonial trade. For his administration of these laws, he was given a salary of £100 and the right to collect fees worth £130 or £140 a year.[66] His collections were small, for the imperial customs system, of which he was the local agent, was designed to regulate trade rather than to raise a revenue. Indeed, the revenue was less than the cost of collecting it. As an imperial officer, Ainslie had no connection with the provincial government. He was responsible to the customs board and his accounts were audited by a local comptroller who was under the same board.

The duality of Ainslie's position lapsed when the merchants successfully refused to pay the old French duties; but it was revived after a fashion by the Quebec Revenue Act, which required him to collect the new duties and turn them over to the receiver general to defray the expenses of the provincial government. For this extra work and responsibility no emolument was provided. The statute merely stated that he could hold back the cost of collection. Before this act came into force on April 5, 1775, Ainslie went to Boston, the seat of the customs board, and there sought directions for the performance of his new task.

The board declined the responsibility as beyond its jurisdiction, and when he returned to Quebec he applied to the governor, who likewise refused to interfere.[67] The problem which the collector was thus left to face by himself was no simple one. As he still had no warehouse in which to store dutiable goods, and as the importers were unable to pay full duties the moment their goods were discharged from the vessels, he had to let them take their goods in return for their notes of hand. For any loss on these notes he was personally responsible. He was put to greater expense because he had to enlarge his staff, for which no extra provision had been made. A further complication arose from an old law which permitted the payment of customs in silver at 5 shillings and 6 pence an ounce, which was somewhat more than it was actually worth.

Ainslie's solution was to charge 5 per cent for collection, on the precedent established in Murray's day, and an additional sum for incidental expenses, under the authority of the Quebec Revenue Act. Also, whenever possible, he collected in gold or bills of exchange and paid the receiver general by the silver rating. These three deductions totaled about 9 per cent of his receipts. Every quarter he delivered the net proceeds to the receiver general's office and sent his accounts home to the treasury, whence he secured a general approval. His accounts of the moneys which he received under the Quebec Revenue Act were not audited at all. He repeatedly refused the comptroller access to them on the ground that they were not under the jurisdiction of the customs board. When the governor and council tried to impose a check upon him, he denied their authority, claiming that the moneys belonged to the treasury, to which alone he was accountable, until he turned them over to the receiver general.[68]

Still worse is the story of the receiver general's office. There was a bewildering succession of officials and an exasperating confusion of accounts. On the establishment of civil government in August, 1764, there was no receiver general. A month later the governor appointed his relative, Walter Murray, who turned the duties over to his son Richard as deputy. Richard Murray acted until July, 1766, when, as will be recalled, Thomas Mills, formerly town major of Quebec, returned with a royal commission as receiver general dated a year previously. Mills remained only until August, 1767. Then, as he asserted, he went home to present the unsatisfactory state of the revenue. Probably he had other reasons, for he did not reappear for twenty years. On Mills' departure, his patent not permitting of a deputy, Carleton named Cramahé acting receiver general. At the end of July, 1770, Thomas Dunn, judge and merchant, took over the office which Cramahé had to vacate on assuming the direction of the government during Carleton's absence. Dunn served for seven years, at the end of which he was obliged to make way for his fellow merchant, William Grant, as deputy receiver general, the latter having been appointed by Mills, now Sir Thomas, who had received a new commission in February, 1777, with power to select a deputy. Grant also served for seven years, until, in July, 1784, difficulties to be explained presently forced him to procure the governor's leave of absence that he might submit his accounts in London. As Grant had no legal authority to appoint a deputy, Haldimand made Henry Caldwell acting receiver general. On September 1, 1787, another member of the council, George Davison, took over the office as Mills' new deputy, and two months later Sir Thomas returned to perform his duties in person. It was not long before unpleasant rumors began to circulate, and then, smelling something wrong, the governor and council discovered that the provincial finances resembled an Augean stable. On August 25, 1789, Dorchester suspended Mills and ordered all incoming public moneys to be delivered to the military paymaster's office.

The trouble sprang from two causes. One was the system of handling public funds. Indeed, it is scarcely true to say that there was a system. In Canada the governor and council had a limited authority in financial matters. They had to pass the contingent accounts of the civil government, and every half year the claims which had been submitted were passed under review. Some were rejected, some were referred to the treasury, and some were allowed. There was no fixed rule for decisions.

Nor was there any close scrutiny until the winter of 1787–88, when Smith, as chairman of the council committee on accounts, with Dorchester's backing began to clean things up.[69] Claims had been granted year after year without proof that the services they represented had actually been performed, that the charges were reasonable, and that they should be paid by the government. Politics seem to have entered into some of the council's decisions on the accounts. The opposition that Monk's claims encountered, as mentioned in a previous chapter, was due to more than their imposing size and the doubtful legality of some of them. He had little chance of fair treatment as long as Mabane's reactionary party was in control. Years before the attorney general was dismissed he undoubtedly suffered in pocket for the political principles he supported.

Another example was that of Dr. Bowman. From about the time of the conquest a certain disease known as the Malbaye or Murray Bay disorder, because it had first been noticed there, had been present in the colony without spreading very much until, under Hamilton's government, it suddenly became a flaming epidemic. Many suspected it to be syphilis, and, judging from the reported symptoms and the treatment that cured it, it probably was that disease, spread extragenitally in the epidemic form it may assume. Faced with this crisis, the lieutenant governor commissioned Dr. Bowman to fight the plague, and the doctor seems to have conquered it. The epidemic did not spread above Lachine, where everyone bound for the west was examined to see that he did not carry the contagion, but from there downward Bowman traveled all over the country from the spring to the end of the summer of 1785, treating some five or six thousand patients.

When the council reviewed his bill, which was considerable because his expenses had been heavy and the mercury medicines he had dispensed in great quantity were costly, there was strong opposition to its payment. The lieutenant governor, who had given the orders that led to this claim, was gone, departed under a cloud, and Bowman was his protégé. Mabane's political animus may also have had a tinge of professional jealousy. The business was not settled when Dorchester arrived, and some months later, Bowman having died, the doctor's father crossed from Ireland to collect the debt.[70]

The receiver general's accounts were never audited in Canada. The only comptroller in the colony was the man who was appointed to check Ainslie's lesser accounts. But the governor and council made a semiannual review of the funds that were supposed to be in the receiver general's office, for the governor issued all warrants on that office and therefore had to know what was there, and they did it with the cooperation of the tenant of the office. This practice led to a deadlock between the provincial government and the office in 1784.

In the previous year the deputy receiver general, William Grant, had begun making deductions that had not been noticed before. Following the example of the collector of customs, he charged the public funds with a sum for his own contingent expenses and with a percentage on all his receipts, 5 per cent on moneys collected in the colony and turned over to him and 2½ per cent on bills on the treasury. The 5 per cent he said was the customary charge of accountants, receivers, and deputy receivers general in the colonies as a recompense for the risk and trouble involved, and he cited the accounts of the receivers and deputy receivers general of Virginia and Barbadoes recorded as a model in Quebec back in 1764. The 2½ per cent he explained as compensation for his trouble in indorsing and selling the bills and as a necessary protection against loss to himself because, like Cochrane, he could not get par value without selling on credit.

It will be observed that the proceeds of the customs duties imposed by the Quebec Revenue Act were thus subject to two stoppages, the first by the collector of customs and the second by the deputy receiver general. This probably added to Haldimand's irritation when the council committee drew his attention to the novelties in Grant's report. The governor objected strenuously but the deputy receiver general asserted his independence of local control. Haldimand then referred the dispute to the treasury, whence he received a reply stating that the three charges could not be allowed. Still was Grant obdurate. He had received no direct orders to this effect and he insisted that he was accountable for everything, including the deductions, only to the treasury and to the audit board in London. He had never been called before the council committee of accounts nor had its reports ever been submitted to him. They were wrong in their statement of the balance on hand.

The deadlock was terminated by the governor's application of a whip which he held in his hand. He informed the deputy receiver general that he would let him have no more bills on the treasury. These would be negotiated through others. Without yielding his point, Grant demanded leave of absence to settle his accounts in England. Haldimand gave it. Grant also wanted to turn over the office to his nephew, but the governor would not allow the deputy to name a deputy, and appointed Caldwell acting receiver general.[71]

In the England of those days, the accounts of the government were in shocking disorder. Public funds were allowed to repose in private possession over long periods. There was a rule that accounts should be audited every seven years, but neither the rule nor the auditing was very strict. When this was true of the large accounts of the various branches of the home government, it is not surprising that the supervision of the much smaller accounts of colonial governments was very loose. On his arrival in Quebec in the fall of 1787,

Mills' last settlement was nine years old, and his quietus of October, 1778, covered only a part of the moneys that had passed through his hands or through the hands of those who had acted for him. Dunn had spent the previous winter in London, missing all the excitement of the famous 1787 legislative session, trying to clear his books, for he had maintained that he acted as a principal and was therefore not answerable to Mills. Both had taken over different parts of Cramahé's accounts. These illustrations may suffice to indicate what had happened as a consequence of the laxity that reigned in London. There was a grand tangle of unsettled accounts and it was almost impossible to tell what were the balances of the successive tenants of the office in Quebec.

Mills had contributed not a little by his neglect, and he was soon to bring things to a miserable climax. His commission of 1777 is curious. Although it had been the home government's policy to terminate sinecure offices attached to the provincial government and to require officials to perform their duties in person after the passage of the Quebec Act, Mills had managed to swim against the tide, securing what he had not possessed before — the right to appoint a deputy. The explanation offered by Grant, in justification of his own financial deductions, was as follows. "Sir Thomas Mills was employed at home and abroad in business and negotiations of state, and as a reward for his services had His Majesty's grant or royal letters patent of the nominal office of receiver general of Quebec with an allowance or salary to himself only of £500 *per annum.*" [72]

We catch glimpses of the absentee moving in fashionable and literary society, and for a while he was away in the Far East. When Caldwell took over the office, of course on the understanding that he could not make the charges that had tripped up Grant, he hoped that he would not have to serve for nothing. Haldimand presented his case to the treasury, whose secretary replied in December, 1784, that "their lordships will lose no time in coming to some determination respecting the office of receiver general in Quebec." In July, 1785, the secretary of the treasury wrote that the man who was acting "in the room of Sir Thomas Mills the patentee now in India" should receive half the salary of the office and that their lordships would consider recommending the revocation of the patent to Mills, "he having been resident for a considerable time in the East Indies." [73] He ought to have died there.

When the receiver general returned from the Orient and crossed the Atlantic to perform his own duties, he was financially embarrassed. This was no new experience for him. Back in the spring of 1779, a few months after some of his accounts had been formally passed, he had written Haldimand a patronizing letter in which he urged him to command Cramahé, who had relinquished the office nine years previously, to send him some money immediately.[74] In 1787 his financial health was apparently much worse. Indeed, it was near the breaking point.

On arriving in Quebec Mills made a great show of applying himself to business, and while he worked with feverish activity the council committee under Smith was laboring to bring order out of chaos. The climax came in the summer of 1789. The receiver general refused to honor several of the governor's warrants upon him, alleging that he had no funds to meet them, though it was formally reported in council that he had a large balance on hand. When asked for an explanation he grew insolent. He asserted that the provincial exchequer was empty but that he would meet all demands when he could collect from the various deputy and acting receivers general. Meanwhile it was whispered about that he was using public moneys to pay private debts. One source of the rumor was at last uncovered when a Quebec merchant named Lees was brought before the council and there, under oath, admitted that he had received from London a private bond of Sir Thomas Mills for £1,135 on which the interest was two years in arrear, that he had applied to Mills to redeem the bond, and that he had secured payment by Mills giving him a draft on Ainslie.[75] Then Dorchester suspended Mills.

Still the receiver general hoped to justify himself. He insisted that he was accountable only to the treasury, and after several weeks of anxious toil he produced, with the aid of what might be called the higher mathematics of finance, a startling account. By charging the government with the portion of his salary which had gone to Caldwell, with a similar salary to Grant, with incidental expenses and the challenged percentages on receipts, and with public payments which had not been properly credited, he showed that the government owed him over £12,000. According to the computations of the council, quite the reverse was true: he owed the govern-

ment a slightly larger amount.[76] Therefore there was a difference
of nearly £25,000.

Both calculations were wrong, if we may trust the official figures
later compiled in London. On November 27, 1793, nine months
after Mills died insolvent, the audit office reported that his books
showed a deficit of £18,500, of which nearly £6,000 could not be
recovered, having been accumulated prior to March 31, 1777, the
date of the bond signed by Grant and deposited by Mills at the
exchequer.[77]

In addition to all this looseness, there was something fundamentally wrong with the provincial government's finances. It was
summed up by Dorchester in a short speech to the council in
March, 1789. The provincial revenue was hopelessly inadequate.
The previous year's expenses amounted to £26,553, of which only
£7,664 were paid from provincial funds. The remaining £18,888
had to come out of the British exchequer.[78] In other words, the
taxpayer in Britain was supporting the chief burden of the Canadian government. This, as will appear in the following chapter,
was perhaps the main reason for the passage of the Constitutional
Act.*

* During the ten years Grant and Caldwell performed the duties of receiver
general, the total amount of the bills drawn on the treasury to meet the needs of
the civil government was over £180,000.[79]

CHAPTER XIX

THE END OF THE OLD PROVINCE OF QUEBEC

DORCHESTER fumbled with the constitutional problem. It was to him a Gordian knot which he had neither the ability to undo nor the courage to cut, and Smith was no great help to him, for he too was baffled by the complicated situation in the colony. Only one change could the governor recommend with assurance. That was the substitution of freehold for feudal tenure in the new districts. Yet he was not satisfied to leave other things as they were. He appreciated the strength of the demand for an assembly and admitted that it would grow, but he could not bring himself to support it. He knew that the Canadians were unprepared for representative government and he feared democracy. As of old he was convinced that this American spirit should not be let loose. Therefore he suggested that one-sixth of every township should be set aside to give the crown the means of rewarding faithful servants and of creating and strengthening an aristocracy. He was afraid to touch the thorny question of the administration of justice; and he was never reconciled to the idea of cutting the province in two. On June 13, 1787, when transmitting the voluminous and conflicting results of the council's investigations, he wrote the secretary of state, "I confess myself as yet at a loss for any plan likely to give satisfaction." [1]

Sydney acknowledged this dispatch on September 20, remarking that the government had no immediate thought of altering the Quebec Act. The establishment of an assembly was not being considered; it would be open to "very great objection." On the matter of jurisprudence, he declared that if the Canadians disliked English commercial laws and clung to their custom of Paris, their will should prevail. He had little sympathy for the racial minority, whose recent behavior he castigated. Though he did not say it, he implied that the cabinet was still contemplating a division of the province. He interpreted its disturbed state as suggesting the separation of its two parts, each with a lieutenant governor, and he gently reproached the governor for having said nothing about it. He also regretted Dorchester's silence on any other possible way of adjusting the difficulties in the colony.[2]

This letter brought little positive reaction from the governor, and that not for some time. In July, 1788, he suggested, possibly on Smith's advice, that the administration of justice might be improved by the creation of one supreme court of common pleas for the whole province, the court to go on circuit periodically.[3] Some weeks later he refuted Sydney's argument from the disturbed state of the province, saying that the animosities that had grown up, being largely confined to Quebec and Montreal, would not be cured by cutting the colony in two. At the same time he admitted that the division might have some good consequences and might even become necessary. The conclusion of this dispatch is striking. He, the man who was to guide the home government but could give no real guidance, said that "an early decision of the business of Canada at home is much to be wished, as the present suspense keeps up some agitation in the minds of people here." [4]

Obviously there was little hope of finding any solution so long as the tory Sydney was allowed to wait on the perplexed Dorchester. Not until he had received a push from parliament did the secretary of state press the governor again.

In the spring of 1786 the opposition in Westminster had urged the immediate amendment of the Quebec Act, only to be voted down after encountering the argument that a thorough study was to be made on the spot by the new governor. For nearly two years this plea sufficed to hold off the London champions of English freedom in the colony.[5] Then the attack was resumed as a consequence of Smith's judicial housecleaning. Adam Lymburner, the leading Quebec merchant mentioned in an earlier chapter, crossed the ocean to plead at the bar of the house of commons in the spring of 1788, and the opposition strongly supported him. Again the government successfully parried the thrust, excusing their inaction on the ground that much fuller information was expected from Dorchester. But they accepted a resolution binding the house to consider the matter early in the next session.[6]

The summer of 1788 passed without any further light coming from across the water, and it began to look as if the government might have to face the coming session with the awkward confession that their hopes of fuller information had been unfounded. This prospect roused the secretary of state to write the governor an urgent dispatch on September 3. He sent it by a special packet boat which was to bear back the reply at once before the navigation season closed. No tory prejudice colors this document. Possibly the government had come to feel the force of the arguments for reform. Dorchester was to give a full and impartial account of the different classes of people who desired a change of government and of those who opposed it, with the arguments on both sides. He was specifically asked to report on the government's proposal to divide the province by a line running along the western boundary of the seigniory of Longueuil, and whether an assembly should not be given to the new settlements right away. That they should have English laws was taken for granted, but the predilections of the Canadian population around Detroit were not to be neglected.[7]

The governor's reply, dated November 8, 1788, was drafted by the chief justice.[8] It added little to the information already gathered at home, except a cursory analysis of the population. The proportion of French to English-speaking people was forty to one in the old parts of the province outside the towns, fifteen to one if the towns were included, and five to one in the whole province. As the total population was then about 130,000,[9] those who spoke English as their native tongue must have numbered a little over 21,000, a third of them living below the mouth of the Ottawa. In the huge extent of the colony Dorchester found a new argument against an assembly. He objected to the proposed division on the ground that the western settlements were "as yet unprepared for any organization superior to that of a county," which they already had in fact though not in name. He was anxious, however, to see a lieutenant governor appointed for the four new western districts,[10] and he was quite willing to let them have an assembly and English laws, with protection for the Canadians at Detroit, should the government reject his advice on the matter of division. He saw no immediate call for any new regulations other than "such as are involved in the subject of the general jurisprudence of the country." [11]

In making this last remark Dorchester was following Smith, who, on the very day he prepared the draft of this dispatch, told him that "a reform of the law and practice of the province " was generally expected as the consequence of the investigation.[12] In singling out this as the most urgent need of the country, the chief justice was not misleading the governor, who leaned on him. He was simply putting first things first. Here was ample reason for their fighting shy of the division of the province and the adoption of representative government. If either or both of these changes were to come without a reform of the laws and their administration being first assured, this reform might never come at all.

In the fall of 1788, lured by the prospect of some final action during the ensuing parliamentary session, Adam Lymburner again set sail for England to inspire the campaign for liberty. His departure was the signal for a renewal of the war of petitions. Both parties memorialized the governor, each trying to prove with many figures and few scruples that the other was neither honest nor representative of the substantial elements of the country. Their effusions were published in the staid and semi-official *Quebec Gazette* and in the more newsy *Herald,* which sprang into existence at this time. This paper, struggling to survive without a government subsidy, sought to increase its circulation by inviting local controversialists to contribute to its columns, and not a few availed themselves of this opportunity. The correspondents expressed themselves with little reserve, because, according to the custom of the day, they concealed their identity, using all manner of pseudonyms from "Junius" to "X Y Z." One enraged reformer declared that the reactionaries were not to be believed, for they would talk "till their tongues were blistered with lies." [13] Another, referring to the vacancy created by the death of Hope in April, 1789, warned the British prime minister to be careful how he filled it. "Of all God's creation," he said, "do not send a military man, but send a law character" [14] — presumably another Smith.

A number of these letters air a grievance that has not yet been mentioned but that should not be ignored, for it was most exasperating. Creditors commonly attached debtors' property only to find that they had grasped a hollow shell. The value of the property had been eaten up by prior and secret obligations, by mortgages, and also by marriage contracts in which the groom transferred to his bride sums he did not possess. The papers of the notaries, who drew and kept such documents, were not open to public inspection. The Roman Catholic church was said to be a particularly bad offender. It was accused of refusing to admit to the priesthood any candidate without a title to real estate proving that he was worth three hundred pounds, thereby coercing tradesmen to give their sons mortgages in order to have them received into orders. As a consequence, it was alleged, priests formed a class of privileged creditors who stepped in to prevent English-speaking merchants collecting from their Canadian debtors. About sixty thousand pounds worth of British property was supposed to be secured to the clergy in this way.[15]

The ugly face of the racial question also peeps through the pages of the *Herald* in 1789. The most outspoken statement, copied from the *London Evening Post,* was by Isaac Ogden, a young Quebec lawyer who was in England at the time. He had come from New England as a loyalist, was politically attached to Smith, had been associated with Monk as legal adviser of the merchants, and, like Monk, was later to mount the bench of Lower Canada. It might have been good policy, he said, for the French government to keep the people of the colony in a "wretched state of ignorance, but it is a question whether it is good policy under the present government. The Canadians are to be considered as attached to their former government. Facts during the late war clearly support this assertion. Nothing will have greater tendency to anglify them than illuminating their understandings, when they will discern the advantages resulting from the mildness of a British government. To effect this, free public schools ought to be established in different parts of the province to teach the inhabitants the English language. The laws of England ought to be introduced; and to make it the interest of the inhabitants to learn the English language, all the proceedings of the courts of law ought to be in English. And every measure should be taken to root out the predilection which they still retain for their former king and government. Great Britain can have but two objects for retaining the province. . . ." One of course was commerce. "The other is founded on policy, from the situation of the province, for whenever it is well settled by inhabitants firmly attached to His Majesty, Great Britain must always hold a rod over the head of the American States and keep them in awe." [16]

Contrary to expectation, the parliamentary session that began in December, 1788, did nothing for Canada. The king had temporarily lost his sanity and Fox his liberalism, with the result that there

This interlude has
Canadian constitu-
session lasted for
have been Sydney,
ed responsibility by
m the prime minis-
ian question again
of ignorance, suc-

In July, Pitt per-
the speaker's chair
e new secretary of
lively sense of his
k. Perhaps the fact
his predecessor had
wever this may be,
government could
ecision, and imme-
l, he plunged into
all the information
ng rapidity. Before
um on what should
his colleagues and
The resulting docu-
ct.

ncial reasons alone
y. The proceeds of
te, and parliament,
elf of the power to
er the British ex-
r the chief burden
y considerable and
of the colony, or a
la. As the former
ative. The problem
d and a nominated
because no one had
it they would un-

The conclusion
duced made a divi
for the whole woul
and difficult to wor
to do was to take a
speaking population
practically all the
give each a legislat
petitions for an asse
be glad to have on
from the Canadian
an assault upon the
they too had an ass
then they would po
work a hardship u
make the necessary
government was la
ready working on t
seigniors' opposition
tion. They were s
numbers were sma
ance of the Canadi
assembly properly,
giving the people a
this defect.

In concluding th
question leaps to the
of gradually assimil
province on the wes
province in the east.
did, he was soon m
weeks later he obser
new districts from t
time for the remova

Having postulate
ernment, Grenville
adjustments were ne
the American Revo
ministration could

was a memorable conflict over the regency bil
been used to explain the delay in revising th
tion, but the king recovered in March and
another five months. The real obstacle seems
who apparently had prepared nothing. He esc
resigning early in June, 1789, having differed f
ter over slavery. Three weeks later the Can
came up and the government, repeating the p
cessfully begged for still another year's grace.[1]

The day of procrastination was now ove
suaded his cousin, William Grenville, to resig
and to accept the office vacated by Sydney.
state, then only twenty-nine years old, had
responsibility and an enormous appetite for w
that he was in the house of commons wherea
been in the lords made a further difference.
the new incumbent was quick to see that t
hardly face another session without some fina
diately parliament was prorogued on August
the Canadian question. He greedily devoure
he could gather and he digested it with ama
the end of the month he produced a memora
be done and why. This he circulated amor
revised in accordance with their suggestions.[1]
ment was the foundation of the Constitutiona

Grenville's analysis was trenchant. For f
there was no practical alternative to an assem
the Quebec Revenue Act were utterly inadec
by the Declaratory Act of 1778, had deprived
raise any further revenue in the colony.
chequer must continue, as it had done, to
of the provincial government, a burden alre
bound to pile up with the rapid developme
taxing authority must be established in Ca
solution was unreasonable, the latter was imp
was thus reduced to a choice between an ele
taxing body. The Canadians had not seen th
put it before them, but the moment they s
doubtedly prefer an assembly.

at representative government must be intro-
n of the province inevitable. One legislature
be difficult to gather, for geographical reasons,
because of racial differences. The only thing
antage of the fact that the bulk of the English-
ved in the upper part of the province, whereas
nch were confined to the lower part, and to
. Though the loyalists had not joined in the
bly, it was taken for granted that they would
f their own. Strenuous objections had come
n other grounds than taxation. They feared
ws on which all their property rested. But if
ably of their own this fear would vanish, for
ss a veto over any proposed change. Lest this
n the mercantile minority, parliament could
eration in the commercial laws before the new
hed. The law officers of the crown were al-
problem and might report at any time. The
an assembly did not merit serious considera-
ply trembling for their own position; their
d their weight was little. Nor was the ignor-
masses, who might not know how to use an
real objection. Experience had shown that
aare in government was calculated to correct

part of Grenville's exposition, an important
ind. Was he turning his back upon the ideal
ng the Canadians? By cutting off an English
e would confirm the French character of the
hether he intended it we do not know. If he
d to make at least a partial retraction. A few
d that the severance of the old subjects in the
new subjects in the old districts was to allow
f ancient prejudices.

two Canadas, each with representative gov-
nt on to consider what further constitutional
sary. Here his whole outlook was colored by
ion. He doubted whether any form of ad-
given to Canada that would prevent its ulti-

mate separation from the empire, but he believed that the evil day might be put off by avoiding the mistakes of the past, the chief of which had been the failure to give the British constitution to the old colonies. They had possessed only part of it. In their constitutions the democratic principle had not been balanced by the principles of monarchy and aristocracy. The true balance should be established in Canada.

To strengthen the aristocratic principle, the secretary of state proposed an important departure from the traditional machinery of British colonial governments. He would create two councils in place of one, separating them according to their functions, legislative and executive. The personnel of the old colonial councils had been controlled by their executive character. The tenure of seats had necessarily depended on the executive will, and this had robbed the upper legislative chambers of any possibility of being permanent and independent bodies, the colonial counterpart of the house of lords. In Canada legislative councilors should be appointed for life or during residence; no salary should be given to them as such, lest it weaken their independence, but marks of honor might be conferred upon them to raise their consequence in the community. Shortly afterward Grenville was more explicit, suggesting that every member of an upper chamber might be made a provincial baronet and that some, after a while, might be elevated to a higher rank.

Less alteration, Grenville observed, was needed to uphold the monarchical principle because an important change had already been made by combining the executive authority and military command over the various colonies in the hands of the king's representative. Yet something more might still be done to strengthen the hands of the executive — by setting aside lands to be held by the crown. These reserves, which would improve in value, would enable the government to maintain its independence of the assembly.

The secretary of state admitted that many believed, as the late revolution suggested, that the colonial self-government he proposed to give the province would be incompatible with imperial unity. But even if he were wrong in running counter to this widespread belief, he insisted that no other policy was possible because American geography would veto it. Because of their proximity to the United States and to the remaining colonies down by the sea, the people of Canada would not long tolerate the system they had nor any other like it. Already the province was very far from being in a tranquil condition, and under the existing management the trouble was likely not only to continue but to increase. Also, Grenville argued, the English political situation dictated the change. If the cabinet decided to maintain the existing form of government, its members would have to speak out and state frankly that their object was to retain the dependence of the colony. Considering the prevailing temper, it was doubtful if they could persuade parliament that such means would attain the object, or that the object itself was worth purchasing at the price of denying to such a large body of British subjects the benefits of the British constitution.[19]

Here it should perhaps be added that the French Revolution, though sometimes linked with the American Revolution as providing the essential background for the new Canadian constitution, had no traceable influence upon its formation. If it helped in any way, it was in the passage of the measure. But it is open to question whether any necessary aid was derived from the argument that the growing disturbances in France gave Britain a freer hand in dealing with Canada.

Heaven prevented the passage of the Constitutional Act in 1790. Having worked out a general solution that satisfied his colleagues, Grenville put it in the form of a bill which he intended to introduce when parliament reassembled in the winter of 1789–90. On October 20, 1789, he sent this draft, and also the memorandum explaining it, to Dorchester to get his comments and to have him fill in certain details that might best be decided in the colony, such as boundaries, the size of the new legislative bodies, and the property qualification for the vote. The ship bearing the bill reached Halifax in due time but was immediately blown out of the harbor and was ultimately obliged to make for New York. The consequence was that it took three months for the papers to reach Quebec. Heavy weather also retarded the reply, which, though written on February 8, did not arrive in London till April 18, 1790. It was then too late in the session to do anything, particularly as the governor had raised some points requiring further consideration and as there was then a fleeting possibility that he might be spending the summer in London, in which event he might be of assistance in perfecting the measure.[20]

Already an important change in Grenville's plans for the new constitution had been forced upon him. The bill was to contain no provision for the reform of the colony's jurisprudence. He much regretted this, but he could not help it, as he explained in a letter of June 5, 1790, acknowledging Dorchester's of February 8. "After much inquiry and consideration, and after receiving the opinions of professional men upon the subject it does not appear to me to be practicable to introduce into the proposed bill any considerable or material articles of commercial law, and the insertion of those of smaller importance would not be desirable." Grenville found some consolation in the conclusion that the complaints of the mercantile minority had their origin more in the uncertainty of the laws than in "the positive defects of any one particular system" and that the uncertainty might be immediately removed by the local legislature and "must ultimately be done away by an uniform and consistent administration of justice," which it would be the duty of the home government to secure after the bill had been passed.

Still Grenville had qualms about French Canadian prejudices against English commercial laws. He did not use the futile argument later advanced by Pitt in the house of commons that the excellent example of English laws in Upper Canada would induce the French of Lower Canada to abandon their old system. He knew that his decision to do nothing for the present would occasion discouragement in the colony, and therefore he threw out a faint ray of hope that this decision might not be final and that Dorchester might be able to supply at least part of the solution that could not be found in London.[21] This suggestion was not likely to bring any response, for William Smith had observed in the fall of 1788 that the change ought to be gradual rather than sudden,[22] and the governor, in his letter of February 8, 1790, had echoed the chief justice's opinion.[23] This opinion was well founded. Some features of the English commercial laws would not fit Canadian conditions. The necessary readjustment would require time, and unfortunately, this was not to be allowed.

Another passage in Grenville's dispatch of June 5, 1790, dealt a hard blow to the hopes of Dorchester and Smith. On receiving the draft of the bill they had been disappointed to find no reference to their cherished project of a general government for all the colonies under the governor general. Both men had dreamed of pulling British North America together, and the government in London had caught enough of the vision to reorganize the colonial administrations, giving all a common governor and each a lieutenant governor. But the union had proved illusory and the British government was about to carry the existing division one stage further. Dorchester's own position was threatened. Unless all the colonies under his nominal authority were really united, he might be suspended in mid-air, a governor without a government. Because he was personally affected, it would hardly have been becoming for him to press the cause of union at this time. Nor did he need to do it. In his faithful friend he had the originator of the idea and the man who could best present it. Without losing any time, Smith drafted additional clauses to effect what he desired, and he wrote a strong letter in support. These documents the governor inclosed in his letter of February 8 with a recommendation for their consideration by the cabinet. In his reply the secretary of state dismissed the subject rather curtly.[24]

At the same time Dorchester met with another disappointment concerning the new governments to be set up. At Grenville's request he had forwarded lists from which the legislative and executive councils of Upper and Lower Canada might be selected, and had taken advantage of the occasion to point out Sir John Johnson, the author of the lists for Upper Canada, as the obvious person for the office of lieutenant governor in Upper Canada.[25] On June 3, 1790, the secretary of state replied that Lieutenant Colonel Simcoe had already been chosen and notified, and that Johnson, for all his merits, would never do. He was too closely identified with the country and had too much property in it for him to fill the office properly. Even if Simcoe should be unable to go, the threat of war with Spain over the Nootka Sound affair suggesting that he might be needed elsewhere, Johnson could not be considered.[26]

Dorchester was plainly much hurt, and with some justification. Back in the spring of 1784, Haldimand had approached Johnson suggesting that he should become lieutenant governor of the new settlements as well as superintendent of Indian affairs.[27] In the summer of 1785 Johnson had conferred with the home government on the matter and had even discussed with Sydney the salary he should receive.[28] Ever since then it had been taken for granted in Canada that the leading loyalist would be His Majesty's representative in the western part of the country. Indeed, Dorchester had regarded the appointment as such an assured fact that he had acted upon it from the time of his arrival in Quebec. He had deferred to Johnson on all matters touching the new settlements. Unfortunately he had never mentioned Johnson's name in his earlier references to the appointment of a lieutenant governor.

Further justification for his feelings may be found in a contrast that must have occurred to him. He had been consulted on the officering of the maritime province governments when he had not the shadow of authority over them, but he was completely ignored in the selection of the most important officer in Upper Canada, which was then under his immediate jurisdiction. Perhaps he suspected that the old confidence in him was shaken. It is doubtful if he restored any of it by the letter which the unpleasant news inspired him to write Grenville on Johnson's behalf. He explained how the appointment had been regarded as settled, he intimated that the supercession of their chief would offend the loyalists, and he suggested that Simcoe might take second place by succeeding Johnson in the Indian department.[29]

The contributions that the governor and the chief justice made to the bill were few and unimportant with the exception of the clauses on tenures. Dorchester and Smith were responsible for the provisions establishing freehold tenure in Upper Canada and permitting freehold grants in Lower Canada, and the elimination of the provision for commutation in Lower Canada was apparently due to their undertaking to deal with the question locally. Even the details they supplied were not all accepted. The franchise, for example, was not what was proposed in Quebec. The governor wanted to prescribe a property qualification that might have excluded a large number of habitants, but he was overruled. What little weight was finally attached to his advice is illustrated by the provision in the bill to permit the crown to attach honors, which might occasionally be hereditary, to seats in the legislative councils. Though this was not in the original draft, Grenville suggested that it might be inserted. The suggestion drew from Dorchester, who had already urged the upbuilding of a colonial aristocracy, a strong denunciation of hereditary honors in Canada on the ground that the fluctuating state of property there would defeat the object of such honors. But the secretary of state paid no attention to this outburst. He did precisely as he had contemplated.

The bill owed even less to parliament. In only two particulars was the measure that received the royal assent on June 10, 1791, different from the measure introduced in the house of commons on March 4, and these particulars were of no moment — the potential life of an assembly was shortened, and the size of Lower Canada's popular chamber was increased. This piece of legislation was so well digested beforehand that parliament could do little with it except pass it. The reports of the speeches throw little additional light upon it. Indeed, the chief interest in the debates on the bill had nothing to do with Canada at all. It was the famous quarrel between Burke and Fox over the French Revolution, which had been dragged into the discussion. Nor, as has sometimes been stated, was it the work of William Pitt. The fact that he sponsored it in the house of commons is the sole ground for supposing that he was its author, and this is explained away by the absence of its undoubted framer, William Grenville, who had been elevated to the house of lords, where he later took charge of his own handiwork.

The Constitutional Act is at once a point of arrival and a point of departure. It terminates the story of the old province of Quebec and it begins the story of Upper and Lower Canada. Therefore a detailed analysis of the measure belongs properly to the history of the new provinces for which it provided the governmental framework. Here the act and its attendant changes should be considered only in a more general way as the winding up of the affairs of the old province of Quebec.

In some important respects the settlement of 1774 was left standing in 1791. The Constitutional Act did not repeal the Quebec Revenue Act nor did it repeal the Quebec Act. It merely repealed that portion of the latter that had provided the colony with a legislature. The position of the Roman Catholic church was not touched. Nor were the laws altered. As before, they could be changed by local legislative authority.

The division of the province, contrary to the oft-repeated statement, was not effected by the Constitutional Act. In its original form the bill did cut Canada in two, and blanks were left for a definition of the boundaries of the new provinces. But Grenville had already seen the difficulty ahead. Because Britain still held territory that the treaty of 1783 recognized as American, this territory could neither be included in Upper Canada nor excluded from it without causing serious trouble. Hence this passage was eliminated from the act, which simply stated the royal intention to divide the colony. This was subsequently carried out by an imperial order-in-council of August 24, 1791.

How the people reacted to the new constitution varied according to their situation. Those in the upper parts of the province were grateful for the assurance that they would hold their lands by free-hold tenure, and they welcomed the division as a deliverance from dependence upon French Canada. Of course they did not object to having an assembly of their own and the right to determine their own jurisprudence. The clergy reserves, which crept into the bill on the eve of its submission to parliament, were not felt as a problem for some years to come.

In the older parts of the province the mass of the people were indifferent because they were not yet politically conscious, and the clergy showed no sign of interest in what was taking place because they were not affected by it. But the few who had been politically awake and active were more or less hostile. Though the seigniors may have seen the reinforcement of their nationality in the division of the province, and though their representation in the old council was to be continued in its two successors, their aristocratic and feudal position was threatened by the creation of a democratically elected chamber and the granting of crown lands in freehold. But their fears were as nothing compared with those of their political foes.

The members of the racial minority had asked for bread and they were being given a stone. Instead of gaining an assembly which they would control, they were to be saddled with an assembly which they could never hope to control. The division of the province would perpetuate their minority position. The combination of division and representative government would raise an insurmountable barrier to the achievement of their hearts' long desire, English commercial laws, and might even smooth the path for the reaction which had alarmed them in the spring of 1787. As of old, they were being delivered a sacrifice on the altar of French Canada.

Their doughty champion, Adam Lymburner, fought their battle in the house of commons during the passage of the measure. He assailed the bill in every way possible, particularly for its failure to establish English commercial laws, the Habeas Corpus Act, and trial by jury in civil causes as unalterable parts of the constitution. His most vehement denunciation was reserved for the proposed division of the colony. Canada was then in such an impoverished condition that to require its people to support two governments was as bad as forcing the Children of Israel in the days of their bondage to make bricks without straw. Upper Canada, with only three or four thousand families scattered over hundreds of miles, would be a mockery of a province, and Lower Canada as well as Upper Canada would be ruined. But the jeremiads of the Quebec merchant might as well have been directed to the moon.

When the sun sank on Christmas Day, 1791, it set on the old province of Quebec. The new constitution was to come into force on the morrow, and the prospect occasioned no rejoicing east of the western boundary of the seigniory of Longueuil.

BIBLIOGRAPHY,
NOTES, AND INDEX

BIBLIOGRAPHY OF PRIMARY SOURCES

Manuscript Material

The Public Archives of Canada, perhaps the greatest archival collection in the British Empire outside London, contain the originals or copies of all the manuscripts upon which this volume is principally based. Some collections have self-explanatory titles; others, including some of the most important, are designated by letters.

The Q series, composed of transcripts of the official correspondence between the provincial government and the home government, is the most valuable of the collections, for in addition to the dispatches both ways it contains a wealth of inclosures. The first two volumes include some correspondence of the military governors. The last volume that deals with the old province of Quebec is 59 B. Some of the volumes are so large that they have been bound in two or three separate parts, and some volumes have been inserted since the series was numbered. These volumes inserted later are designated by capital letters after the numbers. The originals of these supplementary volumes form part of the C. O. 43 series, and the originals of the main volumes form part of the C. O. 42 series in the Public Record Office in London. Q, Volume 1, is the same as C. O. 42, Volume 24. C. O. of course stands for Colonial Office and Q for Quebec or Canada. This unfortunate discrepancy in notation originated half a century ago when the first archivist of the Dominion, Dr. Douglas Brymner, had the transcripts made. At that time the present classification of the originals in the Public Record Office in London had not been adopted. In the Canadian Archives Report for 1890 is a calendar of the volumes covering the period of the old province of Quebec.

The C. O. 42 series, transcripts of the board of trade papers, supplements the Q series throughout the period. The numbers of the volumes, 1 to 23, and the title of the series are the same as those of the originals in the Public Record Office in London. There is a calendar in the Canadian Archives Report for 1921.

The original minutes of the council are also of prime importance. For the period from the establishment of civil government in 1764 to the coming into force of the Quebec Act in 1775 there are three volumes entitled LEGISLATIVE COUNCIL. They record the executive as well as the legislative activities of the council. But they do not record the judicial work of the council, which, as observed in the text, was also the court of appeal in the colony. If, as may be surmised, a minute book of this court of appeals was kept, it has yet to be found. Instead of being numbered, the volumes of the council minutes are distinguished by capital letters, the three just mentioned being A, B, and C. Volumes D, E, and F are confined to the legislative activities of the council from the summer of 1775 to the end of 1791, when the old province of Quebec passed out of existence. These volumes are paralleled by another series entitled STATE BOOK or PRIVY COUNCIL, the volumes of which, D to I, contain the minutes of the council as an executive body. This series has no volume A, B, or C because of the nature of the LEGISLATIVE COUNCIL volumes A, B, and C. From 1787 to the end of 1791 the minutes of the council as a land-granting body were kept separately in what was called the LAND BOOK, of which there are two volumes, A and B. There was still another series known as the REPORT BOOK, which has not yet been discovered. Presumably the loss is not great, for there are few if any reports of consequence that are not entered in the appropriate LEGISLATIVE, STATE, or LAND BOOK or that cannot be found elsewhere if not entered in these books. The council minutes have not been calendared. LAND BOOKS A and B have been published in the Ontario Archives Report for 1928.

The original papers that were laid before the council and filed by its secretary, together with other official papers of the secretary, are preserved in numerous cartons. The binding of these cartons was begun recently. The papers are arranged partly by chronology and partly by subject. Long ago this collection, which like the series does not stop in 1791, was given the title of SUNDRIES and was made a part of the S series, a designation that has been purposely avoided in this volume. Instead, references have been made to particular sections of it, the most important of which is labeled INTERNAL CORRESPONDENCE, PROVINCE OF QUEBEC. Other sections have more precise titles, such as PUBLIC ACCOUNTS and TRADE LICENCES.

The B series, transcripts of the 232 volumes of papers collected by Haldimand, is indispensable for the history of the country from the conquest until shortly before the Constitutional Act was passed. The arrangement of these papers is far from ideal, but their scope is remarkably broad. They throw valuable light on almost every conceivable subject. Even the malicious gossip of the day can there be gleaned. Together with the different series already mentioned, these papers form the most valuable body of manuscript material on the history of the period. The originals are in the British Museum (BRIT. MUS. ADD. MSS. 21661–21892). A two thousand page calendar extends through the Canadian Archives Reports from 1884 to 1889.

The A series, transcripts of Henry Bouquet's papers which came into Haldimand's possession, is of limited value, being confined to the Seven Years' War and the first few years of the British régime in Canada and being concerned chiefly with military and Indian affairs. These papers and the HALDIMAND PAPERS were among the first collected by Dr. Brymner, whose plan was to designate each series by a letter of the alphabet. Hence the A and the B series. The huge C series, military papers, begins only toward the close of the period covered by this volume, as does also the valuable G series, comprising the original dispatches from the home government. The originals of the A series are in the British Museum (BRIT. MUS. ADD. MSS. 21631–21660). The Canadian Archives Report for 1889 contains a calendar of this series.

Among other transcripts of documents in the British Museum, all under the titles of the originals, the HARDWICKE PAPERS, BRIT. MUS. ADD. MSS. 35914–35915, are worthy of special note for their information on policy, trade, and the Labrador boundary, and for some letters of Chief Justice Hey.

The SHELBURNE MANUSCRIPTS, transcripts of the papers of William Petty Fitzmaurice, Earl of Shelburne and Marquess of Lansdowne, since deposited in the William Clements Library in Ann Arbor, Michigan, are a rich miscellaneous collection containing, among other things, many important documents bearing on British policy. There is a calendar in the Canadian Archives Report for 1921. The William Clements Library also possesses the GAGE PAPERS, the GERMAIN PAPERS, and the KNOX PAPERS.

The DARTMOUTH PAPERS, originals presented by Lord Dartmouth to the Public Archives of Canada, resemble the SHELBURNE MANUSCRIPTS in character but are less extensive.

The MURRAY PAPERS, transcripts from originals in the possession of Mrs. Murray of Bath, England, are of great value for Murray's administration. The Canadian Archives Report for 1912 contains a calendar, but it is unsatisfactory because it does not refer to the pages of the different volumes.

The C. O. 5 series, transcripts from originals in the Public Record Office in London, comprises military correspondence of particular value for the military régime. The AMHERST PAPERS, transcripts and photostat copies of originals in the possession of Lord Amherst, embody some interesting material on the beginnings of British rule in Canada.

PLUMATIFS DES AUDIENCES DE LA JURIDICTION DE LA CÔTE DU SUD

DEPUIS SAINT-NICHOLAS JUSQU'À BERTHIER, 1760, transcribed from the
original in Quebec, is the only record yet discovered of Murray's first
courts. REGISTRE D'AUDIENCE DU CONSEIL MILITAIRE DE QUEBEC, 1760–62,
transcribed from the same source, is a record of Murray's court of army
officers. The MONTREAL COURT OF OFFICERS SITTING IN APPEAL, 1761–
64, is a photostat of the original record of this court in Montreal. APPELS
DES JUGEMENTS, MONTREAL, and REGISTRE D'AUDIENCES, CHAMBRE DE
MELICE, MONTREAL, are other judicial records of the same time transcribed from the same source. On the later period, another transcript
from the same source throws much light. It is the REGISTER OF
THE COURT OF QUARTER SESSIONS, MONTREAL. There is also a transcript
of the COURT OF COMMON PLEAS, QUEBEC, 1765–66. For any other of
the judicial records of the period, the student must go to the originals
preserved in the courthouses of Quebec and Montreal.

The LETTER BOOKS of Edward William Gray cover the period from
1774 to 1791. Gray's position as sheriff, as local postmaster, and as a
leading merchant of Montreal give these volumes their importance.

The SMITH PAPERS, photostat copies of originals in the New York
Public Library, are of great value for the period after the American
Revolution. With them should be grouped the portfolio labeled GRAY
V. GRANT, which contains a docket of papers sent by Alexander Gray,
then a Quebec lawyer and later attorney general of the province, to Lord
Melville (Henry Dundas) and tells the story of how Chief Justice Smith
upset the legal system.

In addition to the above-mentioned sources, the archives in Ottawa
contain many other documents, such as the slight volume of FINLAY
PAPERS, which need not be listed here because they were of use to the
author only for incidental points.

PRINTED MATERIAL

A. Shortt and A. G. Doughty, eds., *Documents Relating to the Constitutional History of Canada, 1759–1791,* of which the first edition was
published by the Public Archives of Canada in 1907 and the second in
1918, blazed the trail through what was one of the darkest periods of
Canadian history. The compiling of this great collection of documents
was one of the finest pieces of work ever done in the field of Canadian
history.

W. P. M. Kennedy and G. Lanctot, eds., *Reports on the Laws of
Quebec, 1767–1770* (Ottawa, 1931), another publication of the Dominion Archives, contains the recently discovered reports of the governor and the chief justice.

All the proclamations and ordinances published between the conquest and the Constitutional Act, except some of Murray's issued during the military régime and those ordinances of the civil régime that were disallowed by the home government, have been printed in recent years. The legislation of the military régime is in Appendix B of the Canadian Archives Report for 1918, and the proclamations issued subsequently are in Appendix C of the same volume. The ordinances passed by the governor and council from 1764 to 1767 are in the Canadian Archives Report for 1913, and those passed from 1768 to 1791 are in the Canadian Archives Report for 1914–15.

Miscellaneous groups of documents, some of the first importance, have been printed in the reports of other years down to 1892.

The Ontario Archives Reports for 1904 and 1905 contain material that is invaluable for an understanding of the loyalists and their first settlements.

A. G. Doughty, ed., *The Journal of Captain Knox* (Champlain Society, Toronto, 1916), volumes 2 and 3, which include part of Murray's diary, are of prime importance for the beginning of the military régime.

W. S. Wallace, ed., *The Maseres Letters, 1766–68* (Toronto, 1919), contains interesting letters written by Maseres when he was attorney general of the old province of Quebec.

Of the various publications of Maseres, the most valuable are *A Collection of Several Commissions, and Other Public Instruments . . .* (London, 1772); *An Account of the Proceedings of the British and Other Protestants of the Province of Quebeck . . .* (London, 1775); and the supplement to it, *Additional Papers Concerning the Province of Quebeck* (London, 1776). His long dialogue entitled *The Canadian Freeholder* (3 vols., London, 1776–79) purports to give an insight into contemporary Canadian opinion, but it gives rather an insight into Maseres' Huguenot bias.

The Justice and Policy of the Late Act of Parliament for Making More Effectual Provision for the Government of Quebec . . . (London, 1774) was the anonymous work of William Knox, the under secretary, who stoutly defended the Quebec Act. His *Extra Official State Papers* (2 vols., London, 1789) should not be ignored.

Most of the pamphlet literature of the day, except Knox's defense of the Quebec Act just mentioned and the *State of the Present Form of Government of the Province of Quebec* (London, 1789), which has been attributed to Attorney General James Monk, is of very slight value.

J. Fortescue, ed., *Correspondence of George III* (London, 1927–28), contains, among other things, some interesting letters about Carleton during the early part of the American Revolution.

Sir Henry Cavendish, *Debates of the House of Commons in the Year 1774 on the Bill for Making More Effectual Provision for the Government of the Province of Quebec* (London, 1839), gives the only account of the parliamentary discussion of the Quebec Act. Cavendish was a member of the house of commons and took the notes. Their long-delayed publication was inspired by the renewed interest in Canadian affairs occasioned by the "rebellions" of 1837. The *Parliamentary Register* is better than the *Parliamentary History* for the debates leading up to the passage of the Constitutional Act.

The *Quebec Gazette,* published weekly from June 21, 1764, except during the short duration of the Stamp Tax, continues throughout the period. It is of distinct though limited value. It was the official medium for the publication of official documents and notices. Otherwise it was not a government organ. It expressed no opinions of its own, unless silence be counted expression. It completely ignored the honor paid Governor Carleton in 1776 when he was made a Knight of the Bath. Most of the news it printed came from the outside world, its local news being almost entirely confined to the arrival and departure of ships and of prominent persons. But its paid advertisements, of which there are a goodly number, are a mine of information. In addition to that in the Public Archives of Canada, there is a complete file in the Archives of Quebec. The only other newspapers published in the old province of Quebec were ephemeral — the *Gazette* of Montreal, which appeared during the American Revolution and of which no file has been preserved, and the *Herald* of Quebec, which appeared on November 24, 1788, and of which there is a file in the Public Archives of Canada.

NOTES

I. THE COLONY SURRENDERED

[1] (p. 5). See Dartmouth Papers, vol. 2, p. 60–142, for Lieutenant Marr's remarks upon Quebec during his residence from 1768 to 1772. According to Marr the raising of potatoes became common only after the conquest.

[2] (p. 12). Judge L. F. G. Baby, "L'Exode des classes dirigeantes à la cession du Canada," *Canadian Antiquarian and Numismatic Journal,* third series, vol. 2, p. 97.

II. THE FIRST WINTER OF THE BRITISH IN CANADA

[1] (p. 13). *The Northcliffe Collection* (Publications of the Public Archives of Canada, 1926), p. 131.

[2] (p. 13). Murray's Journal, C. O. 5, vol. 64, p. 38. This interesting document, which covers the period from September 18, 1759, to May 17, 1760, extends to page 115 of this volume. Its sequel to September 17, 1760, is published in *The Journal of Captain Knox* (Champlain Society, Toronto, 1916), vol. 3, p. 306–34.

[3] (p. 13). *Northcliffe Collection,* p. 181.

[4] (p. 13). He died in 1768. *Gentleman's Magazine,* October, 1768.

[5] (p. 15). R. H. Mahon, *Life of General the Honourable James Murray* (London, 1921).

[6] (p. 16). Knox, *op. cit.,* vol. 2, p. 401, 405; Murray's Journal, April 30, 1760.

[7] (p. 16). The navigation of the river was a delicate business.

[8] (p. 17). Murray's Journal, December 31, 1759, quoting Monckton's opinion with approval.

[9] (p. 17). Murray Papers, vol. 1, p. 5. The words in brackets are inserted by the author where the original words of the manuscript are missing and are represented by blanks in the copy deposited in the Public Archives of Canada.

[10] (p. 18). Knox, *op. cit.,* vol. 2, p. 147.

[11] (p. 18). *Ibid.,* p. 260.   [12] (p. 18). *Ibid.,* p. 156.   [13] (p. 19). *Ibid.,* p. 367n.

[14] (p. 19). Murray's Journal, September 21, October 14.

[15] (p. 19). Murray Papers, vol. 1, p. 15.

[16] (p. 20). Murray's Journal, December 8 and 9, 1759.

[17] (p. 20). A. Shortt and A. G. Doughty, eds., *Documents Relating to the Constitutional History of Canada, 1759–1791* (2d ed., Ottawa, 1918), p. 36.

[18] (p. 20). A copy is deposited in the Public Archives of Canada.

[19] (p. 20). *Ibid.,* January 23, 1760.

[20] (p. 21). This is the date in Murray's Journal. The ordinance as published in Canadian Archives Report, 1918, Appendix B, p. 2, is dated November 15.

[21] (p. 21). Knox, *op. cit.,* vol. 2, p. 267, 306, 308.

[22] (p. 22). *Ibid.,* p. 280, 306.

[23] (p. 22). Knox records few other examples.

[24] (p. 22). Can. Arch. Report, 1918, Appendix B, p. 8, 9.

[25] (p. 22). Murray Papers, vol. 1, p. 2.

[26] (p. 22). Murray's Journal, November 25, 1759.

[27] (p. 22). Can. Arch. Report, 1918, Appendix B, p. 3.

[28] (p. 23). Knox, *op. cit.*, vol. 2, p. 306.

[29] (p. 23). Murray's Journal, December 26, 1759.

[30] (p. 23). Can. Arch. Report, 1918, Appendix B, p. 5, 6, January 15, 1760.

[31] (p. 24). Knox, *op. cit.*, vol. 2, p. 454.

[32] (p. 25). Ainslie to Murray, October 28, 1759, in Murray Papers, vol. 3, p. 7; Murray's instructions to Ainslie, June 23, *ibid.*, vol. 1, p. 39; Murray to Colville, June 26, 1760, *ibid.*, p. 41; Murray to Pitt, October 22, 1760, C. O. 5, vol. 64, p. 174.

[33] (p. 25). Can. Arch. Report, 1918, Appendix B, p. 9–11.

III. THE CANADIANS UNDER MILITARY RULE

[1] (p. 26). Disposition of His Majesty's troops, October 4, 1760, C. O. 5, vol. 59, p. 348.

[2] (p. 26). At the head of the rapids a few miles east of the modern Ogdensburg.

[3] (p. 26). Amherst to Pitt, October 19, 1760, *ibid.*, p. 355.

[4] (p. 27). *Ibid.*, p. 250.   [5] (p. 27). *Ibid.*, p. 259.

[6] (p. 27). *Ibid.*, p. 272.   [7] (p. 28). *Ibid.*, p. 276.

[8] (p. 28). A. L. Burt, "Who Was the 'Com[man]d[ant] de la Troupe dans Chaque Coste'?" *Canadian Historical Review*, vol. 7, p. 226 (September, 1926).

[9] (p. 28). Shortt and Doughty, *op. cit.*, p. 38.

[10] (p. 29). Murray Papers, vol. 3, p. 70.

[11] (p. 30). B (Haldimand Papers), vol. 37, p. 10.

[12] (p. 31). C. O. 5, vol. 61–1, p. 327.

[13] (p. 32). Ordinances and Proclamations of the Règne Militaire, Can. Arch. Report, 1918, Appendix B, 228 p., gives practically all the public actions of the three military governments, some of which are quoted below.

[14] (p. 33). Can. Arch. Report, 1918, Appendix B, p. 14.

[15] (p. 33). *Ibid.*, p. 15.   [16] (p. 33). *Ibid.*, p. 16.   [17] (p. 33). *Ibid.*, p. 17.

[18] (p. 33). *Ibid.*, p. 32.   [19] (p. 34). *Ibid.*, p. 48.   [20] (p. 34). *Ibid.*, p. 128.

[21] (p. 35). Registre d' audience du conseil militaire de Quebec, 1760–62, vol. 2, p. 121.

[22] (p. 35). Can. Arch. Report, 1918, Appendix B, p. 58.

[23] (p. 36). C. O. 5, vol. 65, p. 89.

[24] (p. 36). Appels des Jugements (Montreal).

[25] (p. 36). *Supra*, n. 13.

[26] (p. 37). Can. Arch. Report, 1918, Appendix B, p. 37.

[27] (p. 38). *Ibid.*, p. 52, 62, 66, 68–70, 73, 75, 81.

[28] (p. 38). *Ibid.*, p. 76. There may have been some migration into the district of Three Rivers. There the census of 1762 (*ibid.*, p. 159–89) reveals that many new inhabitants had settled since 1760. Only half of these were children.

[29] (p. 38). *Ibid.*, p. 76, 145.

[30] (p. 38). *Ibid.*, p. 41, 122. One of the notaries, one Panet, was appointed receiver of *quints* and *lods et ventes* in Montreal. *Ibid.*, p. 42.

[31] (p. 39). *Ibid.*, p. 23–30.

[32] (p. 39). Registre d'audience, vol. 2, p. 87.

[33] (p. 39). Can. Arch. Report, 1918, Appendix B, p. 102.

[34] (p. 39). *Ibid.*, p. 73, 76. He appointed individuals attested by the Montreal militia chamber.

[35] (p. 39). *Ibid.*, p. 48.   [36] (p. 39). *Ibid.*, p. 66.   [37] (p. 39). *Ibid.*, p. 98.

[38] (p. 39). *Ibid.,* p. 32–35, 46, 54, 55, 103, 114, 116, 122, 135, 139.

[39] (p. 40). *Ibid.,* p. 37.   [40] (p. 40). *Ibid.,* p. 60.   [41] (p. 40). *Ibid.,* p. 102.

[42] (p. 40). *Ibid.,* p. 96.   [43] (p. 40). *Ibid.,* p. 44.

[44] (p. 41). Admiral Saunders gave Murray a list of pilots. Murray Papers, vol. 3, p. 106.

[45] (p. 41). Murray's commission to Rabi and Savard, April 3, 1762, and regulations for masters of vessels, June 24, 1762, in Internal Correspondence, Province of Quebec.

[46] (p. 41). Can. Arch. Report, 1918, Appendix B, p. 134.

[47] (p. 41). *Ibid.,* p. 34.

[48] (p. 41). *Ibid.,* p. 103, 122, 128, 139, 142.

[49] (p. 42). *Ibid.,* p. 52, 121, 139.

[50] (p. 42). *Ibid.,* p. 107.   [51] (p. 42). *Ibid.,* p. 108.

[52] (p. 43). *Ibid.,* p. 113, 126, 141, 155.

[53] (p. 43). *Ibid.,* p. 43, 46, 53.

[54] (p. 43). *Ibid.,* p. 45.   [55] (p. 43). *Ibid.,* p. 50.   [56] (p. 43). *Ibid.,* p. 145.

[57] (p. 43). *Ibid.,* p. 50, 84, 97, 110, 117.

[58] (p. 44). *Ibid.,* p. 97.   [59] (p. 44). *Ibid.,* p. 106.

[60] (p. 44). Registre d'audience, vol. 2, p. 23.

[61] (p. 44). Can. Arch. Report, 1918, Appendix B, p. 31.

[62] (p. 44). *Ibid.,* p. 33.   [63] (p. 45). *Ibid.,* p. 47.   [64] (p. 45). *Ibid.,* p. 75.

[65] (p. 45). *Ibid.,* p. 47.   [66] (p. 46). *Ibid.,* p. 61.

[67] (p. 46). *Ibid.,* p. 77.   [68] (p. 46). *Ibid.,* p. 36.

[69] (p. 46). Registre d'audience, vol. 2, p. 150.

[70] (p. 46). Can. Arch. Report, 1918, Appendix B, p. 65.

[71] (p. 46). *Ibid.,* p. 78–80.   [72] (p. 47). *Ibid.,* p. 33.   [73] (p. 47). *Ibid.,* p. 44.

[74] (p. 47). *Ibid.,* p. 45, 139, 143.   [75] (p. 47). *Ibid.,* p. 32.

[76] (p. 47). *Ibid.,* p. 92, 101, 135.

[77] (p. 47). *Ibid.,* p. 132.   [78] (p. 48). *Ibid.,* p. 85.

[79] (p. 49). B, vol. 8, p. 39–40. There was more jobbing during the summer of 1763. *Ibid.,* vol. 9, p. 40.

[80] (p. 49). Can. Arch. Report, 1918, Appendix B, p. 88.

[81] (p. 49). *Ibid.,* p. 39.   [82] (p. 50). *Ibid.,* p. 58, 134.   [83] (p. 50). *Ibid.,* p. 106.

[84] (p. 50). *Ibid.,* p. 126.   [85] (p. 51). *Ibid.,* p. 58, 60, 78.

[86] (p. 51). B, vol. 8, p. 26–29, 57.

[87] (p. 52). C. O. 42, vol. 6, p. 118.

[88] (p. 52). B, vol. 8, p. 56.   [89] (p. 52). Q, vol. 1, p. 11.

[90] (p. 52). B, vol. 8, p. 24; Murray Papers, vol. 2, p. 224–25.

[91] (p. 53). Can. Arch. Report, 1918, Appendix B, p. 38.

[92] (p. 53). *Ibid.,* p. 97.

[93] (p. 53). *Ibid.,* p. 93.

[94] (p. 53). Murray Papers, vol. 3, p. 49, 111.

[95] (p. 54). Can. Arch. Report, 1918, Appendix B, p. 99.

[96] (p. 54). *Ibid.,* p. 39–42.

[97] (p. 55). B, vol. 2–2, p. 2–19; C. O. 5, vol. 65, p. 49; vol. 83–1, p. 82; Murray Papers, vol. 2, p. 109–22; Q, vol. 2, p. 55–69.

IV. PEACE AND WAR

[1] (p. 57). G. L. Beer, *British Colonial Policy, 1754–1765* (New York, 1907), chap. 8; W. L. Grant, "Canada versus Guadeloupe," *American Historical Review,*

vol. 17, p. 735 (July, 1912); Marjorie Reid, "Pitt's Decision to Keep Canada in 1761," Report of the Canadian Historical Association, 1926.

[2] (p. 59). G. S. Graham, *British Policy and Canada, 1774–1791* (Imperial Studies, no. 4, London, 1930), p. 4, 8, 9.

[3] (p. 59). A. von Ruville, *William Pitt, Earl of Chatham* (Eng. trans., London, 1907), vol. 2, chaps. 15, 16.

[4] (p. 60). The thirty-league limit had been stipulated in the twelfth article of the Treaty of Utrecht, 1713, and was now continued implicitly by a general reference to "former treaties."

[5] (p. 61). F. Parkman, *The Conspiracy of Pontiac* (2 vols., Boston, 1857); T. G. Marquis, *The War Chief of the Ottawas* (Chronicles of Canada series, Toronto, 1915). See also Wisconsin Historical Collections, vol. 18; Michigan Pioneer and Historical Collection, vol. 27; and C. W. Alvord, *The Mississippi Valley in British Politics* (Cleveland, 1917), vol. 1, p. 186–87, for pressure of settlers.

V. The Establishment of Civil Government

[1] (p. 76). Shortt and Doughty, *op. cit.*, p. 127–31.

[2] (p. 76). *Ibid.*, p. 131–63.   [3] (p. 76). *Ibid.*, p. 47–96.

[4] (p. 76). *Ibid.*, p. 163–68.   [5] (p. 76). *Ibid.*, p. 173–81.

[6] (p. 76). *Ibid.*, p. 181–205.

[7] (p. 76). The others were East Florida, West Florida, and Grenada.

[8] (p. 77). For the cutting off of Labrador see the board of trade's report, March 15, 1763, and Egremont to the board of trade, March 24, 1763, C. O. 194, vol. 26.

[9] (p. 77). For the opinion of J. Pownall, secretary of the board of trade, see Shelburne MSS., vol. 49, p. 145, and for that of Lord Barrington, treasurer of the navy, see *ibid.*, vol. 50, p. 23.

[10] (p. 79). This was supplied by the Mutiny Act of 1766.

[11] (p. 80). Not " governor general," as sometimes asserted.

[12] (p. 81). Shortt and Doughty, *op. cit.*, p. 168.

[13] (p. 83). Q, vol. 1, p. 23.

[14] (p. 83). Shortt and Doughty, *op. cit.*, p. 297.

[15] (p. 83). C. W. Alvord, " The Genesis of the Proclamation of 1763," Proceedings of the Michigan Historical Society, 1908; *The Mississippi Valley in British Politics*, vol. 1, p. 174n., 212–13.

[16] (p. 83). Also in the report of June 8, 1763.

[17] (p. 83). Murray Papers, vol. 2, p. 63.

[18] (p. 86). Shelburne MSS., vol. 48, p. 254–56.

[19] (p. 87). C. O. 42, vol. 1–2, p. 396.

[20] (p. 87). Q, vol. 2, p. 132.

[21] (p. 88). *Journals of the Hon. William Hervey* (Bury St. Edmund's, 1906), p. 95.

[22] (p. 88). B, vol. 74, p. 170.

[23] (p. 88). He was appointed by the home government and was commissioned by the governor in Canada.

[24] (p. 89). Shortt and Doughty, *op. cit.*, p. 205–09.

[25] (p. 91). No salaries were provided for them until after they had twice petitioned the council. Then each was allowed £150 per annum. Leg. Coun., vol. B, 75v.

[26] (p. 91). G. E. Hart, *The Quebec Act, 1774* (Montreal, 1891), p. 22; Murray Papers, vol. 2, p. 189, 206.

[27] (p. 92). The original number of the justices of the peace was three dozen, including the councilors whom Murray had selected.

[28] (p. 93). Murray Papers, vol. 3, p. 256.

[29] (p. 93). C. S. S. Higham, " The General Assembly of the Leeward Islands," *English Historical Review,* vol. 41, p. 366 (July, 1926).

[30] (p. 93). Murray Papers, vol. 2, p. 183.

[31] (p. 93). Leg. Coun., vol. B, p. 155.

[32] (p. 94). Cramahé's mission was also to present two important unsettled questions, those of religion and revenue, and possibly to protect the governor's interests at home, where hostile political influences were at work.

[33] (p. 94). Shortt and Doughty, *op. cit.,* p. 236.

[34] (p. 94). Their opinion was dated only three days after Pownall's letter from the board of trade asking for it. In the papers of Lord Dartmouth, who became head of the board of trade a few weeks later, this opinion is immediately followed by an opposite one given sixty years before by Sir Edward Northey with exact references to statutes. Dartmouth Papers, vol. 1, p. 71–73.

[35] (p. 94). Shortt and Doughty, *op. cit.,* p. 247–48.

[36] (p. 94). *Ibid.,* p. 237–46.

[37] (p. 94). Charles Yorke had returned to his old post of attorney general, and was the real author of the following report.

[38] (p. 94). Cramahé and Fowler Walker were the only two men in England who could have given any valuable advice upon the subject.

[39] (p. 95). Shortt and Doughty, *op. cit.,* p. 251–57.

[40] (p. 95). British Museum Add. MSS., vol. 35914 (Hardwicke Papers), p. 72–81.

[41] (p. 95). The instructions referred to in Shortt and Doughty, *op. cit.,* p. 225, n. 1, were never sent. They form part of the instructions pigeonholed in 1766. See also R. A. Humphreys and S. M. Scott, "Lord Northington and the Laws of Canada," *Can. Hist. Rev.,* vol. 14, p. 42–61 (March, 1933), for a fuller study which appeared after this chapter was written.

[42] (p. 96). For a detailed account, including some documents not available elsewhere, see A. Gosselin, *L'Eglise du Canada après la conquête* (Quebec, 1916). Gosselin underestimates Murray's Protestant bias.

[43] (p. 96). Q, vol. 1, p. 253.

[44] (p. 97). *Ibid.,* p. 252.   [45] (p. 97). *Ibid.,* p. 258.

[46] (p. 98). Murray also obliged the Jesuits to make considerable payments to Roubaud.

[47] (p. 99). Murray Papers, vol. 2, p. 139.

[48] (p. 99). Shelburne MSS., vol. 59, p. 30–36.

[49] (p. 99). Q, vol. 18 A, p. 88–103.

[50] (p. 100). In a letter to Briand dated April 20, 1766, Murray asserted that he had done his best to procure his appointment, not only by official dispatches to the government but also by private communications to his clerical brother and to the archbishop of York. Gosselin, *op. cit.,* p. 160–61.

[51] (p. 100). He also urged the appointment of Protestant clergymen for Quebec, Three Rivers, and Montreal, and the establishment of free schools in each of these places to spread the use of the English language. Dartmouth Papers, vol. 1, p. 88.

VI. The Tribulations of Governor Murray

[1] (p. 102). For the quarrel between Murray and Burton see S. M. Scott, "Civil and Military Authority in Canada," *Can. Hist. Rev.,* vol. 9, p. 117–36. This division

of authority tended to produce conditions which resemble those of the French régime when governor and intendant intrigued against each other.

[2] (p. 102). C.O.5, vols. 83–84, contain correspondence relating to the troubles in Florida.

[3] (p. 102). Quebec had eighteen companies and Montreal eleven, making a total of twenty-nine for Canada. The next largest garrison, fourteen companies, was in New York. Halifax and Pensacola each had nine companies, but Nova Scotia had a larger number of settlers than West Florida. C.O.5, vol. 84, p. 392 A.

[4] (p. 103). Knox, op. cit., vol. 2, p. 389.

[5] (p. 104). C.O.5, vol. 59, p. 174–76.

[6] (p. 104). Ibid., p. 361.   [7] (p. 104). Ibid., vol. 60, p. 3.

[8] (p. 104). So said the traders themselves in their petition printed in Shortt and Doughty, op. cit., p. 232. This petition was inclosed in Halifax to the board of trade, June 10, 1765. Q, vol. 2, p. 359.

[9] (p. 104). Q, vol. 2, p. 332, 335.

[10] (p. 104). C.O. 42, vol. 5, p. 28.

[11] (p. 105). Brit. Mus. Add. MSS., vol. 35915 (Hardwicke Papers), p. 19.

[12] (p. 106). C.O.5, vol. 65, p. 89.

[13] (p. 106). See supra, p. 49.

[14] (p. 106). Q, vol. 5, p. 678–79.

[15] (p. 106). An address of the British merchants to Murray, January 17, 1763 (Q, vol. 1, p. 62), reveals no trace of animus. Its words distinctly imply that there was none.

[16] (p. 107). Q, vol. 1, p. 139.

[17] (p. 107). Murray Papers, vol. 2, p. 29, 53; vol. 3, p. 52.

[18] (p. 107). The mutiny was caused by an order announcing the stoppage of fourpence from the pay of all soldiers who wished a continuance of the rations that had been issued free during the war. For some unknown reason, the men in Quebec thought that it emanated from the governor and did not know that it came from England through the commander-in-chief in New York.

[19] (p. 107). Q, vol. 1, p. 162.

[20] (p. 108). Chief Justice Hey's Report of the Enquiry about Mr. Allsopp, April 19, 1768, ibid., vol. 5, p. 626, 633–716.

[21] (p. 108). C.O. 42, vol. 1, p. 180–85.

[22] (p. 109). Montreal Court of Officers Sitting in Appeal, p. 13; Q, vol. 10, p. 95–111; Brit. Mus. Add. MSS., vol. 15491, p. 25–58.

[23] (p. 110). C.O.5, vol. 65, p. 88.

[24] (p. 111). Ibid., p. 89–90.

[25] (p. 112). Q, vol. 5, p. 649, 663–66.

[26] (p. 112). Shortt and Doughty, op. cit., p. 212–19.

[27] (p. 112). Q, vol. 2, p. 255. He later succeeded.

[28] (p. 112). Roman Catholics were not admitted in England.

[29] (p. 113). Leg. Coun., vol. A, p. 122.

[30] (p. 113). The attorney general, George Suckling, ferreted this out. See his memorial of May 3, 1765, C.O. 42, vol. 3, p. 300–11.

[31] (p. 113). A. L. Burt, "The Mystery of Walker's Ear," Can. Hist. Rev., vol. 3, p. 233–55 (September, 1922).

[32] (p. 113). Murray Papers, vol. 2, p. 203–05.

[33] (p. 117). Q, vol. 3, p. 53–119.

[34] (p. 118). C.O. 42, vol. 4, p. 129–30; Murray Papers, vol. 2, p. 209–12; B, vol. 68, p. 81–88.

[35] (p. 118). Leg. Coun., vol. B, p. 123v; B, vol. 8, p. 50.

[36] (p. 119). The above incident probably explains Advocate General Marriott's recondite reference to an assembly in his report. See Shortt and Doughty, *op. cit.*, p. 455.

[37] (p. 121). They are printed in the Can. Arch. Report, 1913, Appendix E. Those which were disallowed, however, do not appear there, but may be found in the council minutes, vol. A, p. 81–86, 91–95, 123–29, 135–39.

[38] (p. 122). From their promulgation they had been decried, particularly in Montreal, as unconstitutional. The billeting trouble was settled under an act of parliament of 1765 which obliged colonial governments to provide quarters for the troops stationed within their respective borders. Since there was no assembly in Canada, the money necessary to rent houses had to be procured by orders on the treasury. One large house then rented for a barracks was burned before it could be occupied by the troops, and the fire was generally supposed to have been of incendiary origin.

[39] (p. 122). The *Quebec Gazette* of March 14, 1765, records a merchants' banquet in his honor.

[40] (p. 122). Leg. Coun., vol. B, p. 44, 110v, 140, 145.

[41] (p. 122). In the publisher's file of the *Quebec Gazette,* now deposited in the Public Archives of Canada, the words "Of no effect" are written over the English version of the first ordinance for billeting troops, and *"Bon pour rien"* over the French version (November 29, 1764). The supplementary ordinance, which appeared a week later, has the written comment, "Damned."

[42] (p. 123). W. S. Wallace, ed., *The Maseres Letters, 1766–1768* (Toronto, 1919), p. 123.

[43] (p. 123). For this campaign and its outcome see A. L. Burt, "Governor Murray and the British Government," Transactions of the Royal Society of Canada, 1928, sec. 2, p. 49–56.

[44] (p. 123). Dartmouth Papers, vol. 1, p. 99–125; Brit. Mus. Add. MSS., vol. 35915 (Hardwicke Papers), p. 114; Murray Papers, vol. 2, p. 226.

[45] (p. 123). B, vol. 8, p. 14–62.

[46] (p. 124). *Quebec Gazette,* July 4, 1765; C. O. 42, vol. 2, p. 109–12.

[47] (p. 126). *Oswald's Memorials* (Edinburgh, 1825), p. 372. Murray's political stock was also elevated by Pitt's recognizing him at a royal levee. B, vol. 68, p. 158.

[48] (p. 126). For the charges against Murray see B, vol. 8, p. 14–17; for his answer see *ibid.,* p. 19–55.

[49] (p. 126). Brit. Mus. Add. MSS., vol. 35915 (Hardwicke Papers), p. 104–11.

[50] (p. 126). *Ibid.,* p. 132.

[51] (p. 127). R. H. Mahon, *op. cit.,* p. 377–78.

VII. Sir Guy Carleton and the Malcontents

[1] (p. 128). Carleton's commission as governor, dated April 12, 1768, was read in council on October 26, 1768. Leg. Coun., vol. C, p. 31.

[2] (p. 129). Apparently he erred in returning the bond covering the liability of the officers sued by Levy. See *supra*, p. 109n.

[3] (p. 130). Dartmouth Papers, vol. 1, p. 185.

[4] (p. 130). The existence of a certain J. Maseres on the staff of the quartermaster general's department since 1763 (C. O. 42, vol. 17, p. 78) suggests that the attorney general was attracted to Canada by a relative.

[5] (p. 130). See especially Brit. Mus. Add. MSS., vol. 35915 (Hardwicke Papers), p. 133. The note by Hardwicke is in the margin of an abstract of Thurlow's report in the beginning of this volume.

[6] (p. 131). Shelburne MSS., vol. 64, p. 117–18.

[7] (p. 132). Leg. Coun., vol. B, p. 192–93v.

[8] (p. 132). C. O. 42, vol. 5, p. 163; Q, vol. 3, p. 326. He admitted him in 1768 after receiving advice. *Ibid.*, p. 330.

[9] (p. 132). A. L. Burt, "Sir Guy Carleton and His First Council," *Can. Hist. Rev.*, vol. 4, p. 321–32 (December, 1923), gives a fuller account of the following incident.

[10] (p. 132). Spread by Eleazar Levy (see *supra*, p. 109n.), who was in favor with Carleton.

[11] (p. 135). Mills lived with Dunn. B, vol. 68, p. 135.

[12] (p. 135). Murray Papers, vol. 3, p. 206.

[13] (p. 135). B, vol. 68, p. 252–53.

[14] (p. 136). Shelburne MSS., vol. 64, p. 416.

[15] (p. 136). Some opposition to this act had appeared in Montreal.

[16] (p. 136). C. O. 42, vol. 5, p. 252.

[17] (p. 136). Q, vol. 3, p. 344.

[18] (p. 136). They are in Brit. Mus. Add. MSS., vol. 35915 (Hardwicke Papers), p. 102–03, 133–37, 286–89, 339–41, and throw much light upon the situation in the colony. The particular passage referred to is on page 340.

[19] (p. 136). H. A. Innis, *The Fur Trade in Canada* (New Haven, 1930), p. 174–79; Brit. Mus. Add. MSS., vol. 35915 (Hardwicke Papers), p. 165–68, 173–91, 201–39, 356–81; Q, vol. 3, p. 420–24; Memorial of Montreal Merchants, February 20, 1765, in Int. Cor. Prov. Que.

[20] (p. 137). *Quebec Gazette.* It was settled in the council on January 18. See Leg. Coun., vol. A, p. 173. The proclamations of this period are published in Can. Arch. Report, 1918, Appendix C, p. 1–68.

[21] (p. 139). A fall in the price of furs in the English market also injured the Canadian trade.

[22] (p. 139). M. G. Reid, "The Quebec Fur-Traders and Western Policy, 1763–1774," *Can. Hist. Rev.*, vol. 6, p. 15–32 (March, 1925).

[23] (p. 140). Q, vol. 4, p. 98–128. The second omitted part of Shelburne to Carleton, June 20, 1767, in Shortt and Doughty, *op. cit.*, p. 281, contains some interesting comments on the trade.

[24] (p. 140). See Brit. Mus. Add. MSS., vol. 35915 (Hardwicke Papers), p. 65–97, 343–50.

[25] (p. 141). For depositions and protests see Int. Cor. Prov. Que., 1765.

[26] (p. 143). In 1768, accused of plotting to loot the post and to hand it over to the French, he was arrested and brought down in irons to be tried by court-martial. The evidence produced was very flimsy and he was found not guilty. His account of the trade and his relations to it are to be found in Brit. Mus. Add. MSS., vol. 35915 (Hardwicke Papers), p. 218–39.

[27] (p. 143). Murray Papers, vol. 2, p. 224–25.

[28] (p. 143). F. Maseres, *A Collection of Several Commissions* (London, 1772), p. 288 ff.; Q, vol. 5, p. 284, 288.

[29] (p. 145). For the argument against it see Brit. Mus. Add. MSS., vol. 35915 (Hardwicke Papers), p. 170–72.

[30] (p. 145). Q, vol. 5, p. 827. This does not appear with the other proclamations published in Can. Arch. Report, 1918.

[81] (p. 145). Q, vol. 3, p. 254.

[82] (p. 146). Maseres, *op. cit.*, p. 288 ff.

[83] (p. 146). In the spring of 1767 he said that the only perquisite he ever accepted was prize money at Havana. Q, vol. 4, p. 176–77.

[84] (p. 147). June 4, 1765.

[85] (p. 147). A number of offices that promised to be particularly lucrative were monopolized by two friends of the government in England. They never set foot in the colony but rented their rights to deputies.

[86] (p. 147). Q, vol. 5, p. 441.

[87] (p. 148). Leg. Coun., vol. B, p. 238–39.

[88] (p. 148). Q, vol. 3, p. 411–13.

[89] (p. 148). Shortt and Doughty, *op. cit.*, p. 298.

[40] (p. 149). Q, vol. 5, p. 245–50, 365–69; Wallace, *op. cit.*, p. 71–74, 125–28. Suckling was later made chief justice of the Virgin Islands. See C. O. 5, vol. 157, p. 25, where he was advised to return to his post.

[41] (p. 149). Shortt and Doughty, *op. cit.*, p. 295; Q, vol. 5, p. 732.

VIII. Toward a New Constitution

[1] (p. 151). Shelburne MSS., vol. 64, p. 137–42.

[2] (p. 152). Shortt and Doughty, *op. cit.*, p. 281.   [3] (p. 152). *Ibid.*, p. 285–87.

[4] (p. 152). Then a clerk in Shelburne's office and later his under secretary of state when Shelburne became home secretary.

[5] (p. 153). C. O. 42, vol. 7, p. 6–10. It is signed by James Marriott, William De Gray, and E. Willes.

[6] (p. 153). Q, vol. 3, p. 411–13.

[7] (p. 154). Shortt and Doughty, *op. cit.*, p. 280.

[8] (p. 154). Chester Martin, *Empire and Commonwealth* (Oxford, 1929).

[9] (p. 155). R. Coupland, *The Quebec Act* (Oxford, 1925).

[10] (p. 155). He was presented to George III.

[11] (p. 156). Can. Arch. Report, 1888, Note C, p. 24–40.

[12] (p. 156). Gosselin, *op. cit.*, p. 193.   [13] (p. 157). Q, vol. 4, p. 320–21.

[14] (p. 158). Shortt and Doughty, *op. cit.*, 281–85.

[15] (p. 159). *Ibid.*, p. 288–91.

[16] (p. 159). "A View of the Civil Government and Administration of Justice in the Province of Canada While It Was Subject to the Crown of France," and "A Plan for Settling the Laws and the Administration of Justice in the Province of Quebec," *Lower Canada Jurist* (Montreal, 1857), vol. 1, appendix, p. 1–48. For Maseres' authorship of these anonymous documents see S. M. Scott, "The Authorship of Certain Papers in the Lower Canada Jurist," *Can. Hist. Rev.*, vol. 10, p. 335–42. A comparison of these documents and Maseres' letters (Wallace, *op. cit.*) with Carleton's dispatches of this time reveals startling similarities of language and argument.

[17] (p. 161). Wallace, *op. cit.*, p. 82–88; Maseres, *op. cit.*, p. 58 ff.

[18] (p. 162). Shortt and Doughty, *op. cit.*, p. 294–96.

[19] (p. 163). *Ibid.*   [20] (p. 163). Q, vol. 5, p. 441–43.

[21] (p. 163). Shortt and Doughty, *op. cit.*, p. 299–301.

[22] (p. 164). Q, vol. 5, p. 344 (partly printed in Shortt and Doughty, *op. cit.*, p. 297–98); Q, vol. 5, p. 376, 602.

[23] (p. 164). *Ibid.*, vol. 6, p. 3–4, 12–13, 67–68; Shortt and Doughty, *op. cit.*, p. 325.

[24] (p. 164). C. O. 42, vol. 7, p. 2–5.

[25] (p. 165). Shortt and Doughty, op. cit., p. 377–95. Important sections are missing in Shortt and Doughty. They may be found in Q, vol. 18 B, p. 64–83.

[26] (p. 166). Adjusted to check the import of rum from New England because only specie was taken in return.

[27] (p. 167). Ibid., vol. 6, p. 67–68.

[28] (p. 168). Ibid., p. 121.   [29] (p. 168). Ibid., p. 127.   [30] (p. 168). Ibid., p. 129.

[31] (p. 168). W. P. M. Kennedy and G. Lanctot, Reports on the Laws of Quebec (Publications of the Public Archives of Canada, no. 12, Ottawa, 1931).

[32] (p. 169). Wallace, op. cit., p. 54.

[33] (p. 169). Ibid., p. 95–96. He had already recommended this in the second of the two documents referred to supra, n. 16.

[34] (p. 169). Ibid., p. 110.

[35] (p. 170). Carleton acknowledged assistance received from Cramahé.

[36] (p. 173). Carleton appointed Henry Kneller, a local lawyer, to act in his place.

[37] (p. 173). He was a member of the cabinet, but the senior secretaries of state were loath to admit him as an equal.

[38] (p. 173). Q, vol. 7, p. 61.

[39] (p. 173). Leg. Coun., vol. C, p. 60–62.

[40] (p. 173). Montreal Justices to Allsopp, July 31, 1769, and Burke to Allsopp, August 6, 1769, in Int. Cor. Prov. Que.

[41] (p. 173). Leg. Coun., vol. C, p. 64v.

[42] (p. 173). Shortt and Doughty, op. cit., p. 395–401.

[43] (p. 173). This epithet was commonly applied. See Walter Murray's Protest, delivered January 10, 1770, in Int. Cor. Prov. Que.

[44] (p. 174). Shortt and Doughty, op. cit., p. 401–16.

[45] (p. 174). See Walter Murray's Protest, supra, n. 43.

[46] (p. 174). Q, vol. 7, p. 89–93.   [47] (p. 174). Leg. Coun., vol. C, p. 97v.

[48] (p. 175). Q, vol. 5, p. 726–28.   [49] (p. 175). Ibid., vol. 6, p. 36.

[50] (p. 176). Gosselin, op. cit., p. 194.   [51] (p. 176). Q, vol. 8, p. 166–68.

IX. The Quebec Act

[1] (p. 177). Shelburne and Hillsborough. The former was now out of office.

[2] (p. 177). Q, vol. 8, p. 1.

[3] (p. 178). Shortt and Doughty, op. cit., p. 423. The decision carried out by this instruction must have been made some time previously.

[4] (p. 178). Q, vol. 8, p. 97–98. On August 7, 1769, when completing his report, Carleton wrote to Hillsborough that he had quashed a Canadian petition "for the reestablishment of the ancient laws of the country, and for some alterations in the administration of justice . . . as I understand the king's intentions are to grant those very concessions and improvements . . . and it is far more eligible that these should take their rise from his paternal attention to their interests than proceed from any solicitation on their part." See Q, vol. 6, p. 115–16. After his departure in 1770, however, Cramahé forwarded him another petition from a number of Canadians praying for the restoration of "the ancient laws and customs which governed all their properties . . . an event on which they consider all their future happiness, and that of their families, entirely to depend, and they already enquire when they may hope to receive some account of your success therein." Q, vol. 7, p. 266.

[5] (p. 178). Cramahé held the matter up. C. O. 42, vol. 16, p. 63.

[6] (p. 179). Leg. Coun., vol. C, p. 48–52v.

[7] (p. 179). *Ibid.*, p. 102v, 104v, 109v–11; Q, vol. 8, p. 82.

[8] (p. 180). *Ibid.*, p. 111–15.

[9] (p. 180). *Ibid.*, p. 160–63.

[10] (p. 181). See Memorial of Charles de Lanaudière, 1777, in Int. Cor. Prov. Que.

[11] (p. 181). Q, vol. 8, p. 217–19.

[12] (p. 181). *Ibid.*, p. 79–80.

[13] (p. 182). Shortt and Doughty, *op. cit.*, p. 445–83.

[14] (p. 183). *Ibid.*, p. 437–45.

[15] (p. 184). *Ibid.*, p. 424–37.

[16] (p. 184). [William Knox], *The Justice and Policy of the Late Act of Parliament for Making More Effectual Provision for the Government of the Province of Quebec* (London, 1774), p. 9.

[17] (p. 185). Sir Henry Cavendish, *Debates of the House of Commons in the Year 1774, on the Bill for Making More Effectual Provision for the Government of the Province of Quebec* (ed. J. Wright, London, 1839).

[18] (p. 186). Shortt and Doughty, *op. cit.*, p. 534n.

[19] (p. 186). *Ibid.*, p. 594–614.

[20] (p. 187). It has been argued that these instructions, dated January 3, 1775, betray a change of mind on the part of the government after the act was passed. See Coupland, *op. cit.*, p. 126. But this is improbable because Carleton, who sailed immediately after the act was passed, must have carried with him a knowledge of the government's intention to allow the merchants no just grievance. Dartmouth's letter of surprise at Carleton's failure to report the satisfaction of the old subjects with the new constitution appears conclusive upon this point. Shortt and Doughty, *op. cit.*, p. 585.

[21] (p. 188). I cannot accept the conclusion of the Hon. T. Chapais in his *Cours d'histoire du Canada* (Quebec, 1919) that this section was an afterthought because it was introduced after the bill had been brought into the house.

[22] (p. 188). The instructions directed the appointment of a Protestant incumbent to any parish in which the majority of the inhabitants desired it, and he was then to collect the tithes payable within that parish.

[23] (p. 188). The *Quebec Gazette,* November 10, 1774, printed a long extract from Knox, *op. cit.*, but ascribed the work, which was anonymous, to Marriott.

[24] (p. 197). Cavendish, *op. cit.*, p. 12.

[25] (p. 197). Hey to the Lord High Chancellor, January 25, 1774, Dartmouth Papers, vol. 1 (unpaged).

[26] (p. 199). Dartmouth Papers, vol. 2, p. 280.

X. The Invasion of Canada

[1] (p. 202). Except where otherwise stated, the authority for the facts related in this chapter may be found in Justin H. Smith, *Our Struggle for the Fourteenth Colony* (2 vols., New York, 1907), a remarkably fine piece of work.

[2] (p. 202). Shortt and Doughty, *op. cit.*, p. 583–84.

[3] (p. 204). F. Maseres, *An Account of the Proceedings of the British and Other Protestants of the Province of Quebec* (London, 1775), p. 231.

[4] (p. 204). Shortt and Doughty, *op. cit.*, p. 586–88.

[5] (p. 207). Grant to Grant, September 20, 1775, Dartmouth Papers (Patshull), vol. 2 (unpaged).

[6] (p. 208). Shortt and Doughty, *op. cit.*, p. 661.

[7] (p. 208). Abbé H. A. Verreau, *Invasion du Canada* (Montreal, 1873), p. 362.

[8] (p. 209). Q, vol. 11, p. 167–68.

[9] (p. 209). *Ibid.*, p. 170–73.

[10] (p. 211). Verreau, *op. cit.*, p. 29 ff.

[11] (p. 213). Hey to [Dartmouth], July 20, 1775, Dartmouth Papers (Patshull), vol. 2.

[12] (p. 214). Q, vol. 11, p. 261.

[13] (p. 214). *Ibid.*, p. 282–83.

[14] (p. 216). Caldwell to Barré, September 19 and 20, 1775, Dartmouth Papers (Patshull), vol. 2.

[15] (p. 217). Articles of Capitulation, Q, vol. 11, p. 278.

[16] (p. 217). Verreau, *op. cit.*, p. 43.

[17] (p. 219). Q, vol. 11, p. 318.

[18] (p. 220). *Ibid.*, p. 324.

[19] (p. 220). *Ibid.*, p. 262–63.

[20] (p. 224). Hey to [Dartmouth], September 11–21, 1775, Dartmouth Papers (Patshull), vol. 2.

[21] (p. 220). F. Maseres, *Additional Papers Concerning the Province of Quebec* (London, 1776), p. 101. Though this Macaulay has the same name as the father of the historian, there is no known connection between them.

[22] (p. 220). Patterson and Grant to John Strettell, September 21, 1775, Dartmouth Papers (Patshull), vol. 2.

[23] (p. 221). Caldwell to Barré, September 19–20, 1775, *ibid.*

[24] (p. 221). Allan McLean to [?], September 21, 1775, *ibid.*

[25] (p. 222). Q, vol. 12, p. 94–101.

[26] (p. 228). Fraser had been taken with the vessels at Sorel but had later been allowed to return to his family. See B, vol. 73, p. 176.

[27] (p. 229). Q, vol. 11, p. 261.

[28] (p. 232). Livius said three small boats, one of which was sunk. His descriptive letter of May 10, 1776, was published anonymously in the *Quebec Gazette*, November 14, 1776.

[29] (p. 240). B, vol. 39, p. 7–8.

[30] (p. 240). *Ibid.*, p. 37.

[31] (p. 240). This included three dozen captured at Ile aux Noix and Ile la Motte at the close of June and the beginning of July.

[32] (p. 240). Q, vol. 12, p. 135.

[33] (p. 241). B, vol. 39, p. 93–94.

[34] (p. 242). J. Fortescue, ed., *Correspondence of King George the Third* (London, 1927–28), vol. 3, p. 386.

[35] (p. 242). *Ibid.*, p. 403.

[36] (p. 242). Jane Clark, "The Command of the Canadian Army for the Campaign of 1777," *Can. Hist. Rev.*, vol. 10, p. 129–35 (June, 1929).

[37] (p. 242). Q, vol. 12, p. 88.

[38] (p. 242). Fortescue, *op. cit.*, vol. 3, p. 196, 236.

[39] (p. 243). *Ibid.*, p. 406.

[40] (p. 243). A. L. Burt, "The Quarrel between Germain and Carleton; An Inverted Story," *Can. Hist. Rev.*, vol. 11, p. 202–22 (September, 1930).

[41] (p. 245). *Ibid.*

[42] (p. 245). Q, vol. 13, p. 369.

XI. A Reactionary Government

[1] (p. 249). Leg. Coun., vol. D, p. 1.

[2] (p. 249). *Ibid.*, p. 4–6.

[3] (p. 249). Shortt and Doughty, *op. cit.*, p. 637–60.

[4] (p. 249). *Ibid.*, p. 671.

[5] (p. 249). Can. Arch. Report, 1918, Appendix C, p. 18. Carleton also announced that he had continued the bailiffs in office until further orders.

[6] (p. 250). Q, vol. 12, p. 119.

[7] (p. 250). Shortt and Doughty, *op. cit.*, p. 674–75.

[8] (p. 250). Q, vol. 14, p. 265–66.

[9] (p. 250). He also issued a commission creating the council presided over by himself, the lieutenant governor, or the chief justice, a court of appeals (Shortt and Doughty, *op. cit.*, p. 672), but no appeal was decided under this instrument (Leg. Coun., vol. D, p. 92). In the absence of the chief justice, who had returned to England just before the siege began, the criminal jurisdiction which he would have exercised had he remained was apparently provided for by a special commission to a civil judge for each case. Livius received at least one such commission.

[10] (p. 250). Q, vol. 12, p. 119.

[11] (p. 250). See Exact State of His Majesty's Legislative Council, *ibid.*, p. 172.

[12] (p. 251). *Ibid.*, p. 170.

[13] (p. 251). State Book (sometimes referred to as Privy Council and sometimes as Executive Council, vol. D, p. 1.

[14] (p. 252). State Book, vol. D, p. 2–4; Can. Arch. Report, 1918, Appendix C, p. 24, 26, 28. The proclamation of 1777 forbade any export except for His Majesty's forces or ships.

[15] (p. 253). Q, vol. 13, p. 297.

[16] (p. 253). To a lesser degree the same was true of the executive council.

[17] (p. 253). He did after he returned as Lord Dorchester.

[18] (p. 253). One in 1777 and another in 1780.

[19] (p. 254). Shortt and Doughty, *op. cit.*, p. 679–82.

[20] (p. 254). *Ibid.*, p. 682–89.

[21] (p. 254). *Ibid.*, p. 690–91.

[22] (p. 254). Leg. Coun., vol. D, p. 9–10.

[23] (p. 257). *Ibid.*, p. 14.

[24] (p. 257). *Ibid.*, p. 22.

[25] (p. 257). Shortt and Doughty, *op. cit.*, p. 677.

[26] (p. 257). The committee was appointed on February 25 and reported on March 29. The session ended on April 29.

[27] (p. 258). The council had adopted this as a rule on February 4, 1768. Leg. Coun., vol. C, p. 3v.

[28] (p. 258). The ordinance of 1764 said "daily." According to the Register of the Court of Quarter Sessions (p. 40, 265), Montreal's market days were Tuesday and Friday in the spring of 1766, and Tuesday, Thursday, and Friday fourteen years later.

[29] (p. 259). *Ibid.*, p. 270.

[30] (p. 259). *Ibid.*, p. 40, 227, 263.

[31] (p. 259). The customary weight of the white loaf was four pounds, and of the brown loaf six pounds.

[32] (p. 259). This clause was not repeated in the 1777 ordinance.

[33] (p. 260). Register of the Court of Quarter Sessions, p. 273.

[34] (p. 260). The justices of the peace wrestled with the problem without aid from the council until February, 1768, when the first ordinance was passed.

[35] (p. 262). Leg. Coun., vol. C, p. 122.

[36] (p. 262). Still another innovation was the use of wooden chimney pots, but this was effectively stopped in 1773. No mention was made of it in the measure of 1777.

[37] (p. 262). Leg. Coun., vol. C, p. 98v.

[38] (p. 262). This was another "objectionable ordinance," but it caused much less criticism than the other two.

[39] (p. 262). Register of the Court of Quarter Sessions, p. 42, 51, 82.

[40] (p. 262). *Ibid.*, p. 175.   [41] (p. 263). *Ibid.*, p. 107.

[42] (p. 263). *Ibid.*, p. 47, 211.   [43] (p. 263). *Ibid.*, p. 55, 132, 307.

[44] (p. 263). *Ibid.*, p. 266, 344.   [45] (p. 263). *Ibid.*, p. 209, 346, 347.

[46] (p. 263). *Ibid.*, p. 42, 271.   [47] (p. 264). *Ibid.*, p. 69.

[48] (p. 264). Government officials, seigniors, and noblesse, retired officers, clergy, students of the seminaries of Quebec and Montreal, and others engaged in "offices of public utility."

[49] (p. 265). A copy of a paper produced in council before the militia ordinance was presented to the governor. Finlay Papers (unpaged).

[50] (p. 266). State of militiamen refusing obedience, March 12 to April 2, 1778, abstract of causes against militiamen, February 19 to April 8, 1783, Int. Cor. Prov. Que.

[51] (p. 266). B, vol. 39, p. 675–76.

[52] (p. 266). *Ibid.*, p. 528.   [53] (p. 266). *Ibid.*, p. 550.

[54] (p. 266). *Ibid.*, p. 554.   [55] (p. 266). *Ibid.*, p. 528.

[56] (p. 266). *Ibid.*, p. 637.   [57] (p. 266). *Ibid.*, p. 564, 655–56, 663.

[58] (p. 266). *Ibid.*, p. 655.   [59] (p. 266). *Ibid.*, vol. 62, p. 329.

[60] (p. 267). A. L. Burt, "The Quarrel between Germain and Carleton; An Inverted Story," *Can. Hist. Rev.*, vol. 11, p. 202–22 (September, 1930).

[61] (p. 267). Q, vol. 13, p. 297. For the story of Peter Livius and his relations with Carleton see A. L. Burt, "The Tragedy of Chief Justice Livius," *Can. Hist. Rev.*, vol. 5, p. 196–212 (September, 1924).

[62] (p. 267). *Ibid.*

[63] (p. 268). Peter Livius was a naturalized citizen. See Q, vol. 74–2, p. 332. See also Haldimand's Diary, Can. Arch. Report, 1889, p. 199.

[64] (p. 268). On promotion to be chief justice, Livius became an ex officio member of the council.

[65] (p. 269). Leg. Coun., vol. D, p. 25.

[66] (p. 269). *Ibid.*, p. 37, 41.

[67] (p. 270). *Ibid.*, p. 30–33.

[68] (p. 270). Finlay's preamble to the motion on April 6, 1778, in Finlay Papers (unpaged).

[69] (p. 270). Leg. Coun., vol. D, p. 35.

[70] (p. 270). *Ibid.*, p. 41.

[71] (p. 270). *Ibid.*, p. 28–30.

[72] (p. 271). *Ibid.*, p. 41, 42.

[73] (p. 271). See Haldimand's later comment in Shortt and Doughty, *op. cit.*, p. 718.

[74] (p. 272). Leg. Coun., vol. D, p. 43.

[75] (p. 272). Of the ordinary council members, he was the senior, ranking immediately after the lieutenant governor and the chief justice.

[76] (p. 273). May 29, 1778, Finlay Papers (unpaged).

[77] (p. 273). The minutes show that he was not admitted to the "privy" council so long as it remained "privy," which was for more than a year after Carleton left.

[78] (p. 273). The attorney general had the right to private practice that did not interfere with his public duties.

XII. A War Raid and Surprises

[1] (p. 276). Jean N. McIlwraith, *Sir Frederick Haldimand* (2d ed., London and Toronto, 1926), is an excellent biography.

[2] (p. 276). To lieutenant general in the army and general in America.

[3] (p. 277). See B, vol. 76, p. 230.

[4] (p. 278). Q, vol. 16–1, p. 292; vol. 19, p. 285.

[5] (p. 278). *Ibid.,* vol. 16–2, p. 388.

[6] (p. 279). *Ibid.,* p. 644.

[7] (p. 280). He reported that it could be bought for £3,000, but the proprietors demanded £5,000, which the home government refused to pay. Haldimand then got permission to purchase through agents in Canada, and in 1780 he acquired it for £3,300. Q, vol. 17–2, p. 736.

[8] (p. 281). *Ibid.,* vol. 16, p. 347.

[9] (p. 281). *Ibid.,* vol. 17–1, p. 76.

[10] (p. 281). *Ibid.,* p. 263–64.

[11] (p. 281). *Ibid.,* p. 133.

[12] (p. 282). *Ibid.,* vol. 18, p. 16.

[13] (p. 282). *Ibid.,* vol. 16–1, p. 296.

[14] (p. 282). *Ibid.,* p. 344; B, vol. 54, p. 96.

[15] (p. 282). *Ibid.,* vol. 57–2, p. 309.

[16] (p. 283). Patrick Campbell, quoted in E. Cruickshank, *Butler's Rangers* (Lundy's Lane Historical Society, 1893), p. 77.

[17] (p. 284). I have been unable to discover what was his relationship, if any, to Sir Guy and Thomas Carleton.

[18] (p. 285). This was the occasion referred to *supra,* page 276.

[19] (p. 287). Oswegatchie was useless, being commanded by a ridge five hundred yards distant. B, vol. 154, p. 29.

[20] (p. 288). Fort Chartres had been destroyed.

[21] (p. 288). Another lieutenant governor, Nicholas Cox, was established at Gaspé.

[22] (p. 289). For his activities there see N. V. Russell, "The Indian Policy of Henry Hamilton," *Can. Hist. Rev.,* vol. 11, p. 20–37 (March, 1930).

[23] (p. 291). J. A. James, *The Life of George Rogers Clark* (Chicago, 1928).

XIII. The Shadow of the War

[1] (p. 292). B, vol. 131, p. 136.

[2] (p. 293). Du Calvet spoke of a hundred suffering like himself, but he named only nineteen, some of whom cannot be traced. See next note.

[3] (p. 293). See William Kingsford, *History of Canada* (Toronto, 1887–88), vol. 7, p. 52–64, and also McIlwraith, *op. cit.,* chap. 14, for good discussions of the prisoners.

[4] (p. 294). B, vol. 62, p. 103.

[5] (p. 294). Montgolfier had also complained of the anti-religious tone of the paper. B, vol. 72–1, p. 177.

[6] (p. 294). Michael Voyer, of whom practically nothing is known.

[7] (p. 294). Q, vol. 20, p. 8.

[8] (p. 295). B, vol. 205, p. 2–4.

[9] (p. 296). On examining the papers taken from a messenger of Du Calvet, Haldimand observed that Du Calvet had signed his own death warrant.

[10] (p. 297). Q, vol. 17, p. 76–77; vol. 20, p. 11.

[11] (p. 297). Ibid., vol. 18, p. 130.

[12] (p. 297). B, vol. 95, p. 94–101.

[13] (p. 297). Ibid., vol. 200–2, p. 277–85, 513–17.

[14] (p. 299). Q, vol. 17–1, p. 195–98.

[15] (p. 299). Ibid., vol. 16–1, p. 345–46; vol. 17–1, p. 76. Valinière died shortly after he reached the country which he hated.

[16] (p. 300). Ibid., p. 195–98; vol. 19, p. 184–85, 220; vol. 20, p. 332.

[17] (p. 300). Ibid., vol. 22, p. 54–72.

[18] (p. 301). Ibid., vol. 21, p. 264–77, 298–302; vol. 22, p. 6–7. On August 8, 1783, Lord North promised to get substitutes from Savoy or some other Catholic country not under Bourbon rule. Ibid., vol. 21, p. 286. On leaving Canada, Haldimand informed Hamilton that four priests from Savoy might soon be expected. Ibid., vol. 24–1, p. 266.

[19] (p. 302). B, vol. 72–1, p. 56.

[20] (p. 303). Freight was paid until 1781. C. O. 42, vol. 16, p. 184.

[21] (p. 303). Q, vol. 17–1, p. 149.

[22] (p. 304). Ibid., vol. 16–2, p. 633; vol. 17–1, p. 140–51.

[23] (p. 304). Ibid., p. 206.

[24] (p. 305). Ibid., vol. 22, p. 91–176. The Niagara representative of Taylor and Forsyth was named Pollard, possibly the man mentioned below.

[25] (p. 305). B, vol. 106, p. 1–7.

[26] (p. 306). Q, vol. 17–1, p. 199–206; vol. 19, p. 26–28, 130, 162, 182, 212, 326, 334–45; vol. 20, p. 272–78, 350–77, 386, 389–95.

[27] (p. 306). It was permitted under special license granted by the governor for such particular purposes as supplying the navy in Halifax. Ibid., vol. 18 B, p. 199; B, vol. 201, p. 16, 18.

[28] (p. 306). B, vol. 54, p. 314; Q, vol. 16–1, p. 296.

[29] (p. 307). Q, vol. 16–1, p. 341–42.

[30] (p. 307). Shortt and Doughty, op. cit., p. 712.

[31] (p. 307). State Book, vol. D, p. 94.

[32] (p. 307). Q, vol. 16–1, p. 289.

[33] (p. 308). Ibid., p. 128.

[34] (p. 308). Ibid., vol. 15, p. 192.

[35] (p. 308). B, vol. 72–1, p. 282.

[36] (p. 308). Ibid., p. 280.

[37] (p. 309). Ibid., vol. 95, p. 79.

[38] (p. 310). Leg. Coun., vol. D, p. 57–60, 66–68, 71–76, 95–102; Shortt and Doughty, op. cit., p. 712–16.

[39] (p. 310). Leg. Coun., vol. D, p. 110–11.

[40] (p. 311). A. R. M. Lower, "Credit and the Constitutional Act," Can. Hist. Rev., vol. 6, p. 123–41 (June, 1925).

[41] (p. 311). Opinion of Yorke and De Gray, March 24, 1766, in David Chisolme Papers.

[42] (p. 312). The above figures are deduced from the Public Accounts of the Province of Quebec. At first glance the entries are misleading, because the bills sold were for sterling and the cash paid, principally in dollars, was calculated in the currency of the province. As £100 sterling were equivalent to £111 1/9 currency, bills entered as sold at 111 1/9 were really negotiated at par, and an entry showing bills sold at 113 meant that exchange stood at 1.7 per cent above par.

[43] (p. 313). Q, vol. 18, p. 72, 82–83.

[44] (p. 313). Ibid., vol. 21, p. 234.

[45] (p. 314). Ibid., vol. 19, p. 23.

[46] (p. 314). Ibid., vol. 18, p. 73.

[47] (p. 314). See "Statistics of the Trade of Quebec," being B, vol. 201, printed in Can. Arch. Report, 1888.

[48] (p. 316). Shortt and Doughty, op. cit., p. 704–05.

[49] (p. 317). Other politics seems to have been involved, for the post which Allsopp coveted went to George, later Sir George, Pownall, a son of John, the under secretary of state.

[50] (p. 319). Leg. Coun., vol. D, p. 71, 73.

[51] (p. 319). Haldimand referred to the office in this way, but it is not mentioned in the establishment prepared at the time of the Quebec Act (Shortt and Doughty, op. cit., p. 613) nor in the list of appointments which Dartmouth sent Carleton on April 15, 1775 (Q, vol. 14, p. 269).

[52] (p. 319). Leg. Coun., vol. D, p. 46.

[53] (p. 320). Ibid., p. 48.

[54] (p. 320). Q, vol. 16–1, p. 341.

[55] (p. 320). Ibid., vol. 18, p. 5. There had been over twenty meetings of the "privy" or "executive" council in each of the years 1777 and 1778, and this was the eighth in 1779. Only one more was held in 1779, none in 1780, only one in 1781, and two in the first eleven months of 1782 — all purely formal sessions. One is reminded of how Henry III in the thirteenth century withdrew business from his council when he lost control of it.

[56] (p. 321). Shortt and Doughty, op. cit., p. 706.

[57] (p. 322). Q, vol. 16–2, p. 621.

[58] (p. 322). Leg. Coun., vol. D, p. 61–65.

[59] (p. 322). Ibid., p. 76–78.

[60] (p. 323). Ibid., p. 78–80.

[61] (p. 324). Though Haldimand was pleased with the document as a whole, for it expressed his own political faith, he sent it back to be toned down in several places. Then were eliminated the slur on Livius, the flat denunciation in the proposed court of appeals, and the insinuation against doctrinaire reforms, for which was substituted a statement that these were no times for "innovations." The amended version is printed in Shortt and Doughty, op. cit., p. 710–11.

[62] (p. 324). Leg. Coun., vol. D., p. 81–89.

[63] (p. 325). Ibid., p. 92–95. The council was now meeting in the Bishop's Palace.

[64] (p. 326). Ibid., p. 104–05.

[65] (p. 326). Q, vol. 18, p. 1–5.

[66] (p. 326). See particularly Q, vol. 17–1, p. 186–93; vol. 17–2, p. 666–71; Shortt and Doughty, op. cit., p. 711–22.

[67] (p. 327). They had caught the point. Q, vol. 18, p. 12.

[68] (p. 327). Ibid., p. 37–40. In another letter of the same date, Germain told Haldimand that he had been right and the majority wrong on the question of price fixing. Ibid., p. 28.

[69] (p. 327). Leg. Coun., vol. D, p. 110–14.

[70] (p. 327). *Ibid.*, p. 115.

[71] (p. 328). *Ibid.*, p. 116–26.

[72] (p. 328). B, vol. 204, p. 109; Q, vol. 21, p. 102–05.

[73] (p. 328). Leg. Coun., vol. D, p. 132–36.

XIV. The Shadow of the Peace

[1] (p. 329). See A. L. Burt, "A New Approach to the Problem of the Western Posts," Report of the Canadian Historical Association, 1931, in which form the greater part of this chapter has already appeared.

[2] (p. 329). For this question see S. F. Bemis, *Jay's Treaty; A Study in Diplomacy and Commerce* (New York, 1923); W. E. Stevens, *The Northwest Fur Trade, 1763–1800* (University of Illinois Studies, Urbana, 1928); and G. W. Brown, "The St. Lawrence in the Boundary Settlement of 1783," *Can. Hist. Rev.,* vol. 9, p. 223–38 (September, 1928).

[3] (p. 331). Fortescue, *op. cit.,* vol. 4, p. 76.

[4] (p. 332). *Parliamentary Register,* vol. 8, p. 248.

[5] (p. 332). Fortescue, *op. cit.,* vol. 6, p. 118.

[6] (p. 332). *Ibid.,* p. 144.   [7] (p. 333). *Ibid.,* p. 172.

[8] (p. 335). F. Wharton, *Revolutionary Diplomatic Correspondence of the United States* (Washington, 1889), vol. 6, p. 603.

[9] (p. 335). See Stevens, *op. cit.,* chap. 3, and Brown, *op. cit.*

[10] (p. 336). The best known presentation of this thesis is A. C. McLaughlin, "The Western Posts and British Debts," Report of the American Historical Association, 1894.

[11] (p. 336). Stevens, *op. cit.*   [12] (p. 336). Q, vol. 21, p. 220–21.

[13] (p. 336). *Ibid.,* p. 229–32.   [14] (p. 337). *Ibid.*

[15] (p. 337). *Ibid.,* p. 402.   [16] (p. 338). *Ibid.,* p. 370.

[17] (p. 338). *Ibid.,* p. 388.   [18] (p. 338). B, vol. 175, p. 227.

[19] (p. 338). Q, vol. 21, p. 405.   [20] (p. 338). *Ibid.,* p. 399.

[21] (p. 338). *Ibid.,* p. 388.   [22] (p. 338). *Ibid.,* p. 390.

[23] (p. 339). B, vol. 105, p. 364.   [24] (p. 339). Q, vol. 21, p. 392–93.

[25] (p. 340). *Ibid.,* vol. 22, p. 5–6.   [26] (p. 340). *Ibid.,* vol. 23, p. 46–47.

[27] (p. 341). *Ibid.,* p. 48.   [28] (p. 342). *Ibid.,* p. 60–62.

[29] (p. 343). *Ibid.,* p. 161–70.   [30] (p. 343). *Ibid.,* p. 164–65.

[31] (p. 343). *Ibid.,* p. 329–38.

[32] (p. 345). This should have been passed earlier. See Shortt and Doughty, *op. cit.,* p. 733.

[33] (p. 345). C. O. 42, vol. 16, p. 114.   [34] (p. 346). Leg. Coun., vol. E, p. 256.

[35] (p. 346). On the North West Company see G. C. Davidson, *The North West Company* (University of California Publications in History, Berkeley, 1918); Innis, *op. cit.,* and *Peter Pond* (Toronto, 1929).

[36] (p. 347). See Stevens, *op. cit.,* p. 106, 120, and documents there cited.

[37] (p. 347). By permitting canoes and bateaux as far as Niagara. See Q, vol. 24, p. 327. In the previous autumn Haldimand had given the North West Company permission to build a vessel at Detroit to be placed on Lake Superior. Can. Arch. Report, 1888, Note E, p. 72.

[38] (p. 350). Some most interesting documents on this subject are published in Can. Arch. Report, 1890, Note E. See particularly p. 108–17.

[39] (p. 350). *Ibid.,* p. 156–57. The identification of the author of the proposal may be found on page xlii.

[40] (p. 352). Shortt and Doughty, *op. cit.*, p. 809.

[41] (p. 353). *Ibid.*, p. 807.

[42] (p. 353). Q, vol. 27, p. 82.

[43] (p. 353). *Ibid.*, p. 86.

[44] (p. 354). *Ibid.*, p. 34–36.

[45] (p. 354). *Ibid.*, p. 44–47; vol. 28, p. 28–30.

[46] (p. 354). *Ibid.*, vol. 43, p. 786–96.

[47] (p. 355). *Ibid.*, vol. 46, p. 395–403, 411–26, 442–540.

[48] (p. 355). *Ibid.*, vol. 26, p. 312, 521, 596; vol. 38, p. 141; vol. 43, p. 784; vol. 46, p. 496.

[49] (p. 356). Can. Arch. Report, 1890, Note E, p. 173–74.

XV. THE LOYALISTS

[1] (p. 357). C. H. Van Tyne, *The Loyalists in the American Revolution* (New York, 1902); L. Sabine, *The Loyalists of the American Revolution* (2 vols, Boston, 1864).

[2] (p. 360). B, vol. 63, p. 212–13.

[3] (p. 360). Sir William Johnson had presented his claim in England.

[4] (p. 360). Q, vol. 26–1, p. 114–18.

[5] (p. 361). Ontario Archives Report, 1904, p. 24.

[6] (p. 361). *Ibid.*, p. 325–488, 913–1124, 1253–85, 1323, 1357–59, 1364.

[7] (p. 361). Int. Cor. Prov. Que. (S. 22).

[8] (p. 362). B, vol. 63, p. 413.

[9] (p. 362). C. O. 42, vol. 16, p. 265.

[10] (p. 363). Ont. Arch. Report, 1928, p. 68.

[11] (p. 363). It is published in *The Centennial of the Settlement of Upper Canada by the United Empire Loyalists, 1784–1884* (Toronto, 1885).

[12] (p. 363). Q, vol. 23, p. 348; vol. 24, p. 66, 163; vol. 26, p. 116. In the winter of 1786–87, Mabane and St. Ours said the loyalists numbered about six thousand. Shortt and Doughty, *op. cit.*, p. 880.

[13] (p. 364). A list of December 2, 1778, shows that there were then 32 men, 42 women, and 117 children at Machiche. See B, vol. 166, p. 2. According to a list of July 1, 1779, 853 refugees were being victualed in or above Sorel. *Ibid.*, p. 9.

[14] (p. 364). *Ibid.*, vol. 129, p. 51.

[15] (p. 364). *Ibid.*, p. 93.

[16] (p. 364). *Ibid.*, vol. 131, p. 31, 62.

[17] (p. 365). Q, vol. 17, p. 189.

[18] (p. 365). *Ibid.*, vol. 20, p. 310–14.

[19] (p. 366). *Ibid.*, vol. 21, p. 257.

[20] (p. 366). *Ibid.*, vol. 23, p. 91–94.

[21] (p. 366). *Ibid.*, p. 1.

[22] (p. 366). B, vol. 64, p. 231–33, 318–20.

[23] (p. 367). Q, vol. 26, p. 116–17. See *supra*, chap. 12, n. 7.

[24] (p. 367). B, vol. 63, p. 269.

[25] (p. 367). *Ibid.*, vol. 64, p. 144, 248; Q, vol. 22, p. 5.

[26] (p. 367). C. O. 42, vol. 16, p. 264.

[27] (p. 367). Q, vol. 23, p. 48–51.

[28] (p. 368). B, vol. 64, p. 145.

[29] (p. 368). Q, vol. 21, p. 220–31.

[30] (p. 369). W. Canniff, *History of the Settlement of Upper Canada* (Toronto, 1869), p. 650.

[31] (p. 369). Q. vol. 22, p. 10.

[32] (p. 370). *Ibid.,* vol. 23, p. 5–8, 33.

[33] (p. 370). B, vol. 158, p. 339.

[34] (p. 370). For settlement up to Cataragua see *ibid.,* vol. 65, p. 20.

[35] (p. 371). *Ibid.,* vol. 115, p. 234.

[36] (p. 371). Q, vol. 25, p. 184; B, vol. 64, p. 364, 392.

[37] (p. 372). Can. Arch. Report, 1891, Note A, p. 7.

[38] (p. 372). B, vol. 115, p. 221, 234.

[39] (p. 372). A very few seem to have gone to the Grand River. *Ibid.,* vol. 65. p. 30–32.

[40] (p. 373). Q, vol. 23, p. 348; vol. 24, p. 163. For further particulars see B, vol. 64, p. 154.

[41] (p. 375). J. F. Pringle, *Lunenburg or the Old Eastern District* (Cornwall, 1890), p. 33, 403–11.

[42] (p. 375). State Book, vol. D, p. 107.

[43] (p. 376). Minutes of an Enquiry in the New Western Settlements, 1787, p. 43, Int. Cor. Prov. Que.

[44] (p. 377). James Croil, *Dundas; or a Sketch of Canadian History* (Montreal, 1861), gives a good description.

[45] (p. 377). A letter from the treasury dated December 20, 1785, authorized a continuance of the issue of full rations till June 30, 1786, and then a smaller allowance till September 30. Leg. Coun., vol. D, p. 277.

[46] (p. 377). Can. Arch. Report, 1891, Note A, p. 13.

[47] (p. 378). Ont. Arch. Report, 1905, p. 463–64.

[48] (p. 378). Canniff, *op. cit.,* used some of them to paint a lurid picture.

[49] (p. 379). State Book, vol. G, p. 437, 468.

[50] (p. 379). *Ibid.,* p. 19.

[51] (p. 379). *Quebec Herald,* July 27, 1789.

[52] (p. 379). Q, vol. 38, p. 164.

[53] (p. 379). *Quebec Herald,* February 23, 1789.

[54] (p. 380). *Quebec Gazette,* May 25, 1789.

[55] (p. 380). *Ibid.,* June 11, 1789.

[56] (p. 380). *Quebec Herald,* June 22, 1789.

[57] (p. 380). *Quebec Gazette,* July 30, 1789.

[58] (p. 380). *Quebec Herald,* June 15, 1789.

[59] (p. 380). This may be traced in the files of the *Quebec Gazette,* where the monthly assize of bread was published. The price was a little higher in Quebec than in Montreal.

[60] (p. 381). State Book, vol. G, p. 1–20.

[61] (p. 381). Gray to Hunter, August 31, 1789, in Letter Book of Edward William Gray.

[62] (p. 382). Gray to John Fraser, January 14, 1790, *ibid.*

[63] (p. 382). State Book, vol. G, p. 421.

[64] (p. 383). There was a surgeon's mate at Cataraqui, another at the Bay of Chaleur, and a garrison surgeon at Detroit to serve the loyalists as well as the troops. Q, vol. 24–1, p. 133. Another reference of the time speaks of the annual visit of a doctor. *Ibid.,* p. 244.

[65] (p. 383). *Ibid.*

[66] (p. 384). Canniff, *op. cit.,* p. 207.

[67] (p. 384). Croil, *op. cit.,* p. 145.

[68] (p. 385). Shortt and Doughty, *op. cit.,* p. 773–77.

[69] (p. 386). Leg. Coun., vol. D, p. 214, 223, 267, 274, 285–87.

[70] (p. 387). State Book, vol. D, p. 237 A (printed).

[71] (p. 389). Minutes of an Enquiry in the New Western Settlements, 1787, Int. Cor. Prov. Que.; Shortt and Doughty, *op. cit.*, p. 938–46, 949–51.

[72] (p. 390). Report of John Collins and William Dummer Powell to Lord Dorchester, August 18, 1787, Int. Cor. Prov. Que.

[73] (p. 391). Shortt and Doughty, *op. cit.*, p. 946–48.

[74] (p. 391). Q, vol. 28, p. 374–79.

[75] (p. 391). *Ibid.*, p. 382–85.

[76] (p. 391). *Ibid.*, vol. 36–1, p. 238.

[77] (p. 392). Shortt and Doughty, *op. cit.*, p. 957.

[78] (p. 392). Q, vol. 36–2, p. 413–14.

[79] (p. 393). Chaplain to the second battalion of Johnson's regiment and formerly missionary to the Mohawks.

[80] (p. 394). W. R. Riddell, *The Life of William Dummer Powell* (Michigan Historical Commission, Lansing, 1924), p. 57–59; Q, vol. 42, p. 136.

[81] (p. 394). This and Land Book, vol. B, have been published in the Ont. Arch. Report, 1928.

[82] (p. 395). *Ibid.*, p. 43–44; also G, vol. 409, Letter Book of Lord Dorchester. According to the latter, the Mecklenburg board was created on August 27, the Luneburg board on September 10, the Montreal board on October 4, 1788, and the Gaspé board on March 10, 1789. I have been unable to discover the dates for the other boards.

[83] (p. 395). C. O. 42, vol. 18, p. 117.

[84] (p. 395). Q, vol. 49, p. 80.

[85] (p. 396). Ont. Arch. Report, 1905, p. 387.

[86] (p. 398). Ont. Arch. Report, 1928, p. 211–23.

[87] (p. 398). January 7, 1789, Int. Cor. Prov. Que.

XVI. A RISING STORM

[1] (p. 401). Finlay to Grant, August 9, 1785, C. O. 42, vol. 17, p. 253.

[2] (p. 402). A. R. M. Lower, *op. cit.*

[3] (p. 402). Q, vol. 22, p. 9.

[4] (p. 403). C. O. 42, vol. 15, p. 29–36.

[5] (p. 404). Q, vol. 22, p. 9–10; Shortt and Doughty, *op. cit.*, p. 736–38.

[6] (p. 404). Leg. Coun., vol. D, p. 144–201.

[7] (p. 404). C. O. 42, vol. 16, p. 13.

[8] (p. 409). Q, vol. 23, p. 58–59.

[8a] (p. 409). Cramahé was given the office of lieutenant governor of Detroit to be held as a sinecure. He died "at his seat near Exeter in Devonshire at an advanced age," on June 9, 1788. See *Quebec Gazette*, September 25, 1788.

[9] (p. 410). Q, vol. 23, p. 389–401; vol. 24, p. 24, 125.

[10] (p. 410). *Ibid.*, vol. 25, p. 162.

[11] (p. 411). *Quebec Gazette*, December 11, 1788.

[12] (p. 411). Shortt and Doughty, *op. cit.*, p. 742–54. The date of the above meetings is unknown, but the petition was dated just eight days after Haldimand sailed and it is almost inconceivable that these meetings could have been held while he was still in Quebec. The petition accumulated more signatures than appear in Shortt and Doughty.

[13] (p. 412). C. O. 42, vol. 17, p. 159.

[14] (p. 412). *Quebec Gazette,* December 11 and 18, 1788. In February, 1786, the London merchants said that the number was over eighteen hundred. Shortt and Doughty, *op. cit.,* p. 797.

[15] (p. 412). *Ibid.,* p. 754–58.   [16] (p. 413). *Ibid.,* p. 762–64.

[17] (p. 413). *Quebec Gazette,* January 15, 1789.

[18] (p. 414). C. O. 42, vol. 17, p. 179–80.

[19] (p. 414). Leg. Coun., vol. D, p. 202–302.

[20] (p. 416). *Quebec Gazette,* June 16, 1785.

[21] (p. 417). C. O. 42, vol. 17, p. 57.

[22] (p. 417). Shortt and Doughty, *op. cit.,* p. 779; State Book, vol. D, p. 173.

[23] (p. 418). Q, vol. 25, p. 247–93.

[24] (p. 419). C. O. 42, vol. 17, p. 111, a dispatch which Nepean drafted for Sydney, but for which the secretary of state, after consulting the premier, substituted the curt note of August 13 printed in Shortt and Doughty, *op. cit.,* p. 780, n. 2.

[25] (p. 419). B, vols. 230–32, printed in Can. Arch. Report, 1889, p. 124–298.

[26] (p. 420). Shortt and Doughty, *op. cit.,* p. 793–96, 805–06.

[27] (p. 421). *Ibid.,* p. 801–05.

XVII. Chief Justice Smith and Lord Dorchester

[1] (p. 422). L. Sabine, *op. cit.;* and M. L. Delafield, "William Smith — the Historian," *Magazine of American History,* vol. 6, p. 418 (June, 1881).

[2] (p. 422). W. M. Whitelaw, *The Maritime Provinces and Canada, a Study in Provincial Rivalries* (Toronto, 1933), p. 54.

[3] (p. 423). Though the summary of these theories has been extracted from documents in the Smith Papers written between his departure from New York and his arrival in Canada, he had conceived them at least a dozen years before, and, as he said in 1790, he had not concealed his ideas. See Shortt and Doughty, *op. cit.,* p. 1019. His conception thus antedated and may have suggested that of Lieutenant Colonel Robert Morse in Can. Arch. Report, 1884, Note C.

[4] (p. 423). Cited by Chester Martin in Report of the Canadian Historical Association, 1928, p. 14.

[5] (p. 424). See *supra,* n. 3.

[6] (p. 425). C. O. 42, vol. 18, p. 147.

[7] (p. 425). Can. Arch. Report, 1894, p. 419.

[8] (p. 425). Q, vol. 26–1, p. 84.

[9] (p. 425). This was taken for granted by Joseph Aplin, a loyalist lawyer who later became attorney general of Prince Edward Island. From Halifax, in March, 1784, Aplin wrote Smith a long letter urging him to use his influence on behalf of the new settlers on the St. John River, who, though grateful for what Sir Guy had done for them, were very discontented with their lot. Aplin wanted the chief justice of the still undivided Nova Scotia to be shipped off to the West Indies and his place to be taken by the man who had presided over the courts of New York. See Can. Arch. Report, 1894, p. 415. What Aplin took for granted is supported by two letters of the following August. One was by Smith to Lord Mahon, Pitt's brother-in-law and supporter, and the other was from Mahon to Sydney inclosing it. They had to do with a not unimportant detail of the Canadian administration. Jenkin Williams was back in his native Wales under a cloud which threatened to prevent his return to Quebec, and Smith advised the appointment of a certain D'Ivernois, a Genevan, on the ground that one of the two legal advisers of the Canadian government should be French. C. O. 42, vol. 18, p. 228–29.

Jenkin Williams was later able to return. His trouble was summed up by Sydney in a memorandum for the prime minister as follows: "The solicitor general is, I believe, a perfectly honest man. Many years ago he was guilty of an act of imprudence and irregularity without the least appearance, in my opinion, of an intent to defraud, but on its being presented to the grand jury of the county in which he lived in Wales a bill was found against him for forgery. He left the country to avoid a trial and went to Canada where he has maintained an unexceptionable character and executed many offices of trust and confidence to his own credit and the advantage of the public. Upon this affair's getting wind in Canada after a residence of between twenty and thirty years he returned to Wales, where all prosecution of the business is stopped and where he was well received, but there remains a doubt whether under all these circumstances a law office of the crown (for which I believe him to be fully competent) ought in propriety to be held by him." *Ibid.*, p. 145.

[10] (p. 426). Smith Papers.

[11] (p. 426). The draft dated June 11, 1785, according to the indorsement.

[12] (p. 427). C. O. 42, vol. 18, p. 144–47. Internal evidence leaves little doubt that the author of this anonymous document was Sydney, and absolutely fixes its date. It was prepared after Hamilton's *faux pas* was known and before his dismissal was decided, i. e., early in August, 1785.

[13] (p. 427). He suggested the supercession of Livius, Monk, and Hamilton, explained the difficulty about Jenkin Williams (*supra*, note 9), and proposed Hope's appointment as lieutenant governor.

[14] (p. 427). According to a letter from Sydney to Hope in the following spring, the ministry had not abandoned the idea of a government for all British North America suggested in the spring of 1784 and were now seriously considering it. Shortt and Doughty, *op. cit.*, p. 810.

[15] (p. 427). C. O. 42, vol. 17, p. 113–14.

[16] (p. 427). Governor Parr of Nova Scotia submitted with a prayer for military promotion to offset his civil demotion. See Can. Arch. Report, 1894, Calendar of Nova Scotia State Papers, p. 442. Thomas Carleton had more cause for disappointment. His step down came on top of a promise that he would step up. He had gone to New Brunswick with Sydney's assurance that he would be governor of Quebec on Haldimand's retirement. He accepted his fate with good grace, encouraged by an advancement to the rank of brigadier general. *Ibid.*, 1895, Calendar of New Brunswick State Papers, p. 10. He refused a solacing offer of Hope's place. This was fortunate, for Hope, who had been told that he might be removed to New Brunswick (Q, vol. 26–1, p. 85), had decided that he would not go. The prospect of being saddled with "an assembly composed of Americans" was to him an "invincible" obstacle. See C. O. 42, vol. 18, p. 90. Moreover, two Carletons in Quebec would not have looked very well, though they had earlier been together in Quebec and also in New York, and the older was relieved by the decision of the younger. *Ibid.*, vol. 18, p. 120.

[17] (p. 428). Smith Papers.

[18] (p. 428). See Can. Arch. Report, 1890, Note E.

[19] (p. 429). Q, vol. 26 A, p. 449, 451. The draft of particular instruction printed in Shortt and Doughty, *op. cit.*, p. 813–15, was altered before it was given to Dorchester on August 26, 1786.

[20] (p. 430). Q, vol. 26 A, p. 449.   [21] (p. 430). *Ibid.*, vol. 26–2, p. 518–79.

[22] (p. 430). *Quebec Gazette*, October 26, 1786. Hope said that he arrived on October 21. Q, vol. 26–2, p. 552. If so, he remained on board for another two days.

[23] (p. 431). See p. 482.   [24] (p. 431). B, vol. 77, p. 216.

[25] (p. 431). Q, vol. 43-2, p. 800.

[26] (p. 432). There are photostat copies in the Canadian Archives, Ottawa.

[27] (p. 432). Smith to Dorchester, November 7, 1788, in the Smith Papers. There is a transcript in Q, vol. 39, p. 117-21.

[28] (p. 433). Q, vol. 38, p. 1.

[29] (p. 433). Shortt and Doughty, op. cit., p. 871.

[30] (p. 434). Ibid., p. 874-97.

[31] (p. 434). No judge could participate in the review of any judgment which he had delivered. Of the three common pleas judges who were members of the council, only Mabane was then present in Quebec and he was excluded by this rule. Fraser was in Montreal and Dunn was in England, whither he had gone to settle his accounts as former acting receiver general. Q, vol. 26-2, p. 511-12.

[32] (p. 434). Gray v. Grant and Grant v. Gray. Photostat copies of the papers relating to this litigation are deposited in the Canadian Archives, Ottawa.

[33] (p. 434). Finlay wrote to Nepean, "I was not a little pleased to find that I had always been of Mr. Smith's opinion." Shortt and Doughty, op. cit., p. 846.

[34] (p. 434). Q, vol. 28, p. 300.

[35] (p. 435). Ibid., vol. 27-1, p. 17.

[36] (p. 435). Shortt and Doughty, op. cit., p. 841-43.

[37] (p. 435). Q, vol. 28, p. 51.

[38] (p. 435). Supra, n. 31.

[39] (p. 436). Shortt and Doughty, op. cit., p. 847-54.

[40] (p. 436). Leg. Coun., vol. E, p. 22.

[41] (p. 436). Shortt and Doughty, op. cit., p. 845.

[42] (p. 436). Leg. Coun., vol. E, p. 2.

[43] (p. 436). Ibid., p. 45.

[44] (p. 437). Shortt and Doughty, op. cit., p. 854. See the Smith Papers for a copy of the bill as printed in March, 1787. It differs in several other particulars, all minor, from the bill as it appears in Shortt and Doughty.

[45] (p. 437). Ibid., p. 844.

[46] (p. 438). Ibid., p. 906, 908.

[47] (p. 438). It should be remembered that the name "Canadian" had only a French connotation until well on in the nineteenth century.

[48] (p. 438). Leg. Coun., vol. E, p. 22.

[49] (p. 439). Ibid., p. 38, 46-52.

[50] (p. 439). Q, vol. 42, p. 48.

[51] (p. 440). Leg. Coun., vol. E, p. 78, 84-91; Finlay's notes on proceedings in the council, C. O. 42, vol. 19, p. 165-79; Shortt and Doughty, op. cit., p. 873-74. Monk also charged the privy council over in London with inconsistency, thereby upholding the English party's contention that final appeals should be submitted to the court of chancery. See Shortt and Doughty, op. cit., p. 745.

[52] (p. 441). Ibid., p. 858-61. Another bill (ibid., p. 863-64) provided for local courts in the old districts. Q, vol. 29-1, p. 1-4. The draft is in the Smith Papers.

[53] (p. 441, 442). The following analysis of the investigation owes much to the valuable assistance of Miss Hilda Neatby of the history department of the University of Minnesota. Needless to say, she is not to be held responsible for any errors that may have crept in.

[54] (p. 442). Q, vols. 29-1 to 34-2.

[55] (p. 442). Ibid., vol. 35, p. 60; C. O. 42, vol. 19, p. 187-88.

[56] (p. 442). In 1777. Q, vol. 48, p. 66.

[57] (p. 444). William Grant, who has sometimes been confused with the William Grant who was merchant, councilor, and deputy receiver general. The lawyer had resided in the colony for only a short while at the beginning of the American troubles. He was then attorney general. On being appealed to by the judges, he wrote Sydney on their behalf. C. O. 42, vol. 19, p. 266–68.

[58] (p. 444). Q, vol. 40, p. 106. After Gray's death, Monk was reinstated on Dorchester's intercession.

[59] (p. 444). An anonymous correspondent in the *Quebec Herald,* March 9, 1789.

[60] (p. 444). *Ibid.,* April 13, 1789. The new ordinance required the judges to give reasons for their judgments.

[61] (p. 444). Q, vol. 38, p. 253.

[62] (p. 444). Gray to Robert Hunter, January 14, 1790, in Letter Book of Edward William Gray.

[63] (p. 445). Q, vol. 43–1, p. 661.

XVIII. Trade, Education, Tenures, and Finance

[1] (p. 446). See Can. Arch. Report, 1890, Note C.

[2] (p. 447). Leg. Coun., vol. E, p. 255–60.   [3] (p. 448). *Ibid.,* p. 168, 205.

[4] (p. 448). G. S. Graham, *British Policy and Canada, 1774–1791* (Imperial Studies, no. 4, London, 1930), chap. 8.

[5] (p. 449). Shortt and Doughty, *op. cit.,* p. 815.

[6] (p. 450). C. O. 42, vol. 16, p. 82.

[7] (p. 450). Shortt and Doughty, *op. cit.,* p. 798.

[8] (p. 450). By the committee of the privy council which had taken over the functions of the board of trade, abolished in 1782.

[9] (p. 450). Leg. Coun., vol. E, p. 166–67, 179–80, 235. Shortt and Doughty, *op. cit.,* p. 733.

[10] (p. 451). Q, vol. 28, p. 4–12; Leg. Coun., vol. E, p. 91.

[11] (p. 451). G, vol. 1, p. 148, 153.

[12] (p. 451). *Quebec Gazette,* January 29, 1789.

[13] (p. 451). Beef, pork, and other kinds of meat, salted, cured, or smoked, could then be imported west of St. John but not through St. John, for some reason which is not clear. By the ordinance of 1788 the governor had power by proclamation to open other channels for the articles that could be imported through St. John.

[14] (p. 451). Q, vol. 41, p. 293.

[15] (p. 451). *Ibid.,* p. 281; 28 George III, cap. 6.

[16] (p. 452). Published in *Quebec Gazette,* September 17, 1789.

[17] (p. 452). State Book, vol. G, p. 295–97; Leg. Coun., vol. F, p. 85–87, 96–105, 110–11.

[18] (p. 452). Q, vol. 45–2, p. 532–34.

[19] (p. 454). Leg. Coun., vol. E, p. 184–86, 236–37.

[20] (p. 454). *Ibid.,* vol. F, p. 4–6, 12, 105–09, 121, 125–27, 160, 171, 189.

[21] (p. 454). Graham, *op. cit.,* chaps. 5 and 6.

[22] (p. 455). In January, 1787, the Quebec merchants' committee said that the average annual import during the previous four years had been 4,514 puncheons, "which if rated high are equal to 540,000 gallons." Leg. Coun., vol. E, p. 175. From other figures given in *ibid.,* p. 436, it would appear that the average annual consumption for the seven years from 1783 to 1790 was about 480,000 gallons.

[23] (p. 455). It had been reduced to this figure by the Rockingham government during the taxation troubles with the old colonies.

[24] (p. 456). I have been unable to discover with certainty the amount of rum imported from England in this year. But the figures mentioned above (note 22) show that nearly half the rum consumed in the colony from 1783 to 1790 paid no duty.

[25] (p. 456). Leg. Coun., vol. E, p. 172–77.

[26] (p. 456). Ibid., p. 160–62.

[27] (p. 457). They would apply this to all British North America, though there were then no distilleries in the maritime provinces.

[28] (p. 457). State Book, vol. D, p. 341–42, 349–50; Q, vol. 28, p. 226–28.

[29] (p. 458). Ibid.

[30] (p. 458). 28 George III, cap. 39.

[31] (p. 459). State Book, vol. G, p. 429, 490.

[32] (p. 459). It has been suggested that this was due to fears for the provincial revenue and for the triangular trade. See Graham, op. cit. This may be the true explanation, but the act was passed in 1788 in spite of the prospect of these consequences, and the purpose of the proposed amendment was merely to prevent the act from remaining virtually a dead letter.

[33] (p. 459). Leg. Coun., vol. E, p. 178–79.

[34] (p. 460). Ibid., p. 163–64.

[35] (p. 461). State Book, vol. F, p. 147–50.

[36] (p. 461). See Petition of Citizens of Quebec, November 19, 1787, ibid., p. 164–93; and Dorchester to Grenville, November 10, 1789, no. 65, Q, vol. 49, p. 1–5.

[37] (p. 462). State Book, vol. G, p. 257.

[38] (p. 462). The old subjects were Dunn, Mabane, Caldwell, and Grant; the new were De Léry, St. Ours, Baby, and Dupré.

[39] (p. 462). Ibid., vol. D., p. 317.

[40] (p. 463). Ibid., vol. H, p. 401–41.

[41] (p. 463). Jean François Hubert, born in Quebec in 1739, ordained in 1766, and consecrated bishop in 1786. He remained coadjutor till 1788, when, on the death of Desglis, he succeeded to the headship of the church.

[42] (p. 463). Ibid., vol. G, p. 235–39.

[43] (p. 464). Ibid., p. 232–43.   [44] (p. 465). Q, vol. 49, p. 21–24.

[45] (p. 465). State Book, vol. H, p. 443–60.

[46] (p. 465). Charles François Bailly, born in Montreal in 1740, ordained in 1767, brought to England in 1778 by Carleton as tutor to his family, and consecrated bishop of Capse in 1789.

[47] (p. 465). Ibid., vol. G, p. 381, 389.

[48] (p. 466). Ibid., vol. H, p. 461–70; Q, vol. 27, p. 28.

[49] (p. 467). Ibid., vol. 49, p. 1–30.

[50] (p. 467). Q, vol. 50–1, p. 13.

[51] (p. 467). State Book, vol. E, p. 55.

[52] (p. 467). Shortt and Doughty, op. cit., p. 999–1000.

[53] (p. 468). Ibid., p. 1004–05, 1014.

[54] (p. 468). Ibid., p. 1026.

[55] (p. 468). Q, vol. 46–1, p. 4–5.

[56] (p. 468). Ibid., vol. 38, p. 348–50.

[57] (p. 469). State Book, vol. H, p. 1–13.

[58] (p. 470). Ibid., p. 130–76.   [59] (p. 470). Ibid., p. 138–40.

[60] (p. 471). Leg. Coun., vol. F, p. 168; Q, vol. 51–2, p. 446–535.

[61] (p. 471). The lieutenant governor and the commandants of Detroit had collected the feudal dues there and had pocketed them as perquisites.

[62] (p. 471). State Book, vol. E, p. 114.

[63] (p. 473). Caldwell to Dorchester, June 1, 1787, in Int. Cor. Prov. Que.; Q, vol. 26–1, p. 219–35.

[64] (p. 473). State Book, vol. E, p. 97.

[65] (p. 473). *Ibid.,* vol. F, p. 97–100.

[66] (p. 474). *Ibid.,* vol. E, p. 127.

[67] (p. 474). *Ibid.,* p. 158.

[68] (p. 475). *Ibid.,* p. 127, 150–61.

[69] (p. 476). *Ibid.,* vol. D, p. 351–97; vol. E, p. 47–49, 56–147, 149–289, 317–36, 362–72; vol. F, p. 44–61, 90–117, 268–319; vol. G, p. 21–67, 75–227, 259–90, 392–408.

[70] (p. 477). *Ibid.,* vol. D, p. 238–59, 315. For a discussion of the disease see J. J. Heagerty, *Four Centuries of Medical History in Canada* (Bristol, 1928), vol. 1, p. 131–60.

[71] (p. 478). The correspondence may be found in the files of the Public Accounts.

[72] (p. 479). State Book, vol. D, p. 366–67.

[73] (p. 479). *Ibid.,* p. 371–72.

[74] (p. 480). B, vol. 72–1, p. 260–69.

[75] (p. 480). State Book, vol. G, p. 64–65.

[76] (p. 481). Dorchester to Grenville, November 10, 1789, Q, vol. 43–2, p. 667–71.

[77] (p. 481). Treasury Papers 29, vol. 65, p. 454–58; Inspector General's Report, November 27, 1793, Audit Office 10, vol. 9.

[78] (p. 481). State Book, vol. F, p. 117.

[79] (p. 481). This figure is deduced from an examination of the Public Accounts.

XIX. THE END OF THE OLD PROVINCE OF QUEBEC

[1] (p. 482). Shortt and Doughty, *op. cit.,* p. 947.

[2] (p. 483). *Ibid.,* p. 863–65.

[3] (p. 483). Q, vol. 36–2, p. 416.

[4] (p. 483). *Ibid.,* vol. 38, p. 164.

[5] (p. 483). *Ibid.,* vol. 35, p. 13.

[6] (p. 483). *House of Commons Journals,* vol. 43, p. 479.

[7] (p. 484). Shortt and Doughty, *op. cit.,* p. 954–58.

[8] (p. 484). Smith Papers.

[9] (p. 484). Haldimand's census of 1784 gave a population of 113,000. In July, 1788, Finlay estimated that there were about 130,000 people in the country. See Q, vol. 38, p. 348. Lymburner's figure was higher, but he had a political motive for it.

[10] (p. 484). I can find no authority for the statement in Shortt and Doughty, *op. cit.,* p. 959, n. 1, that Johnson was appointed to this position. There is good reason to believe that he was not.

[11] (p. 484). *Ibid.,* p. 958–60.   [12] (p. 484). Q, vol. 39, p. 120.

[13] (p. 485). *Quebec Herald,* March 9, 1789.

[14] (p. 485). *Ibid.,* April 27, 1789.

[15] (p. 486). *Ibid.,* October 19, 1789.

[16] (p. 486). *Ibid.,* January 26, 1789.

[17] (p. 487). This may be inferred from the statement in Shortt and Doughty, *op. cit.,* p. 971.

[18] (p. 487). E. Cruickshank, "The Genesis of the Canada Act," Ontario Historical Society Papers and Records, vol. 18, p. 231, 233.

[19] (p. 490). Shortt and Doughty, *op. cit.,* p. 970–87. From internal evidence it is clear that this was written by a member of the cabinet. General Cruickshank says

that this is probably the document which Grenville prepared. It is doubtful if any other member of the cabinet could have done it.

[20] (p. 490). *Ibid.*, p. 1024–25. On August 22, 1789, Dorchester asked for a few months' leave of absence to attend to some private affairs in England. Q, vol. 42, p. 70. A month later he repeated his request. *Ibid.*, p. 167. On October 20 Grenville put him off, saying that he should remain till the new government was "put in motion." Shortt and Doughty, *op. cit.*, p. 970. In his reply on February 8, 1790, Dorchester evidently thought that the delay that had just occurred might make a difference, for he again sought permission to return to look after some private affairs. This time he added that it would give him the opportunity of presenting further explanations to the ministry. *Ibid.*, p. 1005. But Grenville soon had another reason for keeping him at his post. The Nootka Sound affair raised the prospect of war with Spain, which in turn raised the prospect of Spain's inspiring the United States to demand a surrender of the western posts. Britain's necessity of having a wise and prudent governor to watch over her North American possessions in such a crisis would surely induce Dorchester to abandon his desire for the time being. So Grenville wrote him on May 6, 1790. Q, vol. 44–1, p. 84–86. The governor was also tied to Quebec by the death of the lieutenant governor. There was no one competent to act for the governor till a successor to Hope appeared. The position was again offered to Thomas Carleton. On his refusal it was given to Alured Clarke, who had demonstrated his administrative ability in Jamaica. Then, by the very ship in which he dispatched Clarke, Grenville wrote Dorchester on August 4 that he might return unless, of course, conditions seemed to require his continued presence in the colony (Q, vol. 45–2, p. 514). Clarke arrived in Quebec on October 7, 1790 (*ibid.*, vol. 47–1, p. 73), but already his chief had put off his idea of returning that year (*ibid.*, vol. 45–2, p. 516). Not until August 18, 1791, did he sail for home (*ibid.*, vol. 52, p. 317), leaving Clarke to inaugurate the new régime.

[21] (p. 491). Shortt and Doughty, *op. cit.*, p. 1024–27.

[22] (p. 491). Q, vol. 39, p. 120.

[23] (p. 491). Shortt and Doughty, *op. cit.*, p. 1004.

[24] (p. 492). *Ibid.*, p. 1018–24, 1027.

[25] (p. 492). Q, vol. 44–1, p. 130–35.

[26] (p. 492). *Ibid.*, p. 149–51. He also intimated that Dorchester might not have been wise in delegating to Johnson the responsibility for nominating members for the Upper Canadian councils.

[27] (p. 492). C. O. 42, vol. 16, p. 19–21.

[28] (p. 492). *Ibid.*, vol. 18, p. 141; Q, vol. 24–2, p. 456.

[29] (p. 493). *Ibid.*, vol. 46–2, p. 378–83.

INDEX

Abandon, 41

Abbott, Edward, lieutenant governor of Vincennes, 288, 289–90

Acadia of *1713,* contrasted with Canada of *1763,* 75

Acadians, 9, 193

Adolphustown (No. 4 Cataraqui Township), 372

Agriculture, distress in Quebec district, *1760–61,* 53; relief measures, 53, 54; Montreal district Canada's granary, 54; little disturbed by American invasion, 252; disappearance of surplus produce, 306; shortage apparently fictitious, 307, 308; crop shortage, *1788,* 379; among loyalists, 376, 377–79, 383, 384. *See also* Smut

Ainslie, Thomas, in charge of King's Posts, 25; collector of customs, 473–75, 480

Allen, Ethan, capture of Ticonderoga and Crown Point, 210; nearly caught at St. John, 210; retreats up Lake Champlain, 212; tries to enlist Indians, 213; captured, 215, 229; sent to England, 218n.

Allier, ——, judge, 20

Allsopp, George, 136, 161, 274, 308, 323, 400, 407; defiance of lantern order, 107–08, 111–12; relations with Quebec grand jury, 112–13; befriended by Carleton, 132; champion of English laws, 316–20, 326–28; prejudice against, 322, 324–25, 326, 327; protest, *1780,* 324–25; explains trouble over laws, 324–25; dropped from council, 327–28

Amherst, Jeffrey, and capitulation of Montreal, 9; disposal of troops, 26; arrangements for government, 27; issues "placard," 28–29; plans for government not influenced by Murray, 29; departure from Canada, 30; attitude toward natives, 63; invites merchants to Canada, 103–04; seeks Jesuit estates, 460–61; fails to get them, 467

André, executioner of, poses as loyalist, 362n.

Antill, Edward, 221, 228, 230

Appeals, court of, 89, 321, 323; Smith's judgment in, 434–35; proposals to reform, 321, 435

Apsley, Lord Chancellor, 199

Armed Neutrality of the North, 448

Army, relations with Canadians, 17, 26, 29, 30; quarrel with merchants and governor, Chapter VI

Arnold, Benedict, 241, 296; capture of Ticonderoga and Crown Point, 210; secures control of Lake Champlain, 211; marches on Quebec, 217, 222; condition of army of, 222; reaches and retires from Quebec, 222–23; assaults Quebec, 225–27; wounded, 227; action against Forster, 235; retires from Montreal, 238–39

Arrêt of Marly, 38

Ashes, 382, 389, 451

Assembly, royal promise of, 79; Murray's refusal to call, 87, 92, 122, and consequent constitutional miscarriage, 93; of Canadians, 118–19; Carleton discourages agitation for, 149–50; Shelburne on, *1767,* 151; Carleton, Hey, and Maseres opposed to, 162; seigniors opposed to, 162; in instructions of *1768,* 164; abandonment of idea of, 167, 177; Quebec Act revokes promise of, 190; loyalists' interest in, 384, 398–99, 403; demanded by mercantile minority, *1783,* 402; discussed in legislative council, *1784,* 406–08; Finlay and Hamilton doubt value of, 410; denounced by French party, 412–13; anticipated by Smith, 425–26; attitude of Dorchester and Sydney on, 482; Grenville's decision for, 487

Attorney general of Quebec, *see* Suckling, Maseres, Monk, Gray

Augusta (No. 7 Royal Township), 372

Baby, Jacques Duperon, aids Detroit, 69

Baby, Jacques Duperon *fils,* judge, 393

Bailly, Charles François, coadjutor bishop, 465; Chapter XVIII, n. 46

Bakers, 23, 45, 46, 121, 259, 260

Banalité, 387

Barcelona, market for Canadian wheat, 459

Barons' Society (Quebec), 380

Bateau, description of, 286

Bayne, Daniel, 113, 123

533